THE CANONS OF SALISBURY

A RECORD OF THE DIGNITARIES, PREBENDARIES AND OFFICE HOLDERS AND THEIR PLACE IN THE QUIRE OF SALISBURY CATHEDRAL

Compiled by

Christopher Ross

First Published in Great Britain by
The Dean and Chapter of
Salisbury Cathedral
6 The Close, Salisbury SP1 2EF
2000

ISBN 0 9501213 4 7

Cover design Joan Biles, photographs Stephen Wagstaff

Printed in Great Britain at Creeds the Printers
Broadoak, Bridport, Dorset DT6 5NL

CONTENTS

ABBREVIATIONS

ACIB	Associate, Chartered Institute of Bankers
AKC	Associate, King's College, London
ALCD	Associate, London College of Divinity
ARCO	Associate, Royal College of Organists
BA	Bachelor of Arts
BCnL	Bachelor of Canon Law
BCn&CL	Bachelor of Canon & Civil Law
BCL	Bachelor of Civil Law
BD	Bachelor of Divinity
BMus	Bachelor of Music
BSc	Bachelor of Science
Bt	Baronet
BTh	Bachelor of Theology
CB	Commander, Order of the Bath
CBE	Commander, Order of the British Empire
Cert Theol	Certificate in Theology
CMG	Commander, Order of St Michael & St George
DBE	Dame Commander, Order of the British Empire
DCnL	Doctor of Canon Law
DCn&CL	Doctor of Canon & Civil Law
DD	Doctor of Divinity
DipTh	Diploma in Theology
DLitt	Doctor of Letters
DM	Doctor of Medicine
DMus	Doctor of Music
DPhil	Doctor of Philosophy
DSC	Distinguished Service Cross
DTh	Doctor of Theology
FCIB	Fellow, Chartered Institute of Bankers
FCP	Fellow, College of Preceptors
FETC	Further Education Teacher's Cetrtificate
FIMgt	Fellow, Institute of Management
FRCO	Fellow, Royal College of Organists
FRCM	Fellow, Royal College of Music
FRHistS	Fellow, Royal Historical Society
FRICS	Fellow, Royal Institute of Chartered Surveyors
FRS	Fellow, Royal Society
FRSA	Fellow, Royal Society of Arts
FRSL	Fellow, Royal Society of Literature
FSA	Fellow, Society of Antiquaries
JP	Justice of the Peace
LicCnL	Licentiate in Canon Law
LicCL	Licentiate in Civil Law
LicTh	Licentiate in Theology
LLB	Bachelor of Civil Law
LLD	Doctor of Civil Law
LRAM	Licentiate, Royal Academy of Music
LTh	Licentiate in Theology
LVO	Lieutenant, Royal Victorian Order
MA	Master of Arts
MA(Ed)	Master of Arts in Education
MBE	Member, Order of the British Empire
MC	Military Cross
MIPD	Member, Institute of Personnel and Development
MIMgt	Member, Institute of Management
MLitt	Master of Letters
MPhil	Master of Philosophy
OBE	Officer, Order of the British Empire
PGCE	Post Graduate Certificate of Education
PhD	Doctor of Philosophy
RAFVR	Royal Air Force Volunteer Reserve
RNVR	Royal Navy Volunteer Reserve
SchCL	Scholar of Civil Law
SchTh	Scholar of Theology
STh	Scholar in Theology
TD	Territorial Decoration
ThL	Theological Licentiate

Abbreviations used in the Index

bis	appears twice
c.	circa
d.	died
dep.	deprived
res.	resigned
ter	appears three times

PREFACE

The stalls in the quire of the cathedrals of Sarum have been held, either in name or in fact, by more than two thousand four hundred individuals. Many of these are already listed in a number of different places but my purpose here has been to provide in a simple and consolidated form, information about these people and their stalls from the founding of the first cathedral of Sarum until the present day.

Lists of holders of prebends, dignities and offices are so arranged that a person's story can be read without cross referencing. This has of course led to duplication of entries so that, to reduce the size of the document and maintain its simplicity, individual references to original source documents have been omitted and normally, with the exception of dates of resignation or death, only the year is given. To place the information in context however, I have included background information and explanations of the various appointments as well as descriptions of the stalls, their canopies and the arms which they display. Biographical particulars have generally been limited to livings within the diocese and those of particular importance or interest but it is appreciated that there is plenty of material still to be found and additional biographical details and amendments to those existing would be welcomed. Place names are normally given their modern spelling, the main exceptions being Sarum, which is used for the Diocese of Salisbury regardless of the period, and the names of the prebends which are as they appear at the rear of the stalls.

A list of my principal sources is at page 229 but I must thank the Institute of Historical Research, University of London for permission to take most of the material for the period 1066-1857 from the *Fasti Ecclesiæ Anglicanæ* 1066-1300 volume IV, Salisbury, compiled by Professor Diana Greenway and 1300-1541 volume III, Salisbury and 1541-1857 volume VI, Salisbury, compiled by Joyce M Horne. I must also thank the many individuals who have provided me with information about relatives and previous holders of prebends, dignities and livings. In particular I would like to thank Suzanne Eward, the Cathedral Librarian & Keeper of the Muniments for providing me with extracts from the Chapter Acts Books and for undertaking other research, Roy Spring, formerly Clerk of the Works, for information on the stalls, Ronald Mathieson for the depictions and blazons of the armorial bearings, Susan Nicholas for permission to quote from her late husband's researches into the persons represented on the canopies over the stalls, my wife Fiona for her help with the index, Bishop John Cavell who started me on this project and Dr John Gosling for his unfailing support and advice.

31 December 1999 — Christopher Ross

THE CATHEDRAL AND DIOCESE

Hereman was the Bishop of Ramsbury from 1045 to 1055 but he resigned on the refusal of King Edward the Confessor to allow the transfer of the see from Ramsbury to Malmesbury. He was restored to his bishopric in 1058 and was at the same time made Bishop of Sherborne, presiding over these two sees from the monastic cathedral of Sherborne. In 1075 the transfer from Sherborne to Sarum was authorised and Bishop Hereman began to build the first cathedral of the diocese of Sarum at what is now known as Old Sarum. He died in 1078 and the new cathedral was completed in 1091 by his successor, Osmund, Bishop of Sarum 1078-1099. Richard Poore, Bishop of Sarum 1217-1228, decided to move from Old Sarum and build a new cathedral on the site which became known as New Sarum or Salisbury. Work started in 1220 and the cathedral was completed c.1315.

A cathedral is the mother church of the diocese. In 1075 the diocese of Sarum consisted of Dorset, formerly the see of Sherborne, and Wiltshire and Berkshire, formerly the see of Ramsbury. The county of Dorset was transferred to the new see of Bristol on its creation in 1542, however, Bristol was united with the see of Gloucester in 1836 and Dorset was returned to Sarum. Also in 1836 Berkshire was transferred to Oxford diocese and a year later the northern part of Wiltshire became part of Bristol diocese. From that date the diocese has consisted of Wiltshire, except for the northern quarter (Bristol), Dorset, except for an area in the east (Winchester), a small area of Hampshire and a parish in Devon.

From time to time there have been bishops suffragan to assist the Bishop of Sarum, the earliest being recorded in 1315. These held either titular or actual sees, although none within Sarum diocese until the creation of Sherborne as a suffragan see in 1925. The reason for this creation would appear to have been the increase in population and it is known that between the two World Wars consideration was given to dividing the diocese and restoring Sherborne Abbey to its position as the cathedral for Dorset. In 1974 a second suffragan see, of Ramsbury, was created and from this date these two bishops have generally had the care of the Dorset and Wiltshire parts of the diocese, respectively, becoming Area Bishops in 1981.

At the time of Bishop Richard Poore, there are known to have been four archdeacons. The senior Archdeaconry was Dorset which comprised that county. The next senior was the Archdeaconry of Berks, comprising that county. The Archdeaconry of Sarum followed, with the southern part of Wiltshire, while the junior Archdeaconry of Wilts comprised the northern part. There was a break in the diocesan succession in the Archdeaconry of Dorset during its transfer to Bristol diocese between 1542 and 1836, and the western part of the county was removed from it in 1916 to form a new Archdeaconry of Sherborne so as to lighten the burden on the Archdeacon of Dorset and to provide a balance of two Archdeaconries for each county. The Archdeaconry of Berks was transferred to Oxford diocese in 1836.

CANONRIES AND PREBENDS

Canonries

The canons were originally resident at the cathedral but increasingly individuals were away from Sarum, holding royal, papal, or archiepiscopal offices, positions at places of learning, or possibly supervising their prebendal estates from which they drew their income. They were therefore permitted to have periods of absence, sometimes upon payment, while foreign canons were not usually expected to be resident, or even in England. Thus the numbers of those resident, who undertook the day to day management of the cathedral and who became known as "canons residentiary", reduced. There were further reductions at the Reformation and since then the number appears to have been between six and four. Canons residentiary were well supported from the common fund so there was often competition for a vacancy and fees for admission were imposed by the Chapter. In more recent years the canons residentiary normally included, or as now comprise, the Dean, the Precentor, the Chancellor and the Treasurer, otherwise referred to as "the four principal persons". The rest of the clerical canons, described as "non-residentiary", are now mainly found from the parochial clergy of the diocese and, together with the canons residentiary, form the Greater Chapter of the cathedral. Non-residentiary canons have few cathedral duties, although at one time each had to take a 'preaching turn' and also say a specific psalm or piece of scripture each day.

Lay Canonries

There are recorded four lay canons who also held prebends; Sir Thomas Cromwell (Blewbery 1536-1540), Sir Richard Moryson (Yetminster Secunda 1537-1539), Thomas Paston Esq (Blewbery 1540-1542) and William Camden Esq (Ilfracombe 1589-1623). It was not however until the 1968 Statutes of the Cathedral that the position of lay members was formalised and the bishop had the power to establish, with the consent of the Close and Greater Chapters, a College of Lay Canons.

Appointments to the College lay with the bishop and could be for life, or for a term of years, or during the tenure of a particular office. Lay canons were to be concerned to extend the influence of the Cathedral throughout the diocese and perform other functions laid down by the Close Chapter (the four principal persons and three canons non-residentiary elected by the Greater Chapter) after consultation with the Bishop. The appointment of four lay canons in 1988, each to serve an initial period of five years, appears to have been the first creation of a "College".

With the exception of those created in the 16c./17c., lay canons do not hold prebends. In recognition, however, of their position, they were allowed to occupy stalls in the quire as a courtesy, three of the principal persons loaning their prebendal stalls and one unoccupied prebendal stall was also loaned. As the number of lay canons has increased some other prebendal stalls have been allotted for the use of lay canons as "courtesy stalls".

Prebends

The original endowments of the Cathedral were mainly in Dorset and Wiltshire and were derived almost entirely from the possessions of the old bishoprics of Sherborne and Ramsbury. There were also churches and estates in Lincolnshire and Somerset. In c.1131 the cathedral was granted further churches or estates in Wiltshire as well as others in Berkshire, Surrey, Hampshire, Devon, Northamptonshire, Oxfordshire and Gloucestershire, and additional gifts were made from time to time.

These endowments were used to finance the cathedral but from earliest times many of them were given to the canons, as prebends, so as to provide each with sufficient revenue for their needs. The amount of revenue received varied widely and the wealthier prebends, especially those which did not involve the cure of souls, were frequently given by the sovereign or pope to people in their own employ, including at one period a number of foreign cardinals.

The bishop usually held the right to nominate to prebends, although this was sometimes exercised by the pope or the sovereign. From 1617 to 1855 the prebend of Shipton had been used by the sovereign to provide for the Regius Professorship of Civil Law at Oxford.

On occasion the right was gifted or otherwise passed to others. Jocelin de Bohun, Bishop of Sarum 1142-1184, assigned to himself the prebend of Major Pars Altaris, which gave him additional financial support and, most importantly, membership of the Greater Chapter, the governing body of the cathedral, and a voice in its deliberations. In this he was unique being the only bishop in England to take such a step. Major Pars Altaris was exchanged for Horton in 1219, this being exchanged in 1255 for Pottern, which remains the prebend of the Bishop of Sarum to this day.

Certain prebends were also joined to dignities of the cathedral. Calne has been linked to the Treasurer from c.1220, Heytesbury has been held by Deans since 1280, and Bricklesworth has been held by the Chancellor from 1240 to the present day but with a separation between 1864 and 1928. The prebend of Teynton Regis was, from time to time allotted to the Precentor but no prebend was permanently joined to this dignity until 1968 when Shipton was named.

Four prebends were held by the abbots of Benedictine monasteries: Sherborne by the Abbot of Sherborne from early in the 12c. and Ogborne, Loders and Upavon respectively by the Abbots of Le Bec Hellouin, St Mary Monteburg and St Wandrille in Normandy from early in the 13c. The foreign Abbots granted to the cathedral various of their holdings within the diocese, were exempted from the duty of residence but were each required to provide a vicar, usually from a religious house on their lands. Prebends also existed in several of the religious houses such as Wilton, while in the 14c. they also existed in the collegiate churches, like Heytesbury and Wimborne, and colleges such as St Edmund's, Sarum, a growing number of which were being created side by side with the monasteries whose population was slowly declining. These prebends offered their founders a patronage similar to that of secular cathedrals such as Sarum.

By 1226 there were fifty-two prebends at Sarum, making it one of the three largest establishments in England. By 1319 the prebends of Bedminster and Redcliffe had been joined and both Coombe & Harnham and Netherbury had been divided, bringing the total to fifty-three.

In the 15c. the foreign monastic houses in England were dissolved, their estates mainly passing to the Crown. Of these, Ogborne was given to the Dean & Canons of Windsor in 1421, the estate of Loders was given to Sion Abbey and the priory and prebend of Upavon was given to the priory of Ivychurch in Wiltshire. In the time of King Edward VI, the estate of the prebend of Horton was confiscated from the cathedral and granted to Edward Duke of Somerset, and that of Faringdon was bestowed in 1550 on William Henning Esq. Also in the sixteenth century, the prebend of Blewbery, which had been under the nomination of the Knights Templars, was abolished as a prebend and was granted to John Capon, Bishop of Sarum 1539-1557, to be included in the revenues of the bishopric, in exchange for the manor of Godalming. The abbey of Sherborne was also dissolved at the Reformation, as were Sion Abbey and the priory of Ivychurch. The loss of these seven prebends, together with the re-amalgamation of Coombe with Harnham, reduced their number to forty-five.

Under the Dean & Chapter, or Cathedrals, Act of 1840, staff and endowments were reduced, the maximum number of canons residentiary became four, the number of Vicars Choral was reduced, prebendal estates were commuted in exchange for annual grants by the Ecclesiastical Commissioners and all prebends became titular. Four of them, Netherbury in Terra, Netheravon, Durnford and Ufcomb, were however subsequently privately endowed. In 1977 the previously titular prebends of Sherborne, Ogborne, Upavon and Loders were revived and were allocated the stalls previously occupied by the Archdeacons, the Cathedral Statutes now requiring each archdeacon to be inducted into a prebend and given a prebendal stall as soon as possible after appointment. The recreation of these four prebends brought the total to forty-nine, which is the existing number of prebendal stalls. Only Blewbery, Faringdon and Horton remain in suspense so that particulars of these prebends and holders of the prebends are shown after the lists of existing stalls.

Originally, the tenure of appointment to a prebend terminated only on death or resignations. Later it was also on assuming a further prebend, an appointment outside the diocese or otherwise ceasing to reside in the diocese or death. Under George Reindorp, Bishop of Sarum 1973-1981, and his successors, clergy have been required to surrender their prebends on ceasing to hold a living or appointment within this diocese.

DIGNITIES AND OFFICES

Dignities

By the middle of the 12c. the four main dignities were those of the Dean, the Precentor, the Chancellor and the Treasurer, each of which held their own endowments. A direction of the time of Bishop Richard Poore includes, "The stalls of the Four Principal Persons in the choir of Sarum are terminals. In entering the choir from the west the stall of the Dean is on the right hand, that of the Precentor on the left hand. At the east of the choir the stall of the Chancellor is on the right hand, that of the Treasurer on the left hand." The Archdeacons, who were also dignitaries, were seated in order of seniority next to the four principal persons, Dorset beside the Dean, Berks beside the Precentor, Sarum beside the Chancellor and Wilts beside the Treasurer. Since that time, the Archdeaconry of Dorset was moved to Bristol diocese from 1542 to 1586 and in 1919 part was transferred to a new Archdeaconry of Sherborne, while in 1836, the Archdeaconry of Berks was transferred to Oxford diocese.

For many years, to be a member of the chapter and have a place and voice in it, an individual had to hold a prebend. Each of the four principal persons held a prebend, together with its prebendal stall, in addition to the stall of their dignity. There are, however cases of archdeacons and canons residentiary not also holding prebends. At one time there was a requirement that, to be appointed Dean, a candidate had to be already in possession of a prebend, which led at times to some interesting manœuvres. The requirement for the Dean to hold a prebend to be able to have a place and voice in chapter was abolished by Act of Parliament in the 19c., despite the requirement in the Statutes of the Cathedral. Under normal circumstances, the bishop has the right of nomination to all the dignities with the exception of the Dean who, originally elected by the chapter, is now appointed by the Crown.

Offices

Stalls are presently designated for three office holders. The holders of the offices of Subdean and Succentor (or Subchanter) were considered permanent officials of the cathedral, were treated as quasi dignitaries but did not always hold prebends. They had their own stalls in the quire, next but one to the Dean and next but one to the Precentor respectively. The Succentor's stall was later transferred to next but one to the Treasurer. At present there is no Subdean nor Succentor, and the stall of the latter has been redesignated Cathedral Chaplain.

The third stall is for the Vicar Choral. The office originates from the vicars, appointed and funded by each of the canons to assist with their duties in the cathedral, and led to the formation of a College of Vicars Choral with its own independent corporation and endowments and using its own Common Hall in the Close. In 1319 there were always to be thirteen vicars on each side of the quire but numbers reduced as each vicar served a number of canons, until in 1547 lay clerks, or vicars, started to be substituted. In 1686 there were six clergy and in the last century there were only four clergy one of whom was usually the Succentor, together with seven Lay Vicars, including the organist, to substitute for the Vicars Choral. In recent years there have been at the most three or four Vicars Choral at any one time but often only one or even none, as is the present situation. In the absence of the Succentor, or upon the office ceasing to be filled from 1968, services were usually sung from the stall behind the Decani Tenor to the periodic inconvenience of the holder of the stall which belonged to the prebend of Torleton. The stall of Torleton was therefore transferred to that previously held by the Succentor, permitting the Vicar Choral to have a designated stall from which to sing the services.

THE STALLS

In the 13th c., the stalls were generally in their present position but there was a pulpitum, or preaching platform, serving as a screen at the west and there were screens behind the stalls to the north and south. The most senior canons, accompanied by their vicars, occupied the top row in the quire, the more junior the middle row, and the choristers the bottom row. There was no particular allocation of seats other than to the dignitaries, archdeacons and officials until the 14c. when stalls in the back row were allotted to individual prebends. From then onwards, the members of the chapter sat in the back row and, although the abolition of prebends and other causes have introduced changes, the placing of the stalls on the south (decani) or north (cantoris) sides is for the most part as recorded in the fourteenth century.

The principal alteration to the seating has been due to the abolition of the prebends of Blewbery, Faringdon, Horton, Loders, Ogborne, Sherborne and Upavon during the 15c. and 16c., Prior to their abolition., the prebendal stalls of Horton, Blewbery and Ogborne were situated between the present Loders and Grimston, that of Faringdon between the present Slape and Coombe & Harnham, and Upavon, Loders and Sherborne between the present Grantham Borealis and Highworth. Other alterations were caused by the discontinuance of Archdeacons' stalls in 1977 and the revival of the titular prebends of Loders, Ogborne, Sherborne and Upavon.

At the time when the quire was reopened on 1 November 1876, following the restoration by Sir Gilbert Scott, Mr Edmund Street and Sir Arthur Blomfield, the Archdeacons were still seated beside or close to the principal persons; Dorset next to the Dean, Wilts next to the Precentor and Sarum one place away from the Chancellor (an exchange having taken place with Bricklesworth, the Chancellor's prebendal stall). The stall of Berks, next to the Treasurer, had been vacated upon the transfer of the Archdeaconry to Oxford in 1836 until occupied by Sherborne in 1916. Some time in the 16c. or 17c. a place was assigned to the Chancellor of the Diocese whose office in the 15c. to 19c. was mostly exercised by a prebendary or dignitary of the cathedral. A stall plate marked "Cancellarii Dioeces" was fixed to the Treasurer's stall but was removed in 1901.

The inclusion in the Cathedral Statutes of the requirement for the Archdeacons to hold prebends and be given the next available prebendal stall on appointment obviated any further need for the Archdeacons to also hold stalls of their dignities so that in 1977 Ogborne was substituted for Archdeacon of Dorset, Upavon for Archdeacon of Wilts, Loders for Archdeacon of Sarum and Sherborne for Archdeacon of Sherborne, who had succeeded the Archdeacon of Berks, the Archdeaconry of Berks having joined Oxford Diocese. Other changes between 1876 and the present day are the substitution of Vicar Choral for Torleton, Torleton for Succentoris and Succentoris for a vacant stall, which later became Chaplain.

There is space within the quire for sixty-two stalls, as shown below. Of these, fifty-six are named for the four principal persons, the forty-nine prebends, the two officials and the Vicar Choral. The remaining six stalls at the head of gangways are without fronts and with one exception, do not carry any marking to indicate use.

East

	Thesaurarii		Cancellarii Ecclesiae
	Sherborne (previously Archdeacons of Berks and Sherborne)		Bricklesworth
		gangway	
	Chaplain (formerly Succentoris)		Loders (previously Archdeacon of Sarum)
	Winterbourne Earls (formerly Rotesfen)		Grimston
	Calne		Wilsford & Woodford
	Major Pars Altaris		Netheravon
	Highworth		Netherbury in Terra
	Grantham Borealis		Yetminster Prima
	Durnford		Alton Australis
		gangway	
	Fordington & Writhlington		Lyme & Halstock
	Preston		Yatesbury
	Stratford		Ruscomb
	Gillingham Minor (formerly Axford)		Chardstock
	Minor Pars Altaris		Bishopstone
	Yetminster Secunda		Alton Borealis
	Warminster		Vicar Choral
		gangway	
	Coombe & Harnham		Beminster Prima
	Slape		Beminster Secunda
	Hurstbourne & Burbage		Netherbury in Ecclesia
	Stratton		Bedminster & Redcliffe
	Bitton		Chisenbury & Chute
	Gillingham Major (formerly Ramsbury)		Grantham Australis
	Shipton		Heytesbury
	Teynton Regis		Ilfracombe (formerly Bere & Cherminster)
	(Ufcomb (formerly Bedwin)		Pottern
return	(Torleton		Subdecani
stalls	(Upavon (previously Archdeacon of Wilts)		Ogborne (previously Archdeacon of Dorset)
	(Precentoris		Decani

West

The stalls are all 13c., as are the misericords with the exception of one which is a 15c. replacement and were never designed to carry canopies. In the time of Seth Ward, Bishop of Sarum 1667-1689, the level of the stalls was raised and they were refitted and painted, and in the late 18c., with canopies placed above them and doors to the rear, they were made to resemble dark theatre boxes. These were removed in the late 19c. Between 1912 and 1925 the present canopies were produced as a memorial to John Wordsworth, Bishop of Sarum 1885-1911, from designs by C E Ponting with statuettes by Herbert Read of Exeter. Each canopy contains a statuette of a person of distinction wearing dress appropriate to the period. The small brass plates attached to the backs of the stalls mainly date from the restoration completed in 1876 but some have been altered to reflect the majority of the changes already noted. The shields fixed to the rear of the stalls were added in 1952 by Randol Blacking and replace an earlier set.

The shields carry the arms of a Bishop of Sarum or some other person who would have held a stall in the quire, not necessarily the one bearing his arms. With the exception of the stall of Calne, the arms are those held by or attributed to the person depicted on the canopy above. It is generally considered that heraldry, as it is now known, originated in the second quarter of the 12c. but it was at one time fashionable to attribute arms to persons of earlier times. On both the north and south, on either side of the organ case, there are two 'gangway' stalls without arms but on the organ case there are nine shields above seven stalls. The end shield in each case is therefore taken to apply to the seat above the gangways. In the description of stalls and their holders which follow will be found notes on the person commemorated, together with the blazon, or description, of the arms while a depiction of the shields is at pages 224 to 226.

DIVISION OF THE PSALTER

From the middle of the 12c. the Book of Psalms was divided between the canons to be said daily, either corporately or individually, as a work of intercession, one special object being to benefit the souls of the benefactors of the church whether living or dead. Three portions of scripture, not from the psalms, were allotted to the prebends held by the Abbots of the foreign monasteries. The appropriate psalm or reading is given in the description of each prebendal stall.

DIGNITARIES, PREBENDARIES AND OFFICE HOLDERS

The descriptions which follow observe the present layout of the stalls within the quire and start at the west end of the south side with the Dean's stall, and continue along this side from west to east, to the Chancellor's stall.

DECANI

Dignity:- The Dean is appointed by the Crown. He is one of the four principal persons of the Cathedral and although primus inter pares, he is responsible for the performance of the services, for the good order of the Cathedral and for the proper performance of the office holders.

The property of the deanery would appear to have been part of the church of Mere in Wiltshire which was presumably included in the bishop's manor of Chaddenwick, and the chapels of Zeals, Chaddenwick and Kingston Deverill. The church of Sonning in Berkshire which also belonged to the bishopric, was assigned to the deanery together with its chapels of Earley, Sindlesham, Ruscombe, Wokingham, Hurst, Sandhurst and Arborfield. A small estate in Stratford-sub-Castle belonged to the deanery from before 1225.

The house in the Close now known as the Old Deanery which was occupied by Robert de Wickhampton as Dean from 1274 to 1284, was given by him to be the deanery in perpetuity in 1277 when he was Bishop of Sarum. The present Deanery is at No.7 The Close

Stall: This being a return stall, there is no statuette, nor shield.

Holders of the dignity: -

Walter (11c) was, perhaps appointed by Bishop Osmund (1078-1099).

Robert (? -1111) died in 1111.

Serlo (c.1116-c.1122) was Dean of Sarum from c.1116 to c.1122 when he probably resigned to become a canon of Merton Priory. He became Abbot of Cirencester in 1131 and died between 1147 and 1149.

Roger (c.1122-c.1139).

Azo (c.1139-c.1145) may have been Archdeacon of Wilts c.1122/39 and brother of Roger of Ramsbury, his successor. He was Dean of Sarum between c.1139 and c.1145, and held the prebend of Pottern from c.1142 to c.1148.

Robert of Salisbury (c1148-1155) was Dean of Sarum from c.1148 until becoming Bishop of Exeter in 1155. He may be the same person as Robert of Chichester who was a canon of Sarum, with an unidentified prebend, in 1148 and who held a stall at London.

Henry de Beaumont (c.1155-1165) was Dean of Sarum from c.1155 until 1165 when he was consecrated Bishop of Bayeux.

John of Oxford (1165-1175) was a chaplain to King Henry II and one of the royal representatives at the Diet of Wurzburg in 1165. He was said to have sworn support on the King's behalf for anti-Pope Paschal II, but later denied this. He was appointed Dean of Sarum by Jocelin, Bishop of Sarum 1142-1184, at the King's request. His election was, however, annulled by Pope Alexander because of his association with schismatics and on the grounds that some members of the Chapter were in exile with Archbishop Becket, despite Bishop Jocelin's assurance of the election having been by the consent of the unanimous Chapter. He was excommunicated for usurping the deanery but, following an appeal by the Chapter and the surrender of the deanery to the papacy, he formally received it in December 1166, holding it until 1175 when he became Bishop of Norwich. He was present at the coronation of King John.

Jordan (c.1176-c.1193) was an Archdeacon, probably of Sarum, between c.1157 and c.1173, and held a stall at Bayeux, before becoming Dean of Sarum from c.1176 to c.1193. He donated vestments to Sonning church, part of the property of the Deanery.

Eustace (c.1194-1197) was Vice-Chancellor to King Richard I. He was Dean of Sarum from c.1194 to 1197 being appointed by the King in 1196 to the Archdeaconry of Richmond and becoming Treasurer of York and Archdeacon of the East Riding also in 1196. He was consecrated Bishop of Ely in March 1198 and died on 4 February 1215.

Richard Poore (1197-1215) was a brother of Herbert Poore, Bishop of Sarum 1194-1217. He was Dean, holding also the prebend of Bere & Cherminster from 1197 to 1215 and played a large part in the founding of the present cathedral. He became Bishop of Chichester in 1215 and Bishop of Sarum from 1217 to 1228, holding the prebend of Major Pars Altaris from 1217 to 1219, when it was exchanged for the prebend of Horton. He became Bishop of Durham in 1228.

Adam (c.1215-1220) was Archdeacon of Dorset from c.1200 to c.1214 and Dean of Sarum from c.1215 to 1220, holding the prebend of Pottern with both these dignities. He died suddenly on 23 August 1220 at Sonning, was buried in the cathedral at Old Sarum and bequeathed vestments to Sonning and gave ornaments to the cathedral.

William de Waude (1220-1237?) was Precentor of Sarum and held the prebend of Heytesbury from c.1218 to c.1220, continuing to hold the prebend during his time as Dean of Sarum from 1220 to 1237? He gave great assistance to Richard Poore, Bishop of Sarum 1217-1228, in his building of the new cathedral, visiting London to collect alms at the end of 1219.

Robert de Hertford (1237-1257) was Chancellor of Sarum from 1220 to 1236 and Dean of Sarum from 1237 to 1257. He held the prebend of Wilsford & Woodford from 1220 to 1257 and died on 9 December 1257.

Robert de Wickhampton (1258-1271) is thought to have held the prebend of Heytesbury from c.1257 and during his time as Dean of Sarum from 1258 to 1271. He is named as a canon of Sarum in a deed (1245) concerning St Nicholas Hospital, Sarum and his name also appears on the foundation-deed (1269) of the College of St Edmund, Sarum. He was described as a papal chaplain and in 1263 was granted dispensation to be promoted to bishop, notwithstanding his illegitimacy. He was Bishop of Sarum from 1274 to 1284 but he became blind and a coadjutor was appointed in 1282. He appears to have held the office of Master of St Nicholas Hospital, Sarum, in 1271 and he may have been related to Thomas de Wickhampton who was Archdeacon of Sarum (c.1274-c.1307) and held the prebend of Bedwin. He died on 24 April 1284.

Walter Scammel (1271-1284) was Archdeacon of Berks from c.1266 to 1274 and Clerk & Collector to King Henry III from 1267 to 1268. He was Treasurer of Sarum and held the prebend of Calne from 1267 to 1271 when, on becoming Dean from 1271 to 1284, he also held the prebend of Heytesbury. He was elected Bishop of Sarum in 1284, died on 20 September 1286 and was buried at the north side of the presbytery in the cathedral. It is believed to have been in 1280 that the prebend of Heytesbury became permanently joined to the Deanery.

Henry of Braunstone (1284-1287) was Archdeacon of Wilts between c.1275 and c.1279, and of Dorset between 1281 and c.1284. He held the prebend of Bere & Cherminster from c.1274 to 1284 and was Dean of Sarum from 1284 to 1287. He held a stall at Exeter and was Bishop of Sarum from 1287, holding also the office of Master of St Nicholas Hospital, Sarum, until his death on 11 February 1288. He was buried in the lady chapel of the cathedral.

Simon de Micham (or Michelham) (1287-1297) was Chancellor of Sarum from 1272 to 1287, held a stall at Wells in 1284 and was Dean of Sarum from 1287 to 1297. He is believed to have died on 8 June 1297.

Peter of Savoy (1297-1308) held the prebend of Highworth from 1289 to 1297, stalls at York in 1290 and Hereford, was Precentor of Lincoln, Dean of Bridgnorth and of St Martin le Grand, London, and was Treasurer of Llandaff. He was Dean of Sarum from 1297 to 1308 but went to Rome in 1298 and was therefore mostly non-resident. He protested in 1301 against the claim of Simon de Gandavo, Bishop of Sarum 1297-1315, to jurisdiction over the canons and others of the cathedral. In 1304 he was summoned into residence but soon after obtained formal licence to live abroad. He became Archbishop of Lyon in 1308 and had died by November 1332.

William Ruffati (1309-1311) also referred to as William Arcufate or de Farges, was a nephew of Pope Clement V and was created Cardinal-Deacon of St Cosmos and St Damian in 1305 and Cardinal-Priest of St Prudentiana in 1306. He held the prebend of Grantham Australis from 1307 to 1309 and was Dean of Sarum from 1309 to 1311. He is thought to have died on 24 February 1311 in Avignon.

Raymond de Fargis (1311-1346) was also a nephew of Pope Clement V and became Cardinal-Deacon of St Maria Nuova in 1310. The Pope placed him successively into the rich deaneries of St Paul's, Sarum and Lincoln, although not holding more than two at the same time, as well as other benefices. It was said that he was a youth too much beloved by the Pope; he was well disposed but too luxurious. He was Dean of Sarum from 1311 to 1346 and was Archdeacon of Sarum in 1312. He died on 5 October 1346.

Bertrand de Fargis (1346-c.1347) was probably another relation of the Pope and would seem to have held a stall at York in 1308 and to have been Archdeacon of the East Riding in 1310. When Dean of Sarum from 1346 to c.1347, he promised to reside diligently. He died before 26 February 1347.

Raynald Ursinus (1347-1374) was a Protonotary Apostolic, Dean of Sarum from 1347 to 1374 and was made Cardinal-Deacon of St Adrian in 1350. In 1356 he also held stalls at Florence and Pisa, and in 1358 was Archdeacon of Liege and of Perugia. He died at Avignon on 6 June 1374.

James Ursinus (c1376-1379) DCnL, was a Protonotary Apostolic who was made Cardinal-Deacon of St George in Velabro by Pope Gregory XI in 1371. Shortly after the election of Pope Urban VI, whom he crowned, he deserted the Pontif and went over to the rival Pope, Clement VII. He was Dean of Sarum from c.1376 to 1379 and died near Tivoli on 13/15 August 1379 whilst in possession of the deanery.

Thomas Ursinus de Manupello (1379-1390) was nominated to be Dean of Sarum in 1379 but Robert Braybroke was appointed. He became Cardinal-Deacon of St Mary in Dominica c.1380 and died in Rome on 10 January 1390.

Robert Braybrook (1379-1381) BCL, would seem to have held at different times stalls at York and Lincoln and also to have been Archdeacon of Cornwall. He was Dean of Sarum from 1379 until becoming Bishop of London in 1381.

Thomas Montacute (1382-1404) BCL, was the first Dean of Sarum in the 14c. to be resident. He was a kinsman of the Earl of Salisbury and was Dean of Sarum from 1382 to 1404. It was in his time that a dispute arose between John Waltham, Bishop of Sarum 1388-1395, and the Dean & Chapter as to the precise limits of episcopal jurisdiction. An agreement was arrived at in 1392 through the intervention of King Richard II and confirmed by Pope Boniface. He died on 31 August 1404 and requested burial in the cathedral, near his father.

Angelo Acciaiuoli (1390-1391) was to have succeeded after the death of Thomas Ursinus in 1390. He had been consecrated Bishop of Rapolla in 1375 and was translated to Florence in 1383. In 1385 be became Chancellor of the Holy Roman Church, Arch-Priest of the Vatican and Cardinal-Priest of St Laurentius in Damaso. He was nominated to be Dean of Sarum 1390 but he had resigned by 30 July 1391 and Thomas Montacute was nominated. He became Cardinal-Bishop of Ostia in 1397, received a royal licence to take possession of the prebend of Blewbery in 1401 and died on 12 June 1409.

John Chaundeler (1404-1417) held a stall at Lincoln in 1405 and the prebend of Netherbury in Ecclesia from ? to 1394, exchanging it with Henry Harburgh for the dignity of Treasurer of Sarum which he held until 1404. He was Dean of Sarum from 1404 to 1417 and Bishop of Sarum from 1417 until his death on 16 July 1426.

Simon Sydenham (1418-1431) DCL, incorrectly accepted nomination to the Archdeaconry of Berks in 1404 but was pardoned and exchanged it for the Archdeaconry of Sarum which he held from 1404 to 1418. He held the rectory of Sutton Veny from 1417 to 1421 and the prebends of Rotesfen from 1407 to 1415 and Yetminster Secunda from 1415 to 1418 and was Dean of Sarum from 1418 to 1431. Although in 1426 he was elected to the see of Sarum, the Chapter on the recommendation of King Henry VI, gave way to a papal provision in favour of Robert Neville. In 1431 he was consecrated as Bishop of Chichester.

Thomas Brouns (1431-1435) DCn&CL, seems to have been Archdeacon of Stow in 1418. He was Archdeacon of Berks from 1427 to 1431 and early in 1431 held the prebend of Rotesfen. He was the Dean of Sarum from 1431 to 1435, being present in 1433 at the Council of Basle. He became Bishop of Rochester in 1435 and Bishop of Norwich the following year.

Nicholas Bildeston (1435-1441) DCL, held the prebend of Bedwin from 1425 to 1435. Whilst holding the rectory of Bishopstone from 1423 to 1441, he was also Archdeacon of Winchester and Dean of Sarum from 1435 until his death on 31 May 1441.

Adam Moleyns (1441-1445) was Rector of Winterbourne Earls in 1432, held a stall at St Paul's in 1440 and was Archdeacon of Taunton in 1440. He was Archdeacon of Sarum from ? to 1441, held the prebend of Bishopstone from 1440 to 1441, also holding a stall at York in 1441. He was Rector of Stapleford from 1442 to 1445 and Dean of Sarum from 1441 to 1445 when he became Bishop of Chichester. In 1441, he sat as Commissary to try Eleanor Duchess of Gloucester for witchcraft and went to Rome to urge, unsuccessfully, the canonisation of Bishop Osmund. In 1443 he assisted in arranging the marriage of King Henry VI with Margaret of Anjou. In 1450, whilst Bishop of Chichester, he was murdered by some sailors in Portsmouth.

Richard Leyot (1446-1449) DCL, held the prebends of Yetminster Secunda from 1418 to 1422 and Grimston from 1423 to 1446, and was Dean of Sarum from 1446 to 1449. He died on 26 January 1449.

Gilbert Kymer (1449-1463) DM, BCL, was Treasurer of Sarum from 1427 to 1449, Chancellor of Oxford in 1446 and Dean of Sarum from 1449 to 1463. He was also Dean of Wimborne between 1447 and 1463. He died on 16 May 1463 and asked to be buried in the cathedral.

James Goldwell (1463-1472) DCn&CL, held a stall at St Paul's in 1458, was Archdeacon of Essex and had a stall at Hereford in1461. He held the prebend of Stratford from 1462 to 1463 and was Dean of Sarum from 1463 to 1472. He became a Canon of Windsor and Registrar of the Order of the Garter in 1470. On the foundation of the Hungerford chantry he is described as the "Pope's Protonotary-notary". He became Bishop of Norwich in 1472 and died on 15 February 1499.

Stephen Nardini (1473) was Cardinal-deacon of St Adrianus and Archbishop of Milan in 1473. He was to have succeeded James Goldwell but John Davyson was appointed.

John Davyson (1473-1485) was Dean of Windsor in 1471, held the prebend of Bishopstone from 1472 to 1473, a stall at St Paul's in 1473 and was Dean of Sarum from 1473 to 1485. He died 12 October 1485.

Edward Cheyne (1486-1502) DCn&CL, held the prebend of Beminster Secunda from 1475 to 1486 and was Dean of Sarum from 1486 to 1502. He died on 25 July 1502.

Thomas Ruthall (1502-1509) DCnL, held the prebend of Ruscomb from ? to 1503. He was Dean of Sarum from 1502 to 1509 and on his appointment, nominated Richard Newport, Prebendary of Faringdon, as his locum tenens. He was Chancellor of Cambridge University and Archdeacon of Gloucester in 1503, and was created Bishop of Durham in 1509. In 1516 he was Keeper of the Privy Seal and died on 4 February 1523. When asked by Cardinal Wolsey to send him a note of the resources of the bishopric of Durham, he accidentally provided an account of his own inherited estate, which showed his considerable wealth.

William Atwater (1509-1514) DTh, was vicar of Piddlehinton in 1487, held a stall at Windsor in 1449 and was Registrar of the Order of the Garter. He held the prebend of Ruscomb in 1509 and was Dean of Sarum from 1509 to 1514. He was Vice-Chancellor of Oxford University in 1500 and Dean of the Chapel Royal in 1502, becoming Chancellor of Lincoln in 1506 On leaving Sarum, he became Archdeacon of Huntingdon and on 14 September 1514 was appointed Bishop of Lincoln, succeeding Cardinal Wolsey, who held him in high esteem.

John Longland (1514-1521) DTh, was Principal of Magdalen Hall in 1505. He held the prebend of Alton Borealis in 1514 and was Confessor to King Henry VIII. From 1514 to 1521 he was Dean of Sarum, holding a stall at Windsor in 1519, becoming Bishop of Lincoln in 1521 and Chancellor of Oxford in 1532 He died on 7 May 1547.

Cuthbert Tunstal (1521-1522) DCn&CL, held the rectory of Steeple Langford from 1509 to 1511 and became Archdeacon of Chester in 1515. He held a stall at York in 1519 and was Master of the Rolls in 1516. For a brief period in 1521 he held the prebend of Coombe & Harnham, apparently so as to become eligible for election to the Deanery of Sarum which dignity he held from 1521 to 1522. He was consecrated Bishop of London in 1522, becoming Keeper of the Privy Seal in 1523. He moved to the see of Durham in 1530 but in 1551 was deprived by King Edward VI and confined in the Tower. He was restored by Queen Mary I but deprived again by Queen Elizabeth I and placed in honourable custody in Lambeth Palace where he died in 1559 at the age of 89.

Richard Pace (1523-1536) was secretary to King Henry VIII. He held stalls at Southwell from 1510 to 1514 and at York in 1514. He was Archdeacon of Dorset from 1514 to 1523, holding the prebend of Coombe & Harnham from 1521 to 1523 and was Dean of Sarum from 1523 to 1536. He died on 28 June 1536.

Peter Vannes (1536-1563) BTh, held the prebends of Grantham Australis from 1528 to 1529 and Bedwin, as additional to his deanery, from 1529 to 1543. He was Dean of Sarum from 1536 to 1563 and on Bedwin being dissolved by Act of Parliament in 1543, he held the prebend of Shipton from 1544 to 1563 and died early in 1563.

William Bradbridge (1563-1571) BD, held the prebend of Lyme & Halstock from 1554 to 1563, becoming Chancellor of Chichester in 1562. He was a Canon Residentiary from 1561 to 1571 and Dean of Sarum from 1563 to 1571. In 1571 he was consecrated as Bishop of Exeter, being allowed also to hold two benefices due to the impoverished state of that see. On his death on 27 June 1578 however he owed £1,400 to Queen Elizabeth I "and had not wherewith to bury him".

Edmund Freake (1571-1572) DD, became Archdeacon of Canterbury and held stalls at Westminster in 1564, Windsor in 1565 and Canterbury in 1568. He was appointed Dean of Rochester in April 1570, becoming Dean of Sarum and a Canon Residentiary from 1571 to 1572. He was consecrated Bishop of Rochester in 1572, becoming Bishop of Norwich in 1575 and of Worcester in 1584. He died on 21 March 1591.

John Piers (1572-1577) DD, became Dean of Chester in 1567 and Dean of Christ Church. He was Dean of Sarum and a Canon Residentiary from 1572 to 1577. He became Almoner to Queen Elizabeth I and Bishop of Rochester in 1576 and, in the latter capacity, preached before the Queen on the defeat of the Spanish Armada. By royal licence he was permitted to hold the Deanery for life but resigned it upon his translation to the see of Sarum. He was Bishop of Sarum from 1577 until becoming Archbishop of York in 1589. He died on 28 September 1594 and was buried in York Minster.

John Bridges (1577-1604) DD, was Dean of Sarum from 1577 to 1604 and a Canon Residentiary from 1578 to 1604 taking part in the Hampton Court conference which furthered the reform of the Church of England and in 1604 was consecrated Bishop of Oxford. He died on 26 March 1618.

John Gordon (1604-1619) was ordained at the age of 58 and was Dean of Sarum and a Canon Residentiary from 1604 to 1619. He appears to have been in the service of Mary, Queen of Scots, and to have served as a minister in France for Kings of Scotland. He died on 3 September 1619, aged 75 whilst on a visitation of his churches in Dorset, and is buried in the cathedral.

John Williams (1619-1620) DD, was Dean of Sarum and a Canon Residentiary from 1619 to 1620. He was appointed Dean of Westminster in 1620 and in the following year, Bishop of Lincoln. He became Archbishop of York in 1641 and was for a time Keeper of the Great Seal. He died on 25 March 1650.

John Bowle (1620-1630) DD, was Dean of Sarum and a Canon Residentiary from 1620 to 1630 when he was consecrated as Bishop of Rochester. He died on 9 October 1637.

Edmund Mason (1630-1635) DD, was Tutor to Prince Charles, later King Charles II, and was Dean of Sarum and a Canon Residentiary from 1630 to 1635. He was present at the 1634 Metropolitan Visitation by Archbishop Laud to the cathedral. In the same year he was excused residence being called away on His Majesty's service. He died on 24 March 1635.

Richard Bayley (1635-1667) DD, was Archdeacon of Nottingham in 1627 and through being married to the niece of Archbishop Laud, became President of St John's College, Oxford. He held a stall at St Paul's in 1631 and was Dean of Sarum and a Canon Residentiary from 1635 to 1667. He was deprived of both the Deanery and the Presidency for loyalty to King Charles I. He died on 27 July 1667.

Ralph Brideoke (1667-1675) DD, was, in 1659, one of the Commissioners for "the approbation and admission of ministers after the presbyterian mode." Despite this, at the Restoration, he became a Canon of Windsor and Rector of Standish, Lancashire, holding these two together with the Deanery of Sarum and a residentiary canonry from 1667 to 1675. He was consecrated as Bishop of Chichester in 1675 and died on 5 October 1678 at the age of 74. During his tenure as Dean of Sarum, extensive alterations were made to the quire by Bishop Seth Ward.

Thomas Pierce (1675-1691) DD, was a Fellow of Magdalen College, Oxford. On the Restoration, he held stalls at both Lincoln and Canterbury and in 1661 he was elected President of Magdalen College but due to disagreements he resigned in 1675. He was Dean of Sarum and a Canon Residentiary from 1675 to 1691 and engaged in a long, angry and unsuccessful controversy with Bishop Seth Ward as to his right to visitation of the cathedral and to the patronage of the prebends. He died on 28 May 1691.

Robert Woodward (1691-1702) DCL, was Archdeacon of Wilts from 1681 to 1687, holding the rectory of Pewsey from 1685 to 1702. He was Chancellor of Sarum from 1687 to 1691, being also Chancellor of the Diocese, and was Dean of Sarum and a Canon Residentiary from 1691 to 1702. He died on 13 February 1702.

Edward Young (1702-1705) BCL, was a Fellow of New College, Oxford, and of Winchester. He held the prebends of Gillingham Minor from 1682 to 1688 and Coombe & Harnham from 1688 to 1702, and was Dean of Sarum and a Canon Residentiary from 1702 to 1705. He died on 9 August 1705 and was buried in the cathedral.

John Younger (1705-1728) DD, held the living of Bishopstone from 1688 to 1728 and was chaplain to the Princess Anne, later Queen Anne, on her marriage to Prince George of Denmark, and was Keeper of the Bodleian Library He held the prebend of Wilsford & Woodford from 1680 to 1705, was appointed a Canon Residentiary of St Paul's in 1693, holding the latter together with the Deanery of Sarum and a residentiary canonry from 1705 until 1728.. He died on 27 February 1728.

John Clarke (1728-1757) DD, was a distinguished mathematician who spent much of his time in Cambridge. He was Dean of Sarum and a Canon Residentiary from 1728 until his death on 5 February 1757. He was buried in the cathedral.

Thomas Greene (1757-1780) DD, was the son of Bishop Greene who was Bishop of Norwich and then of Ely. He was Chancellor of Lichfield in 1751 and Dean of Sarum and a Canon Residentiary from 1757 to 1780. He died on 23 March 1780.

Rowney Noel (1780-1786) DD, was Dean of Sarum and a Canon Residentiary from 1780 to 1786. He died on 26 June 1786.

John Ekins (1786-1808) DD, was Tutor to the Duke of Rutland and was his chaplain when he was Lord Lieutenant of Ireland. He was Vicar of Stanton Bernard in 1767, Rector of Trowbridge in 1774 and Rector of Newton Tony from 1776 to 1808. He was Dean of Sarum and a Canon Residentiary from 1786 to 1808 and he died on 10 September 1808.

Charles Talbot (1809-1823) BD, was a direct descendant of William Talbot, Bishop of Sarum 1715-1721, and grandson of Lord Chancellor Talbot. He became Dean of Exeter in 1803 and Dean of Sarum and a Canon Residentiary from 1809 to 1823. He appears to have held the office of Master of St Nicholas Hospital, Sarum in 1822. He died on 28 February 1823.

Hugh Nicholas Pearson (1823-1846) DD, was in 1813 a Proctor in Convocation and Domestic Chaplain to King George IV. He was Dean of Sarum and a Canon Residentiary from 1823 to 1846 and was the author of *Christianity in India* and of other works. He resigned on 21 May 1846 and died ten years later.

Francis Lear (1846-1850) BD, was Rector of Chilmark from 1824, holding the prebends of Stratford from 1830 to 1834 and of Netheravon from 1834 to 1846. He was Rector and Vicar of Bishopstone from 1843 and Archdeacon of Sarum from 1836 to 1846. He was Dean of Sarum and a Canon Residentiary from 1846 to 1850, and died on 23 March 1850.

Henry Parr Hamilton (1850-1880) MA, FSA, was a Fellow of Trinity College, Cambridge who very generously supported the restoration of the cathedral. He also bequeathed a large number of books to the cathedral library. He was Dean of Sarum and a Canon Residentiary from 1850 to 1880 and died on 7 February 1880.

[After the death of Henry Parr Hamilton, the Rev John Charles Ryle was to have succeeded him but before he could be installed as Dean, he was appointed the first Bishop of Liverpool.]

George David Boyle (1880-1901) MA, was the son of the Rt Hon David Boyle, Lord Justice General of Scotland, and numbered John Henry Newman amongst his friends. He held a stall at Worcester in 1872. He was Dean of Sarum and a Canon Residentiary from 1880 to 1901, during which time the large sum of £14,000 was spent on the Cathedral under his direction. He was also Precentor of Sarum from 1881 to 1896. He died on 21 March 1901 and is commemorated in both the south choir aisle and the Trinity Chapel.

Alan Becher Webb (1901-1907) DD, was appointed to a fellowship of University College, Oxford in 1863 at the age of twenty four, resigning it four years later. In 1870 he became Bishop of Bloemfontein where he was actively engaged in developing mission and educational work. He resigned in 1898 and was Provost of Inverness and Assistant Bishop in Moray & Brechin before becoming Dean of Sarum and a Canon Residentiary from 1901 to 1907. He died on 12 June 1907 and was buried in the cathedral cloisters.

William Page Roberts (1907-1919) DD, held a stall at Canterbury from 1895 to 1907, and was Dean of Sarum and a Canon Residentiary from 1907 to 1919. He died on 17 August 1928.

Andrew Ewbank Burn (1920-1927) DD, held stalls at Lincoln in 1903 and at Wakefield. He was a Chaplain to King George V and was Dean of Sarum and a Canon Residentiary from 1920 to 1927. He died on 28 November 1927.

John Hugh Granville Randolph (1928-1935) DD, was Bishop Suffragan of Guildford from 1909 to 1927. He was Dean of Sarum and a Canon Residentiary from 1928 until resigning on 1 October 1935. He died on 21 March 1936.

Edward Lowry Henderson (1936-1943) MA, was a Canon Residentiary of Gloucester from 1917 until 1919 when he became Provost of St Mary's Cathedral, Edinburgh. From 1925 to 1935 he was Dean of St Albans and was Dean of Sarum and a Canon Residentiary from 1936 until resigning on 30 June 1943. He died on 26 September 1947.

Henry Charles Robins (1943-1952) MA, held a stall at Chelmsford from 1931 to 1935. He was a Proctor in Convocation from 1932 to 1943 and Chaplain to King George VI from 1939 to 1943. He was Dean of Sarum and a Canon Residentiary from 1943 to 1952 and died on 31 July 1960.

Robert Hamilton Moberly (1952-1960) MA, was Principal of Bishops' College, Cheshunt from 1925 to 1936 when he was consecrated Bishop Suffragan of Stepney, resigning in 1952. He was Dean of Sarum and a Canon Residentiary from 1952 to 1960. He died on 16 September 1978.

Kenneth William Haworth (1960-1971) MA, became Domestic & Diocesan Chaplain to the Bishop of Lichfield, and a lecturer at Lichfield Theological College in 1931. In 1937 he became Chaplain to Wells Theological College before serving as a Chaplain to the Forces from 1939 to 1943. He was Vice Principal and then Principal of Wells Theological College between 1946 and 1960. He held a stall at Wells from 1947 to 1960, was a Proctor in Convocation from 1956 to 1959 and Dean of Sarum and a Canon Residentiary from 1960 until resigning in January 1971. He died on 22 April 1988.

William Fenton Morley (1971-1977) CBE, MA, BD, became a Lecturer and Director of Music at Cuddesdon College, Oxford in 1946. He served as Education Secretary to the Overseas Council of the General Assembly from 1950 to 1956, before becoming a Canon Residentiary and Precentor of Southwark Cathedral. From 1961 to 1971 he held a stall at Ripon and was Dean of Sarum and Canon Residentiary from 1971 to 1977. He was a Proctor in Convocation from 1964 to 1977, Chaplain to Queen Elizabeth II from 1965 to 1971, Chairman of the Deployment and Payment Commission, which produced *The Morley Report*, a Church Commissioner from 1968 to 1977 and Chairman of the Church of England Pensions Board from 1974 to 1980. He died on 9 July 1995.

Sydney Hall Evans (1977-1986) CBE, MA, DD, served as an RAFVR Chaplain 1943-1945, was Warden of the King's College, London, Post Graduate College at Warminster from 1948-1956 and Dean of King's from 1956-1977. He held a stall at Southwark from 1959-1977 and was Dean of Sarum and a Canon Residentiary from 1977 to 1986. It was during his time as Dean that the urgency of a major restoration of the cathedral spire, tower and west front was identified and an appeal was launched under the patronage of HRH The Prince of Wales. He was the first Dean of Sarum to be required to retire by the age of seventy under the Ecclesiastical Offices (Age Limit) Measure 1975, but he was granted an extension of one year by John Austin Baker, Bishop of Sarum 1982-1993, to allow him to see the appeal underway. He died on 6 January 1988. He was the author of *Salisbury Cathedral: a Reflective Guide*.

The Hon Hugh Geoffrey Dickinson (1986-1996) MA, formerly Vicar of St Michaels St Albans from 1977 to 1986, was Dean of Sarum and a Canon Residentiary from 1986 to 1996. During his period of office the Spire Appeal raised £7.5 million, the first Girls Choir was created and Sarum College was founded in the Close. He published a book of Cathedral Prayers and a Pilgrim's Guide.

Derek Richard Watson (1996-) MA, served as Domestic Chaplain to the Bishop of Southwark from 1970 to 1973. He was a Canon Residentiary and Treasurer of Southwark Cathedral from 1978-82, served the parishes of St Luke's and Christ Church Chelsea from 1982 to 1996 and was Area Dean of Chelsea from 1994 to 1996. He became Dean of Sarum and a Canon Residentiary in 1996.

OGBORNE
(previously the stall of the Archdeacon of Dorset)

Until 1977 each Archdeacon had a stall of his dignity in a position of prominence close to one of the four principal persons; these stalls have now been renamed. Particulars of the Archdeacons are given first, followed by the particulars of the prebend the name of which the stall now bears.

Stall: This being a return stall, there is no statuette, nor shield.

ARCHDEACON OF DORSET

The dignity: This is the senior Archdeaconry which was in existence in 1086, covering the entire county of Dorset, formerly the see of Sherborne, with its five deaneries of Bridport, Dorchester, Pimperne, Shaftesbury and Whitchurch (Canonicorum). The county of Dorset was transferred to the new see of Bristol on its creation in 1542 but Bristol was united with the see of Gloucester in 1836 and Dorset was returned to Sarum. In 1916, it was determined that the Archdeaconry had become too large for one person and the county was divided. The rural deaneries of Shaftesbury, Milton, Stalbridge, Sturminster Newton, Blandford, Wimborne, Poole and Purbeck were retained and the rural deaneries of Lyme Bay, Beaminster, Dorchester, Weymouth and Sherborne formed a new Archdeaconry of Sherborne.

8 Archdeacon of Dorset

The property of the Archdeaconry was the church of Gussage All Saints which was granted by Robert de Wickhampton, Bishop of Sarum 1274-1284. The right of presentation to the benefice, a dwelling and two acres were given to Henry of Braunstone, Archdeacon of Dorset 1281-c.1284, by the Prior of Montacute in 1281 and were given by him to the cathedral, to be granted to the Archdeaconry in perpetuity.

Holders of the dignity:-

Adelelm (c.1139-c.1180) was a nephew of Roger le Poer, Bishop of Sarum 1102-1139 and was also Dean of Lincoln from before 1145 until after c. May 1173 but had been succeeded by c.1180.

William (c.1180-c.1193).

Richard (c.1196-c.1198).

Adam (c.1200-c.1214) was Archdeacon of Dorset from c.1200 to c.1214 and Dean of Sarum from c.1215 to 1220, holding the prebend of Pottern with both these dignities. He died suddenly on 23 August 1220 at Sonning and was buried in the cathedral at Old Sarum.

Herbert (c.1222-1225/6).

Humphrey (c.1226-c.1241) held the prebend of Alton Borealis in c.1226 and may have held a stall at Chichester. He had died before 1 May 1244.

Gerard de Bingham (c.1245-c.1255) was probably related to Robert de Bingham, Bishop of Sarum 1229-1246.

Jordan Piruntus (or Conti) (c.1258-?) was a papal notary and vice-chancellor who held the Archdeaconry whilst waiting for a prebend. He held a stall at London in 1259, became Cardinal-Deacon of St Cosma and St Damiano in 1262 and, dying in October 1269, left 11 marks to the altar of the cathedral.

Simon of Bridport (?-1262) may have been a brother of Giles of Bridport, Bishop of Sarum 1257-1262. He was Archdeacon of Dorset from ? to 1262, Archdeacon of Berks from c.1262 to c.1263 and Treasurer of Sarum from c.1265 to c.1267.

John (c.1271).

Gerard de Grandisson (?-1275) held the prebend of Wilsford & Woodford from ?-1275 and was Archdeacon of Dorset before June 1275. He was a papal chaplain and nephew of Otto de Grandisson a royal councillor. He held a stall at York and became Bishop of Verdun in 1276.

Anthony Bek (1275) was bequeathed houses in the Close by Walter Merton in 1276. He was Archdeacon of Durham in 1275, Precentor of York and held stalls at Lichfield, Lincoln, London and Wells. He was Bishop of Durham from 1284 to 1311.

Thomas Bek (1275-1280) was the elder brother of Antony Bek who was nominated to the Archdeaconry in 1275 but does not seem to have occupied it. He held stalls at Lichfield, St David's and Lincoln and was Keeper of the Wardrobe to King Edward 1. He became Bishop of St David's in 1280.

Henry of Braunstone (1281-c.1284) was Archdeacon of Wilts between c.1275 and c.1279, and of Dorset between 1281 and c.1284. He held the prebend of Bere & Cherminster from c.1274 to 1284 and was Dean of Sarum from 1284 to 1287. He held a stall at Exeter and was Bishop of Sarum from 1287, also holding the office of Master of St Nicholas Hospital, Sarum, until his death on 11 February 1288. He was buried in the lady chapel of the cathedral.

William de la Wyle (1287-1297) held the prebend of Teynton Regis from 1275 to 1297 and was Archdeacon of Dorset from 1287 to 1297. He had died by 21 May 1297.

Henry de Bluntesdon (1297-1316) was Archdeacon of Dorset from 1297 to 1316 and became King's Almoner, holding a papal dispensation in 1300 to retain the Archdeaconry and other benefices. He held the prebend of Chisenbury & Chute, stalls at Chichester, London and Wells and had died by 29 September 1316.

Peter de Periton (1316-1321) DCnL, held the prebend of Yetminster Prima from 1303 to 1310. He was appointed but declined the prebend of Durnford in 1309 and held the prebend of Bedminster & Redcliffe from 1310 to 1321. He was Archdeacon of Dorset from 1316 to 1321 and died in 1321.

Thomas de Hotoft (1321-1339) DTh.

John de Kirkeby (1340-1346) was Rector of Keevil in 1333 and held the prebends of Preston from 1334 to 1338 and Minor Pars Altaris from 1338 to ?. He was Master of St Nicholas Hospital, Sarum in 1337 and a Canon Residentiary and Archdeacon of Dorset from 1340 to 1346, holding with the dignity the church of Gussage, and he died in 1346. He was probably the same person who was Precentor of Lichfield from 1332 to 1339.

Bertrand de Deucio (1347,1352) was Provost of Embrun, France and Archbishop of Embrun from 1323 until he was created Cardinal-Priest of St Mark in 1338. He was Archdeacon of Dorset in both 1347 and 1352 and became Cardinal-Bishop of Sabina in 1348, being allowed to visit his Archdeaconry by deputy for a period of five years. He held the prebend of Wilsford & Woodford in 1352 and after being Nuncio to Robert, King of Sicily, and to the Doge of Venice, he died on 21 October 1355.

Robert of Geneva (?-1378) was a Protonotary of the Apostolic See who was made Bishop of Terouane in 1361 and of Cambrai in 1368. He was made Cardinal-Priest of the Twelve Apostles in 1371 and rebelling against Pope Urban VI, he crowned Pope Clement VII in 1378, the first Pope of the great schism. He held the Archdeaconry of Dorset and the Rectory of Gussage in 1373 and in 1378 and died at Avingnon on 16 September 1394.

Thomas Pays (1378-?).

Nicholas Caraccioli (1380) known as the 'Cardinal of Naples', was Cardinal-Priest of St Cyriacus and Inquisitor General of Naples. In 1380 he was Archdeacon of Dorset and Treasurer of Sarum.

Ralph Erghum (1386-?).

Robert Ragenhull (1388-c.1390) was a Canon Residentiary and Archdeacon of Dorset from 1388 to c.1390. He held the prebend of Bishopstone in 1393, exchanging it with Richard Holme for the prebend of Warminster, which he exchanged with John Tydeling in 1406 for the prebend of Major Pars Altaris, holding the latter until 1407. He was Provost of St Edmund's College, Sarum in 1395 and died in 1407.

Adam Easton (?-1397) DTh, was a Benedictine who exchanged the prebend of Yetminster Secunda in 1392 with John de Icklington for the church of Heigham, Norfolk. He was made Archdeacon of Dorset by papal grant in 1396 but he disputed a royal grant to Michael Cergeaux later in the same year and the possession of the dignity was still in dispute on his death. He was created Cardinal-Priest of St Cecilia in 1381/1383 and was one of the six cardinals whom Pope Urban VI had imprisoned and tortured for rebellion. He was spared at the intercession of King Richard II, resigned the cardinalate but was restored by Pope Boniface IX in 1389. He is described as learned, not only in Greek but in Hebrew, and as a voluminous writer. He died at the Vatican shortly before 19 September 1397.

Michael Cergeaux (1396-1397) DCn&CL.

Walter Medford (1397) BCL, was Archdeacon of Dorset in 1397, Chancellor of Sarum from 1402 to 1404 and a brother of Richard Medford, Bishop of Sarum 1396-1407. In 1404 he exchanged the dignity with his successor for the Archdeaconry of Sarum and the prebend of Fordington & Writhlington, exchanging a few days later for the Archdeaconry of Berks. He probably exchanged this Archdeaconry with Peter Alcobasso for the Deanery of Wimborne in 1417. He held the prebends of Major Pars Altaris from 1396 to 1397, Yetminster Prima in 1397, Faringdon from 1397 to 1400, having been excommunicated but later absolved, when he exchanged this prebend for the treasurership of St Paul's. He held the prebend of Netherbury in Ecclesia in 1401, followed by Preston, which he exchanged with Richard Derham for Netherbury in Ecclesia in 1402. He held the prebends of Fordington & Writhlington from 1404 to 1407 and Bedwin from 1407 until his death in 1423.

Nicholas Bubwith (1397-1399, 1400-1406) held a stall at Lincoln, the prebend of Bere & Cherminster from 1402 to ? and was Archdeacon of Dorset from 1397 to 1399 and again from 1400 to 1406 when he became Bishop of London. He was translated to Sarum in 1407 and to Bath & Wells four months later. He was successively Master of the Rolls, Keeper of the Privy Seal and Treasurer of England. He died on 27 October 1424 and was buried at Wells.

Henry Chichele (1397-?) DCL, was appointed to the Archdeaconry of Dorset in 1397 and after two years of litigation at the Curia over the claims of Nicholas Bubwith, he was declared technically an intrusor, but was reinstated in 1399, although Bubwith was appointed a year later. He held the prebends of Rotesfen in 1397, Yetminster Prima from 1397 to 1400, Fordington & Writhlington in 1400, Yetminster Secunda from 1400 to 1402 and Bedminster & Redcliffe from 1402 to 1404, when he exchanged with George Westby for the prebend of Fordington & Writhlington. After litigation, he became Archdeacon of Sarum in 1402, exchanging this and the prebend in 1404 for the dignity of Chancellor of Sarum which, following his consecration as Bishop of St David's in 1407, he continued to hold by papal indulgence until 1409. At one time he held the living of Melcombe Bingham and he became Archbishop of Canterbury in 1414. He was the founder of All Souls College, Oxford and died on 12 April 1443.

John Macworth (1406-1437) was Chancellor of Henry, Prince of Wales, afterwards King Henry V. He held a stall at Lincoln in 1404 and was Archdeacon of Dorset from 1406 until exchanging the dignity in 1437 with John Hody for the church of Tredington, Worcestershire. He held a stall in York in 1436 and is believed to have been Archdeacon of Norfolk in 1408, Dean of Lincoln in 1412 and to have died in 1451.

John Hody (1437-1440) BCL, was uncle to Sir John Hody, Lord Chief Justice of England in the time of King Henry VI; his brother had an estate at Kington Magna. He was Rector of Bishopstrow from 1420 to 1425, Chancellor of Wells in 1426, and held a stall at York from 1426 to 1436. He was Archdeacon of Dorset from 1437 to 1440, in which year he died.

John Stopyndon (1440-1447) held a stall at St Paul's in 1424. He was Archdeacon of Colchester in 1433, was Master of the Rolls in 1438 and was Archdeacon of Dorset from 1440 until his death in 1447.

Robert Aiscough (1447-1449) DTh, held the prebends of Netheravon from 1440 to 1441, Faringdon from 1441 to 1447, Grantham Australis from 1447 to 1448, Chisenbury & Chute in 1448 and Bere & Cherminster from 1448 to 1449. He was Archdeacon of Dorset from 1447 to 1449 and had died by 14 February 1449.

William Ayscough (1449-1486) MA, died in 1486.

Robert Langton (1486-1514) was a nephew of Thomas Langton, Bishop of Sarum 1485-1493, Archdeacon of Dorset from 1486 to 1514 and held the prebends of Fordington and Writhlington from 1485 to 1488 and Bere & Cherminster from 1488 to 1524. He also held stalls at Lincoln from 1483 to 1516, at Southwell from 1514 to 1517 and at York from 1514 to 1524. He appears to have been Treasurer of York from 1509 to 1514 and Chancellor of Lichfield in 1516. He died in 1524.

Richard Pace (1514-1523) was secretary to King Henry VIII. He held stalls at Southwell from 1510 to 1514 and at York in 1514. He was Archdeacon of Dorset from 1514 to 1523, holding the prebend of Coombe & Harnham from 1521 to 1523 and was Dean of Sarum from 1523 to 1536. He died on 28 June 1536.

John Stokesley (1523-1530) DTh, became Bishop of London in 1530.

William Bennet (1530-1533) DCL, died in 1533.

Edward Fox (1533-1535) DTh, was Master of Sherborne Hospital and held a stall at York in 1527. He was Almoner to King Henry VIII who sent him to Rome as his 'Orator', with Stephen Gardiner, in dealings over the validity of the King's marriage with Catherine of Aragon. In 1528 he became Provost of King's College, Cambridge and held the prebend of Major Pars Altaris from ? to 1535. He was Archdeacon of Leicester in 1533 and Archdeacon of Dorset from 1533 to 1535 when he became Bishop of Hereford. He died in 1548.

John Skip (1535?-1542) DTh, may have succeeded Edward Fox. He became Bishop of Hereford in 1539 but held a royal licence to hold the Archdeaconry until All Saints Day 1542.

The Archdeaconry of Dorset was transferred to the diocese of Bristol on 4 June 1542 but was returned to Sarum by Order in Council dated 5 October 1836.

Robert Bentley Buckle (1836-1862) MA, was a Fellow of Sydney Sussex College, Cambridge who held the prebend of Stratton from 1841 to 1893. He was Archdeacon of Dorset in the diocese of Bristol in 1836 and in the diocese of Sarum from 1836 until resigning in 1862. He was Vicar of Upwey from 1836 until resigning in 1888 and he died on 16 September 1893.

Anthony Huxtable (1862) MA, was Rector of Sutton Waldren from 1834 to 1871. He was Archdeacon of Dorset in 1862 for only nine months before resigning. He died on 12 December 1883.

Thomas Sanctuary (1862-1889) was Vicar of Powerstock and Milton and North Poorton from 1840, Archdeacon of Dorset from 1862 and Canon Residentiary from 1857 until his death on 31 May 1889. In 1881 he purchased the Old Workhouse, Crane Street, Salisbury to be the Church House for the Diocese.

Francis Briggs Sowter (1889-1902) MA, was Rector of Corscombe from 1878 to 1884, Vicar of Holy Trinity Weymouth from 1884 to 1890 and of Fleet from 1886 to 1890. He was Rector of Holy Trinity Dorchester and Rural Dean of Dorchester, from 1895 to 1898. He was Archdeacon of Dorset from 1889 to 1902, held the prebend of Highworth from 1903 to 1927 and was a Canon Residentiary from 1910 until resigning in 1916. He died on 10 September 1928 and bequeathed his valuable library to Church House, Salisbury.

Charles Leslie Dundas (1902-1927) was Vicar of Charminster with Stratton from 1895 to 1914. He held the prebend of Ufcomb from 1900 to 1929, was Archdeacon of Dorset from 1902 to 1927, Vicar of Milton Abbas from 1914 to 1917 and a Canon Residentiary from 1914 to 1928. He resigned the prebend in 1929 on it being endowed by Miss Kingsbury and died on 17 March 1932.

Eric James Bodington (1927-1929) MA, was Vicar of Osmington from 1894 to 1899, Vicar of Potterne and Rural Dean of Potterne from 1899 to 1907, Rural Dean of Avebury from 1907 to 1912 and Vicar of Calne from 1907 to 1927. He was Archdeacon of Wilts from 1912 to 1927, held the prebend of Chardstock from 1913 to 1929 and was Archdeacon of Dorset and Canon Residentiary from 1927 to 1929. He died on 25 October 1929.

William Okes Parish (1929-1940)TD, MA, was Vicar of Longfleet from 1885 to 1929 and Rural Dean of Poole from 1893 to 1929. He was Archdeacon of Dorset and a Canon Residentiary from 1929 until resigning on 31 March 1940. He died seven days later.

Harold Nickinson Rodgers (1940-1947) MA, was Archdeacon of Portsmouth from 1927 to 1936, Bishop Suffragan of Sherborne from 1936 to 1947 and Archdeacon of Dorset from 1940 to 1947. He died on 22 June 1947.

Lancelot Farquharson Addison (1947-1956) was Vicar of Cranborne in 1947. He held the prebend of Grimston from 1947 to 1955, was Archdeacon of Dorset from 1947 to 1956 and was Treasurer of Sarum from 1955 until his death in 1956.

Edward Leslie Seager (1956-1974) MA, was Chaplain to the Forces from 1937 to 1946, Vicar of Gillingham from 1946 to 1979, and of Fifehead Magdalen from 1966 to 1979. He held the prebends of Shipton from 1954 to 1968 and Gillingham Major from 1968 to 1979. He was Rural Dean of Shaftesbury from 1951 to 1956 and Archdeacon of Dorset from 1956 to 1974. He was Rural Dean of Blackmore Vale from 1975 to 1979 and a Team Vicar in the Gillingham Team Ministry in 1979. He died on 2 November 1983.

Richard Lloyd Sharp (1975-1982) MA, was Vicar of Portland St John from 1944 to 1949, Vicar of Wootton Bassett from 1949 to 1955 and Perpetual Curate of Broad Town from 1951 to 1955. He was Vicar of St Mark's, Sarum from 1955 to 1964, Vicar of Holy Trinity, Weymouth from 1964 to 1974, held the prebend of Alton Australis from 1968 to 1982 and was Archdeacon of Dorset from 1975 to 1982. He died on 4 July 1982.

(In 1977 the Archdeacons' stalls were discontinued, the stall of the Archdeacon of Dorset being used for the revived prebend of Ogborne.)

OGBORNE

Prebend:- Ogborne takes its name from a priory north of Marlborough in Wiltshire. The Abbot of Le Bec Hellouin in Normandy, who already held a stall at Wells, conveyed churches in the diocese to the Bishop and formed the two Ogbornes, St Andrew and St George, together with Wantage into a prebend which gave Abbots for the time being, through their dependant prior, a seat in choir and a voice in chapter. By 1405 the priory had been dissolved its estates passing in 1421 to the Dean and Canons of St George' Chapel, Windsor. It is understood that Deans of Windsor were admitted as canons and prebendaries from time to time, although there are no records to show who or when.

There are two stalls in the quire named for this prebend. The stall next to the Dean has a plate 'Ogborne', while the gangway stall next to Bricklesworth has a plate 'Okeburne', which is an earlier spelling.

The transfer of prebendal revenues to the Ecclesiastical Commissioners under the Cathedrals Act of 1840 deprived the Deans and Canons of Windsor, in common with the holders of other prebends, of any material ownership, and further legislation at about the same time placed all canonries in the direct patronage of the bishop. In 1997 it was decided to revive this and three other titular prebends, using the Archdeacons' stalls for this purpose.

12 Ogborne

Psalter:- The piece of scripture allotted to the prebend is Deuteronomy 32.

Holders of the prebend:-

The Abbot of Bec for the time being (1208-1405).

The Dean of Windsor for the time being (1421-1840c.?).

Rhys Derrick Chamberlain Walters (1977-1979) OBE, BSc, was Diocesan Missioner of Sarum from 1974 to 1983 and Priest-in-Charge of Burcombe from 1974 to 1979. He held the prebend of Ogborne from 1977 to 1979 and was Treasurer of Sarum and a Canon Residentiary from 1979 to 1983. He was Dean of Liverpool from 1983 to 1999.

Nigel Simeon McCulloch (1979-1986) MA, was Archdeacon of Sarum holding the prebend of Ogborne from 1979 to 1986. From 1978 to 1986 he was successively Priest in Charge and then Rector of Sarum St Thomas and St Edmund. From 1986 to 1992 he was Bishop of Taunton, holding a stall at Wells, and in 1992 he became Bishop of Wakefield.

Barnabas John Hopkinson (1986-1998) MA, was Priest in Charge of Preshute and Team Vicar Marlborough Team from 1975 to 1981, and Rural Dean of Marlborough from 1977 to 1981. From 1981 to 1986 he was Team Rector of Wimborne Minster and Holt, and from 1985 to 1986 was Rural Dean of Wimborne. He was appointed to the prebend of Stratton in 1983. In 1986 he was made Archdeacon of Sarum, surrendering his prebend and receiving instead the prebend of Ogborne. From 1987 to 1998 he also had responsibility for the parish of Stratford-sub-Castle. In 1998 he ceased to be Archdeacon of Sarum and became Archdeacon of Wilts but retained oversight of the Archdeaconry of Sarum, pending the outcome of a review.

SUBDECANI

Office:- At times when the dignity of Dean was held by foreigners, who were frequently non-resident, the office of Subdean became of special importance. It related primarily to the services in the cathedral, the role as Confessor which was abolished at the Reformation, and to the archidiaconal jurisdiction over the city and suburbs of Sarum on behalf of the Dean, who exercised episcopal jurisdiction over these areas. The Subdean was frequently not a canon nor the holder of a prebend and, in the absence of the Dean, did not necessarily assume his duties. He was provided with accommodation - No 16 The Close is known as the Subdeanery, kept residence until released in 1697, and preached in his turn in the cathedral. His archidiaconal functions and revenues were removed by various Acts of Parliament.

Stall: This being a return stall, there is no statuette, nor shield.

Holders of the office:-

William (c.1122-c.1139) probably also held a stall at Hereford.

John the Chanter (c.1180) was Precentor of Exeter in 1154. and was Subdean of Sarum c.1180. He was consecrated Bishop of Exeter in 1186 and died 1 June 1191.

Wimund (c.1193-c.1200).

Thomas of Chobham (c.1201-c.1233) was Subdean of Sarum from c.1201 to c.1233 and held the prebend of Bere & Cherminster in c.1226/7. He was the author of *Summa de Penitencia et Officiis Ecclesiasticis* and other works and was noted in 1228 as not to be elected bishop without a papal indulgence, perhaps due to some defect of birth.

Adam de Essebi (c.1236-c.1237) was Subdean of Sarum from c.1236 to c.1237 and Chancellor of Sarum from 1237/8 to 1240. He held the patronage of Bricklesworth in 1239 and it was at his petition that the prebend of Bricklesworth was permanently joined to the dignity of Chancellor in 1240. He had died by 16 June 1241.

Thomas of Ebbesbourne (c.1237-c.1240) held the prebends of Rotesfen in c.1226/7 and Grantham Australis from 1226/7 to c.1246, and was Subdean of Sarum from c.1237 to c.1240. He died or had resigned by 6 November 1246.

Geoffrey (c.1241).

Nicholas de Lakyng (c.1244-c.1257) was Subdean of Sarum from c.1244 to c.1257 and was also Warden of St Nicholas Hospital, Sarum from 1254. In a deed of 1259 he is styled Rector of Warminster.

John de Burton (c.1262-1269) was Subdean of Sarum from c.1262 to 1269 and Warden of de Vaux College, Sarum from September 1269 until his death. He was Precentor holding also the stall of Grantham Borealis from 1272 to c.1287. He had charge of the diocese during the vacancy in the see before the appointment of Walter Scammel, Bishop of Sarum 1284-1286. He had died by 16 November 1287.

William de Schireborn (c.1271-c.1284) held the prebend of Bishopstone between 1265 and 1284, held the vicarage of Chirton in 1346 and was Subdean of Sarum from c.1271 to c.1284.

Walter of Dorchester (c.1289-c.1291).

Thomas de Staunton (?-1309) was Subdean of Sarum from ? 1309 and had died by 1309.

Robert de Worth (1309-1320) was Subdean of Sarum from 1309 to 1320 and held the prebends of Alton Australis from 1309 to 1313, Durnford from 1313 to 1316 and Chisenbury & Chute from 1316 to 1349. He was a Canon Residentiary, resigning the office of Subdean on 25 November 1320 to become Rector of Bradford-on-Avon. During his time the office of Confessor was permanently added to that of Subdean.

Richard de Potesgrave (1321) was appointed Subdean of Sarum in 1321 but did not accept the office.

Robert de Bluntesdon (1321) held the prebend of Teynton Regis from 1314 and was still occupying it in 1320. He was Subdean of Sarum from April until September 1321. With the office he held the church of "Caundel Haddon". He was Rector of Berwick St John in 1331.

Thomas de Bocton (1321-c.1327) MA, was Subdean of Sarum from 1321 to c.1327 and held the prebends of Minor Pars Altaris from 1325 to 1327 and Warminster from 1327 to 1348. He died in 1348.

William de Lobenham (1329-1330) was Subdean of Sarum and held the prebend of Major Pars Altaris from 1329 to 1330, exchanging both office and prebend with his successor for the rectory of Norton, near Twycross in Lincolnshire.

Ralph de Querendon (1330-?) was Subdean of Sarum and a Canon Residentiary from 1330 to ? and again from 1341 to 1358. He held the prebend of Major Pars Altaris from 1330 to 1358, was Archdeacon of Wilts from 1331 to c.1333 and died in 1358.

William de Ayston (1333) claimed the prebend of Major Pars Altaris in 1332 but it was held by Ralph de Querendon. He claimed the office of Subdean in 1333 but the Chapter considered that he had intruded into it, contrary to statutes.

John de Wotton (1335-?) was Rector of Semley from 1339 to 1344 and Clerk to the Cathedral Chapter.

Nicholas de Wyke (1337-?).

Ralph de Querendon (1341-1358) became Subdean of Sarum for a second time from 1341 to 1358. King Edward III intervened on his behalf when John de Vyse was nominated in 1348 and he received papal confirmation in 1357.

John de Vyse (1348-c.1350) was nominated Subdean in 1348 and died in c.1350.

Nicholas de Mardefield (?-1362) who was appointed Subdean of Sarum by the Archbishop of Canterbury following a lapse, had died by 5 December 1362.

William de Glynton (1362-1396) was Subdean of Sarum from 1362 to 1396 and had died by 13 August 1396.

Edmund Cockerell (1396-1400) was Subdean of Sarum from 1396 to 1400 and held the prebend of Axford from 1399 to 1400. He had died by 16 October 1400 and was buried in the cathedral opposite the chapel of St Edmund.

John Wyther (1400-1407) was Rector of Devizes from 1398 and Subdean of Sarum from 1400 to 1407. He had died by 17 September 1407.

William Somerhill (1407-1410) was Subdean of Sarum from 1407 to 1410, exchanging the office with John Clere (or Smith) for the church of Bentworth, Hampshire.

John Clere (or Smith) (1410-1411) was Subdean of Sarum from 1410 to 1411, exchanging the office after a few months with John Hulling for the church of Limington, Somerset.

John Hulling (1411-1418) was Subdean of Sarum from 1411 to 1418, exchanging the office with John Pedewell for the church of West Dean.

John Pedewell (1418-1452) BCL, held the rectory of West Dean until exchanging it in 1418 for the Subdeanery of Sarum which he held from 1418 to 1452. He had resigned the office by 29 April 1452.

Henry Duke (or Barbour) (1452-1459) BCn&CL, was Subdean of Sarum from 1452 to 1459 and appears to have held the office of Master of St Nicholas Hospital, Sarum in 1457, exchanging the Subdeanery on 25 January 1459 with William Nessingwick for the church of Mottisfont, Hants.

William Nessingwick (1459-1476) was a Notary Public who held the prebends of Preston from 1450 to 1454, Stratton from 1454 to 1459 and Faringdon from 1459 to c.1486. He was Subdean of Sarum from 1459 to 1476, exchanging the office in 1476 with Giles Stanbridge for the church of Milston, which he held until 1487. A Canon Residentiary, he acted as locum tenens for the Dean on more than one occasion, presiding in chapter as locum tenens not Subdean and visiting the prebends in 1463.

Giles Stanbridge (1476-1480) became Vicar of Upavon in 1467, Rector of Donnington in 1468 and he held the living of Milston from 1458 to 1476. He exchanged the living with his predecessor for the office of Subdean of Sarum, which he held from 1476 to 1480. He died in his house in the Close on 20 June 1480.

Nicholas Godfrey (1480-1481) BCn&CL, was Subdean of Sarum from 1480 to 1481 but had resigned by 17 February 1481. He is believed to have attempted to establish for himself a jurisdiction independent of the Dean.

John Hall (1481-?) BCL, was Subdean of Sarum from 1481 to ?

William Branche (?-1486) BCn&CL, was Subdean of Sarum from ? to 1486.

Richard Kelsey (1486-1490) BCL, was Subdean of Sarum from 1486 to 1490, and had died before 23 March 1490.

Thomas Phillips (1490-1505) was Subdean of Sarum from 1490 to 1505 and held the prebend of Yatesbury from 1494 to 1513. He would seem also to have been Vicar of Bray and Rector of Winterslow from 1497 until his death, which was before 23 January 1513.

Thomas Greville (1505-1508) was Subdean of Sarum from 1505 to 1508 and had died by September 1508.

John Robinson (1509-1514) was Subdean of Sarum from 1509 until resigning before 15 September 1514.

Giles Hackluyt (1514-c.1559) who was Subdean of Sarum from 1514 to c.1559 appears to have been in disagreement with the cathedral authorities.

Robert Ellyott (1559-1561).

Thomas Curteys (1561-1564).

John James (1564-c.1577) BCL, held the prebend of Stratford from 1563 to ? and was Subdean of Sarum from 1564 to c.1577.

Thomas Dilworth (c.1577-1589) held the prebend of Fordington & Writhlington from 1572 to 1589 and was Subdean of Sarum from c.1577 to 1589. He was a Canon Residentiary from 1578 to 1589 and acted as locum tenens, by special commission from the Dean. He had died by 23 January 1589.

Nicholas Balgay (1589-1591) MA, held the prebends of Yetminster Prima from 1582 to 1584 and Netheravon from 1584 to 1591. He was Rector of Boscombe and Vicar of Idmiston from 1584 to 1591 and was Subdean of Sarum from 1589 to 1591.

Richard Hooker (1591-1595) MA, was a Fellow of Corpus Christi, Oxford and was described as the ablest living advocate of the Church of England. He was Master of the Temple from 1585 to 1591, Rector of Boscombe, where he wrote part of his *Ecclesiastical Polity*, Subdean of Sarum and held the prebend of Netheravon from 1591 to 1595. He died on 2 November 1600 and was buried in the chancel of Bishopbourne, Kent where he is commemorated.

Thomas Coldwell (1595-1599) MA, was Subdean of Sarum from 1595 to 1599 and held the prebend of Beminster Secunda from 1594 to 1619.

Giles Thornborough (1599-1637) was Rector of Odstock in 1582, a Canon Residentiary from ?-1637, Subdean of Sarum from 1599 to 1637, and held the prebend of Bedminster & Redcliffe from 1593 to 1637. He was Master of a Hospital (St John's?) near Wilton and Rector of Orcheston St Mary from 1588 until his death in 1637. He was buried at Orcheston St Mary.

Alexander Hyde (1637-1661) DCL, was a son of Sir Lawrence Hyde of Sarum and cousin of Lord Chancellor Clarendon. He was a Fellow of New College, Oxford and Subdean of Sarum from 1637 to 1661. He held the prebend of Grantham Australis from 1639 to 1665 and the Rectory of Wylye. He was Rector of Little Langford from 1634 and a Canon Residentiary from 1660 to 1665, being deprived during the Commonwealth. At the Restoration he obtained a canonry and afterwards the Deanery of Winchester, becoming Bishop of Sarum from 1665 until his death on 22 August 1667.

Richard Hyde (1661-1664) DCL, held the prebend of Warminster from 1660 to 1666, the office of Subdean of Sarum from 1661 to 1664 and the prebend of Grantham Borealis in 1666. He held a stall at Winchester in 1662 and died in 1666.

Robert Tutt (1664-1668) was Rector of Barford St Martin and Baverstock in 1662 and Subdean of Sarum from 1664 to 1668, being deprived as a non-juror.

Richard Kent (1668-1692) MA, held the prebends of Major Pars Altaris from 1664 to 1679 and Chisenbury & Chute from 1679 to 1692. He was Subdean of Sarum from 1668 to 1692 and died in 1692.

Thomas Smith (1692-1694) MA, held the prebend of Major Pars Altaris from 1691 to 1694, was Subdean of Sarum from 1692 to 1694 and was Rector of Sarum St Edmund.

Thomas Naish (1694-?) was Subdean of Sarum from 1694 to ? and Rector of Sarum St Edmund 1694-1705.

Charles Tarrant (1755-1759) MA, was Subdean of Sarum from 1755 to 1759 and Succentor of Sarum in 1759. He held the prebend of Yatesbury from 1759 to 1791 and died on 22 February 1791.

James Stirling Sambre (1759-1801) was Rector of Sarum St Edmund in 1754 and Subdean of Sarum from 1759 to 1801.

Thomas Stockwell (1801-1823) was Rector of Stratford Tony in 1788 and Subdean of Sarum from 1801 to 1823.

Matthew Marsh (1824-1840) DD, was Rector of Brinkworth from 1802 to 1840, of Winterslow in 1804 and Chancellor of the Diocese in 1819. He held the prebends of Beminster Prima from 1823 to 1824 and Chisenbury & Chute from 1824 to 1840. He was Subdean of Sarum from 1824 to 1840 and was a Canon Residentiary from 1826 to 1840. He died on 30 July 1840, was buried in the south choir aisle and is commemorated in the south east transept of the cathedral.

Daniel James Eyre (1846-1882) died in 1882.

Edward Slater Browne (1882-1887) MA, was Vicar of St Katharine's, Savernake Forest from 1863 to 1878 and Subdean from 1882 to 1887. He held the prebend of Yetminster Secunda from 1888 to 1897.

George Hugh Bourne (1887-1901) LLD, was Headmaster of St Andrew's School Chardstock from 1866 to 1874, Warden of St Edmund's College, Sarum from 1874 to 1885, Subdean of Sarum from 1887 to 1901 and Treasurer of Sarum from 1901 to 1925. He died on 1 December 1925 and left his property, St Edmund's College, to the diocese for religious purposes..

Robert Rowley Watts (1902-1911?) MA, was Vicar of Stourpaine from 1867, and Rector of Steepleton Iwerne from 1877, to 1902. He was Rural Dean of Pimperne from 1881 to 1903 and Subdean of Sarum from 1902 to 1911?.

Christopher Wordsworth (1911-1917) MA, was a brother of John Wordsworth, Bishop of Sarum 1885-1911, and was a Fellow and Dean of Peterhouse College, Cambridge. He was Rector of Steeple with Tyneham from 1889 to 1897. He held a stall at Lincoln from 1886 to 1911, was Rector of St Peter & St Paul, Marlborough, from 1897 to 1911 and Rural Dean of Marlborough from 1905 to 1911. He was Subdean of Sarum from 1911 to 1917, held the prebend of Ruscomb, from 1911 to 1937, was Librarian from 1913 to 1937 and was Chancellor of Sarum from 1917 to 1928. He was Master of St Nicholas Hospital, Sarum from 1895 to 1938. He was a well known author and editor and died on 30 January 1938.

Charles Myers (1919-1926) MA, held the prebend of Durnford from 1905 to 1926 and was a Canon Residentiary from 1915 to 1927. He was Subdean from 1919 to 1926 and Treasurer of Sarum from 1926 until resigning the dignity in 1937. He died in 1948.

Henry Richard William Farrer (1926-1933) MA, was Vicar of Broadwindsor with Blackdown & Drimpton from 1891 to 1895, Rector of Bridport from 1895 to 1916 and Rural Dean of Bridport from 1898 to 1916. He held the prebend of Gillingham Minor from 1911 to 1933. He was a Canon Residentiary from 1916, Diocesan Canon Missioner from 1918 and Subdean from 1926 until his death on 27 November 1933.

[The office was vacant from 1933 to 1938.]

Anthony Arnold Mayhew (1938-1939) MA, held a stall at St Albans from 1932 to 1935 and was a Canon Residentiary, holding the prebend of Coombe & Harnham, from 1935 to 1939. He was Pro-Prolocutor of the House of Clergy of the Convocation of Canterbury and a Proctor in Convocation from 1936 to 1939. He was Subdean of Sarum from 1938 until his death in 1939.

[The office was vacant from 1939 to 1942.]

Mark Rodolph Carpenter-Garnier (1942-1944) DD, was Bishop of Colombo, Ceylon from 1924 until resigning in 1938. He was Principal of St Boniface College, Warminster, from 1939 to 1942. He held the prebend of Slape from 1938 to 1944 and was Subdean from 1942 until resigning both his prebend and office in 1944. He died on 11 October 1969.

[The office was vacant from 1944 to 1956.]

Guy Vernon Smith (1956-1957) MC, MA, DD, was an Army Chaplain from 1914 to 1918, being awarded the MC in 1917. He was Archdeacon of Colombo from 1925 to 1929, Bishop Suffragan of Willesden from 1929 to 1940 and Bishop of Leicester from 1940 to 1953. He served as Subdean of Sarum from 1956 to 1957 and died on 11 June 1957.

[The office has remained vacant since 1957.]

POTTERN

Prebend:- The manor of Pottern in Wiltshire was part of the pre-Conquest Sherborne episcopal estates, which may have been transferred to the see of Ramsbury c.909. It was seized by King Stephen in 1139 but restored to the bishopric nine years later. The prebend was probably in existence by c.1150 and the tithes of Imber belonged to it c.1226. In the 13th century the name varied between Potterne, Lavington, Potterne & Lavington and Lavington & Potterne. In 1255, with the special sanction of Pope Alexander IV it was linked with the bishopric in the place of the prebend of Horton. The plate at the rear of the stall gives the name as 'Pottern'.

Stall: This being a return stall, there is no statuette, nor shield.

Psalter:- The part of the psalter allotted to the prebend is Psalms 6, 7 and 8

Holders of the prebend:-

Azo (c.1142-c.1148) may have been Archdeacon of Wilts c.1122/39 and brother of Roger of Ramsbury, his successor.. He was Dean of Sarum between c.1139 and c.1145, and held the prebend of Pottern from c.1142 to c.1148.

Adam (c.1200-1220) was Archdeacon of Dorset from c.1200 to c.1214 and Dean of Sarum from c.1215 to 1220, holding the prebend of Pottern with both these dignities. He died suddenly on 23 August 1220 at Sonning and was buried in the cathedral at Old Sarum.

Elias of Derham (c.1226-c.1239) is credited with being the designer architect of the cathedral of New Sarum and was the builder of the original house in the Close called Leadenhall. He was a great friend of Richard Poore, Bishop of Sarum 1217-1228, being referred to as the 'bishop's seneschal', or steward, and as the 'bishop's attorney' in the final concords of 1227 and 1228. He was a canon in September 1222, held the prebend of Pottern from c.1226 to c.1239 and was one of the custodians of the vacant bishopric in 1228, on Bishop Poore's translation to Durham. He also held stalls in Wells and Lincoln and died in 1245.

John de Offington (1245-c.1251) was a Proctor at the Roman Curia from 1242 to 1243, held the prebend of Pottern from 1245 to c.1251, was a papal chaplain by 1247 and died in 1251.

William of York (1254-1256) was Provost of Beverley and held stalls at Lincoln, London and York. He was a royal justice and is described as "a courtier from his childhood, and better versed in the laws of the realm, which he had chiefly studied, than in the laws of God." He appears to have held the office of Master of St Nicholas Hospital, Sarum, in 1246, he was Bishop of Sarum from 1247 to 1256 and held the prebends of Horton from 1247 to 1254 and Pottern from 1254 to 1256. He died on 31 January 1256 and was buried in the cathedral, on the 'south side of the chancel, near St John's altar under a gilt tomb'.

Giles of Bridport (1257-1262) was Archdeacon of Berks from 1237 to c.1255 and Dean of Wells in 1253. He appears to have held the office of Master of St Nicholas Hospital, Sarum from 1259 to 1260, was Bishop of Sarum from 1257 to 1262 and founded de Vaux College, Sarum in 1262. It was during his episcopate that the present cathedral was completed. He died on 13 December 1262 and was buried "in the south side of the choir in the chapel of St Mary Magdalen, under an arch that has a beautiful white marble tomb, wrought as a model of the outside of the tower".

Walter de la Wyle (1263-1271) was Succentor of Sarum from c.1248 to c.1262 and Bishop of Sarum from 1263 until his death on 3 January 1271. In 1269 he founded the College of St Edmund, Sarum for a provost and twelve secular canons, and appears to have held the office of Master of St Nicholas Hospital, Sarum in 1270. He was buried by the altar in the chapel of St Edmund in the cathedral.

Robert de Wickhampton (1271-1284) is thought to have held the prebend of Heytesbury from c.1257 and during his time as Dean of Sarum from 1258 to 1271. He is named as a canon of Sarum in a deed of 1245 concerning St Nicholas' Hospital, Sarum and his name also appears on the 1269 foundation-deed of the College of St Edmund, Sarum. He was described as a papal chaplain and in 1263 was granted dispensation to be promoted to bishop, notwithstanding his illegitimacy. He was Bishop of Sarum from 1274 to 1284 but he became blind and a coadjutor was appointed in 1282. He died 24 April 1284. He appears to have held the office of Master of St Nicholas Hospital, Sarum in 1271 and he may have been related to Thomas de Wickhampton, Archdeacon of Sarum c.1274-c.1307, who held the prebend of Bedwin.

Walter Scammel (1284-1286) was Archdeacon of Berks from c.1266 to 1274 and Clerk & Collector to King Henry III from 1267 to 1268. He was Treasurer of Sarum and held the prebend of Calne from 1267 to 1271 when, on becoming Dean from 1271 to 1284, he also held the prebend of Heytesbury. He was elected Bishop of Sarum in 1284, died on 20 September 1286 and was buried at the north side of the presbytery in the Cathedral. It is believed to have been in 1280 that the prebend of Heytesbury became permanently joined to the deanery.

Henry of Braunstone (1287-1288) was Archdeacon of Wilts between c.1275 and c.1279, and of Dorset between 1281 and c.1284. He held the prebend of Bere & Cherminster from c.1274 to 1284 and was Dean from 1284 to 1287. He held a stall at Exeter and was Bishop of Sarum, holding the office of Master of St Nicholas Hospital, Sarum from 1287 until his death on 11 February 1288. He was buried in the Lady Chapel of the Cathedral.

William de la Corner (1289-1291) had been elected Archbishop of Dublin in 1279 but the election was set aside. He was a papal chaplain, proctor and royal envoy who held the prebends of Teynton Regis from 1270 to 1274 and Highworth in 1284 and was Precentor of York and Archdeacon of Northumberland. He failed to be elected to the see of Sarum in May 1288 but was successful six months later. He was Bishop of Sarum from 1289 until his death probably on 10 October 1291 and appears to have held the office of Master of St Nicholas Hospital, Sarum in 1290. He was buried in the middle of the quire 'nearly under the eagle'.

Nicholas Longespee (1292-1297) was the fourth son of William Longespee, who in the right of his wife Ella, the foundress of Lacock Abbey, became Earl of Salisbury. He was Treasurer of Sarum from before 1275 to 1291 and was Bishop of Sarum from 1292 until his death on 18 May 1297. He was buried in the cathedral, with his heart at Lacock and his viscera at Ramsbury.

Simon de Gandavo (1297-1315) DTh, appears to have held a canonry at Sarum c.1295 and a stall at York. He was Archdeacon of Oxford in 1284 and Bishop of Sarum from 1297 until his death on 2 April 1315. He was one of the officiating bishops at the coronation of King Edward II and wrote to Pope Boniface VIII on the scandal of so many stalls in his church being given to foreigners. He was buried in the cathedral in the southern part of the choir.

Roger de Martival (1315-1330) DTh, was Archdeacon of Huntingdon in 1288 and of Leicester in 1295. In 1293 he became Chancellor of Oxford University and occupied the prebend of Netheravon from 1298 to 1315. He was Dean of Lincoln in 1310 and as Bishop of Sarum from 1315 to 1330 he completed the spire and drew up cathedral statutes in 1319. He died on 14 March 1330, was buried in the cathedral on the north side of the choir under a slab of marble inlaid with brass which has since been removed.

Robert de Wyville (1330-1375) held stalls at Lincoln c.1325, at Lichfield and in 1330 held the prebend of Minor Pars Altaris. He failed to be appointed to the see of Bath & Wells in 1329 but a year later became Bishop of Sarum until his death on 4 September 1375. A contemporary account reads "At the instance of Phillipa, Queen to King Edward III, the Pope preferred Rob. Wyville to the bishopric of Sarum. It is hard to say whether he were more dunce or dwarf, more unlearned or unhansome, insomuch that had the Pope ever *seen* him, as he no doubt *felt* him in his large fees, he would never have conferred the place on him." He recovered Sherborne Castle for the see and it was during his episcopate that the monastery at Edington was founded and the church consecrated. He was buried in the cathedral, in the choir but when the choir was repaved, his remains were removed to the north-east transept.

Ralph Erghum (1375-1388) DCn&CL, was Chancellor of Lancaster. He was the founder of the Hospital of St Michael, near Sarum and was Bishop of Sarum from 1375 to 1388. He was involved in a fierce controversy with the Chapter as to his right of visiting the prebends during a vacancy in the deanery. The matter was referred first to the Archbishop of Canterbury and subsequently to the Pope who decided against the bishop. In 1388 he was translated to Bath & Wells where he died in 1400, being buried in Wells Cathedral.

John de Waltham (1388-1395) held stalls at Lichfield in 1361 and Lincoln in 1382, was Subdean of York in 1381 and Archdeacon of Richmond in 1383. He would appear to have been Master of the Rolls and Keeper of the Privy Seal, and he held the prebend of Chisenbury & Chute in 1384, exchanging it with John de Freton for the prebend of Chalke in Wilton conventual church. He was Bishop of Sarum from 1388 to 1395; in 1390 resisting a metropolitan visitation of Archbishop Courtenay but having been excommunicated, reluctantly yielded. He became Lord Treasurer and also Lord Chancellor in 1391 and the following year, through the intervention of King Richard II, an agreement confirmed by Pope Boniface was arrived at between the Bishop and his Dean and Chapter as to the precise limits of episcopal jurisdiction. He died on 18 September 1395 and was buried by the King's desire in Westminster Abbey.

Richard Medford (1395-1407) received the prebend of Bere & Cherminster in 1386 by royal grant, he having exchanged the prebend with Thomas Stowe for the prebend of Highworth, but the Dean's locum refused to install him. Despite charges of fraudulent exchanges, the exchange between Thomas Stowe and Richard Medford was ratified in 1387, the latter assuming the prebend of Highworth. He held stalls at Windsor in 1381 and at York in 1386. He was imprisoned for some time at Bristol by the Parliament as a supporter of King Richard II. He was Archdeacon of Norfolk in 1385 and in 1390 was appointed by the Pope to the see of Chichester. He was translated to the see of Sarum in 1395 and was Bishop until his death on 3 May 1407. He was buried in St Margaret's Chapel in the south west transept of the cathedral and left a small sum to keep the tower and spire in repair, which indicates that they had been completed before his death.

Nicholas Bubwith (1407) held a stall at Lincoln, the prebend of Bere & Cherminster from 1402 to ? and was Archdeacon of Dorset from 1397 to 1399 and again from 1400 to 1406 when he became Bishop of London. He was translated to Sarum in 1407 and to Bath & Wells four months later. He was successively Master of the Rolls, Keeper of the Privy Seal and Treasurer of England. He died on 27 October 1424 and was buried at Wells.

Robert Hallum (1407-1417) DCnL, held the prebend of Bitton from 1395 to 1406. He was appointed Archdeacon of Canterbury in 1400 and Chancellor of Oxford University in 1403. The King objected to his nomination as Archbishop of York and he was made Bishop of Durham, being translated to Sarum where he was bishop from 1407 to 1417. He was created a Cardinal in 1411, but without title because he did not go to Rome to receive it. At the Council of Constance in 1414 he was leader of the 'English Nation', representatives of the Anglican Church earnestly desiring a thorough reformation of the whole Church and asserting the supremacy of the General Council over the Pope. His death at Gotlieb Castle on 4 September 1417 was regarded as fatal to the cause of many really effective reforms to the Church.

John Chaundeler (1417-1426) held a stall at Lincoln in 1405 and the prebend of Netherbury in Ecclesia from ? to 1394, exchanging it with Henry Harburgh for the dignity of Treasurer of Sarum which he held until 1404. He was Dean of Sarum from 1404 to 1417 and Bishop of Sarum from 1417 until his death on 16 July 1426.

Robert Neville (1427-1438) MA, was a nephew of King Henry IV; his mother being Joan of Lancaster wife of Ralph Neville, Earl of Westmoreland. He held a stall at York and in 1421, at the age of seventeen was Provost of Beverley. He was promoted to the see of Sarum in 1427 by a bull of Pope Martin V, with dispensation on account of his age. In 1438 he was translated to Durham and, dying on 9 July 1457, was buried in Durham cathedral.

William Aiscough (1438-1450) DTh, was secretary and Confessor to King Henry VI. He was Bishop of Sarum from 1438 until his murder at Edington on 29 June 1450, during Jack Cade's Rebellion. Although his will directed that he be buried in the cathedral, his mutilated remains were interred in the religious house of Bonhommes at Edington.

Richard Beauchamp (1450-1481) DCnL was a brother of William Beauchamp, Lord St Amand, and was Archdeacon of Suffolk. In 1448 he was appointed to the see of Hereford, being translated to Sarum in 1450. In 1477 he became also Dean of Windsor, rebuilding the collegiate chapel of St George and receiving the office of Chancellor of the Order of the Garter for him and his successors. Whilst at Sarum he saw the canonisation of St Osmund, he built onto the cathedral the strainer arches and also the Beauchamp chapel, later to be removed, in which he was buried following his death on 18 October 1481.

Lionel Woodville (1482-1484) LicCnL, was brother-in-law to King Edward IV, being the son of Richard, Earl Rivers, whose daughter Elizabeth, co-foundress with Margaret of Anjou of Queens' College, Cambridge, was married to the King. He held a stall at Lincoln in 1465, the prebends of Coombe & Harnham from 1467 to 1478 and Bere & Cherminster from 1478 to 1482. He was also Archdeacon of Oxford and Dean of Exeter, becoming Bishop of Sarum from 1482 to 1484. His death in June 1484 was said to have been hastened by grief at the downfall of his family on the accession of King Richard II, and the execution at Salisbury of Henry Stafford, Duke of Buckingham, his brother-in-law. He was buried in the cathedral.

Thomas Langton (1485-1493) BTh, held a stall at Wells in 1478 and was later Provost of Queen's College, Oxford. He was translated from the see of St David's to that of Sarum in 1485 but it appears that on the accession of King Henry VII, he was imprisoned and deprived of the revenues of the see for a period of less than a month. He was translated to the see of Winchester in 1493 and was elected in 1501 to be Archbishop of Canterbury but died on 27 January, five days afterwards. He was buried in Winchester cathedral.

John Blyth (1493-1499) DCL, was Archdeacon of Stow in 1477 and of Huntingdon in 1478. He held stalls at Lincoln in 1481 and at York in 1484, was Archdeacon of Richmond in 1488 and Master of the Rolls in 1492. His brother, Geoffrey Blyth, was Bishop of Lichfield in 1503 and his uncle, Thomas Rotherham, was Archbishop of York in 1480. He was Bishop of Sarum from 1493 until his death in August 1499. He was buried behind the high altar, beneath the confessional chair and was commonly called the thwart-over bishop, from his body lying north and south, perhaps to allow his body to be under the chair.

Henry Deane (1500-1501) was a member of the order of Augustinian Canons, Prior of Llanthony, near Gloucester, and Chancellor of Ireland in 1499. For his services to King Henry VII, especially with regard to the rebellion by Perkin Warbeck, he was made Bishop of Bangor while also holding the Priory. In 1500 he became Bishop of Sarum, being advanced to the see of Canterbury in May 1501 and appointed Papal Legat. He died of the plague at Lambeth on 15 February 1503 and was buried at Canterbury.

Edmund Audley (1502-1524) DTh, was a member of the family of Tuchet, Barons Audley and Earls of Castlehaven who owned a house, now Church House in Crane Street, Salisbury in 1640. He held a stall at Hereford in 1464, before he was of age for ordination, and then held stalls at Lincoln and Windsor in 1472, Lichfield in 1474, Wells in 1475, London in 1476 and York in 1478. From 1473 to 1475 he held the prebend of Preston, in 1475 he was Archdeacon of the East Riding and while holding that dignity, was appointed to the rectory of Berwick St John. In 1479 he was Archdeacon of Essex and, in 1480, became Bishop of Rochester, only then giving up the remainder of his prebends. He became Bishop of Hereford in 1492 and was translated to Sarum in 1502. He died at Ramsbury on 23 August 1524 and was buried in his chantry chapel in the cathedral.

Laurence Campeggio (1524-1534) was married and had a son who became a cardinal. On the death of his wife he took holy Orders and was made Bishop of Feltre in 1512, of Bologna in 1523, of Huesca in 1530 and of Parenzo in 1533. He was created Cardinal-Priest of St Thomas in Parione in 1518, of St Anastasia in 1519 and of St Maria trans-Tiberim in 1528. He succeeded to the see of Sarum by papal bull in 1524, being enthroned by proxy, and in 1528 was created Papal Legat for England. He was one of the delegates appointed by the Pope to hear the question of the divorce of Henry VIII from Catherine of Aragon and appears in Shakespeare's play King Henry VIII as 'Cardinal Campeius'. In March 1534 he and the Bishop of Worcester were deprived of their sees by Act of Parliament, for non-residence but Campeggio was considered by Rome to be Bishop of Sarum until his death in August 1539. He became Cardinal-Bishop of St Albano in 1534, of Sabina in 1537 and of Praeneste in 1538. He died at the Roman Court on 15 January 1539. For some time after this, an independent succession was maintained by the Pope for both Sarum and Worcester.

Nicholas Shaxton (1535-1539) DTh, was a benefactor of Gonville Hall, Cambridge. He was Treasurer of Sarum from 1533 to 1535 and about the same time held the rectory of Fugglestone with Bemerton. He was Bishop of Sarum from 1535 until resigning in 1539. He had been silenced and afterwards condemned with Latimer but recanted and preached a sermon proclaiming his apostacy when Ann Askew was burnt. He afterwards acted as a bishop suffragan in Ely diocese.

John Salcot (or Capon) (1539-1557) DD, was Abbot of St Benet's, Hulme, Norfolk. He was an active supporter of King Henry VIII in respect of his divorce from Catherine of Aragon, becoming Abbot of Hyde, near Winchester in 1530 and Bishop of Bangor in 1534, whilst still holding the abbey. As King's Commissioner, he sent several people to the stake but he became a Protestant under King Edward VI, changing again under Queen Mary and then sitting as a judge on the trial of Bishop Hooper and John Rogers. He was Bishop of Sarum from 1539 to 1557. King Henry VIII described him as "a great clerk and singularly learned in divinity", and he was no doubt a very able but unscrupulous man, both in the constant change in his opinions and his administration of the estates of the see, impoverishing his bishopric but enriching himself. He died on 24 August 1542 and was buried in the south choir of the cathedral behind the bishop's throne.

John Jewel (1559-1571) BD, was a Fellow of Corpus Christi College, Oxford, from which he was expelled chiefly for his relationship with Peter Martyr, who had been Regius Professor of Divinity. He was Archdeacon of Chichester in 1551 but went to Germany to escape the troubles. He returned in 1557, becoming Bishop of Sarum from 1559 to 1571. He was a friend and patron of Richard Hooker, who regarded him as the "worthiest divine that Christendom had had for the space of some hundreds of years." His best known work was *Apology for the Church of England*. He quarrelled with Dr Thomas Harding, Treasurer of Sarum, over his right to hold a visitation of the Cathedral and died on 23 September 1571, in his 50th year. He was buried in the cathedral before the bishop's throne in the quire.

Edmund Gest (1571-1577) BD, was a Fellow and Vice Provost of King's College, Cambridge, who was Archdeacon of Canterbury. He was made Bishop of Rochester in 1560 and Almoner to the Queen. He had been one of the Protestant disputants along with Bishop Jewel in 1559 and was a prolific author, bequeathing his whole library to the cathedral library. He was Bishop of Sarum from 1571 until his death on 28 February 1577 at the age of 63. He was buried in the centre of the choir between Bishops Jewel and Wyvil. The gravestone was later moved to the north-eastern transept.

John Piers (1577-1589) DD, became Dean of Chester in 1567 and Dean of Christ Church, Oxford. He was Dean of Sarum from 1571 to 1576, becoming a Canon Residentiary in 1572. He was appointed Almoner to Queen Elizabeth I and Bishop of Rochester and in the latter capacity preached before the Queen on the defeat of the Spanish Armada. By royal licence he was permitted to hold the dignity of Dean of Sarum for life but resigned it upon his translation to the see of Sarum. He was Bishop of Sarum from 1577 until becoming Archbishop of York in 1589. He died on 28 September 1594 and was buried in York Minster

John Coldwell (1591-1596) MD, was educated as a physician. He was a domestic chaplain to Archbishop Parker, becoming Dean of Rochester in 1589. He was the first married Bishop of Sarum, serving from 1591 until his death on 14 October 1596. He was buried in the choir of the cathedral beside Bishop Jewel and in the same grave as Bishop Wyvil. He is believed to have wasted the revenues of the see, virtually disposing of the Sherborne estates through the intrigues of Sir Walter Raleigh and through the pressure of Queen Elizabeth I and her agents. He died a very poor man.

Henry Cotton (1598-1615) DD, appears to have been a younger son of Sir Henry Cotton, a Privy Councillor to King Edward VI. He held a stall at Windsor in 1586 and was a chaplain to Queen Elizabeth I, whose godson he was. She is quoted as saying that "she had blessed many godsons but now this godson should bless her." He was Bishop of Sarum from 1598 until his death on 7 May 1615. He left a large family - there had been nineteen children in all to his one wife, aptly named Patience - and was buried in the cathedral.

Robert Abbot (1615-1618) DD, was the elder brother of George Abbot, Archbishop of Canterbury. He was a Fellow of Balliol College, Oxford in 1581 and Master in 1609. He held a stall at Southwell in 1610 and became Regius Professor of Divinity at Oxford in 1612. He was a distinguished theologian, a treatise *De Potestate Regia* inducing King James I to appoint him Bishop of Sarum in 1615. He died on 2 March 1618, at the early age of 58, and was buried in the cathedral opposite the bishop's throne.

Martin Fotherby (1618-1620) DD, was a nephew of John Whitgift, Archbishop of Canterbury, to whom he was chaplain and who gave him a stall at Canterbury where his brother was Dean. He was a chaplain to King James I and is said to have owed his advancement to be Bishop of Sarum in 1618, to the Duke of Buckingham. He died on 11 March 1620 at the age of 60 and was buried in London.

Robert Tounson (1620-1621) DD, was a Fellow of Queens' College, Cambridge. He became Chaplain to King James I in 1617 and soon afterwards Dean of Westminster. In the latter capacity he was present at the execution of Sir Walter Raleigh in Palace Yard. He was Bishop of Sarum for ten months, between 1620 and his death on 15 May 1621, dying of a fever contracted by 'unseasonable sitting up to study', when preparing at short notice to preach before Parliament. He left a widow and fifteen children and was buried in Westminster Abbey.

John Davenant (1621-1641) DD, was a Fellow of Queens' College, Cambridge in 1597 and President in 1614. In 1609 he was appointed the Lady Margaret Professor of Divinity. He was a benefactor of his college, leaving it the advowsons of the livings of Great Cheverell and Newton Tony. In 1619 he was one of the delegates to the Synod of Dort and in 1621 he became Bishop of Sarum. He was chosen for the see by King James I to enable him to befriend the widow and fifteen children left by Bishop Tounson, his predecessor and brother in law. In 1631 he incurred the displeasure of the Court through a sermon showing Calvinistic views and was summoned before the Privy Council. He died on 16 April 1641 and was buried in the south aisle of the choir of the cathedral.

Brian Duppa (1641-1660) DD, was a Fellow of All Souls, Oxford. In 1629 he became Dean of Christ Church, Oxford, and from 1634 to 1638 was Chancellor of Sarum. In about 1636 he became tutor to Prince Charles, later King Charles II, and in 1638 Bishop of Chichester. He was translated to the see of Sarum in 1641 but soon after was deprived of the revenues of the see. A firm friend of King Charles I, he spent much time with him during his imprisonment and after his execution lived for a period in retirement. At the Restoration, in 1660, he was made Lord Almoner and Bishop of Winchester. He died on 26 March 1662 and was buried in Westminster Abbey. Isaak Walton described him as one of "those men in whom there was such a commixture of general learning, of natural eloquence and Christian humility that they deserve a commemoration by a pen equal to their own, which none have exceeded."

Humphrey Henchman (1660-1663) DD, was a Fellow of Clare Hall, Cambridge. He was a son-in-law of Robert Tounson, Bishop of Sarum 1620-1621, becoming Precentor from 1623 to 1660 and Canon Residentiary from 1633 to 1660, although dismissed during the Commonwealth, and holding in succession the prebends of Yatesbury from 1623 to 1629, Grantham Australis from 1629 to 1639 and Teynton Regis from 1639 to 1660. He helped King Charles II to escape after the battle of Worcester; personally escorting him to Heale House and meeting him again at Stonehenge. He was Bishop of Sarum from 1660 until 1663 when he became Bishop of London and Lord Almoner. He died on 7 October 1675 at the age of 83 and was buried at Fulham.

John Earles (1663-1665) DD, was a Fellow of Merton College, Oxford. He was chaplain to Philip, Earl of Pembroke and held the living of Bishopstone from 1639 until resigning in 1662, although deprived and restored in 1660. He was tutor to Prince Charles, was a Canon Residentiary from 1660 to 1662 and was Chancellor of Sarum from 1644 to 1662, although deprived of the revenues during the Commonwealth. At the Restoration he became Dean of Westminster and in 1662 Bishop of Worcester. A year later he was translated to the see of Sarum, dying on 17 November 1665 at Oxford, where he was buried in the chapel of Merton College. Isaak Walton said of him, "None since the death of Mr Hooker had been blessed with more innocent wisdom, more sanctified learning or more pious, peaceable, and primitive temper."

Alexander Hyde (1665-1667) DCL, was a son of Sir Lawrence Hyde of Sarum and cousin of Lord Chancellor Clarendon. He was a Fellow of New College, Oxford and Subdean of Sarum from 1637 to 1661. He held the prebend of Grantham Australis from 1639 to 1665 and the Rectory of Wylye. He was Rector of Little Langford from 1634 and a Canon Residentiary from 1660 to 1665, being deprived during the Commonwealth. At the Restoration he obtained a canonry and afterwards the Deanery of Winchester, becoming Bishop of Sarum from 1665 until his death on 22 August 1667.

Seth Ward (1667-1689) DD, was appointed Savilian Professor of Astronomy at Oxford, ultimately becoming President of Trinity College, Oxford. He first became Precentor and then Dean of Exeter, and in 1667 Bishop of Exeter becoming involved in repairs to the cathedral. In the same year he was translated to the see of Sarum where he reordered the choir, repaired the Palace, which had been damaged during the Commonwealth, and founded the Matrons' College in the Close. He also regained for Bishops of Sarum the Chancellorship of the Order of the Garter after a separation of 150 years. Towards the end of his time at Sarum he was involved with the Dean, Thomas Pierce, in a dispute over his jurisdiction in the cathedral and his right to the patronage of the prebends. He was a founder of the Royal Society, died at Knightsbridge on 6 January 1689 and was buried in the south east transept of the cathedral .

Gilbert Burnet (1689-1715) DD, became Divinity Professor at Glasgow in 1669. He declined the offer of a Scottish bishopric and the living of St Giles, Cripplegate, Edinburgh and became in 1675 Preacher at the Rolls and Lecturer at St Clements. His political opinions and writings brought him into disgrace and, having been deprived of his appointments, he went at the invitation of the Prince of Orange to the Hague. He returned with King William and Queen Mary II and was made Bishop of Sarum in 1689, although Archbishop Sancroft declined to consecrate him personally. He was a historian of his times, an advocate of tolerance, a chairman of committee of the Bill of Rights and an organiser of Queen Ann's Bounty. He was an earnest and diligent diocesan bishop, laying down and strictly enforcing the duties of the clergy. He died on 17 March 1715 and was buried in London.

William Talbot (1715-1721) DD, was born in 1659 in Stourton Castle, Staffordshire becoming Dean of Worcester through the influence of his kinsman Charles, Earl of Shrewsbury. In 1699 he became Bishop of Oxford while still holding the deanery and on the accession of King George I was made Dean of the Chapels Royal. He was Bishop of Sarum from 1715 to 1721 when he was translated to Durham. He died in 1730 and was buried in London.

Richard Willis (1721-1723) DD, was a Fellow of All Souls, Oxford. In 1659 he held a stall at Westminster and in 1701 became Dean of Lincoln. He was made Bishop of Gloucester in 1714 while still holding his deanery and was also Clerk of the Closet and ultimately Lord Almoner. He became Bishop of Sarum in 1721 but was translated to the see of Winchester in 1723. He died at the age of 71 and was buried in Winchester cathedral.

Benjamin Hoadly (1723-1734) DD, was a Fellow of Catherine Hall, Cambridge. He was consecrated Bishop of Bangor in 1716, shortly afterwards preaching at the Chapel Royal on the purely spiritual nature of Christ's kingdom, which gave rise to what was called the 'Bangorian Controversy'. This ultimately caused him to be censured by Convocation. The discussion led to such bitterness that Convocation was virtually suspended for 150 years. He was translated to the see of Hereford in 1721, was Bishop of Sarum from 1723 to 1734, becoming Bishop of Winchester in 1734. He died in 1761 and was buried in Winchester cathedral.

Thomas Sherlock (1734-1748) DD, was the son of Dr W Sherlock, Master of the Temple and Dean of St Paul's. He was educated at Catherine Hall, Cambridge later becoming Master. In 1704 he became himself, at the age of 26, Master of the Temple. He was made Dean of Chichester in 1716, was consecrated Bishop of Bangor in 1728 and was Bishop of Sarum from 1734 to 1748. At both Bangor and Sarum he was a powerful opponent of the views of his predecessor, Bishop Hoadly. He was appointed Lord Almoner in 1743 and is believed to have been depicted by Hogarth in his picture of a bishop receiving from the Devil a mitre filled with coins in exchange for a crucifix. He became Bishop of London in 1749, having previously declined the see of Canterbury and dying in 1761 at the age of 84, was buried in London.

John Gilbert (1748-1757) DCL, held a stall at and was appointed Subdean of Exeter. Two years later he held a stall at Christ Church, Oxford and was appointed Dean of Exeter, being consecrated Bishop of Llandaff in 1740. He was Bishop of Sarum from 1748 to 1757 and early in his time there was in dispute with the Mayor and Corporation respecting the separate jurisdiction of the Cathedral and City authorities. He was promoted to be Archbishop of York in 1757.

John Thomas (1757-1761) DD, was a Fellow of All Souls, Oxford in 1733 and Preceptor to Prince George, afterwards King George III. A Canon Residentiary of St Paul's in 1742 and Chaplain in Ordinary to King George II, he was consecrated Bishop of Peterborough in 1746 and became Bishop of Sarum from 1757 to 1761. He was translated to the see of Winchester in 1761, dying and being buried there in 1781.

The Hon Robert Hay Drummond (1761) DD, was a son of the 7th Earl of Kinnoul. He held a stall at Westminster in 1743 and was consecrated Bishop of St Asaph in 1748. He was Bishop of Sarum from June until September 1761 when he was promoted to be Archbishop of York. He became Lord High Almoner and preached the sermon at the coronation of King George III. He died and was buried at Bishopthorpe, York in 1766.

John Thomas (1761-1766) DD, became Dean of Peterborough in 1740 and held stalls at Westminster and St Paul's in 1742. He was elected Bishop of St Asaph in 1743 but was consecrated to be Bishop of Lincoln in the following year. He became Bishop of Sarum at the age of 80 in 1761, serving until his death on 19 July 1766. He was buried in the south aisle of the cathedral.

John Hume (1766-1782) DD, held a stall at Westminster in 1742, before becoming Bishop of Bristol in 1756 and Bishop of Oxford and Dean of St Paul's in 1758. He was Bishop of Sarum from 1766 until his death on 26 June 1782. He was buried in the south aisle of the cathedral beside his predecessor.

The Hon Shute Barrington (1782-1791) DCL, was the son of the 1st Viscount Barrington. He held stalls at Christ Church, Oxford in 1761 and at St Paul's in 1768, before being consecrated Bishop of Llandaff in 1769. He held a stall at Windsor in 1777 and was Bishop of Sarum from 1782 until his translation to Durham in 1791. He died in 1826.

John Douglas (1791-1807) DD, was tutor to Lord Pulteney, son of the Earl of Bath. He was Chaplain to the 3rd Foot Guards (Scots Guards) at Fontenoy in 1745 and was the author of *'The Criterion (or rules by which true may be distinguished from spurious miracles)'* in 1754. He held a stall at Windsor in 1762 and St Paul's in 1776, before becoming Bishop of Carlisle in 1787 and Dean of Windsor in 1788. He was Bishop of Sarum from 1791 until his death on 18 May 1807 at Windsor, where he was buried.

John Fisher (1807-1825) DD, became a Fellow of St John's College, Cambridge in 1773. A few years later he was appointed a Preceptor to Prince Edward, afterwards Duke of Kent, and in 1781 he became a Chaplain in Ordinary to King George III and Deputy Clerk of the Closet. In 1786 he held a stall at Windsor and in 1803 was consecrated as Bishop of Exeter, becoming a Preceptor to Princess Charlotte, only daughter of the Prince of Wales. He was Bishop of Sarum from 1807 until his death on 8 May 1825.

Thomas Burgess (1825-1837) DD, was a Fellow of Corpus Christi College, Oxford who held the prebend of Wilsford & Woodford from 1787 to 1803 and also a stall at Durham. He became Bishop of St David's in 1803, establishing Lampeter College, and was Bishop of Sarum from 1825 to 1837 during which time he formed and endowed the Church Union Society. He died on 19 February 1837.

Edward Denison (1837-1854) MA, was a brother of the Speaker of the House of Commons who later became Viscount Ossington, a Fellow of Merton College, Oxford and Bishop of Sarum from 1837 to 1854. He was said to have laid the foundations of more than one of those diocesan efforts which, as regards religious education and the general progress of the church, have resulted in so much good. He died on 6 March 1854 and was buried in the cathedral cloisters.

Walter Kerr Hamilton (1854-1869) DD, became a Fellow of Merton College, Oxford in 1833 and the following year he held a stall at Wells. He became a Canon Residentiary, with the house of Leadenhall, and Treasurer of Sarum from 1841 to 1843 and Precentor of Sarum from 1843 to 1854, also holding the prebend of Torleton from 1843 to 1854. He was Bishop of Sarum from 1854 until his death on 1 August 1869. Whilst bishop, he founded Salisbury Theological College and contributed to the debate on cathedral reform. He was buried in the cathedral cloisters beside his predecessor Edward Denison, Bishop of Sarum 1837-1854.

George Moberly (1869-1885) DCL, was a Fellow of Balliol College, Oxford and Headmaster of Winchester College from 1835 until 1866, when he was elected a Fellow of Winchester. He held a stall at Chester in 1868, becoming Bishop of Sarum in 1869; the first high church appointment for many years. His episcopate was marked by the establishment of a Church Synod composed of laity as well as clergy. For sometime before his death on 6 July 1885 his faculties had been decaying and his episcopal duties were discharged by James Butler Knill Kelly, formerly Bishop of Newfoundland. He was buried by the east end of the south choir aisle in the cathedral.

John Wordsworth (1885-1911) DD, DCL, scholar and theologian, was a son of Christopher Wordsworth afterwards Bishop of Lincoln and was the historian of the Lutheran Church of Sweden. He was a Fellow of Brasenose College, Oxford in 1867 and later a Fellow of Oriel College. He held stalls at Lincoln in 1870 and Rochester from 1883 to 1885. He was Bishop of Sarum from 1885 to 1911, founded the Bishop's School, later Bishop Wordsworth's School, Sarum, was a Fellow of the British Academy in 1904 and died on 16 August 1911.

Frederic Edward Ridgeway (1911-1921) MA, became Bishop Suffragan of Kensington in 1901, holding a stall at St Paul's from 1901 to 1903. He was Bishop of Sarum from 1911 until his death on 4 May 1921.

St Clair George Alfred Donaldson (1921-1935) DD, DCL, was Resident Chaplain to the Archbishop of Canterbury from 1888 to 1891. He was Bishop of Brisbane in 1904, becoming Archbishop on the formation of the Province of Queensland, from 1905 to 1921. He was Bishop of Sarum from 1921 until his death on 7 December 1935.

Ernest Neville Lovett (1936-1946) CBE, DD, was Rector of Bishop's Caundle from 1895 to 1898, held a stall at Winchester from 1916 to 1927 and was a Chaplain to King George V. He was Archdeacon of Portsmouth from 1924 to 1927 and was the first Bishop of Portsmouth, serving from 1927 to 1936. He was translated to the see of Sarum in 1936 at the age of 68 and retired on 30 April 1946. He was a man of strong sense of humour, charm and eloquence who communicated well with young people. He died on 8 September 1951

Geoffrey Charles Lester Lunt (1946-1948) MC, DD, was a Chaplain to the Forces during the First World War and was Archdeacon of Egypt and Subdean of Cairo from 1926 to 1928. He held a stall at Portsmouth and was a Proctor in Convocation from 1931 to 1934. He was Bishop of Ripon from 1935 to 1946 when he was translated to the see of Sarum, serving until his death on 17 December 1948.

William Louis Anderson (1949-1963) DSC, DD, served as a Squadron Sergeant Major in the 1st King Edward's Horse from 1914 to 1916 when he was commissioned into the Royal Naval Air Service, being awarded the DSC in 1917. In 1918 he became a Captain in the Royal Air Force. He was ordained in 1920, serving as a Naval Chaplain from 1922 to 1927. He was appointed Bishop Suffragan and Archdeacon of Croydon in 1937 and then Bishop of Portsmouth in 1942. He was Bishop of Sarum from 1949 until his retirement in 1963. He was a beloved Father in God to his clergy and people; he never took kindly to diocesan administration and finance but was an artist of no mean distinction. He died on 5 March 1972.

Joseph Edward Fison (1963-1972) MA, was an Army Chaplain during the Second World War, a Canon Residentiary at Rochester from 1945 to 1952, a Canon Residentiary and Subdean of Truro from 1952 to 1959, Vicar of Great St Mary's, Cambridge from 1959 to 1963 and he held a stall at Ely from 1961 to 1963. He was Bishop of Sarum from 1963 until his death on 2 July 1972. He was a man who fused within his person the prophet, the mystic, the evangelical and the catholic. He was an unforgetable communicator, a most gifted teacher and a man deeply beloved.

George Edmund Reindorp (1973-1981) DD, was a RNVR Chaplain from 1938 to 1946. He was Provost of Southwark from 1957 to 1961 and then Bishop of Guildford from 1961 to 1973. He was translated to Sarum in 1973 and retired in 1981. He was an outstanding and versatile bishop with easy eloquence and a gift for administration and communication; of genuine sincerity and unswerving dedication to his vocation and an energy of such driving force that some of those who served under him did not find life easy. The rewards though were considerable. He was an Assistant Bishop of London from 1982 until his death on 20 April 1990. He was buried in Guildford cathedral.

John Austin Baker (1982-1993) MA, MLitt, DD, was a Lecturer in Old Testament, Cuddesdon Theological College from 1954 to 1957, Fellow, Chaplain and Lecturer in Divinity, Corpus Christi College and lecturer in Divinity, Brasenose and Lincoln Colleges, Oxford from 1959 to 1973. He was Hebrew Lecturer, Exeter College, Oxford from 1969 to 1973, held a stall at Westminster from 1973 to 1982, was Treasurer from 1974 to 1978, Subdean and Lector Theologiæ from 1978 to 1982 and Rector of St Margaret's Westminster and Speaker's Chaplain from 1978 to 1982. He was a member and chairman of many General Synod boards and committees including chairman of the Doctrine Commission. He was author of *The Foolishness of God* (1970) and of other publications and was Bishop of Salisbury from 1982 to 1993.

David Staffurth Stancliffe (1993-) MA, DLitt, was Director of Ordinands and Canon Residentiary of Portsmouth from 1977 to 1982, and Provost of Portsmouth from 1982 until 1993, during which time he completed the transformation of the parish church of St Thomas á Becket into the cathedral. He became Bishop of Sarum and chairman of the Liturgical Commission in 1993.

ILFRACOMBE
(olim Bere & Cherminster)

Prebend:- The church of Bere and the manor of Cherminster, both in Dorset, were part of the pre-Conquest episcopal estates of Sherborne. Both these were given to the canons by Osmund, Bishop of Sarum 1078-1099, and the prebend, known as the golden prebend, was probably in existence by c.1150.

In 1545, the prebend of Bere & Cherminster was dissolved and Ilfracombe substituted by Act of Parliament as a result of an exchange between John Salcot, Bishop of Sarum 1539-1557, and Sir Thomas Wriothesley. The exchange to take place at the next vacancy of Ilfracombe church. Sir Thomas Wriothesley subsequently released the prebendal estates to the Crown.

Canopy statuette and shield:- **Thomas Burgess** DD, was a Fellow of Corpus Christi College, Oxford, who held the prebend of Wilsford & Woodford from 1787 to 1803 and also a stall at Durham. He became Bishop of St David's in 1803, establishing Lampeter College, and Bishop of Sarum from 1825 to 1837 during which time he formed and endowed the Church Union Society. He died on 19 February 1837. (Fig 1.)

Blazon:- Or on a fess gules between in chief three mascles azure and in base a fret of the second five fusils argent the whole within a bordure of the fourth entoyre of bezants (a mullet for difference). [On a gold shield, at the top three blue diamonds with centre holes, at the bottom a red diamond with a hole in it, interlaced with two red strips. Between them five silver elongated diamonds on a red background. The whole shield surrounded by a red border with gold discs on it. (There should also be a pierced five pointed star to indicate a third son)]

Psalter:- The part of the psalter allotted to the prebend is Psalms 15, 16 and 17

Holders of the prebend of Bere & Cherminster:-

Richard Poore (1197-1215) was a brother of Herbert Poore, Bishop of Sarum 1194-1217. He was Dean of Sarum, holding the prebend of Bere & Cherminster from 1197 to 1215 and played a large part in the founding of the present cathedral. He became Bishop of Chichester in 1215 and Bishop of Sarum from 1217 to 1228, holding the prebend of Major Pars Altaris from 1217 to 1219, when it was exchanged for the prebend of Horton. He became Bishop of Durham in 1228.

Thomas of Chobham (c.1226/7) was Subdean of Sarum from c.1201 to c.1233 and held the prebend of Bere & Cherminster in c.1226/7. He was the author of *Summa de Penitencia et Officiis Ecclesiasticis* and was noted in 1228 as not to be elected bishop without a papal indulgence, perhaps due to some defect of birth.

Robert de Lexington (c.1238-?) held the prebend of Bedminster & Redcliffe from c.1227 to c.1238 although it was claimed at intervals by John Romeyn, Subdean of York, on the grounds that the Pope had nominated him for the next vacant prebend. He then held the prebend of Bere & Cherminster from c.1238 to ? and probably also held a stall at Wells.

Ralph of York (?-1263) held the prebend of Bere & Cherminster from ? until his death by 11 January 1263.

Walter of Merton (1263-c.1271) held the prebends of Yatesbury from 1262 to 1263 and Bere & Cherminster from 1263 to c.1271. He was also Archdeacon of Bath and held stalls at Exeter, Lincoln and London. He became Chancellor of England and Bishop of Rochester in 1274 and founded Merton College, Oxford.

Henry of Braunstone (c.1274-1284) was Archdeacon of Wilts between c.1275 and c.1279, and of Dorset between 1281 and c.1284. He held the prebend of Bere & Cherminster from c.1274 to 1284 and was Dean from 1284 to 1287. He held a stall at Exeter and was Bishop of Sarum, holding the office of Master of St Nicholas Hospital, Sarum from 1287 until his death on 11 February 1288. He was buried in the Lady Chapel of the Cathedral.

George of Saluzzo (c.1320-1330) disputed the prebend of Horton with William of Abingdon, his predecessor as Precentor of Sarum, a dignity he held from 1299 to 1319. In 1319 he exchanged the dignity for the Archdeaconry of Buckingham with his brother, Boniface of Saluzzo, but he retained the prebend of Bere & Cherminster from c.1320 until being deprived of all benefices in 1330.

John de Stratford (1322) DCL, was granted the prebend of Bere & Cherminster in 1322 but the grant was revoked later in the year as George of Saluzzo was found to be still alive. He was Rector of Chilmark in the 14c. and was consecrated Bishop of Winchester in 1327.

Robert de Stratford (1327) was granted the prebend of Bere & Cherminster in 1327 but this was revoked in the same year and the prebend given to Thomas de Chaundos. He received the prebend however three years later.

Thomas de Chaundos (1328-1329) was granted the prebend of Bere & Cherminster in 1328 but this was revoked the following year.

Robert de Stratford (1330-1337) finally received the prebend of Bere & Cherminster in 1330 and held it until consecrated as Bishop of Chichester in 1337.

Robert de Turre de Adria (1337-?) claimed the prebend of Bere & Cherminster in 1337 and, although Walter Wyville was appointed in 1338, the Roman Court found in his favour.

Walter Wyville (1338-1340) was Rector of Kingsclere in 1330 and held the prebends of Minor Pars Altaris from 1334 to 1338 and of Bere & Cherminster from 1338 to 1340. While awaiting the ruling of a court in Rome on his dispute with Robert de Turre de Adria, he became Treasurer of Sarum and a Canon Residentiary from 1340 until his death in 1345.

Thomas de Hatfield (1340-1345) was granted the prebend of Bere & Cherminster by King Edward III in 1340 despite Walter Wyville's claim before the Court of Rome. He became Bishop of Durham in 1345.

William de Veyraco (1342-1348) DCL, was nominated to the prebend in 1342 when Robert de Turre de Adria was declared an enemy of the Crown. He was again nominated in 1344, the prebend was taken into the hands of King Edward III in 1347 but he had died by 4 January 1348.

Guy de Pestello (1348-1371) DCnL, held the prebend of Bere & Cherminster from 1348 to 1371 and had died by 16 November 1371.

Henry de Wakefield (1371-1375) received a royal grant of the prebend of Hurstbourne & Burbage in 1371 but this was superseded two months later by a royal grant of the prebend of Bere & Cherminster which he held from 1371 to 1375. He was Archdeacon of Canterbury in 1374 and became Bishop of Worcester in 1375.

William de Agrifolio (1371) was a nephew of Pope Clement VI and was created Cardinal-Priest of St Stephanus in 1367 at the age of 28 years. He returned with Pope Urban V to Avignon in 1370 and became Dean of Anti-Cardinals. He held the prebend of Highworth from ? to 1371, was Archdeacon of Taunton and in both 1371 and 1384 Archdeacon of Berks. He was nominated to the prebend of Bere & Cherminster in 1371 but Henry de Wakefield remained in possession. He held a stall at Lincoln from 1397 to 1384 and died of the plague on 13 January 1401 in the College of St Martial, Rome.

Edward Burnell (1375-?) was Archdeacon of Ely c.1373 and held the prebend of Bere & Cherminster from 1375 to ?.

Nicholas Doberham (1386-1390) was nominated to the prebend of Bere & Cherminster in 1386 and although it was claimed by both Thomas Stowe and William Byde, he was installed. There was then a royal grant of the prebend to Richard Medford with whom Thomas Stowe had made an exchange for the prebend of Highworth. The Dean's locum tenens refused to install Richard Medford but, when the exchange between Thomas Stowe and Richard Medford was ratified, he was installed in 1387. The prebend of Bere & Cherminster became vacant in 1390, either on the consecration of Richard Medford or the resignation of Nicholas Doberham.

Thomas Stowe (?-1387) DCL, as a result of the exchange of the prebend of Highworth with Richard Medford, claimed the prebend of Bere & Cherminster in early 1386 but the Dean's locum tenens refused to install him and Nicholas Doberham was installed. In 1387 he received the prebend of Highworth by royal grant and he had died, whilst holding that prebend, by 19 November 1405.

William Byde (1386) BCL, held the prebend of Warminster from 1361 to 1391 and claimed the prebend of Bere & Cherminster in 1386 but Nicholas Doberham was installed. He was a Canon Residentiary.

Richard Medford (1386-1390) received the prebend of Bere & Cherminster in 1386 by royal grant, having exchanged the prebend with Thomas Stowe for the prebend of Highworth, but the Dean's locum refused to install him. Despite charges by Ralph Ergum, Bishop of Sarum 1375-1388, and Nicholas Doberham against William Byde and Thomas Stowe for intrusion into the two prebends and fraudulent exchanges, the exchange between Thomas Stowe and Richard Medford was ratified in 1387, the latter assuming the prebend of Highworth. He held stalls at Windsor in 1381 and at York in 1386. He was imprisoned for some time at Bristol by the Parliament as a supporter of King Richard II. He was Archdeacon of Norfolk in 1385 and in 1390 was appointed by the Pope to the see of Chichester. He was translated to the see of Sarum in 1395 and was Bishop until his death on 3 May 1407. He was buried in St Margaret's Chapel in the south west transept of the cathedral and left a small sum to keep the tower and spire in repair, which indicates that they had been completed before his death.

William Ashton (?-1390) DCL, claimed the prebend of Bere & Cherminster but following a judicial inquiry, he resigned his claim in 1390. In the same year he was granted the prebend of Wilsford & Woodford but Henry de Winterton retained possession.

Henry Bowet (1390) DCn&CL, was said in 1388 to be Treasurer of Sarum but a Cardinal of Pisa, named Peter, was said to be Treasurer of Sarum in 1390 and Francis Prignani seems to have occupied the dignity in 1391. Henry Bowet also claimed the prebend of Bere & Cherminster in 1390 but three months after John Bloor was installed he was said to be still litigating about prebends.

John Boor (1390-1402) held the prebends of Wilsford & Woodford in 1387 and Bere & Cherminster from 1390 to 1402

Nicholas Bubwith (1402-1406?) held a stall at Lincoln and the prebend of Bere & Cherminster from 1402 to 1406? despite difficulties which included a mandate for the arrest of his disturbers. He was Archdeacon of Dorset from 1397 to 1399 and again from 1400 to 1406 when he became Bishop of London. He was translated to Sarum in 1407 and to Bath & Wells four months later. He was successively Master of the Rolls, Keeper of the Privy Seal and Treasurer of England. He died on 27 October 1424 and was buried at Wells.

John Fraunceys (1402-1404) BCnL, claimed the prebend of Bere & Cherminster in 1402 and received a royal licence to accept nomination in 1404. He was Archdeacon of Berks and held the prebend of Coombe & Harnham, both in 1404.

Thomas Langley (?-1406) held a stall at York in 1400, becoming Dean there in 1401. He was Keeper of the Privy Seal in 1403, Chancellor of England in 1405 and although elected Archbishop of York, was rejected by the Pope in 1405. He held the prebends of Bere & Cherminster from ? to 1406 and Grantham Australis from 1400 to 1406 when he became Bishop of Durham. He was present at the Council of Pisa in 1409 and was made Cardinal in 1411 but without title because he did not go to Rome to be installed. He died on 20 November 1437 and was buried at Durham..

John de Meliorati (1406-1410) was a nephew of Pope Innocent VII. He became Archbishop of Ravenna in 1400 and was created Cardinal-Priest of St Cross in Jerusalem in 1405. He was present at the Council of Pisa and was Dean of the Apostolic See in 1410. He was nominated to the prebend in 1406 but it was in dispute until his death on 14 October 1410, when Anthony de Calvis was nominated.

Richard de Kingston (1406-1418) received a royal grant of the prebend in 1406 but the Chapter refused to install him having received an inhibition from the Official of the Court of Canterbury on behalf of Thomas Stanley. There was a further royal grant in 1407, an archbishop's mandate for an inquiry in 1408 and confirmation to de Kingston in 1410. He died in 1418.

Thomas Stanley (1406) claimed the prebend of Bere & Cherminster in 1406 but the Dean & Chapter refused to admit him. He had already been in dispute over the prebend of Netherbury in Ecclesia for which he had expectations since 1398 but Walter Medford was appointed and installed in 1401. There was a royal declaration against Stanley in 1402.

Anthony de Calvis (1410-1411) was a Canon of St Peter's and Arch-Priest of the Vatican and was Bishop of Imola in 1390 and of Todi in 1395. He was made Cardinal-Priest of St Praxedes in 1405, was present at the Council of Pisa and died at Bologna on 2 October 1411.

Robert Gilbert (1418) DTh, exchanged this prebend, one month after receiving it, with Henry Harburgh for the dignity of Precentor of Sarum. Less than a year later, he exchanged the dignity with Edward Prentys for the prebend of South Newton in Wilton conventual church. He later became Dean of York in 1426 and Bishop of London in 1436. He died in 1448.

Henry Harburgh (1418-1432) had previously been Treasurer of Sarum in 1394, which dignity he exchanged with John Chaundeler for the prebend of Netherbury in Ecclesia. This he exchanged in 1395 with Ralph Selby for the prebend of Alton Borealis. He relinquished this latest prebend in 1403, receiving that of Slape. This he held until 1415 when he received the prebend of Beminster Prima. In 1416 he became Precentor of Sarum. He relinquished his prebend in 1418 and in the same year exchanged the dignity of Precentor for the prebend of Bere & Cherminster, which he held until 1432. He had died by 22 September 1432.

John Castell (1432-1436) DTh, held the prebends of Yetminster Prima from 1428 to 1432, Teynton Regis in 1432 and Bere & Cherminster from 1432 to 1436. He appears to have held the office of Master of St Nicholas Hospital, Sarum in 1425 and he was Archdeacon of Berks from 1431 to 1432?

Nicholas Dixon (1436-1448) exchanged a church and prebend in Yorkshire for this prebend with his predecessor. He died in 1448.

Robert Aiscough (1448-1449) DTh, held the prebends of Netheravon from 1440 to 1441, Faringdon from 1441 to 1447, Grantham Australis from 1447 to 1448, Chisenbury & Chute in 1448 and Bere & Cherminster from 1448 to 1449. He was Archdeacon of Dorset from 1447 to 1449 and had died by 14 February 1449.

Robert Ayscough (1449-1475) BCL, held the prebend of Bere & Cherminster from 1449 to 1475 and Netherbury in Terra from 1475 to 1482. He died in 1482.

Peter Courtenay (1475-1478) DCnL, was the son of Sir Philip Courtenay of Powderham by Elizabeth daughter of Walter, Lord Hungerford KG. In 1453 he was Archdeacon of Exeter, also holding the prebend of Netherbury in Terra from 1448 to 1475 exchanging these for the prebend of Bere & Cherminster, which he held from 1475 to 1478, and the Provostship of St Edmund's College, Sarum. In 1474 he became secretary to King Edward IV, Dean of Windsor in 1476 and Dean of Exeter in 1477. He was Archdeacon of Wilts from 1464 to 1478 when he became Bishop of Exeter, later being translated to Winchester. He died on 22 September 1492.

Lionel Woodville (1478-1482) Lic.CnL, was a brother-in-law to King Edward IV, being the son of Richard, Earl Rivers, whose daughter Elizabeth, co-foundress with Margaret of Anjou of Queens' College, Cambridge, was married to the King. He held a stall at Lincoln in 1465, the prebends of Coombe & Harnham from 1467 to 1478 and Bere & Cherminster from 1478 to 1482. He was also Archdeacon of Oxford and Dean of Exeter, becoming Bishop of Sarum from 1482 to 1484. His death in June 1484 was said to have been hastened by grief at the downfall of his family on the accession of Richard II, and the execution at Salisbury of Henry Stafford, Duke of Buckingham, his brother-in-law. He was buried in the cathedral.

Thomas Danet (1482-1483) DTh, was in 1469, Rector of Brixton Deverill. He held a stall at Windsor and became Dean of Windsor 1481. He died on 18 September 1483.

Robert Boothe (1483?-1488) DCL, had died by 30 January 1488.

Robert Langton (1488-1524) a nephew of Thomas Langton, Bishop of Sarum 1485-1493, he was Archdeacon of Dorset from 1486 to 1514 and held the prebends of Fordington and Writhlington from 1485 to 1488 and Bere & Cherminster from 1488 to 1524. He also held stalls at Lincoln from 1483 to 1516, at Southwell from 1514 to 1517 and at York from 1514 to 1524. He appears to have been Treasurer of York from 1509 to 1514 and Chancellor of Lichfield in 1516. He died in 1524.

Edward Finch (1524-1539) DM, was well endowed with prebends holding in succession those of Yatesbury from 1514 to 1515, Chardstock from 1515 to 1517, Wilsford & Woodford in 1517, Fordington & Writhlington from 1517 to 1518, Grimston from 1518 to 1519 and Faringdon from 1519 to 1521 exchanging the last with William Webbe for the church of Ross on Wye, Hereford. He then held the prebends of Bishopstone from 1521 to 1522, Teynton Regis from 1522 to 1524 and Bere & Cherminster from 1524 to 1539. He was Archdeacon of Wilts from 1522 until 1539. He died in 1539 and was buried in the cathedral.

George Heneage (1539-1546) was the last holder of the prebend of Bere & Cherminster which was dissolved and Ilfracombe substituted by Act of Parliament in 1545. He resigned in 1546.

Holders of the prebend of Ilfracombe:-

George Carew (1555-1556) DD, was the father of George, Earl of Totness and of Sir Peter Carew Kt. He became Dean of Bristol in 1552, was deprived in 1553 and having been restored in 1570, resigned the dignity for the Deanery of Exeter in 1570. He was the first to hold the prebend of Ilfracombe from 1555 to 1556 and he held the prebend of Netherbury in Ecclesia from 1556 to 1583. He was Precentor of Sarum from 1558 to 1583 and a Canon Residentiary from 1556 to 1571. He died in 1583 aged 85.

William Phillips (1557-?) was installed in 1557.

(The prebend of Ilfracombe does not appear in lists of prebendaries of 1564, 1565, 1571 or 1577.)

Thomas Hyde (1583-1588) BD, held the prebend of Ilfracombe from 1583 to 1588 was Chancellor of Sarum and Canon Residentiary from 1588 to 1618 and Rector of Sutton Veny from 1613 to 1618. During his as Chancellor there were new arrangements for the number of Vicars Choral and Lay Vicars and also for the theological lectures to be arranged by the Chancellor. He died in 1618.

John Hotman (1588-?) was installed in July 1588.

William Camden (1589-1623) was a layman who was Second Master of Westminster School in 1575, Headmaster in 1593 and Clarenceaux King of Arms in 1597. He held the prebend of Ilfracombe from 1589 to 1623 and died in 1623.

Edward Davenant (1624-1632) DD, held the prebends of Torleton in 1623, Ilfracombe from 1624 to 1632 and Chisenbury & Chute from 1632 to 1634. He was Treasurer of Sarum from 1634 to 1680, Rector of Poulshot and, in 1625, of Gillingham. He was appointed by his uncle, John Davenant, Bishop of Sarum 1621-1641, to the Archdeaconry of Berks from 1631 to 1634 He died in 1680 at the age of 84.

Nicholas Andrews (1632-1649) MA, died in 1649.

Jeremiah Stephens (1660-1665) BD.

Charles Pickering (1665) MA, held the prebends of Ilfracombe in 1665 and Gillingham Major from 1665 to 1680. He was Rector of Poulshot, where he was buried following his death in 1680.

Thomas Laurence (1665-1671) MA, died in 1671.

Daniel Blyth (1671-1684) MA, was Rector of Upwey where he was buried following his death on 6 May 1684.

John Byrom (1684-1717) MA, was Rector of Stanton St Quintin. He died in 1717.

Thomas Rundle (1717-1721) BCL, held the prebends of Gillingham Minor from 1716 to 1717 and Ilfracombe from 1717 to 1721. He held the Archdeaconry of Wilts from 1720 to 1735 together with the dignity of Treasurer of Sarum from 1721 to 1735 and was consecrated Bishop of Derry in 1735.

Martin Benson (1721-1727) held the prebends of Yetminster Prima from 1720 to 1721 and Ilfracombe from 1721 to 1727. He was Archdeacon of Berks from 1721 to 1735, holding a stall at Durham in 1724. In 1735 he became Bishop of Gloucester and died on 30 August 1752.

Dennis Payne (1727-1753) MA, died on 16 April 1753.

William Hillman (1753-1773) MA, held the prebends of Beminster Prima from 1746 to 1753 and of Ilfracombe from 1753 to 1773. He died on 4 March 1773.

Charles Cooper (1773-1779) DD, was Rector of Trowbridge. He resigned his prebend in 1779 apparently on assuming a stall at Durham.

Charles Everard (later Booth) (1779-1792) MA, died on 7 March 1792.

Charles de Guiffardiere (1792-1810) died on 1 January 1810.

Philip Fisher (1810-1823) DD, held the prebends of Stratton from 1808 to 1810 and Ilfracombe from 1810 to 1823. He was Precentor of Sarum from 1819 to 1842, dying on 19 January 1842 at the age of 92.

William Fisher (1823-1874) MA, was Rector of Poulshot and from 1834 to 1874 a Canon Residentiary. He died on 9 June 1874.

Richard Lowndes (1874-1898) was Rector of Poole Keynes from 1854 to 1862 and of Sturminster Newton from 1862 to 1898. He died on 3 October 1898.

Francis John Huyshe (1898-1905) MA, was Vicar of Wimborne Minster from 1880 to 1905 and was Rural Dean of Wimborne. He died on 13 October 1905.

Charles Albert Bragge (1905-1924) MA, was Vicar of Thorncombe from 1875 to 1924? and Rural Dean of Lyme from 1887 to 1919. He died on 16 December 1924 and was buried at Thorncombe.

Morgan John Walter Morgan (1924-1947) Lic.Th, was Rector of Hazelbury Bryan from 1901 to 1912, Vicar of Yetminster with Chetnole and Rector of Ryme Intrinseca from 1912, and Rural Dean of Sherborne from 1932 to 1934. He died in 1947.

Stanley Baker (1947-1950) MA, DD, was an author who was Vicar Choral from 1897, Chaplain at the Diocesan Training College from 1913 to 1933 and Lecturer from 1903. He was Vicar of Laverstock from 1938 until his death in 1950.

Randall Lionel Bentham Howe (1950-1960) MA, became Rector of Wareham w Arne in 1936. He served as Vicar of Melksham from 1947 to 1954 being also, for the first two years, Rector of Great Chalfield. He was Vicar of Preshute from 1954 until retiring in 1956.

Eric Witham Rogers (1961-1964) AKC, was a minister in India between 1935 and 1949 and Archdeacon of Lucknow for the final two years. On return, he served the parishes of West Dean with East Grimstead from 1949 to 1961 and West Grimstead from 1956 to 1961 when he became Vicar of Alderbury. He retired in 1963.

Cyril Albert Witcomb (1965-1981) was a Chaplain RNVR from 1943 to 1946 when he became Perpetual Curate of St James's Southbroom, Devizes until 1954. He was Vicar of Melksham from 1954 to 1961, held the prebend of Alton Australis from 1960 to 1961 and was Rural Dean of Bradford from 1956 to 1961. He was then Rector of Wilton with Netherhampton from 1963 to 1970, Rural Dean of Wilton from 1964 to 1968 and held the prebend of Ilfracombe from 1965 to 1981. He was Vicar of Calne with Blackland from 1970 to 1976 and Rural Dean of Avebury from 1972 to 1973 and of Calne from 1973 to 1976. He was Vicar of the Woodford Valley from 1976 until his retirement in 1981. He died in January 1993.

Douglas Michael Fidgin (1981) was Rector of Owermoigne with Warmwell from 1970 to 1976 and Rector of Portland with Southwell from 1976 to 1981. Following retirement, he was Priest-in-Charge of Urchfont from 1982 to 1985 and died in September 1991.

John Henry Potter (1983-1991) BA, was Rector of Poole from 1976 to 1987, Rural Dean of Poole from 1980 to 1985 and was Priest in Charge of Charmouth with Catherston Leweston from 1987 until his retirement in 1991.

Barry Walter John Lomax (1991-) STh, was Vicar of New Borough and Leigh St John from 1978 to 1994 when he became Rector of Blandford Forum and Langton Long. He became a Proctor in Convocation in 1990

HEYTESBURY

Prebend:- The churches of the royal manor of Heytesbury in Wiltshire together with three hides, and the churches of Godalming, Surrey, were granted to the cathedral by King Henry I, 1100-1135, and before December 1139 the church of Hill Deverill belonged to the prebend which was listed at the cathedral c.1150.

30 Heytesbury

Heytesbury was a collegiate church, having four canons, originally ordained by Bishop Jocelin c1158, who were endowed with the prebends of Titherington, Horningsham, Hill Deverill and Swallowcliff, and whose appointment lay with the holder of the prebend of Heytesbury. This became permanently joined to the Deanery of Sarum in 1280/1.

Canopy statuette and shield:- **John Fisher** DD, became a Fellow of St John's College, Cambridge in 1773. A few years later he was appointed a Preceptor to Prince Edward, afterwards Duke of Kent and in 1781 he became a Chaplain in Ordinary to King George III and Deputy Clerk of the Closet. In 1786 he held a stall at Windsor and in 1803 was consecrated as Bishop of Exeter, becoming a Preceptor to Princess Charlotte, only daughter of the Prince of Wales. He was Bishop of Sarum from 1807 until his death on 8 May 1825. (Fig. 2.)

Blazon:- Sable on a mount vert two stags salient affrontant argent attired and chained or. [On a black shield, on a green hillock, two silver stags with gold antlers and chains springing forward showing full face and front.]

Psalter:- The part of the psalter allotted to the prebend is Psalms 19, 20 and 21.

Holders of the prebend:-

Ranulph Flambard (c1101/16) was in possession of Godalming church in 1086. He was a senior royal official, Dean of Christchurch, Hants and held stalls at London and Lincoln. He became Bishop of Durham in 1099 and died in September 1128.

Roger of Ramsbury (c.1139-c1150/60) was a brother of Azo, Archdeacon of Wilts c.1122/39 and Dean of Sarum c.1139-c.1145. He was Archdeacon of Wilts from before 1139 to c.1150/60.

Reginald FitzJocelin (1161-1173/74) was the son of Jocelin de Bohun, Bishop of Sarum 1142-1184. He was Archdeacon of Wilts from c.1161 to 1173/74 and was elected Bishop of Bath in 1173

Savaric (c.1183) was a son of Geldwin who was probably second cousin of Jocelin, Bishop of Sarum 1142-1184. He was Archdeacon of Sarum from c.1174 to c.1184 and of Northampton from 1175 to 1192 He held the prebend of Heytesbury c.1183, was Treasurer of Sarum in c.1174/88 and possibly holder of the prebend of Beminster Prima at about the same time. He became Bishop of Bath & Wells in 1192. He held the rectories of Godalming and Hill Deverill in 1180. He died in 1205 and was buried in Bath.

Thomas de Disci (c.1215-c.1218) was Precentor of Sarum from c.1217 to 1218 and died before 2 December 1218. He was clerk to the Archbishop of York in 1202 and was appointed custodian of the bishopric of Sarum during the vacancy of 1217. He is believed to have held the prebend of Heytesbury c.1215-c.1218 and died before 2 December 1218.

William de Waude (c.1218-1237?) was Precentor of Sarum and held the prebend of Heytesbury from c.1218 to 1237?, continuing to hold the latter during his time as Dean from 1220 to 1237? He gave great assistance to Richard Poore, Bishop of Sarum 1217-1228, in his building of the new cathedral; visiting London to collect alms at the end of 1219.

Robert de Wickhampton (c.1257-1271) is thought to have held the prebend of Heytesbury from c.1257 and during his time as Dean of Sarum from 1258 to 1271. He is named as a canon of Sarum in a deed (1245) concerning St Nicholas' Hospital, Sarum and his name also appears on the foundation-deed (1269) of the College of St Edmund, Sarum. He was described as a papal chaplain and in 1263 was granted dispensation to be promoted to bishop, notwithstanding his illegitimacy. He was Bishop of Sarum from 1274 to 1284 but he became blind and a coadjutor was appointed in 1282. He died 24 April 1284. He appears to have held the office of Master of St Nicholas Hospital, Sarum in 1271 and he may have been related to Thomas de Wickhampton, Archdeacon of Sarum c.1274-c.1307, and holder of the prebend of Bedwin.

Walter Scammel (1271-1284) was Archdeacon of Berks from c.1266 to 1274 and Clerk & Collector to King Henry III from 1267 to 1268. He was Treasurer of Sarum and held the prebend of Calne from 1267 to 1271 when on becoming Dean from 1271 to 1284, he also held the prebend of Heytesbury. He was elected Bishop of Sarum in 1284, died on 20 September 1286 and was buried at the north side of the presbytery in the Cathedral. It is believed to have been in 1280 that the prebend of Heytesbury became permanently joined to the deanery.

The Dean of Sarum for the time being (1280-).

[**Jack Rylance Bradshaw** (1987-1994) MA, educationalist and Lay Canon. Following war service in the Royal Corps of Signals (twice mentioned in despatches) he was an educational administrator in Lancashire and Shropshire, Deputy County Education Officer for Dorset from 1953 to 1959, County Education Officer from 1959 to 1974. He was a member of the Church of England Schools Council from 1963 to 1970, the General Synod from 1975 to 1990, on the panel of chairmen from 1980 to 1982 and chairman of the Dioceses Commission from 1986 to 1991. He served on numerous commissions and committees and was on the Central Board of Finance from 1975 to 1986, deputy chairman from 1982 to 1986. He was a member of the Diocesan Conference / Synod from 1964 to 1990, Chairman of the House of Laity and Vice-President from 1979 to 1988, and was a member of a number of its boards, councils and committees including Finance from 1964 to 1988 and Education from 1959 to 1982. He served his parish and deanery, becoming Lay Chairman of Dorchester Deanery from 1970 to 1979 and was a member of the Close Chapter from 1987 to 1994. He occupied Heytesbury as a courtesy stall.]

[**Michael Harry Rex Thompson** (1996-) OBE, FCIB, Lay Canon, Director of Wellington Underwriting since 1996. Served with Lloyds Bank Plc from 1948 to 1995, Deputy Chief Executive from 1987 to 1991 and Deputy Chairman from 1991 to 1995. He was a Director of the National Bank of New Zealand from 1978 to 1982 and again from 1991 to 1995. He became Financial Adviser to the Dean & Chapter in 1995 and a member of the Close Chapter in 1998. He occupies Heytesbury as a courtesy stall.].

GRANTHAM AUSTRALIS

Prebend:- Grantham in Lincolnshire was a royal manor, its churches being given in 1086 to the canons by Osmund, Bishop of Sarum 1078-1099. The two prebends of Grantham Australis and Grantham Borealis were probably in existence before c.1150. Australis comprised the churches of South Grantham and Borealis of North Grantham. Before 1226 they had added to them a piece of land at Stratford-sub-Castle in Wiltshire which was later given to the office of Succentor for making a better provision for the daily mass of the Blessed Virgin. Grantham Australis included the chapels of Gonerby, Harlaxton, Cotsworth, Stoke and Welby.

Canopy statuette and shield:- **John Douglas** DD, was tutor to Lord Pulteney, son of the Earl of Bath. He was Chaplain to the 3rd Foot Guards (Scots Guards) at Fontenoy in 1745 and was the author of *'The Criterion (or rules by which true may be distinguished from spurious miracles)'* in 1754. He held a stall at Windsor in 1762 and St Paul's in 1776, before becoming Bishop of Carlisle in 1787 and Dean of Windsor in 1788. He was Bishop of Sarum from 1791 until his death on 18 May 1807 at Windsor, where he was buried. (Fig. 3.)

Blazon:- Quarterly first and fourth argent a human heart gules imperially crowned or on a chief azure three mullets of the first. Second and third argent three mascles gules on a chief of the last as many lions passant guardant of the first.
[On a silver shield divided into four quarters; top left and bottom right a red human heart with a gold imperial crown, above it on blue, three silver pierced, five pointed stars; top right and bottom left three red diamonds with centre holes, above them on red, three silver erect lions with one hind paw on the ground and the other three paws and the tail in the air, showing full face.]

Psalter:- The part of the psalter allotted to the prebend is Psalms 22, 23 and 24.

Holders of the prebend:-

Walter (1166).

Guy Brito (before 1186).

Geoffrey de Bocland (c.1213-1225) was Archdeacon of Norfolk from before September 1198. He also held a stall at Lincoln, was Dean of St Martin le Grand, London and a Justice in Eye. He had died by 14 September 1225.

Bartholomew de Kemesey (1225-1226/7) first occurs as a canon, prebend unidentified, when acting as the Dean's attorney in 1218/1219. He held the prebend of Grantham Australis from 1225 to 1226/7 and was the Seneschal, or Steward, in c1226.

Thomas of Ebbesbourne (1226/7-c.1246) held the prebends of Rotesfen in c.1226/7 and Grantham Australis from c.1227 to c.1246 and was Subdean of Sarum from c.1237 to c.1240. He died or had resigned by 6 November 1246.

Laurence de Sancto Martino (1246-1252) held a stall at Chichester and was Archdeacon of Coventry. He was elected Bishop of Rochester in 1250 and consecrated in 1251 but he had papal dispensation to retain his benefices for three years. He resigned his interests in 1252.

Nicholas of York (1252-?) was given the prebend by William of York, Bishop of Sarum 1247-1256, but could not occupy it until the resignation of de Sancto Martino. In 1249/1250 he is called rector of the prebend while de Sancto Martino is called custos.

William of Stoke (1264-1296) died before 2 October 1296.

Peter de Gorumville (1296-1298) held the prebends of Grantham Australis from 1296 to 1298 and Bedminster & Redcliffe from 1298 to 1310. He was appointed in 1297 to administer the see, vacant on the death of Nicholas Longespee, Bishop of Sarum 1292-1297. He had died by 28 September 1310.

Richard de Bello (1298) held in turn during 1298 the prebends of Beminster Prima and Grantham Australis, and then Coombe & Harnham from 1298 to 1305. He was given the prebend of Highworth c.1305 although John de Frescobaldis had already been nominated by the Pope. The Pope tried to restore Frescobaldis to the prebend but the Bishop prevented the Dean from oppressing Richard de Bello. Eventually, in 1308 there was a papal dispensation allowing de Bello to retain the prebend, which he did until 1326. He was Archdeacon of Berks in 1313 and in 1315 had charge of the diocese while the see was vacant on the death of Simon de Gandavo, Bishop of Sarum, 1297-1315. He would seem also to have held a stall at Hereford in 1305 and to have been Rector of Poulshot in 1313. He died in 1326.

Henry de Nassington (1298-1307) held the prebends of Beminster Prima in 1298 and Grantham Australis from 1298 to 1307. He had died by 14 July 1307.

William Ruffati (1307-1309) also referred to as William Arcufate or de Farges, was a nephew of Pope Clement V and was created Cardinal-Deacon of St Cosmos and St Damian in 1305 and Cardinal-Priest of St Prudentiana in 1306. He held the prebend of Grantham Australis from 1307 to 1309 and was Dean of Sarum from1309 to 1311. He is thought to have died on 24 February 1311 in Avignon.

Thomas Jorz (1309-1311) was Cardinal-priest of St Sabina.

Pontius de Varesio (1309-1310) claimed the prebend of Horton but it was given to Richard de Abingdon in 1309. The case was taken to the Roman Court but before it was settled, he claimed the prebend of Grantham Australis. This was questioned and he resigned his claim before the end of 1310. Also in 1309 he claimed the dignity of Chancellor of Sarum but Simon de Gandavo, Bishop of Sarum 1297-1315, appealed successfully against this papal grant.

Gilbert Lovel (1311-1332) held the prebends of Preston from 1298 until being succeeded in 1304. He held the prebends of Fordington & Writhlington from ? to 1311 and Grantham Australis from 1311 to 1332. In 1305 Simon de Gandavo, Bishop of Sarum 1297-1315, conceded to Gilbert Lovel the house of residence called 'Aula Plumbea' (Leadenhall) previously occupied by the late William Burnel, Prebendary of Horton.

John de Weston (1332-?).

Richard Swinnerton (1337-?).

Robert de Crull (1375) was Rector of Stepney and Chaplain to King Edward III.

John de Carreu (1375).

John Edward (1375).

William de Gunthorpe (1377?-1400) died in 1400.

Thomas Langley (1400-1406) held a stall at York in 1400, becoming Dean there in 1401. He was Keeper of the Privy Seal in 1403, Chancellor of England in 1405 and was elected Archbishop of York but rejected by the Pope in 1405. He held the prebends of Bere & Cherminster from ? to 1406 and Grantham Australis from 1400 to 1406 when he became Bishop of Durham. He was present at the Council of Pisa in 1409 and was made Cardinal in 1411 but without title because he did not go to Rome to be installed. He died on 20 November 1437 and was buried at Durham..

Edward Prentys (1406) BCL, was Precentor of Sarum from 1419 to 1446. He exchanged the prebend of Grantham Australis, which he held in 1406, with Richard Prentys for the prebend of Stratford which he held from 1406 until 1423. He held the prebend of Durnford from 1423 to his death in 1446. He was a Canon Residentiary and occupied the house called Leadenhall in the Close.

Henry de Minutulis (1406-1410) was Arch-Priest of the Liberian Basilica and Almoner to Pope Gregory XII. He was consecrated Bishop of Bitonto in 1383, became Archbishop of Trani in the same year and was Archbishop of Naples from 1389 to 1403. He was created Cardinal-Priest of St Anastasia in 1389, becoming Cardinal-Bishop of Tusculum in 1403 and of Sabina in 1409. Despite an exchange of prebends between Edward Prentys and Richard Prentys, de Minutulis was nominated in1406 to the prebend of Grantham Australis but he had resigned his claim by early 1410.

Richard Prentys (1406-1416) exchanged the prebend of Stratford which he held from 1404 to 1406, with Edward Prentys for the prebend of Grantham Australis which he held from 1406 to 1416. He died in 1416.

Thomas Enkeston (1416) in the same year, exchanged this prebend for the church of Loughborough, Leicestershire.

John Southam (1416-1441) Lic.CL, received a royal grant of the Archdeaconry of Berks in 1395, apparently holding it until 1404 when he exchanged it with Thomas Southam for the Archdeaconry of Oxford. He held the prebend of Grantham Australis from 1416 to 1441 and had died by March 1441.

John Langton (1441-1447) Lic.CnL, became Bishop of St David's in 1447.

Robert Aiscough (1447-1448) DTh, held the prebends of Netheravon from 1440 to 1441, Faringdon from 1441 to 1447, Grantham Australis from 1447 to 1448, Chisenbury & Chute in 1448 and Bere & Cherminster from 1448 to 1449. He was Archdeacon of Dorset from 1447 to 1449 and had died by 14 February 1449.

Richard Caudray (1448-1458) held a stall at St Paul's in 1425 and held the prebends of Chardstock from 1426 to ? , Chisenbury & Chute from 1433 to 1448 and Grantham Australis from 1448 to 1458.

John Stretton (1458-1471) DCL, held the prebends of Coombe & Harnham from 1452 to 1457, Yatesbury from 1457 to 1458, Grantham Australis from 1458 to 1471, Bedminster & Redcliffe from 1471 to 1474 and Chisenbury & Chute from 1474 to 1475. He was Rector of Poulshot in 1459 and died on 1 January 1475.

John Vernham (1471-1489?) held the prebend of Yatesbury in 1471 and of Grantham Australis from 1471 until apparently resigning in 1489.

Ralph Langton (?-1489) held the prebends of Grantham Australis from ? to 1489 and Bitton in 1492. He died in 1492.

Robert Day (1489-1506) held the prebends of Axford from ? to 1486, Rotesfen from 1486 to 1489 and Grantham Australis from 1489 to 1506. He died in 1506.

John Fotehede (1506-1512) was Rector of Symondsbury and Master of Michael House, Cambridge. He died in 1512.

John Baker (alias Elton) (1512-1514) BCn&CL, held the prebends of Grantham Australis from 1512 to 1514, Grantham Borealis from 1514 to 1519 and Grimston from 1519 until his death in 1547. He was Rector of St Peter's, Marlborough in 1510 and of Sherston in 1511. In 1513 he exchanged the living of Marlborough for the Wardenship of St Catherine's Hospital, Ledbury. He was presented to the living of Mildenhall in 1514. In 1515 he held a stall at Hereford and in 1519 became Rector of Childrey, Berks. In 1534 he gave lands in Oxfordshire and Gloucestershire to found a fellowship at Brazenose College, Oxford, and in the same year was Vicar of Yetminster. Later he became Chancellor of Hereford.

Henry Rawlyns (1514-1519) BCL, was well provided with prebends. He held Yatesbury from 1513 to 1514, Grantham Australis from 1514 to 1519 and Coombe & Harnham 1519 to 1521. He resigned Coombe & Harnham in May 1521, was succeeded by Cuthbert Tunstall who then became Dean of Sarum, and was again appointed to the prebend later in the same year. He then held Faringdon from 1523 to 1524, Hurstbourne & Burbage in 1524 and Teynton Regis, together with the Archdeaconry of Sarum from 1524 to 1526. He was Rector of Christian Malford, died in 1526 and is buried in the cathedral near the Audley chantry.

William Pykenham (1519) BCL, held the prebends of Yatesbury from 1515 to 1517, Ruscomb from 1517 to 1518, Yetminster Secunda from 1518 to 1519, Grantham Australis in 1519 and Grantham Borealis from 1519 to 1535. He died in 1535.

John Dente (1519-1522) died in 1522.

William Burbank (1522-1528) DCnL, held a stall at York in 1512. He was secretary to Cardinals Bainbridge and Wolsey and a friend and correspondent of Erasmus. He died c.1530.

Peter Vannes (1528-1529) BTh, held the prebends of Grantham Australis from 1528 to 1529 and Bedwin, as additional to his deanery, from 1529 to 1543. He was Dean of Sarum from 1536 to 1563 and on Bedwin being dissolved by Act of Parliament in 1543, he held the prebend of Shipton from 1544 to 1563 and died early in 1563.

John Rayne (1529-1537) DCL, died in 1537.

Edward Crome (1537-1562) DD, died in 1562.

Hugh Turnbull (1562-1566) DD, died 23 November 1566.

John Baron (1566-?) MA.

William Barkesdale (1580-1629) MA, died in 1629.

Humphrey Henchman (1629-1639) DD, was a Fellow of Clare Hall, Cambridge. He was a son-in-law of Robert Tounson, Bishop of Sarum 1620-1621, becoming Precentor from 1623 to 1660 and Canon Residentiary from 1633 to 1660 (although dismissed during the Commonwealth) and holding in succession the prebends of Yatesbury from 1623 to 1629, Grantham Australis from 1629 to 1639 and Teynton Regis from 1639 to 1660. He helped King Charles II to escape after the battle of Worcester; personally escorting him to Heale House and then meeting him again at Stonehenge. He became Bishop of London and Lord Almoner in 1663. He died on 7 October 1675 at the age of 83 and was buried at Fulham.

Alexander Hyde (1639-1665) DCL, was a son of Sir Lawrence Hyde of Sarum and cousin of Lord Chancellor Clarendon. He was a Fellow of New College, Oxford and Subdean of Sarum from 1637 to 1661. He held the prebend of Grantham Australis from 1639 to 1665 and the Rectory of Wylye. He was Rector of Little Langford from 1634 and a Canon Residentiary from 1660 to 1665, being deprived during the Commonwealth. At the Restoration he obtained a canonry and afterwards the Deanery of Winchester, becoming Bishop of Sarum from 1665 until his death on 22 August 1667.

Thomas Lambert (1666-1694) BD, was a Canon Residentiary and held the prebend of Grantham Australis from 1666 to 1694. He was Rector of Boyton and of Sherrington from 1677 to 1694 and domestic chaplain to King Charles II. He was Archdeacon of Sarum from 1674 until his death on 29 December 1694, aged 78. He was buried in the cathedral.

Joseph Kelsey (1695-1705) BD, held the prebends of Netherbury in Terra from 1674 to 1695, Grantham Australis from 1695 to 1705 and Highworth from 1705 to 1710. He was Rector of Newton Tony from 1669 to 1710 and of Fugglestone from 1681. He was Warden of St John's Hospital, Heytesbury in 1686 and was a Canon Residentiary and Archdeacon of Sarum from 1695 until his death on 1 November 1710. He was buried in the cathedral.

William Wootton (1705-1727) BD, died in 1727.

John Balguy (1728-1748) MA, died on 20 September 1748.

William Dodwell (1748-1785) MA, held the prebend of Grantham Australis from 1748 to 1785, was a Canon Residentiary from 1754 to 1785, Archdeacon of Berks from 1763 to 1785 and also Vicar of Shottesbrooke cum Waltham and Bucklebury. He died on 23 October 1785 and is buried in the south transept of the cathedral.

Robert Price (1785-1823) DCL, was a Canon Residentiary from 1785 to 1823 and was Vicar of Melksham.. He died on 7 April 1823 and is buried in the cathedral.

Thomas Rennell (1823-1824) BD, was Master of St Nicholas Hospital in 1823 and died on 30 June 1824.

Thomas Henry Mirehouse (1824-1867) MA, died on 7 January 1867.

Sir Talbot Hastings Bendall Baker Bt (1868-1900) was Vicar of Preston with Sutton Poyntz from 1848 to 1877 and Rural Dean of Dorchester from 1870 to 1877. He died on 6 April 1900.

Edwin George Wyld (1900-1920) BA, was Rector of Woodborough from 1873 and Curate in Charge of Manningford Bohun from 1874, to 1881. He was Vicar of Mere from 1881 to 1890 and Vicar of Melksham from 1890 until his death in January 1920.

Joseph William Coulter (1920-1956) MA, was Rector of Langton Matravers from 1900 to 1916, Rector and Rural Dean of Bridport from 1916 to 1927 and Vicar of Calne from 1927 to 1951. He held the prebend of Grantham Australis from 1920 to 1956 and was Archdeacon of Wilts from 1927 to 1951. He died on 10 April 1956.

Theodor Carl Craven Brochner (1956-1970) MA, was Precentor of Liverpool from 1919 to 1921 and of Sheffield from 1923 to 1925. He was Vicar of Milborne St Andrew with Dewlish from 1931 to 1949 and Rural Dean of Bere Regis from 1941 to 1949. He was Vicar of Chickerell with Fleet from 1949 to 1962 and Rural Dean of Weymouth from 1951 to 1962.

Douglas Victor Galloway (1970-1977) was Rector of Bincombe with Broadway from 1949 to 1955, of Westbury with Leigh and Dilton from 1955 to 1962 and of Beaminster from 1962 to 1977. He was Rural Dean of Beaminster from 1966 to 1974 and served as a Proctor in Convocation from 1962 to 1964.

Charles Patrick (Pat) Hanna (1978-1981) MA, was Rector of Hilperton with Whaddon from 1949 to 1955 and Vicar of East & West Harnham from 1955 to 1965. He was Vicar of Bishop's Lavington from 1965 to 1979, Rector of Little Cheverell from 1966 to 1981 and Priest-in-Charge of Erlestoke and Great Cheverell from 1978 until his retirement in 1981. He died in 1988.

Patrick Connor Magee (1982-1984) MA, served as Chaplain RNVR from 1943 to 1946. He was Chaplain of Bryanston School, Blandford for 1960 to 1970, was Vicar of St Michael & All Angels, Bemerton from 1973 to 1975 and Rector of Bemerton Team from 1975 until his retirement in 1984.

John Robert Joughin Kerruish (1985-1986) MA, DipTh, was Vicar of Branksome Park All Saints from 1955 until his retirement in 1986. He died on 29 December 1992.

Allen Edward Henry (Claude) Rutter (1986-1996) MA, was Priest in Charge of Over with Nether Compton, Trent and Sandford Orcas from 1973 to 1980. In 1979 he had charge of Oborne with Poyntington until in 1980 the formation of the benefice of Queen Thorne, of which he was Priest in charge until his retirement in 1996. He was Rural Dean of Sherborne from 1976 to 1987.

Eric John Woods (1998-) MA(Oxon), MA(Cantab), FRSA, became Vicar of Sherborne with Castleton and Rector of Lillington in 1993 and Rural Dean of Sherborne in 1996.

CHISENBURY & CHUTE

Prebend:- The prebend was probably in existence by c.1150. It consisted of estates and tithes at Chisenbury and Chute, and the church of Winterbourne Dauntsey, all in Wiltshire, and the church of Easton in Hampshire.

Canopy statuette and shield:- **The Hon Shute Barrington** DCL, was the son of the 1st Viscount Barrington. He held stalls at Christ Church, Oxford in 1761 and St Paul's in 1768 before being consecrated Bishop of Llandaff in 1769. He held a stall at Windsor in 1777 and was Bishop of Sarum from 1782 until his translation to Durham in 1791. He died in 1826. (Fig. 4.)

Blazon:- Argent three chevronells gules a label of three points azure. [On a silver shield, three red chevrons with above them a blue "label", or horizontal band from which three short pieces depend. (A label usually indicates the eldest son, but here it is an integral part of the arms.)]

Psalter:- The part of the psalter allotted to the prebend is Psalms 56, 57, 58 and 59

Holders of the prebend:-

W------- (?-1217) was Archpriest of Milan who died holding the prebend before 22 April 1217.

Martin de Summis (1217-c.1240) was fined for non-residence in 1227.

Robert de Beauvoir (c.1253-c.1261) was Rector of St Thomas, Sarum.

Gilbert of Bytham (c.1262-1263) held a stall at Wells where he was Precentor, and was Chancellor of Oxford University. He had died holding the prebend by 18 January 1263.

Reimund de Bovisvilla (1263-?) was a kinsman of King Henry III and was a Royal Proctor in the court of France in 1262/3.

Geoffrey de Insula (c.1284 -c.1294).

Henry de Bluntesdon (1297-1316) was Archdeacon of Dorset from 1297 to 1316 and became King's Almoner, holding a papal dispensation in 1300 to retain the Archdeaconry and other benefices. He held the prebend of Chisenbury & Chute, stalls at Chichester, London and Wells and had died by 29 September 1316.

Robert de Worth (1316-1349) was Subdean of Sarum from 1309 to 1320 and held the prebends of Alton Australis from 1309 to 1313, Durnford from 1313 to 1316 and Chisenbury & Chute from 1316 to 1349. He was a Canon Residentiary, resigning the office of Subdean on 25 November 1320 to become Rector of Bradford-on-Avon. During his time the office of Confessor was added to that of Subdean.

Roger Holme (1349-1384) was nominated to the prebend in November 1349 and Thomas Edington was nominated in February 1350. Edington was confirmed in 1351 but in 1366 both were still claiming the prebend. Holme was again confirmed in 1383 and a year later he exchanged the prebend for that of Good Easter in St Martin-le-Grand, London.

Thomas de Edington (1350-?) was nominated to the prebend in February 1350 and confirmed a year later. Roger Holme appeared however to have gained possession.

John de Waltham (1384) held a stall at Lichfield in 1361, was Subdean of York in 1381, held a stall at Lincoln in 1382 and was Archdeacon of Richmond in 1383. He would appear to have been Master of the Rolls and Keeper of the Privy Seal, and to have held the prebend of Chisenbury & Chute in 1384, exchanging it with John de Freton for the prebend of Chalke in Wilton conventual church. He was Bishop of Sarum from 1388 to 1395. In 1390 he resisted a metropolitan visitation of Archbishop Courtenay but having been excommunicated, reluctantly yielded. He became Lord Treasurer and also Lord Chancellor in 1391 and the following year, through the intervention of King Richard II, an agreement confirmed by Pope Boniface was arrived at between the Bishop and his Dean and Chapter as to the precise limits of episcopal jurisdiction. He died on 18 September 1395 and was buried by the King's desire in Westminster Abbey.

John de Freton (1384-?) exchanged the prebend of Chalke in Wilton conventual church for this prebend.

John Chitterne (1385-1415) held the prebends of Chisenbury & Chute from 1385 to 1415 and Hurstbourne & Burbage from 1415 to 1419. He became a Canon Residentiary in 1386, was Rector of Newton Tony from 1415 to 1419 and was Archdeacon of Wilts from 1407 to 1419. He held a stall at St Paul's from 1409 to 1419 and became Archdeacon of Sarum in 1419, dying in the same year.

John Frank (1415-1433) held the prebend of Rotesfen in 1406, exchanging it with Reginald Braybroke for Beminster Prima, which he held from 1406 to 1415. He then held the prebend of Chisenbury & Chute from 1415 to 1433 and Fordington & Writhlington from 1433 to 1438.

Richard Caudray (1433-1448) held a stall at St Paul's in 1425 and the prebends of Chardstock from 1426 to ? , Chisenbury & Chute from 1433 to 1448 and Grantham Australis from 1448 to 1458.

Robert Aiscough (1448) DTh, held the prebends of Netheravon from 1440 to 1441, Faringdon from 1441 to 1447, Grantham Australis from 1447 to 1448, Chisenbury & Chute in 1448 and Bere & Cherminster from 1448 to 1449. He was Archdeacon of Dorset from 1447 to 1449 and had died by 14 February 1449.

William Normanton (1448-1449) held the prebends of Yatesbury from 1443 to 1445, Warminster from 1445 to 1446, Bishopstone from 1446 to 1447, Durnford from 1447 to 1448, Chisenbury & Chute from 1448 to 1449 and Faringdon from 1449 to 1459. He died in 1459.

John Paslewe (1449-1457) BCn&CL, held the prebends of Minor Pars Altaris from 1446 to 1447, Bishopstone from 1447 to 1449, Alton Australis in 1449, and Chisenbury & Chute from 1449 to 1457. He held a stall at Hereford in 1447 and died 1457.

Richard Whitby (1457-1459) BCn&CL, was Treasurer of Sarum from 1462 to 1494 and held the prebends of Slape from 1451 to 1457, Chisenbury & Chute from 1457 to 1459 and Bedwin from 1459 to 1462. He was a Canon Residentiary and not infrequently was locum tenens of the Dean. He died in 1494 and was buried in the Chapel of St Edmund in the cathedral.

William Fydyan (1459-1474) held the prebends of Lyme and Halstock from 1456 to 1459 and Chisenbury & Chute from 1459 to 1474. He died on 24 January 1474.

John Stretton (1474-1475) DCL, held the prebends of Coombe & Harnham from 1452 to 1457, Yatesbury from 1457 to 1458, Grantham Australis from 1458 to 1471, Bedminster & Redcliffe from 1471 to 1474 and Chisenbury & Chute from 1474 to 1475. He was Rector of Poulshot in 1459 and died on 1 January 1475.

William Osgodby (1475-1484) was a Canon Residentiary and in charge of the choir, and was Rector of Codford St Peter in 1476. He held the prebends of Axford from 1459 to 1465 and Bishopstone from 1465 to 1467, exchanging the last with Robert Ampleford for Beminster Secunda which he held from 1467 to 1475. He then held Chisenbury & Chute from 1475 to 1484. He died in 1484.

William Talbot (1484-?) DCnL.

Thomas Rope (?-1486) held the prebends of Chisenbury & Chute from c.1485 to 1486 and Axford from 1486 to 1494. He died in 1494.

Henry Sutton (1486-1495) DM, was the Master of St Nicholas Hospital, Sarum in 1478. He held the prebends of Rotesfen from 1481 to 1486 and Chisenbury & Chute from 1486 to 1495 when he exchanged the latter for the dignity of Treasurer of Sarum which he held from 1495 to 1501.

Geoffrey Blythe (1495-1498) BTh, was a brother of John Blythe, Bishop of Sarum 1494-1499. He was Treasurer of Sarum from 1494 to 1495, exchanging the dignity for the prebend of Chisenbury & Chute which he held from 1495 to 1498. He was Archdeacon of Sarum, holding the prebend of Stratton, from 1499 to 1503 and would seem to have been Dean of York in 1497 and Provost of King's Hall, Cambridge in 1499. In 1503 he was consecrated Bishop of Coventry and Lichfield and died in 1533.

Silvester de Gigliis (1498) became Bishop of Worcester on 1498 and died in 1521.

Peter Carmelian (1498-?) was the King's Latin Secretary.

Florianus Motini (?-1533) died in 1533.

Thomas Bennet (1533-1558) DCL, was Secretary to Cardinal Wolsey, Rector of Sutton Veny from 1502 to 1507, Precentor of Sarum from 1536 to 1558 and held the prebends of Axford from 1529 to 1533 and Chisenbury and Chute from 1533 to 1558. He was Canon Residentiary and Proctor in Convocation for the Chapter, in which capacity he signed the Articles of 1536. For some time he was locum tenens to Peter Vannes, Dean of Sarum, who was non-resident. He died in 1558 and is commemorated at the north side of the choir.

John Fawley (alias Fowler) (1558-1569) was deprived by 18 March 1569.

John Garbrand (alias Herks) (1569-1589) MA, was a Fellow of New College, Oxford. He held the prebends of Minor Pars Altaris from 1564 to 1565, Yatesbury from 1565 to 1569 and Chisenbury & Chute from 1569 to 1589. He was a great friend of John Jewell, Bishop of Sarum 1560-1571, and died in 1589.

Edward Hutchins (1589-1629) MA, was Rector of Brinkworth and a Fellow of Brasenose College, Oxford, where he was an eminent preacher. He died in 1629.

John Thorpe (1629-1632) BD, was Rector of Boscombe and died in 1632.

Edward Davenant (1632-1634) DD, held the prebends of Torleton in 1623, Ilfracombe from 1624 to 1632 and Chisenbury & Chute from 1632 to 1634. He was Rector of Poulshot and in 1625 of Gillingham. He was appointed by his uncle, John Davenant, Bishop of Sarum 1621-1641, to the Archdeaconry of Berks which he held from 1631 to 1634 when he became Treasurer of Sarum from 1634 to 1680, He died in 1680 at the age of 84.

John Rogers (1634-1646) MA, was a nephew by marriage of John Davenant, Bishop of Sarum 1621-1641. He died in 1646 and is buried at Bere Regis.

Joshua Tucker (1660-1679) MA, died in 1679.

Richard Kent (1679-1692) MA, held the prebends of Major Pars Altaris from 1664 to 1679 and Chisenbury & Chute from 1679 to 1692. He was Subdean of Sarum from 1668 to 1692 and died in 1692.

John Stevens (1692-1698) BCL, was Rector of Wylye. He held the prebends of Chisenbury & Chute from 1692 to 1698 and Hurstbourne & Burbage from 1698 to 1701. He died in 1701 and was buried in Wylye.

Augustine Wingfield (1698-1699) MA, was Vicar of Tisbury who died a few months after succeeding to the prebend.

Charles Theophilus Mutel (1699-1701) MA, held the prebends of Chisenbury & Chute from 1699 to 1701 and Hurstbourne & Burbage from 1701 to 1711. He was Vicar of Potterne and died in January 1711.

Ralph Bohun (1701-1716) DCL, was Rector of West Kingston. He died on 12 July 1716.

John Holland (1716-1721) DD, held the prebends of Gillingham Minor in 1716 and Chisenbury & Chute from 1716 to 1721. He resigned the prebend in 1721.

William Colnet (1721-1729) DD, was a Fellow of All Souls, Oxford He died on 16 January 1729.

Samuel Eyre (1729-1742) BCL, died on 2 December 1742.

John Pern (1742-1770) MA, died on 6 April 1770.

Thomas Morgan (1770-1782) DD, died on 1 July 1782.

John Randolph (1782-1783) BD, resigned the prebend on receiving a stall at Christ Church, Oxford. He became Bishop of Oxford in 1799, Bishop of Bangor in 1806 and Bishop of London in 1809.

Herbert Randolph (1783-1803) BCL, died on 2 April 1803.

Robert Charles Blayney (1803-1824) MA, was a Fellow of Worcester College, Oxford. He held the prebends of Beminster Prima from 1797 to 1803 and Chisenbury & Chute from 1803 to 1824. He died on 29 September 1824.

Matthew Marsh (1824-1840) DD, was Rector of Brinkworth from 1802 to 1840, of Winterslow in 1804 and Chancellor of the Diocese in 1819. He held the prebends of Beminster Prima from 1823 to 1824 and Chisenbury & Chute from 1824 to 1840. He was Subdean of Sarum from 1824 to 1840 and was a Canon Residentiary from 1826 to 1840. He died on 30 July 1840, was buried in the south choir aisle and is commemorated in the south east transept of the cathedral..

Fulwar William Fowle (1841-1876) BA, was Rector of Allington from 1816 to 1876 and Perpetual Curate of Amesbury from 1817 to 1868 and Vicar from 1868 to 1876. He died on 28 June 1876.

Charles William Bingham (1876-1881) was a Fellow of New College, Oxford. He was Vicar of Sydling St Nicholas from 1838 to 1840, and of Melcomb Bingham in 1842.

Francis Goddard (1882-1892) MA, JP, was Vicar of Hilmarton from 1858 until his death on 2 November 1892.

The Hon Bertrand Pleydell Bouverie (1894-1926) MA, JP was a son of the fourth Earl of Radnor. He was Rector of Stanton St Quintin from 1870 to 1880 and of Pewsey from 1880 to 1910 and had various overseas winter chaplaincies from 1910 to 1915. He died on 7 November 1926.

John Martyn Fisher (1927-1939) MA, was Vicar of Weymouth St Paul from 1906 to 1939 and died in 1939.

Alfred Vincent Hurley (1939-1948) MA, was Chaplain to HM Borstal, Portland from 1924 to 1928, Deputy Governor from 1925 to 1931. He was Rector of All Saints Portland from 1931, with St George from 1937, to 1934 when he again became Chaplain to the Borstal. He resigned in 1948.

Thomas Western Page-Phillips (1949-1960) was Vicar of Coombe Bissett with Homington from 1938 to 1946, of Wimborne Minster from 1946 to 1956 and of Puddletown with Athelhampton and Burleston from 1956 to 1960.

Herbert Geoffrey Goodall (1961-1974) MA, was Vicar of Farley with Pitton from 1941 to 1947. He was Rector of St Edmund's, Sarum from 1947 to 1959 following which he served as Rector of Blandford Forum and of Langton Long from 1959 to 1972.

Anthony Trevor Johnson (1975-1992) MA, was Rector of Upton Scudamore and Vicar of Warminster St Denys from 1967 to 1985 becoming also Priest-in-Charge of Horningsham from 1976 to 1985. He was Rural Dean of Heytesbury from 1971 to 1976, Priest-in-Charge of Semley & Sedgehill from 1985 to 1986 and Rector of East Knoyle, Semley & Sedgehill from 1986 until his retirement in 1992.

Bruce Duncan (1995-) MBE, BA, FRSA, was a Canon Residentiary of Manchester from 1986 to 1995 when he became Principal of Sarum College, Sarum.

BEDMINSTER & REDCLIFFE

Prebend:- The prebend consisting of Bedminster, with the chapels of St Mary Redcliffe, Leigh, all in Somerset, and Alveston in Gloustershire, was given to the cathedral by King Henry II. It was named as 'Bedminster' in all 12c. documents but 'Radeclive', 'Ratecliv' or 'Radeclive' in the 13c. Even so, there was only the one prebend.

Canopy statuette and shield:- **John Hume** DD, held a stall at Westminster in 1742, before becoming Bishop of Bristol in 1756 and Bishop of Oxford and Dean of St Paul's in 1758. He was Bishop of Sarum from 1766 until his death on 26 June 1782 and was buried in the south aisle of the cathedral beside his predecessor, John Thomas 1761-1766. (Fig.5.)

Blazon:- Vert a lion rampant argent. (On the depiction the lion is shown as or). [On a green shield, an erect silver lion with one hind paw on the ground and the other three paws and the tail in the air, showing full face. (On the depiction the lion is shown as gold)]

Psalter:- The portion of the psalter allotted to the prebend is Psalms 119 (129-176), 120 and 121.

Holders of the prebend:-

Joseph (c.1157).

Walter de Dunstanville (c.1193).

Gilbert de Lacy (c.1226-1227) was probably also Treasurer of Lincoln. He was fined for non-residence in February 1227 and had died by December of that year.

Robert de Lexington (1227-c.1238) held the prebend of Bedminster & Redcliffe from 1227 to c.1238, despite it being claimed at intervals by John Romeyn, Subdean of York, on the grounds of papal nomination to the next vacant prebend. He then held the prebend of Bere & Cherminster from c.1238 to ?. He probably also held a stall at Wells.

Henry Tessun (c.1243-c.1254) was Chaplain to the Abbess of Wilton c.1191 and held the prebends of Durnford from c.1220 to c.1243 and Bedminster & Redcliffe from c.1243 to c.1254. He founded a chantry at St Mary Redcliffe and was successively Archdeacon of Bath by 1243 and Precentor of Wells by 1248. He was a brother of Nicholas Tessun who held the prebend of Blewbery c.1246.

Martin de Littlebury (1264-c.1270) held the prebends of Stratton by 1255-1264 and Bedminster & Redcliffe from 1264 to c.1270.

William Burnel (c.1284-1298) lived in the house called Leadenhall in the Close. He held the prebend of Bedminster & Redcliffe from c.1284 to 1298 and also held stalls at Exeter, Lichfield, St David's and York. He was Provost of Wells by 1289, Dean of Wells from 1292 to c.1295 and Archdeacon of Taunton from 1294 to 1298. He was a nephew of Robert Burnel, Bishop of Bath & Wells 1275-1292. He transferred to the prebend of Horton in 1298, holding it until his death in 1304.

Peter de Gorumville (1298-1310) held the prebends of Grantham Australis from 1296 to 1298 and Bedminster & Redcliffe from 1298 to 1310. He was appointed in 1297 to administer the see, vacant on the death of Nicholas Longespee, Bishop of Sarum 1292-1297. He had died by 28 September 1310.

Peter de Periton (1310-1321) DCnL, held the prebend of Yetminster Prima from 1303 to 1310. He was appointed but declined the prebend of Durnford in 1309 and held the prebend of Bedminster & Redcliffe from 1310 to 1321. He was Archdeacon of Dorset from 1316 to 1321 and died in 1321.

Gerald de Tilheto (1321-1326) DCL, was Archdeacon of Wilts, holding the prebend of Bedminster & Redclyffe, from c.1321 to 1326. He died in 1326.

Robert de Baldock (1326-?1353) DCL, had been given the expectation a canonry in 1322 but William Hale was nominated to this prebend later in the same year. Hale was still not in possession by 1343 when Andrew Offord was nominated, although this was subsequently revoked. It appears that Baldock may have died holding the prebend in 1352/53.

William Hale (1332-1358) was nominated in 1322. A royal mandate was issued in 1333 for the restraint of an armed gathering at Bedminster on his behalf, and although his appointment was ratified, he was still not in possession by 1343 when provision was made to Andrew Offord, although subsequently revoked. He resigned his claim by 13 December 1358.

Andrew de Offord (1343) DCL, was nominated to the prebend of Ramsbury in 1343 but was still not in possession in 1349. He received a royal grant of the prebend of Netherbury in Ecclesia in 1345 but was not admitted. He was nominated to the prebend of Bedminster & Redcliffe in 1343 but this was subsequently revoked.

Richard de Norwich (1353-1361) received a royal grant of this prebend and was admitted in 1353 He died in 1361.

Thomas de Clipston (1358-1361) DCL, was nominated to this prebend on William Hale resigning his claim in 1358. He died in 1361.

William of Wykeham (1361) held the prebend of Yetminster Prima in 1361, before he was in Holy Orders, exchanging it in the same year with Richard de Spridlington for Fordington & Writhlington which he held from 1361 to 1366. He was appointed to the prebend of Bedminster & Redcliffe in 1361 but may have returned to Fordington & Writhlington. He became Bishop of Winchester in 1366 and was the founder of New College, Oxford and Winchester College.

Henry de Winterton (1361-?) BCL, was nominated to the prebend of Bedminster & Redcliffe in 1361. He received the prebend of Wilsford & Woodford c.1385 but a royal grant was made to Robert Bloor in 1387. Title was proved in 1389 but there was then a grant to Walter Pese in 1390, which was revoked in July of the same year. There was then a royal grant to William Ashton in November 1390 but Henry de Winterton retained possession until his death in February 1400.

William de Charlton (1366) BCL, held this prebend in 1366.

Thomas Butiller (?-1402) held the prebend of Bedminster & Redcliffe in 1390 and had died by 19 July 1402. He was Archdeacon of Sarum from c.1381 to 1384. He is believed to have been Archdeacon of Northampton in 1386 and to have held a stall at Lincoln in 1388. He may be the same person who later became Bishop of Chrysopolis.

Henry Chichele (1402-1404) DCL, was appointed to the Archdeaconry of Dorset in 1397 and after two years of litigation at the Curia over the claims of Nicholas Bubwith, he was declared technically an intrusor, but was reinstated in 1399, although Bubwith was appointed a year later. He held the prebends of Rotesfen in 1397, Yetminster Prima from 1397 to 1400, Fordington & Writhlington in 1400, Yetminster Secunda from 1400 to 1402 and Bedminster & Redcliffe from 1402 to 1404, when he exchanged with George Westby for the prebend of Fordington & Writhlington. After litigation, he became Archdeacon of Sarum in 1402 exchanging this and the prebend in 1404 for the dignity of Chancellor of Sarum which, following his consecration as Bishop of St David's in 1407, he continued to hold by papal indulgence until 1409. At one time he held the living of Melcombe Bingham and he became Archbishop of Canterbury in 1414. He was the founder of All Souls College. Oxford and died on 12 April 1443.

William Ashridge (1402) had a royal grant of this prebend but Henry Chichele was installed.

George Westby (1404) held the prebend of Netherbury in Terra from 1403 to 1404, becoming Treasurer of Sarum in 1404. A day later, he exchanged the dignity for the prebend of Fordington & Writhlington and within the same year, exchanged this for the prebend of Bedminster & Redcliffe which he in turn exchanged for Major Pars Altaris which he then exchanged for Axford, resigning the last in the autumn of 1404.

John Lincoln (1404-1415) received a royal grant of the prebend of Ramsbury in 1392 but this was probably ineffective. He held the prebends of Major Pars Altaris from 1397 to 1404 and Bedminster & Redcliffe from 1404 to 1415. He was a Canon Residentiary and also held stalls at Lincoln and Wells. He died in 1415.

John Bathe (1415-1438) received the prebend of Chardstock in 1406 by royal grant, despite John Hacket having already been appointed and held it until 1415. He held the prebend of Bedminster & Redcliffe from 1415 to 1438 and died 1438.

William Percy (1438-1452) became Bishop of Carlisle in 1452.

William Toly (1452-1460) died in 1460.

William Say (1460-1464) DTh, exchanged the prebend of Bedminster & Redcliffe with John Chedworth for the prebend of Wilsford & Woodford which he held from 1464 to 1468. He died in 1468.

John Chedworth (1464-1471) DCL, exchanged the prebend of Wilsford & Woodford, which he held from 1454 to 1464, with William Say for the prebend of Bedminster & Redcliffe which he held from 1464 to 1471. He died in 1471.

John Stretton (1471-1474) DCL, held the prebends of Coombe & Harnham from 1452 to 1457, Yatesbury from 1457 to 1458, Grantham Australis from 1458 to 1471, Bedminster & Redcliffe from 1471 to 1474 and Chisenbury & Chute from 1474 to 1475. He was Rector of Poulshot in 1459 and died on 1 January 1475.

William Chock (1474-1492) held the prebends of Ruscomb from 1473 to 1474 and of Bedminster & Redcliffe from 1474 to 1492. He died in 1492

William Russell (1492-1508) DCnL, was a Canon Residentiary and held the prebends of Wilsford & Woodford from 1489 to 1492 and of Bedminster & Redcliffe from 1492 to 1508. He died in 1508.

Edward Powell (1508-1534) DTh, was a Fellow of Oriel College, Oxford in 1495. He held the prebends of Lyme & Halstock from 1507 to 1508 and of Bedminster & Redcliffe from 1508 to 1534. He was Provost of St Edmund's College, Sarum and the Advocate for Queen Catherine when King Henry VIII sought to divorce her. He was attainted and deprived of his benefices in 1534 and is reported to have been hanged, drawn and quartered on 30 April 1540 for denying the King's supremacy.

Henry Williams (1535-1554) BTh, was deprived in 1554.

Thomas Norman (1554-1555) was a Canon Residentiary from 1554 to 1555 and died in 1555.

John Blaxton (1556-1559) held the prebends of Minor Pars Altaris from 1555 to 1556 and of Bedminster & Redcliffe from 1556 to 1559. He had been deprived by November 1559.

Arthur Saull (1559-1586) MA, held stalls at Bristol and Gloucester and died in 1586.

John Thornborough (1586-1593) held the prebends of Netherbury in Terra from 1575 to 1586 and Bedminster & Redcliffe from 1586 to 1593. He was Rector of Orcheston St Mary from 1575 and of Chilmark from 1577 to 1593. He was a Canon Residentiary from 1583 to c.1593, Chaplain to Queen Elizabeth I, Dean of York in 1589, Bishop of Limerick in 1593, of Bristol in 1603 and of Worcester in 1616. He died on 3 July 1641.

Giles Thornborough (1593-1637) was Rector of Odstock in 1582, a Canon Residentiary from ?-1637, Subdean of Sarum from 1599 to 1637 and held the prebend of Bedminster & Redcliffe from 1593 to 1637. He was Master of a Hospital (St John's?) near Wilton and Rector of Orcheston St Mary from 1588 until his death in 1637. He was buried at Orcheston St Mary.

John Carse (1637-1653) DD, died in 1653.

Francis Horton (1660-1699) MA, held the prebends of Alton Borealis in 1660 and Bedminster & Redcliffe from 1660 to 1699. He was a Canon Residentiary from 1674 to 1699, acting as locum tenens for the Dean. He was successively incumbent of St Martin, Sarum and St Thomas, Sarum and in 1686 was Vicar of Melksham. There were proceedings against him for disrespectful language to the Judge of the Consistory Court. He died in 1699 and was buried at Melksham.

John Gibb (1699-1744) was Vicar of Bedminster cum Redcliffe. He died in 1744.

Thomas Broughton (1744-1774) MA, died on 20 December 1774.

James Hume Spry (1775-1780) DCL, held the prebends of Minor Pars Altaris from 1774 to 1775 and Bedminster & Redcliffe from 1775 to 1780. He was Vicar of Potterne from 1770 to 1780 and also Rector of Brixton Deverill from 1773 to 1780. He died on 27 November 1780.

Richard Whish (1781-1806) MA, resigned in 1806.

Martin Richard Whish (1806-1852) BA, was Vicar of St Mary Redcliffe and died on 7 April 1852.

John Guthrie (1852-1858) MA, was Vicar of Calne from 1835 to 1865 and Vicar of Hilmarton from 1865 until resigning his prebend in 1858 on receiving a stall at Bristol.

Edward Wyndham Tufnell (1858-1859) was Rector of Beechingstoke from 1846 to 1857 and of St Peter's Marlborough from 1857 to 1858. He held the prebends of Major Pars Altaris from 1850 to 1858 and Bedminster & Redcliffe from 1858 to 1859. He was Bishop of Brisbane from 1859 to 1873.

Henry Caswall (1860-1871) MA, DD, was Vicar of Figheldean and died in 1871.

Hugo D Harper (1871-1882) was Master of Sherborne Grammar School from 1851 to 1877 and became Principal of Jesus College, Oxford in 1877.

Charles Humphery Cholmeley (1882-1894) MA, was Vicar of Dinton with Teffont Magna from 1868 to 1885.

Thomas Boughton Buchanan (1894-1924) MA, was Chaplain to Lord Herbert of Lea from 1859 to 1860, Rector of Wishford Magna from 1863 to 1871 and Chaplain to George Moberly, Bishop of Sarum 1869-1885, from 1870 to 1885. He was Vicar of Potterne from 1871 to 1891, Rector of Poulshot from 1891 to 1905 and held the prebend of Bedminster & Redcliffe from 1894 to 1924. He was Archdeacon of Wilts from 1874 to 1911 and a Canon Residentiary from 1895 to 1915. He died on 28 June 1924 and is commemorated in the north choir aisle of the cathedral.

George Frederick Tanner (1924-1927) MA, was Rector of Collingbourne Ducis from 1896 to 1926 and Rural Dean of Marlborough from 1911 to 1926. He died on 6 February 1927 and was buried at Collingbourne Ducis.

Francis Raikes (1927-1932) was Vicar of Figheldean from 1879 to 1895 and Bishopstone from 1895 (with Stratford Tony from 1925) to 1932. He died in 1932.

Edward Henry Hoare Lee (1932-1945) MA, was Vicar of Hilton from 1900 to 1912 and Vicar of Whitchurch Canonicorum with Marshwood, Stanton St Gabriel & Fishpond from 1912 to 1938. He was Curate in Charge of Catherston Leweston from 1930 to 1933 and Rector from 1933 to 1938.

Cyril Henry Meyrick (1945-1951) MA, was Rector of Codford St Mary from 1924, with St Peter from 1930 and Rural Dean of Wylye from 1945 to 1951. He died in 1951.

Richard Laurence Pelly (1952-1966) MA, was Rector of Trowbridge from 1945 to 1954 and Vicar of Farley with Pitton from 1954 to 1957. He was Master of St Nicholas Hospital, Sarum from 1957 to 1968.

John Norman Warne (1967-1980) was Director and Secretary of Religious Education from 1964 to 1970 and was Vicar of St Aldhelm's, Branksome from 1970 until his retirement in 1980.

Brian John Smith (1980-1998) was Vicar of Wilsford & Woodford from 1969 to 1974, Vicar of the Woodford Valley from 1974 to 1976 and Vicar of Mere with West Knoyle and Maiden Bradley from 1976 to 1980. He was Archdeacon of Wilts, holding the prebend of Bedminster & Redcliffe, from 1980 to 1998 and was also Vicar of Bishop's Cannings, All Cannings & Etchilhampton from 1980 to 1983 when he became Diocesan Advisor on Christian Giving from 1983 to 1990. He was Rural Dean of Heytesbury from 1978 to 1980 and Team Vicar in the Redhorn Team from 1990 until his retirement in 1998.

Alan Gordon Gill (1999-) was Rector of Winterbourne Stickland, Turnworth, Winterbourne Houghton, Winterbourne Whitechuch and Winterbourne Clenston from 1978 to 1986 and Vicar of Verwood from 1986.

NETHERBURY IN ECCLESIA

Prebend:- The manor of Netherbury in Dorset was part of the pre-conquest Sherborne episcopal estates granted to the cathedral. The prebend, which was probably in existence by c.1150, consisted of the rectory and the right of presentation to the living of Netherbury, the Perpetual Vicar having been dispossessed for illegitimacy in 1295. In 1291 it was called 'Netherbury & Beaminster'.

Canopy statuette and shield:- **John Thomas** DD, became Dean of Peterborough in 1740 and held stalls at Westminster and St Paul's in 1742. He was elected Bishop of St Asaph in 1743 but was consecrated to be Bishop of Lincoln in the following year. He became Bishop of Sarum, at the age of 80 in 1761 serving until his death on 19 July 1766. He was buried in the south aisle of the cathedral. (Fig. 6.)

Blazon:- Vert a chevron ermine between three wolves' heads erased argent. [On a green shield a chevron of ermine between three silver wolves' heads, as if torn from their bodies.]

Psalter:- The portion of the psalter allotted to the prebend is Psalms 73 and 74.

Holders of the prebend:-

Humphrey of Bassingbourn (c.1226/27) was Archdeacon of Wilts in 1193 and Archdeacon of Sarum c.1193-c.1238. He also held a stall at Lincoln.

Blasius of Anagni (1284?-1315) also referred to as Blasius Romanus, was a nephew and chaplain of Pope Alexander IV who requested Chapter in 1257 to exchange the prebend to which Blasius had been collated to one of his choice. He died in 1315.

Francis Gaetani (?-1329) was a nephew of Pope Boniface VIII and was made Cardinal-Deacon in 1295. He received the prebend from Simon de Gandavo, Bishop of Sarum 1297-1315 but King Edward III later claimed that Gaetani had resigned and he nominated Blasius de Arenna. Gaetani occupied the prebend in 1317 and resigned his benefices on marriage in 1329.

Blasius de Arenna (?-1315) died in 1315.

Parvulus de Monte Florum (1329-1331) received the prebend by royal grant in 1329. Thomas de Luco was installed and the grant was revoked in 1331.

Thomas de Luco (1329-1349) was installed in the prebend of Netherbury in Ecclesia in 1329. Despite a royal grant to Andrew Offord in 1345, he continued in the prebend to 1349. In the same year the prebend of Rotesfen was reserved to him but he died before obtaining it.

Andrew de Offord (1345) DCL, was nominated to the prebend of Ramsbury in 1343 but was still not in possession in 1349. He received a royal grant of the prebend of Netherbury in Ecclesia in 1345 but was not admitted. He was nominated to the prebend of Bedminster & Redcliffe in 1343 but this was subsequently revoked.

Reginald de Brian (1349) BCL, had expectation of a stall in 1348 and unlawfully occupied the prebend of Netherbury in Ecclesia the following year, despite Elias de Pelegrini being nominated to it. He was then nominated to the prebend of Rotesfen and this was confirmed despite it being reserved to Thomas de Luco who died before obtaining it. Later in 1349 he became Bishop of St David's.

Elias de Pelegrini (1349-1351) DCL, was nominated in 1349 but was not installed until 1350. He died in 1351.

Hugh de Pelegrini (1351-1376) DCL, was nominated to the prebend in 1351 but Michael de Northburgh was appointed. Hugh de Pelegrini's nomination was however ratified in the same year although it was revoked in 1376.

Michael de Northburgh (1351) DCL, held the prebend of Lyme & Halstock from 1336 until exchanging it in 1339 for the prebend of Church Withington, Hereford. He was appointed to the prebend of Netherbury in Ecclesia in 1351 but it was already held by Hugh de Pelegrini.

Adam de Hertington (1376-?) held the prebend of Netheravon from 1371 to 1376 and Netherbury in Ecclesia from 1376 to ?.

John Chaundeler (?-1394) held a stall at Lincoln in 1405 and the prebend of Netherbury in Ecclesia from ? to 1394 when he exchanged it with Henry Harburgh for the dignity of Treasurer of Sarum which he held until 1404. He was Dean of Sarum from 1404 to 1417 and Bishop of Sarum from 1417 until his death on 16 July 1426.

Henry Harburgh (1394-1395) was Treasurer of Sarum for three days in 1394 when he exchanged the dignity with John Chaundeler for the prebend of Netherbury in Ecclesia. This he exchanged in 1395 with Ralph Selby for the prebend of Alton Borealis. He relinquished his latest prebend in 1403 receiving that of Slape. This he held until 1415 when he received the prebend of Beminster Prima. In 1416 he became Precentor of Sarum, he relinquished his prebend in 1418 and in the same year exchanged the dignity of Precentor for the prebend of Bere & Cherminster which he held until 1432. He had died by 22 September 1432.

Ralph Selby (1395-1401) DCL, was Warden of King's Hall, Cambridge, in 1391, Archdeacon of Buckingham in 1392, and of Norfolk in 1394. He held the prebends of Alton Borealis from 1392 to 1395 and Netherbury in Ecclesia from 1395 until his resignation in 1401 on becoming a monk at Westminster.

Walter Cook (c.1399) was Archdeacon of Berks from 1395 to 1397 when he was nominated to the prebend of Faringdon but Walter Medford was installed. He may have received the prebend of Netherbury in Ecclesia c.1399 by papal grace but he was deposed in the same year.

Thomas Stanley (1401-1402) had expectations of the prebend of Netherbury in Ecclesia from 1398 but Walter Medford was appointed and installed in 1401. A royal grant to Richard Derham was followed by a royal licence to Thomas Stanley but Richard Derham held the prebend. There was a royal declaration against Stanley in 1402 who claimed the prebend of Bere & Cherminster in 1406 but the Dean & Chapter refused to admit him.

Walter Medford (1401) BCL, was Archdeacon of Dorset in 1397, Chancellor of Sarum from 1402 to 1404 and a brother of Richard Medford, Bishop of Sarum 1396-1407. In 1404 he exchanged the dignity with his successor for the Archdeaconry of Sarum and the prebend of Fordington & Writhlington, exchanging a few days later for the Archdeaconry of Berks. He probably exchanged this Archdeaconry with Peter Alcobasso for the Deanery of Wimborne in 1417. He held the prebends of Major Pars Altaris from 1397 to 1397, Yetminster Prima in 1397, Faringdon from 1397 to 1400, having been excommunicated but later absolved, when he exchanged this prebend for the dignity of Treasurer of St Paul's. He held the prebend of Netherbury in Ecclesia in 1401, followed by Preston which he exchanged with Richard Derham for Netherbury in Ecclesia in 1402. He held the prebends of Fordington & Writhlington from 1404 to 1407 and Bedwin from 1407 until his death in 1423.

Richard Derham (1401-1402) DTh, held the prebend of Netherbury in Ecclesia, despite litigation, from 1401 to 1402 when he exchanged it with Walter Medford for the prebend of Preston, which he held from 1402 to 1412.

Walter Medford (1402) see above.

John Prophete (1402-1416) received a royal grant of the prebend of Bitton in 1395, despite Robert Hallam having already been installed. He held the prebend of Netherbury in Ecclesia from 1402 to 1416 and died in 1416.

Gilbert Hallum (1416-1449) held the prebends of Netherbury in Terra from 1410 to 1413, Highworth from 1413 to 1416 and Netherbury in Ecclesia from 1416 to 1449. He died in 1449.

John Druell (1449-1457) DCn&CL, held the prebends of Alton Australis from 1441 to 1445, Netheravon from 1445 to 1447, Ramsbury from 1447 to 1449 and Netherbury in Ecclesia from 1449 to 1457 exchanging the last with Roger Keyes for the prebend of Blewbery which he held from 1457 until 1469. In 1449 he was Rector of Steeple Langford and he died in 1469.

Roger Keyes (1457-1461) BCnL, held the prebend of Blewbery from 1449 to 1457, exchanging it with John Druell for Netherbury in Ecclesia which he held until 1461. He exchanged this with Fulk Bermyngham for the prebend of Teynton Regis, holding it until 1447 in which year he died.

Fulk Bermyngham (1461-1464) held the prebends of Torleton in 1438, Fordington & Writhlington from 1438 to 1443, Bedwin from 1443 to 1459, Teynton Regis from 1459 to 1461 exchanging the last in 1461 with Roger Keys for Netherbury in Ecclesia, until resigning in 1464.

Malcolm Cosyn (1464-?) was occupying the prebend in 1486.

Hugh Oldham (?-1505) BCn&CL, held the prebends of Alton Borealis from 1495 until resigning in 1500, and Netherbury in Ecclesia from ? to 1505. He was the founder of the Manchester Grammar School and a benefactor of Corpus Christi College, Oxford, becoming Bishop of Exeter in 1505. He died in 1519.

Hugh Dacre (1505-1509) died in 1509

Edward Higgins (1509-1538) Lic.CnL, was Vicar of Steeple Ashton and held the prebends of Axford and Chardstock in 1507, Coombe & Harnham from 1507 to 1509 and Netherbury in Ecclesia from 1509 to 1538. He died in 1538.

Roger Townsend (1538) DCL, received the prebend of Netherbury in Ecclesia and the dignity of Chancellor of Sarum in 1538 and died soon after.

Robert Barns (1538-1540) died in 1540.

Anthony Carsidony (1540-1545) died in 1545.

James Rufforth (1545-1550) died in 1550.

John Arscott (1550-1554) MA, was deprived of the prebend as being a layman in 1554.

John Eryngton (1554-1556) died in 1556.

George Carew (1556-1583) DD, was the father of George, Earl of Totness and of Sir Peter Carew Kt. He became Dean of Bristol in 1552, was deprived in 1553 and having been restored in 1570, resigned it for the Deanery of Exeter in 1570. He was the first to hold the prebend of Ilfracombe, from 1555 to 1556 and held the prebend of Netherbury in Ecclesia from 1556 to 1583. He was Precentor of Sarum from 1558 to 1583 and a Canon Residentiary from 1556 to 1571. He died in 1583 aged 85.

Thomas Aubrey (1583-1609) MA, died in 1609.

John Rawlinson (1609-1631) DD, was a Fellow of St John's College, Oxford and Principal of St Edmund Hall, Oxford in 1608. He was Chaplain to King James I and also to Lord Ellesmere, Chancellor of England. He died on 3 February 1631.

Thomas Fuller (1631-1661) MA, was Vicar of Broadwindsor from 1635 to 1661, although displaced during the Commonwealth. He was a well known author, died on 15 August 1661 and was buried in Cranford, Middlesex..

Thomas Henchman (1661-1674) MA, held the prebends of Slape from 1660 to 1661 and Netherbury in Ecclesia from 1661 to 1674. He held a stall at St Paul's in 1672 and was Archdeacon of Wilts and a Canon Residentiary from 1663 to 1674. He died on 15 December 1674.

Richard Clayton (1675-1676) DD, held the prebends of Minor Pars Altaris from 1661 to 1675 and Netherbury in Ecclesia from 1675 to 1676, and was a Canon Residentiary from 1664 to 1676. He was Master of University College, Oxford and, dying in 1676, was buried in the cathedral.

David Jenner (1676-1693) BA, died in 1693.

Edward Pocock (1693-1726) MA, was Rector of Mildenhall from 1692 to 1726 and held the prebends of Winterbourne Earls from 1675 to 1677, Durnford from 1677 to 1693 and Netherbury in Ecclesia from 1693 to 1726. He died on 27 December 1726.

William Stevenson (1727-1760) died on 12 September 1760.

John Wills (1760-1765) MA, held the prebends of Ruscomb from 1758 to 1760 and Netherbury in Ecclesia from 1760 to 1765. He died on 11 October 1765.

Daniel Dumaresque (1766-1805) DD, died on 28 October 1805.

Edward Dawkins (1805-1816) MA, held the prebends of Ruscomb from 1802 and 1805 and Netherbury in Ecclesia from 1805 to 1816. He died on 1 August 1816.

The Hon Frederick Pleydell Bouverie (1816-1857) MA, was the 3rd son of the 2nd Earl of Radnor. He held the prebend of Netherbury in Ecclesia from 1816 to 1857 and was a Canon Residentiary from 1826 to 1857. He was Rector of Pewsey and died on 6 June 1857.

Richard Seymour Conway Chermside (1857-1867) MA, was Rector of Wilton from 1848 to 1867 and died on 30 July 1867.

George Parker Cleather (1868-1881) was Vicar of Aldbourne from 1852 until his death in 1881.

John Stephenson (1881-1905) MA, was the first Vicar of St John's, Weymouth from 1854 to 1905, and was Rural Dean of Weymouth. He died on 1 April 1905.

Lewen Burton Weldon (1905-1914) MA, DD, was Vicar of Kinson from 1887 to 1891 and Rector of Bridport from 1891 to 1894. He died on 5 January 1914.

William Jacob (1914-1940) MA, was Rector of North Newnton from 1894 to 1898, Vicar of Lyme Regis from 1898 to 1915, Vicar of Warminster from 1915 to 1926 and Rural Dean of Wylye from 1919 to 1922. He was Perpetual Curate of Monkton Wyld from 1926 and Rural Dean of Lyme from 1926. He died in 1940.

Arthur William Stote-Blandy (1941-1951) MA, was Vicar of The Trinity, Trowbridge from 1808 to 1818 and Perpetual Curate of St Michael and All Angels, Colehill from 1818. He died in 1951.

Donald Birkby Eperson (1951-1953) MA, was Vicar of Cherminster and Chaplain Dorset County Mental Hospital from 1938 to 1953.

Eric William Heaton (1953-1956) MA, was a notable theologian. He held the prebend of Netherbury in Ecclesia from 1953 to 1956 was a Canon Residentiary from 1953 to 1960 and Chancellor of Sarum from 1956 to 1960. He was a Fellow of St John's College, Oxford, Dean of Durham from 1974 to 1979, Dean of Christ Church from 1979 to 1991 and Pro-Vice-Chancellor of Oxford University from 1984 to 1991. He died in 1996.

Arthur Donald Frank McKenzie (1956-1968) MA, was Perpetual Curate of Dilton Marsh from 1933 to 1945 and Vicar of St Martin's, Sarum from 1945 to 1966.

Edwin James Greenfield Ward (1968-1985) LVO, MA, was a Chaplain to Queen Elizabeth II from 1955 to 1990 and an Extra Chaplain from 1995, was Archdeacon of Sherborne and Rector of West Stafford with Frome Billet from 1968 to 1984 and held the prebend of Netherbury in Ecclesia from 1968 to 1985. He retired in 1985.

John Keith Oliver (1985-1990) MA, MLitt, was Archdeacon of Sherborne, Priest-in-Charge of West Stafford with Frome Billet and held the prebend of Netherbury in Ecclesia from 1985 to 1990. He became Bishop of Hereford in 1990.

Paul Charles Wheatley (1991-) BA, held a stall at Hereford from 1987 to 1991 when he became Archdeacon of Sherborne, Priest-in-Charge of West Stafford with Frome Billet and occupied the prebend of Netherbury in Ecclesia.

BEMINSTER SECUNDA

Prebend:- The manor of Beaminster in Dorset was part of the pre-Conquest Sherborne episcopal estates given to the cathedral. Two prebends were probably in existence by c.1150, being called in the 1220s 'Beymenistr Rogeri' and 'Beymenistr Valentin' but being given the names of 'Prima' and 'Secunda' in c.1270.

Canopy statuette and shield:- **The Hon Robert Hay Drummond** DD, was a son of the 7th Earl of Kinnoul. He held a stall at Westminster in 1743 and was consecrated Bishop of St Asaph in 1748. He was Bishop of Sarum from June until September 1761, when he was promoted to be Archbishop of York. He became Lord High Almoner and preached the sermon at the coronation of King George III. He died and was buried at Bishopthorpe, York, in 1766. (Fig. 7.)

Blazon:- Quarterly. First and fourth, azure a unicorn salient argent unguled crowned and armed or within a bordure of the last charged with eight thistles proper. Second and third, argent three escutcheons gules. [A shield divided into four quarters: top left and bottom right; on a blue background, a silver unicorn springing forward with crown, hooves and horn of gold, bordered in gold with eight natural coloured thistles upon the border. Top right and bottom left; on a silver background three red shields.]

Psalter:- The portion of the psalter allotted to the prebend is Psalms 64, 65 and 66.

Holders of the prebend:-

Elias (13c) was stated in 1226 to have held a prebend before Valentine and occurs in 1213/14 and 1222. He may have been Elias of Bristol but, if so, he would have held a different prebend.

Valentine (1226/27?-c.1237) held a prebend in 1226/27, the prebend being known as 'Beymenstr Valentine'. He was fined for non-residence in 1227 and was absent in 1228.

William of Ewell (c.1284-c1304) was the nephew of Walter of Merton. He held stalls at London and Bishop Auckland.

John de Bestane (? -1304) was Archdeacon of Salop, held a stall at Hereford and was clerk to Archbishops Pecham and Winchelsey, and Auditor of Causes at the Court of Canterbury. He was alive but infirm on 21 August 1302 but had died by 31 August 1304.

Walter Hervy (1304-1314) held the prebends of Warminster in 1304, Beminster Secunda from 1304 to 1314, Teynton Regis in 1314 and Beminster Secunda again in 1326.

William de Mepham (1314-1316) was appointed to the prebend of Rotesfen in 1313 but this was subsequently revoked as William de Coleshull was already holding it. He held the prebends of Minor Pars Altaris from 1313 to 1316, Beminster Secunda from 1314 to 1316 and Slape in 1316.

Walter Hervy (1326) see above.

William Reymund de Banqueto (?-1330) exchanged the prebend with Richard de Bury in 1330 for a prebend in Crediton collegiate church, Devon.

Richard de Bury (or d'Aungerville) (1330-1333) received a royal grant of the Archdeaconry of Sarum in 1330 but this was revoked and the dignity given to Robert Luffenham. He held the prebend of Beminster Secunda from 1330 to 1333. He was nominated to the prebend of Horton in 1331 but this was already occupied by Peter de Berkeley and he became Bishop of Durham 1333 without having had possession of the prebend. He is also believed to have held a stall at Lichfield in 1330 and been Dean of Wells in 1332. He was Chancellor of England in 1334 and died in 1335.

Edmund Trussel (1334-?).

James Coleman de Havante (1340-1349) died in 1349.

Robert de Wycheford (1366) occupied the prebend in 1366 and is referred to in a Will of 1387.

Philip Thornborough (?-1391) exchanged the prebend with Thomas Haxey for the free chapel of St Radegund in St Paul's crypt in 1391.

Thomas Haxey (1391-1419) received the prebend by exchange with Philip Thornborough but the Chapter initially refused to install him. In 1419 he exchanged it with John Bromsgrove for the prebend of Monkton in Ripon collegiate church.

John Bromsgrove (1419-1429) resigned the prebend in 1429.

John Norton (1429-1431) DCnL, held the prebends of Beminster Secunda from 1429 to 1431 and Horton from 1431 to 1462. He was Archdeacon of Sarum from 1432 to 1433 and Archdeacon of Berks from 1433 until his death in 1462.

Robert Beaumont (1431-1432) BCn&CL held the prebends of Major Pars Altaris in 1431, Beminster Secunda from 1431 to 1432 and Teynton Regis from 1432 until his death in 1459.

Robert Ampleford (1432-1467) MA, held the prebends of Rotesfen from 1431 to 1432 and Beminster Secunda from 1432 to 1467 exchanging the latter with William Osgodby for Bishopstone which he held from 1467 until his death in 1468.

William Osgodby (1467-1475) was a Canon Residentiary in charge of the choir and was Rector of Codford St Peter in 1476. He held the prebends of Axford from 1459 to 1465, Bishopstone from 1465 to 1467, exchanging the latter with Robert Ampleford for Beminster Secunda which he held from 1467 to 1475 He held Chisenbury & Chute from 1475 to 1484 and died in 1484.

Edward Cheyne (1475-1486) DCn&CL, held the prebend of Beminster Secunda 1475 to 1486 and was Dean of Sarum from 1486 to 1502. He died on 25 July 1502.

Richard Hill (1486-1489) BCnL, became Bishop of London in 1489.

John Arundel (1489-1496) BTh, held the prebend of Durnford from 1482 to 1489 and Beminster Secunda from 1489 to 1496. He was Dean of Exeter in 1483, Bishop of Coventry & Lichfield in 1496 and Bishop of Exeter in 1502. He died in 1504.

Edmund Martyn (1496-1499) DCn&CL, died in 1499.

Robert Toneys (1499-?) BCL, held the prebends of Axford from 1494 to 1499 and Beminster Secunda from 1499 to ?.

John Underhill (? -1537) BCnL, held the prebends of Stratton from 1506 to 1510 and Beminster Secunda from ? until his death in 1537.

Richard Wade (1537-1546) MA, died in 1546.

Thomas Burbank (1546-1554) was deprived as a layman in 1554.

Thomas Securis (1554-?) was a scholar of New College, Oxford.

Thomas Burbank (?-1564) see above; had been restored to the prebend in 1562 when he is said to have been excommunicated for two years. He was deprived of the prebend in 1564.

Henry Securis (1564-?) is mentioned in 1565.

Thomas Burbank (c.1568-1578) see above, had again been restored to the prebend in 1568, although he was said not to wear clerical dress nor to behave at all like a priest. He died in 1578.

William Badger (1579-?) BA, held the prebend in 1593.

Thomas Coldwell (1594-1619) MA, was Subdean of Sarum from 1595 to 1599 and held the prebend of Beminster Secunda from 1594 to 1619.

Daniel Birckhead (1619-1620) DD, resigned his prebend in 1620.

Richard Corbett (1620-1631) DD, was Chaplain to King James I. He became Dean of Christ Church, Oxford in 1620 and Bishop of Oxford in 1628 while continuing to hold this prebend until 1631. He became Bishop of Norwich in 1632.

Thomas Lushington (1631-1661) BD, died on 22 December 1661 and is commemorated at Sittingbourne, Kent.

William Hobbes (1662-1670) DD, was Rector of Sherrington from 1657 to 1670 and also Rector of Boyton. He died in 1670.

Joseph Sayer (1670-1693) died in 1693 and was buried in Northchurch, Berkamsted, Hertfordshire.

William Gale (1693-1715) MA, was Vicar of Downton and in 1715 died and was buried there.

Gilbert Burnet (1715-1721) MA, was the second son of Gilbert Burnet, Bishop of Sarum 1689-1715. He held the prebends of Beminster Secunda from 1715 to 1721and Gillingham Major from 1721 to 1726 and died on 17 June 1726. It was said that he would have attained eminence had he not died young.

John Gamage (1721-1747) MA, died in 1747.

Sherlock Willis (1747-1783) MA, was a godson of Thomas Sherlock, Bishop of Sarum 1734-1748. He held a stall at St Paul's in 1749 and died on 21 April 1783.

William Gilpin (1783-1804) MA, wrote on theological subjects and on picturesque landscape. He died on 5 April 1804 at the age of 80.

Thomas Wickham (1804-1829) MA, was Vicar of North Newnton. He died on 25 September 1829.

William Stanley Goddard (1829-1845) DD, was a Fellow of New College, Oxford and Headmaster of Winchester College. He died on 10 October 1845.

Robert Grant (1845-1886) BCL, was a Fellow of New College, Oxford, a Fellow of Winchester and Vicar of Bradford Abbas, Dorset. He resigned the prebend on 4 December 1886.

George Charles Bell (1886-1913) MA, was Head Master of Christ's Hospital from 1868 to 1876, Master of Marlborough College from 1876 to 1903 and Principal of Queen's College, London from 1903 to 1913. He died on 6 January 1913.

Frederick Wallis (1913-1928) DD, was a Fellow of Caius College, Cambridge, and Dean of Caius from 1878 to 1891. He was Bishop of Wellington, New Zealand from 1895 to 1911, Archdeacon of Wilts from 1911 to 1912, held the prebend of Beminster Secunda from 1913 to 1928 and was the first Archdeacon of Sherborne from 1916 to 1919. He died on 24 June 1928.

William Harrington McCann Clarke (1928-1937) BD, was Vicar of Stratford-sub-Castle from 1906 to 1912, Vicar of Westbury with Dilton & Leigh from 1912 to 1921 and of Bradford on Avon from 1921 to 1937. He was Rural Dean of Bradford from 1930 to 1937. He died in January 1937.

Daniel Frederic Slemeck (1937-1960) MA, was Vicar of Alderholt from 1913 to 1921, Vicar of Charminster (with Stratton to 1931) from 1921 to 1938, Rector of Maiden Newton with Frome Vauchurch from 1938 to 1958 and Rural Dean of Dorchester from 1929 to 1938. He was Rector of Compton Valence from 1947 to 1957, Rector of Compton Abbas with Wynford Eagle & Toller Fratrum from 1949 to 1950 and Rural Dean of Abbotsbury from 1947 to 1955.

Edward Brewer Brooks (1961-1986) was Vicar of Rowde from 1946 to 1956 and of Fordington St George from 1956 to 1970. He was Vicar of St Edmund's, Sarum from 1970 to 1974 and Rector of St Thomas and St Edmund, Sarum from 1974 to 1978.

Bede Robert Cooper (1988-) BA, was Priest-in-Charge of Broad Town from 1974 to 1979 and Vicar of Wootton Bassett from 1974 to 1986. He became Rector of Wilton with Netherhampton and Fugglestone in 1986.

BEMINSTER PRIMA

Prebend:- The manor of Beaminster in Dorset was part of the pre-Conquest Sherborne episcopal estates given to the cathedral. Two prebends were probably in existence by c.1150, being called in the 1220s 'Beymenistr Rogeri' and 'Beymenistr Valentin' but being given the names of 'Prima' and 'Secunda' in c.1270.

Canopy statuette and shield:- **John Thomas** DD, was a Fellow of All Souls, Oxford in 1733 and Preceptor to Prince George, afterwards King George III. A Canon Residentiary of St Paul's in 1742 and Chaplain in Ordinary to George II, he was consecrated Bishop of Peterborough in 1746 and became Bishop of Sarum from 1757 to 1761. He was translated to the see of Winchester in 1761, dying and being buried there in 1781. (Fig. 8.)

Blazon:- Argent on a chevron engrailed azure two griffins combattant of the first gorged with two bars gules on a chief of the second three cinquefoils of the first. [On a silver shield, a blue chevron with 'scooped' edges and on it two rampant silver griffins, with double red collars. Above it, on a blue background, three silver five petalled flowers.]

Psalter:- The portion of the psalter allotted to the prebend is Psalms 60, 61, 62 and 63.

Holders of the prebend:-

Savaric (late 12c.) was a son of Geldwin who was probably second cousin of Jocelin, Bishop of Sarum 1142-1184. He was Archdeacon of Sarum from c.1174 to c.1184 and of Northampton from 1175 to 1192 He held the prebend of Heytesbury c.1183, was Treasurer of Sarum in c.1174/88 and possibly holder of the prebend of Beminster Prima at about the same time. He became Bishop of Bath & Wells in 1192. He held the rectories of Godalming and Hill Deverill in 1180. He died in 1205 and was buried in Bath.

Roger de Worth (c.1225-c.1228) held the prebend referred to as 'Beymenistr Rogeri' from c.1225 to c.1228.

Thomas de Ripton (c.1284-?) held the prebend of Beminster Prima from c.1284 to ?. He was a Canon Residentiary in 1285 and held the prebend of Coombe & Harnham from ? until his death by 11 August 1298.

John de Polbergh (alias Medicus) (?-1298) held the prebend of Warminster from c.1284 to ? when he transferred to the prebend of Beminster Prima, holding it until his death before 3 March 1298.

Richard de Bello (1298) held in turn during 1298 the prebends of Beminster Prima and Grantham Australis, and also Coombe & Harnham from 1298 to 1305. He was then given the prebend of Highworth although John de Frescobaldis had already received a papal nomination. The Pope tried to restore Frescobaldis to the prebend but the Bishop prevented the Dean from oppressing Richard de Bello. Eventually, in 1308, there was a papal dispensation allowing de Bello to retain the prebend of Highworth which he did until 1326. He was Archdeacon of Berks in 1313 and in 1315 had charge of the diocese while the see was vacant on the death of Simon de Gandavo, Bishop of Sarum, 1297-1315. He would seem also to have held a stall at Hereford in 1305 and to have been Rector of Poulshot in 1313. He died in 1326.

Henry de Nassington (1298) held the prebends of Beminster Prima in 1298 and Grantham Australis from 1298 to 1307. He had died by 14 July 1307.

William de Braybrok (1298-?) held the prebends of Alton Australis from c.1297 to 1298 and Beminster Prima from 1298 to c.1319.

Robert Luffenham (?-1348) was a notary public, Archdeacon of Sarum and a Canon Residentiary from ? to 1348 and held the prebend of Beminster Prima from c.1330 to 1348, also holding a stall at Wells. He had died by 6 October 1348.

Peter de Wotton (1349. 1351) who had expectations of a prebend since 1343, occupied this prebend in 1349. Peter de Gildesburgh was appointed in 1351 but there was a royal grant to Peter de Wotton six months later.

Peter de Gildesburg (1351) was granted the prebend of Beminster Prima in 1351 but Peter Wotton appeared to be occupying it. He held the prebend of Rotesfen from 1357 to 1362, when he exchanged it with Robert Walsham for the prebend of St Martin-le-Grand, London.

Ralph Restwald (?-1361) exchanged the prebend with John de Downton for the church of Westbourne, Sussex.

John de Downton (1361-?).

Roger de Freton (1372) DCL.

Reginald Braybroke (?-1406) held the prebend of Beminster Prima from ? to 1406 when he exchanged it with John Frank for the prebend of Rotesfen which he held from 1406 to 1407. He then exchanged this prebend with Roger Attehurn for St Radegund's chapel in St Paul's crypt.

Roger Walden (1389) received a royal grant of the prebend of Beminster Prima in 1389 and held the prebends of Bishopstone from 1391 to 1392 and Horton from 1392 to 1397. He was consecrated Archbishop of Canterbury in 1397 but his claim was refused by King Henry IV. He became Bishop of London in 1405 and died a year later.

John Frank (1406-1415) held the prebend of Rotesfen in 1406, exchanging it with Reginald Braybroke for Beminster Prima which he held from 1406 to 1415. He then held the prebend of Chisenbury & Chute from 1415 to 1433 and Fordington & Writhlington from 1433 to 1438.

Henry Harburgh (1415-1418) was Treasurer of Sarum for three days in 1394 when he exchanged the dignity with John Chaundeler for the prebend of Netherbury in Ecclesia. This he exchanged in 1395 with Ralph Selby for the prebend of Alton Borealis. He relinquished this latest prebend in 1403 receiving that of Slape. This he held until 1415 when he received the prebend of Beminster Prima. In 1416 he became Precentor of Sarum, he relinquished his prebend in 1418 and in the same year exchanged the dignity of Precentor for the prebend of Bere & Cherminster, which he held until 1432. He had died by 22 September 1432.

John Tydeling (1418-1420) BCL, was a Canon Residentiary and held the prebend of Axford from 1401 to 1404 when he exchanged it with George Westby for the prebend of Major Pars Altaris. He held this prebend until 1406. He then held the prebends of Warminster from 1406 to 1418, Yetminster Secunda in 1418, Beminster Prima from 1418 to 1420, Stratton from 1420 to 1437, exchanging it with John Symondsburgh for the prebend of Yatesbury in 1437. This he exchanged with John Morton for the prebend of North Leverton in Southwell collegiate church, Nottinghamshire.

John Ixworth (1420-1431) DCL, was appointed to the prebend of Highworth in 1406 but apparently failed to gain possession. He was Archdeacon of Worcester in 1412, held stalls at St Paul's and Chichester and held the prebend of Beminster Prima from 1420 until his resignation in 1431.

Walter Sherrington (1431-1436) held the prebend of Minor Pars Altaris in 1420, exchanging it with Richard Richman for the prebend of Decem Librarum at Lincoln. He held the prebends of Beminster Prima from 1431 to 1436 and Shipton from 1436 until his death in 1449. He held stalls at York and Chichester and was Chancellor of the Duchy of Lancaster and a Canon Residentiary of St Paul's.

John Payne (1436-1467) held the prebends of Shipton from 1435 to 1436 and Beminster Prima from 1436 to 1467. He died in 1467.

John Curteys (1467-1471) DM, died in 1471.

William Moreland (1471-1482) exchanged the prebend in 1482 with David Hopton for a prebend at St Stephen's, Westminster.

David Hopton (1482-?) held the prebends of Beminster Prima from 1482 to c.1487 and Bitton from 1487 to 1492. He may have held a stall at, and been Archdeacon of, Exeter. He died in 1492.

James Stanley (1493-1506) was a son of Thomas, Earl of Derby. He held the prebends of Yetminster Prima in 1477, again from 1492 to 1493, and Beminster Prima from 1493 to 1506. He was Archdeacon of Richmond in 1500, Precentor of Sarum from 1485 to 1506 and became Bishop of Ely in 1506.

Francis Meryng (1507-1509) died in 1509.

William Barton (1509-1515) was Succentor of Sarum from 1502 to 1509. He was consecrated Bishop Suffragan of Saloniensis c.1509 to assist Edmund Audley, Bishop of Sarum 1502-1524, within the diocese which he did from 1509 to 1517. He held the prebends of Ruscomb in 1509, Beminster Prima from 1509 to 1515 and of Grimston from 1515 to 1518. He died in 1518.

Thomas Martyn (1515-1517) DCnL, held the prebends of Chardstock from 1507 to 1515, Beminster Prima from 1515 to 1517 and Wilsford & Woodford from 1517 to 1524. He died in 1524.

John Woodroff (1517-?) held the prebends of Axford from 1508 to 1509, Ruscomb from 1509 to 1517 and Beminster Prima from 1517 to ? He also held a stall at Hereford.

Edward Baker (or Elton) (? -1533) died in 1533.

Richard Coren (1533-1543) DTh, died in 1543.

Stephen Cheston (1543-1572) LLB, died in 1572.

Robert Pinkeney (1572-1636) BA, was summoned more than once before the Chapter for failing to pay his Vicar his stipend and for failing to take his own preaching turn. He was Rector of Berwick St John and died in 1636.

Gilbert Hynde (1636-1658) MA, died in 1658.

Thomas Lockey (1660) BD, held the prebends of Beminster Prima in 1660, and Alton Australis from 1660 until resigning in 1672. He held a stall at Christ Church, Oxford in 1665 and died in 1679.

Thomas Bowerman (1660-1671) DD, died in 1671.

Charles Mason (1671-1677/8) DD, was a Fellow of King's College, Cambridge and Rector of Stour Provost. A return to the Commissioners in 1650 reported that 'the parsonage of Stower Provost was worth £70 per annum, Charles Mason receiving the profits, but not being a sufficiently able minister nor serving the cure himself above two or three Sabbaths together, but putting in disaffected ministers in his place.' He died in 1677/8.

The Hon John Feilding (1678-1682) MA, DD, was the 4th son of the 1st Earl of Desmond. He was a Chaplain to King William III and was Vicar of Piddlehinton. He was a Canon Residentiary from 1680 to 1698 and was Archdeacon of Dorset in the diocese of Bristol from 1683 to 1697. He held the prebends of Yatesbury from 1677 to 1678, Beminster Prima from 1678 to 1682 and Gillingham Major from 1682 to 1698, dying in 1698.

Giles Thornburgh (1682-?) MA, held the prebends of Gillingham Minor from 1677 to 1682 and Beminster Prima from 1682 to ? It was vacant at 28 March 1693. He held a stall at Winchester in 1684.

Edward Chubb (1693-1710) MA, was Rector of Warminster and of Brixton Deverill in 1710, in which year he died.

John Foster (1710-1724) MA, was Vicar of Longbridge Deverill from 1685 to 1724 and was buried at that church.

Abdias Taylor (1724-1745) died in 1745.

William Hillman (1746-1753) MA, held the prebends of Beminster Prima from 1746 to 1753 and of Ilfracombe from 1753 to 1773. He died on 4 March 1773.

John Allen (1753-1757) MA, held the prebends of Beminster Prima from 1753 to 1757 and Fordington & Writhlington from 1757 to 1765. He died in 1765.

James Sparrow (1757-1770) MA, was Rector of Brinkworth. He resigned in 1770.

James Sparrow (1770-1797) BD, was the son of his predecessor. He died on 1 March 1797.

Robert Charles Blayney (1797-1803) MA, was a Fellow of Worcester College, Oxford. He held the prebends of Beminster Prima from 1797 to 1803 and Chisenbury & Chute from 1803 to 1824. He died on 29 September 1824.

Richard Francis Onslow (1803-1823) MA, was Archdeacon of Worcester in 1815. He held the prebends of Beminster Prima from 1803 to 1823 and Highworth from 1823 to 1849. He died on 18 October 1849.

Matthew Marsh (1823-1824) DD, was Rector of Brinkworth from 1802 to 1840, of Winterslow in 1804 and Chancellor of the Diocese in 1819. He held the prebends of Beminster Prima from 1823 to 1824 and Chisenbury & Chute from 1824 to 1840. He was Subdean of Sarum from 1824 to 1840 and was a Canon Residentiary from 1826 to 1840. He died on 30 July 1840, was buried in the south choir aisle and is commemorated in the south east transept of the cathedral.

Henry William Majendie (1824-1869) MA, was Vicar of Speen, Berkshire, and also held a stall at Bangor. He died on 17 December 1869.

Robert Francis Wilson (1870-1888) died on 8 October 1888.

Edward Inman (1889-1924) MA, was Rector and Vicar of West Knoyle from 1872 to 1882. He was Rector of Gillingham with East & West Stour, Milton, Motcombe and Enmore Green from 1882 to 1891, Vicar of Potterne from 1891 to 1899 and Rural Dean of Potterne from 1892 to 1900. He died on 15 May 1924.

Edward Denny (1924-1928) MA, was Rector of Codford St Peter from 1915 to 1928. He died on 18 May 1928 and was buried at Codford St Peter.

Charles Hawkins Syndercombe Bower (1928-1961) was Vicar of Hinton St Mary from 1899 to 1909, Rector of Childe Okeford from 1909 to 1938 and of Hanford from 1913 to 1938. He was Rural Dean of Sturminster Newton from 1922 to 1929 and Curate in Charge of Fifehead Magdalen from 1938 to 1939 and of East Orchard with St Margaret's Marsh from 1939 to 1950. He died in 1961.

Harry George Green (1961-1971) was Vicar of Christ Church, Warminster from 1943 to 1965 and Curate-in-Charge of Bishopstrow from 1953 to 1956. He was Vicar of Abbotsbury from 1965 to 1971 and died in July 1994.

John Henry Rumens (1972-1986) AKC, was Vicar of Alderholt from 1954 to 1959, Rector of St Edmund's, Sarum from 1959 to 1972, Rural Dean of Sarum from 1969 to 1972 and Vicar of The Trinity, Trowbridge from 1972 to 1979. He was Priest-in-Charge of Sturminster Marshall from 1979 to 1983 and Vicar from 1983 until his retirement in 1985.

Richard Andrew Babington (1988-1993) was Rector of Blandford Forum and also of Langton Long from 1972 to 1993. He was Rural Dean of Milton & Blandford from 1986 to 1993 and died in July 1993.

[John Hugh Charles Privett (1995-) Lay Canon and solicitor. He joined Porter Bartlett & Mayo, now Porter Dodson, of Somerset and Dorset, in 1973 and the Diocesan Board of Finance in 1974, becoming Chairman in 1989, whilst also holding parochial and deanery appointments. He occupies Beminster Prima as a courtesy stall.**]**

(Gangway)

Shield:- **John Colet** held the prebend of Durnford from 1503 to 1519. He was Dean of St Paul's in 1505 and founded its school. He died in 1519. (Fig. 9.)

Blazon:- Sable a chevron between three bucks trippant or. [On a black shield, a gold chevron between three golden walking bucks.]

VICAR CHORAL

Shield:- **William Camden** was a layman who was Second Master of Westminster School in 1575, Headmaster in 1593 and Clarenceaux King of Arms in 1597. He held the prebend of Ilfracombe from 1589 to 1623 and died in 1623. (Fig. 10.)

Blazon:- Azure a fess engrailed between six crosses crosslet fitchee or. [Across the centre of a blue shield, a broad, horizontal gold band with 'scooped' edges between six gold crosses with pointed base and the top and arms crossed.]

ALTON BOREALIS

Prebend:- The Manor of Alton Pancras in Dorset was part of the pre-Conquest episcopal estates of Sherborne. By c.1150 two prebends were probably in existence. In the 1220s these were called 'Awelton arch[idiaconi]', and 'Awelton', while both were called 'Awelton' without distinction in 1226. In 1284 the names were 'Awelton Sancti Pancratii' and 'Awelton', while in 1291 there was a distinction between 'Aulton in Southbury', later Australis, and 'Aulton in Northbury', later Borealis. From 1329, the holders of the prebends can certainly be distinguished and can be traced back to 1297 but for the purpose of the earlier succession in the prebends, 'Alton Pancras' is taken to be Alton Australis and 'Alton Archidiaconi' to be Alton Borealis.

Shield:- **William Lyndwood** DCn&CL, was a celebrated author and Dean of the Court of Arches. He was employed by King Henry V in various missions to Spain, Portugal and elsewhere, and was at one time Keeper of the Privy Seal. He held the prebends of Ruscomb from 1412 to 1424 and Bishopstone from 1424 to 1434. He was nominated by the Pope to the see of St David's and was consecrated in 1442. (Fig. 11.)

Blazon:- Argent a fess crenelly between three fleurs-de-lys sable. [Across the centre of a silver shield, a broad, horizontal battlemented black band between three black fleurs-de-lys.]

Psalter:- The portion of the psalter allotted to the prebend is Psalms 83, 84 and 85.

Holders of the Prebend:-

Humphrey (c.1226/7) was Archdeacon of Dorset c.1226 to c.1241 and may have held a stall at Chichester. He had died before 1 May 1244.

Wimund (c.1284-c.1288).

John de Langeton (c.1297-1305) was Royal Chancellor from 1292 to 1302, Treasurer of Wells from 1296, Bishop-elect of Ely in 1298, Archdeacon of Canterbury from 1299 and Bishop of Chichester from 1305. He held stalls at Chichester, Lichfield, Lincoln, Dublin and Lanchester and died in 1337.

Richard Inge (1305-?) was holding the prebend in 1320 when he was fined for non-residence.

Thomas Owayn (1340-?).

Thomas de Pulteneye (1353) Lic.Cn&CL.

John de Gormonchester (?-1388) held a papal grant to hold this and other prebends at the same time.

Thomas Swyndon (1388-1392) BTh, died in 1392.

Ralph Selby (1392-1395) DCL, was Warden of King's Hall, Cambridge in 1391, Archdeacon of Buckingham in 1392, and of Norfolk in 1394. He held the prebends of Alton Borealis from 1392 to 1395 and Netherbury in Ecclesia from 1395 until his resignation in 1401 on becoming a monk at Westminster.

Henry Harburgh (1395-1403) was Treasurer of Sarum for three days in 1394 when he exchanged the dignity with John Chaundeler for the prebend of Netherbury in Ecclesia. This he exchanged in 1395 with Ralph Selby for the prebend of Alton Borealis. He relinquished this latest prebend in 1403, receiving that of Slape. This he held until 1415 when he received the prebend of Beminster Prima. In 1416 he became Precentor of Sarum. He relinquished his prebend in 1418 and in the same year exchanged the dignity of Precentor for the prebend of Bere & Cherminster, which he held until 1432. He had died by 22 September 1432.

William Dennis (1403-1407) died in 1407.

John Everdon (1407-1420) died in 1420.

John Forrest (1420-1446) held a stall at Lincoln in 1401 and was Dean of Wells in 1425. He died in 1446.

Robert Ayscough (1446-1459) DCnL, held the prebends of Warminster from 1440 to 1441, Bishopstone from 1441 to 1446 and Alton Borealis from 1446 to 1459. He had resigned by 9 April 1459.

Thomas Estington (1459-1469) Sch.Th, held the prebends of Alton Borealis from 1459 to 1469 and Yetminster Secunda from 1469 to 1471. He died on 3 January 1471.

John Alcock (1469-1472) DCL, was the founder of Jesus College, Cambridge. He was Master of the Rolls and later Lord Chancellor. He became Bishop of Rochester in 1472, of Worcester in 1476 and of Ely in 1486. He died on 1 October 1500.

John Gunthorpe (1472-?) MA, held the prebends of Alton Borealis from 1472 to ? and Bitton from 1492 to 1498. He was Almoner to King Edward IV and in 1468 Warden of King's Hall, Cambridge. He held a stall at St Paul's in 1468, was Archdeacon of Essex and was Dean of Wells in 1472. He had died by July 1498.

John Coryngdon (?-1495) BCnL, died in 1495.

Hugh Oldham (1495-1500) BCn&CL, held the prebends of Alton Borealis from 1495 until resigning in 1500, and Netherbury in Ecclesia from ? to 1505. He was the founder of the Manchester Grammar School and a benefactor of Corpus Christi College, Oxford, becoming Bishop of Exeter in 1505. He died in 1519.

James Straytbarell (1500-1506) exchanged the prebend with John Veysey in 1506 for the church of St Mary upon the Hill, Chester.

John Veysey (1506-1514) DCL, was Chancellor of Lichfield and Canon, Precentor and ultimately Dean, of Exeter. He also held the Deaneries of Windsor and Wolverhampton. In 1519 he became Bishop of Exeter. He vacated the prebend for eleven days in December 1514 to permit John Longland to be eligible for the dignity of Dean of Sarum.

John Longland (1514) DTh, was Principal of Magdalen Hall, Oxford in 1505 and Confessor to King Henry VIII. He held the prebend of Alton Borealis for ten days in 1514 before becoming Dean of Sarum, holding the dignity from 1514 to 1521. He held a stall at Windsor in 1519, became Bishop of Lincoln in 1521 and Chancellor of Oxford in 1532 He died on 7 May 1547.

John Veysey (1514-1519) see above.

John Hone (1519-?) MA.

John Booth (?-1542) DTh, died in 1542.

John Crayford (1542-1544) DD, held the prebend of Alton Borealis from 1542 to 1544 and was permitted to be simultaneously Chancellor of Sarum from 1544 to 1547 and Archdeacon of Berks from 1545 to 1547, becoming Master of University College, Oxford in 1546. He became a Canon Residentiary in 1547 and died the same year.

Roland Swynbourne (1544-1557) MA, died in 1557.

Thomas Lewen (1557-?) was appointed to the prebend in October 1557, was instituted by the Archbishop and despite a counter claim was installed in 1558.

Robert Burton (1557) BCL, was appointed in November 1557 and although he petitioned the Archbishop in April 1558 for institution instead of Thomas Lewen, he died soon after and his rival claimant was installed.

George Harvey (1559-1564) BA, died in 1564.

John Bolde (1564-1589) DD, was a Canon Residentiary from 1570 to 1602 and held the prebends of Alton Borealis from 1564 to 1589 and Ufcomb from 1589 to 1602. He died in 1602.

John Case (1589-1600) MA, was a Fellow of St John's College, Oxford who died on 23 January 1600.

Ralph Hulton (1600-1619) DM, died in 1619.

John Lynch (1619-1630) MA, resigned in 1630.

Richard Steward (1630-1651) DCL, was a Fellow of All Souls' College, Oxford. He held the livings of Aldbourne from 1629 to 1639, Alton Barnes in 1630 and of Mildenhall, and became Clerk of the Closet to King Charles I. He was Dean of Chichester in 1634, Provost of Eton in 1639 and in 1640 was chosen to be the Prolocutor of Convocation. In 1642 he was nominated Dean of St Paul's and afterwards Dean of Westminster but was never installed. He was deprived of all his preferments and died in Paris on 14 November 1651

Francis Horton (1660) MA, held the prebends of Alton Borealis in 1660 and Bedminster & Redcliffe from 1660 to 1699. He was Canon Residentiary from 1674 to 1699, acting in 1683 as locum tenens for the Dean. He was in succession incumbent of St Martin, Sarum, and St Thomas, Sarum, and was Vicar of Melksham in 1686. He corresponded about the Bishop's Visitations and a letter from Canon Robert Woodward, Dean of Sarum 1691-1702 to Archbishop Sancroft reported on the proceedings against Francis Horton for disrespectful language to the Judge of the Consistory Court. He died in 1699 and was buried at Melksham.

Richard Drake (1660-1663) DD, held the prebend of Alton Borealis from 1660 to 1663 and was Chancellor of Sarum from 1663 to 1681. He was a Canon Residentiary from 1666 to 1681, catalogued the muniments in the cathedral and died in 1681.

John Durell (1663-1683) MA, held a stall at Durham in 1668 and was Dean of Windsor in 1677. He died on 6 June 1683.

Richard Hill (1683-1695) MA, was Rector of East Knoyle from 1662 to 1695. He held the prebends of Grantham Borealis from 1666-1683 and Alton Borealis from 1683 to 1695. He was a Canon Residentiary from 1665 to 1671, died on 20 March 1695 and was buried in the cathedral near the door of the Consistory Court.

Charles Trippett (1695-1707) MA, was Rector of East Knoyle from 1695 to 1707. He died on 7 July 1707 and is commemorated at East Knoyle.

William Jackson (1707-1723) was Vicar of Aldbourne from 1681 to 1723. He died in 1723 and was buried at Aldbourne.

Arthur Ashley Sykes (1724-1756) MA, held the prebend of Alton Borealis from 1724 to 1756 and was Precentor of Sarum from 1726 to 1756. He died on 23 November 1756.

William Barford (1756-1780) was Vicar of North Newnton from 1722 to1731, Rector of Chilmark from 1723 to 1747 and Rector and Vicar of Bishopstone from 1747 to 1780. He died on 8 June 1780.

Thomas Eyre (1780-1812) DCL, held the prebends of Stratford from 1778 to 1780 and Alton Borealis from 1780 to 1812. He was Rector of Chilmark from 1770 to 1812, was also Rector of Fovant and was a Canon Residentiary from 1797 to 1812. He died on 26 March 1812.

Robert Morres (1812-1841) MA, held the prebends of Netherbury in Terra from 1805 to 1812 and Alton Borealis from 1812 to 1841. He was Vicar of Britford and died on 18 October 1841.

James Venables (1842-1850) MA, was Vicar of Buckland Newton, Dorset. He died on 18 December 1850.

Newton Smart (1851-1879) MA, was Vicar of Alderbury in 1843. He died on 23 June 1879.

Martin Johnson Green (1879-1889) BD, was a Fellow of Lincoln College, Oxford, Rector of Winterbourne Abbas from 1848 to 1889 and Rural Dean of Bridport from 1868 to 1885. He died on 17 September 1889.

George Herbert Moberly (1889-1895) MA, was a historian and son of George Moberly, Bishop of Sarum 1869-1885. He was Master of St Nicholas Hospital from 1878 to 1895 and died on 30 April 1895.

Walter Francis Short (1895-1896) MA, was a Fellow of New College, Oxford and Chaplain at the Royal Military Academy, Woolwich from 1870 to 1875. He was Rector of Donhead St Mary with Charlton from 1882 to 1896 and Rural Dean of Chalke from 1888 to 1896.

Henry Clark Powell (1896-1901) MA, was Provost of Inverness from 1869 to 1876, Vicar of Stanton St Bernard from 1877 to 1882 and of Wylye from 1882 to 1901. He died on 5 May 1901.

Charles Rowland Haydock Hill (1901-1911) MA, was Rector of Evershot with Frome St Quintin and Melbury Bubb from 1885 to 1889 and of West Fordington from 1889 to 1894. He was Vicar of Lyme Regis from 1894 to 1898 and Rector of Holy Trinity, Dorchester with Frome Whitfield from 1898 to 1911. He died on 15 July 1911.

Charles Lloyd Sanctuary (1912-1934) MA, was Vicar of West Fordington from 1880 to 1889, Vicar of Powerstock with Milton from 1889 to 1898, Rector of North Poorton from 1890 to 1898 and Rural Dean of Bridport from 1894 to 1898. He was Vicar of St Thomas, Sarum from 1898 to 1914 and Vicar of Frampton from 1917 to 1920. He died in 1934.

Reginald Ernest Pennington Gorringe (1935-1959) MA, was Rector of Manston from 1910 to 1928 and Vicar of St Thomas, Sarum from 1928 to 1937. He was Custos of St John's Hospital Heytesbury from 1937 to 1959 and Rural Dean of Heytesbury from 1944 to 1946. He died in 1959.

Edward John Mackie (1959-1974) was Rector of Charmouth from 1945 to 1962 and of Catherston-Leweston from 1958 to 1962. He was Vicar of Whiteparish from 1962 to 1968.

Patrick Thomas Ashton (1975-1977) LVO, MA, was Domestic Chaplain to Queen Elizabeth II from 1955 to 1970. He was Rector in the Swanborough Group from 1970 to 1973, Curate-in-Charge of Avebury with Winterbourne Monkton and Berwick Basset from 1974 to 1975 and Team Rector of Upper Kennet from 1975 until his retirement in 1977. He died in April 1994.

Denis Walter Shaw (1977-1985) was Rector of Tarrant Rushton, of Tarrant Keynstone and of Tarrant Crawford from 1970 to 1976, Rural Dean of Milton & Blandford from 1973 to 1981, Priest-in-Charge of Bere Regis from 1976 to 1977, and Vicar of Bere Regis and Affpuddle with Turners Puddle from 1978 until his retirement in 1985. He died in May 1997.

Peter Robert Oades (1985-1989) MA, was Vicar Choral and also Chaplain of the Cathedral School from 1968 to 1974. He was Vicar of Sturminster Newton and Hinton St Mary from 1974 to 1981, Rector of Stock Gaylard with Kings Stag and Lydlinch from 1975 to 1981 and Rural Dean of Blackmore Vale from 1978 to 1981. He was Vicar of the Woodford Valley from 1981 until his retirement in 1989 and Chaplain to the Deaf in Salisbury from 1982 to 1992.

Philip Anthony Crowe (1991-1995) MA, was a tutor and the last Principal of Salisbury & Wells Theological College from 1988 to 1995 and a Proctor in Convocation from 1990 to 1995.

David Kingsley Callard (1995-) MA, was Team Rector of Swanage and Studland Team Ministry, from 1983 to 1993 and Team Rector of Oakdale St George from 1993.

BISHOPSTONE

Prebend:- Bishopstone in north Wiltshire was a part of the bishop's manor of Ramsbury in 1066 and 1086. and may have been included in the grant of Ramsbury church to the canons of the cathedral by Osmund, Bishop of Sarum 1078-1099. The prebend, consisting of the church of Bishopstone was probably in existence by c.1150. It should not be confused with the parish of Bishopstone near Salisbury.

Shield:- **George Moberly** DCL, was a Fellow of Balliol College, Oxford and Headmaster of Winchester College from 1835 until 1866 when he was elected a Fellow of Winchester. He held a stall at Chester in 1868, becoming Bishop of Sarum in 1869; the first high church appointment for many years. His episcopate was marked by the establishment of a Church Synod composed of laity as well as clergy. For some time before his death on 6 July 1885 his faculties had been decaying and his episcopal duties were discharged by the Rt Revd James Butler Knill Kelly, formerly Bishop of Newfoundland. He was buried by the east end of the south choir aisle in the cathedral. (Fig. 12.)

Blazon:- Or two chevrons gules on a canton of the second a cross crosslet fitchee argent. [On a gold shield, two red chevrons. On a red square in the top left corner, a silver cross with pointed base and the top and arms crossed.]

Psalter:- The portion of the psalter allotted to the prebend is Psalms 67 and 68.

Holders of the prebend:-

Henry of Bishopstone (c.1226/7-c.1246) on occasion taught canon law at Oxford. He was fined for non-residence and was also abroad on business for King Henry III in 1227.

William de Schireborn (?-1284) was Proctor of Scholars of De Vaux College in 1269, held the prebend of Bishopstone between ? and 1284, held the vicarage of Chirton in 1346 and was Subdean of Sarum from c.1271 to c.1284.

John de Havering (?-1306) was a papal chaplain and Archdeacon of Dublin who had died at the Papal Curia by 12 October 1306.

Richard de Havering (?-1341) was fined for non-residence in 1320 and died in 1341.

Peter de Inkpen (1341) was Rector of Chiseldon in1324 and held the prebends of Bishopstone in 1341 and Wilsford & Woodford from 1341 to ?

Peter Raymund de Rapistagno (1342-1350) was nominated to the prebend in 1342 and was installed in 1343. He died in 1350.

Walter de Brian (1343) was granted the prebend in 1343 although it was already occupied by Peter Raymund de Rapistagno.

Ramond Pelegrini (1350) held the prebend of Bishopstone in 1350. He was nominated to the prebend of Highworth in 1350 but Henry Walton was also appointed. He exchanged the prebend of Highworth in February 1365 with Peter Boniface for the chapel in the Bishop of London's palace but it appears that the exchange was out of order as the prebend was later said to be vacant due to his death on 16 September 1365.

Arnold Pelegrini (1350-1363) disputed William de Okeborne's right to the prebend and died in 1363.

William de Okeborne (1351-?) received a royal grant of the prebend in 1351 despite it having already been reserved to the Pope and been granted to Arnold Pelegrini. On Pelegrini's death in 1363 he received the prebend and was holding it in 1366.

William Fullborne (? -1391) was in possession of the prebend in 1387 and had died by 6 August 1391.

Roger Walden (1391-1392) received a royal grant of the prebend of Beminster Prima in 1389 and held the prebends of Bishopstone from 1391 to 1392 and Horton from 1392 to 1397. He was consecrated Archbishop of Canterbury in 1397 but his claim was refused by King Henry IV. He became Bishop of London in 1405 and died a year later.

Robert Ragenhull (1393) was a Canon Residentiary and Archdeacon of Dorset from 1388 to c.1390. He held the prebend of Bishopstone in 1393, exchanging it with Richard Holme for the prebend of Warminster which he exchanged with John Tydeling in 1406 for the prebend of Major Pars Altaris, holding the latter until 1407. He was Provost of St Edmund's College, Sarum in 1395 and died in 1407.

Richard Holme (1393-1424) held the prebend of Warminster from 1391 to 1393, exchanging it with Robert Ragenhull in 1393 for the prebend of Bishopstone which he held until 1424. He died in 1424.

William Lyndwood (1424-1434) DCn&CL, was a celebrated author and Dean of the Court of Arches. He was employed by Henry King V in various missions to Spain, Portugal and elsewhere, and was at one time Keeper of the Privy Seal. He held the prebends of Ruscomb from 1412 to 1424 and Bishopstone from 1424 to 1434. He was nominated by the Pope to the see of St David's and was consecrated in 1442.

Stephen Wilton (1434-?) DCnL, was Archdeacon of Sarum from 1433 until after 1435 and held the prebends of Bishopstone from 1434 to? and Chardstock from 1441 to 1442. He held a stall at Lincoln, exchanging it in 1433 for a stall at St Paul's. He was Archdeacon of Middlesex in 1441 and of Cleveland in 1454. He died in 1457.

Adam Moleyns (?-1441) was Rector of Winterbourne Earls in 1432 and held a stall at St Paul's as well as the dignity of Archdeacon of Taunton in 1440. He was Archdeacon of Sarum and held the prebend of Bishopstone from c.1440 to 1441. He held a stall at York in 1441, was Dean of Sarum from 1441 to 1445 becoming Bishop of Chichester. He sat in 1441 as Commissary to try Eleanor Duchess of Gloucester for witchcraft and went to Rome to urge, unsuccessfully, the canonisation of Bishop Osmund. In 1443 he assisted in arranging the marriage of King Henry VI with Margaret of Anjou. In 1450, whilst Bishop of Chichester, he was murdered by some sailors in Portsmouth.

Robert Ayscough (1441-1446) DCnL, held the prebends of Warminster from 1440 to 1441, Bishopstone from 1441 to 1446 and Alton Borealis from 1446 to 1459. He had resigned by 9 April 1459.

William Normanton (1446-1447) held the prebends of Yatesbury from 1443 to 1445, Warminster from 1445 to 1446, Bishopstone from 1446 to 1447, Durnford from 1447 to 1448, Chisenbury & Chute from 1448 to 1449 and Faringdon from 1449 to 1459. He died in 1459.

John Paslewe (1447-1449) BCn&CL, held the prebends of Minor Pars Altaris from 1446 to 1447, Bishopstone from 1447 to 1449, Alton Australis in 1449, and Chisenbury & Chute from 1449 to 1457. He held a stall at Hereford in 1447 and died 1457.

Richard Trove (1449) held the prebends of Axford from 1447 to 1449, Bishopstone and Alton Australis in 1449 and Netheravon from 1449-?

Richard Hayman (1449) held the prebends of Axford and Bishopstone in 1449 and Alton Australis from 1449 to 1461, exchanging it with John Waynefleet for a canonry at St Stephen's, Westminster.

John Hethe (1449-1465) MA, died in 1465.

William Osgodby (1465-1467) was a Canon Residentiary in charge of the choir and was Rector of Codford St Peter in 1476. He held the prebends of Axford from 1459 to 1465, Bishopstone from 1465 to 1467, exchanging the latter with Robert Ampleford for the prebend of Beminster Secunda which he held from 1467 to 1475. He then held the prebend of Chisenbury & Chute from 1475 to 1484 and died in 1484.

Robert Ampleford (1467-1468) MA, held the prebends of Rotesfen from 1431 to 1432 and Beminster Secunda from 1432 to 1467, exchanging the latter with William Osgodby for Bishopstone which he held from 1467 until his death in 1468.

John Pemberton (1468-1472) held the prebend of Bishopstone from 1468 to 1472, exchanging it with John Davyson for the prebend of Cadington Major in St Paul's.

John Davyson (1472-1473) was Dean of Windsor in 1471, held the prebend of Bishopstone from 1472 to 1473, a stall at St Paul's in 1473 and was Dean of Sarum from 1473 to 1485. He died 12 October 1485.

John Barnaby (1473-1482) exchanged the prebend in 1482 with John Blakwyn for the church of Barwick in Elmet, Yorkshire.

John Blakwyn (1482-?) MA.

Richard Fox (?-1486) BCL, held the prebends of Bishopstone from ? to 1486 and Granthan Borealis from 1486 to 1487, founding schools at Taunton and Grantham. He became Bishop of Exeter in 1487, of Bath in 1492, of Durham in 1494 and of Winchester in 1501. He was the Keeper of the Great Seal to King Henry VII and King Henry VIII and founded Corpus Christ College, Oxford. He died in 1528.

William Elliott (1486-?) BCL, held the prebend of Bishopstone from 1486 possibly until 1501. He was probably Archdeacon of Barnstable in 1492 and was Chancellor of Sarum from 1501 to 1507. He was Provost of St Edmund's College, Sarum and, dying in 1507, asked to be buried in the cathedral.

Eliseus Ruthyn (?-1511) BCn&CL, died in 1511.

Thomas Randolph (1511-1521) Lic.CnL, held the prebends of Warminster from 1497 to 1511 and Bishopstone from 1511 to 1521. He died in 1521.

Edward Finch (1521-1522) DM, was well endowed with prebends holding in succession those of Yatesbury from 1514 to 1515, Chardstock from 1515 to 1517, Wilsford & Woodford in 1517, Fordington & Writhlington from 1517 to 1518, Grimston from 1518 to 1519, Faringdon from 1519 to 1521 exchanging the latter with William Webbe for the church of Ross on Wye, Hereford. He then held the prebends of Bishopstone from 1521 to 1522, Teynton Regis from 1522 to 1524 and Bere & Cherminster from 1524 to 1539. He was Archdeacon of Wilts from 1522 until 1539, died in 1539 and was buried in the cathedral.

Edward Molineux (1522-1524) held the prebends of Minor Pars Altaris from 1519 to 1522, Bishopstone from 1522 to 1524 and Faringdon from 1524 to 1535.

Bernard Holden (1524-1531) died in 1531.

John Wafer (1531-1538) died in 1538.

John Macalpine (1538-?).

Paul Bush (?-1554) was a Canon Residentiary and became the first Bishop of Bristol in 1542, whilst continuing to hold the prebend until 1554.

Lawrence Hussey (1554-?) Lic.CL.

John Disley (1560-1563) had resigned by 29 June 1563.

James Harbert (1563-1568) had resigned by 8 July 1568.

John Watkins (1568-1594) MA, died in May 1594.

Peter Sharpe (?-1601) BD, had resigned by 23 March 1601.

John Barnston (1601-1645) MA, was a Fellow of Brasenose College, Oxford and the founder of a Hebrew Lecture there. For some time he was Chaplain to Lord Chancellor Egerton. He was Rector of Everley in 1598, a Canon Residentiary from c.1614 to 1645 and acted as locum tenens for the Dean. He died on 30 May 1645 and was buried at the east end of the cathedral.

Henry Kininmond (1660-1678) MA, was Rector of All Cannings and dying in 1678 was buried at All Cannings.

Isaac Walton (1679-1681) MA, was a son of Isaak Walton. He held the prebends of Yatesbury from 1678 to 1679, Bishopstone from 1679 to 1681 and Netheravon from 1681 to 1719. He was Rector of Boscombe in 1679 and Rector of Poulshot in 1680. He was a Canon Residentiary from 1698 to 1719, living in what is now known as the Walton Canonry in the Close, he died on 29 December 1719 and was buried in the cathedral.

Richard Bowman (1681-1691) BCL, held the prebends of Bishopstone from 1681 to 1691 and Ufcomb from 1691 to 1692. He died in 1692 and was buried in Potterne.

Cornelius Yeate (1691-1696) MA, held the prebend of Bishopstone from 1691 to 1696 and was Archdeacon of Wilts from 1696 to 1720. He had considerable controversy with Seth Ward, Bishop of Sarum 1667-1689, over the disposal of the prebends and owed his promotion to both the prebend and the Archdeaconry to Gilbert Burnet, Bishop of Sarum 1689-1715. He died on 12 April 1720.

Thomas Coker (1696-1741) MA, was a Canon Residentiary from 1713 to 1741. He was Rector of Little Hinton from 1684 to 1741 and died in 1741.

Angel Chauncy (1741-1762) MA, died on 28 April 1762.

John Taylor (1762-1765) DD, held the prebends of Bishopstone from 1762 to 1765 and Fordington & Writhlington from 1765 to 1772, and was a Canon Residentiary with the house of Leadenhall from 1766 to 1772. He was well known in the literary world, was Chancellor of the Diocese of Lincoln in 1744, Archdeacon of Buckingham in 1753 and held a stall at St Paul's from 1757 to 1766. He died on 29 August 1772.

Norman Mead (1765-1766) MA, died on 3 June 1766.

William Whitworth (1766-1804) MA, was Archdeacon of Sarum, holding the prebend of Bishopstone from 1766 to 1804. He died on 14 May 1804.

Edward Rogers (1804-1821) MA, resigned in 1821.

Whittington Landon (1821-1838) DD, became Vicar of Bishopstone in 1817. He held a stall at Norwich and was Provost of Worcester College, Oxford and Dean of Exeter. He died on 29 December 1838.

William Dansey (1841-1856) MA, was an historian whose works included *Horæ Decaniæ Rurales*, and Rector of Donhead St Andrew from 1820 to 1856. He died on 7 June 1856.

Francis Lear (1856-1861) MA, was Rector and Vicar of Bishopstone from 1850 to 1914. He held the prebend of Bishopstone from 1856 to 1861, was Chancellor of Sarum from 1861 to 1864, a Canon Residentiary from 1862 to 1914, Precentor of Sarum from 1864 to 1875 and Archdeacon of Sarum from 1875 to 1914. He held the prebend of Bricklesworth from 1861 to 1914 and dying on 19 February 1914 was buried in the cloisters.

James Fraser (1861-1870) was a Fellow of Oriel College, Oxford and was Rector of Cholderton from 1857 to 1859. He was Chancellor of Sarum from 1858 to 1860 and held the prebend of Bishopstone from 1861 until 1870, when he became Bishop of Manchester. He died on 22 October 1885.

Matthew Wilkinson (1870-1876) MA, DD, was a Fellow of Clare College, Cambridge. He was Head Master of Kensington School from 1840, Master of Marlborough College from 1843 to 1852, Vicar of West Lavington from 1852 to 1873 and Vicar of Melksham from 1873 to 1876. He died in March 1976.

Robert Sparke Hutchings (1876-1910) was Vicar of Monkton Wyld from 1850 to 1865, of Alderbury from 1865 to 1910 and of Pitton with Farley from 1865 to 1874. He was Rural Dean of Alderbury from 1869 to 1910 and a Proctor in Convocation from 1886 to 1906. He died on 6 November 1910.

Douglas Macleane (1910-1924) MA, author, was Rector of Codford St Peter from 1884 to 1915 and Vicar of Branksome 1915 to 1922. He was a Proctor in Convocation, died on 2 September 1925 and is commemorated in the north choir aisle of the cathedral.

Percy John Dale (1925-1957) OBE, MA, held the prebend of Bishopstone from 1925 to 1957. He was Rector of Fittleton from 1911 to 1920, Rector of West Dean with East Grimstead from 1920 to 1938 and Master of St Nicholas's Hospital from 1938 to 1957. He was Treasurer & Secretary of the Diocesan Board of Finance from 1919 to 1933, Honorary Secretary of the Diocesan Conference from 1933 to 1939, Archdeacon of Sarum from 1936 to 1950, a Proctor in Convocation from 1935 to 1937 and a Church Commissioner and member of its Board of Governors from 1948 to 1953. He died on 22 April 1957.

Jeffrey Stanley Maples (1957-1960) MA, held a stall at Lincoln before becoming Diocesan Director of Religious Education from 1956 to 1963, holding the prebend of Bishopstone from 1957 to 1960. He was a Proctor in Convocation from 1958 to 1969 and was Chancellor of Sarum and a Canon Residentiary from 1960 to 1967. He was Director of the Bible Reading Fellowship from 1963 to 1967 and Archdeacon of Swindon and a Proctor in Convocation from 1974 to 1982.

Philip Humphrey Hall (1960-1968) was Vicar of Ramsbury with Axford from 1938 to 1947. He was Rector of Bishopstone with Stratford Tony from 1951 to 1965, held the prebend of Bishopstone from 1960 to 1968, was Chaplain of Newbridge Hospital, Sarum, from 1965 to 1970 and Vicar of the Close with the prebend of Ufcomb from 1968 to 1980.

Angus Campbell MacInnes (1968-1977) CMG, MA, DD, was Archdeacon in Palestine and Trans-Jordan from 1943 to 1950 and of Jerusalem from 1950 to 1951. From 1953 to 1957 he was Bishop Suffragan of Bedford and then Archbishop of Jerusalem from 1957 to 1968. He was Chaplain and Sub-Prelate of the Order of St John of Jerusalem and was Assistant Bishop of Sarum from 1968 to 1973. He was Master of St Nicholas Hospital, Sarum from 1968 to 1977 and he died on 29 April 1977.

John Frederick Alexander Ellis (1977-1980) was Vicar of Harnham from 1965 to 1980 and Rural Dean of Sarum from 1977 to 1980.

David Bailey (1980-1983) MA, was Vicar of Bothenhampton with Walditch from 1962 to 1969 and Rector of Swanage with Herston from 1969 to 1983.

Percy Frank Chapman (1983-1988) BSc, MA, was Assistant Chaplain of Marlborough College from 1941 to 1965. He was Vicar of Aldbourne and Baydon, and Rector of Whitton, from 1965 to 1972. He was Vicar of Coombe Bissett with Homington from 1972 to 1981, Priest in Charge of Bishopstone with Stratford Tony from 1980 to 1981 and Rector of Chalke Valley East from 1981 to 1988. He died on 18 July 1999 at the age of 93.

Robert Andrew Willis (1988-1992) BA, was Vicar Choral from 1975 to 1978, Team Rector of Tisbury from 1978 to 1987, Vicar of Sherborne with Castleton & Lillington from 1987 to 1992 , a Proctor in Convocation from 1985 to 1992 and Dean of Hereford from 1992.

Gwyneth Mary Evans (1996-) became Chaplain to Salisbury Hospitals in 1989.

CHARDSTOCK

Prebend:- The manor of Chardstock in Devon, formerly in Dorset, belonged to the bishop in 1066 and 1086 and was from time to time subject to disputes. The prebend consisted of the church of Chardstock and later the chapel of Wambrook, Somerset.

Shield:- **Walter Kerr Hamilton** DD, was in 1833 a Fellow of Merton College, Oxford and in 1834 he held a stall at Wells. He became a Canon Residentiary, with the house of Leadenhall, and Treasurer of Sarum from 1841 to 1843 and Precentor of Sarum from 1843 to 1854 also holding the prebend of Torleton from 1843 to 1854. He was Bishop of Sarum from 1854 until his death on 1 August 1869. Whilst bishop, he founded Salisbury Theological College and contributed to the debate on cathedral reform. He was buried in the cathedral beside his predecessor Edward Denison, Bishop of Sarum 1837-1854. (Fig. 13.)

Blazon:- Quarterly. First and fourth, gules three cinquefoils argent a mullet for difference. Second, gules three cinquefoils argent in fesspoint a heart or. Third, gules three doves close with a bordure argent. [A shield in four quarters: top left and bottom right; on a red background three silver five petalled flowers with a pierced five pointed star to indicate a third son. Top right; on a red background three silver five petalled flowers with a gold heart in the centre. Bottom left; on a red background three silver doves with their wings to their sides, within a silver border.]

Psalter:- The portion of the psalter allotted to the prebend is Psalms 147, 148 and 149.

Holders of the prebend:-

Abraham of Winchester (between 1215 & 1220) was Treasurer of Sarum from 1214 to c.1222 and held the prebend of Chardstock between 1215 & 1220.

Gilbert de Sandford (c.1226/7-c.1233).

Henry de Esse (before 1281-c.1297) held the prebends of Chardstock from before 1281 to c.1297 and Horton from 1289 to 1297/98. He had died by 20 January 1298.

William de Chaddleshunt (1309-?) DCL, was Archdeacon of Wilts from 1304 to 1320. He held the prebends of Alton Australis from 1304 to 1309 and Chardstock from 1309 to ?. He held stalls at Lichfield and St Paul's and one of his name was Rector of Dauntsey in 1303. He died before 3 February 1320.

Raterius de Miramonte (c.1318-?) held the prebend in 1318 and became Bishop of Vaison in 1336.

John Piers (1336-?) held the prebend in 1344.

John de Mota (1348) had expectations of a prebend in 1343 and held the prebend of Chardstock in 1348 but John Gogh subsequently received it.

John Gogh (1350-1352) received a royal grant of the prebend of Chardstock in 1350, King Edward III having recovered the right of appointment from Roger Wyville, Bishop of Sarum 1330-1375, and he was installed in 1351. He was nominated to the prebend of Preston in 1351and despite other claimants, was installed in1352. It was claimed again 1357 but he held it in 1360 and probably died in 1361.

Martin Monlyshe (1352-?) held the prebend in 1366.

William de Osmundeston (?-1373) exchanged the prebend of Chardstock with John Cheyne in 1373.

John Cheyne (1373-1406) held the prebend of Bedwin from 1366 to 1373?. He received the prebend of Chardstock in 1373 by exchange but was reported to have died abroad by November 1390. Despite counter claims, he still held the prebend on his death in 1406.

Richard Felde (1389) received a royal grant of the prebend in 1389, which was probably ineffective since John Cheyne had incorrectly been reported dead. He received the prebend of Highworth by royal grant in 1392 but then received the prebend of Lyme & Halstock a month later, resigning it in 1400.

William Glym (1402) was excommunicated in 1399 for disobeying a decision of the papal court which confirmed John Cheyne's possession of the prebend and for preventing him gaining possession. He received however, a royal grant of the prebend in 1402 but appears to have failed to gain possession. In 1404 he claimed the dignity of Treasurer of Sarum by virtue of a royal licence of May 1404. There was an inquiry in 1408 at which he was imprisoned but he was pardoned in 1410.

John Haket (1406) DCL, was appointed to the prebend of Chardstock in 1406 but a royal grant was made to John Bathe. He held the prebends of Major Pars Altaris from 1413 to 1423 and Yetminster Secunda from 1423 to 1442. He died in 1442.

John Bathe (1406-1415) received the prebend of Chardstock in 1406 by royal grant, despite John Hacket having been appointed and held it until 1415. He held the prebend of Bedminster & Redcliffe from 1415 to 1438, and died 1438.

William Werkeman (1415-1426) was Rector of Stourton from 1403 to 1407. He held the prebends of Axford from 1411 to 1415 and Chardstock from 1415 to 1426. He died in 1426.

Richard Caudray (1426-?) held a stall at St Paul's in 1425 and held the prebends of Chardstock from 1426 to ? , Chisenbury & Chute from 1433 to 1448 and Grantham Australis from 1448 to 1458.

William Booth (?-1441) exchanged this prebend with Stephen Wilton in 1441 for the church of Prescot, Lancs.

Stephen Wilton (1441-1442) DCnL, was Archdeacon of Sarum from 1433 until after 1435 and held the prebends of Bishopstone from 1434 to ? and Chardstock from 1441 to 1442. He held a stall at Lincoln, exchanging it in 1433 for a stall at St Paul's. He was Archdeacon of Middlesex in 1441 and of Cleveland in 1454. He died in 1457.

George Neville (1442-1456) was the youngest son of Richard Neville, Earl of Salisbury, who was beheaded in 1460 and brother of Richard, Earl of Salisbury and Warwick known as the King-maker. He was Chancellor of Oxford in 1453 and became Bishop of Exeter in 1456, at the age of twenty-seven. He held the great seal under King Henry V in 1460 and having been dispossessed of it, was shortly after reappointed by King Edward IV.

John Lax (1457-?) DCL, was private secretary to Pope Calixtus III. He was Chancellor of the Hospital of St Thomas of Canterbury at Rome.

John Walbrond (?1464) BCL, exchanged this prebend in 1464 with Robert Stillington for a prebend at St Stephen's, Westminster.

Robert Stillington (1464) DCL, held the prebend of Chardstock in 1464 and was Archdeacon of Berks from 1464 to 1465 when he became Bishop of Bath & Wells.

Leyson Geffray (1464-1475) was Rector of St Mary, Corn Street, Wilton, and died in 1475.

John Dogget (1475-?) DTh, DCnL, was a nephew of Cardinal Bourchier. He held the prebends of Ruscomb from 1474 to 1475, Chardstock from 1475 to ? and Bitton from 1479 to 1486. A native of Sherborne, he founded a chapel on the south side of the churchyard there. He held a stall at Lincoln, was Treasurer of Chichester in 1479, Chaplain to King Richard III in 1483, Chancellor of Sarum from 1486 to 1501, a Canon Residentiary and Vicar General of Sarum, and Chancellor of Lichfield in 1488. In 1490 he held the rectory of Winterborne Shelston. He became Archdeacon of Chester and Provost of King's College, Cambridge in 1499. He died on 4 March 1501/2 and was buried in the cathedral.

William Sheriff (1481) MA, held the prebends of Major Pars Altaris from 1472 to ? and Chardstock in 1481.

Ralph Heathcott (?-1486) BCn&CL, held the prebends of Chardstock from ? to 1486, Bitton from 1486 to 1487, Faringdon from 1487? to 1492 and Hurstbourne & Burbage from 1492 to 1493, exchanging the latter with Adrian de Bardis in 1493 for the prebend of Ramsbury and the church of Wroughton. He held the prebend of Ramsbury from 1493 until his death in 1499. He was Rector of St Peter's, Marlborough in 1481.

Christopher Bainbridge (1486) LLD, held the prebends of Grantham Borealis from ? to 1486, Chardstock in 1486 and Horton from 1486 to 1508. He was Master of the Rolls in 1504. After holding many preferments, amongst them those of Provost of Queen's College, Oxford and Dean of York, he was made Bishop of Durham in 1507 and Archbishop of York in 1508. He was created Cardinal-Priest of St Marcellinus & St Peter in 1508 and of St Praxedes in 1511. He led a military expedition against Ferrara, was poisoned by his steward, an Italian priest on 14 July 1514 and was buried at the English College, Rome. Sylvester Gigliis, Bishop of Worcester, was suspected of having instigated the murder but was declared innocent by the Pope.

Thomas Mades (1489-1500) died in 1500.

John Hobbull (1501-1505) DTh, died in 1505.

Christopher Twyneho (1505-1507) held the prebends of Axford from 1504 to 1505 and Chardstock from 1505 to 1507 and the Archdeaconry of Berks, together with the prebend of Highworth, from 1507 to 1509. He appears also to have held a stall at Hereford from 1480 to 1509. He had died by 20 December 1509.

Edward Higgins (1507) Lic.CnL, was Vicar of Steeple Ashton and held the prebends of Axford in 1507, Chardstock in 1507, Coombe & Harnham from 1507 to 1509 and Netherbury in Ecclesia from 1509 to 1538. He died in 1538.

Thomas Martyn (1507-1515) DCnL, held the prebends of Chardstock from 1507 to 1515, Beminster Prima from 1515 to 1517 and Wilsford & Woodford from 1517 to 1524. He died in 1524.

Edward Finch (1515-1517) DM, was well endowed with prebends holding in succession those of Yatesbury from 1514 to 1515, Chardstock from 1515 to 1517, Wilsford & Woodford in 1517, Fordington & Writhlington from 1517 to 1518, Grimston from 1518 to 1519 and Faringdon from 1519 to 1521 exchanging the latter with William Webbe for the church of Ross on Wye, Hereford. He then held the prebends of Bishopstone from 1521 to 1522, Teynton Regis from 1522 to 1524 and Bere & Cherminster from 1524 to 1539. He was Archdeacon of Wilts from 1522 to 1539, died in 1539 and was buried in the cathedral.

John Stone (1517-1524) BCL, held the prebends of Axford from 1509 to 1511, Warminster from 1511 to 1517, Chardstock from 1517 to 1524 and Fordington & Writhlington from 1524 to ?.

John Pinnock (1524-1537) was consecrated Bishop Suffragan of Syene in 1518 to assist Edmund Audley, Bishop of Sarum 1502-1524, within the diocese which he did until 1535. He held the prebend of Durnford from 1519 to 1520, exchanging it with Nicholas Inglescent for the vicarage of Highworth and the prebend of Axford. He held the prebend of Axford from 1520 to 1524, exchanging it in 1524 for the prebend of Chardstock which he held until 1537. He died in 1537.

Robert Bysse (1537-1546) DCn&CL, practised law at the Court of Rome in 1513. He was Principal of Henxsey Hall in 1514 and in 1524 was Vicar-General to the Bishop of Bath & Wells. He had died by 20 December 1546.

Innocent Reade (1546-1564) had resigned by 29 March 1564.

Robert Hooper (1564-?) MA, was a Canon Residentiary from 1569 to 1571. He held the prebend of Chardstock from 1564 until at least 1568, and is thought to have held the prebend of Winterbourne Earls from ? to 1571. He died in 1571 whilst holding a prebend but this may have been Chardstock. He was Rector of Fyfield.

Edward Dering (1571-1576) BD, died on 26 June 1576.

John Swone (1576-1613) had resigned by 8 December 1613.

William Osborne (1613-1646) DD, was a Canon Residentiary from ? until 1646. He died on 1 April 1646.

William Payne (1660-1689) MA, died on 26 September 1689.

Robert Pierce (1689-1707) was Rector of North Tidworth from 1680 to 1707 and owned Zouche manor. He was described by the bishop as 'a very ill man of a turbulent spirit and loose behaviour that had given him much trouble and uneasiness in the county.' He died in 1707.

Charles Wroughton (1707-1729) MA, was Rector of Codford St Peter where he is commemorated following his death on 28 October 1729.

Richard Hele (1729-1756) MA, was Vicar of Britford, Master of the Choristers' School and author of *Devotions for the Clergy*. He died on 25 July 1756 and was buried in the cathedral.

Edward Blake (1756-1765) DD, was Vicar of St Thomas', Sarum and died on 11 June 1765.

John King (1765-1770) BA, died on 25 July 1770.

John Huish (1770-1802) BA, died in 1802.

Edward Tew (1802-1818) MA, was a Fellow of King's College, Cambridge and in 1781 a Fellow of Eton. He held the prebends of Yatesbury from 1799 to 1802 and Chardstock from 1802 to 1818. He died on 30 August 1818 aged 82.

Henry Woodcock (1818-1840) DD, held the prebends of Stratford from 1805 to 1818 and Chardstock from 1818 to 1840. He held a stall at Christ Church, Oxford in 1824 and died on 8 August 1840.

The Hon Charles Amyand Harris (1841-1863) MA, was a son of the second Earl of Malmesbury. He was a Fellow of All Souls, Oxford from 1835 to 1837, Rector of Shaftesbury from 1839 to 1840 and Rector of Wilton and Bulbridge and Vicar of Ditchampton from 1840 to 1848. From 1841 to 1863 he held the prebend of Chardstock and was Domestic Chaplain to Edward Denison, Bishop of Sarum 1837-1854, and Walter Kerr Hamilton, Bishop of Sarum 1854-1869. He was Archdeacon of Wilts and Vicar of Bremhill with Highway from 1863 to 1868, Bishop of Gibraltar from 1868 to 1873, died on 16 March 1874 and was buried at Bremhill.

John Wilkinson (1863-1876) MA, was Rector of Broughton Gifford from 1848 to 1876 and was Secretary to the Diocesan Board of Education. He died in 1876.

John Duncan (1876-1907) was Vicar of Lyneham from 1859 to 1865, during which time he built a new church at Bradenstoke. He was Vicar of Calne from 1865 to 1907, his appointment leading to the establishment of a Free Church in the town. He was Rural Dean of Calne in 1898 and was Private Chaplain to the Marquis of Lansdowne. He died on 28 January 1907.

Robert Crowther Abbott (1907-1913) MA, was an Assistant Master of Marlborough College from 1892 to 1907 and Principal of Sarum Theological College from 1907 to 1913. He was Vicar of Holy Trinity, Weymouth and Rural Dean of Weymouth from 1914 to 1916, Vicar of Gillingham with East & West Stour from 1916 to 1925 and Rural Dean of Gillingham from 1917 to 1925. He held the prebends of Chardstock from 1907 to 1913 and Grantham Borealis from 1918 to 1927. He was a Proctor in Convocation and was the first Bishop Suffragan of Sherborne from 1925 to 1927, dying on 25 November 1927.

Eric James Bodington (1913-1929) MA, was Vicar of Osmington from 1894 to 1899, Vicar of Potterne and Rural Dean of Potterne from 1899 to 1907, Rural Dean of Avebury from 1907 to 1912 and Vicar of Calne from 1907 to 1927. He was Archdeacon of Wilts from 1912 to 1927, held the prebend of Chardstock from 1913 to 1929 and was Archdeacon of Dorset and Canon Residentiary from 1927 to 1929. He died on 25 October 1929.

Ernest Clement Eddrup (1930-1961) MA, was Rector of Corfe Mullen from 1916 to 1959. He resigned his prebend in 1961.

George Bertram Gerrish (1961-1964) was Rector of Portland and Chaplain to the Verne Prison from 1952 to 1964.

John Percy Hinton (1965-1974) was Vicar of Westbury with Dilton Marsh and Westbury Leigh from 1941 to 1955 and Rector of Bridport from 1955 to 1974. He died in 1991.

Philip Roberts (1975-1987) was Vicar of Westbury from 1963 to 1973, Team Rector of Dorchester from 1973 to 1980 and Vicar of the Close from 1989 to 1995.

Christopher Bryant (1987-) AKC, was Vicar of Chirton & Marden and Rector of Patney from 1971 to 1976, also Charlton and Wilsford until 1978. He was then Rector of St John with St Mary, Devizes from 1978 to 1997 and Rural Dean of Devizes from 1983 to 1992. In 1997 he became Master of St Nicholas Hospital, Sarum.

RUSCOMB

Prebend:- Ten hides of land at Ruscomb in Berkshire, were given to the canons of the cathedral in 1099 by Osmund, Bishop of Sarum 1078-1099. The prebend, also referred to as Ruscomb Southbury, Rotescombe or even Rotescamp, was probably in existence by c.1150.

Shield:- **Edward Denison** MA, was a brother of a Speaker of the House of Commons later Viscount Ossington, and a Fellow of Merton College, Oxford, who became Bishop of Sarum from 1837 to 1854. He was said to have laid the foundations of more than one of those diocesan efforts which, as regards religious education and the general progress of the church, have resulted in so much good. He died on 6 March 1854 and was buried in the cathedral cloisters. (Fig. 14.)

Blazon:- Ermine a bend cotised between in chief a unicorn's head erased and in base a cross crosslet fitchee all gules. [On an ermine shield, a red band from top left to bottom right, with a narrow red band on either side of it. On the top right of this a red unicorn's head, as if torn from the body, and on the bottom left a red cross with pointed base and the top and arms crossed.]

Psalter:- The portion of the psalter allotted to the prebend is Psalm 106.

Holders of the prebend:-

John (c.1197/1215) was Succentor between c.1193 and 1197/1215 and held the prebend of Ruscomb c.1197/1215. He gave a cope and ornaments to the cathedral.

Luke (of Winchester) des Roches (c.1223-c.1226) was a nephew of Peter des Roches, Bishop of Winchester 1205-1238 and held the prebends of Ruscomb from c.1223 to c.1226, Coombe & Harnham from c.1226/7 to 1231 and Hurstbourne & Burbage from 1231 to c.1253. He held a stall at London, was Archdeacon of Surrey c.1245, Rector of Hurstbourne in 1249 and probably died c.1253.

Stephen of Ecton (c.1226/7-1228) was fined for non-residence in 1227. He was a clerk to King Henry III, held a papal dispensation to hold an additional benefice and resigned in 1228 to become a monk.

Ranulph Brito (1228-1246) was installed in 1229 after some difficulty, the prebend having been claimed by John Romeyn, Subdean of York. He was Dean of Windsor, held a stall at St Paul's, and had died before 10 December 1246.

Robert Passelewe (c.1246-?) was a clerk to King Henry III, held a stall at London, was bishop-elect of Chichester in 1244 and was Archdeacon of Lewes from 1244 to 1252. He died on 6 June 1252.

Laurence de Hakeburne (c.1284-1288?) was ordained priest in 1288 and was elected Bishop of Sarum in the same year but died three months later on 8 August 1288, before receiving the archbishop's confirmation.

William de Ripariis (?-1317) was a clerk to King Edward III and died whilst holding this prebend on 29 May 1317.

Thomas de Bek (1317-1339) exchanged this prebend with William be Feriby in 1339 for the church of Brompton, Yorkshire.

William Feriby (1339) held the prebend of Ruscomb in 1339, exchanging it with Alan Coningsburgh for the prebend of Sharow in Ripon collegiate church, and later the prebend of Netheravon which he held from 1366 to 1369. He also held a stall at York.

Alan Coningsburgh (1339-1362) DCL.

Richard de Ravenser (1362-?) held the prebends of Ruscomb from 1362 to ? and, having had expectations of a prebend in 1363, appears to have held the prebend of Preston from 1366? to 1367. He exchanged this with John de Withornwick for the free chapel of Tickhill, Yorks. He was Chaplain to King Edward III, held stalls at St Paul's, Hereford, St David's and the collegiate church of St Stephen, Westminster and was Provost of Beverley.

Nicholas de Newton (?-1368) BCnL, exchanged this prebend with John de Corf for the prebend of Coombe Prima at Wells.

John de Corf (1368-?) held a stall at Wells and the prebends of Ruscomb from 1368 to ? and Netherbury in Terra from 1373 to ?

John Croume (?-1370) exchanged this prebend with Thomas Spert for the vicarage of St Nicholas, Bristol.

Thomas Spert (1370-1398) DCL, died in 1398.

William Spaldwick (1398-1410) was a Canon Residentiary and Custos of the Hospital of St Nicholas, Sarum in 1397. He died in 1410.

John Fyton (1410-1412) MA, BTh, was Archdeacon of Stafford and held the prebends of Ruscomb from 1410 to 1412, Granthan Borealis from 1412 to 1416 and Highworth from 1416 to 1422. He exchanged the last with John Stafford for the dignity of Chancellor of Sarum, which he held from 1422 to 1432, dying in 1432.

William Lyndwood (1412-1424) DCn&CL, was a celebrated author and Dean of the Court of Arches. He was employed by King Henry V in various missions to Spain, Portugal and elsewhere, and was at one time Keeper of the Privy Seal. He held the prebends of Ruscomb from 1412 to 1424 and Bishopstone from 1424 to 1434. He was nominated by the Pope to the see of St David's and was consecrated in 1442.

Thomas Bekyngton (1424-1435) DCL, held the prebends of Ruscomb from 1424 to 1435 and Bedwin from 1435 to 1443, when he became Bishop of Bath & Wells.

Nicholas Caraunt (1435-1446) BCL, held the prebends of Ruscomb from 1435 to 1446 and Grimston from 1446 to 1467. He died in 1467.

Robert Langrish (1446-1448) held the prebends of Ruscomb from 1446 to 1448 and Durnford from 1448 to 1454. He was a Canon Residentiary and Rector of Newbury and he died in 1454.

William Brygon (1448-1454) BCn&CL, held the prebends of Minor Pars Altaris from 1447 to 1448, Ruscomb from 1448 to 1454, Durnford from 1454 to 1459 and Stratton from 1459 to 1469. He died in 1469.

Simon Huchyns (1454-1468) BCL, was sent to Rome as a Procurator for the Chapter concerning the canonisation of Bishop Osmund.

William Hermer (1468-?).

William Chock (1473-1474) held the prebends of Ruscomb from 1473 to 1474 and Bedminster & Redcliffe from 1474 to 1492. He died in 1492

John Dogget (1474-1475) DTh, DCnL, was a nephew of Cardinal Bourchier. He held the prebends of Ruscomb from 1474 to 1475, Chardstock from 1475 to ? and Bitton from 1479 to 1486. A native of Sherborne, he founded a chapel on the south side of the churchyard there. He held a stall at Lincoln, was Treasurer of Chichester in 1479, Chaplain to King Richard III in 1483, Chancellor of Sarum from 1486 to 1501, a Canon Residentiary and Vicar General of Sarum, and Chancellor of Lichfield in 1488. In 1490 he held the rectory of Winterborne Sheltston. He became Archdeacon of Chester and Provost of King's College, Cambridge in 1499. He died on 4 March 1501/02 and was buried in the cathedral.

George Dawne (1475-?) held the prebend in 1486.

Thomas Ruthall (?-1503) DCnL, held the prebend of Ruscomb from ? to 1503. He was Dean of Sarum from 1502 to 1509 and on his appointment nominated Richard Newport, Prebendary of Faringdon, as his locum tenens. He was Chancellor of Cambridge University, Archdeacon of Gloucester in 1503, and was created Bishop of Durham in 1509. In 1516 he was Keeper of the Privy Seal and died on 4 February 1523. When asked by Cardinal Wolsey to send a note of the resources of the bishopric of Durham, he accidentally provided an account of his own inherited estate which showed his considerable wealth!

Richard Surland (1503-1509) resigned in 1509.

William Atwater (1509) DTh, was Vicar of Piddlehinton in 1487, held the prebend of Ruscomb in 1509 and was Dean of Sarum from 1509 to 1514. He held a stall at Windsor in 1449 and was Registrar of the Order of the Garter. He was Vice-Chancellor of Oxford University in 1500 and Dean of the Chapels Royal in 1502, becoming Chancellor of Lincoln in 1506 On leaving Sarum, he became Archdeacon of Huntingdon and on 14 September 1514 was appointed Bishop of Lincoln, succeeding Cardinal Wolsey, who held him in high esteem.

William Barton (1509) was Succentor of Sarum from 1502 to 1509. He was consecrated Bishop Suffragan of Saloniensis c.1509 to assist Edmund Audley, Bishop of Sarum 1502-1524, within the diocese, which he did from 1509 to 1517. He held the prebends of Ruscomb in 1509, Beminster Prima from 1509 to 1515 and Grimston from 1515 to 1518. He died in 1518.

John Woodroff (1509-1517) held the prebends of Axford from 1508 to 1509, Ruscomb from 1509 to 1517 and Beminster Prima from 1517 to ?. He also held a stall at Hereford.

William Pykenham (1517-1518) BCL, held the prebends of Yatesbury from 1515 to 1517, Ruscomb from 1517 to 1518, Yetminster Secunda from 1518 to 1519, Grantham Australis in 1519 and Grantham Borealis from 1519 to 1535. He died in 1535.

Reginald Pole (1518-1519) BA, son of Sir Richard Pole and a relative of King Henry VIII, was a Fellow of Corpus Christi College, Oxford and was on friendly terms with Ignatius Loyola. He held the Deanery of Wimborne in 1518 and the prebends of Ruscomb from 1518 to 1519 and Yetminster Secunda from 1519 to 1537 but was deprived in 1537. He held the Vicarage of Piddlehinton in 1532. He was ordained deacon in 1536 being created Cardinal-Deacon of St Nereus & St Achilles, Cardinal of St Vitus & St Modestus in the following year, and in 1540 of St Mary in Cosmedin. Also in 1540, as Papal Legate, he reconciled England to Rome He was ordained priest in 1556 and in the same year was consecrated Archbishop of Canterbury but died twenty months later, at the age of 58, on 17 November 1558, the same day as Queen Mary I, and was buried at Canterbury. Erasmus wrote of him 'as deserving a principal place among my friends' and the Emperor Charles VI was urged to persuade him to seek marriage with Princess Mary when she was heir to the throne. He was however too deeply attached to learning to be dazzled by the glamour.

John Fox (1519-1530) was Archdeacon of Winchester and died before 6 August 1530.

Thomas Lupsett (1530-1531) MA, distinguished himself as a lecturer in rhetoric at Oxford. He was a member of various embassies and had died by 12 January 1531.

William Chamberlain (1531-1546) MA, had died by 16 September 1546.

Thomas Knight (1546-1547) resigned by 20 April 1547.

Humphrey Brockehurst (1547-?).

John Everode (1550-?) held the prebends of Yatesbury from 1547 to ? and Ruscomb from 1550 to ?

Robert Hope (1558) died before 29 December 1558.

John Acanthim (1559-1566) died before 18 December 1566.

Alexander Wimshurst (1566-1568) MA, died before 9 December 1568.

Ezekial Taylor (1568-1594) died before 23 August 1594

Samuel Marsh (1594-1636) MA, resigned by 9 July 1636.

Samuel Marsh (1636-1657) BD, was Rector of Patney and died in August 1657.

John Sellick (1660-1690) MA, died on 23 June 1690 and is commemorated in Wells Cathedral.

William Lake (1690-1704) MA, was Rector of Great Somerford from 1702 to 1704 and also Vicar of Chippenham and Rector of Hardenhuish. He died on 9 March 1704 and is commemorated in Chippenham church.

Nathaniel Shute (1704-1712) BD, had died by 3 March 1712 and was buried at Great Cheverell.

James Ligertwood (1712-1742) MA, was Rector of Brixton Deverill and Vicar of Warminster. He died on 24 October 1742 and was buried at Brixton Deverill.

Francis Powell (1742-1758) MA, died on 6 December 1758 and is commemorated at Britford.

John Wills (1758-1760) MA, held the prebends of Ruscomb from 1758 to 1760 and Netherbury in Ecclesia from 1760 to 1765. He died on 11 October 1765.

Humphrey Humphreys (1761-1783) MA, died on 30 April 1783.

Barfoot Colton (1783-1799) MA, held the prebends of Ruscomb from 1783 to 1799 and Coombe & Harnham from 1799 to 1803. He was a Canon Residentiary from 1788 to 1803 and died in 1803.

John Montgomery (1799-1802) MA, held the prebend of Ruscomb from 1799 to 1802 and Ufcomb in 1802. He died in 1802.

Edward Dawkins (1802-1805) MA, held the prebends of Ruscomb from 1802 to 1805 and Netherbury in Ecclesia from 1805 to 1816. He died on 1 August 1816.

John Henry Jacob (1805-1828) MA, was Rector of North Tidworth and died on 13 January 1828.

George Augustus Montgomery (1828-1842) MA, was Rector and Vicar of Bishopstone. He died on 1 December 1842.

Richard Crawley (1843-1869) MA, was Vicar of Steeple Ashton from 1828 to 1869. He died on 9 December 1869.

Solomon Cæsar Malan (1870-1875) MA, DD, was Vicar of Broadwindsor from 1845 to 1875. He was a noted orientalist, linguist, fluently speaking twenty languages, author, painter, collector and musician who, in the absence of a doctor in the parish, ministered to the minor ailments of his people. He died on 25 November 1894.

Reginald Southwell Smith (1875-1895) was Rector of West Stafford from 1836 to 1895 and Rural Dean of Dorchester from 1870 to 1886. He died on 28 December 1895.

Harry William Carpenter (1896-1911) OBE, MA, held the prebends of Ruscomb from 1896 to 1911 and Netherbury in Terra from 1911 to 1936. He was Vice Principal of Sarum Theological College from 1879 to 1880, a Vicar Choral from 1879 to 1914, Precentor of Sarum from 1896 to 1936, Archdeacon of Sarum from 1914 to 1936, and a Canon Residentiary from 1915 to 1936. He died on 20 July 1936.

Christopher Wordsworth (1911-1937) MA, was a brother of John Wordsworth, Bishop of Sarum 1885-1911 and was a Fellow and Dean of Peterhouse College, Cambridge. He was Rector of Steeple with Tyneham from 1889 to 1897. He held a stall at Lincoln from 1886 to 1911, was Rector of St Peter & St Paul, Marlborough from 1897 to 1911 and Rural Dean of Marlborough from 1905 to 1911. He was Subdean of Sarum from 1911 to 1917, holding the prebend of Ruscomb from 1911 to 1937, Librarian from 1913 to 1937 and Chancellor of Sarum from 1917 to 1928. He was Master of St Nicholas Hospital, Sarum from 1895 to 1938. He was a well known author and editor and died on 30 January 1938.

Arnold Brian Burrowes (1937-1949) OBE, MA, served with the Irish Fusiliers from 1916 to 1919, was a Fellow, Lecturer, Dean and Chaplain of Pembroke College, Oxford from 1921 to 1937 and Senior Proctor from 1931 to 1932. He was Principal of Sarum Theological College from 1937 to 1949 and Bishop of St Andrew's, Dunkeld & Dunblane from 1950 to 1955. He died on 15 November 1963.

Charles Gordon Tulloch Colson (1950-1956) MA, was Rector of Winterslow from 1938 to 1943 and Vicar of Warminster from 1943 to 1956. He was Rural Dean of Heytesbury from 1946 to 1954 and Rector of Upton Scudamore from 1947 to 1956.

Claud Stanley Green (1956-1974) was in charge of Holy Angels, Parkstone from 1940 to 1944, Vicar of Bradford-on-Avon from 1944 to 1956 and Rural Dean of Bradford-on-Avon from 1952 to 1956.. He was Vicar of Sturminster Newton and Perpetual Curate of Hinton St Mary from 1956 to 1965 and Rural Dean of Sturminster Newton from 1958 to 1965.

William George Rowley (1975-1978) was Vicar of Allington St Swithun from 1964 to 1973 and Priest-in-Charge of Powerstock with West Milton, Witherstone and North Poorton from 1973 to 1978. He died in March 1992.

William (Bill) Henry Barnard (1979-1993) was Rector of Hinton Martel from 1953 to 1993 and Rural Dean of Wimborne from 1975 to 1979.

[Henry Charles Head (1995-) MA, taught at Rugby School from 1963 to 1977 and was Assistant Director of Education, Jersey from 1983 to 1992. He became Director of Education of the Diocese in 1992 and was appointed a Lay Canon in 1995. He occupies Ruscomb as a courtesy stall.**]**.

YATESBURY

Prebend:- The prebend consisted of land at Yatesbury in Wiltshire and is presumed to have been in existence by c.1150.

Shield:- **Thomas Sherlock** DD, was the son of Dr W Sherlock, Master of the Temple and Dean of St Paul's. He was educated at Catherine Hall, Cambridge, later becoming Master. In 1704 he became himself, at the age of 26, Master of the Temple. He was made Dean of Chichester in 1716, was consecrated Bishop of Bangor in 1728 and was Bishop of Sarum from 1734 to 1748. At both Bangor and Sarum he was a powerful opponent of the views of his predecessor, Bishop Hoadly. He was appointed Lord Almoner in 1743 and is believed to have been depicted by Hogarth in his picture of a bishop receiving from the Devil a mitre filled with coins in exchange for a crucifix. He became Bishop of London in 1749, having previously declined the see of Canterbury, and died in 1761 at the age of 84, being buried in London. (Fig.15.)

Blazon:- Per pale argent and azure three fleurs-de-lys counterchanged. [On a shield divided down the centre, silver to the left and blue to the right, three fleurs-de-lys blue on silver and silver on blue.]

Psalter:- The portion of the psalter allotted to the prebend is Psalms 108 and 109.

Holders of the prebend:-

Peter of Blois (c.1198) was non-resident although holding a prebend c.1198, which was probably Yatesbury as it was the only one of the specific, known value. He was Archdeacon of Bath by 1182, Archdeacon of London by 1202 and held a stall at Rouen. He died in 1212.

Hugh of Wells (c.1226-c.1234) was Archdeacon of Bath by 1215, held a stall at Lincoln and died in late 1234 or early 1235.

Walter of Merton (1262-1263) held the prebends of Yatesbury from 1262 to 1263 and Bere & Cherminster from 1263 to c.1271. He was also Archdeacon of Bath and held stalls at Exeter, Lincoln and London. He became Chancellor of England and Bishop of Rochester in 1274. He founded Merton College, Oxford.

John Maunsel (1263-c.1265) was a kinsman of John Maunsel who was keeper of the Great Seal to King Henry III. He was a royal clerk who also held stalls at Wells and York and had died by August/September 1265.

John de Middleton (c.1268-c.1291) is named in the 1268 foundation charter of the College of St Edmund, Sarum, as the Rector of St Thomas, Sarum. He held the prebend of Yatesbury and was Succentor of Sarum from c.1268 to c.1290/1.

Robert Luterel (?-1315) had vacated the prebend by 10 May 1315.

Nicholas Hengate (c.1315-1318) exchanged the prebend with Roger de Northburgh for the prebend of Piona Parva, Hereford.

Roger de Northborough (1318-1322) was presented by King Edward II to the prebend of Blewbery in 1316 but a legal dispute ensued. He held the prebend of Yatesbury from 1318 to 1322 when he became Bishop of Lichfield.

William de Selton (1322) was given the prebend of Yatesbury in 1322 but Peter de Credonio took possession. He held the prebend of Coombe & Harnham from 1331? to 1354 and was Rector of Nettleton in 1328 and of Longbridge Deverill. He died in 1354.

Peter de Credonio (1322-?) held the prebend in 1338.

John de Eccleshale (1340-?) received a royal grant of the prebend of Hurstbourne & Burbage in 1338 but it was already held by John de Abingdon. He received the prebend of Yatesbury in 1340.

Peter FitzWaryn (1361-?).

John de Eyli (1366) BCL, held the prebend in 1366.

Adam de Lakenhyth (?-1378) exchanged this prebend with John Clerevaus for the church of Banham, Nottinghamshire.

John Clerevaus (1378-?).

Walter Easton (?-1399) held the prebend in 1387 and died in 1399.

Robert Bush (1399-1416) died in 1416.

Oliver Dyneley (1416-1423) held the prebends of Yatesbury from 1416 to 1423 and Major Pars Altaris from 1423 to 1431. He was a Canon Residentiary and Rector of Fittleton. He died in 1431.

John Symondesburgh (1423-1437) BCL, was Archdeacon of Wilts from 1423 to 1449 and Treasurer of Sarum from 1449 to 1454. He held the prebend of Yatesbury from 1423 to 1437, exchanging it with John Tydeling for the prebend of Stratton which he held from 1437 to 1449. He held the rectory of Dinton in 1433 and was Treasurer of St Paul's from 1420 to 1423. He died in 1454 and asked to be buried before St Margaret's altar in the cathedral.

John Tydeling (1437) BCL, was a Canon Residentiary and held the prebends of Axford from 1401 to 1404, until exchanging it with George Westby for the prebend of Major Pars Altaris, which he held from 1404 to 1406. He then held the prebends of Warminster from 1406 to 1418, Yetminster Secunda in 1418, Beminster Prima from 1418 to 1420 and Stratton from 1420 to 1437, exchanging the last with John Symondsburgh for the prebend of Yatesbury. This he exchanged four months later with John Morton for the prebend of North Leverton in Southwell collegiate church, Notts.

John Moreton (1437-1440) MA, died in 1440.

John Chedworth (1440-1443) DTh, held the prebends of Yatesbury from 1440 to 1443, Stratford from 1443 to 1445, Netherbury in Terra from 1445 to 1447 and Hurstbourne & Burbage from 1447 to 1452. He held a stall at Lincoln and was at different times Archdeacon of Northampton and of Lincoln. He was Provost of King's College, Cambridge in 1446, Archdeacon of Wilts from 1449 to 1452 and was consecrated Bishop of Lincoln in 1452. He died on 23 November 1471.

William Normanton (1443-1445) held the prebends of Yatesbury from 1443 to 1445, Warminster from 1445 to 1446, Bishopstone from 1446 to 1447, Durnford from 1447 to 1448, Chisenbury & Chute from 1448 to 1449 and Faringdon from 1449 to 1459. He died in 1459.

Thomas Kirkeby (1445-1446) held the prebends of Yatesbury from 1445 to 1446, Warminster from 1446 to 1448, Netheravon from 1448 to 1449, Ramsbury from 1449 to 1464 and Highworth from 1464 to 1476. He also held the prebend of Stanton Berners under the Abbey of Wilton and died in 1476.

Walter Colles (1446-1453) BCn&CL, exchanged the prebend with Ralph Drew for a prebend in St Crantock's collegiate church, Cornwall.

Ralph Drew (1453) BCn&CL, held the prebends of Yatesbury in 1453 and Lyme & Halstock from 1453 to 1456. He died in 1456.

Richard Wetton (1453-1457) DCL, resigned in 1457.

John Stretton (1457-1458) DCL, held the prebends of Coombe & Harnham from 1452 to 1457 , Yatesbury from 1457 to 1458, Grantham Australis from 1458 to 1471, Bedminster & Redcliffe from 1471 to 1474 and Chisenbury & Chute from 1474 to 1475. He was Rector of Poulshot in 1459 and died on 1 January 1475.

Robert Parker (1458-1461) died in 1461.

John Russell (1461-1462) DCnL, held the prebends of Yatesbury from 1461 to 1462 and Horton from 1462 to 1476. He was Archdeacon of Berks from 1466 to 1476 and held a stall at St Paul's in 1474. He became Bishop of Rochester in 1476 and of Lincoln in 1480. He was Chancellor of Oxford from 1483 to 1494 and Chancellor of England under Kings Edward V and Richard III. He died in 1494.

John Paynot (1462-1471) died in 1471.

John Vernham (1471) held the prebends of Yatesbury in 1471 and Grantham Australis from 1471 to 1489?.

Roger Rotherham (1471-?) DCL, held the prebend in 1473 and died in 1477.

Leonard Say (1477-1493) died in 1493.

Henry Carnebull (1493-1494) resigned in 1494.

Thomas Phillips (1494-1513) was Subdean of Sarum from 1490 to 1505 and held the prebend of Yatesbury from 1494 to 1513. He would seem also to have been Vicar of Bray, and Rector of Winterslow from 1497 until his death which was before 23 January 1513.

Henry Rawlyns (1513-1514) BCL, was well provided with prebends. He held Yatesbury from 1513 to 1514, Grantham Australis from 1514 to 1519 and Coombe & Harnham 1519 to 1521. He resigned the last in May 1521, was succeeded by Cuthbert Tunstall, who then became Dean of Sarum, and was again collated to the prebend about two weeks later. The prebend then passed to Richard Pace but was assumed by Henry Rawlyns for the third time in 1523. He then held Faringdon from 1523 to 1524, Hurstbourne & Burbage in 1524 and Teynton Regis, together with the Archdeaconry of Sarum from 1524 to 1526. He was Rector of Christian Malford, died in 1526 and is buried in the cathedral near the Audley chantry.

Edward Finch (1514-1515) DM, was well endowed with prebends holding in succession those of Yatesbury from 1514 to 1515, Chardstock from 1515 to 1517, Wilsford & Woodford in 1517, Fordington & Writhlington from 1517 to 1518, Grimston from 1518 to 1519, Faringdon from 1519 to 1521 exchanging the last with William Webbe for the church of Ross on Wye, Hereford. He then held the prebends of Bishopstone from 1521 to 1522, Teynton Regis from 1522 to 1524 and Bere & Cherminster from 1524 to 1539. He was Archdeacon of Wilts from 1522 to 1539. He died in 1539 and was buried in the cathedral.

William Pykenham (1515-1517) BCL, held the prebends of Yatesbury from 1515 to 1517, Ruscomb from 1517 to 1518, Yetminster Secunda from 1518 to 1519, Grantham Australis in 1519 and Grantham Borealis from 1519 to 1535. He died in 1535.

Richard Dudley (1517-?) DTh, was Precentor of Sarum from 1507 to 1536 and held the prebends of Minor Pars Altaris from 1508 to 1517, Yatesbury from 1517 to ? and Durnford from ? (holding it in 1535) to 1536. He died in 1536.

John Bigges (?-1524) BCn&CL, held the prebend of Yatesbury from ? to 1524, exchanging it with John Cockes for the church of Moulton, Suffolk, and Minor Pars Altaris from 1524 to 1544. He was Vicar of Tisbury and Rector of Chilmark. He died in 1544 and asked to be buried in the cathedral.

John Cockes (1524-1546) DCL, died in 1546.

John Bodenham (1546-1547) held the prebends of Minor Pars Altaris from 1544 to 1546 and Yatesbury from 1546 to 1547. He was Rector of St Peter's, Marlborough and died in 1547.

John Everode (1547-?) held the prebends of Yatesbury from 1547 to ? and Ruscomb from 1550 to ?.

Thomas Nelson (1549-?) MA.

Thomas White (1553-1565) DCL, held the prebends of Yatesbury from 1553 to 1565 and Ufcomb from 1565 to 1571. He was Warden of New College, Oxford from 1553 to 1573, Chancellor of Sarum from 1571 to 1588, Archdeacon of Berks from 1557 to 1588 and Chancellor of the Diocese. He died on 12 June 1588 and was buried in the Morning Chapel of the cathedral.

John Garbrand (alias Herks) (1565-1569) MA, was a Fellow of New College, Oxford. He held the prebends of Minor Pars Altaris from 1564 to 1565, Yatesbury from 1565 to 1569 and Chisenbury & Chute from 1569 to 1589. He was a great friend of John Jewell, Bishop of Sarum 1560- 1571 and died in 1589.

Edmund Weston (1569-1570) BCn&CL, died in 1570.

William Overton (1570-1580) DD, was a Fellow of Magdalen College, Oxford in 1551 and held stalls at Chichester and Winchester. He became Bishop of Coventry & Lichfield in 1580 and died in 1609.

Hugh Langley (1580-1591) died in 1591.

John Hopkinson (1591-?).

Richard Mulcaster (1592-1611) MA, was Headmaster of St Paul's School, London in 1596 and died on 15 April 1611.

Hugh Gough (?-1623) MA, was Rector of Little Cheverell from 1584 to 1625 and Rector of All Cannings from 1593 to 1625. He resigned the prebend in 1623.

Humphrey Henchman (1623-1629) DD, was a Fellow of Clare Hall, Cambridge. He was a son-in-law of Robert Tounson, Bishop of Sarum 1620-1621, becoming Precentor of Sarum from 1623 to 1660 and Canon Residentiary from 1633 to 1660 (although dismissed during the Commonwealth). He held in succession the prebends of Yatesbury from 1623 to 1629, Grantham Australis from 1629 to 1639 and Teynton Regis from 1639 to 1660. He helped King Charles II to escape after the battle of Worcester; personally escorting him to Heale House and meeting him again at Stonehenge. He became Bishop of London and Lord Almoner in 1663. He died on 7 October 1675 at the age of 83 and was buried at Fulham.

Edward Gough (1629-1668) MA, was Rector of Great Cheverell and editor of Camden's Britannia. He died on 8 October 1668.

Daniel Whitby (1668) DD, was Precentor of Sarum from 1672 to 1726. He held the prebends of Yatesbury in 1668, Hurstbourne & Burbage from 1668 to 1696 and Teynton Regis from 1696 to 1726. He was Chaplain to Seth Ward, Bishop of Sarum 1667-1689, a Canon Residentiary from 1676 to 1726 and Rector of St Edmund's, Sarum. He caused excitement by publishing *The Protestant Reconciler* and similar writings, which advocated general religious tolerance. This brought upon him the wrath of the authorities, Chief Justice Jeffreys even directing his indictment. He died on 21 March 1726 aged 90.

John Martin (1668-1677) MA, held the prebends of Yatesbury from 1668 to 1677 and Preston from 1677 until he was deprived as a non-juror in 1690. Because of his learning and temperament, Gilbert Burnet, Bishop of Sarum 1689-1715, gave him the equivalent of a stipend for life, from his own pocket. He died on 10 November 1693.

The Hon John Feilding (1677-1678) MA, DD, was the 4th son of the 1st Earl of Desmond. He was a Chaplain to King William III and was Vicar of Piddlehinton. He was a Canon Residentiary from 1680 to 1698 and was Archdeacon of Dorset in the diocese of Bristol from 1683 to 1697. He held the prebends of Yatesbury from 1677 to 1678, Beminster Prima from 1678 to 1682 and Gillingham Major from 1682 to 1698, dying in 1698.

Isaac Walton (1678-1679) MA, was a son of Isaak Walton the author and fisherman. He held the prebends of Yatesbury from 1678 to 1679, Bishopstone from 1679 to 1681 and Netheravon from 1681 to 1719. He was Rector of Boscombe in 1679 and Rector of Poulshot in 1680. He was Canon Residentiary, living in what is now known as the Walton Canonry in the Close from 1698 to 1719, died on 29 December 1719 and was buried in the cathedral.

Timothy Morton (1679) MA, held the prebends of Yatesbury in 1679 and Major Pars Altaris from 1679 until resigning in 1687. He was Vicar of St Martin's, Sarum.

Thomas Barford (1679-1701) MA, was Rector of Chilmark from 1685 to 1701 and a Canon Residentiary from 1690 to 1701. He died on 29 November 1701 and was buried in the south choir aisle of the cathedral.

Henry Rogers (1701-1721) MA, died in 1721.

John Squire (1721-1759) MA, held the prebend of Yatesbury from 1721 to 1759 and was Succentor of Sarum from 1727 to 1759. He died on 2 July 1759.

Charles Tarrant (1759-1791) MA, was Subdean of Sarum from 1755 to 1759 and Succentor of Sarum from 1759 to 1791. He held the prebend of Yatesbury from 1759 to 1791 and died on 22 February 1791.

John Harrington (1791-1795) DD, died on 10 June 1795.

Thomas Henry Hume (1795-1799) MA, was the only son of John Hume, Bishop of Sarum 1766-1782 and nephew of Nathaniel Hume, Precentor of Sarum 1774-1804. He held the prebends of Yatesbury from 1795 to 1799 and Bitton from 1799 to 1806. He was a Canon Residentiary from 1803 to 1834 and Treasurer of Sarum from 1806 to 1834 Amongst others, he held the livings of Broad Hinton, Stratford-sub-Castle and Brixton Deverill. He died on 6 January 1834 and is buried in the south transept of the cathedral.

Edward Tew (1799-1802) MA, was a Fellow of King's College, Cambridge and in 1781 a Fellow of Eton. He held the prebends of Yatesbury from 1799 to 1802 and Chardstock from 1802 to 1818. He died on 30 August 1818 aged 82.

Charles Francis (1802-1805) MA, held the prebends of Yatesbury from 1802 to 1805 and Lyme & Halstock from 1805 to 1819, exchanging the latter with Robert James Carr for the prebend of Hurstbourne & Burbage, which he held from 1819 to 1821. He died in 1821,

Kenrick Francis Saunders (1805-1853) MA, died on 9 June 1853.

Arthur Fane (1854-1872) MA, was Vicar of Warminster in 1841. He died on 11 June 1872.

Eldon Surtees Bankes (1872-1915) was Rector of Corfe Castle from 1854 to 1898 and was a Canon Residentiary from 1898 until his death on 1 February 1915.

Albert Ernest Joscellyne (1915-1941) DD, was Co-adjutor Bishop of Jamaica from 1905 to 1913. He was Vicar of St Mark's, Sarum, from 1913 to 1919, held the prebend of Yatesbury from 1915 to 1941, was Archdeacon of Sherborne from 1919 to 1941, Vicar of Chardstock from 1919 to 1930 and Vicar of Preston from 1930 to 1937. He resigned his Archdeaconry in 1941 and died on 3 May 1945.

John Challoner Chute (1941-1961) MA, was Rector of Piddlehinton from 1938 to 1957 and Archdeacon of Sherborne, holding the prebend of Yatesbury from 1941 to 1961. He died on 12 September 1961.

Maurice Heath Garner (1961-1970) MA, was Rector of St Mary's, Weymouth, from 1947 to 1970 and Chaplain to Weymouth District Hospital from 1958 to 1961. He was a Proctor in Convocation from 1964 to 1970. He died in December 1993.

John Treharne Davies (1972-1981) BA, was Vicar of Bradpole from 1952 to 1959, Vicar of Potterne from 1959 to 1973 and Vicar of Worton from 1967 to 1973, and Rural Dean of Devizes from 1965 to 1973. He was Curate-in-Charge of Ramsbury with Axford from 1973 to 1974 and Rector of Whitton Team from 1974 to 1981.

David John Tizzard (1984-1985) LRAM, was Team Vicar of Bemerton from 1975 to 1979 and Diocesan Adviser on Social Responsibility and Chaplain to the Deaf from 1979 to 1985. He held a stall at Carlisle from 1994 to 1996 when he returned to the diocese, becoming a Team Vicar of Beaminster until his retirement in 1999.

Ian Keith Wrey Savile (1986-1988) MA, was Rector of Canford Magna from 1981 to 1988 and Rural Dean of Wimborne from 1985 to 1988. He was Patronage Secretary of the Church Pastoral Aid Society from 1988 until his retirement in 1993.

Peter St George Vaughan (1989-1998) MA, was Precentor of Auckland Cathedral from 1972 to 1975, Principal of Crowther Hall, CMS Training College Selly Oak from 1975 to 1983 and Archdeacon of Westmorland & Furness holding a stall at Carlisle from 1983 to 1989. He was Area Bishop of Ramsbury from 1989 to 1998 when he became Assistant Bishop of Bradford, holding a stall at Bradford.

Peter Fearnley Hullah (1999-) BD, AKC, FRSA, is a Freeman of the City of London and was Housemaster of the International Centre, Sevenoaks School from 1982 to 1987, Senior Chaplain of King's School, Canterbury from 1987 to 1992 and Head Master Chetham's School of Music, Manchester from 1992 to 1999. He became Bishop Suffragan and Area Bishop of Ramsbury in 1999.

LYME & HALSTOCK

Prebend:- Lands in Lyme and Halstock, both in Dorset, were among the early endowments of the church of Sherborne, both churches being granted by the abbot to the cathedral in 1191, to form a prebend, .

Shield:- **Gilbert Burnet** DD, became Divinity Professor at Glasgow in 1669. He declined the offer of a Scottish bishopric and the living of St Giles, Cripplegate, Edinburgh and became in 1675 Preacher at the Rolls and Lecturer at St Clements. His political opinions and writings brought him into disgrace and, having been deprived of his appointments, he went, at the invitation of the Prince of Orange, to the Hague. He returned with King William and Queen Mary II and was made Bishop of Sarum in 1689, although Archbishop Sancroft declined to consecrate him personally. He was a historian of his times, an advocate of tolerance, a chairman of committee of the Bill of Rights and an organiser of Queen Ann's Bounty. He was an earnest and diligent diocesan bishop, laying down and strictly enforcing the duties of the clergy. He died on 17 March 1715 and was buried in London. (Fig. 16.)

Blazon:- Argent a buglehorn sable garnished gules within the baldrick a mullet in chief three holly leaves proper. [On a silver shield, a black buglehorn with red mounts and sling. Within the sling a pierced five point star and, at the top, three natural coloured holly leaves.]

Psalter:- The portion of the psalter allotted to the prebend is Psalm 150.

Holders of the prebend:-

Simon of Wells (c.1193-?) was the son of Robert, alias de Camera, and held the prebend in both 1193 and 1200. He was a royal clerk who became Archdeacon of Wells and Provost of Beverley and held a stall in London. He became Bishop of Chichester in 1204.

Stephen de Normandis dei Conti (c.1226/7-?) was married and had a son Philip, a Minorite. He was a nephew of Pope Innocent III, a friend of Pope Alexander IV and was Vicar of Rome to two Popes and Auditor of Cases. He restored discipline among the Lateran and Vatican canons, quieted sedition in Perugia and Tuscany and was Legate in Sicily to publish the excommunication of the Emperor Frederick and to absolve the Sicilians from their allegiance. He was Governor of Sabina, the Maritime Provinces and the Campagna, he was present at the conclaves of four Popes, was Cardinal-Deacon of St Adriano from 1216 to 1228 and Cardinal-Priest of St Maria trans-Tiberim from 1229 to 1254. He held the prebend of Lyme & Halstock from c.1226/7 to ? and also held a stalls at Lincoln and York. He died on 8 December 1254 and was buried in St Peter's, Rome..

Henry de la Estane (c.1257) held the prebend in 1257.

Jordan of Wimborne (c.1284-c.1288) was Archdeacon of Derby from 1278 to 1279 and of Chester from 1280 to 1282 and was one of the Chamberlains of the Exchequer.

James of Spain (?-1330) was the illegitimate son of Alfonso X, King of Castile and half-nephew of Queen Elinor. He held this prebend in 1302 until exchanging it with John de Melbourne in 1330 for the prebend of Chester-le-Street Collegiate church, Co Durham. He held stalls at London, Exeter, Lichfield, Wells, York and Dublin.

John de Melbourne (1330-1336) exchanged this prebend in 1336 with Michael de Northburgh for the prebend of Eccleshall in Lichfield.

Michael de Northburgh (1336-1339) DCL, held the prebend of Lyme & Halstock from 1336 until exchanging it with Robert Chickewell in 1339 for the prebend of Church Withington, Hereford. He was appointed to the prebend of Netherbury in Ecclesia in 1351 but it was already in the possession of Hugh de Pelegrini.

Robert Chickewell (1339-?) received this prebend from his predecessor and occupied it in 1345. He held a stall at Hereford and was Dean of the Chapel of St Clement in Pontefract Castle.

John Barne (?-1362) BCnL, was Archdeacon of Wilts from 1343 to 1361. He held the prebend of Lyme & Halstock from ? until his death in 1362.

Simon Cloune (1362-?).

Bartholomew de Bourne (1366) held a stall at Lincoln from 1329 to 1369. He had expectation of a canonry in 1353 and held this prebend in 1366.

William Walsham (?-1389) had his appointment ratified in 1386 but he died in 1389.

John Dunwich (1389-1392) was installed in 1389 and although others were granted the prebend or attempted to occupy it, he died holding the prebend in 1392.

Thomas Martyn (1390) was granted the prebend in 1390 but did not appear to occupy it.

John Wardeyn (1390) attempted to occupy the prebend in 1390 but it was held by John Dunwich in 1392.

Richard Felde (1392-1400) received a royal grant of the prebend of Chardstock in 1389, which was probably ineffective since John Cheyne had incorrectly been reported dead. He received the prebend of Highworth by royal grant in 1392 but he received the prebend of Lyme & Halstock a month later, resigning it in 1400.

John Colman or Colles (1400-1418) died in 1418.

John Stokes (1418-1431) Lic.CL, resigned in 1431.

Thomas Circester (1431-1453) BTh, was a Canon Residentiary and a great benefactor of the cathedral library. He died in 1453.

Ralph Drew (1453-1456) BCn&CL, held the prebends of Yatesbury in 1453 and Lyme & Halstock from 1453 to 1456. He died in 1456.

William Fydyan (1456-1459) held the prebends of Lyme and Halstock from 1456 to 1459 and Chisenbury & Chute from 1459 to 1474. He died on 24 January 1474.

John Lovibond (1459-1477) died in 1477.

Richard Hayward (1477-1493) DCL, held the prebends of Major Pars Altaris from 1464 to 1472, Axford from 1472 to 1477 and Lyme & Halstock from 1477 to 1493. He died in 1493.

Robert Hussee (1493-1497) resigned in 1497.

Henry Babington (1497-1507) BTh, died in 1507.

Edward Powell (1507-1508) DTh, was a Fellow of Oriel College, Oxford in 1495. He held the prebends of Lyme & Halstock from 1507 to 1508 and of Bedminster & Redcliffe from 1508 to 1534. He was Provost of St Edmund's College, Sarum and the Advocate for Queen Catherine when King Henry VIII sought to divorce her. He forfeited his estates and was deprived of his benefices in 1534 for denying the King's supremacy and is reported to have been hanged, drawn and quartered in Smithfield on 30 April 1540 .

Walter Blount (1508-1509) BCL, held the prebends of Minor Pars Altaris in 1508, Lyme & Halstock from 1508 to 1509 and Alton Australis from 1509 until resigning in 1530.

Hugh Ashton (1509-1517) BCL, in 1517.

Thomas Larke (1517-1518) MA, resigned in 1518.

Richard Parker (1518-?).

Robert Bone (?-1554) died in 1554.

William Bradbridge (1554-1563) BD, held the prebend of Lyme & Halstock from 1554 to 1563 and was a Canon Residentiary from 1561 to 1571. He became Chancellor of Chichester and was Dean of Sarum from 1563 to 1571. In 1571 he was consecrated as Bishop of Exeter, being allowed also to hold two benefices due to the impoverished state of the see. On his death on 27 June 1578 however he owed Queen Elizabeth I £1,400 "and had not wherewith to bury him".

Thomas Coveney (1563-?) DMus, held the prebend in 1565.

David Yale (1571-?) MA, held the prebend in 1593 but it was vacant in 1615.

Walter Curle (1615-1630) DD, was a Canon Residentiary from before 1623 to 1630. He was Rector of Mildenhall from 1619 to 1629 and of Fuggleston St Peter. He became Bishop of Rochester in 1628 but was allowed to continue to hold this prebend. He became Bishop Bath & Wells in 1629 and of Winchester in 1632.

Roger Bates (1630-1634) DD, was a Chaplain to King James I. He died on 15 March 1634.

Richard Chandler (1634-?) MA, was Rector of Wilton.

William Creed (1660-1663) DD, was a Fellow of St John's College, Oxford and a Proctor in 1644. He became Rector of Codford St Mary in 1660 and Archdeacon of Wilts and a Canon Residentiary, holding the prebend of Lyme & Halstock from 1660 until 1663. He was Regius Professor of Divinity at Oxford in 1661 and held a stall at Christ Church, Oxford. He also held the Rectory of Stockton and died on 19 July 1663.

Francis Bayly (1663-1667) MA, was Rector of Woodborough, where he died on 14 May 1667 and was buried.

John Nicholas (1667-1712) MA, was Master of St Nicholas Hospital, Sarum in 1661 and Warden of Winchester. He died on 27 February 1712 and is commemorated in Winchester Cathedral.

Thomas Burnet (1712-1750) was Rector of West Keynton and Master of St Nicholas Hospital, Sarum in 1711. He died on 28 May 1750.

George Woodward (1750-1755) MA, held the prebends of Lyme & Halstock from 1750 to 1755 and Stratton from 1755 to 1790. He died on 5 May 1790.

Thomas Seward (1755-1790) MA, died on 4 March 1790.

Robert Holmes (1790-1805) DD, was Public Orator, Professor of Poetry and in 1782 Bampton Lecturer at Oxford University. He died on 12 November 1805.

Charles Francis (1805-1819) MA, held the prebends of Yatesbury from 1802 to 1805 and Lyme & Halstock from 1805 to 1819, exchanging the latter with Robert James Carr for the prebend of Hurstbourne & Burbage which he held from 1819 to 1821. He died in 1821,

Robert James Carr (1819-1824) MA, DD, held the prebend of Hurstbourne & Burbage in 1819, exchanging it with Charles Francis for the prebend of Lyme & Halstock, which he held until 1824. He was Dean of Hereford from 1820 to 1824, Bishop of Chichester from 1824 to 1831 and Bishop of Worcester from 1831 to 1841. He held a stall at St Paul's and was Clerk to the Closet but was dismissed on account of strict adherence to his political principles on the accession of Queen Victoria. He died on 24 April 1841.

Edward Fane (1824-1862) MA, held a stall at Lincoln and died on 28 December 1862.

William David Morrice (1863-1898) was Vicar of Longbridge Deverill from 1852 to 1874 and Rural Dean of Wylye from 1860 to 1874. He was Vicar of St Thomas, Sarum from 1874 and Rural Dean of Wilton from 1880, until resigning in 1885. He died on 16 January 1898.

Montagu Hankey (1898-1919) MA, was Rector of Maiden Newton from 1868, Rural Dean of Bridport from 1885 and was a Proctor in Convocation. He died in 1919.

William George Barclay (1919-1931) was Rector of Minterne from 1887 to 1914, Rector of Hillfield and Vicar of Hermitage from 1898 to 1914 and Rural Dean of Whitchurch from 1907 to 1914. He was Vicar of Charminster with Stratton from 1914 to 1921, Rural Dean of Dorchester from 1919 to 1921 and Rector of Zeals from 1921. He died in 1931.

Arthur Gordon Robertson (1931-1940) MA, was Headmaster of Sarum Choir School from 1900 to 1930, Vicar Choral from 1900 to 1937 and Succentor of Sarum from 1931 to 1937. He held the prebend of Lyme & Halstock from 1931 until his death in 1940.

Sydney James Nisbet Wallace (1941-1942) was Rector of Trowbridge from 1929 to 1942 and Rural Dean of Bradford from 1939 to 1942.

Bertram Thomas Rosson (1943-1973) Lic.Th, MA, JP, was Rector of Bryanston with Durweston from 1924 to 1943, Rector & Vicar of Blandford Forum from 1943, also Rector of Long Langton from 1951 to 1958. He was Rural Dean of Milton from 1939 to 1943 and of Blandford from 1943 to 1954.

John Robert Geoffrey Neale (1974-1988) AKC, held a stall at Guildford from 1968 to 1974, was Archdeacon of Wilts from 1974 to 1980, Bishop Suffragan of Ramsbury from 1974 to 1981 and Area Bishop of Ramsbury from 1981 to 1988. He held the prebend of Lyme & Halstock from 1974 to 1988 and was Secretary for Partners for World Mission and Assistant Bishop of London (Stepney) 1989 to 1991. He became an Assistant Bishop of Bristol and of Bath & Wells in 1992 and of Gloucester in 1994.

Stephen Squires Venner (1989-1994) MA, was Vicar of Studley from 1976 to 1982, Vicar of Weymouth Holy Trinity from 1982 to 1994 and a Proctor in Convocation from 1985 to 1994. He was Bishop Suffragan of Middleton from 1994 to 1999 and Bishop Suffragan of Dover from 1999.

Derek Michael Ryder (1997-1999) MA, was Team Rector of Wexcombe from 1987 to 1999 and Rural Dean of Pewsey from 1989 to 1999. He retired on 31 January 1999.

Edward Gregory Ambrose Wilford Page-Turner (1999-) was Vicar of Seend from 1970 to 1971 and Vicar of Seend and Bulkington from 1971 to 1979. He became Rector of Askerswell, Loders and Powerstock in 1989, Rural Dean of Lyme Bay in 1992 and of Beaminster in 1994.

(Gangway)

Shield:- **Seth Ward** DD, was appointed Savilian Professor of Astronomy at Oxford, ultimately becoming President of Trinity College, Oxford. He first became Precentor and then Dean of Exeter, and in 1667 Bishop of Exeter becoming involved in repairs to the cathedral. In the same year he was translated to the see of Sarum where he reordered the choir, repaired the Palace, which had been damaged during the Commonwealth, and founded the Matrons' College in the Close. He also regained for Bishops of Sarum the Chancellorship of the Order of the Garter after a separation of 150 years. Towards the end of his time at Sarum he was involved with the Dean, Thomas Pierce, in a dispute over his jurisdiction in the cathedral and his right to the patronage of the prebends. He was a founder of the Royal Society, died at Knightsbridge on 6 January 1689 and was buried in the south east transept of the cathedral . (Fig. 17.)

Blazon:- Azure a cross patonce or. (The cross is variously recorded as flory, moline and patee). [On a blue shield a gold cross with the ends spreading into trefoils. (The cross is variously recorded as the ends spreading into fleur-de-lyse, into two parts and as a square.)]

ALTON AUSTRALIS

(Alton Pancras)

Prebend:- The Manor of Alton Pancras in Dorset was part of the pre-Conquest episcopal estates of Sherborne. By c.1150 two prebends were probably in existence. In the 1220s these were called 'Awelton arch[idiaconi], and 'Awelton', while both were called 'Awelton' without distinction in 1226. In 1284 the names were 'Awelton Sancti Pancratii' and 'Awelton', while in 1291 there was a distinction between 'Aulton in Southbury', later Australis, and 'Aulton in Northbury', later Borealis. From 1329, the holders of the prebends can certainly be distinguished and can be traced back to 1297 but for the purpose of the earlier succession in the prebends, 'Alton Pancras' is taken to be Alton Australis and 'Alton Archidiaconi' to be Borealis.

Canopy statuette and shield:- **Humphrey Henchman** DD, was a Fellow of Clare Hall, Cambridge. He was a son-in-law of Robert Tounson, Bishop of Sarum 1620-1621, becoming Precentor from 1623 to 1660 and Canon Residentiary from 1633 to 1660 (although dismissed during the Commonwealth) and holding in succession the prebends of Yatesbury from 1623 to 1629, Grantham Australis from 1629 to 1639 and Teynton Regis from 1639 to 1660. He was a Canon Residentiary from 1633 to 1660 and helped King Charles II to escape after the battle of Worcester; personally escorting him to Heale House and meeting him again at Stonehenge. He became Bishop of London and Lord Almoner in 1663. He died on 7 October 1675 at the age of 83 and was buried at Fulham. (Fig. 18.)

Blazon:- Or a chevron between three buglehorns sable on a chief gules three lions rampant of the first. [On a gold shield, a black chevron between three black buglehorns. Above them on a red background three erect golden lions with one hind paw on the ground and the other three paws and the tail in the air, showing full face.]

Psalter:- The portion of the psalter allotted to the prebend is Psalms 79, 80, 81 and 82.

Holders of the prebend:-

Gilbert de Axminstre (c.1226/27-c.1236) was the parson of Stalbridge in 1222.

Roger Baret (c.1284-c.1288) had died by 6 October 1292.

William de Braybrok (c.1297-1298) held the prebends of Alton Australis from c.1297 to 1298 and Beminster Prima from 1298 to c.1319.

Walter Burdon (1298-1304) MA, was a distinguished theologian and a former Chancellor of Oxford University who was Archdeacon of Gloucester from 1295. He held the prebends of Alton Australis from 1298 to 1304 and Horton from 1304 to 1308.

William de Chaddleshunt (1304-1309) DCL, was Archdeacon of Wilts from 1304 to 1320. He held the prebends of Alton Australis from 1304 to 1309 and Chardstock from 1309 to ?. He held stalls at Lichfield and St Paul's and one of his name was Rector of Dauntsey in 1303. He died before 3 February 1320.

Robert de Worth (1309-1313) was Subdean of Sarum from 1309 to 1320 and held the prebends of Alton Australis from 1309 to 1313, Durnford from 1313 to 1316 and Chisenbury & Chute from 1316 to 1349. He was a Canon Residentiary and resigned the office of Subdean on 25 November 1320 to become Rector of Bradford-on-Avon. During his time, the office of Confessor was permanently added to that of Subdean.

Hugh de Spineto (1313-1329) held the prebends of Minor Pars Altaris from 1311 to 1313 and Alton Australis from 1313 to 1329 . He was fined for non-residence in 1320 and died in 1329.

Hugh de Knossyngton (1329-1351) died in 1351.

William de Nassington (1351-1359) died by June 1359

John Maydenhyth (1386-1407) BCL, was a Canon Residentiary. He was Dean of Chichester in 1400, being rebuked by his bishop in 1403 for the lax discipline which he had allowed in his cathedral. He died in 1407.

Simon Marchford (1407-1420) held a stall at Lincoln in 1411 and died in 1420.

Thomas Morton (1420-1423) exchanged in 1423 this prebend and the prebend of Bonehill in Tamworth, Staffordshire with John Prentys for the prebend of North Newbald in York.

John Prentys (1423-1441) held the prebends of Alton Australis from 1423 to 1441 and Netheravon from 1441 to 1445. He held a stall at St Paul's from 1439 to 1445, in which year he died.

John Druell (1441-1445) DCn&CL, held the prebends of Alton Australis from 1441 to 1445, Netheravon from 1445 to 1447, Ramsbury from 1447 to 1449 and Netherbury in Ecclesia from 1449 to 1457, exchanging the last with Roger Keyes for the prebend of Blewbery which he held from 1457 until 1469. In 1449 he was Rector of Steeple Langford and he died in 1469.

Nicholas Cecill (1445-1447) held the prebends of Warminster from 1442 to 1445 and Alton Australis from 1445 to 1447. He died in 1447.

William Hende (1447-1449) held the prebends of Axford from 1426 to 1447 and Alton Australis from 1447 to 1449. He was Archdeacon of Worcester in 1443 and died in 1449.

John Paslewe (1449) BCn&CL, held the prebends of Minor Pars Altaris from 1446 to 1447, Bishopstone from 1447 to 1449, Alton Australis in 1449, and Chisenbury & Chute from 1449 to 1457. He held a stall at Hereford in 1447 and died 1457.

Richard Trove (1449) held the prebends of Axford from 1447 to 1449, Bishopstone and Alton Australis in 1449 and Netheravon from 1449-?.

Richard Hayman (1449-1461) held the prebends of Axford and Bishopstone in 1449 and Alton Australis from 1449 to 1461, exchanging it with John Waynefleet for a canonry at St Stephen's, Westminster.

John Waynflete (1461-1479) BCnL, held a stall at St Paul's from 1454-1465 and died in 1479.

Edmund Albone (1479-1485) DMus, died in 1485.

George Hardgill (1490) MA, appears to have died in 1499.

John Chymew (?-1509) died in 1509.

Walter Blount (1509-1530) BCL, held the prebends of Minor Pars Altaris in 1508, Lyme & Halstock from 1508 to 1509 and Alton Australis from 1509 until resigning in 1530.

Edward Walshe (1530-?) was deprived of a stall at Hereford in 1554 and may have been deprived of this prebend also.

Gilbert Coren (1554-?).

Peter Bizzari (or Perusinus) (1561-?) died in 1558.

William Arnold (1588-1616) died in 1616.

John Lee (1616-1624) BD, held the prebend of Alton Australis from 1616 to 1624, was Treasurer of Sarum from 1624 to 1634 and was a Canon Residentiary from ?-1634. He was Rector of Wylye from 1619 to 1634 and in 1629 that of Little Langford, both of which he held with the Treasurership. He died on 16 November 1634.

Thomas Mason (1624-1649) BD, was a Canon Residentiary from 1634 until deprived in 1649 of office and house (Leadenhall) by the Parliamentarians.

Thomas Lockey (1660-1672) BD, held the prebends of Beminster Prima in 1660, and Alton Australis from 1660 until resigning in 1672. He held a stall at Christ Church, Oxford in 1665 and died in 1679.

Timothy Topping (1672-1696) MA, held the prebends of Alton Australis from 1672 to 1696 and Durnford from 1696 to 1708. He was Rector of Chilton Foliat and died and was buried there in 1708.

Henry Austin (1696-1710) MA, was Vicar of Chalk and held the prebends of Alton Australis from 1696 to 1710 and Stratton from 1710 to 1730. He died in 1730.

Roger Kay (1710-1731) MA, was Rector of Fittleton from 1689 to 1731. He died in 1731.

George Maddocks (1731-1744) MA, became Chancellor of Llandaff in 1737 and died in 1744.

Martin Annesley (1744-1749) MA, died on 4 June 1749.

Robert Gilbert (1749-1753) MA, was Chancellor of Llandaff in 1744, and Rector of Compton Basset and West Kington in 1750. He held the prebends of Alton Australis from 1749 to 1753 and Highworth from 1753 to 1776. He died on 30 November 1776 and is commemorated in the cathedral.

Frederick Toll (1754-1756) MA, resigned the prebend in 1756.

John Lumby (1756-1758) MA, was Rector of St Martin's, Sarum. He held the prebends of Minor Pars Altaris from 1751 to 1756 and Alton Australis from 1756 to 1758. He died on 9 January 1758.

John Mulso (1758-1791) MA, held a stall at Winchester between 1770 and 1791 and died on 21 September 1791.

William Coxe (1791-1792) MA, was Rector of Bemerton in 1788 and Rector of Stourton. He held the prebends of Alton Australis from 1791 to 1792, Bitton from 1792 to 1799, Grimston from 1799 to 1801 and Netheravon from 1801 to 1828. He was a Canon Residentiary and Archdeacon of Wilts from 1804 to 1828 and died on 8 June 1828.

Walter John Kerrich (1792-1842) BA, died on 31 August 1842.

Henry Deane (1842-1882) BCL, was a Fellow of New College, Oxford. He was Vicar of Gillingham and died on 6 April 1882.

John Smith (1882-1904) BA, was Rector of Kington Magna from 1866 to 1880, Vicar of Lyme Regis from 1880 to 1883, Vicar of Motcombe with Enmore Green from 1883 to 1892 and Rural Dean of Shaftesbury. He died in 1904.

Edward Wyndham Goodden (1904-1924) was Rector of Nether with Over Compton from 1884 until his death on 19 May 1924.

Thomas John Woodall (1924-1929) was Chaplain to Sarum Infirmary from 1888 to 1894, Chaplain to the Earl of Radnor from 1894 to 1900 and Vicar of Britford from 1894 to 1929. He was Chaplain to Sarum Workhouse from 1895 to 1929 and Rural Dean of Chalke from 1923 to 1930. He held the prebends of Alton Australis from 1924 to 1929 and Ufcomb from 1929 to 1940. He died in 1940.

William Norman Willson (1930-1952) MA, was Vicar of Redlynch from 1909 to 1915, Vicar of Lyme Regis from 1915 to 1927, Rural Dean of Lyme from 1919 to 1927, Rector of St Martin's, Sarum, from 1927 to 1939 and Rural Dean of Wilton from 1932 to 1934. He resigned his prebend in 1952, due to ill health.

Harold Arthur Blair (1953-1960) MA, BD, was Vicar of Winterbourne Earls with Dauntsey & Winterbourne Gunner from 1945 to 1954 and Perpetual Curate of Southbroom from 1954 to 1960. He was a Canon Residentiary and Chancellor of Truro from 1960 to 1975.

Cyril Albert Witcomb (1960-1961) was a Chaplain RNVR from 1943 to 1946 when he became Perpetual Curate of St James's Southbroom, Devizes until 1954. He was Vicar of Melksham from 1954 to 1961, held the prebend of Alton Australis from 1960 to 1961 and was Rural Dean of Bradford from 1956 to 1961. He was then Rector of Wilton with Netherhampton from 1963 to 1970, Rural Dean of Wilton from 1964 to 1968, and held the prebend of Ilfracombe from 1965 to 1981. He was Vicar of Calne with Blackland from 1970 to 1976 and Rural Dean of Avebury from 1972 to 1973 and of Calne from 1973 to 1976. He was Vicar of the Woodford Valley from 1976 until his retirement in 1981. He died in January 1993.

Jesse Lees (1961-1967) was Rector of Fovant from 1942 to 1951. He was Minister of St George's Conventual District of Oakdale from 1951 to 1960, Vicar from 1960 to 1963 and Rural Dean of Poole from 1955 to 1959. He was Vicar of Market Lavington from 1963 to 1967. He died in April 1995.

Richard Lloyd Sharp (1968-1982) MA, was Vicar of Portland St John from 1944 to 1949, Vicar of Wootton Bassett from 1949 to 1955 and Perpetual Curate of Broad Town from 1951 to 1955. He was Vicar of St Mark's, Sarum from 1955 to 1964, Vicar of Holy Trinity, Weymouth from 1964 to 1974 and Archdeacon of Dorset from 1975 to 1982. He died on 4 July 1982.

Paul Bunday (1983-1995) MA, ALCD, was Rector of Landford with Plaitford from 1966 to 1977 and Rural Dean of Alderbury from 1973 to 1977. He was Team Rector of Radipole and Melcome Regis from 1977 to 1986 and Rural Dean of Weymouth from 1982 to 1985. He served in the Whitton Team as Team Vicar from 1986 to 1991 and Team Rector from 1991 to 1995.

David Dicker (1995-1996) MA, was Vicar of Tisbury from 1964 to 1971, Rector of Shaston Team from 1986 to 1996 and Rural Dean of Blackmore Vale from 1990 to 1995.

Victor (Vic) Robert Barron (1998-) became Team Rector of Kinson in 1989 and Rural Dean of Poole in 1994.

YETMINSTER PRIMA

Prebend:- Yetminster in Dorset was part of the pre-Conquest Sherborne episcopal estates. By c.1150 two prebends were probably in existence, which were called 'Ethemenstr W de Len' and 'Ethemenstr Tancre' in the 1220s. These later became Yetminster Prima, otherwise Superior or Overbury or Upbury and Yetminster Secunda, otherwise Inferior, or Southbury.

Canopy statuette and shield:- **Brian Duppa** DD, became in 1612 a Fellow of All Souls, Oxford. In 1629 he became Dean of Christ Church, Oxford, and from 1634 to 1638 was Chancellor of Sarum. In about 1636 he became tutor to Prince Charles and in 1638 Bishop of Chichester. He was translated to the see of Sarum in 1641 but soon after was deprived of the revenues of the see. A firm friend of King Charles I, he spent much time with him during his imprisonment and after his execution lived for a period in retirement. At the Restoration in 1660 he was made Lord Almoner and Bishop of Winchester. He died on 26 March 1662 and was buried in Westminster Abbey. Isaak Walton described him as one of "those men in whom there was such a commixture of general learning, of natural eloquence and Christian humility that they deserve a commemoration by a pen equal to their own, which none have exceeded." . (Fig. 19.)

Blazon:- Azure a lion's jamb erased in fess between two chains or on a canton of the last a rose gules barbed and seeded proper. [On a blue shield, horizontally across the centre a gold lion's leg, as if torn from the body, with beside it above and below, a gold chain. On a gold square in the top left corner, a red rose with natural coloured leaf petals and seeds.]

Psalter:- The portion of the psalter allotted to the prebend is Psalms 86, 87 and 88.

Holders of the prebend:-

William de Lenn (c.1226/27-c.1243).

Roger de la Grene (c.1243-c.1271) held the prebend of Yetminster Prima from c.1243 to c.1271, was Rector of Preshute and was Archdeacon of Wilts from c.1258 to c.1271.

Tedisius de Camilla (c.1284-c.1291) was a clerk to King Edward I and received royal appointment to the Archdeaconry of York in 1266; this proved ineffective and he became Dean of Wolverhampton. He was excommunicated in 1282 and there was a case against him in the Papal Curia in 1284. He later, however, became a papal chaplain. He was a kinsman of Pope Adrian V and was probably related to Gabriel de Camilla who held the prebend of Grimston (c.1297-?).

William de Sancto Johanne (?-1297) held the prebends of Yetminster Prima from ? to 1297 and Ramsbury in 1297 and from 1307 to c.1323. He was fined for non-residence in 1320 and there is a memorial brass to him in Ramsbury church.

Richard de Wynton (1297-1303) DTh, held the prebends of Yetminster Prima from 1297 to 1303 and Bitton from 1303 to 1304. He was Subdean of Wells and died in 1304.

Peter de Periton (1303-1310) DCnL, held the prebend of Yetminster Prima from 1303 to 1310, was appointed but declined the prebend of Durnford in 1309 and held the prebend of Bedminster & Redcliffe from 1310 to 1321. He was Archdeacon of Dorset from 1316 to 1321 and died in 1321.

Bochard de Vernon (1311-1315) resigned in 1315.

William de Melton (1315-1316) held the prebends of Yetminster Secunda in 1315 and Yetminster Prima from 1315 to 1316. He resigned his prebend in 1316 on becoming Archbishop of York.

Bochard de Vernon (1316-?).

John de Offord (?-1348) DCL, became Archbishop of Canterbury in 1348.

Henry de Walton (1348-1358) was nominated to the prebend of Yetminster Prima in 1348, installed in 1352 and had resigned by 25 June 1358, the same date that Dalmacius de Monte Florum was also said to have resigned. He held the prebend of Highworth from 1350 to 1352.

Dalmacius de Monte Florum (?-1358) was said to have resigned the prebend by 25 June 1358.

Philip Bernardini (1358-?) DCL.

William of Wykeham (1361) held the prebend of Yetminster Prima in 1361 before he was in holy Orders, exchanging it in the same year with Richard de Spridlington for Fordington & Writhlington, which he held from 1361 to 1366. He was appointed to the prebend of Bedminster & Redcliffe in 1361 but may have returned to Fordington & Writhlington. He became Bishop of Winchester in 1367 and was the founder of New College, Oxford and Winchester College.

Richard de Spridlington (1361-1376) held the prebend of Fordington & Writhlington from ? to 1361, exchanging it with William of Wykeham for the prebend of Yetminster Prima which he held from 1361 until exchanging it in 1376 with John Turk for the prebend of Offley, Lichfield.

John Turk (1376-1397) DTh, was a Canon Residentiary and Custos Puerorum in 1391 and died in 1397.

Walter Medford (1397) BCL, was Archdeacon of Dorset in 1397, Chancellor of Sarum from 1402 to 1404 and a brother of Richard Medford, Bishop of Sarum 1396 to 1407. In 1404 he exchanged the dignity with Henry Chichele for the Archdeaconry of Sarum and the prebend of Fordington & Writhlington, exchanging the dignity a few days later for the Archdeaconry of Berks. He probably exchanged this Archdeaconry with Peter Alcobasso for the deanery of Wimborne in 1417. He held the prebends of Major Pars Altaris from 1396 to 1397, Yetminster Prima in 1397, Faringdon from 1397 to 1400, having been excommunicated but later absolved, when he exchanged this prebend for the Treasurership of St Paul's. He held the prebend of Netherbury in Ecclesia in 1401, followed by Preston, which he exchanged with Richard Derham for Netherbury in Ecclesia in 1402. He held the prebends of Fordington & Writhlington from 1404 to 1407 and Bedwin from 1407 until his death in 1423.

Henry Chichele (1397-1400) DCL, was appointed Archdeacon of Dorset in 1397. After two years' litigation at the Curia over the claims of Nicholas Bubwith, he was declared technically an intrusor, but was reinstated in 1399, although Bubwith was appointed a year later. He held the prebends of Rotesfen in 1397, Yetminster Prima from 1397 to 1400, Fordington & Writhlington in 1400, Yetminster Secunda from 1400 to 1402 and Bedminster & Redcliffe from 1402 to 1404, when he exchanged with George Westby for the prebend of Fordington & Writhlington. After litigation, he became Archdeacon of Sarum in 1402, exchanging this and the prebend in 1404 for the dignity of Chancellor of Sarum which, following his consecration as Bishop of St David's in 1407, he continued to hold by papal indulgence until 1409. At one time he held the living of Melcombe Bingham and he became Archbishop of Canterbury in 1414. He was the founder of All Souls, Oxford, and died on 12 April 1443.

Ralph Lovell (1402-1405) held the prebends of Yetminster Prima from 1402 to 1405 and Highworth from 1405 to 1413.

John Medford (1405-1407) was Rector of Huish in 1401 and held the prebends of Coombe & Harnham in 1404, Highworth in 1405 and Yetminster Prima from 1405 to 1407. He died in 1407

William Pilton (1407) was granted the prebend of Yetminster Prima early in 1407 but Laurence de Gomecii was appointed nine days later. He then received the prebend of Bitton in 1407 by royal grant but it was already occupied by Geoffrey Crukadan. He was then appointed to the prebend of Grimston and installed in 1408 but there was papal intervention on behalf of Thomas Polton.

Laurence Gomecii (1407-1428) received a royal grant of the prebend and was installed in 1408. Despite pressure to resign, he was still holding the prebend at his death in 1428 .

Richard Clifford (1409) was, as a result of a commission of the Bishop of London in 1409, to receive the prebend on the resignation of Laurence Gomecii. The latter, however, died while still holding the prebend in 1428.

John Castell (1428-1432) DTh, held the prebends of Yetminster Prima from 1428 to 1432, Teynton Regis in 1432 and Bere & Cherminster from 1432 to 1436. He was Archdeacon of Berks from 1431 to 1432?

John Stopyndon (1432-1442) held a stall at St Paul's in 1424. He was Archdeacon of Colchester in 1433, Master of the Rolls in 1438 and Archdeacon of Dorset from 1440 until his death in 1447.

William Crowton (1442-1477) MA, was Rector of All Cannings. He died in 1477 and asked to be buried in the cathedral.

James Stanley (1477-?) was a son of Thomas, Earl of Derby. He held the prebends of Yetminster Prima from 1477 to ? and again from 1492 to 1493, and Beminster Prima from 1493 to 1506. He was Archdeacon of Richmond in 1500, Precentor of Sarum from 1485 to 1506 and became Bishop of Ely in 1506.

William Smith (?-1492) may well have been the person of the same name who became Bishop of Lincoln in 1492.

James Stanley (1492-1493) see above.

Richard Bray (1493-1497) resigned in 1497.

Edward Bray (1497-1503) resigned in 1503.

William Stillington (1503-1510) died in 1510.

John Keyton (1510-1537) died in 1537.

Thomas Thirlby (1537-1540) DCn&CL, was Fellow of Trinity Hall, Cambridge, Prolocutor of Convocation and Provost of St Edmund's College, Sarum. He became Bishop of Westminster in 1540, of Norwich in 1550 and of Ely in 1554.

Thomas Myntryn (1540-?) MA.

Nicholas Balgay (1582-1584) MA, held the prebends of Yetminster Prima from 1582 to 1584 and Netheravon from 1584 to 1591. He was Rector of Boscombe and Vicar of Idmiston from 1584 to 1591 and was Subdean of Sarum from 1589 to 1591.

Abraham Conham (1584) BD, held the prebends of Yetminster Prima in 1584 and Grantham Borealis from 1584 to 1613. He was Rector and Vicar of Bishopstone and died in 1613.

Richard Eedes (1584-1604) BD, died in 1604.

John FitzJames (1605-1611) died in 1611.

John Still (1611-1613) MA, was a son of Bishop Still of Bath & Wells and held the prebends of Yetminster Prima from 1611 to 1613 and Grantham Borealis from 1613-1662 He was Rector of Christian Malford and held a stall at Wells. He died in 1662.

Henry Good (1613-1660) MA, held the livings of Fisherton Anger and of Woodford cum Wilsford. He died in 1660.

Henry Carpenter (1660-1662) MA, died in 1662.

Joseph Matthews (1662-1664) BD, died in 1664.

Joshua Childrey (1664-1670) DD, held the prebend of Yetminster Prima, was Rector of Upwey and Archdeacon of Sarum from 1664 until his death in 1670. He was buried at Upwey.

John Sherman (1670-1671) DD, held the prebend of Yetminster Prima and was Archdeacon of Sarum from 1670 until his death on 27 March 1671. He is commemorated in the chapel of Jesus College, Cambridge.

Isaac Barrow (1671-1675) DD, was Master of Trinity College, Cambridge in 1673.

William Corker (1675-1702) MA, was a Fellow of Trinity College, Cambridge. He died on 30 April 1702.

John Colbatch (1702-1720) BD, resigned in 1720.

Martin Benson (1720-1721) held the prebends of Yetminster Prima from 1720 to 1721 and Ilfracombe from 1721 to 1727. He was Archdeacon of Berks from 1721 to 1735, holding a stall at Durham in 1724. In 1735 he became Bishop of Gloucester and died on 30 August 1752.

Joseph Butler (1721-1739) BA, was the author of *'The Analogy of Religion'*. He was Bishop of Bristol in 1738, Dean of St Paul's from 1740 to 1750 and Bishop of Durham in 1750.

George William Harris (1739-1777) MA, died on 23 August 1777.

Nathaniel Hume (1777-1804) MA, was Precentor of Sarum from 1774 to 1804. He held the prebends of Winterbourne Earls from 1770 to 1777, Yetminster Prima from 1777 to 1804 and the livings of Bremhill in 1782 and Brixton Deverill in 1799. He died on 28 April 1804.

John White (1804-1833) BCL, was a Fellow of New College, Oxford. He died on 18 July 1833.

George Radcliffe (1833-1849) DD, was Chaplain to Thomas Burgess, Bishop of Sarum 1825-1837. He died on 26 July 1849.

John Leyborne Popham (1849-1872) MA, was Rector of Chilton Foliat from 1835 to 1872. He died on 24 September 1872.

Henry Thomas Glyn (1872-1900) was Rector of Melbury Abbas from 1847 to 1880 and of Fontmell Magna with West Orchard from 1880 to 1900 (West Orchard to 1893). He died on 22 January 1900.

Frederick Brooke Westcott (1900-1909) MA, DD, was a Fellow of Trinity College, Cambridge, Assistant Master at Rugby School from 1884 to 1892 and Head Master of Sherborne School from 1892 to 1908. He held the prebend of Yetminster Prima from 1900 to 1909, was Archdeacon of Norwich from 1910 to 1918 and was a Chaplain in Ordinary to the Sovereign. He died on 24 February 1918.

William Okes Parish (1909-1940) TD, MA, was Vicar of Longfleet from 1885 to 1929 and Rural Dean of Poole from 1893 to 1929. He was Archdeacon of Dorset and a Canon Residentiary from 1929 until resigning on 31 March 1940. He died seven days later.

Lindsay Bartlett (1940-1960) Lic.Th, was a Chaplain to the Forces from 1918 to 1919, Vicar of Preshute from 1920 to 1931 and Rural Dean of Marlborough from 1930 to 1931. He was Rector and Rural Dean of Bridport from 1931 to 1947, Rector of Fugglestone with Bemerton from 1947 to 1956 and Rural Dean of Wilton from 1954 to 1964. He held the prebends of Yetminster Prima from 1940 to 1960 and Ufcomb, together with the office of Vicar of the Close, from 1960 to 1968. He died in 1968.

Arthur William White (1960-1972) MA, was Perpetual Curate of Poole St James from 1938 to 1943 and Curate in Charge of Canford Magna from 1943 to 1945. He was Perpetual Curate of St Michael & All Angels, Sarum from 1945 to 1965 and Vicar of Broadstone from 1965 to 1971.

George Thomas Brett (1972-1977) was Rector of Trowbridge from 1961 to 1973 and Rural Dean of Bradford from 1969 to 1973. He was Vicar of Potterne and of Worton from 1973 to 1977.

Colin Charles Perry (1977-1982) MA, was Vicar of Aldbourne from 1956 to 1964 and of Baydon from 1957 to 1964. He was Perpetual Curate of St Francis, Sarum from 1964 to 1971, Vicar of Preston with Sutton Poyntz from 1971 to 1981, Team Rector of Preston with Sutton Poyntz and Osmington with Poxwell from 1981 to 1982 and Rural Dean of Weymouth from 1975 to 1979.

Keith Alan Hugo (1984-) BA, was Diocesan Communications Officer from 1977 to 1989, Vicar of Worton and of Potterne from 1977 to 1984, and Vicar of Potterne with Worton and Marston from 1984 to 1989. He became Rector of Wyke Regis in 1989 and Rural Dean of Weymouth in 1994.

NETHERBURY IN TERRA

Prebend:- The manor of Netherbury in Dorset was part of the pre-conquest Sherborne episcopal estates granted to the cathedral. The prebend, which was probably in existence by c.1150, consisted of land in Netherbury, and was otherwise known as 'Yondover"

This stall was endowed with £1,000 by Canon Robert Rowley Watts, Prebendary of Netherbury in Terra 1887-1911, under a declaration of trust dated 7 November 1891.

Canopy statuette and shield:- **John Davenant** DD, was a Fellow of Queen's College, Cambridge in 1597 and President in 1614. In 1609 he was appointed Margaret Professor of Divinity. He was a benefactor of his college, leaving it the advowsons of the livings of Great Cheverell and Newton Tony. In 1619 he was one of the delegates to the Synod of Dort and in 1621 he became Bishop of Sarum. He was chosen for the see by King James I to enable him to befriend the widow and fifteen children left by Bishop Tounson, his predecessor and brother in law. In 1631 he incurred the displeasure of the Court through a sermon showing Calvinistic views and was summoned before the Privy Council. He died on 16 April 1641 and was buried in the south aisle of the choir of the cathedral. (Fig. 20.)

Blazon:- Gules crusilly fitchee or between three escallops ermine. [On a red shield strewed with gold crosses having pointed bases and the ends crossed, three ermine scallop shells.] (These arms were confirmed to the Bishop's father in 1588 and it is thought that the arms of Robert Tounson, Bishop of Sarum 1620-1621, (Fig.21) were derived from them.)

Psalter:- The portion of the psalter allotted to the prebend is Psalm 88.

Holders of the prebend:-

Robert Scot (c.1226/27-c.1233) went to Scotland in 1219 to collect alms for the new cathedral. He was fined for non-residence in 1227 and was again in Scotland in 1228.

Albert of Lavagna (c.1284-?1308) held a stall at York from 1289 to 1293 and at Lincoln from c.1267 until his death on 11 May 1308.

William de Bosco (?-1311) DTh, was a distinguished theologian and a former Chancellor of Oxford University. He held the prebend of Netherbury in Terra from ? to 1311 and was Chancellor of Sarum from 1309 to 1313. He died in March 1313.

Robert de Winchcomb (1311-1335) was Rector of Boscombe and held the prebend of Netherbury in Terra from 1311 to 1335, with a brief interval in 1313 when he received the prebend of Slape for four months, Netherbury in Terra having been given to William Coleshull for the same period.

William Coleshulle (1313) MA, held the prebend of Rotesfen from 1311 to 1316, although receiving the prebend of Netherbury in Terra for a four month period in 1313. He was Rector of St Peter's, Old Sarum, in 1298 and died in 1335.

John Rivers (?-1343) exchanged the prebend in 1343 with Robert de Burton for the church of Ripley, Hants.

Robert de Burton (1343-1358) exchanged the prebend of Netherbury in Terra in 1358 with John de Blewbery for the office of deacon in Wilton monastery. He held the prebend of Shipton from 1358 to 1361 and died in 1361.

John de Blewbury (1358-1372) died in 1372.

John de Corf (1373-?) held the prebends of Ruscomb from 1368 to ? and Netherbury in Terra from 1373 to ?.

William Burghbrigg (?-1392) died in 1392.

John de Ravenser (1392-1393) died in 1393.

George Louthorp (1393-1403) was Rector of St Thomas, Sarum and held the prebend of Netherbury in Terra from 1393 to 1403. He exchanged this with George Westby for the prebend of Fordington & Writhlington in 1403 and in 1404 exchanged this for the dignity of Treasurer of Sarum which he held until 1427. He was a Canon Residentiary.

George Westby (1403-1404) held the prebend of Netherbury in Terra from 1403 to 1404, becoming Treasurer of Sarum in 1404. A day later, he exchanged the dignity for the prebend of Fordington & Writhlington and, within the same year, exchanged this for the prebend of Bedminster & Redcliffe, which he in turn exchanged for Major Pars Altaris, which he then exchanged for Axford, resigning the last in the autumn of the same year.

Thomas Wisbech (1404-1410) held the prebends of Stratford from 1403 to 1404 and Netherbury in Terra from 1404 to 1410. He died in 1410.

Gilbert Hallum (1410-1413) held the prebends of Netherbury in Terra from 1410 to 1413, Highworth from 1413 to 1416 and Netherbury in Ecclesia from 1416 to 1449. He died in 1449.

Roger Basset (1413-1416) DCn&CL, died in 1416.

William Clynt (1416-1425) died in 1425.

William Swyft (1425-1445) BCL, was a Canon Residentiary who held the prebends of Stratford from 1423 to 1425 and Netherbury in Terra from 1425 to 1445. He died in 1445.

John Chedworth (1445-1447) DTh, held the prebends of Yatesbury from 1440 to 1443, Stratford from 1443 to 1445, Netherbury in Terra from 1445 to 1447 and Hurstbourne & Burbage from 1447 to 1452. He held a stall at Lincoln and was at different times Archdeacon of Northampton and of Lincoln. He was Provost of King's College, Cambridge in 1446, Archdeacon of Wilts from 1449 to 1452 and was consecrated Bishop of Lincoln in 1452. He died on 23 November 1471.

Peter Courtenay (1448-1475) DCnL, was the son of Sir Philip Courtenay of Powderham by Elizabeth daughter of Walter Lord Hungerford KG. In 1453 he was Archdeacon of Exeter, also holding the prebend of Netherbury in Terra from 1448 to 1475 exchanging these for the prebend of Bere & Cherminster which he held from 1475 to 1478, and the Provostship of St Edmund's College, Sarum. In 1474 he became secretary to King Edward IV, Dean of Windsor in 1476 and Dean of Exeter in 1477. He was Archdeacon of Wilts from 1464 to 1478 when he became Bishop of Exeter, later being translated to Winchester. He died on 22 September 1492.

Robert Ayscough (1475-1482) BCL, held the prebends of Bere & Cherminster from 1449 to 1475 and Netherbury in Terra from 1475 to 1482. He died in 1482.

Richard Salter (1483-1508) DCnL, resigned the prebend in 1508.

James Rogers (1508-1545) BCL, died in 1546.

Edward Seymour (1546-1555) resigned in 1555.

Symon Harbyn (1555-1575) resigned in 1575.

John Thornborough (1575-1586) held the prebends of Netherbury in Terra from 1575 to 1586 and Bedminster & Redcliffe from 1586 to 1593. He was Rector of Orcheston St Mary from 1575 and of Chilmark from 1577 to 1593. He was a Canon Residentiary from 1583 to c.1593, Chaplain to Queen Elizabeth I, Dean of York in 1589, Bishop of Limerick in 1593, of Bristol in 1603 and of Worcester in 1616. He died on 3 July 1641.

William Souch (1586-1589) DD, was Precentor of Sarum from 1584 to 1608. He held the prebends of Netherbury in Terra from 1586 to 1589 and Fordington & Writhlington from 1589 to 1608. He appears to have been the subject of a Visitation over the Precentor's rights to the common fund and a house of residence.

Matthew Bust (1589-1593) MA, resigned in 1593.

John Chamber (1593-1604) MA, died in 1604 and was commemorated in St George's Chapel, Windsor.

Thomas Elye (1604-?) MA, may have died in 1615.

Barnabas Holloway (1615-?) MA, was presented by King James I, the prebend being allegedly vacant by Thomas Elye's death, but there are no records.

John Priaulx (1660-1674) DD, held the prebend of Netherbury in Terra from 1660 to 1674, was a Canon Residentiary from 1661 to 1674 and Archdeacon of Sarum from 1671 to 1674. He died on 4 June 1674 and was buried and commemorated in the cathedral.

Joseph Kelsey (1674-1695) BD, held the prebends of Netherbury in Terra from 1674 to 1695, Grantham Australis from 1695 to 1705 and Highworth from 1705 to 1710. He was Rector of Newton Tony from 1669 to 1710 and of Fugglestone from 1681. He was Warden of St John's Hospital, Heytesbury in 1686 and was a Canon Residentiary and Archdeacon of Sarum from 1695 until his death on 1 November 1710. He was buried in the cathedral.

Thomas Hawes (1695-1717) MA, died in 1717 and was buried at Ramsbury.

Samuel Dunster (1717-1720) DD, held the prebends of Netherbury in Terra from 1717 to 1720 and Grimston from 1720 to 1748. He resigned in 1748.

John Taylor (1720-1767) MA, died in 1767.

William Talbot (1767-1771) MA, held the prebend of Netherbury in Terra from 1767 to 1771 and was Chancellor of Sarum from 1771 to 1811. He died on 25 November 1811.

Arthur Coham (1771-1772) MA, held the prebends of Netherbury in Terra from 1771 to 1772 and Fordington & Writhlington from 1772 to 1799. He was Vicar of Potterne from 1781 to 1793, Rector of Brixton Deverill and Archdeacon of Wilts from 1779 to 1799. He died on 14 February 1799 and is commemorated at Brixton Deverill.

Richard Dickson Lillington (1773-1786) DCL, died in 1786.

John Honeywood (1786-1788) MA, was Rector of Barford St Martin. He held the prebends of Netherbury in Terra from 1786 to 1788 and Netheravon from 1788 to 1800. He died on 21 December 1800.

Charles Sturges (1789-1805) MA, died on 22 April 1805.

Robert Morres (1805-1812) MA, held the prebends of Netherbury in Terra from 1805 to 1812 and Alton Borealis from 1812 to 1841. He was Vicar of Britford and died on 18 October 1841.

Herbert Hawes (1812-1830) held the prebends of Netherbury in Terra from 1812 to 1830 and Grimston from 1830 to 1837. He was Rector of St Edmund's, Sarum, and died on 17 January 1837.

George Stanley Faber (1830-1854) BD, died on 27 January 1854.

Lundy Foot (1854-1873) MA, was Rector of Long Bredy where he was buried following his death early in 1873.

Edward Meade (1873-1887) was Rector of Winkfield, Wilts, in 1842. He died in 1887.

Robert Rowley Watts (1887-1911) MA, was Vicar of Stourpaine from 1867 to 1902 and Rector of Steepleton Iwerne from 1877 to 1902. He was Rural Dean of Pimperne from 1881 to 1903, held the prebend of Netherbury in Terra from 1887 to 1911 and was Subdean of Sarum from 1902 to 1911. He endowed this stall in 1891 and died on 10 January 1911.

Harry William Carpenter (1911-1936) OBE, MA, held the prebends of Ruscomb from 1896 to 1911 and Netherbury in Terra from 1911 to 1936. He was Vice Principal of Sarum Theological College from 1879 to 1880, a Vicar Choral from 1879 to 1914, Precentor of Sarum from 1896 to 1936, Archdeacon of Sarum from 1914 to 1936, and a Canon Residentiary from 1915 to 1936. He died on 20 July 1936.

William Harold Ferguson (1936-1947) MA, was Precentor of Sarum, a Canon Residentiary and held the prebend of Netherbury in Terra from 1936 until he resigned the prebend and dignity on 30 April 1947. He died in 1950.

Cyril Jackson (1947-1968) was Precentor of Sarum, a Canon Residentiary, held the prebend of Netherbury in Terra and was a Proctor in Convocation from 1947 until his resignation on 15 November 1968.

Harold Wilson (1972) MA, DD, was Principal of Sarum Theological College from 1965 to 1971, a Canon Residentiary from 1968 to 1973, Chancellor of Sarum from 1971 to 1972 and Principal of Salisbury & Wells Theological College from 1971 to 1973. He held the prebends of Winterbourne Earls from 1965 to 1970 and Netherbury in Terra in 1972. He was a Canon Residentiary and Chancellor of St Paul's from 1973 to 1975 and died on 2 November 1975.

John Victor Skinner (1973-1982) BA, was Diocesan Director of Education from 1970 to 1982. He died in 1986.

Henry Graham Jack (1983-1987) AKC, BD, was Rector of Trowbridge St James from 1974 until his retirement in 1987.

Samuel John Thomas Buffrey (1987-1993) MA, was Rector of Gussage St Michael and Vicar of Gussage All Saints from 1961 to 1969, Vicar of Amesbury from 1969 to 1980 and Rural Dean of Avon from 1977 to 1980. He was Priest-in-Charge of Broadstone from 1980 to 1982 and Vicar from 1982 to 1993. He retired in 1993.

Christopher John Francis Rutledge (1995-) BSc, Cert Theol, FETC, MPhil, DPhil, was Priest-in-Charge of Derry Hill from 1976 to 1978, Vicar from 1978 to 1981, Priest-in-Charge of Talbot Village from 1981 to 1982 and Vicar from 1982.

NETHERAVON

Prebend:- The church of Netheravon in Wiltshire was granted to the cathedral by King Henry I some time between 1107 and 1135 and the prebend was probably in existence c.1150.

This stall was endowed with £800 by the Rev the Hon Sidney Meade under a deed of endowment dated 26 August 1897

Canopy statuette and shield:- **Robert Tounson** DD, was a Fellow of Queens' College, Cambridge. He became Chaplain to King James I in 1617 and soon afterwards Dean of Westminster. In the latter capacity he was present at the execution of Sir Walter Raleigh in Palace Yard. He was Bishop of Sarum for ten months, between 1620 and his death on 15 May 1621, dying of a fever contracted by 'unseasonable sitting up to study', when preparing at short notice to preach before Parliament. He left a widow and fifteen children and was buried in Westminster Abbey. (Fig. 21.)

Blazon:- Gules five crosses crosslet fitchee in saltire or between four escallops ermine. [On a red shield, five crosses with pointed bases and top and arms crossed, in the form of an X, between four ermine scallop shells.] (It is thought that these arms were derived from those of John Davenant, Bishop of Sarum 1621-1641, (Fig. 20).)

Psalter:- The portion of the psalter allotted to the prebend is Psalms 70, 71 and 72.

Holders of the prebend:-

Roger of Sarum (c.1226/27-1236) was Precentor of Sarum from c.1227 to 1244. He held the prebends of Netheravon from c.1226/27 to 1236 and Teynton Regis from c.1236 to 1244, the latter being joined to the dignity of Precentor for a time. He was consecrated as Bishop of Bath & Wells in 1244, although the Chapter of Wells refused to concur with his election and, dying on 21 December 1247, he was buried in Bath.

Hugh de la Penne (c.1284-?1295) may have been the person of the same name who was a royal clerk and Queen's Treasurer who had died by 22 April 1295.

Roger de Martival (1298-1315) DTh, was Archdeacon of Huntingdon in 1288 and of Leicester in 1295. In 1293 he became Chancellor of Oxford University and occupied the prebend of Netheravon from 1298 to 1315. He was Dean of Lincoln in 1310 and as Bishop of Sarum from 1315 to 1330 he completed the spire and drew up cathedral statutes in 1319. He died on 14 March 1330, was buried in the cathedral on the north side of the choir under a slab of marble inlaid with brass which has since been removed.

Gilbert de Middleton (1315-1322) held the prebends of Netheravon from 1315 to 1322 and Horton from 1322 to 1330. He was also well endowed with other prebends, simultaneously holding stalls at St Paul's, Lincoln, Chichester, Hereford and Wells. He became Archdeacon of Northampton in 1316 and held the church of Edington. In 1321 King Edward II "granted him that he should not be disturbed in any of his benefices." He died in 1330/31.

John de Fonteneye (1322-?) held the prebend of Horton in 1322, exchanging it with Gilbert de Middleton for the prebend of Netheravon.

Innocent de Fieschi (1327) was granted the prebend of Grimston in 1319 but it was held by Thomas Staunton. He occupied the prebend of Netheravon in 1327.

Manuel de Fieschi (?-1343) occupied the prebend in 1335 and became Bishop of Vercelli in 1343.

William of Edington (1343-1345) was the founder of the religious house at Edington and the builder of the present church. He received a royal grant of this prebend in 1343 but about one month later Walter de Burley was appointed. He became Bishop of Winchester in 1345.

Walter de Burley (1343-1344) DTh, exchanged the prebend in 1344 with William of Edington for the chapel of Imber.

Stephen la Porta (1346-1351) was installed in 1346 but John de Wolvesey, who had previous expectations, was installed in 1348. He died in 1351.

John de Wolvesey (1348-?) received the prebend in 1348 but on Stephen la Porta's death William de Melborne was appointed. A royal grant in 1351 however confirmed his position.

William de Melborne (1351-?) was appointed to the prebend in 1351. Thomas de Bredon was also appointed in the same year but a royal commission called for the arrest of all those prosecuting appeals against William de Melborne. In a dispute with William Feriby in the Court of Canterbury in 1369 however, he was outlawed but pardoned in 1371.

Thomas de Bredon (1351) was appointed to the prebend in 1351 but William de Melborne appeared to have had a better case. He may have held the dignity of Treasurer of Sarum in 1350.

Robert de Derby (1358-?) held the prebend from 1358 until his death.

William Feriby (1366.1369) held the prebend of Ruscomb in 1339, exchanging it with Alan Coningsburgh for the prebend of Sharow in Ripon collegiate church and the prebend of Netheravon which he held in 1366 and 1369. He held a stall at York.

Adam de Hertington (1371-1376) held the prebends of Netheravon from 1371 to 1376 and Netherbury in Ecclesia from 1376 to ?

John de Bishopstone (1376-?).

William Croiser (?-1388) exchanged the prebend in 1388 with Roger Gray for the chapel of St Mary & St Leonard of the Rood by Tarporley, Cheshire.

Roger Gray (1388-1408) died in 1408.

Nicholas de Ryssheton (1408-1413) DCn&CL, died in 1413.

Nicholas Calton (1413-1440) died in 1440.

Robert Aiscough (1440-1441) DTh, held the prebends of Netheravon from 1440 to 1441, Faringdon from 1441 to 1447, Grantham Australis from 1447 to 1448, Chisenbury & Chute in 1448 and Bere & Cherminster from 1448 to 1449. He was Archdeacon of Dorset from 1447 to 1449 and had died by 14 February 1449.

John Prentys (1441-1445) held the prebends of Alton Australis from 1423 to 1441 and Netheravon from 1441 to 1445. He held a stall at St Paul's from 1439-1445, in which year he died.

John Druell (1445-1447) DCn&CL, held the prebends of Alton Australis from 1441 to 1445, Netheravon from 1445 to 1447, Ramsbury from 1447 to 1449 and Netherbury in Ecclesia from 1449 to 1457, exchanging the last with Roger Keyes for the prebend of Blewbery which he held from 1457 until 1469. In 1449 he was Rector of Steeple Langford and he died in 1469.

William Byconyll (1447-1448) DCL, held the prebends of Durnford from 1446 to 1447 and Netheravon from 1447 to 1448. He died in 1448.

Thomas Kirkeby (1448-1449) held the prebends of Yatesbury from 1445 to 1446, Warminster from 1446 to 1448, Netheravon from 1448 to 1449, Ramsbury from 1449 to 1464 and Highworth from 1464 to 1476. He also held the prebend of Stanton Berners under the Abbey of Wilton and died in 1476.

Richard Trove (1449-?) held the prebends of Axford from 1447 to 1449, Bishopstone and Alton Australis in 1449 and Netheravon from 1449 to ?.

Richard Caunton (?-1465) DCn&CL, held the prebend of Netheravon from ? to 1465 and was Archdeacon of Sarum from 1446 to 1465. He died in 1465.

Thomas Rotherham (1465-1468) DTh, was one of the original Fellows of King's College, Cambridge. In 1465 he was Chaplain to King Edward IV and he became Provost of Beverley, Bishop of Rochester in 1468 and of Lincoln in 1471. In 1473 he was Lord Chancellor and in 1480 Archbishop of York, combining with that dignity the Mastership of Pembroke Hall.

Thomas Bonifant (1468-1470) DTh, was a Chantry-Priest of St Catherine, Wanborough and died in 1470.

John Segden (1470-1476) DTh, was Master of Balliol College, Oxford and Archdeacon of Gloucester. He held the prebends of Netheravon from 1470 to 1476 and Highworth from 1476 to 1482?. He also held a stall at Worcester. He died in 1482.

John Emwell (1476-1478) BCnL, was Precentor of Sarum from 1479 to 1480. He held the prebends of Netheravon from 1476 to 1478 and Coombe & Harnham from 1478 to 1485. He resigned the dignity in 1480 and died in 1485.

Edward Pole (1478-1479) appears to have been a son of the Duke of Suffolk. He was Precentor of Sarum from 1480 to 1485 and held the prebends of Netheravon from 1478 to 1479 and Hurstbourne & Burbage from 1479 to ?. He became Archdeacon of the East Riding in 1480 and of Richmond in 1484.

Laurence Cokkys (1479-?) DCnL, held the prebends of Durnford from 1478 to 1479, Netheravon from 1479 to ? and Grimston in 1490. He was Rector of Winterbourne Basset in 1485 and Fisherton Anger in 1490 and was a Canon Residentiary in 1497. He died in 1501.

John Peyrson (1490) was present in chapter in 1490.

John Withers (?-1534) DCnL, held the prebend until his death in 1534.

Simon Symonds (1534-1551) was a Fellow of King's College, Cambridge and afterwards Vicar of Bray from 1535-1551. In 1535 he held a stall at Windsor and was Chaplain to King Henry VIII. He also held stalls at Lincoln and Lichfield, being removed from the latter in 1546 for not paying his dues. He died in 1551.

Jerome Barnaby (1551-1584) was Rector of Boscombe in 1565 and Vicar of Idmiston. He died in 1584.

Nicholas Balgay (1584-1591) MA, held the prebends of Yetminster Prima from 1582 to 1584 and Netheravon from 1584 to 1591. He was Rector of Boscombe and Vicar of Idmiston from 1584 to 1591 and was Subdean of Sarum from 1589 to 1591.

Richard Hooker (1591-1595) MA, was a Fellow of Corpus Christi, Oxford and was described as the ablest living advocate of the Church of England. He was Master of the Temple from 1585 to 1591, Rector of Boscombe, where he wrote part of his *Ecclesiastical Polity*, Subdean of Sarum and held the prebend of Netheravon from 1591 to 1595. He died on 2 November 1600 and was buried in the chancel of Bishopbourne, Kent where he is commemorated.

Thomas Ivye (1595-1623) MA, was Vicar of Enford and Rector of Fittleton. He died in 1623.

Anthony Gulson (1623-1626) MA, died in 1626.

Robert Pearson (1626-1639) DD, resigned his prebend in 1639. He was Archdeacon of Suffolk from 1613 to 1639.

John Vincent (1639) MA, died in 1639.

John Pearson (1639-1662) MA, was Archdeacon of Surrey in 1660. He resigned his prebend on becoming Master of Trinity College, Cambridge in 1662 and he became Bishop of Chester in 1673

Ralph Sanderson (1662-1679) MA, died in 1679 and was buried at Weyhill, Hampshire.

Thomas Ward (1679-1681) LLD, was a nephew of Seth Ward, Bishop of Sarum 1667-1689, and in 1679 was ordained deacon and priest in one day. A month later he received the prebend of Netheravon, holding it from 1679 to 1681. He held the prebends of Gillingham Major from 1681 to 1682 and Teynton Regis from 1682 to 1696. He was Archdeacon of Wilts from 1687 until his death on 20 March 1696. His appointment to a prebendal stall at a very early age and his rapid advancement led to a controversy between Bishop and Dean.

Isaac Walton (1681-1719) MA, was a son of Isaak Walton the author and fisherman. He held the prebends of Yatesbury from 1678 to 1679, Bishopstone from 1679 to 1681 and Netheravon from 1681 to 1719. He was Rector of Boscombe in 1679 and Rector of Poulshot in 1680. He was a Canon Residentiary from 1698 to 1719, living in what is now known as the Walton Canonry in the Close, died on 29 December 1719 and was buried in the cathedral.

John Laurence (1720-1732) MA, died on 18 May 1732.

William Lane (1732-1752) MA, was Rector of St Edmund's, Sarum. He died on 14 July 1752.

John James Majendie (1752-1783) held stalls at Worcester in 1769 and at Windsor in 1774. He died on 7 August 1783.

Edward Innes (1783-1788) was Rector of Stockton from 1772 to 1778 and Rector of Devizes from 1774 until his death on 18 November 1788. He was buried at Devizes.

John Honeywood (1788-1800) MA, was Rector of Barford St Martin. He held the prebends of Netherbury in Terra from 1786 to 1788 and Netheravon from 1788 to 1800. He died on 21 December 1800.

William Coxe (1801-1828) MA, was Rector of Bemerton in 1788 and Rector of Stourton. He held the prebends of Alton Australis from 1791 to 1792, Bitton from 1792 to 1799, Grimston from 1799 to 1801 and Netheravon from 1801 to 1828. He was a Canon Residentiary and Archdeacon of Wilts from 1804 to 1828, dying on 8 June 1828.

Liscombe Clarke (1828-1834) MA, held a stall at Hereford in 1821. He was Archdeacon of Sarum from 1827 to 1836, a Canon Residentiary from 1832 to 1841and Treasurer of Sarum from 1834 to 1841. He held the prebends of Minor Pars Altaris from 1827 to 1828 and Netheravon from 1828 to 1834 and was Vicar of Downton. He died on 17 April 1841.

Francis Lear (1834-1846) BD, was Rector of Chilmark from 1824, holding the prebends of Stratford from 1830 to 1834 and of Netheravon from 1834 to 1846. He was Rector and Vicar of Bishopstone from 1843 and Archdeacon of Sarum from 1836 to 1846. He was Dean of Sarum and a Canon Residentiary from 1846 to 1850, dying on 23 March 1850.

John Watts (1846-1872) MA, was a Fellow of University College, Oxford and Rector of Tarrant Gunville from 1828 until his death on 5 June 1872.

William Henry Rich Jones (1872-1885) MA, FSA, antiquary and author, was Vicar of Bradford-on-Avon from 1851 to 1885 and Rural Dean of Potterne from 1861 to 1873. He restored the Saxon church in Bradford-on-Avon and wrote, amongst other books on the diocese, *'Fasti Ecclesiae Sarisberiensis, or a Calendar of the Bishops, Deans, Archdeacons and Members of the Cathedral Body at Salisbury from the Earliest Times to the Present'* published in 1881. In 1883 he prefixed his wife's maiden name of Rich and he died on 28 October 1885.

Thomas Henry Tait (1886-1888) MA, was Rector of Hilperton with Whaddon from 1861 to 1888 and died in November 1888.

Arthur Baynham (1888-1892) MA, was Rector of Potterne from 1871 to 1873, Vicar of Bishop's Lavington from 1873 to 1892 and Rural Dean of Potterne from 1874 to 1892.

The Hon Sidney Meade (1892-1916) MA, JP, was the 3rd son of the 3rd Earl of Clanwilliam. He was Rector of Wylye from 1869 to 1882 and was clerical secretary of the Diocesan Synod. He died on 11 February 1917.

Ernest Edward Dugmore (1917-1925) MA, author, was Vicar of Parkstone from 1872 to 1910 and Succentor from 1909 to 1925. He held the prebends of Gillingham Major from 1890 to 1917 and Netheravon from 1917 to 1925 and died in 1925.

Henry Robert Whytehead (1925-1937) MA, was Rector of St Peter & St Paul, Marlborough from 1887 to 1897, Vicar of Warminster from 1897 to 1915 and Rural Dean of Heytesbury from 1914 to 1919. He held the prebends of Minor Pars Altaris from 1917 to 1925 and Netheravon from 1925 to 1937, and was Succentor from 1925 to 1931. He died in 1937.

Archibald Leslie Keith (1938-1948) MA, was Vicar of Wimborne Minster from 1920 to 1946 and Rural Dean of Wimborne from 1928 to 1946. He held the prebends of Grantham Borealis from 1929 to 1937 and Netheravon from 1938 until resigning in 1948. He died in 1956.

Cecil Andrew Plaxton (1948-1993) MA, was Vicar of Southbroom from 1932 to 1937, Vicar of Holy Trinity, Weymouth from 1937 to 1951 and Rural Dean of Weymouth from 1944 to 1951. He held the prebend of Netheravon from 1948 to 1993, was Rector of Pewsey from 1951 to 1956 and Archdeacon of Wilts from 1951 to 1974. He died on 2 February 1993.

Stella Vivian Collins (1993-1997) was Deaconess and Deacon at Harnham from 1977 to 1988, Diocesan Lay Ministry Adviser and Advisor on Women's Ministry from 1982 to 1997, Deacon at Wilton with Netherhampton and Fugglestone from 1988 to 1994 and Curate from 1994 to 1997. She was on the staff of the Southern Dioceses' Ministerial Training Scheme from 1981 to 1990, was Rural Dean Wylye & Wilton from 1989 to 1994 and was the first woman canon of the cathedral, holding the prebend of Netheravon from 1993 to 1997 .

Christopher Francis Brown (1998-) was Priest-in-Charge of Wylye, Fisherton Delamere & the Langfords from 1977 to 1979, Rector of Yarnbury from 1979 to 1982, Rector of Portland All Saints with St Peter from 1982 to 1988 and Rural Dean of Weymouth from 1985 to 1988. He became Rector of Trowbridge St James in 1988 and a Proctor in Convocation in 1993.

WILSFORD & WOODFORD

Prebend:- In 1086 Wilsford in Wiltshire was part of the lands of Hugh, Earl of Chester which were granted to the canons in 1091 by Osmund, Bishop of Sarum 1078-1099. It would appear that Wilsford was by 1153 a chapel of Woodford, now Middle Woodford, which by c.1210 was part of the bishop's manor. The prebend was probably in existence c.1150, being called Woodford in 1187 and mainly during the 12 c., although Wilsford c.1270. The prebend comprised the church of Woodford with the chapel of Wilsford, lands and tithes and possibly land at Stratford-sub-Castle.

Canopy statuette and shield:- **Martin Fotherby** DD, was a nephew of John Whitgift, Archbishop of Canterbury, to whom he was chaplain and who gave him a stall at Canterbury where his brother was Dean. He was a chaplain to King James I and is said to have owed his advancement to be Bishop of Sarum in 1618, to the Duke of Buckingham. He died on 11 March 1620 at the age of 60 and was buried in London. (Fig. 22.)

Blazon:- Gules a cross flory lozengy or (in dexter chief a crescent for difference). [On a red shield, a gold cross made of diamond shapes with fleur-de-lyse at the points. (There should be a crescent, indicating a second son, at the top left.)]

Psalter:- The portion of the psalter allotted to the prebend is Psalms 98, 99, 100, 101 and 102.

Holders of the prebend:-

Roger (before 1153) was Succentor of Sarum before 1153 and held the prebend of Wilsford & Woodford.

Robert de Hertford (1226/7-?) was sent to the diocese of Ely to collect alms for the new cathedral in 1219. He was Chancellor of Sarum from 1220 to 1236 and Dean of Sarum from 1237 to 1257. He held the prebend of Wilsford & Woodford from 1226/7 to ?1257 and died on 9 December 1257.

Gerard de Grandisson (?-1265) was Archdeacon of Dorset before June 1275. He was a papal chaplain and nephew of Otto de Grandisson who was a royal councillor. He held a stall at York and became Bishop of Verdun in 1276.

Matthew de Carazolis (1265-1305) was a nephew of Berard of Naples and died before 2 November 1305.

Matthew de Carazolis (1305-?) is alleged to have succeeded to the prebend before he was 15 years old. In 1309 it was said that he was dead and a royal licence was granted to Thomas de Lugore. This grant was revoked in 1310 since Matthew de Carazolis was found to be still alive!

Thomas de Lugore (1309-1310) DCL.

Arnoloto de Custornio (1313-?) was fined for non-residence in 1320.

Nicholas de la Wyle (1324-1341) was a distinguished theologian and Precentor of Sarum from 1323 to 1341. He held the prebend of Wilsford & Woodford from 1324 to 1341 and a stall at Wells.. He was a Canon Residentiary and was locum tenens of the Dean in 1340. He died in 1341.

Peter de Inkpen (1341-?) was Rector of Chiseldon in 1324 and held the prebends of Bishopstone in 1341 and Wilsford & Woodford from 1341 to ?.

Bertrand de Deucio (1352) was Provost of Embrun, France and Archbishop of Embrun from 1323 until he was created Cardinal-Priest of St Mark's in 1338. He was Archdeacon of Dorset in 1347 and 1352, and became Cardinal-Bishop of Sabina in 1348 being allowed to visit his Archdeaconry by deputy for a period of five years. He held the prebend of Wilsford and Woodford in 1352. After being Nuncio to Robert, King of Sicily, and to the Doge of Venice he died on 21 October 1355.

Raymund ? (1363) is believed to have occupied the prebend in 1363.

Humphrey de Aldeburgh (1378-?) BCn&CL.

Henry de Winterton (1385-1400) Lic.CL, was nominated to the prebend of Bedminster & Redcliffe in 1361. He received the prebend of Wilsford & Woodford in 1385 but a royal grant was made to Robert Bloor in 1387. Title was proved in 1389 but there was then a royal grant to Walter Pese in 1390 which was revoked in July of the same year. There was a further royal grant to William Ashton in November 1390 but de Winterton kept possession until his death in February 1400.

John Boor (1387) was granted the prebend of Wilsford & Woodford in 1387 and held the prebend of Bere & Cherminster from 1390 to 1402

Walter Pese (1390) received a royal grant of the prebend in January 1390 but this was revoked six months later.

William Ashton (1390) DCL, claimed the prebend of Bere & Cherminster from ? to 1390 but following a judicial inquiry, he resigned his claim in 1390. In the same year he was granted the prebend of Wilsford & Woodford but Henry de Winterton retained possession.

Ralph Repyngton (1398-1416) had a royal grant of the Archdeaconry of Berks in 1395 but John Southam was holding it in 1404. He also received the prebend of Wilsford & Woodford by royal grant in 1398 but Henry de Winterton did not vacate it until his death in 1400.

Hugh Holbach (1416-1417) DCnL, died in 1417.

Henry Ware (1417-1418) Lic.Cn&CL, became Bishop of Chichester in 1418.

William Hayton (1419-1425) held the prebends of Wilsford & Woodford from 1419 to 1425 and Highworth from 1426 to 1435. He died in 1435.

Thomas Bubwith (1425-1428) BCn&CL, held the prebends of Wilsford & Woodford from 1425 to 1428 and Bitton from 1428 to 1447. He resigned in 1447.

Richard Harewell (1428-1435) died in 1435.

William Gray (1435-1454) MA, became Bishop of Ely in 1454.

John Chedworth (1454-1464) DCL, exchanged the prebend of Wilsford & Woodford, which he held from 1454 to 1464, with William Say for the prebend of Bedminster & Redcliffe, holding the latter from 1464 to 1471. He died in 1471.

William Say (1464-1468) DTh, exchanged the prebend of Bedminster & Redcliffe with John Chedworth for the prebend of Wilsford & Woodford which he held from 1464 to 1468. He died in 1468.

Henry Sharp (1468-1489) DCL, held the prebends of Torleton from 1463 to 1468 and Wilsford & Woodford from 1468 to 1489. He died in 1489.

William Russell (1489-1492) DCnL, was a Canon Residentiary and held the prebends of Wilsford & Woodford from 1489 to 1492 and of Bedminster & Redcliffe from 1492 to 1508. He died in 1508.

Richard Newport (1492) BCL, held the prebends of Major Pars Altaris from 1490 to 1492, Wilsford & Woodford in 1492 and Faringdon from 1492 to 1514. He was Rector of Mildenhall and Vicar General to Edmund Audley, Bishop of Sarum 1502-1524. He died in 1514 and desired to be buried in the cathedral.

Richard Lichfield (1493-1497) DCn&CL, was a Canon Residentiary. He held a stall at St Paul's and the Archdeaconries of Middlesex and Bath, dying in 1497.

Edward Crome (1497-1517) DTh, died in 1517.

Edward Finch (1517) DM, was well endowed with prebends holding in succession those of Yatesbury from 1514 to 1515, Chardstock from 1515 to 1517, Wilsford & Woodford in 1517, Fordington & Writhlington from 1517 to 1518, Grimston from 1518 to 1519, Faringdon from 1519 to 1521 exchanging the last with William Webbe for the church of Ross on Wye, Hereford. He then held the prebends of Bishopstone from 1521 to 1522, Teynton Regis from 1522 to 1524 and Bere & Cherminster from 1524 to 1539. He was Archdeacon of Wilts from 1522 to 1539, died in 1539 and was buried in the cathedral.

Thomas Martyn (1517-1524) DCnL, held the prebends of Chardstock from 1507 to 1515, Beminster Prima from 1515 to 1517 and Wilsford & Woodford from 1517 to 1524. He died in 1524.

Miles Willen (1524-?).

Anthony Denys (?-1538) the prebend became vacant through his marriage.

William Latimer (1538-?) BTh, was a Fellow of All Souls, Oxford in 1489.

William Garnet (1538-?) received another prebend in 1543.

Christopher Hales (1543-1554) MA, was in 1539, a Fellow of St John's College, Cambridge. He was deprived in 1554 on the accession of Queen Mary I as being a layman and went to live in Frankfurt.

Peter Weaver (1554-?).

William Marwood (1559-1581) MA, died in August 1581.

Thomas Paynter (1581-1583) MA, held the prebends of Wilsford & Woodford from 1581 to 1583, Slape from 1583 to 1587 and Shipton from 1587 to 1614. He died in 1614.

Ralph Smith (1584-1616) BD, resigned in 1616.

John Moseley (1616-?) DD.

Thomas Gorges (1643-1667) was a Fellow of All Souls, Oxford, Archdeacon of Winchester and held a stall at Westminster. He died in 1667 and was buried in Westminster Abbey.

William Lloyd (1667-1680) DD, was Dean of Bangor and then Archdeacon of Merioneth before becoming Bishop of St Asaph in 1680 and then of Lichfield in 1692. He was one of the seven bishops to be sent to the Tower in the reign of King James II.

John Younger (1680-1705) DD, held the living of Bishopstone from 1688 to 1728 and was chaplain to the Princess Anne, later Queen Anne, on her marriage to Prince George of Denmark, and was Keeper of the Bodleian Library He held the prebend of Wilsford & Woodford from 1680 to 1705, was appointed a Canon Residentiary of St Paul's in 1693, holding the latter together with the Deanery of Sarum and a residentiary canonry from 1705 until 1728. He died on 27 February 1728.

John Hoadley (1706-1713) MA, was Chancellor of Sarum from 1713 to 1727. He was a brother of Benjamin Hoadly, Bishop of Sarum 1723-1734, and chaplain to Gilbert Burnet, Bishop of Sarum 1689-1715, the latter appointing him to the prebend of Wilsford & Woodford from 1706 to 1713 and the Archdeaconry of Sarum from 1710 to 1727. He became a Canon Residentiary and Rector of St Edmund, Sarum. He was consecrated as Bishop of Ferns and Leighlin in 1727, becoming Archbishop of Dublin in 1729 and of Armagh in 1742.

Francis Fox (1713-1730) MA, held the prebends of Wilsford & Woodford from 1713 to 1730 and Stratton from 1730 to 1738. He was Vicar of Potterne and died on 6 July 1738.

John Scott (1730-1756) MA, died in 1756.

The Hon George Hamilton (1756-1787) MA, died on 26 November 1787.

Thomas Burgess (1787-1803) DD, was a Fellow of Corpus Christi College, Oxford who held the prebend of Wilsford & Woodford from 1787 to 1803 and also a stall at Durham. He became Bishop of St David's in 1803, establishing Lampeter College, and Bishop of Sarum from 1825 to 1837 during which time he formed and endowed the Church Union Society. He died on 19 February 1837.

John Brereton (1803-1811) MA, died on 12 March 1811.

William Ward (1811-1838) BD, became Bishop of Sodor and Man in 1828 but continued to hold this prebend until his death on 26 January 1838.

George Anthony Denison (1841-1848) MA, was a Fellow of Oriel College, Oxford, Vicar of Broadwindsor from 1838 to 1845 and in 1849 held a stall at Wells. He was appointed Archdeacon of Taunton in 1851 but in 1853, having been charged with unsound doctrine, he preached three sermons in Wells Cathedral which affirmed the real presence in the elements and led to court proceedings by the Evangelical Alliance. He was sentenced to deprivation but in 1857 the Court of Arches reversed the finding on a technical point. He died on 21 March 1896 at East Brent, Somerset, where he was buried.

The Hon William Hugh Scott (1848-1868) was the 2nd son of the 6th Baron Polwarth & 11th Baron Harden. He was Rector of Maiden Newton in 1837 and died on 17 April 1868.

Frederick Bennett (1868-1899) was Vicar of the parishes of Maddington from 1851 and of Shrewton from 1853 until their union in 1870 and of the united benefice until 1895. He died on 1 July 1903.

Louis George Mylne (1899-1905) DD, author, was Bishop of Bombay from 1876 to 1897 and Vicar of St Mary's, Marlborough from 1897 to 1905. He held a stall at Worcester from 1917 until his death on 19 February 1951.

Robert Ewing (1905-1908) MA, DD, was an educationalist who was Rector of Winterslow from 1888 to 1894 and Vicar of The Trinity, Trowbridge from 1894 to 1908. He died in 1908.

Edgar Nembhard Thwaites (1908-1919) was Rector of Fisherton Anger from 1873 until resigning in 1914. He died on 30 April 1919.

Thomas Joseph Lawrence (1919) MA, LLD, JP, lawyer and author, was a Fellow of Downing College, Cambridge, Tutor, Chaplain and Dean from 1876 to 1877. He was Warden of Cavendish College, Cambridge, from 1876 to 1877 and Rector of Upton Lovel from 1902 to 1919. He died on 16 August 1919.

Henry Herbert Mogg (1919-1929) BA, was Vicar of Chittoe from 1886 to 1907 and Vicar of Bishop's Cannings from 1907 to 1927. He was Rural Dean of Avebury from 1919 to 1927 and was a Proctor in Convocation. He died on 30 July 1929.

Auriol Giffard Ruddle (1930-1935) AKC, was Rector of Durrington from 1911 to 1935 and Rural Dean of Amesbury from 1920 to 1935. He died on 29 January 1935.

Charles Pigott Edmonds (1936-1949) BA, was Rector of Fontmell Magna with West Orchard from 1903 to 1949 and Rural Dean of Sturminster Newton from 1930 to 1943.

Oswald Rochfort Yerburgh (1950-1966) MA, was Rector of Maperton from 1930 to 1932, Vicar of Steeple Ashton with Semmington from 1932 to 1959 and Rural Dean of Bradford-on-Avon from 1942 to 1952. He was Rector of Studland from 1959 to 1966 and Rural Dean of Purbeck from 1961 to 1966. He died on 25 June 1966.

John Charles Wallis (1966-1980) DSC, Lic.Th, MA, was a Chaplain RNVR from 1941 to 1946, Vicar of Allington from 1946 to 1948, Chaplain of University College and Hatfield College, Durham from 1948 to 1957, and Rector of Bloxworth with Winterborne Anderson, Zelstone and Tomson from 1957 to 1961. He was Rector of Wareham with Arne from 1961 to 1979 and of East Holme from 1976 to 1979. He was Rural Dean of Purbeck from 1966 to 1973 and died in December 1992.

Keith Richard Scott Rintoul (1980-1982) MA, was Vicar of Collingbourne Kingstone from 1949 to 1954 and Perpetual Curate of The Trinity, Trowbridge from 1954 to 1964. He was Perpetual Curate of West Fordington from 1964 to 1973, Priest-in-Charge of Allington St Swithun from 1973 to 1979, Team Vicar of Bridport from 1979 to 1982 and Rural Dean of Bridport from 1979 until his retirement in 1982. He had died in 1990.

John James Fuller (1983-1997) BA, was a tutor at Cuddesdon Theological College from 1971 to 1975 and at Ripon College, Cuddesdon from 1975 to 1977. He was Principal of the Southern Dioceses Ministerial Training Scheme from 1977 to 1997.

[**John Darlington** (1997-) MIMgt; Lieutenant Colonel and Lay Canon. He served in the Royal Tank Regiment from 1950 to 1986, was Bursar of Salisbury & Wells Theological College from 1986 to 1994, and Bursar of Sarum College from 1994 to 1996. He was elected to the General Synod in 1990, holds parochial, deanery and diocesan positions and was appointed to the Close Chapter in 1998. He occupies Wilsford & Woodford as a Courtesy Stall]

GRIMSTON

Prebend:- Grimston is a small hamlet in the parish of Stratton in Dorset, which was probably part of the pre-Conquest Sherborne episcopal estates.

Canopy statuette and shield:- **Robert Abbot** DD, was the elder brother of George Abbot, Archbishop of Canterbury. He was a Fellow of Balliol College, Oxford in 1581 and Master in 1609. He held a stall at Southwell in 1610 and became Regius Professor of Divinity at Oxford in 1612. He was a distinguished theologian, a treatise *De Potestate Regia* inducing King James I to appoint him Bishop of Sarum in 1615. He died on 2 March 1618, at the early age of 58, and was buried in the cathedral opposite the bishop's throne. (Fig. 23.)

Blazon:- Gules a chevron between three pears pendant stalked or. [On a red shield, a gold chevron between three gold hanging pears with stalks.]

Psalter:- The portion of the psalter allotted to the prebend is Psalm 89.

Holders of the prebend:-

Richard de Maupudre (c.1226/27-c.1233) also held a stall at Chichester and died before 23 February 1246.

Robert de Strode (c.1284-c.1297) was infirm but still alive in 1298.

Gabriel de Camilla (1297-1318) went abroad in 1309 and died at Orleans on 26 August 1318. He was probably related to Tedisius de Camilla who held the prebend of Yetminster Prima c.1284-c.1291.

Thomas de Staunton (1318-?) received a royal grant of the prebend of Grimston in 1318 and despite a papal grant to Innocent de Fieschi, he appears to have held it until at least 1324. He was Precentor of Sarum from 1344 to 1347.

Innocent de Fieschi (1319) was granted the prebend of Grimston in 1319 but it was held by Thomas Staunton. He occupied the prebend of Netheravon in 1327.

John de Woodford (1333-1350) held the prebend despite support for Thomas de Staunton by the chapter in 1334. He was Surgeon and Chaplain to King Edward III, held a stall at St Paul's and had died by 27 June 1350.

Roger de Cloune (1350-?) held the prebend of Faringdon from 1349 until it was given to John de Edington by royal grant in 1350, when he received the prebend of Grimston, holding it until at least 1366. He was Archdeacon of Sarum from 1361 until at least 1375 and was a Canon Residentiary.

Simon de Borsano (1379) held the prebends of Grimston and Yetminster Secunda in 1379.

Thomas Worston (?-1408) may have held the prebend from 1390. He died in 1408.

William Pilton (1408) received the prebend of Yetminster Prima early in 1407 but Laurence de Gomecii received it nine days later. He then received the prebend of Bitton in 1407 by royal grant but it was already occupied by Geoffrey Crukadan. He was then appointed to the prebend of Grimston and installed in 1408 but there was papal intervention on behalf of Thomas Polton.

Thomas Polton (1408-1418) BCn&CL, was an Austin Friar who held the prebend despite the appointment of William Pilton in 1408. He became Bishop of Hereford in 1420, of Chichester in 1421 and of Worcester in 1426. He was at the Council of Constance in 1417 and in 1432, as ambassador at Rome, was appointed by King Henry VI to attend the Council of Basle. He died in 1433.

Thomas Cranley (1418-1423) BCnL, died in 1423.

Richard Leyot (1423-1446) DCL, held the prebends of Yetminster Secunda from 1418 to 1423 and Grimston from 1423 to 1446. He was Dean of Sarum from 1446 to 1449 and died on 26 January 1449.

Nicholas Caraunt (1446-1467) BCL, held the prebends of Ruscomb from 1435 to 1446 and Grimston from 1446 to 1467. He died in 1467.

Hugh Pavy (1467-1471) BCL, held the prebends of Grimston from 1467 to 1471, becoming a Canon Residentiary in 1471, and Bedwin from 1471 to 1485. In 1479 he became Archdeacon of Wilts and in 1485 Bishop of St David's, while continuing to hold his Archdeaconry.

John Peese (1471-1487) DCL, held the prebends of Yetminster Secunda in 1471 and Grimston from 1471 to 1487. He died in 1487.

Laurence Cokkys (1490) DCnL, held the prebends Durnford from 1478 to 1479, Netheravon from 1479 to? and Grimston in 1490. He was Rector of Winterbourne Basset in 1485 and Fisherton Anger in 1490, and was a Canon Residentiary in 1497. He died in 1501.

William Wilton (?-1507) DCnL, held the prebend of Grimston from ? to 1507, resigning it to become Chancellor of Sarum from 1507 to ?, and was Master of St Nicholas Hospital, Sarum in 1501. In his will, he left legacies to Symondsbury and Marnhull churches. He died in 1526 and there is a large monument to his memory against the wall, near the south east end, of the cathedral.

James Bromwich (1507-1515) BCnL, held the prebends of Axford from 1505 to 1507, Coombe & Harnham in 1507, Grimston from 1507 to 1515, Faringdon from 1515 to 1519 and Hurstbourne & Burbage from 1519 to 1524. He was Chancellor of Hereford in 1518 and became Archdeacon of Sarum in 1524, dying a month after his appointment.

William Barton (1515-1518) was Succentor of Sarum from 1502 to 1509. He was consecrated Bishop of Saloniensis c.1509 to assist Edmund Audley, Bishop of Sarum 1502-1524, within the diocese, which he did from 1509 to 1517. He held the prebends of Ruscomb in 1509, Beminster Prima from 1509 to 1515 and Grimston from 1515 to 1518. He died in 1518.

Edward Finch (1518-1519) DM, was well endowed with prebends holding in succession those of Yatesbury from 1514 to 1515, Chardstock from 1515 to 1517, Wilsford & Woodford in 1517, Fordington & Writhlington from 1517 to 1518, Grimston from 1518 to 1519, Faringdon from 1519 to 1521 exchanging the last with William Webbe for the church of Ross on Wye, Hereford. He then held the prebends of Bishopstone from 1521 to 1522, Teynton Regis from 1522 to 1524 and Bere & Cherminster from 1524 to 1539. He was Archdeacon of Wilts from 1522 until 1539. He died in 1539 and was buried in the cathedral.

John Baker (alias Elton) (1519-1547) BCn&CL, held the prebends of Grantham Australis from 1512 to 1514, Grantham Borealis from 1514 to 1519 and Grimston from 1519 until his death in 1547. He was Rector of St Peter's, Marlborough in 1510 and of Sherston in 1511. In 1513 he exchanged the living of Marlborough for the Wardenship of St Catherine's Hospital, Ledbury. He was presented to the living of Mildenhall in 1514. In 1515 he held a stall at Hereford and in 1519 became Rector of Childrey, Berks. In 1534 he gave lands in Oxfordshire and Gloucestershire to found a fellowship at Brazenose College, Oxford and in the same year was Vicar of Yetminster. Later he became Chancellor of Hereford.

William Hutton (1547-?) BD,

Richard Chaundeler (1558-1582/3) was Rector of Cheverell Magna and held the prebends of Major Pars Altaris from 1546 to 1558 and Grimston from 1558 to 1582/3. From 1554 to 1582/3 he was Archdeacon of Sarum and from 1557 to 1582/3 a Canon Residentiary. He died in 1582/3 and was buried in the cathedral.

Thomas Busfield (1583-1621) MA, held the prebends of Stratford from 1577 to 1583 and Grimston from 1583 to 1621. He died in 1621.

John Cooth (1621-1660) MA, held a stall at Wells. He died on 20 September 1660.

John Price (1660-1691) was appointed to this prebend by special gift of King Charles II and was a Fellow of Eton. He was chaplain to General Monk in Scotland in 1659 and died in 1691.

John Hinton (1691-1720) held the prebends of Ufcomb from 1683 to 1691 and Grimston from 1691 to 1720. He died in 1720.

Samuel Dunster (1720-1748) DD, held the prebends of Netherbury in Terra from 1717 to 1720 and Grimston from 1720 to 1748. He resigned in 1748.

Charles Dunster (1748-1750/1) MA, died in 1750/1.

The Hon Robert Sherard (1751-1799) MA, became the 4th Earl of Harburgh in 1770. He was a Canon Residentiary from 1757 until resigning in 1773. He died on 21 April 1799.

William Coxe (1799-1801) MA, was Rector of Bemerton in 1788 and Rector of Stourton. He held the prebends of Alton Australis from 1791 to 1792, Bitton from 1792 to 1799, Grimston from 1799 to 1801 and Netheravon from 1801 to 1828. He was Master of St Nicholas Hospital, Sarum in 1792 and a Canon Residentiary and Archdeacon of Wilts from 1804 to 1828. He died on 8 June 1828.

Phineas Pett (1801-1830) DD, was Archdeacon of Oxford in 1797 and held a stall at Christ Church, Oxford in 1815. He died on 4 February 1830.

Herbert Hawes (1830-1837) held the prebends of Netherbury in Terra from 1812 to 1830 and Grimston from 1830 to 1837. He was Rector of St Edmund's, Sarum and died on 17 January 1837.

William Edward Hony (1841-1875) BD, was a Fellow of Exeter College, Oxford and Rector of Baverstock in 1827. He held the prebend of Grimston from 1841 to 1875, was Archdeacon of Sarum from 1846 to 1875 and was a Canon Residentiary from 1857 to 1875. He died on 7 January 1875.

Alfred Codd (1875-1896) was Rector of Beaminster from 1857 to 1890 and died in January 1896.

Sidney Edmund Davies (1896-1917) MA, was Vicar of Broadwindsor from 1885 to 1891, Vicar of Gillingham with East & West Stour and Milton from 1891 to 1899 and Rural Dean of Shaftesbury from 1893 to 1899. He was Rector of Wyke Regis from 1899 until his death on 10 July 1917.

Edgar William James Hellins (1918-1947) MA, BCL, was Rector of Marnhull from 1908 to ?. He was a Proctor in Convocation from 1918 and Pro-Prolocutor of the Lower House of the Convocation of Canterbury from 1926 to 1936. He died in 1947.

Lancelot Farquharson Addison (1947-1955) was Vicar of Cranborne in 1947. He held the prebend of Grimston from 1947 to 1955. He was Archdeacon of Dorset from 1947 to 1956 and was Treasurer of Sarum from 1955 until his death in 1956.

Stephen Basil Wingfield-Digby (1955-1971) MBE, MA, was Curate-in-Charge of St George's Conventual District of Oakdale from 1938 to 1946 and Minister from 1946 to 1947. He was Chaplain to the Forces from 1940 to 1945 and was mentioned in despatches. He was Vicar of Sherborne with Castleton and Lillington from 1947 to 1968 and held the prebend of Grimston from 1955 to 1971. He was Archdeacon of Sarum and Canon Residentiary from 1968 to 1979 and Treasurer of Sarum from 1971 to 1978. He died on 22 January 1996.

John Clifford Townsend (1972-1990) MA, was Vicar of Branksome St Aldhelm from 1960 to 1970, Vicar of Melksham from 1970 to 1973 and Team Rector from 1973 to 1980. He was Rural Dean of Bradford from 1973 to 1980, Priest-in-Charge of Harnham from 1980 to 1981, Vicar from 1981 to 1990 and Rural Dean of Sarum from 1980 to 1985. He retired in 1990.

Martin Anthony Shallcross (1993-) FRICS, farmer and land agent, was a non-stipendiary minister for Landford with Plaitford and also for Bramshaw from 1978 to 1981. He joined the Tisbury Team Ministry in 1981 and became the first non-stipendiary canon of the cathedral, receiving the prebend of Grimston in 1993.

LODERS
(previously the stall of the Archdeacon of Sarum)

Until 1977 each Archdeacon had a stall of his dignity in a position of prominence close to one of the four principal persons; these stalls have now been renamed. Particulars of the Archdeacons are given first, followed by the particulars of the prebend the name of which the stall now bears.

Canopy statuette and shield:- **Henry Cotton** DD, appears to have been a younger son of Sir Henry Cotton, a Privy Councillor to King Edward VI. He held a stall at Windsor in 1586 and was a chaplain to Queen Elizabeth I, whose godson he was. She is quoted as saying that "she had blessed many godsons but now this godson should bless her." He was Bishop of Sarum from 1598 until his death on 7 May 1615. He left a large family - there had been nineteen children in all to his one wife, aptly named Patience - and was buried in the cathedral. (Fig. 24.)

Blazon:- Azure a chevron between three hanks of cotton erect argent. [On a blue shield, a silver chevron between three, upstanding, silver hanks of cotton.]

ARCHDEACON OF SARUM

The dignity:- The third Archdeaconry, covering the deaneries of Amesbury, Chalke, Pottern, Wilton and Wylye.

Holders of the dignity:-

Ernald (c.1133-c.1139).

Henry (c.1142/53-c.1154/55) was sent from Evreux by the Papal Legates to give notice to Archbishop Becket of the appeal to the Pope against his sentences. He was Precentor of Sarum from c.1142 to c.1164 and Archdeacon of Sarum from c.1142/53 to c.1154/55.

Jordan (c.1156/7-c.1173) was an Archdeacon, probably of Sarum, between c.1157 and c.1173, and held a stall at Bayeux, before becoming Dean of Sarum from c.1176 to c.1193. He donated vestments to Sonning church.

Savaric (c.1174/84) was a son of Geldwin who was probably second cousin of Jocelin, Bishop of Sarum 1142-1184. He was Archdeacon of Sarum from c.1174 to c.1184 and of Northampton from 1175 to 1192 He held the prebend of Heytesbury c.1183, was Treasurer of Sarum in c.1174/88 and possibly holder of the prebend of Beminster Prima at about the same time. He became Bishop of Bath & Wells in 1192. He held the rectories of Godalming and Hill Deverill in 1180. He died in 1205 and was buried in Bath.

Azo (?-c.1194/5) was said to have died by 1194/5.

Humphrey of Bassingbourn (c.1193-c.1238) was Archdeacon of Wilts in 1193, Archdeacon of Sarum c.1193-c.1238 and held the prebend of Netherbury in Ecclesia in c.1226/27. He also held a stall at Lincoln.

Stephen (c.1241-c.1244).

Nicholas de Capella (c.1245-c.1271).

Thomas de Wickhampton (alias de Grano) (c.1275-c.1307) held the prebend of Bedwin c.1284 and died between January 1307 and March 1309.

Walter Hervy (1309,1328) occupied the dignity in 1309 although Raymond de Planell had been nominated. In 1312 Raymond de Fargis is called archdeacon but Walter Hervy was still in occupation in 1328.

Raymond de Planell (?-1309) was nominated Archdeacon of Sarum but the dignity was occupied by Walter Hervy.

Raymond de Fargis (1312) was a nephew of Pope Clement V and became Cardinal-Deacon of St Maria Nuova in 1310. The Pope placed him successively into the rich deaneries of St Paul's, Sarum and Lincoln, although not holding more than two at the same time, as well as other benefices. "He was a youth too much beloved by the Pope; he was well disposed but too luxurious." He was Dean of Sarum from 1311 to 1346 and was Archdeacon of Sarum in 1312. He died on 5 October 1346.

Robert Luffenham (?-1348) was a notary public, Archdeacon of Sarum and a Canon Residentiary from ? to 1348. He held the prebend of Beminster Prima from c.1330 to 1348, also holding a stall at Wells. He had died by 6 October 1348.

Richard de Bury (or d'Aungerville) (1330) received a royal grant of the Archdeaconry of Sarum in 1330 but this was revoked and the dignity given to Robert Luffenham. He held the prebend of Beminster Secunda from 1330 to 1333. He was nominated to the prebend of Horton in 1331 but this was already occupied by Peter de Berkeley and he became Bishop of Durham 1333 without having had possession of the prebend. He is also believed to have held a stall at Lichfield in 1330 and been Dean of Wells in 1332. He was Chancellor of England in 1334 and died in 1335.

Roger de Kington (1348-1361) DTh, died in 1361.

Roger de Cloune (1361-?) held the prebend of Faringdon from 1349 until it was given to John de Edington by royal grant in 1350 when he then received the prebend of Grimston, holding it until at least 1366. He was Archdeacon of Sarum from 1361 until at least 1375 and was a Canon Residentiary.

Thomas Butiller (?-1384) held the prebend of Bedminster & Redcliffe in 1390 and had died by 19 July 1402. He was Archdeacon of Sarum from c.1381 to 1384. He is believed to have been Archdeacon of Northampton in 1386 and to have held a stall at Lincoln in 1388. He may be the same person who later became Bishop of Chrysopolis.

William Potyn (1384-1402) received the dignity in exchange with Thomas Butiller for the church of Lyminge, Kent. He died in 1402.

Walter FitzPiers (1400-1402) received the dignity by royal grant in 1400 but William Potyn was in possession of it at his death in 1402.

Henry Chichele (1402-1404) DCL, was appointed to the Archdeaconry of Dorset in 1397 and after two years of litigation at the Curia over the claims of Nicholas Bubwith, he was declared technically an intrusor but was reinstated in 1399, although Bubwith was appointed a year later. He held the prebends of Rotesfen in 1397, Yetminster Prima from 1397 to 1400, Fordington & Writhlington in 1400, Yetminster Secunda from 1400 to 1402 and Bedminster & Redcliffe from 1402 to 1404, when he exchanged with George Westby for the prebend of Fordington & Writhlington. After litigation, he became Archdeacon of Sarum in 1402, exchanging this and the prebend in 1404 for the dignity of Chancellor of Sarum which, following his consecration as Bishop of St David's in 1407, he continued to hold by papal indulgence until 1409. At one time he held the living of Melcombe Bingham and he became Archbishop of Canterbury in 1414. He was the founder of All Souls, Oxford and died on 12 April 1443.

Walter Medford (1404) BCL, was Archdeacon of Dorset in 1397, Chancellor of Sarum from 1402 to 1404 and a brother of Richard Medford, Bishop of Sarum 1396-1407. In 1404 he exchanged the dignity with his successor for the Archdeaconry of Sarum and the prebend of Fordington & Writhlington, exchanging a few days later for the Archdeaconry of Berks. He probably exchanged this Archdeaconry with Peter Alcobasso for the deanery of Wimborne in 1417. He held the prebends of Major Pars Altaris from 1397 to 1397, Yetminster Prima in 1397, Faringdon from 1397 to 1400, having been excommunicated but later absolved, when he exchanged this prebend for the treasurership of St Paul's. He held the prebend of Netherbury in Ecclesia in 1401 followed by Preston which he exchanged with Richard Derham for Netherbury in Ecclesia in 1402. He held the prebends of Fordington & Writhlington from 1404 to 1407 and Bedwin from 1407 until his death in 1423.

Simon Sydenham (1404-1418) DCL, incorrectly accepted nomination to the Archdeaconry of Berks in 1404 but was pardoned and exchanged it for the Archdeaconry of Sarum which he held from 1404 to 1418. He held the rectory of Sutton Veny from 1417 to 1421 and the prebends of Rotesfen from 1407 to 1415 and Yetminster Secunda from 1415 to 1418 and was Dean of Sarum from 1418 to 1431. Although in 1426 he was elected to the see of Sarum, the Chapter on the recommendation of King Henry VI, gave way to a papal provision in favour of Robert Neville. In 1431 he was consecrated as Bishop of Chichester.

John Holand (1418-1419) DCL, died in 1419.

John Chitterne (1419) held the prebends of Chisenbury & Chute from 1385 to 1415 and Hurstbourne & Burbage from 1415 to 1419. He became a Canon Residentiary in 1386, was Rector of Newton Tony from 1415 to 1419 and was Archdeacon of Wilts from 1407 to 1419. He held a stall at St Paul's from 1409 to 1419 and became Archdeacon of Sarum in 1419, dying in the same year.

John Stafford (1419-1420) DCL, was Archdeacon of Sarum from 1419 to 1420 and Chancellor of Sarum from 1420 to 1422. He exchanged the dignity of Chancellor for the prebend of Highworth, holding it from 1422 to 1424 when he became Bishop of Bath & Wells. He became Archbishop of Canterbury in 1443 and died on 25 May 1452.

William Alnwick (1420-1426) became Bishop of Norwich in 1426.

Alexander Sparrow (1426-1432) BCn&CL, held the prebends of Axford from 1423 to 1426 and Fordington & Writhlington from 1426 to 1433. He was Archdeacon of Sarum from 1426 to 1432 when he became Archdeacon of Berks until 1433. He was Treasurer of St Paul's in 1423 and died in 1433.

John Norton (1432-1433) DCnL, held the prebends of Beminster Secunda from 1429 to 1431 and Horton from 1431 to 1462. He was Archdeacon of Sarum from 1432 to 1433 and Archdeacon of Berks from 1433 until his death in 1462.

Stephen Wilton (1433-?) DCnL, was Archdeacon of Sarum from 1433 until after 1435 and held the prebends of Chardstock from 1441 to 1442 and Bishopstone from 1434 until before 1440. He held a stall at Lincoln, exchanging it in 1433 for a stall at St Paul's. He was Archdeacon of Middlesex in 1441 and of Cleveland in 1454. He died in 1457.

Adam Moleyns (?-1441) was Rector of Winterbourne Earls in 1432, held a stall at St Paul's in 1440 and was Archdeacon of Taunton in 1440. He was Archdeacon of Sarum, held the prebend of Bishopstone from 1440 to 1441 and held a stall at York in 1441. He was Dean of Sarum from 1441 to 1445 when he became Bishop of Chichester. In 1441, he sat as Commissary to try Eleanor Duchess of Gloucester for witchcraft and went to Rome to urge, unsuccessfully, the canonisation of Bishop Osmund. In 1443 he assisted in arranging the marriage of King Henry VI with Margaret of Anjou. In 1450, whilst Bishop of Chichester, he was murdered by some sailors in Portsmouth.

Richard Andrew (1441-1444) DCL, was Archdeacon of Sarum from 1441 until resigning in 1444. He held the prebends of Faringdon from 1447 to 1449, Stratton from 1449 to 1454 and Grantham Borealis from 1454 to 1477. He was a friend of Archbishop Chichele and was the first Warden of All Souls, founded by him in 1437. He was Dean of York in 1451 and Chancellor of Canterbury. He died in 1477.

Peter Barbo (1444 -1446) was born in Naples, the son of Nicholas Barbo by Polixena, sister of Pope Eugenius IV. He became Canon of Padua, Archdeacon of Bologna, Bishop of Servia in Middle Italy in 1440, Bishop of Vicenza in Upper Italy in 1451 and of Padua in 1459. He held the Archdeaconry of Sarum from 1444 to 1446. He was made Cardinal-Deacon of St Mary Nova in 1440, Cardinal-Priest of St Mark in 1451 and was crowned as Pope Paul II in 1464. He was noted for his generosity and for his imposing appearance, he delighted in display and promoted splendid carnival festivities. He died on 26 July 1471.

Richard Caunton (1446-1465) DCn&CL, held the prebend of Netheravon from ? to 1465 and was Archdeacon of Sarum from 1446 to 1465. He died in 1465.

Roger Radclyffe (1465-1471) DCL, died in 1471.

William Eure (1471-?) MA, died in 1482, possibly as Archdeacon of Sarum.

Edmund Chaderton (?-1499) held the prebend of Stratton from 1479 to 1499 and was Archdeacon of Sarum from ? until his death in 1499.

Geoffrey Blythe (1499-1503) BTh, was a brother of John Blythe, Bishop of Sarum 1494-1499. He was Treasurer of Sarum from 1494 to 1495, exchanging the dignity for the prebend of Chisenbury & Chute which he held from 1495 to 1498. He was Archdeacon of Sarum, holding the prebend of Stratton, from 1499 to 1503 and would seem to have been Dean of York in 1497 and Provost of King's Hall, Cambridge in 1499. In 1503 he was consecrated Bishop of Coventry and Lichfield and died in 1533.

George Sydenham (1503-1524) BCn&CL, held the prebends of Yetminster Secunda from 1502 to 1518 and Fordington & Writhlington from 1518 to 1524. He was Archdeacon of Sarum from 1503 to 1524 and was Chaplain to King Henry VII and King Henry VIII. He died in 1524 and was buried in the cathedral.

James Bromwich (1524) BCnL, held the prebends of Axford from 1505 to 1507, Coombe & Harnham in 1507, Grimston from 1507 to 1515, Faringdon from 1515 to 1519 and Hurstbourne & Burbage from 1519 to 1524. He was Chancellor of Hereford in 1518 and became Archdeacon of Sarum in 1524, dying a month after his appointment.

Henry Rawlyns (1524-1526) BCL, was well provided with prebends. He held Yatesbury from 1513 to 1514, Grantham Australis from 1514 to 1519 and Coombe & Harnham 1519 to 1521. He resigned Coombe & Harnham in May 1521, was succeeded by Cuthbert Tunstall who then became Dean of Sarum, and was again appointed to the prebend later in the same year. He then held Faringdon from 1523 to 1524, Hurstbourne & Burbage in 1524 and Teynton Regis, together with the Archdeaconry of Sarum from 1524 to 1526. He was Rector of Christian Malford, died in 1526 and is buried in the cathedral near the Audley chantry.

Richard Duck (?-1539) DTh, was Vice-Chancellor of Oxford in 1517, held a prebend at Wells in 1537 and was Archdeacon of Sarum from ? to 1539. He died in 1539.

Edward Layton (1539-1546) BTh, resigned on 20 July 1546.

Robert Okinge (1546-1554) LLD, was Archdeacon of Sarum from 1546 to 1554 and a Canon Residentiary from 1547 to 1554. He had been Commissary to John Salcot, Bishop of Sarum 1539-1557, when Bishop of Bangor. In the convocation of 1547, he voted against allowing the marriage of clergy but married as soon as this was permissible. He held the prebend of Rotesfen from 1544 to 1545, when the prebend was dissolved by Act of Parliament, and the prebend of Winterbourne Earls, upon its substitution in 1545 until he was deprived of his livings in 1554.

Richard Chaundeler (1554-1582/3) was Rector of Cheverell Magna and held the prebends of Major Pars Altaris from 1546 to 1558 and Grimston from 1558 to 1582/3. From 1554 to 1582/3 he was Archdeacon of Sarum and from 1557 to 1582/3 a Canon Residentiary. He died in 1582/3 and was buried in the cathedral.

Ralph Pickover (1583-1615) MA, held the prebends of Stratford from 1583 to 1586 and Gillingham Major from 1586 to 1615. He was Rector of Winterbourne Gunner and was Archdeacon of Rochester from 1576 to 1593. He would seem to have held a stall at Christ Church, Oxford in 1580 and was Archdeacon of Sarum and a Canon Residentiary from 1583 to 1615. He died on 8 March 1615 and was buried in the cathedral.

William Barlow (1615-1625) BD, died on 25 May 1625.

Thomas Marler (1625-1643) BD, died in 1643.

William Buckner (1643-?) MA.

Anthony Hawles (1658-1664) DD, held the prebend of Bitton from 1660 to 1664, was Archdeacon of Sarum from 1658 to 1664, a Canon Residentiary from 1660 to 1664 and held a stall at Windsor in 1660. He was Rector and Vicar of Bishopstone in 1662 and died on 16 January 1664.

Joshua Childrey (1664-1670) DD, held the prebend of Yetminster Prima, was Rector of Upwey and Archdeacon of Sarum from 1664 until his death in 1670. He was buried at Upwey.

John Sherman (1670-1671) DD, held the prebend of Yetminster Prima and was Archdeacon of Sarum from 1670 until his death on 27 March 1671.

John Priaulx (1671-1674) DD, held the prebend of Netherbury in Terra from 1660 to 1674, was a Canon Residentiary from 1661 to 1674 and Archdeacon of Sarum from 1671 to 1674. He died on 4 June 1674 and was buried and commemorated in the cathedral.

Thomas Lambert (1674-1694) BD, was a Canon Residentiary and held the prebend of Grantham Australis from 1666 to 1694. He was Rector of Boyton and of Sherrington from 1677 to 1694 and domestic chaplain to King Charles II. He was Archdeacon of Sarum from 1674 until his death on 29 December 1694, aged 78. He was buried in the cathedral.

Joseph Kelsey (1695-1710) BD, held the prebends of Netherbury in Terra from 1674 to 1695, Grantham Australis from 1695 to 1705 and Highworth from 1705 to 1710. He was Rector of Newton Tony from 1669 to 1710 and of Fugglestone from 1681. He was Warden of St John's Hospital, Heytesbury in 1686 and was a Canon Residentiary and Archdeacon of Sarum from 1695 until his death on 1 November 1710. He was buried in the cathedral.

John Hoadley (1710-1727) MA, was Chancellor of Sarum from 1713 to 1727. He was a brother of Benjamin Hoadly, Bishop of Sarum 1723-1734, and chaplain to Gilbert Burnet, Bishop of Sarum 1689-1715, the latter appointing him to the prebend of Wilsford & Woodford from 1706 to 1713 and the Archdeaconry of Sarum from 1710 to 1727. He became a Canon Residentiary and Rector of St Edmund's, Sarum. He was consecrated as Bishop of Ferns and Leighlin in 1727, becoming Archbishop of Dublin in 1729 and of Armagh in 1742.

Joseph Sager (1727-1732) MA, held the prebends of Warminster from 1726 to 1732 and Gillingham Major from 1732 to 1757. He was a Canon Residentiary from 1726 to 1757 and Archdeacon of Sarum from 1727 until resigning in 1732. He died on 18 July 1757 and was buried in the cathedral.

Samuel Rolleston (1732-1766) MA, held the prebend of Teynton Regis from 1731 to 1766, was Archdeacon of Sarum from 1732 to 1766 and, as a Canon Residentiary from 1756 to 1766, lived at Leadenhall. He held a stall at Winchester in 1744, was Rector of St Edmund's, Sarum and from 1745 to 1746, of East Knoyle. He died on 2 May 1766 and was buried in the cathedral where he is commemorated in the south choir aisle.

William Whitworth (1766-1804) MA, was Archdeacon of Sarum, holding the prebend of Bishopstone, from 1766 to 1804. He died on 14 May 1804.

Charles Daubeny (1804-1827) DCL, held the prebend of Minor Pars Altaris from 1784 to 1827, was Vicar of North Bradley from 1777 to 1827 and Archdeacon of Sarum from 1804 until his death on 10 July 1827.

Liscombe Clarke (1827-1836) MA, held a stall at Hereford in 1821. He was Archdeacon of Sarum from 1827 to 1836, a Canon Residentiary from 1832 to 1841and Treasurer of Sarum from 1834 to 1841. He held the prebends of Minor Pars Altaris from 1827 to 1828 and Netheravon from 1828 to 1834 and was Vicar of Downton. He died on 17 April 1841.

Francis Lear (1836-1846) BD, was Rector of Chilmark from 1824, holding the prebends of Stratford from 1830 to 1834 and of Netheravon from 1834 to 1846. He was Rector and Vicar of Bishopstone from 1843 and Archdeacon of Sarum from 1836 to 1846. He was Dean of Sarum and a Canon Residentiary from 1846 to 1850 and died on 23 March 1850.

William Edward Hony (1846-1875) BD, was a Fellow of Exeter College, Oxford and Rector of Baverstock in 1827. He held the prebend of Grimston from 1841 to 1875, was Archdeacon of Sarum from 1846 to 1875 and was a Canon Residentiary from 1857 to 1875. He died on 7 January 1875.

Francis Lear (1875-1914) MA, was Rector and Vicar of Bishopstone from 1850 to 1914. He held the prebend of Bishopstone from 1856 to 1861, was Chancellor of Sarum from 1861 to 1864, a Canon Residentiary from 1862 to 1914, Precentor of Sarum from 1864 to 1875 and Archdeacon of Sarum from 1875 to 1914 . He died on 19 February 1914 and was buried in the cloisters.

Harry William Carpenter (1914-1936) OBE, MA, held the prebends of Ruscomb from 1896 to 1911 and Netherbury in Terra from 1911 to 1936. He was Vice Principal of Sarum Theological College from 1879 to 1880, a Vicar Choral from 1879 to 1914, Precentor of Sarum from 1896 to 1936, Archdeacon of Sarum from 1914 to 1936, and a Canon Residentiary from 1915 to 1936. He died on 20 July 1936.

Percy John Dale (1936-1950) OBE, MA, held the prebend of Bishopstone from 1925 to 1957. He was Rector of Fittleton from 1911 to 1920, Rector of West Dean with East Grimstead from 1920 to 1938 and Master of St Nicholas's Hospital from 1938 to 1957. He was Secretary of the Diocesan Board of Finance from 1919 to 1932, Honorary Secretary of the Diocesan Conference from 1933 to 1939, Archdeacon of Sarum from 1936 to 1950, a Proctor in Convocation from 1935 to 1937 and a Church Commissioner and member of its Board of Governors from 1948 to 1953. He died on 22 April 1957.

Frank McGowan (1951-1967) MBE, MA, DipTh, served in the Army from 1915 to 1918, was Rector of Cholderton from 1929 to 1954 and held the prebend of Gillingham Major from 1944 to 1967. He was a Proctor in Convocation from 1948 to 1951 and Archdeacon of Sarum from 1951 to 1967. He was Prior of St John's Hospital, Burcombe from 1954 to 1966 and died on 21 February 1968.

Stephen Basil Wingfield-Digby (1968-1979) MBE, MA, was Curate-in-Charge of St George's Conventual District of Oakdale from 1938 to 1946 and Minister from 1946 to 1947. He was Chaplain to the Forces from 1940 to 1945 and was mentioned in despatches. He was Vicar of Sherborne with Castleton and Lillington from 1947 to 1968 and held the prebend of Grimston from 1955 to 1971. He was Archdeacon of Sarum and Canon Residentiary from 1968 to 1979 and Treasurer of Sarum from 1971 to 1978. He died on 22 January 1996.

(In 1977 the Archdeacons' stalls were discontinued, the stall of the Archdeacon of Sarum being used for the prebend of Loders.)

LODERS

Prebend:- The church of Loders and the chapel of Bradpole, both in Dorset which were already in the possession of the Norman abbey of St Mary Montebergh and its dependent priory of Loders, were created a prebend by Herbert Poore, Bishop of Sarum 1194-1217. The abbey gave to the bishop and cathedral the churches of Powerstock and Fleet and the Abbots of Montebergh became canons of the cathedral, holders of this prebend and had a voice in chapter.

In the 15c. the foreign monasteries were dissolved and the estate at Loders became part of the endowments of Sion Abbey until the dissolution of the monasteries when the prebend became extinct. In 1997 it was decided to revive this and three other titular prebends, using the Archdeacons' stalls for this purpose.

Psalter:- The portion of scripture allotted to the prebend is Exodus 15 and Habakuk 3.

Holders of the prebend:-

The Abbot of St Mary Montebergh for the time being (1213-15c.).

The Abbot of Sion Abbey for the time being (15c.-1540).

Kenneth George William Prior (1977-1982) BA, was Perpetual Curate and then Vicar of Longfleet from 1955 until his retirement in 1982, and Rural Dean of Poole from 1975 to 1980.

John Roberton Stewart (1983-1990) was Rector of Langton Matravers from 1970 to 1984 and Rector of Kingston, Langton Matravers and Worth Matravers from 1984 to 1990., and Rural Dean of Purbeck from 1982 to 1989. He held the prebend of Loders from 1983 to 1990 and was Treasurer of Sarum and a Canon Residentiary from 1990 to 1995.

David Rea Price (1992-) was Team Rector of Wimborne Minster & Holt from 1986 to 1996 becoming Rector of Wimborne Minster in 1996 and Rural Dean of Wimborne in 1988.

(Gangway)
(carries name plate of "Okeburne"; see Ogborne)

Canopy statuette and shield:- **John Coldwell** MD, was educated as a physician. He was domestic chaplain to Archbishop Parker, becoming Dean of Rochester in 1589. He was the first married Bishop of Sarum, serving from 1591 until his death on 14 October 1596. He was buried in the choir of the cathedral beside Bishop Jewel and in the same grave as Bishop Wyvil. He is believed to have wasted the revenues of the see, virtually disposing of the Sherborne estates through the intrigues of Sir Walter Raleigh and through the pressure of Queen Elizabeth I and her agents. He died a very poor man. (Fig. 25.)

Blazon:- Chequy argent and sable on a chief or three quivers gules banded of the third each holding five arrows of the first. [At the top of a shield comprising alternate squares of silver and black, on a gold background, three red, gold banded, quivers each with five silver arrows.]

BRICKLESWORTH

Prebend:- The church of Bricklesworth, otherwise called Brixworth, in Northamptonshire, and Shipton under Wychwood, Oxfordshire, were part of royal manors in the 11.c. Two prebends were created, one before 1099 for G...., the eldest son of Arnulph the falconer and a second before 1116 for his younger son Humphrey. Two prebends were probably in existence by c.1150 but may have been held jointly until full separation between 1226 and 1227. The dependent chapels of Swinbrook, Idbury and Fifield formed part of the Bricklesworth prebend while Shipton under Wychwood with the chapel of Lyneham formed the prebend of Shipton.

On 6 November 1240 the prebend of Bricklesworth was permanently joined to the dignity of Chancellor of Sarum. On 8 January 1864 however, the revenue having been transferred to the Ecclesiastical Commissioners in 1858, it was considered that the purpose for which the prebend was annexed to the Chancellorship had ceased to exist. The holder of the prebend, Chancellor Francis Lear, "urged for divers good causes and considerations" that the prebend be disunited and disannexed from the dignity of Chancellor and this separation was agreed under an ordinance of the Dean, Canons Residentiary and Chancellor and confirmed by the Bishop. Chancellor Francis Lear was appointed to the higher dignity of Precentor of Sarum and continued to hold the prebend of Bricklesworth. His successor as Chancellor, Edward Paroissien Eddrup, who had been appointed to the prebend of Durnford in 1861, continued to hold it with this dignity. With the appointment of Charles Tunnacliffe Dimont to the prebend of Bricklesworth in 1914 and to the dignity of Chancellor in 1928, the dignity and prebend were reunited.

Canopy statuette and shield:- **John Piers** DD, became Dean of Chester in 1567 and Dean of Christ Church, Oxford. He was Dean of Sarum from 1571 to 1576, becoming a Canon Residentiary in 1572. He was appointed Almoner to Queen Elizabeth I and Bishop of Rochester and in the latter capacity preached before the Queen on the defeat of the Spanish Armada. By royal licence he was permitted to hold the dignity of Dean of Sarum for life but resigned it upon his translation to the see of Sarum. He was Bishop of Sarum from 1577 until becoming Archbishop of York in 1589. He died on 28 September 1594 and was buried in York Minster (Fig. 26.)

Blazon:- Azure a pelican in piety or standing on a globe argent. [On a blue shield, a gold pelican pecking her breast to feed her young, standing on a silver globe. (the globe has been omitted from the depiction, causing confusion with the arms of Bishop Fox of Exeter - see Fig. 39, Minor Pars Altaris)]

Psalter:- The portion of the psalter allotted to the prebend is Psalms 9 and 10

Holders of the prebend:-

Humphrey (before1115-?) was the son of Arnulf the falconer.

Richard of Brimpton (c.1133/69) may have been the father of Robert of Brimpton.

Robert of Brimpton (after 1215-c.1222) who held the prebend of Shipton from c.1215 to c.122, was probably Robert, Canon of Sarum, parson of Shipton, who held the prebend of Bricklesworth from after 1215 to c.1222

Adam de Essebi (1223/24-1241) held the prebend of Bricklesworth from c.1223/24 to 1241. He was Subdean of Sarum from c.1236 to c.1237 and Chancellor of Sarum from 1237/8 to 1240. He held the patronage of Bricklesworth in 1239 and it was at his petition that the prebend of Bricklesworth was permanently annexed to the dignity of Chancellor in 1240. He had died by 16 June 1241.

The Chancellor of Sarum for the time being (1240-1864).

Francis Lear (1861-1914) MA, was Rector and Vicar of Bishopstone from 1850 to 1861. He held the prebend of Bishopstone from 1856 to 1861, was Chancellor of Sarum from 1861 to 1864, a Canon Residentiary from 1862 to 1914, Precentor of Sarum from 1864 to 1875 and Archdeacon of Sarum from 1875 to 1914. He died on 19 February 1914.

Charles Tunnacliffe Dimont (1914-1953) MA, DD, was Vice Principal of Wells Theological College from 1909 to 1913 and Principal of Sarum Theological College from 1913 to 1937. He held the prebend of Bricklesworth from 1914 to 1953. He was Chancellor of Sarum from 1928, in which year the dignity and prebend were reunited, until 1953. He was a Canon Residentiary from 1928 to 1953, Prior of The Hospital of St John, Burcombe from 1936 to 1953, a Proctor in Convocation from 1938 to 1945 and Sub Chaplain of the Order of St John of Jerusalem from 1941 to 1953. He died on 6 November 1953.

The Chancellor of Sarum for the time being (1928-)

CANCELLARII ECCLESIAE

Dignity:- The Chancellor has to possess a competent knowledge of theology and is to seek to promote religious and theological education in the diocese. He has the general supervision of the Cathedral Library. The prebend of Bricklesworth was assigned to the dignity on 6 November 1240 but was separated from the dignity in 1864. It was reunited in 1928.

Canopy statuette and shield:- **Edmund Gest** BD, was a Fellow and Vice Provost of King's College, Cambridge who was Archdeacon of Canterbury. He was made Bishop of Rochester in 1560 and Almoner to the Queen. He had been one of the Protestant disputants along with Bishop Jewel in 1559 and was a prolific author, bequeathing his whole library to the cathedral library. He was Bishop of Sarum from 1571 until his death on 28 February 1577 at the age of 63. He was buried in the centre of the choir between Bishops Jewel and Wyvil. The gravestone was later moved to the north-eastern transept. (Fig. 27.)

Blazon:- Azure a chevron between three swans heads argent beaked or. [On a blue shield, a silver chevron between three silver swans' heads with gold beaks.]

Holders of the dignity:-

Philip (c.1155/61) may have been the chancellor of Archbishop Theobald during c.1152 to c.1161, or Philip of Salisbury who was a clerk to the Archbishop during 1150 to 1152.

Baldwin (c.1182-1197/1205) was the donor of a cope to the cathedral.

Hugh de Garherst (c.1206/7-c.1220) was a delegate from the Chapter to the diocese of Winchester in 1219 to collect funds for the new cathedral.

Robert de Hertford (1220-1236) was Chancellor of Sarum from 1220 to 1236 and Dean of Sarum from 1237 to 1257. He held the prebend of Wilsford & Woodford from 1220 to 1257 and died on 9 December 1257.

Richard (1236) might have been the Richard de Bremble who held the prebend of Bitton from c.1226 to c.1233.

Adam de Essebi (1237/8-1240) held the prebend of Bricklesworth from c.1223/24 to 1240. He was Subdean of Sarum from c.1236 to c.1237 and Chancellor of Sarum from 1238 to 1240. He held the patronage of Bricklesworth in 1239 and it was at his petition that the prebend of Bricklesworth was permanently annexed to the dignity of Chancellor in 1240. He had died by 16 June 1241.

Ralph de Hecham (or Heytham) (c.1240/1-c.1271) was Vicar of Bricklesworth between 1240 and 1241. He went to Rome in 1270 as a Proctor for the Chapter in respect of the election of Robert Wickhampton as Bishop and appears to have returned with the large silver head standing on a pedestal containing relics of St Catherine which was amongst the cathedral treasures in 1536. He probably died on 21 November 1271.

Simon de Micham (or Michelham) (1272-1287) was Chancellor of Sarum from 1272 to 1287, held a stall at Wells in 1284 and was Dean of Sarum from 1287 to 1297. He is believed to have died on 8 June 1297.

Ralph of York (1288-1309) was a Canon of Sarum as early as 1244 when he witnessed the foundation deed of the Hospital of St Nicholas, Sarum and was a great benefactor of the cathedral library. From c.1273 to c.1288 he held the prebend of Horton and was Chancellor of Sarum from 1288 to 1309. He became Archdeacon of Sudbury, Norfolk, in 1284 and died on 21 November 1309.

William de Bosco (1309-1313) DTh, was a distinguished theologian and a former Chancellor of Oxford University. He held the prebend of Netherbury in Terra from ? to 1311 and was Chancellor of Sarum from 1309 to 1313. He had died by 1 March 1313.

Pontius de Varesio (1309-1311) claimed the prebend of Horton in 1309 although it had been given to Richard de Abingdon. The case was taken to the Roman Court but before it was settled he claimed the prebend of Grantham Australis. This was questioned and he resigned his claim before the end of 1310. Also in 1309 he claimed the dignity of Chancellor of Sarum but Simon de Gandavo, Bishop of Sarum 1297-1315, appealed against this papal grant. Protection was granted to William de Bosco in 1310 and, following the death of Pontius de Varesio, Tydo de Varesio received the dignity.

Tydo de Varesio (1311) was given the dignity of Chancellor of Sarum in 1311 although William de Bosco was in occupation. He held the prebend of Grantham Borealis from 1313 to 1331 and, on appointment by the Pope, was Archdeacon of Berks from 1313 to 1331, despite an ineffective royal grant being made to Gilbert de Stapleton in 1317. He died in 1331.

Henry de la Wyle (1313-1329) DTh, held the prebends of Minor Pars Altaris in 1309, Durnford from 1309 to 1311 and Fordington & Writhlington from 1311 to 1313. He was Chancellor of Sarum from 1313 to 1329 and in 1326 he founded a chantry at the altar of St Peter and the rest of the Apostles at the east end of the north aisle of the cathedral. In 1329 he left to the Chapter his house near Leadenhall in the Close and died in June 1329.

Richard de Ayremynne (1329-1340) was Chaplain to King Edward III and Master of the Rolls. He acted for a time as locum tenens for the Dean and was Vicar-General of Norwich diocese in 1325.

Elias de Sancto Albano (1340-?) held the prebend of Durnford from 1334 to 1340 when he became a Canon Residentiary and Chancellor of Sarum. He was wrongly reported dead in 1350 so that Thomas de Trillek was appointed Chancellor. In 1352 the Pope permitted him to resign the dignity in exchange for the prebend of Stratford, which he does not appear to have occupied, and the church of St Thomas, Sarum, held by John de Wilton.

Thomas de Trillek (1350) was appointed but the holder of the dignity, Elias de Sancto Albano had not died, as had been reported.

Simon of Sudbury (?-1361) DCL, claimed the dignity of Chancellor of Sarum in 1353 and was occupying it in 1356. He was a domestic chaplain to Pope Innocent VI who gave him the dignity, becoming Bishop of London in 1361 and Archbishop of Canterbury in 1375. He was beheaded in Wat Tyler's rebellion in 1381.

John de Wilton (1355) held the dignity in 1355 although Simon of Sudbury had claimed it in 1353.

John Norton (1361-1402) DCL, was a Canon Residentiary and Proctor for the Chapter at the Visitation in 1395 of John Waltham, Bishop of Sarum 1388-1395. He died in 1402 and was buried in the cathedral.

Walter Medford (1402-1404) BCL, was Archdeacon of Sarum in 1397, Chancellor of Sarum from 1402 to 1404 and a brother of Richard Medford, Bishop of Sarum 1396 to 1407. In 1404 he exchanged the dignity with Henry Chichele for the Archdeaconry of Sarum and the prebend of Fordington & Writhlington, exchanging this dignity a few days later for the Archdeaconry of Berks. He probably exchanged this Archdeaconry with Peter Alcobasso for the deanery of Wimborne in 1417. He held the prebends of Major Pars Altaris from 1396 to 1397, Yetminster Prima in 1397, Faringdon from 1397 to 1400, having been excommunicated but later absolved, when he exchanged this prebend for the Treasurership of St Paul's. He held the prebend of Netherbury in Ecclesia in 1401, followed by the prebend of Preston, which he exchanged with Richard Derham for the prebend of Netherbury in Ecclesia in 1402. He held the prebends of Fordington & Writhlington from 1404 to 1407 and Bedwin from 1407 until his death in 1423.

Henry Chichele (1404-1409) DCL, was collated to the Archdeaconry of Dorset in 1397 and after two years' litigation at the curia over the claims of Nicholas Bubwith, he was declared technically an intrusor but was reinstated in 1399, although Bubwith was appointed a year later. He held the prebends of Rotesfen in 1397, Yetminster Prima from 1397 to 1400, Fordington & Writhlington in 1400, Yetminster Secunda from 1400 to 1402 and Bedminster & Redcliffe from 1402 to 1404, when he exchanged the last with George Westby for the prebend of Fordington & Writhlington. After litigation, he became Archdeacon of Sarum in 1402, exchanging this and the prebend in 1404 for the dignity of Chancellor of Sarum which, following his consecration as Bishop of St David's in 1407, he continued to hold by papal indulgence until 1409. At one time he held the living of Melcombe Bingham and he became Archbishop of Canterbury in 1414. He was the founder of All Souls, Oxford and died on 12 April 1443.

William Faringdon (1408-1409) DTh, was granted the dignity of Chancellor of Sarum by King Henry IV in 1408 but it was given to William Chichele in 1410.

William Chichele (1410-1420) was Archdeacon of Canterbury in 1420 and died at Rome in 1424.

John Stafford (1420-1422) DCL, was Archdeacon of Sarum from 1419 to 1420 and Chancellor of Sarum from 1420 to 1422. He exchanged the dignity of Chancellor for the prebend of Highworth, holding it from 1422 to 1424 when he became Bishop of Bath & Wells. He became Archbishop of Canterbury in 1443 and died on 25 May 1452.

John Fyton (1422-1432) MA, BTh, was also Archdeacon of Stafford and held the prebends of Ruscomb from 1410 to 1412, Granthan Borealis from 1412 to 1416 and Highworth from 1416 to 1422. He exchanged the last with John Stafford for the dignity of Chancellor of Sarum, which he held from 1422 to 1432, dying in 1432.

Richard Praty (1432-1438) DTh, became a Fellow of Oriel College, Oxford and Chancellor of Oxford University in 1438. In the same year he became Bishop of Chichester following commendation to Pope Eugenius IV by Henry VI, with whom he was in high favour.

Andrew Holes (1438-1470) Lic.CnL, was also Archdeacon of the West Riding in 1442. In 1445 the residentiary house of Leadenhall was granted to him and he became Archdeacon of Wells in 1450. He died in the Leadenhall on 1 April 1470 and requested to be buried in the cathedral, in St Mary Magdalen Chapel, on the south side of the choir.

William Ive (1470-1486) DTh, died in 1486 and was buried in the cathedral.

John Dogget (1486-1501) DTh, DCnL, was a nephew of Cardinal Bourchier. He held the prebends of Ruscomb from 1474 to 1475, Chardstock from 1475 to ? and Bitton from 1479 to 1486. A native of Sherborne, he founded a chapel on the south side of the churchyard there. He held a stall at Lincoln, was Treasurer of Chichester in 1479, Chaplain to King Richard III in 1483, Chancellor of Sarum from 1486 to 1501, a Canon Residentiary and Vicar General of Sarum, and Chancellor of Lichfield in 1488. In 1490 he held the rectory of Winterborne Sheltston. He became Archdeacon of Chester and Provost of King's College, Cambridge in 1499. He died on 4 March 1501/02 and was buried in the cathedral.

William Elliott (1501-1507) BCL, held the prebend of Bishopstone from 1486, possibly until 1501. He was Chancellor of Sarum from 1501 to 1507 and was probably Archdeacon of Barnstable in 1492. He was Provost of St Edmund's College, Sarum and, dying in 1507, asked to be buried in the cathedral.

William Wilton (1507-?) DCL, held the prebend of Grimston from ? to 1507, resigning it to become Chancellor of Sarum from 1507 to ?, and was Master of St Nicholas Hospital, Sarum in 1501. In his will, he left legacies to Symondsbury and Marnhull churches. He died in 1526 and there is a large monument to his memory against the wall, near the south east end of the cathedral.

Thomas Winter (?-1530) was said to be a son of Cardinal Wolsey, obtaining before he was of age the prebend of Bedwin, which he held from 1522 to 1529, the Archdeaconries of Richmond, Suffolk and Cornwall and the Deanery of Wells. He was Chancellor of Sarum from ? to 1530. At the time of Wolsey's fall he gave up or lost most of his dignities.

Edward Lee (1530-1531) DTh, held the prebend of Rotesfen from 1510 to 1530 and was Chancellor of Sarum from 1530 to 1531. He was Archdeacon of Colchester in 1523, later becoming Almoner to King Henry VIII and being consecrated Archbishop of York in 1531. He is described as a furious papist and opponent of the Reformation. He died in 1544 and was buried in York Cathedral.

Edward Carne (1531-1537) DCL, resigned c. 20 March 1537.

Thomas Parker (1537-1538) DCnL, was Precentor of Hereford in 1531 and Chancellor of Lichfield Diocese. He died on 22 August 1538.

Roger Townsend (1538) DCL, received the prebend of Netherbury in Ecclesia and the dignity of Chancellor of Sarum in 1538, and died soon after.

John Edmunds (1538-1544) DTh, DD, was Master of Peterhouse, Cambridge in 1522 and Vicar of Aldbourne from 1524 to 1544. He was one of the compilers of *The Institution of a Christian Man* and died in 1544.

John Crayford (1544-1547) DD, held the prebend of Alton Borealis from 1542 to 1544 and was permitted to be simultaneously Chancellor of Sarum from 1544 to 1547 and Archdeacon of Berks from 1545 to 1547, becoming Master of University College, Oxford in 1546. He became a Canon Residentiary in 1547 and died the same year.

Henry Parry (1547-1554) was a Canon Residentiary from 1549 to 1554. He was deprived by March 1554 but restored in 1559 on the accession of Queen Elizabeth I. He asked in his will to be buried under the pulpit in the cathedral.

William Geffre (1554-1558) was probably Archdeacon of Northampton in 1554. In 1557 he was appointed Warden of Heytesbury Hospital. He is described as a cruel man, helping to send martyrs to heaven in chariots of fire. He died in 1588.

Thomas Heskins (1558-1559) DD, was vicar of Bricklesworth and held the prebend of Torleton from 1554 to 1558. He was Chancellor of Sarum from 1558 to 1559 and a Canon Residentiary from 1559 to 1571. He had been appointed by Queen Mary I in 1558 to be a preacher in the diocese during the vacancy in the see. This was during her struggle with the Pope over his attempt to appoint Cardinal Peto to the see of Sarum. He was deprived for refusing to acknowledge the supremacy of Queen Elizabeth I and retired to Flanders.

Henry Parry (1559-1571) see above, was Chancellor of Sarum and a Canon Residentiary again, from 1559 to 1571. He died in 1571.

Thomas White (1571-1588) DCL, held the prebends of Yatesbury from 1553 to 1565 and Ufcomb from 1565 to 1571. He was Warden of New College, Oxford from 1553 to 1573, Chancellor of Sarum from 1571 to 1588, Archdeacon of Berks from 1557 to 1588 and was Chancellor of the Diocese. He died on 12 June 1588 and was buried in the cathedral near the west wall of the north-east transept.

Thomas Hyde (1588-1618) BD, held the prebend of Ilfracombe from 1583 to 1588 was Chancellor of Sarum and Canon Residentiary from 1588 to 1618 and Rector of Sutton Veny from 1613 to 1618. During his time there were new arrangements for the number of Vicars Choral and Lay Vicars and also for the theological lectures to be arranged by the Chancellor. He died in 1618.

Francis Dee (1618-1634) DD, became also Dean of Chichester in 1630 and was consecrated Bishop of Peterborough in 1634. He died in October 1638.

Brian Duppa (1634-1638) DD, became in 1612 a Fellow of All Souls, Oxford. In 1629 he became Dean of Christchurch and from 1634 to 1638 was Chancellor of Sarum. In about 1636 he became tutor to Prince Charles, later King Charles II, and in 1638 Bishop of Chichester. He was translated to the see of Sarum in 1641 but soon after was deprived of the revenues of the see. A firm friend of King Charles I, he spent much time with him during his imprisonment and after his execution lived for a period in retirement. At the Restoration, in 1660, he was made Lord Almoner and Bishop of Winchester. He died on 26 March 1662 and was buried in Westminster Abbey. Isaak Walton described him as one of "those men in whom there was such a commixture of general learning, of natural eloquence and Christian humility that they deserve a commemoration by a pen equal to their own, which none have exceeded."

William Chillingworth (1638-1644) MA, was the author of *The Religion of Protestants - a safe way of Salvation*. He died in Chichester in 1644, just after its siege in which he had taken part and was buried there. There is a monument to his memory in the south-east transept of the cathedral.

John Earles (1644-1662) DD, was a Fellow of Merton College, Oxford. He was chaplain to Philip, Earl of Pembroke and held the living of Bishopstone from 1639 until resigning in 1662, although deprived and restored in 1660. He was tutor to Prince Charles, was a Canon Residentiary from 1660 to 1662 and was Chancellor of Sarum from 1644 to 1662, although deprived of the revenues during the Commonwealth. At the Restoration he became Dean of Westminster and in 1662 Bishop of Worcester. A year later he was translated to the see of Sarum, dying on 17 November 1665 at Oxford, where he was buried in the chapel of Merton College. Walton said of him, "None since the death of Mr Hooker had been blessed with more innocent wisdom, more sanctified learning or more pious, peaceable, and primitive temper."

Richard Drake (1663-1681) DD, held the prebend of Alton Borealis from 1660 to 1663 and was Chancellor of Sarum from 1663 to 1681. He was a Canon Residentiary from 1666 to 1681, catalogued the muniments in the cathedral and died in 1681.

Seth Ward (1681-1687) MA, was a nephew of Seth Ward, Bishop of Sarum 1667-1689. He was Archdeacon of Wilts from 1675 to 1681, Chancellor of Sarum from 1681 to 1687 and Treasurer of Sarum from 1687 to 1690. He held the prebend of Coombe & Harnham from 1672 to 1681. He died on 11 May 1690, aged 43, and was buried in the cathedral near the grave of his uncle.

Robert Woodward (1687-1691) DCL, was Archdeacon of Wilts from 1681 to 1687, holding the rectory of Pewsey from 1685 to 1702. He was Chancellor of Sarum from 1687 to 1691, and also Chancellor of the Diocese, and Dean of Sarum and Canon Residentiary from 1691 to 1702. He died on 13 February 1702.

Michael Geddes (1691-1713) DCL, was a Canon Residentiary from 1699 to 1713. He presented a verge to the cathedral in 1712 and died on 12 April 1713.

John Hoadley (1713-1727) MA, was Chancellor of Sarum from 1713 to 1727. He was a brother of Benjamin Hoadly, Bishop of Sarum 1723-1734, and chaplain to Gilbert Burnet, Bishop of Sarum 1689-1715, the latter appointing him to the prebend of Wilsford & Woodford from 1705 to 1713 and the Archdeaconry of Sarum from 1710 to 1727. He became a Canon Residentiary and Rector of St Edmund, Sarum. He was consecrated as Bishop of Ferns and Leighlin in 1727, becoming Archbishop of Dublin in 1729 and of Armagh in 1742.

Witting Colton (1727-1755) MA, died on 21 December 1755.

Philip Walton (1756-1771) MA, died in April 1771.

William Talbot (1771-1811) MA, held the prebend of Netherbury in Terra from 1767 to 1771and was Chancellor of Sarum from 1771 to 1811. He died on 25 November 1811.

The Hon Hugh Percy (1812-1856) MA, DD, was the 3rd son of the 1st Earl of Beverley. He married the daughter of Manners Sutton, Archbishop of Canterbury, was Chancellor of Exeter from 1810 to 1816, held stalls at St Paul's and Canterbury from 1816 to 1856, was Archdeacon of Canterbury from 1822 to 1825 and Dean of Canterbury from 1825 to 1827. He was Bishop of Rochester from 1827, and of Carlisle later in the same year until 1856. He was allowed to continue to hold the dignity of Chancellor of Sarum until his death on 5 February 1856.

James Fraser (1858-1860) was a Fellow of Oriel College, Oxford, and was Rector of Cholderton from 1857 to 1859. He was Chancellor of Sarum from 1858 to 1860 and held the prebend of Bishopstone from 1861 until 1870 when he became Bishop of Manchester.

Francis Lear (1861-1864) MA, was Rector and Vicar of Bishopstone from 1850 to 1861. He held the prebend of Bishopstone from 1856 to 1861, was Chancellor of Sarum from 1861 to 1864, a Canon Residentiary from 1862 to 1914, Precentor of Sarum from 1864 to 1875 and Archdeacon of Sarum from 1875 to 1914 . He died on 19 February 1914 and was buried in the cloisters. [The prebend of Bricklesworth, which had been joined to the dignity of Chancellor since 1240, was retained by Francis Lear on his becoming Precentor of Sarum.]

Edward Paroissien Eddrup (1864-1868) was the first Principal of Sarum Theological College from 1861 to 1868. He held the prebend of Durnford from 1861 to 1905, which included the period 1864 to 1868 during which he was Chancellor of Sarum and should have received the prebend of Bricklesworth. This had however been retained by Francis Lear upon his move to the dignity of Precentor. He was Vicar of Bremhill with Foxham and Highway from 1868 to ? and was Rural Dean of Avebury. He died on 13 November 1905 and is commemorated in the north choir aisle of the cathedral..

John Daubney (1868-1877) MA, was Succentor of Sarum from 1865, Chancellor of Sarum from 1868 to 1877, Principal of Sarum Theological College from 1868 to 1878, and Precentor of Sarum from 1877 to 1881.

Robert George Swayne (1877-1894) was Rector of St Edmund's, Sarum from 1863 to 1876. He held the prebend of Gillingham Major from 1870 to 1874, was a Canon Residentiary from 1874 to 1894, was Chancellor of Sarum from 1877 until resigning in 1894 and held the prebend of Slape from 1894 to 1895. He died on 22 April 1901.

Edward Russell Bernard (1894-1917) MA, was a Fellow of Magdalen College, Oxford and was Vicar of Tarrant Monkton with Tarrant Launceston from 1870 to 1876, a Canon Residentiary from 1889 to 1909, Chancellor of Sarum from 1894 to 1917, a Chaplain in Ordinary to Queen Victoria from 1899 to 1901 and subsequently to Kings Edward VII and George V. He was Rural Dean of Wimborne from 1905 to 1907. He held the prebend of Coombe & Harnham from 1886 until his death on 22 April 1921.

Christopher Wordsworth (1917-1928) MA, was a brother of John Wordsworth, Bishop of Sarum 1885-1911, and was a Fellow and Dean of Peterhouse College, Cambridge. He was Rector of Steeple with Tyneham from 1889 to 1897. He held a stall at Lincoln from 1886 to 1911, was Rector of St Peter & St Paul, Marlborough, from 1897 to 1911 and Rural Dean of Marlborough from 1905 to 1911. He was Subdean of Sarum from 1911 to 1917, holding the prebend of Ruscomb from 1911 to 1937, was Librarian from 1913 to 1937 and was Chancellor of Sarum from 1917 to 1928. He was Master of St Nicholas Hospital, Sarum from 1895 to 1938. He was a well known author and editor and died on 30 January 1938.

Charles Tunnacliffe Dimont (1928-1953) DD, was Vice Principal of Wells Theological College from 1909 to 1913 and Principal of Sarum Theological College from 1913 to 1937. He held the prebend of Bricklesworth from 1914 to 1953. In 1928 he became Chancellor of Sarum, in which year the dignity and prebend were reunited, to 1953. He was a Canon Residentiary from 1928 to 1953 and Prior of The Hospital of St John, Burcombe from 1936 to 1953. He died in 1953.

Arthur Frederick Smethurst (1953-1956) MA, DPhil, BSc, held the prebend of Shipton from 1949 to 1953. He was Canon Residentiary from 1949 to 1957, Chancellor of Sarum from 1953 to 1956 and Treasurer of Sarum from 1956 until his death on 15 September 1957.

Eric William Heaton (1956-1960) MA, was a notable theologian. He held the prebend of Netherbury in Ecclesia from 1953 to 1956 was a Canon Residentiary from 1953 to 1960 and Chancellor of Sarum from 1956 to 1960. He was a Fellow of St John's College, Oxford, Dean of Durham from 1974 to 1979, Dean of Christ Church from 1979 to 1991 and Pro-Vice-Chancellor of Oxford University from 1984 to 1991. He died in 1996.

Jeffrey Stanley Maples (1960-1967) MA, held a stall at Lincoln before becoming Diocesan Director of Religious Education from 1956 to 1963, holding the prebend of Bishopstone from 1957 to 1960. He was a Proctor in Convocation from 1958 to 1969 and was Chancellor of Sarum and a Canon Residentiary from 1960 to 1967. He was Director of the Bible Reading Fellowship from 1963 to 1967 and Archdeacon of Swindon and a Proctor in Convocation from 1974 to 1982.

William Moelwyn Merchant (1967-1970) MA, DLitt, FRSL, was a Lecturer at University College, Cardiff, from 1939 to 1950, Senior Lecturer from 1950 to 1961 and Reader in 1961. He was Professor of English at Exeter University from 1961 to 1973, Chancellor of Sarum from 1967 to 1970, a Canon Residentiary from 1967 to 1973 and held the prebend of Slape from 1971 to 1973. He died in April 1997.

Harold Wilson (1971-1972) MA, DD, was Principal of Salisbury Theological College from 1965 to 1971, a Canon Residentiary from 1968 to 1973, Chancellor of Sarum from 1971 to 1972 and Principal of Salisbury & Wells Theological College from 1971 to 1973. He held the prebends of Winterbourne Earls from 1965 to 1970 and Netherbury in Terra in 1972. He was a Canon Residentiary and Chancellor of St Paul's from 1973 to 1975 and died on 2 November 1975.

Ian Geoffrey David Dunlop (1972-1992) MA, FSA, a noted author on French architecture and history, was a Canon Residentiary and Chancellor of Sarum from 1972 to 1992. He was a Lecturer at the Theological College and was from 1975 to 1985 a Proctor in Convocation.

David Michael Karl Durston (1992-) MA, held a stall at Lichfield from 1989 to 1992 and became Chancellor of Sarum and a Canon Residentiary in 1992.

This concludes the south side of the quire and the descriptions which now follow start at the west end of the north side with the Precentor's stall, and continue along this side from west to east, to the Treasurer's stall.

PRECENTORIS

Dignity:- The Precentor is second in dignity to the Dean, reflecting the importance placed on divine worship. The Precentor has to have a competent knowledge of music and of liturgy, is Master of the Music, directs the Organist and Choir in their duties and is responsible for their performance, subject to the right of supervision reserved to the Dean. The Precentor has charge of the music and other books used in the services.

The dignity of Precentor was endowed with the church of Westbury in Wiltshire. This was originally conferred on the cathedral by King Henry I and was probably assigned to the Precentor by Robert, Bishop of Sarum 1107-1139. Unlike the other three principal persons, the dignity was not permanently connected to a particular prebend until 1968 when the prebend of Shipton was joined to this dignity. There is however only one recorded case, Boniface de Saluzzo, Precentor of Sarum 1319-1323, where a Precentor has not also held some prebend and therefore had no voice in chapter.

Stall: This being a return stall, there is no statuette, nor shield.

Holders of the dignity:-

Godwin (c.1122) was the author of *Meditaciones Godwini* and was buried and commemorated at Old Sarum.

Hubert (c.1122/1139).

Henry (c.1142/53-1151/c.1164) was sent from Evreux by the Papal Legates to give notice to Archbishop Becket of the appeal to the Pope against his sentences. He was Archdeacon of Sarum from c.1142 to -c.1154/55.

Walter (c.1165-c.1194) held the dignity in 1194.

Robert (c.1213/14-c.1215).

Thomas de Disci (c.1217-1218) was Precentor of Sarum from c.1217 to 1218 and died before 2 December 1218. He was clerk to the Archbishop of York in 1202 and was appointed custodian of the bishopric of Sarum during the vacancy of 1217. He is believed to have held the prebend of Heytesbury c.1215-c.1218 and died before 2 December 1218.

William de Waude (1218-1220) was Precentor of Sarum and held the prebend of Heytesbury from 1218 to 1220, continuing to hold the latter during his time as Dean of Sarum from 1220 to 1237? He gave great assistance to Richard Poore, Bishop of Sarum 1217-1228, in his building of the new cathedral, visiting London to collect alms at the end of 1219.

William de Badeston (c.1221-c.1222) was a canon in 1219 when he was sent to Canterbury diocese to collect alms for the new cathedral.

Richard (c.1222).

Geoffrey (c.1224-c.1226/7) was Precentor of Sarum from c.1224 to c.1226 and witnessed a deed c.1224 by which the prebend of Calne was joined to the dignity of Treasurer of Sarum. He held the prebend of Highworth from? to 1226/27.

Roger of Sarum (c.1227-1244) was Precentor of Sarum from c.1227 to 1244. He held the prebends of Netheravon from c.1226/27 to 1236 and Teynton Regis from c.1236 to 1244, the latter being joined to the dignity of Precentor for a time. He was consecrated as Bishop of Bath & Wells in 1244, although the Chapter of Wells refused to concur with his election and dying on 21 December 1247, he was buried in Bath.

Andrew of Lavagna (c.1244-1270) was a nephew of Pope Innocent IV. He was Precentor of Sarum and held the prebend of Teynton Regis from 1244 to 1270. He also held a stall at Chartres and was provost of estates in Normandy. He died in February 1270.

Stephen de Gurunvile (1270-1272) held a stall at Hereford and was Precentor of Sarum from 1270 to 1272. He briefly held the prebend of Teynton Regis, then joined to the dignity, from 1270 to 1271. After this he held the prebend of Grantham Borealis from 1271 to 1272 and had died by 30 August 1272.

John de Burton (1272-c.1287) was Subdean of Sarum from c.1262 to 1269 and Warden of de Vaux College, Sarum from September 1269 until his death. He was Precentor, holding also the stall of Grantham Borealis from 1272 to c.1287. He had charge of the diocese during the vacancy in the see prior to the appointment of Walter Scammel, Bishop of Sarum 1284-1286. He had died by 16 November 1287.

Ralph le Waleys of Brightwell (c.1288-c.1294/5) was Precentor of Sarum from c.1288 to c.1294/5 although only in deacon's orders at the time of his appointment. He received a papal dispensation, notwithstanding his being the son of a subdeacon, to become Archdeacon of Wilts from c.1283 to c. 1287, although the Archdeaconry was probably already in the hands of Ralph of Leicester in 1283. He held the prebend of Fordington and Writhlington from c.1275 to c.1284.

William of Abingdon (c.1296-1298) was Precentor of Sarum from c.1296 to 1298 and held the prebend of Horton for less than four months in 1298 despite it having been given by the Pope to George Saluzzo, his successor as Precentor. He was Archdeacon of Wilts from ? to c.1295/6 and had died before 5 May 1298.

George of Saluzzo (1299-1319) disputed the prebend of Horton with William of Abingdon, his predecessor as Precentor of Sarum, a dignity he held from 1299 to 1319. In 1319 he exchanged the dignity for the Archdeaconry of Buckingham with his brother, Boniface of Saluzzo, but he retained the prebend of Bere & Cherminster from c.1320 until being deprived of all benefices in 1330.

Boniface of Saluzzo (1319-1323) assumed the dignity of Precentor of Sarum by exchange for the Archdeaconry of Buckingham with his cousin, George of Saluzzo. He appears not to have held a prebend.

Iswin de Gandavo (1323) was Rector of Beechingstoke in 1304 and of Preshute in 1312. He held the prebends of Major Pars Altaris from 1312 to 1314 and Coombe & Harnham from 1314 to ?. He was Precentor of Sarum in 1323, holding the dignity with the church of Westbury annexed to it, and was Archdeacon of Wilts from 12 March 1326 until resigning fifteen days later.

Nicholas de la Wyle (1323-1341) was Precentor of Sarum from 1323 to 1341, held the prebend of Wilsford & Woodford from 1324 to 1341 and a stall at Wells. He was a Canon Residentiary and in 1340 was locum tenens of the Dean. He died in 1341.

Thomas de Welewick (1341-1343) died in 1343.

Gerard de Daumario (1343) was a nephew of Pope Clement VI and a Dominican friar who became Vicar General of the Order in 1340. He was created Cardinal-Priest of St Sabina in 1342 and Precentor of Sarum in 1343. He failed to take possession of the dignity of Precentor but the income from it was reserved to pay his debts, despite his holding several incumbencies including the rectory of Tisbury. He died at Avignon on 27 September 1343.

Thomas de Staunton (1344-1347) received a royal grant of the prebend of Grimston in 1318 and, despite it being granted to Innocent de Fieschi, he appears to have held it until at least 1324. He was Precentor of Sarum from 1344 to 1347.

John de la Chambre (1347-?) held the prebend of Minor Pars Altaris from 1340 to 1365 and was Precentor of Sarum from 1347 to c.1360. He was admitted as a Canon Residentiary in 1340.

Philip Codeford (1361.1364) DCL.

Robert Walsham (?-1385) held the prebend of Rotesfen from 1362 to c.1372 and was Precentor of Sarum from ? to 1385. He died in 1385.

John Welborne (?-1397) DCL, was Precentor of Sarum from ? to 1397. He held the prebend of Hurstbourne & Burbage from 1386 to 1397, but exchanged the dignity, the prebend and the church of Crewkerne, Somerset, with Adam Mottrum in 1397 for the Archdeaconry of Ely, the prebend of Fenton at York and a portion of St Probus church, Cornwall.

Adam Mottrum (1397-1415) was Archdeacon of Ely, exchanging this and other benefices with John Welbourn. He was Precentor of Sarum and held the prebend of Hurstbourne & Burbage from 1397 to 1415 and was also Rector of South Newton. He was appointed Vicar General of the diocese in 1408 and in his Will asked to be buried in the Cathedral.

Arnold de Monte St Silvestri (1415).

Thomas Faukys (1415-1416) was Precentor of Sarum from 1415 to 1416, exchanging the dignity with Henry Harburgh for the church of St Bride, London.

Henry Harburgh (1416-1418) was Treasurer of Sarum for three days in 1394 when he exchanged the dignity with John Chaundeler for the prebend of Netherbury in Ecclesia. This he exchanged in 1395 with Ralph Selby for the prebend of Alton Borealis. He relinquished this latest prebend in 1403, receiving that of Slape. This he held until 1415 when he received the prebend of Beminster Prima. In 1416 he became Precentor of Sarum, he relinquished his prebend in 1418 and in the same year exchanged the dignity of Precentor for the prebend of Bere & Cherminster, which he held until 1432. He had died by 22 September 1432.

Robert Gilbert (1418-1419) DTh, exchanged the prebend of Bere & Cherminster one month after receiving it, with Henry Harburgh for the dignity of Precentor. Less than a year later, he exchanged the dignity with Edward Prentys for the prebend of South Newton in Wilton conventual church. He later became Dean of York in 1426 and Bishop of London in 1436. He died in 1448.

Edward Prentys (1419-1446) BCL, was Precentor of Sarum from 1419 to 1446. He exchanged the prebend of Grantham Australis, which he held in 1406, with Richard Prentys for the prebend of Stratford which he held from 1406 until 1423. He held the prebend of Durnford from 1423 to his death in 1446. He was a Canon Residentiary and occupied the house called Leadenhall in the Close.

Nicholas Upton (1446-1457) BCn&CL, was co-author of *Survey of churches, lands and tenements belonging to the church of Sarum* and was an author of treatises on war and heraldry. He received the prebend of Major Pars Altaris in 1431 and still held it in 1435. He was Rector of Stapleford from 1434 to 1442, Master of St Nicholas Hospital, Sarum in 1442 and Precentor of Sarum from 1446 to 1457. He died in 1457.

John Stokes (1457-1467) DCL, held a stall at St Paul's in 1430. From 1457 to 1467 he was Precentor of Sarum and held the prebend of Coombe & Harnham, receiving the prebend from John Stretton in exchange for the Treasurership of Chichester. He was probably Archdeacon of Ely in 1445 and a Prebendary of Hereford. He died in 1467.

Thomas St Just (1467) DMus, was Warden of King's College, Oxford in 1463. He died in 1467.

Robert Kirkham (1467-1471) was Precentor of Sarum, also holding the prebend of Bedwin, from 1467 to 1471. He was Master of the Rolls in 1462 and died in 1471.

Thomas Hawkins (1471-1479) MA, was Precentor of Sarum from 1471 to 1479. He held the prebends of Minor Pars Altaris from 1471 to 1474 and Hurstbourne & Burbage from 1474 to 1479. He was also Provost of Oriel College, Oxford and Archdeacon of Worcester. He died in 1479 and was buried in the Cathedral.

John Emwell (1479-1480) BCnL, was Precentor of Sarum from 1479 to 1480. He held the prebends of Netheravon from 1476 to 1478 and Coombe & Harnham from 1478 to 1485. He resigned the dignity in 1480 and died in 1485.

Edward Pole (1480-1485) appears to have been a son of the Duke of Suffolk. He was Precentor of Sarum from 1480 to 1485 and held the prebends of Netheravon from 1478 to 1479 and Hurstbourne & Burbage from 1479 to ?. He became Archdeacon of the East Riding in 1480 and of Richmond in 1484.

James Stanley (1485-1506) was a son of Thomas, Earl of Derby. He held the prebends of Yetminster Prima in 1477, again from 1492 to 1493, and Beminster Prima from 1493 to 1506. He was Archdeacon of Richmond in 1500, Precentor of Sarum from 1485 to 1506 and became Bishop of Ely in 1506.

Simon Stalworth (1506-1507) MA, held the prebend of Warminster from 1494 to 1495 and was Precentor of Sarum from 1506 to 1507. He died in 1511.

Richard Dudley (1507-1536) DTh, was Precentor from 1507 to 1536 and held the prebends of Minor Pars Altaris from 1508 to 1517, Yatesbury from 1517 to ? and Durnford from ? (holding it in 1535) to 1536. He died in 1536.

Thomas Bennet (1536-1558) DCL, was Secretary to Cardinal Wolsey, Rector of Sutton Veny from 1502 to 1507, Precentor of Sarum from 1536 to 1558 and held the prebends of Axford from 1529 to 1533 and Chisenbury and Chute from 1533 to 1558. He was Canon Residentiary and Proctor in Convocation for the Chapter, in which capacity he signed the Articles of 1536. For some time he was locum tenens to Peter Vannes, Dean of Sarum, who was non-resident. He died in 1558 and is commemorated at the north side of the choir.

George Carew (1558-1583) DD, was the father of George, Earl of Totness and of Sir Peter Carew Kt. He became Dean of Bristol in 1552, was deprived in 1553 and having been restored in 1570, resigned it for the Deanery of Exeter in 1570. He was the first to hold the prebend of Ilfracombe, from 1555 to 1556 and held the prebend of Netherbury in Ecclesia from 1556 to 1583. He was Precentor of Sarum from 1558 to 1583 and a Canon Residentiary from 1556 to 1571. He died in 1583 aged 85.

Tobias Matthew (1583) DD, was Precentor of Sarum in 1583. He held the prebend of Teynton Regis from 1572 to 1589, becoming President of St John's College, Oxford and in 1577 Dean of Christ Church Oxford, Dean of Durham in 1583, Bishop of Durham in 1595 and Archbishop of York in 1606. He was one of the divines employed in the Hampton Court Conference.

William Souch (1584-1608) DD, was Precentor of Sarum from 1584 to 1608. He held the prebends of Netherbury in Terra from 1586 to 1589 and Fordington & Writhlington from 1589 to 1608. He appears to have been the subject of a Visitation over the Precentor's rights to the common fund and a house of residence.

Walter Benet (1608-1614) BD, was Precentor of Sarum from 1608 to 1614 and held the prebends of Yetminster Secunda from 1610 to 1614 and Stratton in 1614. He was Archdeacon of Wilts from 1610 to 1614, holding with this the rectory of Mynty. He died in 1614.

Henry Cotton (1614-1622/23) MA, was a son of Henry Cotton, Bishop of Sarum 1598-1615. He was appointed Precentor of Sarum in 1614 but Francis Souch was presented by the King and instituted by the Archbishop in 1620. He held the prebends of Fordington & Writhlington from 1608 to 1612, Bitton from 1612 to 1615 and Highworth from 1615 to his death, while still Precentor, in 1622/23.

Francis Souch (1620) BCL, was appointed by King James I and instituted by the Archbishop of Canterbury, despite the dignity being already held by Henry Cotton.

Humphrey Henchman (1623-1660) DD, was a Fellow of Clare Hall, Cambridge. He was a son-in-law of Robert Tounson, Bishop of Sarum 1620-1621, becoming Precentor from 1623 to 1660 and Canon Residentiary from 1633 to 1660 (although dismissed during the Commonwealth) and holding in succession the prebends of Yatesbury from 1623 to 1629, Grantham Australis from 1629 to 1639 and Teynton Regis from 1639 to 1660. He was a Canon Residentiary from 1633 to 1660 and helped King Charles II to escape after the battle of Worcester; personally escorting him Heale House and meeting him again at Stonehenge. He became Bishop of London and Lord Almoner in 1663. He died on 7 October 1675 at the age of 83 and was buried at Fulham.

Thomas Hyde (1660-1666) DD, held the prebend of Stratford from 1639 to 1660. He was appointed Precentor of Sarum by King Charles II in 1660, serving until 1666, and held the prebend of Teynton Regis from 1660 until his death in 1666.

John South (1666-1672) BCL, was a Fellow of New College, Oxford and Regius Professor of Greek in 1622. He died in 1672.

Daniel Whitby (1672-1726) DD, held the prebends of Yatesbury in 1668, Hurstbourne & Burbage from 1668 to 1696 and Teynton Regis from 1696 to 1726. He was Chaplain to Seth Ward, Bishop of Sarum 1667-1689, Precentor of Sarum from 1672 to 1726, a Canon Residentiary from 1676 to 1726, and Rector of St Edmund's, Sarum. He caused excitement by publishing the *Protestant Reconciler* and similar writings, which advocated general religious tolerance. This brought upon him the wrath of the authorities, Chief Justice Jeffreys even directing his indictment. He died on 21 March 1726 aged 90.

Arthur Ashley Sykes (1726-1756) MA, held the prebend of Alton Borealis from 1724 to 1756 and was Precentor of Sarum from 1726 to 1756. He died on 23 November 1756.

William Herring (1756-1774) DD, was Precentor of Sarum from 1756 to 1774. He was also Dean of St Asaph from 1751 to 1774. He died on 23 May 1774.

Nathaniel Hume (1774-1804) MA, was Precentor of Sarum from 1774 to 1804 and Master of St Nicholas Hospital, Sarum in 1770. He held the prebends of Winterbourne Earls from 1770 to 1777, Yetminster Prima from 1777 to 1804 and the livings of Bremhill in 1782 and Brixton Deverill in 1799. He died on 28 April 1804.

William Douglas (1804-1819) MA, was a son of John Douglas, Bishop of Sarum 1791-1807. He was Archdeacon of Wilts from 1799 to 1804, a Canon Residentiary from 1799 to 1819 and Precentor of Sarum from 1804 to 1819. He held the prebends of Coombe & Harnham from 1792 to 1799 and Fordington & Writhlington from 1799 to 1819. He was also Chancellor of the Diocese, Master of St Nicholas Hospital in 1792, Rector of Brixton Deverill and Vicar of Potterne. He died on 19 March 1819.

Philip Fisher (1819-1842) DD, held the prebends of Stratton from 1808 to 1810 and Ilfracombe from 1810 to 1823. He was Precentor of Sarum from 1819 to 1842, dying on 19 January 1842 at the age of 92.

Walter Kerr Hamilton (1843-1854) DD, was a Fellow of Merton College, Oxford in 1833. In 1834 he held a stall at Wells, becoming a Canon Residentiary with the house of Leadenhall from 1841 to 1854, Treasurer of Sarum from 1841 to 1843 and Precentor of Sarum from 1843 to 1854, also holding the prebend of Torleton from 1843 to 1854. He was Bishop of Sarum from 1854 until his death on 1 August 1869. Whilst at Sarum he founded Sarum Theological College and contributed to the debate on cathedral reform. He was buried in the cathedral beside his predecessor, Edward Denison, Bishop of Sarum 1837-1854.

William Beadon Heathcote (1854-1862) BCL, was Precentor of Sarum from 1854 to 1862 and held the prebend of Winterbourne Earls from 1856 to 1862. He was Vicar of Sturminster Marshall in 1858 and died on 21 August 1862.

Francis Lear (1864-1875) MA, was Rector and Vicar of Bishopstone from 1850 to 1861. He held the prebend of Bishopstone from 1856 to 1861, was Chancellor of Sarum from 1861 to 1864, a Canon Residentiary from 1862 to 1914, Precentor of Sarum from 1864 to 1875 and Archdeacon of Sarum from 1875 to 1914 . He died on 19 February 1914 and was buried in the cloisters. [The prebend of Bricklesworth, which had been joined to the dignity of Chancellor since 1240, was retained by Francis Lear on his becoming Precentor of Sarum.]

John Daubney (1877-1881) MA, was Succentor of Sarum from 1865, Chancellor of Sarum from 1868 to 1877, Principal of Sarum Theological College from 1868 to 1878, and Precentor of Sarum from 1877 to 1881.

George David Boyle (1881-1896) MA, was the son of the Rt Hon David Boyle, Lord Justice General of Scotland, and numbered John Henry Newman amongst his friends. He held a stall at Worcester in 1872. He was Dean of Sarum and a Canon Residentiary from 1880 to 1901, during which time the large sum of £14,000 was spent on the Cathedral under his direction. He was also Precentor of Sarum from 1881 to 1896. He died on 21 March 1901 and is commemorated in both the south choir aisle and the Trinity Chapel.

Harry William Carpenter (1896-1936) OBE, MA, held the prebends of Ruscomb from 1896 to 1911 and Netherbury in Terra from 1911 to 1936. He was Vice Principal of Sarum Theological College from 1879 to 1880, a Vicar Choral from 1879 to 1914, Precentor of Sarum from 1896 to 1936, Archdeacon of Sarum from 1914 to 1936, and a Canon Residentiary from 1915 to 1936. He died on 20 July 1936.

William Harold Ferguson (1936-1947) MA, was Precentor of Sarum, a Canon Residentiary and held the prebend of Netherbury in Terra from 1936 until he resigned the prebend and dignity on 30 April 1947. He died in 1950.

Cyril Jackson (1947-1968) was Precentor of Sarum, a Canon Residentiary, held the prebend of Netherbury in Terra and was a Proctor in Convocation from 1947 until his resignation on 15 November 1968.

Cyril Vincent Taylor (1969-1975) held the prebend of Shipton from 1969 to 1974 and was Precentor of Sarum and a Canon Residentiary from 1969 until 1975. He was a composer, hymn editor and broadcaster. He died in 1991 and is commemorated in the north cloister of the cathedral.

Charles Moxon (1975-1985) was a minor canon of St Paul's from 1946 to 1952 and Sacristan from 1947 to 1952. He was Precentor of Sarum and a Canon Residentiary, holding the prebend of Shipton from 1975 to 1985. He died soon after his retirement.

David Jeremy Christopher Davies (1985-) MA, was Chaplain to Queen Mary College (now QMC and Westfield College) from 1974 to 1978 and Senior Chaplain to the University of Wales (Cardiff) from 1978 to 1985. He became Precentor of Sarum and a Canon Residentiary, holding the prebend of Shipton in 1985 and a Proctor in Convocation in 1993.

UPAVON
(previously the Archdeacon of Wilts)

Until 1977 each Archdeacon had a stall of his dignity in a position of prominence close to one of the four principal persons; these stalls have now been renamed. Particulars of the Archdeacons are given first, followed by the particulars of the prebend the name of which the stall now bears.

Stall: This being a return stall, there is no statuette, nor shield.

ARCHDEACON OF WILTS

The dignity:- The fourth Archdeaconry covered the deaneries of Avebury, Cricklade, Malmesbury and Marlborough. The church of Minety, part of the pre-Conquest endowment of Malmesbury Abbey, was tied to the Archdeaconry in 1276.

Holders of the dignity:-

Azo (c.1122/39) may have been Archdeacon of Wilts c.1122/39 and brother of Roger of Ramsbury who succeeded him. He was Dean of Sarum between c.1139 and c.1145, and held the prebend of Pottern from c.1142 to c.1148.

Roger of Ramsbury (1139-c.1150/60) was a brother of Azo, Archdeacon of Wilts c.1122/39 and Dean of Sarum c.1139-c.1145. He was Archdeacon of Wilts and held the prebend of Heytesbury from 1139 to c.1150/60.

Reginald FitzJocelin (c.1161-1173/4) was the son of Jocelin de Bohun, Bishop of Sarum 1142-1184. He was Archdeacon of Wilts, holding the prebend of Heytesbury, from c.1161 to 1173/4 and was elected Bishop of Bath in 1173.

William (c.1170).

Richard of Wilton (before 1179-c.1189/90) was Sheriff of Wilts from 1164 to 1179.

Humphrey of Bassingbourn (c.1193) was Archdeacon of Wilts in 1193, Archdeacon of Sarum c.1193-c.1238 and held the prebend of Netherbury in Ecclesia in c.1226/27. He also held a stall at Lincoln.

William of Ste-Mère-Eglise (c.1193-1198) was a clerk of the royal chamber by 1183, was Dean of Mortain and of St Martin le Grand, London and was elected Bishop of London in 1198.

Richard Grosseteste (c.1199-c.1222/3) was Archdeacon of Wilts from c.1199 to c.1222/3 and held the prebend of Calne c. 1121.

William de Merston (c.1223-c.1205/24).

Stephen of Tisbury (c.1226-1246) held the prebend of Axford from c.1225-1226/27. He was Archdeacon of Wilts from c.1226 to 1246 and had died by 1 August 1246.

Roger of Buscot (1246-1247) was Clerk to Robert Grossetester, Bishop of Lincoln and died in 1247.

Nicholas of York (c.1247-c1257).

Roger de la Grene (c.1258-c.1271) held the prebend of Yetminster Prima from c.1243 to c.1271, was Rector of Preshute and was Archdeacon of Wilts from c.1258 to c.1271.

Henry of Braunstone (c.1275-c.1279) was Archdeacon of Wilts between c.1275 and c.1279, and of Dorset between 1281 and c.1284. He held the prebend of Bere & Cherminster from c.1274 to 1284 and was Dean of Sarum from 1284 to 1287. He held a stall at Exeter and was Bishop of Sarum, holding the office of Master of St Nicholas Hospital, Sarum from 1287 until his death on 11 February 1288. He was buried in the lady chapel of the cathedral.

Ralph le Waleys of Brightwell (c.1283-c.1287) was Precentor of Sarum from c.1288 to c.1294/5 although only in deacon's orders at the time of his appointment. He received a papal dispensation, notwithstanding his being the son of a subdeacon, to become Archdeacon of Wilts from c.1283 to c.1287, although the Archdeaconry was probably already in the hands of Ralph of Leicester in 1283. He held the prebend of Fordington and Writhlington from c.1275 to c.1284.

Ralph of Leicester (c.1283) DCL, occurs only once, in 1283 and would appear to have been Chancellor of Cambridge University

William of Abingdon (?-c.1295/6) was Precentor of Sarum from c.1296 to 1298 and held the prebend of Horton for less than four months in 1298 despite it having been given by the Pope to George Saluzzo, his successor as Precentor. He was Archdeacon of Wilts from ? to c.1295/6 and died in 1298.

Richard de Sotwell (?-1303) held the prebend of Bitton from 1289 to 1296 and was Archdeacon of Wilts from c.1299 to c.1303 when he went to Rome with Walter de Langeton, Bishop of Coventry & Lichfield. He died in 1303.

Thomas of Savoy (?-1304) had expectations of the Archdeaconry of Wilts in 1301. He held it but his position was uncertain and he was deprived of it on 28 February 1304.

William de Chaddleshunt (1304-1320) DCL, was Archdeacon of Wilts from 1304 to 1320. He held the prebends of Alton Australis from 1304 to 1309 and Chardstock from 1309 to ?. He held stalls at Lichfield and St Paul's, and one of his name was Rector of Dauntsey in 1303. He died before 3 February 1320.

Gerald de Tilheto (?-1326) DCL, was Archdeacon of Wilts, holding the prebend of Bedminster & Redclyffe, from c.1321 to 1326. He died in 1326.

Iswin de Gandavo (1326) was Rector of Beechingstoke in 1304 and of Preshute in 1312. He held the prebends of Major Pars Altaris from 1312 to 1314 and Coombe & Harnham from 1314 to ?. He was Precentor of Sarum in 1323, holding the dignity with the church of Westbury annexed to it and was Archdeacon of Wilts from 12 March 1326 until resigning fifteen days later.

Robert de Baldock (1326) DCL, had expectations of the Archdeaconry of Wilts since 1322 and accepted it in 1326 but he renounced it a few days later.

Robert de Ayleston (1326-1331) held the prebend of Major Pars Altaris from 1321 to 1322, exchanging it in 1322 with John de Winchelsea for the prebend of Bitton. He was Archdeacon of Wilts from 1326 to 1331 and of Berks from 1331 to c.1333 and was in the same year Archdeacon of Bath. He was Rector of Wootton Basset in 1322 and held a stall at Lincoln in 1331.

Ralph de Querendon (1331-?) was Subdean of Sarum and a Canon Residentiary from 1330 to ? and held the prebend of Major Pars Altaris from 1330 to 1358. He was Archdeacon of Wilts from 1331 to c.1333 and died in 1358.

John de Whitchurch (1333-1343) BCn&CL, was Archdeacon of Wilts from 1333 to 1343 when he exchanged the dignity with John Barne for the church of Sedgefield, Co. Durham. He held the prebend of Axford from 1335 to 1338, exchanging it with John de Abingdon for the prebend of Hurstbourne & Burbage, which he held until his death in 1358. He was a Canon Residentiary.

John Barne (1343-1361) BCnL, was Archdeacon of Wilts from 1343 to 1361. He held the prebend of Lyme & Halstock from ? until his death in 1362.

John Lineden (1361) received the dignity by 26 December 1361 and exchanged it the following day with John Silvestre for the church of Fugglestone.

John Silvestre (or Codeford) (1361-?) held the dignity in 1379.

Nicholas Wykeham (1388-1407) Lic.CL, was Principal of Hart Hall, Oxford. He held the prebend of Bedwin from 1388 to 1406, became Archdeacon of Winchester in 1372 and was Warden of New College, Oxford c.1379. He was Archdeacon of Wilts from 1388 to 1406 and died in 1407.

William Magot (1407) received the Archdeaconry of Wilts on 17 March 1407 and exchanged it with John Chitterne on 21 April 1407 for the church of Berwick St John.

John Chitterne (1407-1419) held the prebends of Chisenbury & Chute from 1385 to 1415 and Hurstbourne & Burbage from 1415 to 1419. He became a Canon Residentiary in 1386, was Rector of Newton Tony from 1415 to 1419 and was Archdeacon of Wilts from 1407 to 1419. He held a stall at St Paul's from 1409 to 1419 and became Archdeacon of Sarum in 1419, dying in the same year.

Simon Gaunstede (1419-1423) died in 1423.

John Symondesburgh (1423-1449) BCL, was Archdeacon of Wilts from 1423 to 1449 and Treasurer of Sarum from 1449 to 1454. He held the prebend of Yatesbury from 1423 to 1437, exchanging it with John Tydeling for the prebend of Stratton which he held from 1437 to 1449. He held the Rectory of Dinton in 1433 and was Treasurer of St Paul's from 1420 to 1423. He died in 1454 and asked to be buried before St Margaret's altar in the cathedral.

John Chedworth (1449-1452) DTh, held the prebends of Yatesbury from 1440 to 1443, Stratford from 1443 to 1445, Netherbury in Terra from 1445 to 1447 and Hurstbourne & Burbage from 1447 to 1452. He held a stall at Lincoln and was at different times Archdeacon of Northampton and of Lincoln. He was Provost of King's College, Cambridge in 1446, Archdeacon of Wilts from 1449 to 1452 and was consecrated Bishop of Lincoln in 1452. He died on 23 November 1471.

Marinus Ursinus (1452-?) occupied the Archdeaconry of Wilts in 1454.

Vincent Clement (1457-1464) DTh, resigned in 1464.

Peter Courtenay (1464-1478) DCnL, was the son of Sir Philip Courtenay of Powderham by Elizabeth daughter of Walter, Lord Hungerford KG. In 1453 he was Archdeacon of Exeter, also holding the prebend of Netherbury in Terra from 1448 to 1475 exchanging these for the prebend of Bere & Cherminster, which he held from 1475 to 1478, and the Provostship of St Edmund's College, Sarum. In 1474 he became secretary to King Edward IV, Dean of Windsor in 1476 and Dean of Exeter in 1477. He was Archdeacon of Wilts from 1464 to 1478 when he became Bishop of Exeter, later being translated to Winchester. He died on 22 September 1492.

Hugh Pavy (1479-?) BCL, held the prebends of Grimston from 1467 to 1471, becoming a Canon Residentiary in 1471, and Bedwin from 1471 to 1485. In 1479 he became Archdeacon of Wilts and in 1485 Bishop of St David's, while continuing to hold his Archdeaconry.

Christopher Urswick (?-1522) was Warden of King's Hall, Oxford resigning in 1488 when he became Dean of York. He was Archdeacon of Richmond in 1493 and Archdeacon of Wilts from c.1493 to 1522, during which time he became Dean of Windsor in 1495, Archdeacon of Huntingdon in 1496 and Archdeacon of Winchester in 1501, holding a stall at Southwell in 1509. He held the prebend of Bedwin from ? to 1522 and was Chaplain and Almoner to King Henry VII and to the Countess of Richmond.

Edward Finch (1522-1539) DM, was well endowed with prebends holding in succession those of Yatesbury from 1514 to 1515, Chardstock from 1515 to 1517, Wilsford & Woodford in 1517, Fordington & Writhlington from 1517 to 1518, Grimston from 1518 to 1519 and Faringdon from 1519 to 1521 exchanging the last with William Webbe for the church of Ross on Wye, Hereford. He then held the prebends of Bishopstone from 1521 to 1522, Teynton Regis from 1522 to 1524 and Bere & Cherminster from 1524 to 1539. He was Archdeacon of Wilts from 1522 until 1539. He died in 1539 and was buried in the cathedral.

John Pollard (1539-1554) MA, was Archdeacon of Wilts from 1539 until being deprived in 1554.

John Lawrence (1554-1564) BCn&CL, was deprived in 1564.

Giles Lawrence (1564-1577) BCL.

John Sprint (1577-1590) DD, was Dean of Bristol in 1571. He held the prebend of Bitton from 1573 to 1578, was Archdeacon of Wilts from 1577 to 1590 and was also Treasurer of Sarum from 1584 to 1590. He died in 1590.

Edmund Lilly (1590-1610) DD, died in 1610 and was buried at St Mary the Virgin, Oxford.

Walter Benet (1610-1614) BD, was Precentor of Sarum from 1608 to 1614 and held the prebends of Yetminster Secunda from 1610 to 1614 and Stratton in 1614. He was Archdeacon of Wilts from 1610 to 1614, holding with the dignity the Rectory of Mynty. He died in 1614.

Thomas Leche (1614-1646) MA, was Rector of Pewsey and Archdeacon of Wilts from 1614 to 1646 and held the prebend of Bitton from 1615 to 1646. He died in 1646 and was buried at Pewsey.

William Creed (1660-1663) DD, was a Fellow of St John's College, Oxford and a Proctor in 1644. He became Rector of Codford St Mary in 1660 and Archdeacon of Wilts and a Canon Residentiary, holding the prebend of Lyme & Halstock, from 1660 until his death in 1663. He was Regius Professor of Divinity at Oxford in 1661 and held a stall at Christ Church, Oxford. He also held the Rectory of Stockton and died on 19 July 1663.

Thomas Henchman (1663-1674) MA, held the prebends of Slape from 1660 to 1661 and Netherbury in Ecclesia from 1661 to 1674. He held a stall at St Paul's in 1672 and was Archdeacon of Wilts and a Canon Residentiary from 1663 to 1674. He died on 15 December 1674.

Seth Ward (1675-1681) MA, was a nephew of Seth Ward, Bishop of Sarum 1667-1689. He was Archdeacon of Wilts from 1675 to 1681, Chancellor of Sarum from 1681 to 1687 and Treasurer of Sarum from 1687 to 1690. He held the prebend of Coombe & Harnham from 1672 to 1681. He died on 11 May 1690 aged 43 and was buried in the cathedral near the grave of his uncle.

Robert Woodward (1681-1687) DCL, was Archdeacon of Wilts from 1681 to 1687, holding the rectory of Pewsey from 1685 to 1702. He was Chancellor of Sarum from 1687 to 1691, being also Chancellor of the Diocese, and was Dean of Sarum and a Canon Residentiary from 1691 to 1702. He died on 13 February 1702.

Thomas Ward (1687-1696) LLD, was a nephew of Seth Ward, Bishop of Sarum 1667-1689, and in 1679 was ordained deacon and priest in one day. A month later he received the prebend of Netheravon, holding it from 1679 to 1681. He held the prebends of Gillingham Major from 1681 to 1682 and Teynton Regis from 1682 to 1696. He was Archdeacon of Wilts from 1687 until his death on 20 March 1696. His appointment to a prebendal stall at a very early age and his rapid advancement led to a controversy between Bishop and Dean.

Cornelius Yeate (1696-1720) MA, held the prebend of Bishopstone from 1691 to 1696 and was Archdeacon of Wilts from 1696 to 1720. He had considerable controversy with Seth Ward, Bishop of Sarum 1667-1689, over the disposal of the prebends and owed his promotion to both the prebend and the Archdeaconry to Gilbert Burnet, Bishop of Sarum 1689-1715. He died on 12 April 1720.

Thomas Rundle (1720-1735) BCL, held the prebends of Gillingham Minor from 1716 to 1717 and Ilfracombe from 1717 to 1721. He held the Archdeaconry of Wilts from 1720 to 1735 together with the dignity of Treasurer of Sarum from 1721 to 1735 and was consecrated Bishop of Derry in 1735.

Henry Stebbing (1735-1763) DD, was also Chancellor of the Diocese. He died on 2 January 1763 and is commemorated in the south aisle of the cathedral.

Charles Weston (1763-1768) MA, resigned in 1768.

Richard Brickenden (1768-1779) DD, died in 1779.

Arthur Coham (1779-1799) MA, held the prebends of Netherbury in Terra from 1771 to 1772 and Fordington & Writhlington from 1772 to 1799. He was Vicar of Potterne from 1781 to 1793, Rector of Brixton Deverill and Archdeacon of Wilts from 1779 to 1799. He died on 14 February 1799 and is commemorated at Brixton Deverill.

William Douglas (1799-1804) MA, was a son of John Douglas, Bishop of Sarum 1791-1807. He was Archdeacon of Wilts from 1799 to 1804, a Canon Residentiary from 1799 to 1819 and Precentor of Sarum from 1804 to 1819. He held the prebends of Coombe & Harnham from 1792 to 1799 and Fordington & Writhlington from 1799 to 1819. He was also Chancellor of the Diocese, Master of St Nicholas Hospital in 1792, Rector of Brixton Deverill and Vicar of Potterne. He died on 19 March 1819.

William Coxe (1804-1828) MA, was Rector of Bemerton in 1788 and Rector of Stourton. He held the prebends of Alton Australis from 1791 to 1792, Bitton from 1792 to 1799, Grimston from 1799 to 1801 and Netheravon from 1801 to 1828. He was a Canon Residentiary, Archdeacon of Wilts from 1804 to 1828 and died on 8 June 1828.

William Macdonald (1828-1862) MA, was Vicar of Chitterne in 1812 and Vicar of Bishop's Cannings in 1815. He held the prebend of Bitton from 1807 to 1862, was a Canon Residentiary from 1823 to 1862 and Archdeacon of Wilts from 1828 to 1862. He died on 24 June 1862.

Henry Drury (1862-1863) was Vicar of Bremhill in 1845, held the prebend of Shipton from 1855 to 1863, was Chaplain to the House of Commons in 1857 and Archdeacon of Wilts from 1862 to 1863. He died on 25 January 1863.

The Hon Charles Amyand Harris (1863-1868) MA, was a son of the second Earl of Malmesbury. He was a Fellow of All Souls, Oxford from 1835 to 1837, Rector of Shaftesbury from 1839 to 1840 and Rector of Wilton and Bulbridge and Vicar of Ditchampton from 1840 to 1848. From 1841 to 1863 he held the prebend of Chardstock and was Domestic Chaplain to Edward Denison, Bishop of Sarum 1837-1854, and Walter Kerr Hamilton, Bishop of Sarum 1854-1869, and was Archdeacon of Wilts and Vicar of Bremhill with Highway from 1863 to 1868. He was Bishop of Gibraltar from 1868 to 1873, died on 16 March 1874 and was buried at Bremhill.

Thomas Stanton (1868-1874) was Rector of Shaftesbury in 1846 and Vicar of Burbage in 1852. He held the prebend of Ufcomb from 1859 to 1875, was Archdeacon of Wilts from 1868 to 1874 and died in 1875.

Thomas Boughton Buchanan (1874-1911) MA, was Chaplain to Lord Herbert of Lea from 1859 to 1860, Rector of Wishford Magna from 1863 to 1871 and Chaplain to George Moberly, Bishop of Sarum 1869-1885, from 1870 to 1885. He was Vicar of Potterne from 1871 to 1891, Rector of Poulshot from 1891 to 1905 and held the prebend of Bedminster & Redcliffe from 1894 to 1924. He was Archdeacon of Wilts from 1874 to 1911 and a Canon Residentiary from 1895 to 1915. He died on 28 June 1924 and is commemorated in the north choir aisle of the cathedral.

Frederick Wallis (1911-1912) DD, was a Fellow of Caius College, Cambridge, and Dean of Caius from 1878 to 1891. He was Bishop of Wellington, New Zealand from 1895 to 1911, Archdeacon of Wilts from 1911 to 1912, held the prebend of Beminster Secunda from 1913 to 1928 and was Archdeacon of Sherborne from 1916 to 1919. He died on 24 June 1928.

Eric James Bodington (1912-1927) MA, was Vicar of Osmington from 1894 to 1899, Vicar of Potterne and Rural Dean of Potterne from 1899 to 1907, Rural Dean of Avebury from 1907 to 1912 and Vicar of Calne from 1907 to 1927. He was Archdeacon of Wilts from 1912 to 1927, held the prebend of Chardstock from 1913 to 1929 and was Archdeacon of Dorset and Canon Residentiary from 1927 to 1929. He died on 25 October 1929.

Joseph William Coulter (1927-1951) MA, was Rector of Langton Matravers from 1900 to 1916, Rector and Rural Dean of Bridport from 1916 to 1927 and Vicar of Calne from 1927 to 1951. He held the prebend of Grantham Australis from 1920 to 1956 and was Archdeacon of Wilts from 1927 to 1951. He died on 10 April 1956.

Cecil Andrew Plaxton (1951-1974) MA, was Vicar of Southbroom from 1932 to 1937, Vicar of Holy Trinity, Weymouth from 1937 to 1951 and Rural Dean of Weymouth from 1944 to 1951. He held the prebend of Netheravon from 1948 to 1993, was Rector of Pewsey from 1951 to 1956 and Archdeacon of Wilts from 1951 to 1974. He died on 2 February 1993.

John Robert Geoffrey Neale (1974-1980) AKC, held a stall at Guildford from 1968 to 1974, was Archdeacon of Wilts from 1974 to 1980, Suffragan Bishop of Ramsbury from 1974 to 1981 and Area Bishop of Ramsbury from 1981 to 1988. He held the prebend of Lyme & Halstock from 1974 to 1988. He was Secretary of Partners for World Mission and an Assistant Bishop of Southwark from 1989 to 1991 and an Assistant Bishop of Bristol from 1992.

(In 1977 the Archdeacons' stalls were discontinued, the stall of the Archdeacon of Wilts being used for the prebend of Upavon.)

UPAVON

Prebend:- The church of Upavon in Wiltshire was already in the possession of the Norman abbey of St Wandrille when it was created a prebend by Herbert Poore, Bishop of Sarum 1194-1217. The Abbots of St Wandrille became canons of the cathedral, probably in exchange for a grant to the cathedral of the churches of Whitchurch, Sherston and Wilsford. The prebend consisted of the church of Upavon, the chapel of Charlton and part of the chapel of Rushall, all in Wilts, as well as income from the churches of Boughton and Moulton in Northamptonshire, and Bridport in Dorset. The Prior of Upavon acted as the proctor of the Abbot.

In 1423 the priory of Upavon, together with the prebend, was granted to the priory of Ivychurch in Wiltshire which itself passed to the Crown at the dissolution of the monasteries. In 1997 it was decided to revive this and three other titular prebends, using the Archdeacons' stalls for this purpose.

Stall: This being a return stall, there is no statuette, nor shield.

Psalter:- The portion of scripture allotted to the prebend is Isaiah 12 and Isaiah 38 v 10.

Holders of the prebend:-

The Abbot of St Wandrille for the time being (c1226-1423).

The Prior of Ivychurch for the time being (1423-c.1540).

Philip Rigby Rounds (1977-1989) was Vicar of Laverstock from 1956 to 1967 and Rector of Wyke Regis from 1967 until his retirement in 1989.

Philip David Slater (1991-) was Vicar of Bulford, Figheldean and Milston from 1982 to 1993, Vicar of Avon Valley from 1993 to 1995 and Rural Dean of Avon from 1985 to 1995. He became Vicar of the Close in 1995.

TORLETON

Prebend:- The manor of Torleton, sometimes called Tarlton or Torlington, is in Gloucestershire. It was given to the cathedral by Walter of Salisbury some time after 1142. The prebend consisted of the chapel of Torleton in the parish of Rodmarton.

Stall: This being a return stall, there is no statuette, nor shield.

Psalter:- The portion of the psalter allotted to the prebend is Psalms 132, 133, 134, 135, 136 and 137.

Holders of the prebend:-

Geoffrey of Devon (c.1226/7-c.1244).

Hugh Lavent (c.1284).

Geoffrey de Pecorariis (?-1311) exchanged the prebend in 1311 with John de Everdon for the prebend of Wrottesley in Tettenhall royal free chapel, Staffordshire.

John de Everdon (1311-1322) was Baron of the Exchequer in 1307, Chancellor of Lincoln in 1308 and Dean of Wolverhampton in 1311. He exchanged this prebend in 1322 with Vitalis de Testa for the dignity of Dean of St Paul's and the prebend of Newington in St Paul's.

Vitalis de Testa (1322-1346) received the prebend by exchange in 1322 and despite royal grants to others, he continued to hold it until exchanging it in 1346 with John de Leche for the prebend of Hova Ecclesia at Chichester.

John de Brian (1343) received the prebend of Torleton by royal grant in 1343 but a grant was subsequently made to John de Makelesfeld. He was nominated to the prebend of Grantham Borealis in 1350 but a royal grant of that prebend was made to William de Retford.

John de Makelesfeld (1343-1344) received a royal grant of this prebend in both 1343 and 1344 but they were revoked in 1344.

John de Lech (1346-1361) DCnL, received the prebend by exchange and died in 1361.

William Benet (1361-?).

John Wormonhale (1366-1369) DCL.

William Loring (?-1416) was a Canon Residentiary and both a theologian and lawyer. He repaired and extended his house in the Close, known as 'Hemingsby'.

Edmund Dutton (1416) held the prebends of Torleton in 1416 and Grantham Borealis from 1416 to 1450, exchanging the latter with John Reedhill in 1450 for a prebend in St Chad's collegiate church, Shrewsbury.

Thomas Burton (1416-1427) BCn&CL, held the prebend of Torleton from 1416 to 1427 when he exchanged it with William Ingram for the prebend of Moreton and Whaddon in Hereford.

William Ingram (1427-1435) was a Canon Residentiary and Comunar in 1456. He held the prebends of Torleton from 1427 to 1435 and Highworth from 1435 to 1464. He died in 1464.

William Prentys (1435-1436) DTh, held the prebend of Torleton from 1435 to 1436 when he exchanged it with William Croucheston for the precentorship of St Mary's, Southampton.

William Croucheston (1436-1438) DCL, died in 1438.

Fulk Bermyngham (1438) held the prebends of Torleton in 1438, Fordington & Writhlington from 1438 to 1443, Bedwin from 1443 to 1459 and Teynton Regis from 1459 to 1461 exchanging the last with Roger Keys for Netherbury in Ecclesia which he held from 1461 until resigning in 1464.

John Depeden (1438-1457) held stalls at Chichester and in 1449 at Windsor. He was Registrar of the Order of The Garter.

William Mitchell (1457-1463) BCL, died in 1463.

Henry Sharp (1463-1468) DCL, held the prebends of Torleton from 1463 to 1468 and Wilsford & Woodford from 1468 to 1489. He died in 1489.

Edward Pownyngs (1468-1484) BCL, died in 1484.

William Guyon (1484-1493) BCnL, died in 1494.

Thomas Burchold (1494-?) BCnL.

Henry Wilcocks (?-1518) DCL, died in 1518.

Richard Gardiner (1518) MA, held the prebends of Stratford from 1507 to 1518 and Torleton in 1518. He died in 1518.

William Fleshmonger (1518-1541) DCnL, died in 1541.

William Capon (1541-1550) DTh, was a brother of John Salcot (or Capon), Bishop of Sarum 1539-1557. He was Master of Jesus College, Cambridge in 1517 and chaplain to Cardinal Wolsey. He held a stall at Wells in 1537 and was Archdeacon of Anglesea in 1543. He died in 1550.

Edward Keble (1550-1554) MA, was a Canon Residentiary from 1551 to 1554. Despite rival claims on behalf of Thomas Heskins, he held the prebend of Torleton from 1550 until being deprived of it in 1554.

Thomas Heskins (1554-1558) DD, was Vicar of Bricklesworth who held the prebend of Torleton from 1554 to 1558, was Chancellor of Sarum from 1558 to 1559 and a Canon Residentiary from 1559 to 1571. He had been appointed by Queen Mary I in 1558 to be a preacher in the diocese during the vacancy in the see. This was during her struggle with the Pope over his attempt to appoint Cardinal Peto to the see of Sarum. He was deprived of the dignity in 1559 for refusing to acknowledge the supremacy of Queen Elizabeth I and retired to Flanders.

Henry Hervie (1558-1571/2) LLD.

John Ebden (1572-1612) DD, was probably the same person who held a stall at St Paul's and was Archdeacon of Winchester from 1571 to 1575.

William Harward (1612-1623) MA, died on 25 June 1623.

Edward Davenant (1623) DD, held the prebends of Torleton in 1623, Ilfracombe from 1624 to 1632 and Chisenbury & Chute from 1632 to 1634. He was Treasurer of Sarum from 1634 to 1680, Rector of Poulshot and in 1625 of Gillingham. He was appointed by his uncle, John Davenant, Bishop of Sarum 1621-1641, to the Archdeaconry of Berks from 1631 to 1634 and died in 1680 at the age of 84.

William Hicks (1623-1637) MA, died in 1637.

John Gandy (1637-1672) MA, was a Fellow of Oriel College, Oxford and Chaplain to John Davenant, Bishop of Sarum 1621-1641. He died in 1672.

Robert Frampton (1672-1683) was borne at Pimperne, educated at the free school at Gillingham and held livings at both Fontmell and Okeford Fitzpaine. He held a stall at Gloucester and was Dean there in 1673 and Bishop in 1680. He was deprived as a non-juror, having previously been one of the seven bishops sent to the Tower in the time of King James II.

John Stubbs (1683-1699) MA, held the prebends of Gillingham Minor in 1682 and Torleton from 1683 to 1699. He died in 1699.

Richard Barford (1699-1735) was Rector of Chilmark. He died in 1735 and was buried in Wilton.

Nicholas Webb (1735-1775) MA, was Vicar of Downton from 1721 to 1775 and held stalls at both Lincoln and St Pauls. He died on 15 January 1775 and was commemorated at Downton.

Charles Jasper Selwyn (1775-1794) MA, died on 10 September 1794.

Browne Grisdale (1794-1814) DD, held the prebends of Stratford in 1794 and Torleton from 1794 to 1814. He died in 1814.

George Frederick Nott (1814-1841) MA, DD, FSA,was a Fellow of All Souls, an author on 16c. literature, a translator from Italian and Bampton Lecturer in 1802. He held a stall at Chichester in 1802, was Vicar of Broadwindsor from 1808 to 1813, held a stall at Winchester in1810 and died on 25 October 1841.

John George Majendie (1841-1842) BD, was Rector of Heddington and died on 2 November 1842.

Walter Kerr Hamilton (1843-1854) DD, was in 1833 a Fellow of Merton College, Oxford. In 1834 he held a stall at Wells, becoming a Canon Residentiary, with the house of Leadenhall, and Treasurer of Sarum from 1841 to 1843 and Precentor of Sarum from 1843 to 1854, also holding the prebend of Torleton from 1843 to 1854. He was Bishop of Sarum from 1854 until his death on 1 August 1869. Whilst at Sarum he founded Salisbury Theological College and contributed to the debate on cathedral reform. He was buried in the cathedral beside his predecessor, Edward Denison, Bishop of Sarum 1837-1854.

Robert Bickersteth (1854) MA, held the prebend of Torleton in 1854. He was Treasurer of Sarum and a Canon Residentiary from 1854 to 1857 and Bishop of Ripon from 1857 to 1884. He died on 15 April 1884.

Anthony Huxtable (1854-1883) MA, was Rector of Sutton Waldren from 1834 to 1871. He was Archdeacon of Dorset in 1862 for only nine months before resigning. He died on 12 December 1883

William Hector Lyon (1884-1911) MA, was Rector of Oborne from 1854 to 1868, Perpetual Curate of Castleton from 1854 to 1908 and Vicar of Sherborne with Castleton from 1868 to 1908. He died on 30 August 1911.

John Colvile Morton Mansel-Pleydell (1911-1938) MA, was Vicar of Sturminster Newton from 1899 to 1915 and Rural Dean of Shaftesbury from 1903 to 1915. He died in 1938.

Ernest Cross (1938-1951) MA, was Vicar Choral, also Domestic Chaplain and Private Secretary to St Clair George Alfred Donaldson, Bishop of Sarum 1921-1935, from 1920 to 1932. He was a lecturer at Sarum Theological College from 1924 to 1933, a Proctor in Convocation from 1931 to 1935 and was Rector of East Knoyle from 1932 to 1951. He died in 1956.

Wilfred Thomas Clayton (1951-1964) AKC, was Vicar of Bulford from 1916 to 1954 and of Alderbury from 1954 to 1960.

John Bertram Phillips (1965-1970) MA, DD, author, broadcaster and translator of the *New Testament in Modern English*, was in the diocese from 1955 to 1964, held a stall at Chichester from 1957 to 1960 and died on 21 July 1982.

Kenneth Walter Meiklejohn (1971-1975) MA, BD, was Rector of St Peter and All Saints, Dorchester from 1960 to 1973, and Rural Dean of Dorchester from 1967 until his retirement in 1975.

Frederick Paul Preston Goddard (1975-1987) MA, was Vicar of Sherborne with Castleton and Lillington from 1969 to 1987 and Rural Dean of Sherborne from 1973 to 1977. He retired in 1987.

William Andrew Matthews (1988-) MA, was Priest-in Charge of Winsley from 1973 to 1975, Vicar of Winsley from 1975 to 1981, Vicar of Bradford-on-Avon from 1981 and Rural Dean of Bradford from 1984 to 1994.

UFCOMB
(olim Bedwin)

Prebend:- The church of Great Bedwin in Wiltshire, was held by Bristoard the priest in 1086 and by his father in 1066. It was given to the canons by Osmund, Bishop of Sarum 1078-1099, in 1091. The prebend, which was probably in existence by c.1150, consisted of the churches of both Great and Little Bedwin. A mill at Ford and land at Stoke may have been subsequently added to the prebend.

The prebend of Bedwin was dissolved by Act of Parliament in 1543, it having been surrendered by John Salcot, Bishop of Sarum 1539-1557, to King Henry VIII who granted it, together with the patronage of the parish church of Ufcomb in Devon, to the Earl of Hertford, presumably on condition that a prebend be formed out of it.

This stall was endowed with £1,000 under the Will of Miss Helen Mary Kingsbury, who died 20 February 1929, in memory of her father, the Revd Canon Thomas Luck Kingsbury, Prebendary of Ufcomb 1875-1899.

Stall: This being a return stall, there is no statuette, nor shield.

Psalter:- The portion of the psalter allotted to the prebend is Psalms 29, 30 and 31.

Holders of the prebend of Bedwin:-

Herbert (c.1170/1184).

Herbert of Bedwyn (c.1226/7-c.1258).

Thomas de Wickhampton (alias de Grano) (c.1284) was Archdeacon of Sarum c.1275 to c.1307 and died between January 1307 and March 1309.

Peter of Savoy (?-1312) died in September 1312 while holding the prebend.

Nicholas Tyngewicke (1312-?) MA, held the prebend of Major Pars Altaris from 1309 to 1312 and in 1312 was appointed to the prebend of Bedwin. He was in possession of Bedwin in 1320 despite the appointment of both Rigaud and Bertrand de Asserio.

Rigaud de Asserio (1312-1319) was appointed to the prebend in 1312 and received a royal grant in 1319. He became Bishop of Winchester in the same year.

Bertrand de Asserio (1319-?) received a royal grant of the prebend in 1319, upon Rigaud de Asserio becoming Bishop of Winchester. He was appointed in 1321, had the grant revoked in 1322 and was licensed to prosecute his claims in 1331.

Robert de Taunton (1333-1335) received the prebend by royal grant in 1333 and had died by 22 February 1335.

Richard Bentworth (1337-1338) DCL, became Bishop of London in 1338 and Chancellor of England.

John de Gynewell (1338-1347) became Bishop of Lincoln in 1347 and is believed to have died on 5 August 1532.

John de Welborne (1347-1366) was deprived of the prebend by the Pope on 13 October 1366.

John Cheyne (1366-?) held the prebend of Bedwin from 1366 to 1373?. He received the prebend of Chardstock in 1373 by exchange but was reported to have died abroad by November 1390. Despite counter claims, he still held the prebend when he died in 1406.

Nicholas Wykeham (1388-1407) Lic.CL, was Principal of Hart Hall, Oxford. He held the prebend of Bedwin from 1388 to 1407, became Archdeacon of Winchester in 1372 and was Warden of New College, Oxford c.1379. He was Archdeacon of Wilts from 1388 to 1407 and died in 1407.

Robert Uppy (1407).

John Wakering (1407) held the prebend of Bedwin in 1407, exchanging it in the same year with Walter Medford for the prebend of Fordington & Writhlington which he held from 1407 to 1415. He became Bishop of Norwich in 1416.

Walter Medford (1407-1423) BCL, was Archdeacon of Dorset in 1397, Chancellor of Sarum from 1402 to 1404 and a brother of Richard Medford, Bishop of Sarum 1396 to 1407. In 1404 he exchanged the dignity with his successor for the Archdeaconry of Sarum and the prebend of Fordington & Writhlington, exchanging a few days later for the Archdeaconry of Berks. He probably exchanged this Archdeaconry with Peter Alcobasso for the deanery of Wimborne in 1417. He held the prebends of Major Pars Altaris from 1396 to 1397, Yetminster Prima in 1397, Faringdon from 1397 to 1400, having been excommunicated but later absolved, when he exchanged this prebend for the treasurership of St Paul's. He held the prebend of Netherbury in Ecclesia in 1401, followed by the prebend of Preston, which he exchanged with Richard Derham for the prebend of Netherbury in Ecclesia in 1402. He held the prebends of Fordington & Writhlington from 1404 to 1407 and Bedwin from 1407 until his death in 1423.

Richard de Cordon (or Brown) (1423) DCL, was appointed in 1423 but Simon de Teramo received the prebend.

Simon de Teramo (1423-1425) held the prebend from 1423 until resigning in 1425.

Nicholas Bildeston (1425-1435) DCL, held the prebend of Bedwin from 1425 to 1435. Whilst holding the rectory of Bishopstone from 1423 to 1441, he was also Archdeacon of Winchester and Dean of Sarum from 1435 until his death on 31 May 1441.

Thomas Bekyngton (1435-1443) DCL, held the prebends of Ruscomb from 1424 to 1435 and Bedwin from 1435 to 1443 when he became Bishop of Bath & Wells.

Fulk Bermyngham (1443-1459) held the prebends of Torleton in 1438, Fordington & Writhlington from 1438 to 1443, Bedwin from 1443 to 1459, Teynton Regis from 1459 to 1461 exchanging the last with Roger Keys for Netherbury in Ecclesia in 1461 until resigning in 1464.

Richard Whitby (1459-1462) BCn&CL, was Treasurer of Sarum from 1462 to 1494 and held the prebends of Slape from 1451 to 1457, Chisenbury & Chute from 1457 to 1459 and Bedwin from 1459 to 1462. He was a Canon Residentiary and not infrequently was locum tenens of the Dean. He died in 1494 and was buried in the chapel of St Edmund in the cathedral.

Peter de Testa (1462-1467) died in 1467.

Robert Kirkham (1467-1471) was Precentor of Sarum, also holding the prebend of Bedwin, from 1467 to 1471. He was Master of the Rolls in 1462 and died in 1471.

Hugh Pavy (1471-1485) BCL, held the prebends of Grimston from 1467 to 1471, becoming a Canon Residentiary in 1471, and Bedwin from 1471 to 1485. In 1479 he became Archdeacon of Wilts and in 1485 Bishop of St David's, while continuing to hold his Archdeaconry.

Christopher Urswick (?-1522) was Warden of King's Hall, Oxford, resigning in 1488 when he became Dean of York. He was Archdeacon of Richmond in 1493 and Archdeacon of Wilts from 1493 to 1522, during which time he became Dean of Windsor in 1495, Archdeacon of Huntingdon in 1496 and Archdeacon of Winchester in 1501, holding a stall at Southwell in 1509. He held the prebend of Bedwin from ? to 1522 and was Chaplain and Almoner to King Henry VII and to the Countess of Richmond.

Thomas Winter (1522-1529) was said to be a son of Cardinal Wolsey, obtaining before he was of age the prebend of Bedwin from 1522 to 1529, the Archdeaconries of Richmond, Suffolk and Cornwall and the Deanery of Wells. He was Chancellor of Sarum from ? to 1530. At the time of Wolsey's fall he gave up or lost most of his dignities.

Peter Vannes (1529-1543) BTh, held the prebends of Grantham Australis from 1528 to 1529 and Bedwin, as additional to his deanery, from 1529 to 1543. He was Dean of Sarum from 1536 to 1563 and on Bedwin being dissolved by Act of Parliament in 1543, he held the prebend of Shipton from 1544 to 1563 and died early in 1563.

Holders of the prebend of Ufcomb:-

John Warner (1554-1565) DM, was Regius Professor of Medicine and Warden of All Souls, Oxford in 1536. He held stalls at St Paul's in 1547 and Winchester in 1549, and was in succession the Archdeacon of Cleveland and of Ely. He was Dean of Winchester in 1559 and died in March 1565.

Thomas White (1565-1571) DCL, held the prebends of Yatesbury from 1553 to 1565 and Ufcomb from 1565 to 1571. He was Warden of New College, Oxford from 1553 to 1573, Chancellor of Sarum from 1571 to 1588, Archdeacon of Berks from 1557 to 1588 and was Chancellor of the Diocese. He died on 12 June 1588 and was buried in the Morning Chapel of the cathedral.

Adrian Hawthorne (1571-1577) BD.

William Hayte (1577-1589) MA, died in 1589.

John Bolde (1589-1602) DD, was a Canon Residentiary from 1570 to 1602 and held the prebends of Alton Borealis from 1564 to 1589 and Ufcomb from 1589 to 1602. He died in 1602.

Christopher Perin (1602-1612) MA, died on 13 October 1612 and is commemorated in Winchester cathedral.

Nicholas Fuller (1612-1623) MA, was secretary to Bishops Horne and Watson of Winchester. He was Rector of Allington (Wilts) in 1584 and died in 1623, being buried at Allington .

Thomas Clarke (1623-1634) DD, resigned the prebend in 1634.

Thomas Clarke (1634-1683) MA, was Rector of Manningford Abbots from 1624 to 1683, although ejected before 1658 but restored in 1660. He died in 1683 at Manningford Abbots where he was buried.

John Hinton (1683-1691) held the prebends of Ufcomb from 1683 to 1691 and Grimston from 1691 to 1720. He died in 1720.

Richard Bowman (1691-1692) BCL, held the prebends of Bishopstone from 1681 to 1691 and Ufcomb from 1691 to 1692. He died in 1692 and was buried at Potterne.

Abraham Brooksbank (1692-1711) MA, died in 1711.

Francis Eyre (1711-1738) MA, was a Canon Residentiary from 1720 to 1738 He died on 28 October 1738 and was buried in the cathedral.

John Fountayne (1739-1802) MA, held a stall at Windsor. He died on 14 February 1802.

John Montgomery (1802) MA, held the prebend of Ruscomb from 1799 to 1802 and Ufcomb in 1802. He died in 1802.

John Frederick Browning (1802-1823) DD, held the prebends of Warminster in 1802 and Ufcomb from 1802 to 1823. He died on 19 August 1823.

Frederick Browning (1823-1858) BD, died on 3 December 1858

Thomas Stanton (1859-1875) was Rector of Shaftesbury in 1846 and Vicar of Burbage in 1852. He held the prebend of Ufcomb from 1859 to 1875, was Archdeacon of Wilts from 1868 to 1874 and died in 1875.

Thomas Luck Kingsbury (1875-1899) MA, was a theologian, Perpetual Curate of Savernake from 1854 to 1861 and of Easton Royal from 1869 to 1875. He was Vicar of Burbage from 1875 to 1879 and of Kingston Deverill from 1879 to 1885. He was Vicar of Coombe Bissett from 1885 to 1892. He was a Proctor in Convocation and contributed largely to the repair of the cathedral tower and spire. He died on 4 December 1899. (In 1929 the prebend was endowed by Miss Kingsbury in her father's memory.)

Charles Leslie Dundas (1900-1929) was Vicar of Charminster with Stratton from 1895 to 1914. He was Archdeacon of Dorset from 1902 to 1927, Vicar of Milton Abbas from 1914 to 1917 and a Canon Residentiary from 1914 to 1928. He resigned the prebend in 1929 on it being endowed by Miss Kingsbury and died on 17 March 1932.

Thomas John Woodall (1929-1940) was Chaplain to Sarum Infirmary from 1888 to 1894, Chaplain to the Earl of Radnor from 1894 to 1900 and Vicar of Britford from 1894 to 1929. He was Chaplain to Sarum Workhouse from 1895 to 1929 and Rural Dean of Chalke from 1923 to 1930. He held the prebends of Alton Australis from 1924 to 1929 and Ufcomb from 1929 to 1940. He died in 1940.

Herbert William Allen (1940-1944) BA, ARCO, was Curate in Charge of Broadstone, Canford Magna, from 1901 to 1904 and Rector of South Perrott with Mosterton from 1904 to 1917. He was Vicar of St Paul's, Fisherton Anger, from 1917 to 1930, Rural Dean of Wilton from 1929 to 1930 and Vicar of Alderbury from 1936 to 1940. He was Succentor of Sarum from 1938 to 1944 and held the prebends of Winterbourne Earls from 1925 to 1940 and Ufcomb from 1940 to 1944. He was Vicar of the Close from 1940 until his death in 1944.

Thomas Haworth Jervis (1945-1955) MA, was Vicar of Rowde from 1804 to 1811 and was Vicar of Alderbury from 1911 to 1924. He was Rector of Woodborough from 1924 and Rural Dean of Cannings from 1927. He held the prebend of Yetminster Secunda from 1932 to 1945 when he became Vicar of the Close and held the prebend of Ufcomb from 1945 to 1955. He died in 1955.

Francis Earle Trotman (1956-1959) MA, was Vicar of Mere from 1909 to 1927 and was Rural Dean of Heytesbury from 1925 to 1927. He was Rector of Long Bredy with Little Bredy from 1927 to 1947 and was Rural Dean of Abbotsbury from 1929 to 1947. He was Vicar of the Close from 1956 to 1959. He held the prebends of Warminster from 1930 to 1956 and Ufcomb from 1956 to 1959. He died in 1959.

Lindsay Bartlett (1960-1968) Lic.Th, was a Chaplain to the Forces from 1918 to 1919, Vicar of Preshute from 1920 to 1931 and Rural Dean of Marlborough from 1930 to 1931. He was Rector and Rural Dean of Bridport from 1931 to 1947, Rector of Fugglestone with Bemerton from 1947 to 1956 and Rural Dean of Wilton from 1954 to 1964. He held the prebends of Yetminster Prima from 1940 to 1960 and Ufcomb, while Vicar of the Close, from 1960 to 1968. He died in 1968.

Philip Humphrey Hall (1968-1980) was Vicar of Ramsbury with Axford from 1938 to 1947. He was Rector of Bishopstone with Stratford Tony from 1951 to 1965, held the prebend of Bishopstone from 1960 to 1968, was Chaplain of Newbridge Hospital, Sarum, from 1965 to 1970 and held the prebend of Ufcomb, while Vicar of the Close from 1968 to 1980.

Dudley Alban Hodges (1980-1989) MA, was a Canon Residentiary and Precentor of Lichfield from 1965 until retiring in 1976. He was Vicar of the Close, holding the prebend of Ufcomb from 1987 to 1989. He died in November 1994.

John Curtiss Whettem (1991-1992) MA, was Team Rector of Swanborough from 1980 to 1992 and Rural Dean of Pewsey from 1984 to 1989. He retired in 1992.

Clive Ronald Franklin Cohen (1992 -) ACIB, became Rector of Winterslow in 1985 and was Rural Dean of Alderbury from 1989 to 1993.

TEYNTON REGIS

Prebend:- Teynton Regis, sometimes described as Teynton Regis cum Yalmeton et Preston, is near Plympton, in Devon. Serlo, 'Collector of Devon', gave the churches of Kingsteignton, Harberton, East Allington and West Allington to the cathedral. This was confirmed by Pope Eugenius III in 1146 when the church of Kenton was added. In c.1226, the prebend consisted of the church of Kingsteignton with the chapel of Highweek and the church of East Allington with a chapel.

Canopy statuette and shield:- **Giles of Bridport** was Archdeacon of Berks from 1237 to c.1255 and Dean of Wells in 1253. He was Bishop of Sarum from 1257 to 1262 and founded de Vaux College, Sarum in 1262. It was during his episcopate that the present cathedral was completed. He died on 13 December 1262 and was buried "in the south side of the choir in the chapel of St Mary Magdalen, under an arch that has a beautiful white marble tomb, wrought as a model of the outside of the tower". (Fig. 28.)

Stall plate:- Engraved "The canopy of this stall was presented by the parishioners of Southbroom in memory of their vicar, William Gardiner, Canon 1910 - 1925".

Blazon:- Azure a cross between four bezants or. [On a blue shield, a gold cross between four gold coins.]

Psalter:- The portion of the psalter allotted to the prebend is Psalms 122, 123, 124, 125, 126, 127, 128, 129, 130 and 131.

Holders of the Prebend :-

Richard (c.1122).

Martin de Pateshull (c.1224/28-c.1229) was a Justice to King Henry III from 1218 to 1229. He held a stall at Lincoln, was Archdeacon of Norfolk by 1228 and became Dean of St Paul's. He died on 14 November 1229.

Roger of Sarum (c.1236-1244) was Precentor of Sarum from c.1227 to 1244. He held the prebends of Netheravon from c.1226/27 to 1236 and Teynton Regis from c.1236 to 1244, the latter being joined to the dignity of Precentor of Sarum for a time. He was consecrated as Bishop of Bath & Wells in 1244, although the Chapter of Wells refused to concur with his election and, dying on 21 December 1247, he was buried in Bath.

Andrew of Lavagna (1244-1270) was a nephew of Pope Innocent IV. He was Precentor of Sarum and held the prebend of Teynton Regis from 1244 to 1270. He was held a stall at Chartres and was provost of estates in Normandy. He died in February 1270.

Stephen de Gurunvile (1270-1271) held a stall at Hereford and was Precentor of Sarum from 1270 to 1272. He briefly held the prebend of Teynton Regis, then joined to this dignity, from 1270 to 1271. He then held the prebend of Grantham Borealis from 1271 to 1272 and had died by 30 August 1272.

William de la Corner (1270-1274) had been elected Archbishop of Dublin in 1279 but the election was set aside. He was a papal chaplain, proctor and royal envoy and held the prebends of Teynton Regis from 1270 to 1274 and Highworth from c.1284 to 1288, and was Precentor of York and Archdeacon of Northumberland. He failed to be elected to the see of Sarum in May 1288 but was successful six months later. He was Bishop of Sarum from 1289 until his death probably on 10 October 1291. He was buried in the middle of the quire 'nearly under the eagle'.

John of Leicester (1274-1275) held the prebends of Teynton Regis from 1274 to 1275 and Hurstbourne & Burbage from 1275 to c.1288) He was the Chancellor to Robert Wickhampton, Bishop of Sarum 1274-1284, and may have died in c.1290.

William de la Wyle (1275-1297) was Archdeacon of Dorset from 1287 to 1297. He had died by 21 May 1297.

John of Binsted (1297-1308) was the Controller of the King's Wardrobe. He renounced holy Orders in 1308 and married in or before 1311.

Walter Hervy (1314) held the prebends of Warminster in 1304, Beminster Secunda from 1304 to 1314, Teynton Regis in 1314 and Beminster Secunda again in 1326.

Robert de Jorz (?-1314) exchanged this prebend in 1314 with Robert de Bluntesdon for the church of Skirpenbeck, Yorks.

Robert de Bluntesdon (1314-?) held the prebend of Teynton Regis from 1314, still occupying it in 1320. He was Subdean of Sarum from April until September 1321. With the office he held the church of "Caundel Haddon". He was Rector of Berwick St John in 1331.

John de Fieschi (1334-1349) became Bishop of Vercelli in 1349.

William Dighton (?-1391) was Chaplain to King Richard II and held a stall at St Paul's. He died in 1391.

William de Waltham (1391-1398) exchanged the prebend in 1398 with Thomas Feriby for the prebend of St Martin's altar in Beverley collegiate church, Yorks.

Thomas Feriby (1398-1432) died in 1432.

John Castell (1432) DTh, held the prebends of Yetminster Prima from 1428 to 1432, Teynton Regis in 1432 and Bere & Cherminster from 1432 to 1436. He was Archdeacon of Berks from 1431 to 1432?

Robert Beaumont (1432-1459) BCn&CL, held the prebends of Major Pars Altaris in 1431, Beminster Secunda from 1431 to 1432 and Teynton Regis from 1432 until his death in 1459.

Fulk Bermyngham (1459-1461) held the prebends of Torleton in 1438, Fordington & Writhlington from 1438 to 1443, Bedwin from 1443 to 1459, Teynton Regis from 1459 to 1461 exchanging the last with Roger Keys for Netherbury in Ecclesia in 1461 until resigning in 1464.

Roger Keyes (1461-1477) BCnL, held the prebend of Blewbery from 1449 to 1457, exchanging it with John Druell for Netherbury in Ecclesia, which he held from 1457 until 1461 when he exchanged it with Fulk Bermyngham for the prebend of Teynton Regis, holding the last until 1477, in which year he died.

Thomas Austell (1477-1515) BCnL, died in 1515.

William Gray (1515-1522) MA, would appear not to have been ordained before 1550 when he became Archdeacon of Berks, holding the dignity until 1522. He held the prebends of Grantham Borealis from 1508 to 1514, Horton in 1514, Faringdon from 1514 to 1515 and Teynton Regis from 1515 to 1522. He held a stall at Hereford from 1512 to 1522. He died in 1522 and asked to be buried in Ramsbury church.

Edward Finch (1522-1524) DM, was well endowed with prebends holding in succession those of Yatesbury from 1514 to 1515, Chardstock from 1515 to 1517, Wilsford & Woodford in 1517, Fordington & Writhlington from 1517 to 1518, Grimston from 1518 to 1519, Faringdon from 1519 to 1521 exchanging the last with William Webbe for the church of Ross on Wye, Hereford. He then held the prebends of Bishopstone from 1521 to 1522, Teynton Regis from 1522 to 1524 and Bere & Cherminster from 1524 to 1539. He was Archdeacon of Wilts from 1522 until 1539. He died in 1539 and was buried in the cathedral.

Henry Rawlyns (1524-1526) BCL, was well provided with prebends. He held Yatesbury from 1513 to 1514, Grantham Australis from 1514 to 1519 and Coombe & Harnham 1519 to 1521. He resigned the last in May 1521, was succeeded by Cuthbert Tunstall who then became Dean of Sarum, and was again collated to the prebend later in the same year. The prebend then passed to Richard Pace but was assumed by Henry Rawlyns for the third time in 1523. He then held Faringdon from 1523 to 1524, Hurstbourne & Burbage in 1524 and Teynton Regis, together with the Archdeaconry of Sarum from 1524 to 1526. He was Rector of Christian Malford, died in 1526 and was buried in the cathedral near the Audley chantry.

Stephen Gardiner (?-1531) DCn&CL, was appointed by Cardinal Wolsey, acting on behalf of Lorenzo Campegio, Bishop of Sarum 1525-1534. He was secretary to Wolsey, ambassador to Rome and defended King Henry VIII in his book *De Vera Obedientia*. He resigned the prebend in 1531 to become Bishop of Winchester. He died in 1555.

John Olyver (1531-1552) DCL, died in 1552.

Leonard Bilson (1552-1571/2) MA, was a Canon Residentiary from 1560 to 1561?. He was put in the pillory in 1562 and was in prison in 1568 but he still held the prebend in 1571.

Tobias Matthew (1572-1589) DD, was Precentor of Sarum in 1583. He held the prebend of Teynton Regis from 1572 to 1589, became President of St John's College, Oxford and Dean of Christ Church in 1557, Dean of Durham in 1583, Bishop of Durham in 1595 and Archbishop of York in 1606. He was one of the divines employed in the Hampton Court Conference.

Samuel Proctor (1589-1638/9) MA, died by 5 January 1639.

Humphrey Henchman (1639-1660) DD, was a Fellow of Clare Hall, Cambridge. He was a son-in-law of Robert Tounson, Bishop of Sarum 1620-1621, becoming Precentor from 1623 to 1660 and Canon Residentiary from 1633 to 1660 (although dismissed during the Commonwealth) and holding in succession the prebends of Yatesbury from 1623 to 1629, Grantham Australis from 1629 to 1639 and Teynton Regis from 1639 to 1660. He helped King Charles II to escape after the battle of Worcester; personally escorting him to Heale House and meeting him again at Stonehenge. He became Bishop of London and Lord Almoner in 1663. He died on 7 October 1675 at the age of 83 and was buried at Fulham.

Thomas Hyde (1660-1666) DD, held the prebend of Stratford from 1639 to 1660. He was appointed Precentor of Sarum by King Charles II in 1660 serving until 1666, and held the prebend of Teynton Regis from 1660 until his death in 1666.

Gabriel Thistlethwayt (1666-1682) BCL, died in 1682.

Thomas Ward (1682-1696) LLD, was a nephew of Seth Ward, Bishop of Sarum 1667-1689, and in 1679 was ordained deacon and priest on the same day. A month later he received the prebend of Netheravon, holding it from 1679 to 1681. He held the prebends of Gillingham Major from 1681 to 1682 and Teynton Regis from 1682 to 1696. He was Archdeacon of Wilts from 1687 until his death on 20 March 1696. His appointment to a prebendal stall at a very early age and his rapid advancement led to a dispute between Bishop and Dean.

Daniel Whitby (1696-1726) DD, was Precentor of Sarum from 1672 to 1726. He held the prebends of Yatesbury in 1668, Hurstbourne & Burbage from 1668 to 1696 and Teynton Regis from 1696 to 1726. He was Chaplain to Seth Ward, Bishop of Sarum 1667-1689, a Canon Residentiary from 1676 to 1726, and Rector of St Edmund's, Sarum. He caused excitement by publishing the *Protestant Reconciler* and similar writings, which advocated general religious tolerance. This brought upon him the wrath of the authorities, Chief Justice Jeffreys even directing his indictment. He died on 21 March 1726 aged 90.

William Wake (1726-1731) MA, died on 25 September 1731.

Samuel Rolleston (1731-1766) MA, held the prebend of Teynton Regis from 1731 to 1766, was Archdeacon of Sarum from 1732 to 1766 and, as a Canon Residentiary from 1756 to 1766, lived at Leadenhall. He was Rector of St Edmund's, Sarum and from 1745 to 1746 of East Knoyle. He held a stall at Winchester in 1744 and dying on 2 May 1766, was buried in the Cathedral where he is commemorated in the south choir aisle.

Glocester Ridley (1766-1774) BCL, died on 3 November 1774.

Benjamin Spry (1774-1806) MA, held the prebends of Warminster from 1773 to 1774 and Teynton Regis from 1774 to 1806. He died on 1 October 1806.

Jarvis Kenrick (1806-1838) LLB, died on 21 November 1838.

Robert Moore (1841-1865) MA, was Rector of Wimborne St Giles and died on 26 January 1865.

Robert Farquharson (1865-1881) was Rector of Langton Long and died on 13 May 1881.

James John Jacob (1881-1909) MA, was Chaplain to Sarum Infirmary from 1850, Curate in Charge of St Paul's, Fisherton Anger, from 1853 to 1858 and Vicar of Horningsham from 1858 to 1900. He was Rural Dean from 1874 and was Chaplain to the Marquis of Bath. He died on 21 November 1909.

William Gardiner (1910-1925) MA, BD, was Vicar of St Mary, Marlborough from 1887 to 1897 and Rural Dean of Marlborough from 1891 to 1897. He was Vicar of Southbroom from 1897 to 1919 and Rural Dean of Avebury from 1906 to 1919. He died on Good Friday 1925 and the canopy of the stall was presented by the parishioners of Southbroom in his memory.

Arthur Savile Beresford Freer (1925-1936) MA, was Vicar of Gussage All Saints from 1901 to 1936, Rural Dean of Pimperne from 1919 to 1928 and a Proctor in Convocation from 1927 to 1936.

Stephen Montague Douglas Davys (1937-1955) MA, was Vicar of Urchfont with Stert from 1915 to 1929 and Rural Dean of Enford from 1925 to 1929. He was Vicar of North Bradley with Southwick & Brokers Wood from 1929 to 1955.

Percival Sexty (1955-1968) was Chaplain to the Forces from 1916 (mentioned in despatches 1917) to 1918. He was Rector of Evershot with Frome St Quinton & Melbury Bubb from 1923 to 1926, Vicar of Bishop's Lavington (with Little Cheverell to 1958) from 1926 to 1960, Rector of Great Cheverell from 1936 to 1958 and Rural Dean of Devizes from 1953 to 1965. He retired in 1968.

Edward John Townroe (1969-1993) MA, was Warden of King's College, London, at St Boniface College, Warminster from 1956 to 1969 and became a Fellow of King's College in 1959. He retired in 1993.

Colin Michael Day (1994-) BSc, AKC, MA, was Diocesan Adviser on Mission and Evangelism from 1990 to 1995, when he became Vicar of Branksome Park All Saints.

SHIPTON

Prebend:- The church of Bricklesworth, otherwise called Brixworth in Northamtonshire, and Shipton under Wychwood in Oxfordshire, were part of royal manors in the 11.c. Two prebends were created, one before 1099 for G....., the eldest son of Arnulph the falconer and a second before 1116 for his younger son Humphrey. Two prebends were probably in existence by c.1150 but may have been held jointly until full separation between 1226 and 1227. The dependent chapels of Swinbrook, Idbury and Fifield formed part of the Bricklesworth prebend while Shipton under Wychwood with the chapel of Lyneham formed the prebend of Shipton.

It would appear that from an early period the prebend of Shipton was within the gift of the Sovereign who, in 1617, joined it to the Regius Professorship of Civil Law at Oxford. This continued until 1855 when all canonries were placed under the direct patronage of the bishop by Act of Parliament.

Canopy statuette and shield:- **Walter de la Wyle** was Succentor of Sarum from c.1248 to c.1262 and Bishop of Sarum from 1263 until his death on 3 January 1271. In 1269 he founded the College of St Edmund, Sarum for a provost and twelve secular canons. He was buried by the altar in the chapel of St Edmund in the cathedral. (Fig. 29.)

Blazon:- Azure a chevron between three castles or. [On a blue shield, a gold chevron between three gold castles.]

Psalter:- The portion of the psalter allotted to the prebend is Psalms 37, 38 and 39.

Holders of the prebend:-

G...... (c.1099) was the eldest son of Arnulph the falconer who founded the prebend.

Robert of Brimpton (after 1215-c.1222) held the prebend of Shipton from c.1215 to c.1222 and was probably Robert, Canon of Sarum and parson of Shipton, who held the prebend of Bricklesworth from after 1215 to c.1222

Elias Ridel (c.1226/7-c.1236).

Manser (c1247/8) was Rector of Shipton and presumably of this prebend, when making presentation to the vicarage in 1247/48.

William of Brimpton (1267-c.1278/9).

Roger de Fromton (c.1284-c.1297) still held the prebend in July 1297.

John Hoesee (alias Huesey) (1300-1315) had died by 16 November 1315.

William de Brimpton (1315-1324) resigned in 1324.

William Aylmer (1323-?) was nominated in 1323 and had died by October 1328.

Rhys ap Howell (1326) received a royal grant of the prebend in 1326 although Richard Elsfield was also nominated.

Richard de Elsfield (1326) was nominated to the prebend but was prevented from occupying it by a royal writ received the same day.

Edmund de Bereford (1328-?).

James de Beaufort (1354-1358) exchanged a portion of the church of Wighton, Norfolk in 1347 with Thomas de Brembre for the prebend of Stratton and was installed the same day. He exchanged it back however, five months later and Thomas de Brembre was installed the following day. He held the prebend of Shipton from 1354 to 1358. He was Rector of Steeple Lavington and died in 1358.

Robert de Burton (1358-1361) exchanged the prebend of Netherbury in Terra in 1358 with John de Blewbury for the office of deacon in Wilton monastery. He held the prebend of Shipton from 1358 to 1361 and died in 1361.

Thomas de Keynes (1361-1367) died in 1367.

Robert Whitbergh (1367-1389) died in 1389.

Thomas More (1389-1421) was a Fellow of Pembroke Hall, Cambridge, Treasurer to the Queen-Consort and received this prebend from King Richard III. He also held a stall at St Paul's and was Archdeacon of Colchester. He became Dean of St Paul's in 1407 and had died by 4 January 1421.

Robert Rolleston (1422-1428) exchanged the prebend in 1426 with John Bernyngham for the prebend of Wetwang in York but the exchange was apparently ineffective and he resigned the prebend by 1 January 1428.

John Bernyngham (1426) briefly held the prebend on exchange with Robert Rolleston.

Thomas Bouchier (1428-1435) MA, was a son of William, Earl of Ewe and a great grandson of King Edward III. He held the deanery of St Martin le Grand and a stall at Hastings in 1427 and being in his sixteenth year and 'of a race of great nobles' was allowed to take possession of a hospital at York. He became Bishop of Worcester in 1435, was translated to Ely in 1443 and became Archbishop of Canterbury in 1454. He was Lord Chancellor in 1455 and Cardinal-Priest of St Cyriac in 1467. He crowned Kings Edward IV and Richard II, married King Henry VII and dying on 6 April 1486 was buried in Canterbury Cathedral..

John Payne (1435-1436) held the prebends of Shipton from 1435 to 1436 and Beminster Prima from 1436 to 1467. He died in 1467.

Robert Sherrington (1436).

Walter Sherrington (1436-1449) held the prebend of Minor Pars Altaris in 1420, exchanging it with Richard Richman for the prebend of Decem Librarum in Lincoln. He held the prebends of Beminster Prima from 1431 to 1436 and Shipton from 1436 until his death in 1449. He held stalls at York and Chichester, was Chancellor of the Duchy of Lancaster and a Canon Residentiary of St Paul's.

William Westbury (1449-1477) BCL, died in 1477.

Oliver Dinham (1477-1479) MA, resigned in 1479.

Nicholas Goldwell (1479-1506) BCL, died in 1506.

Roger Lupton (1506-1540) DTh, was Provost of Eton and died in 1540.

John London (1540-1543) DCL, held stalls at York and Lincoln. He was Domestic Chaplain to Archbishop Warham, became Warden of New College, Oxford in 1526, later holding a stall at Windsor and became Dean of Osney and of Wallingford. He was a Visitor for the Removing of Images and Relics on the suppression of the monasteries but afterwards changed course and helped to convict several persons who were burnt at Windsor under the Six Articles. He fell into disgrace, was convicted of perjury and died in the Fleet Prison in 1543.

Peter Vannes (1544-1563) BTh, held the prebends of Grantham Australis from 1528 to 1529 and Bedwin, as additional to his deanery, from 1529 to 1543. He was Dean of Sarum from 1536 to 1563 and on Bedwin being dissolved by Act of Parliament in 1543, he held the prebend of Shipton from 1544 to 1563 and died early in 1563.

John Foxe (1563-1587) MA, was a Fellow of Magdalen College, Oxford, but was expelled as a heretic and went abroad in 1545. He returned at the accession of Queen Elizabeth I and was famous as author of *Acts and Monuments (1563)* ('Foxe's Book of Martyrs'). He died on 18 April 1587.

Thomas Paynter (1587-1614) MA, held the prebends of Wilsford & Woodford from 1581 to 1583, Slape from 1583 to 1587 and Shipton from 1587 to 1614. He died in 1614.

George Proctor (1614-1633) MA, died in 1633.

Richard Zouch (1633-1661) DCL, was Regius professor of Civil Law at Oxford and died on 1 March 1661.

Giles Sweit (1661-1672) DCL, was Regius Professor of Civil Law at Oxford and died in 1672.

Thomas Bouchier (1672-1713) DCL, was Regius Professor of Civil Law at Oxford and having resigned c.22 March 1713 was succeeded by his son.

James Bouchier (1714-1736) DCL, succeeded his father to the prebend and the Regius Professorship of Civil Law at Oxford and died on 19 August 1736.

Henry Brooke (1737-1752) DCL, was Regius Professor of Civil Law at Oxford and died on 24 March 1752.

Robert Jenner (1754-1767) DCL, was Regius Professor of Civil Law at Oxford and died in July 1767.

Robert Vansittart (1767-1789) DCL, was Regius Professor of Civil Law at Oxford and died on 31 January 1789.

Thomas Francis Wenman (1789-1796) DCL, was Regius Professor of Civil Law at Oxford and died on 8 April 1796.

French Laurence (1796-1809) DCL, was Regius Professor of Civil Law at Oxford and died on 27 February 1809.

Joseph Phillimore (1809-1855) DCL, was Regius Professor of Civil Law at Oxford and died on 24 February 1855.

Henry Drury (1855-1863) was Vicar of Bremhill in 1845, held the prebend of Shipton from 1855 to 1863, was Chaplain to the House of Commons in 1857 and Archdeacon of Wilts from 1862 to 1863. He died on 25 January 1863.

Charles Onslow (1863-1884) was Priest-Vicar of Wimborne Minster in 1850 and Vicar of Holt from 1870 to 1884.

John Parr (1884-1887) MA, was Vicar of Parkstone from 1858 to 1872 and Rural Dean of Whitchurch. He was Vicar of St Mary's Marlborough and Rural Dean of Marlborough from 1872 to 1887. He died on 9 August 1889 and was buried at Parkstone.

Benjamin Whitefoord (1887-1910) MA, DD, was Principal of Salisbury Theological College from 1883 to 1907 and Vicar of Potterne from 1907 to 1910. He died on 29 November 1910.

Selwyn Blackett (1911-1937) was Rector of Wareham with Arne from 1888 to 1937 and Rural Dean of Purbeck from 1914 to 1929.

Walter John Barton (1937-1949) MA, held the prebend of Shipton from 1937 to 1949 and was Treasurer of Sarum from 1949 until resigning in 1955. He was a Canon Residentiary from 1944 but resigned in 1951 as the donor, believed to be his sister, who had made it financially possible to revive the canonry for seven years had not been able to renew the donation.

Arthur Frederick Smethurst (1949-1953) MA, DPhil, BSc, held the prebend of Shipton from 1949 to 1953. He was Canon Residentiary from 1949 to 1957, Chancellor of Sarum from 1953 to 1956 and Treasurer of Sarum from 1956 until his death on 15 September 1957.

Edward Leslie Seager (1954-1968) MA, was Chaplain to the Forces from 1937 to 1946, Vicar of Gillingham from 1946 to 1979, and of Fifehead Magdalen from 1966 to 1979. He held the prebends of Shipton from 1954 to 1968 and Gillingham Major from 1968 to 1979. He was Rural Dean of Shaftesbury from 1951 to 1956 and Archdeacon of Dorset from 1956 to 1974. He was Rural Dean of Blackmore Vale from 1975 to 1979 and a Team Vicar in the Gillingham Team Ministry in 1979. He died on 2 November 1983.

The Precentor of Sarum for the time being (1968 -)

[**William Hanbury Saumarez Smith** (1987-1992) OBE, MA, Lay Canon, served in the Indian Civil Service from 1935 until the partition of India in 1947. He was Diocesan Secretary of Sarum and Secretary & Treasurer of the Diocesan Board of Finance from 1947 to 1957. He was Secretary of the Central Board of Finance and General Secretary of the Central Administrative Council for the Church's Ministry from 1958 to 1965 and Archbishops' Appointments Secretary from 1965 to 1977. He was a member of the Close Chapter from 1987 to 1992, occupied Shipton as a courtesy stall and died on 28 April 1994.]

[**Janet Mason Henderson** (1993-1997) MA, BD, PGCE, Lay Canon, Lay Reader, held posts in education from 1951 to 1960, was Editorial Assistant SPG/USPG from 1960 to 1966 and was on the staff of Christian Aid from 1966 to 1971. She was Deputy Director of the British Council of Churches Race Relations Unit from 1971 to 1977 and held posts, including Project Co-ordination Manager of the British & Foreign Bible Society. She was a member of the Church Assembly/General Synod from 1965 to 1981 and a Church Commissioner from 1973 to 1978. She served on various diocesan and deanery organisations, including being Lay Chairman of Marlborough Deanery from 1988 to 1996 . She was a member of the Close Chapter from 1993 to 1997 and occupied Shipton as a courtesy stall.]

GILLINGHAM MAJOR
(olim Ramsbury)

Prebend:- Ramsbury in Wiltshire was originally the seat of the ancient bishopric for Wiltshire and Berkshire, which was created c.909. The prebend, which was probably in existence c.1150, consisted of the church of Ramsbury and the chapel of Baydon. This prebend and the prebend of Axford, were dissolved by Act of Parliament of 1545, as a result of an exchange between the Earl of Hertford and John Salcot, Bishop of Sarum 1539-1557, the Bishop receiving the prebend of Gillingham, formerly of Shaftesbury Abbey in Dorset. From this he was required to form two prebends; Gillingham Major replacing Ramsbury and Gillingham Minor replacing Axford.

Canopy statuette and shield:- **Henry of Braunstone** was Archdeacon of Wilts between c.1275 and c.1279, and of Dorset between 1281 and c.1284. He held the prebend of Bere & Cherminster from c.1274 to 1284 and was Dean of Sarum from 1284 to 1287. He held a stall at Exeter and was Bishop of Sarum from 1287 to his death on 11 February 1288. He was buried in the Lady Chapel of the Cathedral. (Fig. 30.)

Blazon:- Quarterly per pale and per chevron or and azure. [A shield divided into four quarters: top left, gold; top right, blue. Bottom left, divided diagonally; top left gold, bottom right blue. Bottom right; divided diagonally, top right blue, bottom left gold.]

Psalter:- The portion of the psalter allotted to the prebend is Psalms 11, 12, 13 and 14.

Holders of the prebend of Ramsbury:-

Robert Coterel (c.1226/27-c.1233).

Thomas of Bridport (c.1284-1296) was a candidate for the see of Sarum in 1288, when William de la Corner, Bishop of Sarum 1289-1291, was elected. He was the Warden of de Vaux College, Sarum in 1289 and at his death by 23 July 1296.

William de Sancto Johanne (1297. 1307-c.1323) held the prebends of Yetminster Prima from ? to 1297 and Ramsbury in 1297 and from 1307 to c.1323. He was fined for non-residence in 1320 and there is a memorial brass to him in Ramsbury church.

William de Grandisson (1325, 1329) held the prebend in 1325 and 1329.

Simon de Montacute (1330-1333) received the prebend by royal grant in 1330 and became Bishop of Worcester in 1333.

William de Lardo (1334-?) was nominated in 1334 but Thomas de Shrewsbury having been appointed, he died in 1343 without possession of the prebend.

Thomas de Shrewsbury (1335) was appointed to the prebend but because Edmund de Beche received a royal grant, he resigned within four months of his appointment.

Edmund de la Beche (1335-?) received the prebend of Ramsbury by royal grant in 1335 but in 1355 there was a papal mandate for his removal and the appointment of John de Stretley. He was Rector of Compton Chamberlain in 1315 and Archdeacon of Berks in 1334 and 1359.

Andrew de Offord (1343-?) DCL, was nominated to the prebend of Ramsbury in 1343, but was still not in possession in 1349. He received a royal grant of the prebend of Netherbury in Ecclesia in 1345 but was not admitted. He was nominated to the prebend of Bedminster & Redcliffe in 1343 but this was subsequently revoked.

John de Stretley (1355-1368/9) DCL, died in 1368 or 1369.

Hugh de Wymondeswold (?-1378) Sch.CL, claimed the prebend of Coombe & Harnham in 1366 and held the prebend of Ramsbury from ? until exchanging it in 1378 with Thomas de Oldington for the prebend of Warthill in York.

Thomas de Oldington (1378-?) held the prebend in 1383.

Richard Wyche (1388-1414).

John Lincoln (1392) received a royal grant of the prebend of Ramsbury in 1392 but this was probably ineffective. He held the prebends of Major Pars Altaris from 1397 to 1404 and Bedminster & Redcliffe from 1404 to 1415. He was a Canon Residentiary and held also stalls at Lincoln and Wells. He died in 1415.

John Hurlegh (1414-1425) BCnL, died in 1425.

Robert Broun (1425-1438) BTh, was Rector of Donhead St Mary from 1399 to 1434 and held the prebends of Coombe & Harnham from 1404 to 1425 and Ramsbury from 1425 to 1438. He died in 1438.

William Estcourt (1438-1447) Sch.Th, is said to have held the prebend of Major Pars Altaris in 1438. He held the prebend of Ramsbury from 1438 until his death to 1447.

John Druell (1447-1449) DCn&CL, held the prebends of Alton Australis from 1441 to 1445, Netheravon from 1445 to 1447, Ramsbury from 1447 to 1449 and Netherbury in Ecclesia from 1449 to 1457, exchanging the last with Roger Keyes for the prebend of Blewbery which he held from 1457 until 1469. He was Rector of Steeple Langford in 1449 and died in 1469.

Thomas Kirkeby (1449-1464) held the prebends of Yatesbury from 1445 to 1446, Warminster from 1446 to 1448, Netheravon from 1448 to 1449, Ramsbury from 1449 to 1464 and Highworth from 1464 to 1476. He also held the prebend of Stanton Berners under the Abbey of Wilton and died in 1476.

Robert Hall (1464-1481) DCnL, held the prebends of Major Pars Altaris from? to 1464 and Ramsbury from 1464 to 1481.

Adrian de Bardis (1481-1493) was a Florentine who held the prebend of Ramsbury from 1481 to 1493 exchanging it and the church of Wroughton with Ralph Heathcott for the prebend of Hurstbourne & Burbage which he held from 1493 to 1519, in which year he died. He was Rector of St Peter's Marlborough and of 'Elyngdon', and held a stall at Lincoln.

Ralph Heathcott (1493-1499) BCn&CL, held the prebends of Chardstock from ? to 1486, Bitton from 1486 to 1487, Faringdon from 1487? to 1492 and Hurstbourne & Burbage from 1492 to 1493, exchanging the last with Adrian de Bardis in 1493 for the church of Wroughton and the prebend of Ramsbury, holding this prebend from 1493 until his death in 1499. He was Rector of St Peter's, Marlborough in 1481.

Richard Mayew (1500-1504) DTh, was President of Magdalen College, Oxford, in 1480 and Archdeacon of Oxford from 1492. He was also Chaplain and Almoner to King Henry VII. He succeeded to the see of Hereford in 1504 and died in 1516.

Bernard Boerio (1505-1514) resigned in 1514.

Robert Audley (1514-1545) held the prebend of Ramsbury from 1514 to 1545 and was Archdeacon of Berks from 1522 to 1545. He died in 1545 and asked to be buried in the cathedral near his uncle Edmund Audley, Bishop of Sarum 1502-1524.

Holders of the prebend of Gillingham Major:-

Richard Vernon (1555-1556) MA, died in 1556.

John FitzJames (1557-1559) MA, was deprived by 10 November 1559.

John Spithoveus (1559-1564) DD, died in 1564.

Henry Ryley (1564-?) BD, was a Canon Residentiary from 1564 until resigning in1571.

Ralph Pickover (1586-1615) MA, held the prebends of Stratford from 1583 to 1586 and Gillingham Major from 1586 to 1615. He was Rector of Winterbourne Gunner and was Archdeacon of Rochester from 1576 to 1593. He would seem to have held a stall at Christ Church, Oxford, in 1580 and was Archdeacon of Sarum and a Canon Residentiary from 1583 to 1615. He died on 8 March 1615 and was buried in the cathedral.

John Jessop (1615-1626) BD, died on 21 February 1626.

John Ryves (1626-1665) BCL, was a son-in-law of Robert Tounson, Bishop of Sarum 1620-1621. He held the prebend of Gillingham Major from 1626 to 1665, was Archdeacon of Berks from 1634-1665 and a Canon Residentiary from 1662 to 1665. He also held a stall at Winchester. He was Rector of Tarrant Gunville where he is commemorated following his death on 19 August 1665.

Charles Pickering (1665-1680) MA, held the prebends of Ilfracombe in 1665 and Gillingham Major from 1665 to 1680. He was Rector of Poulshot, where he was buried following his death in 1680.

Thomas Ward (1681-1682) LLD, was a nephew of Seth Ward, Bishop of Sarum 1667-1689, and in 1679 was ordained deacon and priest in the same day. A month later he received the prebend of Netheravon, holding it from 1679 to 1681. He held the prebends of Gillingham Major from 1681 to 1682 and Teynton Regis from 1682 to 1696. He was Archdeacon of Wilts from 1687 until his death on 20 March 1696. His appointment to a prebendal stall at a very early age and his rapid advancement led to disagreement between Bishop and Dean.

The Hon John Feilding (1682-1698) MA, DD, was the 4th son of the 1st Earl of Desmond. He was a Chaplain to King William III and was Vicar of Piddlehinton. He was a Canon Residentiary from 1680 to 1698 and was Archdeacon of Dorset in the diocese of Bristol from 1683 to 1697. He held the prebends of Yatesbury from 1677 to 1678, Beminster Prima from 1678 to 1682 and Gillingham Major from 1682 to 1698, dying in 1698.

William Craig (1698-1721) MA, died on 19 February 1721.

Gilbert Burnet (1721-1726) MA, was the second son of Gilbert Burnet, Bishop of Sarum 1689-1715. He held the prebends of Beminster Secunda from 1715 to 1721and Gillingham Major from 1721 to 1726. He died on 17 June 1726 and would have attained eminence had he not died young.

John Craig (1726-1732) MA, held the prebends of Durnford from 1708 to 1726 and Gillingham Major from 1726 to 1732. He died in 1732.

Joseph Sager (1732-1757) MA, held the prebends of Warminster from 1726 to 1732 and Gillingham Major from 1732 to 1757. He was a Canon Residentiary from 1726 to 1757 and Archdeacon of Sarum from 1727 until resigning in 1732. He died on 18 July 1757 and was buried in the cathedral.

Newton Ogle (1757-1758) was married to a daughter of John Thomas, Bishop of Sarum 1757-1761 and later Bishop of Winchester. He held the prebends of Gillingham Major from 1757 to 1758, Stratford from 1758 to 1759 and Gillingham Major again from 1759 to 1794. He became Dean of Winchester in 1769 and held the prebend of Stratford from 1794 until his death on 6 January 1804.

John Nichol (1758-1759) MA, died in 1759.

Newton Ogle (1759-1794) see above.

John Savile Ogle (1794-1828) MA, was the son of Newton Ogle and resigned the prebend in 1828. He was a Canon Residentiary from 1812 until resigning in 1826, and also held a stall at Durham.

Edward Challoner Ogle (1828-1869) MA, died on 7 November 1869.

Robert George Swayne (1870-1874) was Rector of St Edmund's, Sarum from 1863 to 1876. He held the prebend of Gillingham Major from 1870 to 1874, was a Canon Residentiary from 1874 to 1894, was Chancellor of Sarum from 1877 until resigning in 1894 and held the prebend of Slape from 1894 to 1895. He died on 22 April 1901.

Charles Tower (1877-1890) was Rector of Chilmark from 1843 to 1880, Rural Dean of Chalke from 1863 to 1872 and Succentor of Sarum from 1869 to 1877. He held the prebend of Gillingham Major from 1877 to 1890. He died on 12 June 1890 and was buried at Chilmark.

Ernest Edward Dugmore (1890-1917) MA, author, was Vicar of Parkstone from 1872 to 1910 and Succentor of Sarum from 1909 to 1925. He held the prebends of Gillingham Major from 1890 to 1917 and Netheravon from 1917 to 1925. He died in 1925.

Edward Ponsonby Knubley (1917-1931) MA, was Vicar of Steeple Ashton with Semmington from 1897 to 1931 and Rural Dean of Potterne from 1923 to 1931. He died on 8 November 1931.

James Senior Stuart (1932-1943) MA, was Vicar of Christ Church, Warminster in 1899. He died on 5 October 1943.

Frank McGowan (1944-1967) MBE, MA, DipTh, served in the Army from 1915 to 1918, was Rector of Cholderton from 1929 to 1954 and held the prebend of Gillingham Major from 1944 to 1967. He was a Proctor in Convocation from 1948 to 1951 and Archdeacon of Sarum from 1951 to 1967. He was Prior of St John's Hospital, Burcombe from 1954 to 1966 and died on 21 February 1968.

Edward Leslie Seager (1968-1979) MA, was Chaplain to the Forces from 1937 to 1946, Vicar of Gillingham from 1946 to 1979, and of Fifehead Magdalen from 1966 to 1979. He held the prebends of Shipton from 1954 to 1968 and of Gillingham Major from 1968 to 1979. He was Rural Dean of Shaftesbury from 1951 to 1956 and Archdeacon of Dorset from 1956 to 1974. He was Rural Dean of Blackmore Vale from 1975 to 1979 and a Team Vicar in the Gillingham Team Ministry in 1979. He died on 2 November 1983.

Linley Dennys Blathwayt (1979-1981) MA, was Vicar of Shalbourne with Bagshot, Ham & Buttermere from 1959 to 1966, Rector of Gussage St Michael with All Saints from 1969 to 1971, Rector of Corscombe and Curate-in -Charge of Evershot with Frome St Quintin with Melbury Bubb from 1971 to 1975 and Rector, also with Melbury Osmund with Melbury Sampford, from 1975 to 1979. He was Team Rector of the Melbury Team from 1975 to 1981 and Rural Dean of Beaminster from 1975 until retiring in 1981

Geoffrey Elmer Walton (1981-) BA, Dip.Th, was Recruitment Secretary to the Advisory Council for the Church's Ministry from 1969 to 1975 and Vicar of Weymouth Holy Trinity from 1975 to 1982. He became Archdeacon of Dorset and Priest-in Charge of Witchampton and Hinton Parva, Long Crichel & Moor Crichel in 1982.

BITTON

Prebend:- The prebend comprising the church of Bitton in Gloucestershire, was probably in existence by c.1150.

Canopy statuette and shield:- **Nicholas Longespee** was the fourth son of William Longespee, who in the right of his wife Ella, the foundress of Lacock Abbey, became Earl of Salisbury. He was Treasurer of Sarum from before 1275 to 1291 and was Bishop of Sarum from 1292 until his death on 18 May 1297. He was buried in the cathedral, with his heart at Lacock and his viscera at Ramsbury. (Fig. 31.)

Blazon:- Azure six lioncels or. [On a blue shield, six erect young lions with one hind paw on the ground and the other three paws and the tail in the air, showing full face.]

Psalter:- The portion of the psalter allotted to the prebend is Psalms 40, 41, 42 and 43.

Holders of the prebend:-

John de Kenovill (c.1200) was the donor of a silk cloth to the cathedral and may have held a stall at Rouen in 1206.

Richard de Bremble (c.1226/7-c.1233) may have been the Richard who was Chancellor of Sarum in 1236.

Adenulf dei Conti of Anagni (c.1274-c.1289) was a nephew of Pope Gregory IX and a papal chaplain who held stalls at Paris, Bayeux, Lincoln, London and York. He had died by 8 April 1289.

Richard de Sotwell (1289-1296) held the prebend of Bitton from 1289 until resigning in 1296 and was Archdeacon of Wilts from c.1299 to c.1303 when he went to Rome with Walter de Langeton, Bishop of Coventry & Lichfield. He died in 1303.

William de Sardene (1296-1303) held this prebend in 1299. He was Archdeacon of Oxford and held stalls at Lincoln, Hereford, Lichfield and Wells. He died on 5 November 1303.

Richard de Wynton (1303-1304) DTh, held the prebends of Yetminster Prima from 1297 to 1303 and Bitton from 1303 to 1304. He was Subdean of Wells and died in 1304.

John de Winchelsea (1304-1322) MA, exchanged the prebend of Bitton in 1322 with Robert de Ayleston for the prebend of Major Pars Altaris which he held from 1322 to 1326, when he became a Franciscan friar at Sarum.

Robert de Ayleston (1322-?) held the prebend of Major Pars Altaris from 1321 to 1322, exchanging it in 1322 with John de Winchelsea for the prebend of Bitton. He was Archdeacon of Wilts from 1326 to 1331 and of Berks from 1331 to c.1333 and was in the same year Archdeacon of Bath. He also held a stall at Lincoln in 1331 and was Rector of Wotton Basset in 1322.

Edmund de Ramsbury (1338,1343) held the prebend in 1338 and 1343.

John de Winckley (?-1347) exchanged this prebend in 1347 with Walter Waleys for the church of Shalfleet, Isle of Wight.

Walter Waleys (1347-?) was holding this prebend in 1360 and was Rector of Spettisbury.

John Godewyke (?-1395) resigned in 1395.

Robert Hallum (1395-1406) DCnL, held the prebend of Bitton from 1395 to 1406. He was appointed Archdeacon of Canterbury in 1400 and Chancellor of Oxford in 1403. The King objected to his nomination as Archbishop of York and he was made Bishop of Durham, being translated to Sarum where he was bishop from 1407 to 1417. He was created a Roman Cardinal in 1411 but without title because he did not go to Rome to receive it. At the Council of Constance in 1414 he was leader of the 'English Nation', representatives of the Anglican Church earnestly desiring a thorough reformation of the whole Church and asserting the supremacy of the General Council over the Pope. His death at Gotlieb Castle on 4 September 1417 was regarded as fatal to the cause of many really effective reforms in the Church.

John Prophete (1395) received a royal grant of the prebend of Bitton in 1395, despite Robert Hallam having already been installed. He held the prebend of Netherbury in Ecclesia from 1402 to 1416 and died in 1416.

Geoffrey Crukadan (1406-1420) BCnL, Lic.CL, received the prebend of Bitton in 1406 and despite the appointment of William Pilton, continued to hold the prebend until his death in 1420.

William Pilton (1407) received the prebend of Yetminster Prima early in 1407 but Laurence de Gomecii received it nine days later. He then received the prebend of Bitton in 1407 by royal grant but it was already occupied by Geoffrey Crukadan. He was then appointed to the prebend of Grimston and installed in 1408 but there was papal intervention on behalf of Thomas Polton.

Roger Harewell (1420-1428) held the prebends of Stratton from 1407 to 1420 and Bitton from 1420 to 1428. He resigned the latter in 1428.

Thomas Bubwith (1428-1447) BCn&CL, held the prebends of Wilsford & Woodford from 1425 to 1428 and Bitton from 1428 to 1447. He resigned in 1447.

William Vauce (1447-1479) BCn&CL, died in 1479.

John Dogget (1479-1486) DTh, DCnL, was a nephew of Cardinal Bourchier. He held the prebends of Ruscomb from 1474 to 1475, Chardstock from 1475 to ? and Bitton from 1479 to 1486. A native of Sherborne, he founded a chapel on the south side of the churchyard there. He held a stall at Lincoln, was Treasurer of Chichester in 1479, Chaplain to King Richard III in 1483, Chancellor of Sarum from 1486 to 1501, a Canon Residentiary and Vicar General of Sarum, and Chancellor of Lichfield in 1488. In 1490 he held the rectory of Winterborne Sheltston. He became Archdeacon of Chester and Provost of King's College, Cambridge in 1499. He died on 4 March 1501/02 and was buried in the cathedral.

Ralph Heathcott (1486-1487) BCn&CL, held the prebends of Chardstock from ? to 1486, Bitton from 1486 to 1487, Faringdon from 1487? to 1492 and Hurstbourne & Burbage from 1492 to 1493, exchanging the last with Adrian de Bardis in 1493 for the prebend of Ramsbury and the church of Wroughton, holding this prebend from 1493 until his death in 1499. He was Rector of St Peter's, Marlborough in 1481.

David Hopton (1487-1492) held the prebends of Beminster Prima from 1482 to c.1487 and Bitton from 1487 to 1492. He may have held a stall at and been Archdeacon of Exeter. He died in 1492.

Ralph Langton (1492) held the prebends of Grantham Australis from ? to 1489 and Bitton in 1492. He died in 1492.

John Gunthorpe (1492-1498) MA, held the prebends of Alton Borealis from 1472 to ? and Bitton from 1492 to 1498. He was the King's Almoner and in 1468 Warden of King's Hall, Cambridge. He held a stall at St Paul's in 1468, was Archdeacon of Essex and in 1472 Dean of Wells. He died by July 1498.

Thomas Holes (1498-1531) BCL, held the prebends of Rotesfen from 1489 to 1498 and Bitton from 1498 to 1531. He was Rector of Dinton and died in 1531.

George Wolfet (1531-?, 1546-1554) DCnL, was deprived for non-payment of royal subsidy but pardoned in 1546 and reinstated. He died in 1554.

Robert Ryve (1554-1573) BCL, held the prebends of Minor Pars Altaris from 1546 to 1554 and Bitton from 1554 to 1573. He died in 1573.

John Sprint (1573-1578) DD, was Dean of Bristol in 1571. He held the prebend of Bitton from 1573 to 1578, was Archdeacon of Wilts from 1577 to 1590 and was also Treasurer of Sarum from 1584 to 1590. He died in 1590.

Meredith Morgan (1578-1612) MA, was Rector of Pewsey who died in 1612.

Henry Cotton (1612-1615) MA, was a son of Henry Cotton, Bishop of Sarum 1598-1615. He was appointed Precentor of Sarum in 1614 but Francis Souch was presented by King James I and instituted by the Archbishop in 1620. He held the prebends of Fordington & Writhlington from 1608 to 1612, Bitton from 1612 to 1615 and Highworth from 1615 to his death, while still Precentor, in 1622/3.

Thomas Leche (1615-1646) MA, was Rector of Pewsey and Archdeacon of Wilts from 1614 to 1646 and held the prebend of Bitton from 1615 to 1646. He had died by 15 January 1646 and was buried at Pewsey.

Anthony Hawles (1660-1664) MA, DD, held the prebend of Bitton from 1660 to 1664, was Archdeacon of Sarum from 1658 to 1664, a Canon Residentiary from 1660 to 1664 and held a stall at Windsor in 1660. He was Rector and Vicar of Bishopstone in 1662 and died on 16 January 1664.

Thomas Hill (1664-1671) MA, was Rector of Bishopstone and a Canon Residentiary from 1665 to 1671. He died on 28 November 1671.

Richard Watson (1671-1685) DD, held the prebends of Warminster from 1666 to 1671 and Bitton from 1671 to 1685. He was Rector of Pewsey and donated a valuable collection of books to the cathedral library. He died on 13 January 1685 and is commemorated at Pewsey.

Benjamin Johnson (1685-1685/6) BD, died in 1685/6.

Edmund Jeffrey (1686-1692) MA, resigned in 1692.

Richard Eyre (1692-1745) MA, was a Canon Residentiary from 1710 to 1745. He died in 1745.

Ralph Freeman (1746-1772) DD, died on 29 June 1772.

Matthew Spry (1772-1792) MA, died on 8 June 1792.

William Coxe (1792-1799) MA, was Rector of Bemerton in 1788 and Rector of Stourton. He held the prebends of Alton Australis from 1791 to 1792, Bitton from 1792 to 1799, Grimston from 1799 to 1801 and Netheravon from 1801 to 1828. He was a Canon Residentiary and Archdeacon of Wilts from 1804 to 1828 and died on 8 June 1828.

Thomas Henry Hume (1799-1806) MA, was the only son of John Hume, Bishop of Sarum 1766-1782, and nephew of Nathaniel Hume, Precentor of Sarum 1774-1804. He held the prebends of Yatesbury from 1795 to 1799 and Bitton from 1799 to 1806. He was a Canon Residentiary from 1803 to 1834 and Treasurer of Sarum from 1806 to 1834 Amongst others, he held the livings of Broad Hinton, Stratford-sub-Castle and Brixton Deverill. He died on 6 January 1834 and is buried in the south transept of the cathedral.

William Lewis Rham (1806-1807) BA, was a leading agriculturist and Vicar of Broad Hinton from 1804. He resigned the prebend in 1807.

William Macdonald (1807-1862) MA, was Vicar of Chitterne in 1812 and Vicar of Bishop's Cannings in 1815. He held the prebend of Bitton from 1807 to 1862, was a Canon Residentiary from 1823 to 1862 and Archdeacon of Wilts from 1828 to 1862. He died on 24 June 1862.

Edward Arthur Dayman (1862-1890) MA, was a Fellow of Exeter College, Oxford, an author and Rector of Shillingstone from 1842 to 1890. He was a Proctor in Convocation in 1852 and served as Rural Dean of Whitchurch. He died in October 1890.

Edward Nallet Young (1890-1895) MA, was a Fellow of Trinity College, Cambridge and Head Master of Sherborne School from 1878 to 1892.

Charles Herbert Mayo (1895-1929) MA, DLitt, author, was Vicar of Long Burton with Holnest from 1872 to 1912 and Rural Dean of Shaftesbury from 1882 to 1912. He died in 1929.

Charles Philip Stewart Clarke (1929-1934) MA, was Rector of Donhead St Andrew from 1916 to 1932, Rural Dean of Tisbury from 1926 to 1932 and Proctor in Convocation from 1926 to 1934. He was Rector of North Stoneham with Bassett from 1932 to 1934, becoming Archdeacon of Chichester with a stall at Chichester from 1934.

Arnold Mortimer Sharp (1934-1938) MA, was Vicar of Kinson (with Newtown to 1904 and with Talbot Village to 1919) from 1892 to 1931. He was a Proctor in Convocation from 1905 to 1929 and was Rural Dean of Poole from 1929 to 1938? He died in 1938.

Harry Barton (1938-1958) was perpetual curate of St Luke's, Parkstone from 1920 to 1958, a Proctor in Convocation from 1929 to 1945 and Rural Dean of Poole from 1937 to 1949. He died in 1958.

Francis Bernard Ross Browne (1958-1970) was a Chaplain to the Forces (being twice mentioned in despatches) from 1931 to 1942. He was Rector of Marlborough from 1952 to 1966 and Rural Dean of Marlborough from 1953 to 1963. He died in 1970.

George Vivian Syer (1970-1971) MA, ThL, was Vicar of Whitechurch Canonicorum with Stanton St Gabriel from 1959 to 1971, Rector of Wooton Fitzpaine from 1966 to 1971 and Rural Dean of Lyme Bay from 1962 to 1971. He died in December 1995.

Alan George Kett Fairbairn Mackenzie (1972-1977) OBE, BSc, was Chaplain and Secretary to the Diocesan Association for the Deaf and Hard of Hearing from 1959 to 1974. He was Priest-in-Charge of Corscombe from 1975 to 1977 and of Halstock and East & West Chelborough in 1977. He retired in 1977 and died in March 1997..

Hugh Raymond Mumford (1977-1989) was Vicar of Nether Cerne from 1969 to 1971, Rector of Godmanstone and of Cerne Abbas with Upcerne and of Minterne Magna from 1969 to 1971, and Vicar of Cerne Abbas with Godmanstone and Minterne Magna from 1971 to 1989. He was Rural Dean of Dorchester from 1975 to 1979 and retired in 1989.

John Raymond Sargant (1992-) MA, was Vicar of Christ Church Bradford-on-Avon from 1976 to 1990, Ecumenical Officer for Wilts Archdeaconry from 1976 to 1990 and founding Secretary of the county ecumenical body for Wiltshire. He became a Team Vicar in the Marlborough Team and Diocesan Inter-Faith Adviser in 1990.

STRATTON

Prebend:- The prebend, which was probably in existence by c.1150 consisted of land at Stratton in Dorset, which appeared to be part of the royal manor of Dorchester.

Canopy statuette and shield:- **Roger de Martival** was Archdeacon of Huntingdon in 1288 and of Leicester in 1295. In 1293 he became Chancellor of Oxford University and occupied the prebend of Netheravon from 1298 to 1315. He was Dean of Lincoln in 1310 and as Bishop of Sarum from 1315 to 1330 he completed the spire and drew up cathedral statutes in 1319. He died on 14 March 1330, was buried in the cathedral on the north side of the choir under a slab of marble inlaid with brass which has since been removed. (Fig 32.)

Blazon:- Argent a cinquefoil pierced sable. [On a silver shield, a black five petalled flower with a hole in the centre.]

Psalter:- The portion of the psalter allotted to the prebend is Psalms 49, 50 and 51.

Holders of the prebend:-

Daniel de Longo Campo (c.1226/7-c.1233) was fined for non-residence in 1227, held a stall at Exeter and died on 10 May 1241.

Martin de Littlebury (1255-1264) held the prebends of Stratton by 1255 to 1264 and Bedminster & Redcliffe from c.1264 to c.1270.

Stephen de la Wyle (c.1284-c.1301) probably died before 13 June 1301.

Aymeric de Sancto Cirico (?-1319) held the prebend in 1316.

Bernand de Cucinaco (1319-1347) died in 1347

Thomas de Brembre (1343-1347,1347-?) was Chaplain to King Edward III who appointed him to the prebend of Stratton in 1343, although it was occupied by Bernand de Cucinaco. He exchanged it in 1347 with James Beaufort for a portion in the church of Wighton, Norfolk, exchanging it back however five months later and was installed the following day. He held a stall at St Paul's in 1354 and became Dean of Wimborne where he established a foundation for a Warden and four chaplains.

James de Beaufort (1347) exchanged a portion of the church of Wighton, Norfolk in 1347 with Thomas de Brembre for the prebend of Stratton and was installed the same day. He exchanged it back five months later and held the prebend of Shipton from 1354 to 1358. He was Rector of Steeple Lavington and died in 1358.

Bertrand de Budocio (1347) was appointed to the prebend on the death of Bernand de Cucinaco but John de Thursteyn was also appointed.

John Thursteyn (1347-?) was appointed to the prebend but royal support was given to Thomas de Brembre. Papal confirmation was however given in 1355 to an exchange of the prebend with Thomas de Brembre for a prebend in Abergwili collegiate church and the prebend of Thorney at Chichester.

John de Buckingham (1361-1362) was appointed to the prebend of Preston in 1351 but it was claimed by two others. He then held the prebend of Stratton from 1361 to 1362 before becoming Bishop of Lincoln in 1362.

Robert Sumpter (1362-?) DCL, probably failed to gain possession of the prebend.

John Hanneye (1366) held the prebend in 1366.

Thomas Grene (?-1387) died, while still holding the prebend in 1387.

Thomas Bekyngham (1387-1407) died in 1407.

Roger Harewell (1407-1420) held the prebends of Stratton from 1407 to 1420 and Bitton from 1420 to 1428. He resigned the prebend in 1428.

John Tydeling (1420-1437) BCL, was a Canon Residentiary and held the prebend of Axford from 1401 to 1404, exchanging it with George Westby for the prebend of Major Pars Altaris in 1404, which he held until 1406. He then held the prebends of Warminster from 1406 to 1418, Yetminster Secunda in 1418, Beminster Prima from 1418 to 1420, Stratton from 1420 to 1437, exchanging the last with John Symondsburgh for the prebend of Yatesbury in 1437. This he exchanged with John Morton for the prebend of North Leverton in Southwell collegiate church, Notts.

John Symondesburgh (1437-1449) BCL, was Archdeacon of Wilts from 1423 to 1449 and Treasurer of Sarum from 1449 to 1454. He held the prebend of Yatesbury from 1423 to 1437, exchanging it with John Tydeling for the prebend of Stratton which he held from 1437 to 1449. He held the Rectory of Dinton in 1433 and was Treasurer of St Paul's from 1420 to 1423. He died in 1454 and asked to be buried before St Margaret's altar in the cathedral.

Richard Andrew (1449-1454) DCL, was Archdeacon of Sarum from 1441 to 1444 when he resigned. He held the prebends of Faringdon from 1447 to 1449, Stratton from 1449 to 1454 and Grantham Borealis from 1454 to 1477. He was a friend of Archbishop Chichele and the first Warden of All Souls, Oxford founded by him in 1437. He was Dean of York in 1451 and Chancellor of Canterbury. He died in 1477.

William Nessingwick (1454-1459) was a Notary Public who held the prebends of Preston from 1450 to 1454, Stratton from 1454 to 1459 and Faringdon from 1459 to c.1486. He was Subdean of Sarum from 1459 to 1476, exchanging the office in 1476 with Giles Stanbridge for the church of Milston which he held until 1487. A Canon Residentiary, he acted as locum tenens for the Dean on more than one occasion, presiding in chapter as locum tenens not Subdean and visiting the prebends in 1463.

William Brygon (1459-1469) BCn&CL, held the prebends of Minor Pars Altaris from 1447 to 1448, Ruscomb from 1448 to 1454, Durnford from 1454 to 1459 and Stratton from 1459 to 1469. He died in 1469.

Adam Copendale (1469-1479) DCL, held the prebends of Yetminster Secunda from 1466 to 1469, and Stratton from 1469 until exchanging the latter in 1479 with Edmund Chaderton for the prebend of St Katharine's altar in Beverley collegiate church, Yorks.

Edmund Chaderton (1479-1499) held the prebend of Stratton from 1479 to 1499 and was Archdeacon of Sarum from ? until his death in 1499.

Geoffrey Blythe (1499-1503) BTh, was a brother of John Blythe, Bishop of Sarum 1494-1499. He was Treasurer of Sarum from 1494 to 1495, exchanging the dignity for the prebend of Chisenbury & Chute which he held from 1495 to 1498. He was Archdeacon of Sarum, holding the prebend of Stratton, from 1499 to 1503 and would seem to have been Dean of York in 1497 and Provost of King's Hall, Cambridge in 1499. In 1503 be was consecrated Bishop of Lichfield, dying in 1533.

John Hall (1503-1506) resigned in 1506

John Underhill (1506-1510) BCnL, held the prebends of Stratton from 1506 to 1510 and Beminster Secunda from ? until his death in 1537.

John Kite (1510-1518) BCnL, was Rector of Boscombe from 1499 to 1504. He held a stall at Exeter and was Archbishop of Armagh and Apostolic Legate in Ireland from 1513 to 1521 when he became Bishop of Carlisle. In 1518 he resigned his prebend and became Ambassador to Spain and in 1521 titular bishop of Thebes. He died on 19 June 1537.

Richard Eden (1518-1551) died in 1551.

Richard Rosse (1551-1558) died in 1558.

John Williams (1558) DCL, was instituted by the Archbishop of Canterbury in 1558 but Francis Mallet was presented and instituted a month later. He died in December 1558, probably whilst still holding the prebend.

Francis Mallet (1558) was appointed to the prebend in 1558 but John Williams appears to have continued to hold it. He was granted in 1558 the temporalities as Bishop-nominate of Sarum by Queen Mary I but on her death in December, Queen Elizabeth I declined to accept him.

Philip Baker (1559) BD.

Thomas Key (1560-?) MA, was a Fellow of All Souls, Oxford and became Master of University College and Registrar of the University. He died in May 1572.

John Colcell (1565-1599) was a Canon Residentiary from 1566 to 1599 and died in 1599.

John Torksey (1600-1614) BD, died on 10 January 1614.

Walter Benet (1614) BD, was Precentor of Sarum from 1608 to 1614 and held the prebends of Yetminster Secunda from 1610 to 1614 and Stratton in 1614. He was Archdeacon of Wilts from 1610 to 1614 also holding the rectory of Mynty. He died in 1614.

John Harward (1614-1666) MA, was Vicar of Wanborough.

James Gardiner (1666-1671) MA, resigned in 1671, apparently on becoming Subdean of Lincoln. He became Bishop of Lincoln in 1695.

Gregory Hascard (1671-1708) DD, died in 1708.

George Stevens (1708-1710) MA, held the prebends of Stratton from 1708 to 1710 and Highworth from 1710 to 1733. He died in 1733.

Henry Austin (1710-1730) MA, was Vicar of Chalk and held the prebends of Alton Australis from 1696 to 1710 and Stratton from 1710 to 1730. He died in 1730.

Francis Fox (1730-1738) MA, held the prebends of Wilsford & Woodford from 1713 to 1730 and Stratton from 1730 to 1738. He was Vicar of Potterne and died on 6 July 1738.

Hugh Wynne (1738-1754) LLD, held the prebends of Warminster from 1737 to 1738 and Stratton from 1738 to 1754. He was a Canon Residentiary from 1739 to 1754 and died on 13 October 1754.

George Woodward (1755-1790) MA, held the prebends of Lyme & Halstock from 1750 to 1755, and Stratton from 1755 to 1790. He died on 5 May 1790.

Benjamin Pye (1790-1808) DCL, died on 26 March 1808.

Philip Fisher (1808-1810) DD, held the prebends of Stratton from 1808 to 1810 and Ilfracombe from 1810 to 1823. He was Precentor of Sarum from 1819 until his death on 19 January 1842 at the age of 92.

The Hon Thomas Alfred Harris (1810-1823) MA, was the 2nd son of the 1st Earl of Malmesbury. He held a stall at York and a benefice in Hampshire and died on 15 December 1823.

John Still (1824-1839) BCL, was Rector of Cricklade and of Fonthill Gifford from 1797 to 1839 and was Vicar of Inglesham. He died on 1 April 1839.

Robert Bentley Buckle (1841-1893) MA, was a Fellow of Sydney Sussex College, Cambridge. He was Archdeacon of Dorset in the diocese of Bristol in 1836 and in the diocese of Sarum from 1836 until resigning in 1862. He was Vicar of Upwey from 1836 until resigning in 1888 and he died on 16 September 1893.

William Gildea (1893-1918) MA, was Vicar of West Lulworth from 1862 to 1879, Vicar of Netherbury with Solway Ash from 1879 and Rural Dean of Bridport from 1890. He resigned the prebend in 1918.

Herbert Chidley Coote (1918-1919) MA, was Vicar of St Paul's, Poole, from 1889 to 1892, Vicar of St John the Evangelist, Wimborne from 1894 (and Rector of Stanbridge from 1896) to 1905, and Rector of Trowbridge from 1905. He was Rector of St Peter's Dorchester from ? to 1919. He died in May 1919.

Stephen Harold Wingfield-Digby (1919-1932) MA, was Chaplain, Royal Military Academy Woolwich from 1907 to 1911 and Vicar of Sherborne with Castleton (and Lillington from 1921) from 1916. He was Rural Dean of Sherborne from 1920 and a Proctor in Convocation from 1922 to 1924. He resigned in 1932.

Sydney Clement Winterton (1934-1940) BA, was Chaplain to Bishop Wordsworth's School, Sarum from 1911 to 1915, Rector of Orcheston St Michael from 1918 to 1920, Diocesan Director of Education from 1926 to ? and Vicar of Charlton All Saints with Standlynch from 1930.

Alfred Wilkinson Markby (1940-1966) MA, was Rector of St Peter's Dorchester from 1930 to 1956 and Chaplain to Dorchester Prison from 1930 to 1947.

David Wynne-Owen (Fr. David) (1966-1970) BA, DipTh, joined the Society of St Francis in 1947. He was Minister from 1957 to 1968 and Minister General from 1968 to 1970. He worked in the USA from 1970 to 1980 and died in 1994.

Charles Perry Smith (1971-1980) was Rector of Hawkchurch from 1954 to 1959 and Warden of Pilsdon House from 1959 to 1980.

Frank Smedley (1980-1982) was Vicar of Overton with Fyfield & East Kennet from 1957 to 1964 and Perpetual Curate of The Trinity, Trowbridge from 1964 to 1968, Vicar from 1968 to 1971. He was Vicar of Wool with East Burton & Coombe Keynes from 1971 (and of East Stoke from 1976) to 1982. He was Rural Dean of Purbeck from 1976 until his retirement in 1982. He died in April 1992.

Barnabas John Hopkinson (1983-1986) MA, was Priest in Charge of Preshute and Team Vicar Marlborough Team 1975-1981, and Rural Dean of Marlborough from 1977 to 1981. From 1981 to 1986 he was Team Rector of Wimborne Minster and Holt, and from 1985 to 1986 was Rural Dean of Wimborne. He was appointed to the prebend of Stratton in 1983. In 1986 he was made Archdeacon of Sarum, surrendering his prebend and receiving instead the prebend of Ogborne. From 1987 to 1998 he also had responsibility for the parish of Stratford-sub-Castle. In 1998 he ceased to be Archdeacon of Sarum and became Archdeacon of Wilts but retaining oversight of the Archdeaconry of Sarum, pending the outcome of a review.

Geoffrey Barton (1986-1992) MA, was the Chaplain to Roundway Hospital, Devizes from 1977 to 1992. He retired in 1992.

John McNeish (1992-1999) was Precentor of St John's Cathedral, Aberdeen from 1964 to 1966, Chaplain RAF from 1966 to 1972, Priest-in-Charge of Stour Provost with Todber from 1975 to 1979 and Team Rector Gillingham from 1979 until retiring in 1999. He was Rural Dean of Blackmore Vale from 1981 to 1986.

HURSTBOURNE & BURBAGE

Prebend:- The churches of Hurstbourne Tarrant in Hampshire and Burbage in Wiltshire, were both held by Vitalis the priest in 1086 and were subsequently given to the cathedral. The prebend was probably in existence c.1150.

Canopy statuette and shield:- **Robert de Wyville** held stalls at Lincoln c.1325, at Lichfield and in 1330 held the prebend of Minor Pars Altaris. He failed to be appointed to the see of Bath & Wells in 1329 but a year later became Bishop of Sarum until his death on 4 September 1375. A contemporary account reads "At the instance of Phillipa, Queen to King Edward III, the Pope preferred Rob. Wyville to the bishopric of Sarum. It is hard to say whether he were more dunce or dwarf, more unlearned or unhansome, insomuch that had the Pope ever *seen* him, as he no doubt *felt* him in his large fees, he would never have conferred the place on him." He recovered Sherborne Castle for the see and it was during his episcopate that the monastery at Edington was founded and the church consecrated. He was buried in the cathedral, in the choir but when the choir was repaved his remains were removed to the north-east transept. . (Fig. 33.)

Blazon:- Gules a cross or fretty azure between four mullets pierced of the second. [On a red shield, a gold cross with a fretwork of blue diagonals, between four gold, pierced five pointed stars.]

Psalter:- The portion of the psalter allotted to the prebend is Psalm 69.

Holders of the prebend:-

Richard Barre (c.1175-c.1208) held the dignities of Archdeacon of Lisieux and Archdeacon of Ely. He held the prebend in 1200 and was still alive in 1202 but had been succeeded as Archdeacon of Ely by 1215.

Bartholomew des Roches (c.1215-1230) was fined for non-residence in 1227. He was Archdeacon of Winchester, held stalls at London and Exeter and died on 12 December 1230. He is believed to have donated a cope to the cathedral.

Luke (of Winchester) des Roches (1231-c.1253) was a nephew of Peter des Roches, Bishop of Winchester 1205-1238 and held the prebends of Ruscomb from c.1223 to c.1226, Coombe & Harnham from c.1226/7 to 1231 and Hurstbourne & Burbage from 1231 to c.1253. He held a stall at London, was Archdeacon of Surrey c.1245, Rector of Hurstbourne in 1249 and probably died c.1253.

Giles de Forda (?-1272) occurs as a canon and was Vicar of Hurstbourne c.1260. He may have held this prebend.

John of Leicester (?1275-c.1289) held the prebends of Teynton Regis from 1274 to 1275 and Hurstbourne & Burbage from ?1275 to 1288) He was the Chancellor to Robert Wickhampton, Bishop of Sarum 1274-1284 and may have died in c.1290.

John Oreby (?-1316) was nominated to a prebend in 1303, held this prebend in 1307 and died in 1316.

Alexander de Hemingby (1316-?) held the prebend of Slape from 1304 and, although Robert de Winchcombe was appointed in 1313, this was revoked four months later and he continued to hold the prebend until 1316. He was appointed to the prebend of Grantham Borealis in 1313 but this was also revoked four months later on the appointment of Tydo de Varesio. He held the prebend of Hurstbourne & Burbage from 1316 to c.1328.

John de Oxendon (1334,1335).

John de Abingdon (?-1338) DTh, held the prebends of Hurstbourne & Burbage from ? to 1338 when, despite a royal grant to John de Eccleshale, he exchanged it with John de Whitchurch for the prebend of Axford, which he held from 1338 to 1343. He died in 1343.

John de Eccleshale (1338) received a royal grant of the prebend of Hurstbourne & Burbage in 1338 but it was already held by John de Abingdon. He received the prebend of Yatesbury in 1340.

John de Whitchurch (1338-1358) BCn&CL, was Archdeacon of Wilts from 1338 to 1343 when he exchanged the dignity with John Barne for the church of Sedgefield, Co. Durham. He held the prebend of Axford from 1335 to 1338, exchanging it with John de Abingdon for the prebend of Hurstbourne & Burbage, which he held until his death in 1358. He was a Canon Residentiary.

Saladin de Fallecis (1358-?) had papal confirmation of the grant of this prebend in 1358. He exchanged it in 1363 with Richard Thorne for the prebend of Wisborough in Chichester, but this was revoked.

Richard de Thorne (1363) received the prebend by exchange which was revoked.

Henry de Wakefield (1371) received a royal grant of the prebend of Hurstbourne & Burbage in 1371 but this was superseded two months later by a royal grant of the prebend of Bere & Cherminster which he held from 1371 to 1375. He was Archdeacon of Canterbury in 1374 and became Bishop of Worcester in 1375.

Thomas de Swaby (1371) received a royal grant of this prebend in 1371 but a further royal grant was made to John de Glaston three months later.

John de Glaston (1371-1382) died in 1382.

John Welbourn (?-1397) DCL, was Precentor of Sarum from ? to 1397. He held the prebend of Hurstbourne & Burbage from c.1386 to 1397 but exchanged the dignity, the prebend and the church of Crewkerne, Somerset, with Adam Mottrum in 1397 for the Archdeaconry of Ely, the prebend of Fenton at York and a portion of St Probus church, Cornwall.

Adam Mottrum (1397-1415) was Archdeacon of Ely, exchanging this and other benefices with John Welbourn. He was Precentor of Sarum and held the prebend of Hurstbourne & Burbage from 1397 to 1415 and was also Rector of South Newton. He was appointed Vicar General of the diocese in 1408 and in his Will asked to be buried in the Cathedral.

John Luke (1415) held the prebends of Hurstbourne & Burbage in 1415, Slape from 1415 to 1425 and Coombe & Harnham from 1425 to 1435. He died in 1435.

John Chitterne (1415-1419) held the prebends of Chisenbury & Chute from 1385 to 1415 and Hurstbourne & Burbage from 1415 to 1419. He became a Canon Residentiary in 1386, was Rector of Newton Tony from 1415 to 1419 and was Archdeacon of Wilts from 1407 to 1419. He held a stall at St Paul's from 1409 to 1419 and became Archdeacon of Sarum in 1419, dying in the same year.

Thomas Rudborne (1419-1433) Sch.Th, was Warden of Merton College, Oxford in 1416, Archdeacon of Sudbury in 1413 and Bishop of St David's in 1433.

John de la Bere (1433-1447) became Bishop of St David's in 1447.

John Chedworth (1447-1452) DTh, held the prebends of Yatesbury from 1440 to 1443, Stratford from 1443 to 1445, Netherbury in Terra from 1445 to 1447 and Hurstbourne & Burbage from 1447 to 1452. He held a stall at Lincoln and was at different times Archdeacon of Northampton and of Lincoln. He was Provost of King's College, Cambridge in 1446, Archdeacon of Wilts from 1449 to 1452 and was consecrated Bishop of Lincoln in 1452. He died on 23 November 1471.

John Cranborne (1452-1474) BCL, held the prebends of Rotesfen from 1432 to 1435, Coombe & Harnham from 1435 to 1452 and Hurstbourne & Burbage from 1452 to 1474. He died in 1474.

Thomas Hawkins (1474-1479) MA, was Precentor of Sarum from 1471 to 1479. He held the prebends of Minor Pars Altaris from 1471 to 1474 and Hurstbourne & Burbage from 1474 to 1479. He was Provost of Oriel College, Oxford and Archdeacon of Worcester. He died in 1479 and was buried in the Cathedral.

Edward Pole (1479-?) appears to have been a son of the Duke of Suffolk. He was Precentor of Sarum from 1480 to 1485 and held the prebends of Netheravon from 1478 to 1479 and Hurstbourne & Burbage from 1479 to ?. He became Archdeacon of the East Riding in 1480 and of Richmond in 1484.

John Taylor (1485-1492) DTh, died in 1492.

Ralph Heathcott (1492-1493) BCn&CL, held the prebends of Chardstock from ? to 1486, Bitton from 1486 to 1487, Faringdon from 1487? to 1492 and Hurstbourne & Burbage from 1492 to 1493, exchanging the last with Adrian de Bardis in 1493 for the prebend of Ramsbury and the church of Wroughton, holding this prebend from 1493 until his death in 1499. He was Rector of St Peter's, Marlborough in 1481.

Adrian de Bardis (1493-1519) was a Florentine who held the prebend of Ramsbury from 1481 to 1493 exchanging it and the church of Wroughton with Ralph Heathcott for the prebend of Hurstbourne & Burbage, which he held from 1493 to 1519 in which year he died. He was Rector of St Peter's Marlborough and of 'Elyngdon', and held a stall at Lincoln.

James Bromwich (1519-1524) BCnL, held the prebends of Axford from 1505 to 1507, Coombe & Harnham in 1507, Grimston from 1507 to 1515, Faringdon from 1515 to 1519 and Hurstbourne & Burbage from 1519 to 1524. He was Chancellor of Hereford in 1518 and became Archdeacon of Sarum in 1524, dying a month after his appointment.

Henry Rawlyns (1524) BCL, was well provided with prebends. He held Yatesbury from1513 to 1514, Grantham Australis from 1514 to 1519 and Coombe & Harnham 1519 to 1521. He resigned the last in May 1521, was succeeded by Cuthbert Tunstall who then became Dean of Sarum, and was again collated to the prebend later in the same year. The prebend then passed to Richard Pace but was assumed by Henry Rawlyns for the third time in 1523. He then held Faringdon from 1523 to 1524, Hurstbourne & Burbage in 1524 and Teynton Regis, together with the Archdeaconry of Sarum from 1524 to 1526. He was Rector of Christian Malford, died in 1526 and is buried in the cathedral near the Audley Chantry.

Richard Arche (1524-1552) BCL, held the prebend of Preston from ? to 1524, resigning to assume the prebend of Faringdon in 1524, which he resigned a month later. He then received the prebend of Hurstbourne & Burbage which he held from 1524 until resigning in 1552. Two years later he was appointed to the prebend of Minor Pars Altaris but may not have received it before being deprived of all benefices early in 1555. He was Vicar of Avebury and held a stall at Windsor from 1538 until deprived in 1555. He was a Canon Residentiary from 1527 to 1554 and Treasurer of Sarum from 1551 to 1555 during which time the Commissioners appointed to survey Church Goods and Chantries visited the cathedral.

Henry Iden (1552-1556) resigned in 1556.

John Pollard (1556-1558) MA, was Archdeacon of Wilts from 1539 to 1554 and held the prebend of Hurstbourne & Burbage from 1556 to 1558. He is believed to have died in 1558.

David Powell (1558) MA, was apparently deprived of his prebend early in the reign of Queen Elizabeth I.

John Jeffrys (1559-1590) BA, resigned in 1590.

Richard Jeffrys (1590-?) MA, held the prebend in 1593.

Peter Lilly (1594) MA, BD, received the prebend of Hurstbourne & Burbage in 1594 and held it for less than a year. He held a stall at St Paul's in 1599, was Archdeacon of Taunton and occupied the prebend of Highworth from 1604 until his death in 1615.

William Pritchard (1595-1629) MA, died in 1629.

James White (1629-1661) BD, was Rector of Boscombe from 1632 to 1661, of Rolleston until 1644 and Rector of Newton Tony from 1660 to 1661. He held a stall at Winchester and died in 1661.

Samuel Rogers (1661-1668) BD, was Rector of Boscombe. He died in 1668.

Daniel Whitby (1668-1696) DD, was Precentor of Sarum from 1672 to 1726. He held the prebends of Yatesbury in 1668, Hurstbourne & Burbage from 1668 to 1696 and Teynton Regis from 1696 to 1726. He was Chaplain to Seth Ward, Bishop of Sarum 1667-1689, a Canon Residentiary from 1676 to 1726, and Rector of St Edmund's, Sarum. He caused excitement by publishing the *Protestant Reconciler* and similar writings, which advocated general religious tolerance. This brought upon him the wrath of the authorities, Chief Justice Jeffreys even directing his indictment. He died on 21 March 1726 aged 90.

James Canaries (1696-1698) held the prebends of Durnford from 1693 to 1696 and Hurstbourne & Burbage from 1696 to 1698.

John Stevens (1698-1701) BCL, was Rector of Wylye. He held the prebends of Chisenbury & Chute from 1692 to 1698 and Hurstbourne & Burbage from 1698 to 1701. He died in 1701 and was buried at Wylye.

Charles Theophilus Mutel (1701-1711) MA, held the prebends of Chisenbury & Chute from 1699 to 1701 and Hurstbourne & Burbage from 1701 to 1711. He was Vicar of Potterne and died in January 1711.

Benjamin D'Aranda (1711-1739) BA, died on 27 December 1739 and is commemorated at Bremhill.

Charles Moss (1740-1786) MA, held the prebends of Warminster from 1738 to 1740 and Hurstbourne & Burbage from 1740 to 1786. He was Rector of Boscombe from 1738 to 1750 a Canon Residentiary from 1746 to 1786 although becoming Bishop of St David's in 1766 and of Bath & Wells in 1774. He died in 1802.

Charles Moss (1786-1811) MA, was a Canon Residentiary from 1786 to 1797. He became Bishop of Oxford in 1807 but continued to hold the prebend until his death on 16 December 1811.

John Fisher (1812-1819) BA, was a nephew of John Fisher, Bishop of Sarum 1817-1825, who received the prebend of Hurstbourne & Burbage in 1812, one month after his ordination as a deacon. He continued to hold this prebend to 1819 and Fordington & Writhlington from 1819 to 1832, and was Vicar of Osmington and Vicar of Gillingham. He was Archdeacon of Berks from 1817 to 1832 and a Canon Residentiary, occupying the house of Leadenhall from 1819 to 1832. He died on 25 August 1832 and is commemorated at Osmington.

Robert James Carr (1819) MA, DD, held the prebend of Hurstbourne & Burbage in 1819, exchanging it with Charles Francis for the prebend of Lyme & Halstock, which he held until 1824. He was Dean of Hereford from 1820 to 1824, Bishop of Chichester from 1824 to 1831 and Bishop of Worcester from 1831 to 1841. He held a stall at St Paul's and was Clerk to the Closet but dismissed on account of strict adherence to his political principles on the accession of Queen Victoria. He died on 24 April 1841.

Charles Francis (1819-1821) MA, held the prebends of Yatesbury from 1802 to 1805 and Lyme & Halstock from 1805 to 1819, exchanging the latter with Robert James Carr for the prebend of Hurstbourne & Burbage, which he held from 1819 to 1821. He died in 1821,

James Thomas Hurlock (1821-1847) DD, died on 2 February 1847.

Francis Dyson (1847-1858) MA, was Rector of North and South Tidworth from 1829 to 1858. He became Vicar of Cricklade in 1849 and died on 30 November 1858.

Nathaniel Bond (1859-1889) was Rector of Steeple and Tyneham from 1852 until his death in 1889.

Harry Everett Ravenhill (1889-1913) MA, was Vicar of Buckland Newton with Plush from 1860 to 1907 and Rural Dean of Whitchurch from 1882 to 1906. He died on 12 May 1913 and was buried at Buckland Newton.

John Marshall Collard (1913-1917) MA, was Vicar of Christ Church, West Fordington from 1894 until his death in June 1917.

George Cyril Hutchings (1917-1950) MA, was Vicar of Broadwindsor from 1896 to 1912 and Vicar of Burstock from 1902 to 1912. He was Vicar of St Michael with Holy Trinity Beaminster from 1912, Rural Dean of Bridport from 1912 and a Proctor in Convocation from 1929 to 1936.

Hugh Vaughan White (1950-1967) was Vicar of Broad Hinton from 1919 to 1966, Rural Dean of Winterbourne Bassett from 1952 to 1966 and Rural Dean of Avebury from 1939 to 1955.

Brian Cyril Aldis (1968-1994) was Rector of Hamworthy from 1951 to 1983 and a Proctor in Convocation from 1975 to 1983. He died in November 1994.

Richard Sydney Double (Bro Samuel) (1995-) BD, AKC, joined the Society of St Francis in 1975 and became Guardian of Hillfield Friary in 1992.

SLAPE

Prebend:- Slape in the parish of Netherbury in Dorset was part of the pre-Conquest Sherborne episcopal estates. The prebend was probably in existence by c.1150.

Canopy statuette and shield:- **Ralph Erghum** DCn&CL, was Chancellor of Lancaster and Bishop of Sarum from 1375 to 1388. He was the founder of the Hospital of St Michael, near Sarum and was involved in a fierce controversy with the Chapter as to his right of visiting the prebends during a vacancy in the Deanery. The matter was referred first to the Archbishop of Canterbury and subsequently to the Pope who decided against the bishop. In 1388 he was translated to Bath & Wells where he died in 1400, being buried in Wells Cathedral. (Fig. 34.)

Blazon:- Argent a griffin segreant gules. [On a silver shield, a red griffin with wings displayed.]

Psalter:- The portion of the psalter allotted to the prebend is Psalms 75, 76 and 77.

Holders of the prebend:-

Robert de Bingham (c.1226/27-1229) was fined for non-residence in 1227. He was the founder of St Nicholas Hospital, Sarum and is said to have built the bridge over the River Avon beside it. He held the prebend of Slape from c.1226/7 to 1229 when he became Bishop of Sarum from 1229 to 1246, holding with the bishopric the prebend of Horton. He died on 2 November 1246 and was buried in the still unfinished cathedral.

John le Bel (1263-?) is presumed to have been a royal clerk, having custody of the sees of Chichester to 1262 and Sarum to 1263.

William le Deneys (alias Dacus) (?-1304) held the prebend in 1284 and died whilst holding it before 16 April 1304.

Alexander de Hemingby (1304-1316) held the prebend of Slape from 1304 and, although Robert de Winchcombe was appointed in 1313, this was revoked four months later and he continued to hold the prebend until 1316. He was appointed to the prebend of Grantham Borealis in 1313 but this was also revoked four months later on the appointment of Tydo de Varesio. He held the prebend of Hurstbourne & Burbage from 1316 to c.1328.

Robert de Winchcomb (1313) was Rector of Boscombe and held the prebend of Netherbury in Terra from 1311 to 1335 with a brief interval in 1313 when he received the prebend of Slape for four months, Netherbury in Terra having been given to William Coleshull for the same period.

William de Mepham (1316-?) was appointed to the prebend of Rotesfen in 1313 but this was subsequently revoked as William Coleshull was already holding it. He held the prebends of Minor Pars Altaris from 1313 to 1316, Beminster Secunda from 1314 to 1316 and Slape from 1316 to ?; still holding the last in 1320.

William de Crouthorne (1334-1349) DCnL, died in 1349.

Richard de Netheravon (1349-?) received the prebend in 1349 and, although Thomas David was appointed, papal confirmation was given in 1350.

Thomas David (1349) was appointed in 1349 but Richard de Netheravon received papal confirmation..

Roger le White (1366) held the prebend in 1366.

Richard Haxton (1373) held the prebend in 1373 but his arrest was ordered in November.

John de Ludham (?-1378) exchanged this prebend with Peter de Barton for a prebend in Wherwell conventual church, Hampshire.

Peter de Barton (1378-1403) held a stall at Wells. He asked to be buried in the cathedral and died in 1403.

Henry Harburgh (1403-1415) was Treasurer of Sarum for three days in 1394 when he exchanged the dignity with John Chaundeler for the prebend of Netherbury in Ecclesia. This he exchanged in 1395 with Ralph Selby for the prebend of Alton Borealis. He relinquished this latest prebend in 1403, receiving that of Slape. This he held until 1415 when he received the prebend of Beminster Prima. In 1416 he became Precentor of Sarum, he relinquished his prebend in 1418 and in the same year exchanged the dignity of Precentor for the prebend of Bere & Cherminster, which he held until 1432. He had died by 22 September 1432.

John Luke (1415-1425) held the prebends of Hurstbourne & Burbage in 1415, Slape from 1415 to 1425 and Coombe & Harnham from 1425 to 1435. He died in 1435.

John Conge (1425-?) received the prebends of Stratford in March 1425 and Slape in July 1425. He still held the latter in 1449.

Richard Whitby (1451-1457) BCn&CL, was Treasurer of Sarum from 1462 to 1494 and held the prebends of Slape from 1451 to 1457, Chisenbury & Chute from 1457 to 1459 and Bedwin from 1459 to 1462. He was a Canon Residentiary and not infrequently was locum tenens of the Dean. He died in 1494 and was buried in the chapel of St Edmund in the cathedral.

Thomas Swyft (1457-1465) BCn&CL, held the prebends of Axford from 1449 to 1457 and Slape from 1457 until exchanging it in 1465 with John Bedale for the church of Hollingbourne, Kent.

John Bedale (1465-1483) BCnL, died in 1483.

Henry Howton (?-1505) held the prebend in 1486 and died in 1505.

John Dowman (1505-?) DCL.

Roger Edgeworth (?-1560) DD, was a Fellow of Oriel College, Oxford, a noted preacher in the university and defender of the old unreformed faith. He held stalls at Bristol and Wells and was Chancellor of the latter from 1554 to 1560. He died in 1560.

William Hemerford (1560-1583) BD, was installed in 1560 and, although Roger Marbeck was presented by Queen Mary I, he appears to have remained in possession until his death on 4 October 1583.

Roger Marbeck (1560) MA, although presented by Queen Mary I, failed to gain possession.

Thomas Paynter (1583-1587) MA, held the prebends of Wilsford & Woodford from 1581 to 1583, Slape from 1583 to 1587 and Shipton from 1587 to 1614. He died in 1614.

William Goodwin (1587-1620) MA, died on 11 June 1620.

John Prideaux (1620-1641) was Rector of Exeter College, Oxford, in 1612, Regius Professor of Divinity, Oxford, in 1615 and Chaplain to both King James I and King Charles I. He was appointed Bishop of Worcester in 1641.

Christopher Prior (1641-?) MA, was Principal of New Inn Hall, Oxford. He held a stall at Wells and was Rector of Collingbourne Ducis. He died in 1658.

Thomas Henchman (1660-1661) MA, held the prebends of Slape from 1660 to 1661, and Netherbury in Ecclesia from 1661 to 1674. He held a stall at St Paul's in 1672 and was Archdeacon of Wilts and a Canon Residentiary from 1663 to 1674. He died on 15 December 1674.

Edmund Sly (1661-1663) MA, held the prebends of Slape from 1661 to 1663 and Durnford from 1663 until his death on 19 August 1677. He was Rector of Sherrington from 1670 to 1677 and is commemorated in the cathedral.

Stephen Constable (1663-1684) MA, died in 1684 and was buried at Mildenhall.

Hananiah Gifford (1684-1693) MA, resigned in 1693.

Thomas Green (1693-1720) DD, died on 25 February 1720.

Henry Thorpe (1720-1764) MA, was Vicar of Preshute from 1711 to 1723 and died on 1 May 1764.

Walter Kerrich (1764-1803) MA, was a Fellow of St Catherine's Hall, Cambridge. He was a Canon Residentiary from 1777 to 1803, and was Vicar of Stratford-sub-Castle. He died on 21 July 1803 and is commemorated in the cathedral.

Charles Ekins (1803) MA, was a Fellow of King's College, Cambridge. He held the prebends of Slape in 1803 and Coombe & Harnham from 1803 to 1826. He was a Canon Residentiary from 1804 to 1826 and died in 1826.

John Guard (1804-1829) BD, died on 5 October 1829.

Edward Berens (1829-1859) MA, held the prebend of Slape from 1829 to 1859, was Archdeacon of Berks in Sarum diocese from 1832 to 1836 and in Oxford diocese from 1836 until his resignation in 1855. He was Vicar of Shrivenham in 1804 and Rector of Englefield Green in 1818. He died on 7 April 1859.

Frederick John Rooke (1859-1894) was Rector of Rampisham from 1843 until his death in 1894.

Robert George Swayne (1894-1895) was Rector of St Edmund's, Sarum from 1863 to 1876. He held the prebend of Gillingham Major from 1870 to 1874, was a Canon Residentiary from 1874 to 1894, was Chancellor of Sarum from 1877 until resigning in 1894 and held the prebend of Slape from 1894 to 1895. He died on 22 April 1901.

John David Morrice (1901-1933) MA, was Vicar of Longbridge Deverill with Monkton Deverill & Crockerton from 1875 to 1890 and was Honorary Secretary of the Diocesan Board of Education from 1889 to 1894. He was Rector of St Edmund's, Sarum, from 1890 to 1919, Rural Dean of Sarum and Wilton from 1897 to 1914 and Rector of Monkton Farleigh from 1919 to 1925.

Edward Courtenay West (1934-1938) MA, was Chancellor of Grahamstown Cathedral, South Africa, from 1911 to 1913 and held a stall there from 1911 to 1919. He was Archdeacon of Port Elizabeth from 1917 to 1919 and Principal of St Boniface College, Warminster, from 1929 to 1938. He died in 1938.

Mark Rodolph Carpenter-Garnier (1938-1944) DD, was Bishop of Colombo, Ceylon, from 1924 until resigning in 1938. He was Principal of St Boniface College, Warminster from 1939 to 1942. He held the prebend of Slape from 1938 to 1944 and was Subdean from 1942 until resigning both his prebend and office on 12 July 1944. He died on 11 October 1969.

James Carey (1945) BA, was Rector of Collingbourne Ducis.

George Clare Morrow (1945-1953) MA, was Rector of Moreton from 1920 to 1930 and Rector of Holy Trinity, Dorchester with Frome Whitfield from 1939 to 1950. He was Rector of Bradford Peverell with Stratton from 1950 to ? and Rural Dean of Dorchester from 1942. He died in 1953.

William Strowan Algernon Amherst Robertson (Fr. Algy) (1953-1955) MA, joined Christian Seva Sangha Indian Franciscan community in 1928 and became the first Guardian of the Society of St Francis at Cerne Abbas in 1937, serving until his death in 1955.

Ernest Steward Merriman (1956-1971) BA, was a Chaplain to the Forces from 1917 to 1920 and Rector of Stalbridge from 1925 to 1958. He was Rural Dean of Stalbridge from 1940 to 1954 and of Sturminster Newton from 1954 to 1958. He was Master of St John's Hospital, Heytesbury from 1959 to 1970 and died in 1971..

William Moelwyn Merchant (1971-1973) MA, DLitt, FRSL, Professor, was a Lecturer at University College, Cardiff, from 1939 to 1950, Senior Lecturer from 1950 to 1961 and Reader in 1961. He was Professor of English at Exeter University from 1961 to 1973, Chancellor of Sarum from 1967 to 1970, a Canon Residentiary from 1967 to 1973 and held the prebend of Slape from 1971 to 1973. He died in April 1997.

Geoffrey David Jeremy Walsh (1973-1976) MA, was Rector of Marlborough from 1966 to 1976, a Proctor in Convocation from 1970 to 1975, Archdeacon of Ipswich from 1976 to 1986 and Bishop Suffragan of Tewkesbury from 1986 to 1995.

Herbert John Treasure (1976-1982) MA, was Vicar of Ramsbury with Axford from 1947 to 1958 and of Broadchalke with Bowerchalke from 1958 to 1969. He was Vicar of Puddletown with Athelhampton and Burleston from 1969 to 1975 and Priest-in-Charge of Barford St Martin and of Baverstock and of Dinton and of Compton Chamberlayne from 1975 to 1980, becoming the Rector of all these from 1981 to 1982. He died in January 1993.

Timothy Mark Frowde Biles (1983-) DipTh, was Chaplain to St Francis School, Hooke from 1966-1972, Priest-in-Charge of Toller Porcorum with Hooke from 1972 to 1979, Priest-in-Charge Melplash with Mapperton from 1974 to 1979, Priest-in-Charge Beaminster from 1977 to 1979 and became Team Rector of Beminster in 1979. He was Rural Dean of Beaminster from 1984 to 1989.

COOMBE & HARNHAM

Prebend:- The churches of Coombe Bissett and Harnham in Wiltshire were granted to the cathedral by King Henry I and confirmed by King Henry II in 1158. The prebend was probably in existence by c.1150 and consisted of the churches of Coombe Bissett and Harnham and land at Boscombe. In 1281 it was called Coombe, Harnham & Boscombe but it became Coombe & Harnham in 1291.

Canopy statuette and shield:- **Richard Medford** received the prebend of Bere & Cherminster in 1386 by royal grant, he having exchanged the prebend with Thomas Stowe for the prebend of Highworth, but the Dean's locum refused to install him. Despite charges of fraudulent exchanges, the exchange between Thomas Stowe and Richard Medford was ratified in 1387, the latter assuming the prebend of Highworth. He held stalls at Windsor in 1381 and at York in 1386. He was imprisoned for some time at Bristol by the Parliament as a supporter of King Richard II. He was Archdeacon of Norfolk in 1385 and in 1390 was appointed by the Pope to the see of Chichester. He was translated to the see of Sarum in 1395 and was Bishop until his death on 3 May 1407. He was buried in St Margaret's Chapel in the south west transept of the cathedral and left a small sum to keep the tower and spire in repair, which indicates that they had been completed before his death. (Fig. 35.)

Blazon:- Barry dancetty of four, or and sable, or and azure. [Four equal width, transverse parts with zig-zag edges, from the top: gold, black, gold, blue.]

Psalter:- The portion of the psalter allotted to the prebend is Psalm 105.

Holders of the prebend:-

Luke (of Winchester) des Roches (c.1226/7-1231) was a nephew of Peter des Roches, Bishop of Winchester 1205-1238 and held the prebends of Ruscomb from c.1223 to c.1226, Coombe & Harnham from c.1226/7 to 1231 and Hurstbourne & Burbage from 1231 to c.1253. He held a stall at London, was Archdeacon of Surrey c.1245, Rector of Hurstbourne in 1249 and probably died c.1253.

Thomas of Warwick (1231-?) was a clerk to Robert Bingham, Bishop of Sarum 1220-1246, and was holding the prebend in 1233.

Geoffrey de Meleborn (alias Brito) (before 1281-c.1287) died before 2 February 1290.

Thomas de Ripton (?-c.1298) held the prebend of Beminster Prima from c.1284 to ?. He was a Canon Residentiary in 1285 and held the prebend of Coombe & Harnham from ? to his death by 11 August 1298.

Richard de Bello (1298-?) held in turn during 1298 the prebends of Beminster Prima and Grantham Australis, and also Coombe & Harnham from 1298 to 1305?. He was then given the prebend of Highworth although John de Frescobaldis had already been nominated by the Pope. The Pope tried to restore Frescobaldis to the prebend but the bishop prevented the Dean from oppressing Richard de Bello. Eventually in 1308 there was a papal dispensation allowing de Bello to retain the prebend which he did until 1326. He was Archdeacon of Berks in 1313 and in 1315 had charge of the diocese while the see was vacant on the death of Simon de Gandavo, Bishop of Sarum, 1297-1315. He would seem also to have held a stall at Hereford in 1305 and to have been Rector of Poulshot in 1313.

Richard de Wanetyngg (?-1314) resigned the prebend in 1314.

Iswin de Gandavo (1314-?) was Rector of Beechingstoke in 1304 and of Preshute in 1312. He held the prebends of Major Pars Altaris from 1312 to 1314 and Coombe & Harnham from 1314 to ?. He was Precentor of Sarum in 1323, holding the dignity with the church of Westbury joined to it, and was Archdeacon of Wilts from 12 March 1326 until resigning fifteen days later.

Peter de Vernon (1330) is understood to have received the prebend in 1330 and to have died in 1331.

William de Selton (?-1354) was given the prebend of Yatesbury in 1322 but Peter de Credonio took possession. He held the prebend of Coombe & Harnham from 1331? to 1354 and was Rector of Nettleton in 1328 and of Longbridge Deverill. He died in 1354.

John de Badby (1354-?) held the prebend in 1354.

Hugh de Wymondeswold (1366) Sch.CL, claimed the prebend of Coombe & Harnham in 1366 and held the prebend of Ramsbury from ? until exchanging it in 1378 with Thomas de Oldington for the prebend of Warthill in York.

John de Feriby (1372) held the prebend in 1372.

Richard Beverley (1372-?) received the prebend by royal grant in 1372 and held the prebend of Preston from ? until exchanging it in 1387 with John Carp for the prebend of Whitgreave Parva in the royal free chapel of Stafford.

Thomas Southam (?-1404) Lic.CL, held the prebend of Coombe & Harnham from ? to 1404. He exchanged the Archdeaconry of Oxford for the Archdeaconry of Berks two months before his death on 15 March 1404.

John Medford (1404) was Rector of Huish in 1401 and held the prebends of Coombe & Harnham in 1404, Highworth in 1405 and Yetminster Prima from 1405 to 1407. He died in 1407

John Fraunceys (1404) BCnL, held the prebend of Bere & Cherminster from 1402 to 1404, was Archdeacon of Berks and held the prebend of Coombe & Harnham in 1404.

Robert Broun (1404-1425) BTh, was Rector of Donhead St Mary from 1399 to 1434 and held the prebends of Coombe & Harnham from 1404 to 1425 and Ramsbury from 1425 to 1438. He died in 1438.

John Luke (1425-1435) held the prebends of Hurstbourne & Burbage in 1415, Slape from 1415 to 1425 and Coombe & Harnham from 1425 to 1435. He died in 1435.

John Cranborne (1435-1452) BCL, held the prebends of Rotesfen from 1432 to 1435, Coombe & Harnham from 1435 to 1452 and Hurstbourne & Burbage from 1452 to 1474. He died in 1474.

John Stretton (1452-1457) DCL, held the prebends of Coombe & Harnham from 1452 to 1457, Yatesbury from 1457 to 1458, Grantham Australis from 1458 to 1471, Bedminster & Redcliffe from 1471 to 1474 and Chisenbury & Chute from 1474 to 1475. He was Rector of Poulshot in 1459. He died on 1 January 1475.

John Stokes (1457-1467) DCL, held a stall at St Paul's in 1430. From 1457 to 1467 he was Precentor of Sarum and held the prebend of Coombe & Harnham, receiving the prebend from John Stretton in exchange for the Treasurership of Chichester. He was probably Archdeacon of Ely in 1445 and held a stall at Hereford. He died in 1467.

Lionel Woodville (1467-1478) LicCnL, was a brother-in-law to King Edward IV, being the son of Richard, Earl Rivers, whose daughter Elizabeth, co-foundress with Margaret of Anjou of Queens' College, Cambridge, was married to the King. He held a stall at Lincoln in 1465, the prebends of Coombe & Harnham from 1467 to 1478 and of Bere & Cherminster from 1478 to 1482. He was also Archdeacon of Oxford and Dean of Exeter, becoming Bishop of Sarum from 1482 to 1484. His death in June 1484 was said to have been hastened by grief at the downfall of his family on the accession of King Richard II, and the execution at Salisbury of Henry Stafford, Duke of Buckingham, his brother-in-law. He was buried in the cathedral.

John Emwell (1478-1485) BCnL, was Precentor of Sarum from 1479 to 1480. He held the prebends of Netheravon from 1476 to 1478 and Coombe & Harnham from 1478 to 1485. He resigned the dignity in 1480 and died in 1485.

Geoffrey Ellis (1485-1507) BCL, died in 1507 and desired to be buried in the cathedral.

James Bromwich (1507) BCnL, held the prebends of Axford from 1505 to 1507, Coombe & Harnham in 1507, Grimston from 1507 to 1515, Faringdon from 1515 to 1519 and Hurstbourne & Burbage from 1519 to 1524. He was Chancellor of Hereford in 1518 and became Archdeacon of Sarum in 1524, dying a month after his appointment.

Edward Higgins (1507-1509) Lic.CnL, was Vicar of Steeple Ashton and held the prebends of Axford and of Chardstock in 1507, Coombe & Harnham from 1507 to 1509 and Netherbury in Ecclesia from 1509 to 1538. He died in 1538.

John Estmond (1509-1514) MA, held the prebends of Axford from 1507 to 1508, Rotesfen from 1508 to 1509, Coombe & Harnham from 1509 to 1514 and Minor Pars Altaris from 1517 to 1519 He died in 1519.

William Creting (1514-1519) MA, died in 1519.

Henry Rawlyns (1519-1521) BCL, was well provided with prebends. He held Yatesbury from1513 to 1514, Grantham Australis from 1514 to 1519 and Coombe & Harnham 1519 to 1521. He resigned the last in May 1521, was succeeded by Cuthbert Tunstall who then became Dean of Sarum, and was again collated to the prebend later in the same year. The prebend then passed to Richard Pace but was assumed by Henry Rawlyns for the third time in 1523. He then held Faringdon from 1523 to 1524, Hurstbourne & Burbage in 1524 and Teynton Regis, together with the Archdeaconry of Sarum from 1524 to 1526. He was Rector of Christian Malford, died in 1526 and is buried in the cathedral near Bishop Audley's chantry.

Cuthbert Tunstal (1521) DCn&CL, was Rector of Steeple Langford and became Archdeacon of Chester in 1515, held a stall at York in 1519 and was Master of the Rolls in 1516. For a brief period in 1521 he held the prebend of Coombe & Harnham, apparently so as to become eligible for the dignity of Dean of Sarum which he held from 1521 to 1522. He was consecrated Bishop of London in 1522, becoming Keeper of the Privy Seal in 1523. He was transferred to the see of Durham in 1530 but in 1551 was deprived by King Edward VI and confined in the Tower. He was restored by Queen Mary I but deprived again by Queen Elizabeth I and placed in honourable custody in Lambeth Palace where he died in 1559 at the age of 89.

Henry Rawlyns (1521) see above.

Richard Pace (1521-1523) was secretary to King Henry VIII. He held stalls at Southwell from 1510 to 1514 and at York in 1514. He was Archdeacon of Dorset from 1514 to 1523, holding the prebend of Coombe & Harnham from 1521 to 1523 and was Dean of Sarum from 1523 to 1536. He died on 28 June 1536.

Henry Rawlyns (1523) see above.

John Chamber (1523-1549) DM, held the prebends of Stratford from 1518 until resigning in 1519, and Coombe & Harnham from 1523 to 1549. He was most probably physician to King Henry VIII and Archdeacon of Meath. If so, he was Dean of Westminster and one of the first members of the College of Physicians. He may well have been Warden of Merton College, Oxford from 1525 to 1544 and Archdeacon of Bedford from 1524 until his death in 1549.

Thomas Mille (1549-1554) was deprived as a layman in 1554. He was restored c.1559 but died in 1566.

Robert Kynsey (1554-?) MA.

Thomas Mille (?-1566) see above, was restored c.1559.

Leonard Parry (1566-1614) died in 1614.

John Chappell (1614-1672) MA, died in 1672.

Seth Ward (1672-1681) MA, was a nephew of Seth Ward, Bishop of Sarum 1667-1689. He was Archdeacon of Wilts from 1675 to 1681, Chancellor of Sarum from 1681 to 1687 and Treasurer of Sarum from 1687 to 1690. He held the prebend of Coombe & Harnham from 1672 to 1681, died on 11 May 1690 aged 43 and was buried in the cathedral near the grave of his uncle.

William Samm (1681-1687/8) MA, was a nephew of Seth Ward, Bishop of Sarum 1667-1689. He had died by 14 January 1688.

Edward Young (1688-1702) BCL, was a Fellow of New College, Oxford, and a Fellow of Winchester. He held the prebends of Gillingham Minor from 1682 to 1688 and Coombe & Harnham from 1688 to 1702, and was Dean of Sarum and a Canon Residentiary from 1702 to 1705. He died on 9 August 1705 and was buried in the cathedral.

White Kennett (1702-1720) DD, became Bishop of Peterborough in 1718 but continued to hold the prebend of Coombe & Harnham until 1720.

Abraham Frank (1720-1733) MA, died on 1 September 1733 and is commemorated at West Dean, Wiltshire.

Thomas Woodford (1733-1779) LLB, was the author of *Paraphrase on the Psalms* and died in 1779.

John Hume (1779-1782) MA, was Master of St Nicholas Hospital, Sarum in 1774. He held the prebend of Coombe & Harnham from 1779 until exchanging it in 1782 with Edward Emily for the Vicarage of Bishop's Lavington and the Mastership of St Nicholas Hospital, Sarum.

Edward Emily (1782-1792) MA, was Vicar of Bishop's Lavington and Master of St Nicholas Hospital, Sarum in 1782. He left an estate at Woking valued at £6,000 to Shute Barrington, Bishop of Sarum 1782-1791, who added it to the endowment of St Nicholas Hospital. He died on 20 June 1792 and is commemorated at the Hospital.

William Douglas (1792-1799) MA, was a son of John Douglas, Bishop of Sarum 1791-1807. He was Archdeacon of Wilts from 1799 to 1804, a Canon Residentiary from 1799 to 1819 and Precentor of Sarum from 1804 to 1819. He held the prebends of Coombe & Harnham from 1792 to 1799 and Fordington & Writhlington from 1799 to 1819. He was also Chancellor of the Diocese, Master of St Nicholas Hospital, Sarum in 1792, Rector of Brixton Deverill and Vicar of Potterne. He died on 19 March 1819.

Barfoot Colton (1799-1803) MA, held the prebends of Ruscomb from 1783 to 1799 and Coombe & Harnham from 1799 to 1803. He was a Canon Residentiary from 1788 to 1803 and died in 1803.

Charles Ekins (1803-1826) MA, was a Fellow of King's College, Cambridge. He held the prebends of Slape in 1803 and Coombe & Harnham from 1803 to 1826. He was a Canon Residentiary from 1804 to 1826 and died in 1826.

John Bright (1826-1833) MA, died on 27 July 1833.

Lord Charles Paulet (1833-1870) MA, was the 2nd son of the 13th Marquis of Winchester. He died on 23 July 1870.

Henry Blackstone Williams (1870-1880) MA, was a Fellow of New College, Oxford and in 1849 a Fellow of Winchester. He was Rector of Bradford Peverell from 1850 until his death in 1880.

Charles King (1880-?) MA, was Priest-Vicar from 1835 to 1880 and was Vicar of Stratford-sub-Castle in 1852.

Edward Russell Bernard (1886-1921) MA, was a Fellow of Magdalen College, Oxford and was Vicar of Tarrant Monkton with Tarrant Launceston from 1870 to 1876, a Canon Residentiary from 1889 to 1909, Chancellor of Sarum from 1894 to 1917, a Chaplain in Ordinary to Queen Victoria from 1899 to 1901 and subsequently to Kings Edward VII and George V. He was Rural Dean of Wimborne from 1905 to 1907. He held the prebend of Coombe & Harnham from 1886 until his death on 22 April 1921.

Frederick Phipps (1921-1934) BA, was Vicar of Frome Vauchurch with Batcombe from 1885 to 1901 and Vicar of St Peter's, Devizes, from 1901. He died on 9 October 1934.

Anthony Arnold Mayhew (1935-1939) MA, held a stall at St Albans from 1932 to 1935 and was a Canon Residentiary, with the prebend of Coombe & Harnham from 1935 to 1939, Pro-Prolocutor of the House of Clergy of the Convocation of Canterbury and a Proctor in Convocation from 1936 to 1939 and Subdean of Sarum from 1938 until his death in 1939.

John Jones (1939-1941) BA, was Rector of Marlborough from 1929 to 1941 and Rural Dean of Marlborough from 1931 to 1941. He resigned his prebend on leaving the diocese.

Alfred Swann (1941-1952) DSC, MA, was Dean and Archdeacon of Hong Kong from 1927 to 1935. He was Vicar of Potterne and Rural Dean of Potterne from 1935 to 1941, Rector of Marlborough from 1941 to 1952, Perpetual Curate of Christ Church, Savernake, from 1941 to 1947 and Rural Dean of Marlborough from 1942 to 1952.

Arthur Robert Dittmer (1953-?) LTh, was Rector of Pimperne from 1923 to 1936 and Rural Dean of Blandford from 1935 to 1936. He was Rector of Burton Bradstock with Shipton Gorge (with Chilcombe from 1954) from 1936, a Proctor in Convocation from 1947 to 1960 and Rural Dean of Bridport from 1952.

William David Conwyl Williams (1974-1986) OBE, BA, was Chaplain to the Forces from 1935 to 1960 and Honorary Chaplain to Queen Elizabeth II from 1957 to 1960. He was Rector of Devizes St John with St Mary from 1960 to 1977, Rural Dean of Devizes from 1973 to 1977, Master of St Nicholas Hospital, Sarum from 1977 to 1986 and died on 15 April 1995.

[Dame Muriel Diana Reader Harris (1987-1992) DBE, BA, FRSA, FCP, Lay Canon, was Headmistress Sherborne School for Girls from 1950 to 1975, President of the Association of Headmistresses from 1953 to 1958 and of the Association of Headmistresses of Boarding Schools from 1960 to 1962. Among her many concerns, she served on the Archbishop's Council on Evangelism from 1966 to 1968, on the General Synod Broadcasting Panel from 1975 to 1986, and on King George's Jubilee Trust from 1949 to 1979. She was a member of the board, later chairman, of Christian Aid from 1976 to 1983, President of the Church Missionary Society from 1969 to 1982, a member of the Council of Westminster Abbey Choir School from 1976 to 1988 and a Governor of Godolphin School, Sarum from 1975 to 1986. She was a member, later vice-president, of the Council of the Royal Society of Arts from 1975 to 1989. She occupied Coombe & Harnham as a courtesy stall and died on 7 October 1996.]

[Lionel Dakers (1993-1998) CBE, DMus, FRCO, FRCM, Mus.B, Lay Canon, was Assistant Organist St George's Chapel, Windsor from 1950 to 1954, Organist Ripon Cathedral from 1954 to 1957, Organist Exeter Cathedral from 1957 to 1972 and Director of the Royal School of Church Music from 1972 to 1989. An author, he was Chairman of the Diocesan Advisory Committee from 1990 to 1998 and a co-opted member of the Close Chapter from 1993 to 1998. He occupied Coombe & Harnham as a courtesy stall.]

Henry Gervis Pearson (1999-) MA, became Team Rector of Marlborough Team Ministry in 1991 and Rural Dean of Marlborough in 1994.

(Gangway)

Shield:- **Stephen Gardiner** DCn&CL, was appointed by Cardinal Wolsey, acting on behalf of Lorenzo Campegio, Bishop of Sarum 1525-1534, to the prebend of Teynton Regis which he held from after 1526 until 1531. He was secretary to Wolsey and ambassador to Rome. He resigned the prebend in 1531 to become Bishop of Winchester. (Fig. 36.)

Blazon:- Azure on a cross or between four griffins' heads erased argent a cinquefoil pierced gules. [On a blue shield, a gold cross with a red, pierced five petalled flower in its centre between four silver griffins' heads, as if torn from the body.]

WARMINSTER

Prebend:- Warminster in Wiltshire was a royal manor in 1066 and 1086. Two hides of land held by Walter, son of Edward, were given to the cathedral by King Henry I, confirmed in 1146 by the Pope and in 1158 by King Henry II. The prebend comprising this land was probably in existence c.1150.

Shield:- **William of Wykeham** held the prebend of Yetminster Prima in 1361, before he was in Holy Orders, exchanging it in the same year with Richard de Spridlington for the prebend of Fordington & Writhlington, which he held from 1361 to 1366. He was appointed to the prebend of Bedminster & Redcliffe in 1361 but may have returned to Fordington & Writhlington. He became Bishop of Winchester in 1367 and was the founder of New College, Oxford and Winchester College. (Fig. 37.)

Blazon:- Argent two chevrons sable between three roses pierced gules. [On a silver shield, two black chevrons between three red pierced roses.]

Psalter:- The portion of the psalter allotted to the prebend is Psalms 116, 117 and 118.

Holders of the prebend:-

Peter Picot (c.1226/7-c.1232) was Clerk to the Dean & Chapter of Sarum and may have held a stall at Exeter.

Robert Foliot (c.1242/3-?) held the prebend in 1257 and had died by 28 June 1286.

Hugh de Albiniaco (?-c.1263) had resigned the prebend by 15 March 1263.

Walter de Albiniaco (1263-?) was 'Custodian of the Queen's Lands' from 1264 to 1367.

John de Polbergh (alias Medicus) (c.1284-?) held the prebend of Warminster from c.1284 to ?, when he transferred to the prebend of Beminster Prima, holding the latter until his death in 1298.

Osbert de Baggeston (?-1304) held the prebend in 1297 and died holding it by 22 January 1304.

Walter Hervy (1304) held the prebends of Warminster in 1304, Beminster Secunda from 1304 to 1314, Teynton Regis in 1314 and Beminster Secunda again in 1326.

John de Abbotsbury (?-1328) held the prebend in 1320 and died in 1328.

Thomas de Bocton (1327-1348) MA, was Subdean of Sarum from 1321 to c.1327 and held the prebends of Minor Pars Altaris from 1325 to 1327 and Warminster from 1327 to 1348. He died in 1348.

Itherius de Concoreto (1328) BCn&CL, was nominated to the prebend of Warminster in 1328 although Thomas de Bocton had received it a year earlier. Six months later he was nominated to the prebend of Faringdon which he was holding in 1337, despite a royal grant in 1335 to William de Excestre. He was Archdeacon of London, held a stall at St Paul's, and was Chancellor of Ely. He had married by June 1343.

Thomas de Tughall (1348-?) was nominated to the prebend in 1348 but Thomas de Bocton was still holding it.

Baldwin de Mohun (1348) received the prebend by royal grant in July 1348 but died within five months.

Bartholomew de Bradden (?-1361) held the prebend of Axford from 1344 to 1350 and claimed the dignity of Treasurer of Sarum in 1351 but the claim was passed to the Courts. He received papal confirmation of the prebend of Warminster in 1350 and resigned it in 1361. He was Rector of St Peter's Marlborough from 1334 to 1336, Rector of Barford St Martin and in 1342 was Master of St Nicholas Hospital, Sarum.

William Byde (1361-1391) BCL, held the prebend of Warminster from 1361 to 1391 and unsuccessfully claimed the prebend of Bere & Cherminster in 1386. He was a Canon Residentiary.

Richard Holme (1391-1393) held the prebend of Warminster from 1391 to 1393, exchanging it with Robert Ragenhull in 1393 for the prebend of Bishopstone which he held until 1424. He died in 1424.

Robert Ragenhull (1393-1406) was a Canon Residentiary and Archdeacon of Dorset from 1388 to c.1390. He held the prebend of Bishopstone in 1393, exchanging it with Richard Holme for the prebend of Warminster, which he exchanged with John Tydeling in 1406 for the prebend of Major Pars Altaris, which he held until 1407. He was Provost of St Edmund's College, Sarum in 1395 and died in 1407.

John Tydeling (1406-1418) BCL, was a Canon Residentiary and held the prebend of Axford from 1401 to 1404 and exchanged it with George Westby for the prebend of Major Pars Altaris in 1404, which he held until 1406. He then held the prebends of Warminster from 1406 to 1418, Yetminster Secunda in 1418, Beminster Prima from 1418 to 1420 and Stratton from 1420 to 1437, exchanging the last with John Symondsburgh for the prebend of Yatesbury in 1437. This he exchanged with John Morton for the prebend of North Leverton in Southwell collegiate church, Notts.

William Milton (1418-1424) Lic.CL, held the prebends of Minor Pars Altaris from 1400 to 1418 and Warminster from 1418 to 1424. He died in 1424.

John Hody (1424-1440) BCL, was uncle to Sir John Hody, Lord Chief Justice of England in the time of King Henry VI; his brother had an estate at Kington Magna. He was Rector of Bishopstrow from 1420 to 1425, Chancellor of Wells in 1426, and held a stall at York from 1426 to 1436. He was Archdeacon of Dorset from 1437 to 1440, in which year he died.

Robert Ayscough (1440-1441) DCnL, held the prebends of Warminster from 1440 to 1441, Bishopstone from 1441 to 1446 and Alton Borealis from 1446 to 1459. He had resigned by 9 April 1459.

John Pyville (1441-1442) BTh, held the prebends of Warminster from 1441 to 1442 and Yetminster Secunda from 1442 until resigning in 1446. He was Provost of St Edmund's College, Sarum.

Nicholas Cecill (1442-1445) held the prebends of Warminster from 1442 to 1445 and Alton Australis from 1445 to 1447. He died in 1447.

William Normanton (1445-1446) held the prebends of Yatesbury from 1443 to 1445, Warminster from 1445 to 1446, Bishopstone from 1446 to 1447, Durnford from 1447 to 1448, Chisenbury & Chute from 1448 to 1449 and Faringdon from 1449 to 1459. He died in 1459.

Thomas Kirkeby (1446-1448) held the prebends of Yatesbury from 1445 to 1446, Warminster from 1446 to 1448, Netheravon from 1448 to 1449, Ramsbury from 1449 to 1464 and Highworth from 1464 to 1476. He also held the prebend of Stanton Berners under the Abbey of Wilton and died in 1476.

John Bolde (1448-1451) BCnL, died in 1451.

Henry Trevilian (1451-1472) BCL, died in 1472.

William Chauntry (1472-1475) held the prebend of Warminster from 1472 until resigning in 1475. He then held the prebend of Fordington & Writhlington from 1482 until his death in 1485.

Thomas Burley (1475-?) held the prebend in 1486.

Robert Sherborne (?-1494) BM, resigned the prebend in 1494, was Dean of St Paul's in 1499, Bishop of St David's in 1505 and Bishop of Chichester in 1508.

Simon Stalworth (1494-1495) MA, held the prebend of Warminster from 1494 to 1495 and was Precentor of Sarum from 1506 to 1507. He died in 1511.

William Oldham (1495-1497) resigned the prebend in 1497.

Thomas Randolph (1497-1511) Lic.CnL, held the prebends of Warminster from 1497 to 1511 and Bishopstone from 1511 to 1521. He died in 1521.

John Stone (1511-1517) BCL, held the prebends of Axford from 1509 to 1511, Warminster from 1511 to 1517, Chardstock from 1517 to 1524 and Fordington & Writhlington from 1524.

Alexander Audley (1517) died only six months after receiving the prebend.

Thomas Wever (1517-1520) MA, resigned the prebend in 1520.

Peter Roderic (1520-1524) resigned the prebend in 1524.

John Quarre (1524-?) held the prebend in 1539, was still alive as Archdeacon of Llandaff in 1545 but had been succeeded in the prebend in 1558.

Richard Domynycke (1558-?) was firmly opposed to the Reformation and was deprived of his livings under Queen Elizabeth I.

John Percey (1561-1563) was summoned at the Visitation of the cathedral in 1563 by John Jewell, Bishop of Sarum 1560-1571, and was deprived for preaching and celebrating divine service while excommunicate.

William Bennett (1563-?) was deprived of the prebend.

Lewis Evans (1584-1600) resigned the prebend in 1600.

Edward Evans (1600-1626) was excommunicated for failing to pay the stipend of his Vicar and resigned the prebend in 1626.

Francis Matkin (1626-?) BCL, held the prebend in 1634.

Richard Hyde (1660-1666) DCL, held the prebend of Warminster from 1660 to 1666, the office of Subdean of Sarum from 1661 to 1664 and the prebend of Grantham Borealis in 1666. He held a stall at Winchester in 1662 and died in 1666.

Richard Watson (1666-1671) DD, held the prebends of Warminster from 1666 to 1671 and Bitton from 1671 to 1685. He was Rector of Pewsey and donated a valuable collection of books to the cathedral library. He died on 13 January 1685 and is commemorated at Pewsey.

Robert Hawkins (1672) BD, was Rector of Trowbridge. He died in 1672 and was buried in Trowbridge.

Paul Latham (1672-1687) MA, author of a theological work and a preacher of considerable note was Vicar of Warminster in 1660. He died in 1687 and was buried at Warminster.

Thomas Lessey (1687-1726) MA, died on 2 March 1726.

Joseph Sager (1726-1732) MA, held the prebends of Warminster from 1726 to 1732 and Gillingham Major from 1732 to 1757. He was a Canon Residentiary from 1726 to 1757 and Archdeacon of Sarum from 1727 until resigning in 1732. He died on 18 July 1757 and was buried in the cathedral.

John Straight (1732-1736) BD, died in 1736.

Hugh Wynne (1737-1738) LLD, held the prebends of Warminster from 1737 to 1738 and Stratton from 1738 to 1754. He was a Canon Residentiary from 1739 to 1754 and died on 13 October 1754.

Charles Moss (1738-1740) MA, held the prebends of Warminster from 1738 to 1740 and Hurstbourne & Burbage from 1740 to 1786. He was a Canon Residentiary from 1746 to 1786 whilst becoming Bishop of St David's in 1766 and of Bath & Wells in 1774. He died in 1802.

John Clarke (1740-1741) MA, died on 19 June 1741.

William Miles (1741-1748) MA, died in 1748.

William Miles (1748-1773) died in 1773.

Benjamin Spry (1773-1774) MA, held the prebends of Warminster from 1773 to 1774 and Teynton Regis from 1774 to 1806. He died on 1 October 1806.

George Watson Hand (1775-1802) MA, held a stall at St Paul's in 1775 and was Archdeacon of Dorset in the diocese of Bristol, holding a stall at Bristol, from 1780 to 1801. He died on 3 February 1802.

John Frederick Browning (1802) held the prebends of Warminster in 1802 and Ufcomb from 1802 to 1823.

Henry Hetley (1802-1832) BD, was Vicar of South Newton and also became Vicar of Aldworth, Berkshire in 1782, dying on 12 March 1832.

William Dalby (1832-1861) MA, was Rector of Compton Basset and Vicar of Warminster. He died on 3 December 1861.

Richard Payne (1861-1890) BCL, was a Fellow of New College, Oxford. He was Vicar of Downton from 1841 to 1882, Rural Dean of Wilton from 1848 to 1879 and Proctor in Convocation from 1879 to 1882. He died on 8 November 1890.

Edward Steward (1890-1930) was Chaplain & Lecturer at Sarum Training College from 1880 to 1889 and Principal from 1889 to 1913. He was Rector of Boyton (with Sherrington from 1909) from 1907 to 1924. He died on 11 April 1930.

Francis Earle Trotman (1930-1956) MA, was Vicar of Mere from 1909 to 1927 and was Rural Dean of Heytesbury from 1925 to 1927. He was Rector of Long Bredy with Little Bredy from 1927 to 1947 and was Rural Dean of Abbotsbury from 1929 to 1947. He held the prebends of Warminster from 1930 to 1956 and Ufcomb, together with the living of Vicar of the Close, from 1956 to 1959. He died in 1959.

David Rokeby Maddock (1956-1967) MA, was Vicar of Wilton from 1943 to 1947, Rector of Wareham with Arne from 1947 to 1961, Curate-in-Charge of Grange from 1950 to 1961 and Rural Dean of Purbeck from 1948 to 1961. He held the prebend of Warminster from 1956 to 1967, was Archdeacon of Sherborne and Rector of Bradford Peverell with Stratton from 1961 to 1966, Bishop Suffragan of Dunwich from 1967 to 1976 and Provost of Bury St Edmund from 1976 to 1980. He died on 14 August 1984.

William Ancell Martin Langdon (1968-1981) MA, was Chaplain of HM Borstal, Portland from 1945 to 1949 and Rector of All Saints with St Peter, Portland from 1948 to 1951. He was Rector of Langton Matravers from 1951 to 1961. He was Vicar of Melksham from 1961 to 1969, Rural Dean of Bradford from 1967 to 1969 and Vicar of Charminster from 1969 to 1981.

Michael John Apps (Bro Bernard) (1981-1989) MA, joined the Society of St Francis in 1958. He was the Guardian of Hillfield Friary from 1978 to 1989 and a Proctor in Convocation from 1980 to 1990.

Roger Sharpe (1989-) MA, was Vicar of Redlynch and Morgan's Vale from 1968 to 1986 and Rural Dean of Alderbury from 1982 to 1986. He was Vicar of Warminster St Denys, Rector of Upton Scudamore and Priest in Charge of Horningsham from 1986 to 1988, Rector of Warminster St Denys, Upton Scudamore & Horningsham from 1988 to 1995, Rural Dean of Heytesbury from 1989 to 1995, Priest in Charge of Corsley and Chapmanslade from 1992 to 1995 and Rector of Cley Hill Warminster Team from 1995.

YETMINSTER SECUNDA

Prebend:- Yetminster in Dorset was part of the pre-Conquest Sherborne episcopal estates. By c.1150 two prebends were probably in existence, which were called 'Ethemenstri W de Len' and 'Ethemenstr Tancre' in the 1220s. These later became Yetminster Prima, otherwise Superior, or Overbury, or Upbury, and Yetminster Secunda, otherwise Inferior, or Southbury.

Shield:- **Henry Chichele** DCL, was appointed Archdeacon of Dorset in 1397 and after two years' litigation at the Curia over the claims of Nicholas Bubwith, he was declared technically an intrusor but was reinstated in 1399 although Bubwith was appointed a year later. He held the prebends of Rotesfen in 1397, Yetminster Prima from 1397 to 1400, Fordington & Writhlington in 1400, Yetminster Secunda from 1400 to 1402 and Bedminster & Redcliffe from 1402 to 1404, when he exchanged the last with George Westby for the prebend of Fordington & Writhlington. After litigation, he became Archdeacon of Sarum in 1402, exchanging this and the prebend in 1404 for the dignity of Chancellor of Sarum which, following his consecration as Bishop of St David's in 1407, he continued to hold by papal indulgence until 1409. At one time he held the living of Melcombe Bingham and he became Archbishop of Canterbury in 1414. He was the founder of All Souls, Oxford and died on 12 April 1443. (Fig. 38.)

Blazon:- Or a chevron between three cinquefoils pierced gules. [On a gold shield a red chevron between three red pierced five petalled flowers.]

Psalter:- The portion of psalms allotted to the prebend is Psalm 107.

Holders of the prebend:-

Tancred (c.1226/7) was Archdeacon of Bologna in 1226, fined for non-residence in 1227 and was recorded as 'a Roman, absent abroad' in 1228. He was a canonist and compiler of *Compilatio Quinta*.

Richard Coleshulle (c.1284-c.1291) held the prebend in 1291 and had charge of the spiritualities of the diocese during the vacancy following the death of William de la Corner, Bishop of Sarum 1289 to 1291 and held the prebend in 1291.

William de Melton (1315) held the prebends of Yetminster Secunda in 1315 and Yetminster Prima from 1315 to 1316. He resigned his prebend in 1316 on becoming Archbishop of York.

Nicholas Lambert (1322,1326) was holding the prebend in both 1322 and 1326.

William Nadale (?-1339) DTh, resigned the prebend in 1339.

John Gifford (1339-1349) died in 1349.

John de Wynwyk (1349-1359) exchanged the prebend in 1359 with John de Welwyk for the prebend of Monkton in Ripon collegiate church.

John de Welwyk (1359-?).

Richard de Spridlington (1366) held the prebend in 1366.

Simon de Borsano (1379) held the prebends of Grimston and Yetminster Secunda in 1379.

Peter de Erghum (1386-?).

William Litlyngton (1387,1389) received the prebend in 1387 and despite a royal grant to Guy Mone in 1388, produced in 1389 royal letters of confirmation.

Guy Mone (1388-?) was granted the prebend of Yetminster Secunda in 1388, He held the prebends of Grantham Borealis from 1395 until resigning in 1396, and Faringdon in 1397. He held a stall at St Paul's and was Treasurer of that cathedral from 1394 to 1397, when he became Bishop of St David's. He twice held the office of Treasurer of England.

Adam Easton (?-1392) DTh, was a Benedictine who exchanged the prebend of Yetminster Secunda in 1392 with John de Icklington for the church of Heigham, Norfolk. He was made Archdeacon of Dorset by papal grant in 1396 and although he disputed a royal grant to Michael Cergeaux later in the same year, the possession of the dignity was still in dispute on his death. He was created Cardinal-Priest of St Cecilia in 1381/1383 and was one of the six cardinals whom Pope Urban VI had imprisoned and tortured for rebellion. He was spared at the intercession of King Richard II, resigning the cardinalate but was restored by Pope Boniface IX in 1389. He is described as learned, not only in Greek but in Hebrew and as a voluminous writer. He died at the Vatican shortly before 19 September 1397.

John Icklington (1392) resigned in 1392.

Richard Pittes (1392-1415) was a notary public and a Canon Residentiary.

Henry Chichele (1400-1402) DCL, was appointed to the Archdeaconry of Dorset in 1397 and after two years' litigation at the Curia over the claims of Nicholas Bubwith, he was declared technically an intrusor, but was reinstated in 1399, although Bubwith was appointed a year later. He held the prebends of Rotesfen in 1397, Yetminster Prima from 1397 to 1400, Fordington & Writhlington in 1400, Yetminster Secunda from 1400 to 1402 and Bedminster & Redcliffe from 1402 to 1404, when he exchanged with George Westby for the prebend of Fordington & Writhlington. After litigation, he became Archdeacon of Sarum in 1402, exchanging this and the prebend in 1404 for the dignity of Chancellor of Sarum which, following his consecration as Bishop of St David's in 1407, he continued to hold by papal indulgence until 1409. At one time he held the living of Melcombe Bingham and he became Archbishop of Canterbury in 1414. He was the founder of All Souls, Oxford and died on 12 April 1443.

Simon Sydenham (1415-1418) DCL, incorrectly accepted nomination to the Archdeaconry of Berks in 1404 but was pardoned and exchanged it for the Archdeaconry of Sarum which he held from 1404 to 1418. He held the rectory of Sutton Veny from 1417 to 1421 and the prebends of Rotesfen from 1407 to 1415 and Yetminster Secunda from 1415 to 1418 and was Dean of Sarum from 1418 to 1431. Although in 1426 he was elected to the see of Sarum, the Chapter on the recommendation of King Henry VI, gave way to a papal provision in favour of Robert Neville. In 1431 he was consecrated as Bishop of Chichester.

John Tydeling (1418) BCL, was a Canon Residentiary and held the prebend of Axford from 1401 to 1404, exchanging it with George Westby for the prebend of Major Pars Altaris in 1404, which he held until 1406. He then held the prebends of Warminster from 1406 to 1418, Yetminster Secunda in 1418, Beminster Prima from 1418 to 1420, Stratton from 1420 to 1437, exchanging the last with John Symondsburgh for the prebend of Yatesbury in 1437. This he exchanged with John Morton for the prebend of North Leverton in Southwell collegiate church, Notts.

Richard Leyot (1418-1423) DCL, held the prebends of Yetminster Secunda from 1418 to 1423 and Grimston from 1423 to 1446, and was Dean of Sarum from 1446 to 1449. He died on 26 January 1449.

John Haket (1423-1442) DCL, received the prebend of Chardstock in 1406 but a royal grant was made to John Bathe. He held the prebends of Major Pars Altaris from 1413 to 1423 and Yetminster Secunda from 1423 to 1442. He died in 1442.

John Pyville (1442-1466) BTh, held the prebends of Warminster from 1441 to 1442 and Yetminster Secunda from 1442 until resigning in 1466. He was Provost of St Edmund's College, Sarum.

Adam Copendale (1466-1469) DCL, held the prebends of Yetminster Secunda from 1466 to 1469, and Stratton from 1469 until exchanging it in 1479 with Edmund Chaderton for the prebend of St Katharine's altar in Beverley collegiate church, Yorks.

Thomas Estington (1469-1471) Sch.Th, held the prebends of Alton Borealis from 1459 to 1469 and Yetminster Secunda from 1469 to 1471. He died on 3 January 1471.

John Peese (1471) DCL, held the prebends of Yetminster Secunda in 1471 and Grimston from 1471 to 1487. He died in 1487.

William Dudley (1471-1476) MA, held a stall at St Paul's and was Archdeacon of Middlesex in 1475. He became Dean of Windsor in 1473 and Bishop of Durham in 1476.

John Seymour (1476-1502) died in 1502.

George Sydenham (1502-1518) BCn&CL, held the prebends of Yetminster Secunda from 1502 to 1518 and Fordington & Writhlington from 1518 to 1524. He was Archdeacon of Sarum from 1503 to 1524 and was Chaplain to Kings Henry VII and Henry VIII. He died in 1524 and was buried in the cathedral.

William Pykenham (1518-1519) BCL, held the prebends of Yatesbury from 1515 to 1517, Ruscomb from 1517 to 1518, Yetminster Secunda from 1518 to 1519, Grantham Australis in 1519 and Grantham Borealis from 1519 to 1535. He died in 1535.

Reginald Pole (1519-1537) BA, son of Sir Richard Pole and a relative of King Henry VIII, was a Fellow of Corpus Christi College, Oxford and was on friendly terms with Ignatius Loyola. He held the Deanery of Wimborne in 1518 and the prebends of Ruscomb from 1518 to 1519 and Yetminster Secunda from 1519 to 1537 but was deprived in 1537. He held the Vicarage of Piddlehinton in 1532. He was ordained deacon in 1536 being created Cardinal-Deacon of St Nereus & St Achilles, Cardinal of St Vitus & St Modestus in the following year, and in 1540 of St Mary in Cosmedin. Also in 1540, as Papal Legate, he reconciled England to Rome He was ordained priest in 1556 and in the same year was consecrated Archbishop of Canterbury but died twenty months later, at the age of 58, on 17 November 1558, the same day as Queen Mary I, and was buried at Canterbury. Erasmus wrote of him 'as deserving a principal place among my friends' and the Emperor Charles VI was urged to persuade him to seek marriage with Princess Mary when she was heir to the throne. He was however too deeply attached to learning to be dazzled by the glamour.

Sir Richard Moryson (1537-1539) MA, was a lawyer, not in holy Orders, who resigned the prebend in 1539. He was a member of Parliament and secretary to Cromwell. He was employed in various embassies, knighted in 1550 and died at Strasbourg in 1556.

Henry Cole (1539-?) was ordained deacon in 1542 whilst already holding this prebend, a rectory and a stall at St Paul's. He became Warden of New College, Oxford in 1542, Provost of Eton in 1554 and Dean of St Paul's in 1556. He was deprived of his benefices early in the reign of Queen Elizabeth I and died in January 1580.

Thomas Handford (1559).

Henry Willett (1562-1563) was summoned for simony and perjury at the Visitation of the cathedral in 1563 by John Jewell, Bishop of Sarum 1560-1571, and was deprived.

Richard Bennet (1563-1592).

Edward Grant (1592-?) DD, held the prebend in 1593.

John Fennell (1595-?) MA.

Walter Benet (1610-1614) BD, was Precentor of Sarum from 1608 to 1614 and held the prebends of Yetminster Secunda from 1610 to 1614 and Stratton in 1614. He was Archdeacon of Wilts from 1610 to 1614, holding with this the rectory of Mynty. He died in 1614.

Simon Holdip (1614-?) BA, held the prebend in 1634.

John Wall (1644-1666) DD, died on 20 October 1666. He held a stall at Christ Church, Oxford where he is commemorated.

Thomas Hyde (1666-1703) MA, was a distinguished Oriental scholar. In 1665 he was Chief Keeper of the Bodleian and he became Professor of Arabic in 1691 and Regius Professor of Hebrew in 1697. He was also Archdeacon of Gloucester in 1678. He was one of the editors of the Polyglott Bible and died in 1703.

John Gane (1703-1738) MA, died in 1738.

George Conway (1738-1753) MA, died on 1 July 1753.

Abraham le Moine (1753-1757) DD, died in 1757.

Gregory Sharpe (1757-1771) LLD, died on 8 January 1771.

Edward Rolle (1771-1791) BD, died on 30 June 1791.

Archibald Alison (1791-1839) BCL, died on 17 May 1839

Gorges Paulin Lowther (1841-1881) was Rector of Orcheston St George in 1830 and a Proctor in Convocation from 1835 to 1868. He died on 25 April 1881.

Lionel Digby Dawson-Damer (1881-1888) MA, was a grandson of the first Earl of Portarlington. He was Rector of Winterbourne Came from 1858 to 1862 and Rector of Cheddington from 1862 to 1869. He was Vicar of Canford Magna from 1869 until retiring through ill health in 1884. He was twice Rural Dean. In retirement he helped with the building of the church of St John the Baptist, Broadstone and died on 2 July 1888.

Edward Slater Browne (1888-1897) MA, was Vicar of St Katharine's, Savernake Forest from 1863 to 1878 and Subdean from 1882 to 1887. He held the prebend of Yetminster Secunda from 1888 to 1897.

George Briscoe Oldfield (1897-1932) MA, was Rector of Berwick-in-Tisbury with Sedgehill-in-Mere from 1872 to 1908. He was Secretary to the Diocesan Board of Finance from 1884 to 1901 and of the Diocesan Board of Education from 1890 to 1904. He was Secretary of the Diocesan Voluntary Schools Association from 1897 to 1920 and died on 5 February 1932.

Thomas Haworth Jervis (1932-1945) MA, was Vicar of Rowde from 1904 to 1911 and was Vicar of Alderbury from 1911 to 1924. He was Rector of Woodborough from 1924 and Rural Dean of Cannings from 1927. He held the prebend of Yetminster Secunda from 1932 to 1945 when he became Vicar of the Close, holding the prebend of Ufcomb from 1945 to 1955. He died in 1955.

Vernon Herbert Jones (1945-1946) MA, was a Chaplain to the Deaf & Dumb.

Roland Ralph Bailey (1947-1957) PhD, was Diocesan Director of Religious Education from 1941 to 1955, a Proctor in Convocation from 1944 to 1955 and General Secretary of the National Society and Secretary of the Schools Council of the General Synod from 1955 until his death in 1957.

Walter Bertram Hughes (1958-1959) OBE, MA, was a Chaplain to the Forces from 1916 to 1941. He was Rector of Odstock with Nunton & Bodenham from 1943 and Rural Dean of Alderbury from 1953, until his death in 1959.

Percy Anderson (1959-1973) was Vicar of Chisledon with Draycott Foliat from 1946 to 1953, Rural Dean of Marlborough in 1953, Vicar of Charminster from 1953 to 1969 and Rural Dean of Dorchester from 1953 to 1967.

Giles Clayton (1973-1992) was Rector of Durrington from 1952 to 1970, a Proctor in Convocation from 1965 to 1985 and Rural Dean of Avon from 1967 to 1970. He was Rector of St Martin's, Sarum, from 1970 to 1986, Rural Dean of Salisbury from 1972 to 1977 and Master of St Nicholas Hospital, Sarum from 1986 to 1992.

Alan Geoffrey Woods (1992-1996) was Priest-in-Charge Cherminster from 1981 to 1983, Vicar of Cherminster & Stinsford from 1983 to 1990 and Vicar of Calne from 1990 to 1996. He became Sub Chaplain of Malta and Gozo and Chancellor of Malta Cathedral in 1996.

Stanley Charles Holbrooke-Jones (1996-1998) MA, DipTh, was Rector of Poole from 1988 to 1998.

Richard Darrell George Weyman (1999-) BA, PhD, became Diocesan Director of Post Ordination Training and Priest in Charge of Marnhull in 1992

MINOR PARS ALTARIS

Prebend:- A portion of the gifts at the high altar were included in a grant by Osmund, Bishop of Sarum 1078-1099, to the cathedral. From this Jocelin de Bohun, Bishop of Sarum 1142-1184, created two prebends, the greater being Major Pars Altaris and the lesser Minor Pars Altaris.

Shield:- **Richard Fox** BCL, held the prebends of Bishopstone from ? to 1486 and Granthan Borealis from 1486 to 1487. He became Bishop of Exeter in 1487, of Bath in 1492, of Durham in 1494 and of Winchester in 1501. He was the Keeper of the Great Seal to King Henry VII and King Henry VIII and founded Corpus Christ College, Oxford. He died in 1528. (Fig. 39.)

Blazon: Azure a pelican or vulned proper. [On a blue shield, a gold pelican pecking her breast to feed her young with natural colour blood.]

Psalter:- The portion of the psalter allotted to the prebend is Psalm 138, 139, 140, 141 and 142.

Holders of the prebend:-

Henry de Sancto Edmundo (c.1226/7-?) held the prebend in 1238.

Edmund de Mortimer (1284) may have held this prebend in 1284. He also held a stall at Hereford, was Treasurer of York from 1265 to c.1282, inherited a family estate in 1282 and married c.1285.

William de Marchia (c.1284-?) was a royal clerk and Controller of the Wardrobe to King Edward I from 1283 to 1290, when he served as Treasurer of the Exchequer until 1295. He was also Dean of St Martin le Grand, London. He held stalls at Chichester and Wells and became Bishop of Bath & Wells in 1293.

Richard de Abingdon (1305-1309) held the prebends of Minor Pars Altaris from 1305 to 1309 and Horton from 1309 to 1322 and died in 1322.

Henry de la Wyle (1309) DTh, held the prebends of Minor Pars Altaris in 1309, Durnford from 1309 to 1311 and Fordington & Writhlington from 1311 to 1313. He was Chancellor of Sarum from 1313 to 1329 and in 1326 he founded a chantry at the altar of St Peter and the rest of the Apostles at the east end of the north aisle in the cathedral. In 1329 he left to the Chapter his house near Leadenhall in the Close and died in June 1329.

Robert de Scoville (1309-?).

Hugh de Spineto (1311-1313) held the prebends of Minor Pars Altaris from 1311 to 1313 and Alton Australis from 1313 to 1329 . He was fined for non-residence in 1320 and died in 1329.

William de Mepham (1313-1316) was appointed to the prebend of Rotesfen in 1313 but this was subsequently revoked as William de Coleshull was already holding it. He held the prebends of Minor Pars Altaris from 1313 to 1316, Beminster Secunda from 1314 to 1316 and Slape from 1316 to ?.

John de Rosse (1316-1325) DCL, became Bishop of Carlisle in 1325.

Thomas de Bocton (1325-1327) MA, was Subdean of Sarum from 1321 to c.1327, holding the prebends of Minor Pars Altaris from 1325 to 1327 and Warminster from 1327 to 1348. He died in 1348.

Robert de Wyville (1330) held stalls at Lincoln c.1325, at Lichfield and in 1330 held the prebend of Minor Pars Altaris. He failed to be appointed to the see of Bath & Wells in 1329 but a year later became Bishop of Sarum until his death on 4 September 1375. A contemporary account reads "At the instance of Phillipa, Queen to King Edward III, the Pope preferred Rob. Wyville to the bishopric of Sarum. It is hard to say whether he were more dunce or dwarf, more unlearned or unhansome, insomuch that had the Pope ever *seen* him, as he no doubt *felt* him in his large fees, he would never have conferred the place on him." He recovered Sherborne Castle for the see and it was during his episcopate that the monastery at Edington was founded and the church consecrated. He was buried in the choir of the cathedral but when the choir was repaved, his remains were removed to the north-east transept.

Richard de Hale (1331-1334) died in 1334.

Walter Wyville (1334-1338) was Rector of Kingsclere in 1330 and held the prebends of Minor Pars Altaris from 1334 to 1338 and of Bere & Cherminster from 1338 to 1340. He was Treasurer of Sarum and a Canon Residentiary from 1340 to 1345 and died in 1345.

John de Kirkeby (1338-?) was Rector of Keevil in 1333 and held the prebends of Preston from 1334 to 1338 and Minor Pars Altaris from 1338 to ?. He was Master of St Nicholas Hospital, Sarum in 1337 and a Canon Residentiary and Archdeacon of Dorset from 1340 to 1346, holding with the dignity the church of Gussage, and he died in 1346. He was probably the same person who was Precentor of Lichfield from 1332 to 1339.

John de la Chambre (1340-1365) held the prebend of Minor Pars Altaris from 1340 to 1365 and was Precentor of Sarum from 1347 to c.1360. He was admitted as a Canon Residentiary in 1340.

John Haverbergh (1365-?) received the prebend in 1365 by royal grant but this was disputed with Ralph de Olneye the following year.

Ralph de Olneye (1366).

Richard Treton (1387, 1390) held the prebend in both 1387 and 1390.

John Scarle (1395-1400) held the prebends of Minor Pars Altaris from 1395 to 1400 and Fordington & Writhlington from 1400 to 1403. He died in 1403.

William Milton (1400-1418) Lic.CL, held the prebends of Minor Pars Altaris from 1400 to 1418 and Warminster from 1418 to 1424. He died in 1424.

Nicholas Godwin (1418-?).

Walter Sherrington (1420) held the prebend of Minor Pars Altaris in 1420, exchanging it with Richard Richman for the prebend of Decem Librarum in Lincoln. He held the prebends of Beminster Prima from 1431 to 1436 and Shipton from 1436 until his death in 1449. He held stalls at York and Chichester and was Chancellor of the Duchy of Lancaster and a Canon Residentiary of St Paul's.

Richard Richman (1420-?) held the prebend in 1435.

John Lound (1438-1445) BCn&CL, exchanged the prebend in 1445 with William Kirkeby for the church of St John the Baptist, in Walbrook, London.

William Kirkeby (1445-1446) died in 1446.

John Paslewe (1446-1447) BCn&CL, held the prebends of Minor Pars Altaris from 1446 to 1447, Bishopstone from 1447 to 1449, Alton Australis in 1449 and Chisenbury & Chute from 1449 to 1457. He held a stall at Hereford in 1447 and died 1457.

William Brygon (1447-1448) BCn&CL, held the prebends of Minor Pars Altaris from 1447 to 1448, Ruscomb from 1448 to 1454, Durnford from 1454 to 1459 and Stratton from 1459 to 1469. He died in 1469.

Thomas Passhe (1448-1471) MA, held a stall at Windsor in 1449 and resigned this prebend in 1471.

Thomas Hawkins (1471-1474) MA, was Precentor of Sarum from 1471 to 1479. He held the prebends of Minor Pars Altaris from 1471 to 1474 and Hurstbourne & Burbage from 1474 to 1479. He was also Provost of Oriel College, Oxford and Archdeacon of Worcester. He died in 1479 and was buried in the Cathedral.

William Long (1474-?).

John Bostock (?-1490) BCnL, held the prebends of Minor Pars Altaris from? to 1490 and Durnford from 1490 to 1500. He was Rector of Okeford Fitzpaine, a Canon Residentiary and the Commissary of the Chapter for visiting various prebends during a vacancy in the Deanery. He died in 1500.

Richard Payne (1490-1506) resigned in 1506.

John Denby (1506-1508) MA, died in 1508.

Walter Blount (1508) BCL, held the prebends of Minor Pars Altaris in 1508, Lyme & Halstock from 1508 to 1509 and Alton Australis from 1509 until resigning in 1530.

Richard Dudley (1508-1517) DTh, was Precentor from 1507 to 1536 and held the prebends of Minor Pars Altaris from 1508 to 1517, Yatesbury from 1517 to ? and of Durnford from ? (holding it in 1535) to 1536. He died in 1536.

John Estmond (1517-1519) MA, held the prebends of Axford from 1507 to 1508, Rotesfen from 1508 to 1509, Coombe & Harnham from 1509 until resigning in 1514 and Minor Pars Altaris from 1517 to 1519 He had died by 9 May 1519.

Edward Molineux (1519-1522) held the prebends of Minor Pars Altaris from 1519 to 1522, Bishopstone from 1522 to 1524 and Faringdon from 1524 to 1535.

John Viall (1522-?).

William Canning (?-1524) held the prebends of Minor Pars Altaris from ? to 1524, Axford in 1524 and Stratford from 1524 to 1554. He died in 1554.

John Bigges (1524-1544) BCn&CL, held the prebend of Yatesbury from ? to 1524, exchanging it with John Cockes for the church of Moulton, Suffolk and Minor Pars Altaris from 1524 to 1544. He was Vicar of Tisbury and Rector of Chilmark, died in 1544 and asked to be buried in the cathedral.

John Bodenham (1544-1546) held the prebends of Minor Pars Altaris from 1544 to 1546 and Yatesbury from 1546 to 1547. He was Rector of St Peter's, Marlborough and died in 1547.

Robert Ryve (1546-1554) BCL, held the prebends of Minor Pars Altaris from 1546 to 1554 and Bitton from 1554 to 1573. He died in 1573.

Richard Arche (1554) BCL, held the prebend of Preston from ? to 1524, resigning to assume the prebend of Faringdon in 1524, which he resigned a month later. He then received the prebend of Hurstbourne & Burbage which he held from 1524 until resigning in 1552. Two years later he was appointed to the prebend of Minor Pars Altaris but may not have received it before being deprived of all benefices early in 1555. He was Vicar of Avebury and held a stall at Windsor from 1538 until deprived in 1555. He was a Canon Residentiary from 1527 to 1554 and Treasurer of Sarum from 1551 to 1555 during which time the Commissioners appointed to survey Church Goods and Chantries visited the cathedral.

John Blaxton (1555-1556) held the prebends of Minor Pars Altaris from 1555 to 1556 and of Bedminster & Redcliffe from 1556 to 1559. He had been deprived by November 1559.

John Thompson (1556) BD, held the prebend for less than two months.

Laurence Vawse (1556-1559) BD, was deprived of his offices early in the reign of Queen Elizabeth I.

John Smith (1559-1564) was probably Archdeacon of Llandaff and died in 1564.

John Garbrand (alias Herks) (1564-1565) MA, was a Fellow of New College, Oxford. He held the prebends of Minor Pars Altaris from 1564 to 1565, Yatesbury from 1565 to 1569 and Chisenbury & Chute from 1569 to 1589. He was a great friend of John Jewell, Bishop of Sarum 1560- 1571, and died in 1589.

William Merrick (1565-?) received the prebend in 1565, was occupying it in 1571 and still held it in 1577, although Samuel Mott was installed in 1574.

Samuel Mott (1574).

William Tooker (1587-1622) MA, was a Fellow of New College, Oxford in 1577. He was Archdeacon of Barnstaple, held a stall at Exeter and in 1602 was Dean of Lichfield. He was Chaplain to Elizabeth I and a Canon Residentiary from ? to 1622. He died at Sarum on 19 March 1622 and was buried in the cathedral.

William Tounson (1622-1639) MA, resigned in 1639.

Herbert Croft (1639-1644) BD, resigned the prebend in 1644, apparently on becoming Dean of Hereford. He held stalls at Windsor and Worcester and in 1662 became Bishop of Hereford.

Robert Raynsford (1644-1649) BD, died in 1649.

Richard Clayton (1661-1675) DD, held the prebends of Minor Pars Altaris from 1661 to 1675 and Netherbury in Ecclesia from 1675 to 1676 and was a Canon Residentiary from 1664 to 1676. He was Master of University College, Oxford and dying in 1676, was buried in the cathedral.

Marmaduke Good (1675-1678) MA, died in 1678 and was buried at Ufton, Berkshire.

Lancelot Addison (1678-1703) DD, author of theological and devotional books, was Rector of Milston from 1670 to 1703 but did not reside after he became Dean of Lichfield in 1683. He became Archdeacon of Coventry in the following year and died on 20 April 1703, being commemorated in Lichfield cathedral.

Edward Chandler (1703-1717) DD, became Bishop of Lichfield in 1717 and of Durham in 1730. He died in 1750.

John Bampton (1718-1751) MA, was Rector of Stratford Tony and founder of the Bampton Lectures. He was a Canon Residentiary from 1726 to 1751, died on 2 June 1751 and was buried in the north choir aisle of the cathedral.

John Lumby (1751-1756) MA, was Rector of St Martin's, Sarum. He held the prebends of Minor Pars Altaris from 1751 to 1756 and Alton Australis from 1756 to 1758. He died on 9 January 1758.

Henry Gresley (1756-1774) MA, died in 1774.

James Hume Spry (1774-1775) DCL, held the prebends of Minor Pars Altaris from 1774 to 1775 and Bedminster & Redcliffe from 1775 to 1780. He was Vicar of Potterne from 1770 to 1780 and Rector of Brixton Deverill from 1773 to 1780. He died on 27 November 1780.

Humphrey Henchman (1775-1779) BD, was Rector of Barford St Martin and Rector of Great Cheverell and died on 8 August 1779.

Edward Foyle (1779-1784) MA, died on 7 May 1784.

Charles Daubeny (1784-1827) DCL, held the prebend of Minor Pars Altaris from 1784 to 1827, was Vicar of North Bradley from 1777 to 1827 and Archdeacon of Sarum from 1804 until his death on 10 July 1827.

Liscombe Clarke (1827-1828) MA, held a stall at Hereford in 1821. He was Archdeacon of Sarum from 1827 to 1836 and Treasurer of Sarum from 1834 to 1841. He held the prebends of Minor Pars Altaris from 1827 to 1828 and of Netheravon from 1828 to 1834 and was Vicar of Downton. He died on 17 April 1841.

Charles Grove (1828-1868) MA, was Rector of Odstock. He died on 28 May 1868.

John Hemery Carnegie (1868-1872) was Vicar of Cranborne from 1842 to 1872.

William Henry Teale (1872-1874) was Rector of Devizes in 1861 and died in 1878.

Francis Warre (1875-1917) was Vicar of Bere Regis with Winterbourne Kingston from 1864 to 1876, Vicar of Melksham from 1876 to 1890 and Rural Dean of Bradford from 1888 to 1890. He was Rector of Fugglestone with Bemerton from 1890 and was Secretary of the Diocesan Board of Finance from 1882 to 1913. He died in 1917.

Henry Robert Whytehead (1917-1925) MA, was Rector of St Peter & St Paul, Marlborough from 1887 to 1897, Vicar of Warminster from 1897 to 1915 and Rural Dean of Heytesbury from 1914 to 1919. He held the prebends of Minor Pars Altaris from 1917 to 1925 of Netheravon from 1925 to 1937 and was Succentor from 1925 to 1931. He died in 1937.

Walter Hercules Kewley (1925-1950) MA, was Rector of Fittleton from 1886 to 1911 and Rural Dean of Enford from 1896 to 1911. He was Vicar and Rural Dean of Potterne from 1911 to 1935.

Horace Henry Coley (1950-1961) Lic.Th, was Vicar of Alderholt from 1921 to 1927, Rector of Shaftesbury from 1927 to 1954 and Rural Dean of Shaftesbury from 1945 to 1951. He died in 1961.

Howard Littleton Philp (1961-1975) BA, PhD, DLitt, was Vicar of Froxfield from 1940 to 1944, Yetminster with Chetnole & Ryme Intrinseca from 1944 to 1958 and Ramsbury with Axford from 1958 to 1972. He died on 29 May 1978.

Alfred Loughlin (1975-1981) was Vicar of Kinson from 1954 to 1981.

George Muxlow (1981-1984) was Vicar of Oakdale St George from 1963 to 1979 and Team Rector from 1979 to 1984. He died in January 1997.

Peter Richard Huxham (1985-1992) MA, was Vicar of St Osmund's Parkstone from 1970 to 1975, Team Rector of Parkstone St Peter with Branksea and St Osmund from 1975 to 1992 and Rural Dean of Poole from 1985 to 1992.

Tobias (Toby) Salisbury (1992-1997) was Vicar of Urchfont with Stert from 1967 to 1973, Rector of Burton Bradstock with Shipton Gorge and Chilcombe from 1973 to 1979, Priest-in-Charge of Long Bredy with Little Bredy and Kingston Russell from 1975 to 1979, Team Rector of Bride Valley from 1979 to 1986 and Vicar of Great and Little Bedwin and Savernake Forest from 1986 to 1997.

[**Diana Katharine Witts** (1998-) OBE, BSc, Cross of St Augustine, Lay Canon, was Senior Mistress Gordonstoun School from 1970 to 1975, served with the Church Mission Society, as a Mission Partner in Kenya and Zaire from 1976 to 1985, as Africa Secretary from 1985 to 1995 and as General Secretary from 1995. She occupies Minor Pars Altaris as a courtesy stall.]

GILLINGHAM MINOR
(olim Axford)

Prebend:- Axford is a hamlet in the parish of Ramsbury in Wiltshire and was therefore part of the Bishop's manor of Ramsbury of 1066 and 1086, which was presumably given to the canons by Osmund, Bishop of Sarum 1078-1099. The prebend was probably in existence by c.1150 and certainly by 1186. In 1291 it was called 'Axford & Haydon', Haydon being near Sherborne in Dorset. The prebends of Axford and Ramsbury, were dissolved by Act of Parliament of 1545 as a result of an exchange between the Earl of Hertford and John Salcot, Bishop of Sarum 1539-1557, the Bishop receiving the prebend of Gillingham, formerly of Shaftesbury Abbey in Dorset. From this he was required to form two prebends; Gillingham Major replacing Ramsbury and Gillingham Minor replacing Axford.

Shield:- **Walter of Merton** held the prebends of Yatesbury from 1262 to 1263 and Bere & Cherminster from 1263 to c.1271. He was also Archdeacon of Bath and held stalls at Exeter, Lincoln and London. He became Chancellor of England and Bishop of Rochester in 1274. He founded Merton College, Oxford. (Fig. 40.)

Blazon:- Or three chevronells per pale, one gules and azure, between two azure and gules. [On a gold shield, three chevrons with their colours divided in the centre. One red on the left, blue on the right between two blue on the left, red on the right.]

Psalter:- The portion of the psalter allotted to the prebend is Psalms 110, 111, 112, 113, 114 and 115.

Holders of the prebend of Axford:-

Walter (c.1155/1189) held the office of Succentor of Sarum and the prebend of Axford during c.1155/1189.

Gregory (1200) held the prebend in 1200.

Stephen of Tisbury (?-1226/7) was Archdeacon of Wilts from c.1226 to 1246 and died in 1246.

John of Derby (?-1319) held a stall at Wells and was elected Dean of Lichfield in 1280. He held this prebend in 1284 and died on 12 October 1319.

John Luttrell (1319-1335) DTh, may have been Chancellor of Oxford from 1317 to 1322 and held a stall at York in 1334. He died in 1335.

John de Whitchurch (1335-1338) BCn&CL, was Archdeacon of Wilts from 1338 to 1343 when he exchanged the dignity with John Barne for the church of Sedgefield, Co. Durham. He held the prebend of Axford from 1335 to 1338, exchanging it with John de Abingdon for the prebend of Hurstbourne & Burbage which he held until his death in 1358. He was a Canon Residentiary.

John de Abingdon (1338-1343) DTh, held the prebends of Hurstbourne & Burbage from ? to 1338 when, despite a royal grant to John de Eccleshale, he exchanged it with John de Whitchurch for the prebend of Axford, which he held from 1338 to 1343. He died in 1343.

John Bateman (or de Vienna) (1343-1349) was nominated in 1343 and although Bartholomew de Bradden was installed, he was again nominated in 1345. He died in 1349.

Bartholomew de Bradden (1344-1350) held the prebend of Axford from 1344 to 1350, claimed the dignity of Treasurer of Sarum in 1351 but the case was referred for judgement. He received papal confirmation of the prebend of Warminster in 1350 and resigned it in 1361. He was Rector of St Peter's Marlborough from 1334 to 1336 and was Rector of Barford St Martin.

Roger de Shipbrok (1349-?) was nominated to the prebend on the death of John Bateman and although it was given to Gervase de Wilford, he received a pardon in 1355 and held the prebend in 1366.

Gervase de Wilford (1350-?) received the prebend by royal grant in 1350, confirmed by the Pope in 1351 and was appointed in 1361. Roger de Shipbrok still held the prebend in 1366.

Richard Croxton (?-1380) exchanged the prebend in 1380 with Thomas Banaster of Eltisley for the prebend of Dunham & Newport at Lincoln.

Thomas Banaster of Eltisley (1380-1399) BCL, held a stall at Lincoln and died in 1399.

Edmund Cockerell (1399-1400) was Subdean of Sarum from 1396 to 1400 and held the prebend of Axford from 1399 to 1400. He had died by 16 October 1400 and was buried in the cathedral opposite the chapel of St Edmund.

John Tydeling (1401-1404) BCL, was a Canon Residentiary and held the prebend of Axford from 1401 until exchanging it in 1404 with George Westby for the prebend of Major Pars Altaris in 1404, which he held until 1406. He then held the prebends of Warminster from 1406 to 1418, Yetminster Secunda in 1418, Beminster Prima from 1418 to 1420, Stratton from 1420 to 1437, exchanging the last with John Symondsburgh for the prebend of Yatesbury in 1437. This he exchanged with John Morton for the prebend of North Leverton at Southwell collegiate church, Notts.

George Westby (1404) held the prebend of Netherbury in Terra from 1403 to 1404, becoming Treasurer of Sarum in 1404. A day later, he exchanged the dignity for the prebend of Fordington & Writhlington and within 1404 he exchanged this for Bedminster & Redcliffe, which he in turn exchanged for Major Pars Altaris, which he then exchanged for Axford, resigning the last in the autumn of the same year.

John Longville (1404-1411) held the prebend of Axford from 1404 until exchanging it in 1411 with William Werkeman for the prebend of Bedford Major at Lincoln cathedral. He also held the prebend of Fordington & Writhlington from 1416 to 1426. He held a stall at Windsor and died in 1426.

William Werkeman (1411-1415) was Rector of Stourton from 1403 to 1407. He held the prebends Axford from 1411 to 1415 and Chardstock from 1415 to 1426. He died in 1426.

Edmund Bekenham (1415-1416) died in 1416.

Richard Ullerston (1416-1423) DTh, may have been Chancellor of Oxford in 1407. He died in 1423 and asked to be buried in the cathedral.

Alexander Sparrow (1423-1426) BCn&CL, held the prebends of Axford from 1423 to 1426 and Fordington & Writhlington from 1426 to 1433. He was Archdeacon of Sarum from 1426 to 1432 when he became Archdeacon of Berks until 1433. He was Treasurer of St Paul's in 1423 and died in 1433.

William Hende (1426-1447) held the prebends of Axford from 1426 to 1447 and Alton Australis from 1447 to 1449. He was Archdeacon of Worcester in 1443 and died in 1449.

Richard Trove (1447-1449) held the prebends of Axford from 1447 to 1449, Bishopstone and Alton Australis in 1449 and Netheravon from 1449-?

Richard Hayman (1449) held the prebends of Axford and Bishopstone in 1449 and Alton Australis from 1449 to 1461, exchanging the last with John Waynefleet for a canonry at St Stephen's, Westminster.

Thomas Swyft (1449-1457) BCn&CL, held the prebends of Axford from 1449 to 1457 and Slape from 1457 until exchanging it in 1465 with John Bedale for the church of Hollingbourne, Kent.

John Arundel (1457-1459) DM, was a Fellow of Exeter College, Oxford. He was both Physician and Chaplain to King Henry VI. He held stalls at various times at Wells, Lichfield, Hereford, Lincoln, York and St Paul's. One of his name would seem to have held the Rectory of Trowbridge from 1456 to 1458. He was consecrated Bishop of Chichester in 1459.

William Osgodby (1459-1465) was a Canon Residentiary in charge of the choristers, and was Rector of Codford St Peter in 1476. He held the prebends of Axford from 1459 to 1465 and Bishopstone from 1465 to 1467, exchanging the latter with Robert Ampleford for Beminster Secunda, which he held from 1467 to 1475. He then held the prebend of Chisenbury & Chute from 1475 to 1484 and died in 1484.

Thomas Boleyn (1465-1472) was Master of Gonville and Caius College, Cambridge from 1454 to 1472. He was Subdean and Precentor of Wells and died in 1472.

Richard Hayward (1472-1477) DCL, held the prebends of Major Pars Altaris from 1464 to 1472, Axford from 1472 to 1477 and Lyme & Halstock from 1477 to 1493. He died in 1493.

Ralph Stourton (1477-?).

Robert Day (? -1486) held the prebends of Axford from ? to 1486, Rotesfen from 1486 to 1489 and Grantham Australis from 1489 to 1506. He died in 1506.

Thomas Rope (1486-1494) held the prebends of Chisenbury & Chute from c.1485 to 1486 and Axford from 1486 to 1494. He held a stall at Lincoln in 1490 and was Rector of Symondsbury. He died in 1494.

Robert Toneys (1494-1499) BCL, held the prebends of Axford from 1494 to 1499 and Beminster Secunda from 1499 to ?.

Hugh Peynthwyn (1499-1504) DCL, became Archdeacon of Canterbury and died in 1504.

Christopher Twyneho (1504-1505) held the prebends of Axford from 1504 to 1505 and Chardstock from 1505 to 1507 and the Archdeaconry of Berks, together with the prebend of Highworth, from 1507 to 1509. He appears also to have held a stall at Hereford from 1480 to 1509. He had died by 20 December 1509.

James Bromwich (1505-1507) BCnL, held the prebends of Axford from 1505 to 1507, Coombe & Harnham in 1507, Grimston from 1507 to 1515, Faringdon from 1515 to 1519 and Hurstbourne & Burbage from 1519 to 1524. He was Chancellor of Hereford in 1518 and became Archdeacon of Sarum in 1524, dying a month after his appointment.

Edward Higgins (1507) Lic.CnL, was Vicar of Steeple Ashton and held the prebends of Axford in 1507, Chardstock in 1507, Coombe & Harnham from 1507 to 1509 and Netherbury in Ecclesia from 1509 to 1538. He died in 1538.

John Estmond (1507-1508) MA, held the prebends of Axford from 1507 to 1508, Rotesfen from 1508 to 1509, Coombe & Harnham from 1509 to 1514 and Minor Pars Altaris from 1517 to 1519 He died in 1519.

John Woodroff (1508-1509) held the prebends of Axford from 1508 to 1509, Ruscomb from 1509 to 1517 and Beminster Prima from 1517 to ? He also held a stall at Hereford.

John Stone (1509-1511) BCL, held the prebends of Axford from 1509 to 1511, Warminster from 1511 to 1517, Chardstock from 1517 to 1524 and Fordington & Writhlington from 1524.

Nicholas Inglesent (1511-1520) MA, held the prebend of Axford from 1511, exchanging it and the vicarage of Highworth in 1520 with John Pinnock for the prebend of Durnford.

John Pinnock (1520-1524) was consecrated Bishop Suffragan of Syene in 1518 to assist Edmund Audley, Bishop of Sarum 1502-1524, within the diocese which he did until 1535. He held the prebend of Durnford from 1519 to 1520, exchanging it with Nicholas Inglescent for the vicarage of Highworth and the prebend of Axford. He held the prebend of Axford from 1520 to 1524, exchanging it in 1524 for the prebend of Chardstock which he held until 1537. He died in 1537.

William Canning (1524) held the prebends of Minor Pars Altaris from ? to 1524, Axford in 1524 and Stratford from 1524 to 1554. He died in 1554.

Thomas Bennet (1529-1533) DCL, was Secretary to Cardinal Wolsey, Rector of Sutton Veny from 1502 to 1507, Precentor of Sarum from 1536 to 1558 and held the prebends of Axford from 1529 to 1533 and Chisenbury and Chute from 1533 to 1558. He was Canon Residentiary and Proctor in Convocation for the Chapter, in which capacity he signed the Articles of 1536. For some time he was locum tenens to Peter Vannes, Dean of Sarum, who was non-resident. He died in 1558 and is commemorated at the north side of the choir.

William Betts (1533-1535) was Rector of Fuggleston and Bemerton in 1534 and died in 1535.

Charles Smith (1535-1545) was the last holder of the prebend of Axford.

Holders of the prebend of Gillingham Minor:-

John Aprice (1555-1558) died in 1558.

Robert Glasmond (1558-1559) is presumed to have died in 1559.

Christopher Rookes (1559-?) MA, is said to have been the Rector of Stour Provost. He held the prebend in 1577.

Adam Hill (1582-1595) MA, was a Fellow of Balliol College, Oxford in 1568, held the prebend of Gillingham Minor from 1582 to 1595 and was Succentor of Sarum in 1584. He was a noted an eloquent preacher, becoming the Vicar of Westbury and Rector of Gussage St Michael. He died c.16 February 1595.

Thomas Crump (1595-1604) was Succentor of Sarum from 1595 until resigning in 1602. He held the prebend of Gillingham Minor from 1595 until resigning the prebend in 1604.

John Odell (1604-1628) MA, was Vicar of St Martin's, Sarum in 1606 and died in 1628.

Matthew Nicholas (1628-1661) DCL, was Rector of West Dean and a Canon Residentiary from ? (serving in 1638) to 1661. He was Dean of Bristol, held a stall at Westminster and was Warden of St Nicholas' Hospital, Sarum in 1630. He was appointed Dean of St Paul's by King Charles I but failing to take up the dignity, was re-granted it at the Restoration. He was a great friend of John Davenant, Bishop of Sarum 1621-1641. He died on 13 or 14 August 1661 and is commemorated at Winterbourne Earls.

John Houghton (1662-1677) BD, died on 7 August 1677.

Giles Thornburgh (1677-1682) MA, held the prebends of Gillingham Minor from 1677 to 1682 and Beminster Prima from 1682 to c.1693. He held a stall at Winchester in 1684 and had died by March 1693.

John Stubbs (1682) MA, held the prebends of Gillingham Minor in 1682 and Torleton from 1683 to 1699. He died in 1699.

Edward Young (1682-1688) BCL, was a Fellow of New College, Oxford and a Fellow of Winchester. He held the prebends of Gillingham Minor from 1682 to 1688 and Coombe & Harnham from 1688 to 1702. He was Dean of Sarum and Canon Residentiary from 1702 to 1705, died on 9 August 1705 and was buried in the cathedral.

Thomas Morer (1688-1715) MA, died on 22 December 1715.

John Holland (1716) DD, held the prebends of Gillingham Minor in 1716 and Chisenbury & Chute from 1716 until resigning the prebend in 1721.

Thomas Rundle (1716-1717) BCL, held the prebends of Gillingham Minor from 1716 to 1717 and Ilfracombe from 1717 to 1721. He held the Archdeaconry of Wilts from 1720 to 1735 together with the dignity of Treasurer of Sarum from 1721 until 1735 when he was consecrated Bishop of Derry.

Thomas Henchman (1717-1746) MA, was Vicar of St Martin's, Sarum in 1661 and of St Thomas', Sarum in 1667 He died on 14 October 1746 and was buried in the cathedral.

John Pocock (1746-1773) MA, died on 13 July 1773.

Charles Green (1773-1803) MA, died in 1803.

Hugh Owen (1803-1827) BA, was Archdeacon of Salop in 1821. He died on 23 December 1827.

Thomas Tyrwhitt (1828-1849) MA, was Vicar of Turnworth and of Winterborne Whitechurch. He died on 10 or 11 August 1849 and is commemorated at Winterborne Whitechurch.

Richard Waldy (1849-1869) MA, was Vicar of Affpuddle. He died on 19 December 1869.

George Lloyd Nash (1869-1893) was Vicar of Tolpuddle from 1852 to 1893 and was Rural Dean of Whitchurch. He died on 7 August 1893.

Percival Hart Dyke (1893-1910) MA, was Rector of Compton Abbas from 1871 until retiring through ill health in 1896. He was a devoted advocate to the cause of temperance and died on 14 December 1910.

Henry Richard William Farrer (1911-1933) MA, was Vicar of Broadwindsor with Blackdown & Drimpton from 1891 to 1895, Rector of Bridport from 1895 to 1916 and Rural Dean of Bridport from 1898 to 1916. He held the prebend of Gillingham Minor from 1911 to 1933, was a Canon Residentiary from 1916, Diocesan Canon Missioner from 1918 and Subdean from 1926 until his death on 27 November 1933.

Kenneth Donald Mackenzie (1934-1935) MA, author, Fellow, Dean & Chaplain Pembroke College, Oxford, was a Canon Residentiary from 1934 to 1935, Bishop of Brechin from 1935 to 1943 and President of the Church Union from 1951 to 1956. He died on 1 October 1966.

Sherburne Porah Tregelles Prideaux (1936-1950) MA, DD, was a Lecturer at St Boniface College, Warminster, and Sarum Theological College from 1919.

Frederick Cryer Tindall (1950-1981) AKC, BD, was a Fellow of King's College, London. He was a Lecturer and Bursar of Chichester Theological College from 1928 to 1930 and Vice Principal from 1930 to 1936. He was a Proctor in Convocation from 1936 to 1945, held a stall at Chichester from 1948 to 1950, was Principal of Sarum Theological College from 1950 to 1965, Proctor in Convocation from 1950 to 1975, Pro-Prolocutor of the Lower House of Canterbury from 1959 to 1975 and a Clerical Judge of the Court of Arches from 1969 to 1980. He died in December 1995.

William Hugh Andrew (1981-1986) was Rector of Weymouth St Mary from 1971 to 1976, Vicar of Heatherlands St John from 1976 to 1982, Rector of Alderbury and West Grimstead from 1982 to 1986 and Proctor in Convocation from 1975 to 1985.

Peter George Hardman (1987-) BSc, was Assistant Chaplain, later Chaplain, of Marlborough College, Wilts, from1967 to 1979 and became Team Rector of Wareham in 1979.

STRATFORD

Prebend:- The gift to the canons of land at Stratford-sub-Castle near Salisbury by Osmund, Bishop of Sarum 1078-1099, was confirmed by the Pope in 1146 and the prebend was probably in existence by c.1150.

Shield:- **Robert de Bingham** was fined for non-residence in 1227. He was the founder of St Nicholas Hospital, Sarum and is said to have built the Ayleswade Bridge beside the Hospital. He held the prebend of Slape from c.1226/7 until 1229 when he became Bishop of Sarum from 1229 to 1246, holding with the bishopric the prebend of Horton. He died on 2 November 1246 and was buried in the still unfinished cathedral. (Fig. 41.)

Blazon:- Azure a bend between two cotises and six crosses patee or. (Not cross crosslet fitchee as shown in the depiction.) [On a blue shield, a gold band from the top left to the bottom right, with a narrow gold band on either side of it, between six gold square crosses. (Not crosses with pointed base, and top and arms crossed as shown in the depiction.]

Psalter:- The portion of the psalter allotted to the prebend is Psalm 119 (1-48)

Holders of the prebend:-

Hugo de Templo (c.1220-1226) also held a stall at Heytesbury collegiate church and died holding the prebend on 11 April 1226.

Anastasius (?-c.1226/7) held first an unidentified prebend and then the prebend of Stratford from ? to c.1226/27. He was Succentor of Sarum from c.1209/15 to c.1226/27.

Robert de Waye (1284) held the prebend in 1284.

Nicholas de Fighino (1319-1321) exchanged the prebend in 1321 with Robert de Patrica for the church of Havant, Hampshire.

Robert de Patrica (1321-1327) was granted the prebend of Preston in 1320 but this was revoked in the same year. He then held the prebend of Stratford from 1321 until exchanging it in 1327 with Nicholas de Lodelowe for the prebend of Stretton in the royal free chapel of Penkridge, Staffordshire.

Nicholas de Lodelowe (1327-1333) received the prebend by exchange. On his death in 1333 the Chapter asked the Pope to nominate John de Sarum but John Piers received the prebend.

John Piers (1334-1344) DCL, died in 1344.

John de Sarum (1344-1350) died in 1350.

John de Wilton (1350-1380) was Rector of St Thomas', Sarum, and Chancellor of Sarum in 1355. He held the prebend of Stratford from 1350 to 1380, despite papal confirmation in 1351 of Richard de Haversham. Papal permission of an exchange in 1352 with Elias de Sancto Albano, Chancellor of Sarum, was ineffective and he exchanged the prebend in 1380 with Robert Croucheston for the church of Stratfieldsaye, Hampshire.

Richard de Haversham (1351) was confirmed in the prebend by the Pope in 1351 but this was apparently ineffective as John de Wilton continued to hold it.

Robert Croucheston (1380-1397) was a Canon Residentiary who died in 1397.

John Walrond (1397-1403) died in 1403.

Thomas Wisbech (1403-1404) held the prebends of Stratford from 1403 to 1404 and Netherbury in Terra from 1404 to 1410. He died in 1410.

Richard Prentys (1404-1406) exchanged the prebend of Stratford, which he held from 1404 to 1406, with Edward Prentys for the prebend of Grantham Australis holding the latter from 1406 to 1416. He died in 1416.

Edward Prentys (1406-1423) BCL, was Precentor of Sarum from 1419 to 1446. He exchanged the prebend of Grantham Australis, which he held in 1406, with Richard Prentys for the prebend of Stratford which he held from 1406 until 1423. He held the prebend of Durnford from 1423 to his death in 1446. He was a Canon Residentiary and occupied the house called Leadenhall in the Close.

William Swyft (1423-1425) BCL, was a Canon Residentiary who held the prebends of Stratford from 1423 to 1425 and Netherbury in Terra from 1425 to 1445. He died in 1445.

John Conge (1425) received the prebends of Stratford in March 1425 and Slape in July 1425. He held the latter in 1449.

John Whittemer (1425-?) held the prebend in 1435.

John Cariter (?-1443) died in 1443 and asked to be buried in the cathedral.

John Chedworth (1443-1445) DTh, held the prebends of Yatesbury from 1440 to 1443, Stratford from 1443 to 1445, Netherbury in Terra from 1445 to 1447 and Hurstbourne & Burbage from 1447 to 1452. He held a stall at Lincoln and was at different times Archdeacon of Northampton and of Lincoln. He was Provost of King's College, Cambridge in 1446, Archdeacon of Wilts from 1449 to 1452 and was consecrated Bishop of Lincoln in 1452. He died on 23 November 1471.

Walter Bayliff (1445-?) held the prebend in 1454.

James Goldwell (1462-1463) DCn&CL, held a stall at St Paul's in 1458, was Archdeacon of Essex and had a stall at Hereford in 1461. He held the prebend of Stratford from 1462 to 1463 and was Dean of Sarum from 1463 to 1472. He became a Canon of Windsor and Registrar of the Order of the Garter in 1470. On the foundation of the Hungerford chantry he is described as the Pope's Proto-notary. He became Bishop of Norwich in 1472 and died on 15 February 1499.

William Attingham (1463-?) held the prebend in 1473.

Maurice ap David (1486).

Richard Skry (?-1507) died, holding the prebend, in 1507.

Richard Gardiner (1507-1518) MA, held the prebends of Stratford from 1507 to 1518 and Torleton in 1518. He died in 1518.

John Chamber (1518-1519) DM, held the prebends of Stratford from 1518 until resigning in 1519 and Coombe & Harnham from 1523 to 1549. He was most probably physician to King Henry VIII and Archdeacon of Meath. If so, he was Dean of Westminster and one of the first members of the College of Physicians. He may well have been Warden of Merton College, Oxford from 1525 to 1544 and Archdeacon of Bedford from 1524 until his death in 1549.

John Edgar (1519-1523) resigned in 1523.

John Mason (1523-1524) BMus, held the prebends of Stratford from 1523 to 1524 and Preston from 1524 to 1548. He died in 1548.

William Canning (1524-1554) held the prebends of Minor Pars Altaris from ? to 1524, Axford in 1524 and Stratford from 1524 to 1554. He died in 1554.

Stephen Templer (1554-1563) MA, died in 1563.

John James (1563-?) BCL, held the prebend of Stratford from 1563 to ? and was Subdean of Sarum from 1564 to c.1577.

Thomas Busfield (1577-1583) MA, held the prebends of Stratford from 1577 to 1583 and Grimston from 1583 to 1621. He died in 1621.

Ralph Pickover (1583-1586) MA, held the prebends of Stratford from 1583 to 1586 and Gillingham Major from 1586 to 1615. He was Rector of Winterbourne Gunner and was Archdeacon of Rochester from 1576 to 1593. He would seem to have held a stall at Christ Church, Oxford in 1580 and was Archdeacon of Sarum and a Canon Residentiary from 1583 to 1615. He died on 8 March 1615 and was buried in the cathedral.

John Pryme (1586-1596) BD, died in 1596.

Benjamin Russell (1596-1633) BD, was a friend and pupil of Richard Hooker. He was Rector of Boscombe in 1595 and died in 1633.

Charles Robson (1633-1639) MA, resigned in 1639.

Thomas Hyde (1639-1660) DD, held the prebend of Stratford from 1639 to 1660. He was appointed Precentor of Sarum by King Charles II and held the prebend of Teynton Regis from 1660 to 1666. He died in 1666.

Aylmer Lynch (1660-1692) BD, died on 24 January 1692 and is commemorated at Langley Burrell.

Edward Hardwick (1692-1706) MA, was a Canon Residentiary from 1701 to 1706. He died on 13 July 1706 and was buried in the cathedral.

Rice Adams (1706-1737) MA, was Rector of Donhead St Mary from 1689 until his death and burial there in 1737.

William Periam (1738-1744) DD, died in 1744.

Edmund Aubery (1744-1757) BCL, died on 7 November 1757.

Newton Ogle (1758-1759) was married to a daughter of John Thomas, Bishop of Sarum 1757-1761. He held the prebends of Gillingham Major from 1757 to 1758, Stratford from 1758 to 1759 and Gillingham Major again from 1759 to 1794. He became Dean of Winchester in 1769 and again held the prebend of Stratford from 1794 until his death on 6 January 1804 (see below).

Pulter Forester (1759-1778) DD, also held a stall at St Paul's and died on 20 July 1778.

Thomas Eyre (1778-1780) DCL, held the prebends of Stratford from 1778 to 1780 and Alton Borealis from 1780 to 1812. He was Rector of Chilmark from 1770 to 1812, was also Rector of Fovant and was a Canon Residentiary from 1797 to 1812. He died on 26 March 1812.

John Chafy (1780-1782) MA, died on 8 February 1782.

Humphrey Sumner (1782-1794) DD, held the prebends of Stratford from 1782 to 1794 and Winterbourne Earls from 1794 to 1814. He was Provost of King's College, Cambridge from 1797 to 1814 and died on 23 March 1814.

Browne Grisdale (1794) DD, held the prebends of Stratford in 1794 and Torleton from 1794 to 1814. He died in 1814.

Newton Ogle (1794-1804) see above.

William Lisle Bowles (1804-1805) MA, poet and antiquary, held the prebends of Stratford from 1804 to 1805 and Major Pars Altaris from 1805 to 1850. He was Rector of Chicklade from 1795 to 1797, Vicar of Bremhill and was a Canon Residentiary from 1828 to 1850. He died on 7 April 1850 and was buried in the south choir aisle of the cathedral.

Henry Woodcock (1805-1818) DD, held the prebends of Stratford from 1805 to 1818 and Chardstock from 1818 to 1840. He held a stall at Christ Church, Oxford in 1824 and died on 8 August 1840.

Thomas Davies (1818-1830) BCL, died on 21 April 1830.

Francis Lear (1830-1834) BD, was Rector of Chilmark from 1824, holding the prebends of Stratford from 1830 to 1834 and of Netheravon from 1834 to 1846. He was Rector and Vicar of Bishopstone from 1843 and Archdeacon of Sarum from 1836 to 1846. He was Dean of Sarum and Canon Residentiary from 1846 to 1850, dying on 23 March 1850.

William Short (1834-1878) MA, was Vicar of Chippenham who died on 16 February 1878.

John Dryden Hodgson (1878-1896) MA, was a Fellow of St Peter's College, Cambridge. He was Vicar of East Grafton from 1850 to 1896, of Great Bedwin from 1855 to 1896 and Rector of Collingbourne Ducis from 1875 to 1896. He died on 19 August 1896.

Robert Newman Milford (1896-1912) was Rector of East Knoyle from 1865 to 1912 ? and was Rural Dean of Chalke from 1872 to 1912?. He resigned in 1912.

James Michael John Fletcher (1912-1940) MA, FRHistS, was an author and editor. He was Vicar of Wimborne Minster from 1906 to 1919 and Rural Dean of Pimperne from 1907 to 1919. He was Assistant Cathedral Librarian from 1932 to 1936, and Librarian from 1936 until his death on 23 February 1940.

Rupert Edward Gascoigne Newman (1940-1945) MC(& bar), MA, was a Chaplain to the Forces from 1919 to 1921, Vicar of Gillingham with East & West Stour and Milton from 1925 to ? and Rural Dean of Shaftesbury from 1928 to 1945 and Rural Dean of Shaftesbury from 1928 to 1945.

William Leonard Bertram Caley (1946-1948) MA, LTh, was Rector of St Paul's Fisherton Anger from 1940 to 1948, Rural Dean of Wilton from 1944 to 1948 and a Proctor in Convocation from 1945 to 1948 He resigned the prebend in 1948.

Walter Archibald Prideaux (1948-1961) MA, was Chaplain to the Forces from 1917 to 1919, Archdeacon of Damaraland from 1927 to 1931 and Rector of St Edmund's, Sarum, from 1932 to 1940. He was Rector of Pewsey from 1940 to 1951 and Curate-in-Charge of Huish with Oare from 1945 to 1950. He was Rural Dean of Pewsey from 1945 to 1950 and was Vicar of Charlton All Saints with Standlynch from 1951 to 1958. He died on 26 August 1965

William <u>Douglas</u> O'Hanlon (1961-1982) MA, was Chaplain RAFVR from 1939 to 1946, Rector of Langton Matravers from 1946 to 1951, Vicar of Calne (with Blacklands from 1963) from 1951 to 1972, Curate-in Charge of Heddington from 1953 to 1963, and Incumbent of Studland from 1972 to 1982.

Michael Thomas Christian-Edwards (1987-1992) MA, was Vicar of Trowbridge St Thomas from 1967 to 1975, Rector of Wingfield with Rowley 1967 to 1975, Priest-in-Charge Fisherton Anger from 1975 to 1981, Rector from 1981 to 1992 and Industrial Chaplain, Sarum from 1985 to 1992.

Gerald Stephen Miles Squarey (1992-) was Vicar of Bradford Abbas with Clifton Maybank from 1967 to 1974, Priest-in-Charge Corfe Castle from 1974 to 1979, Rector from 1979 to 1984, Rector of Steeple with Tyneham, Church Knowle and Kimmeridge from 1979 to 1984 and Rector of Corfe Castle, Church Knowle, Kimmeridge & Steeple with Tyneham from 1984 to 1990. He was Priest-in-Charge of Pimperne from 1990 to 1991, Priest-in-Charge of Stourpaine, Durweston and Bryanston from 1990 to 1991 and became Rector of Pimperne, Stourpaine, Durweston and Bryanston and Rural Dean of Milton & Blandford in 1991.

PRESTON

Prebend:- Sutton Poyntz was part of the royal estate of Dorchester in Dorset and it is presumed that Preston was also. The prebend, which was probably in existence by c.1150 consisted of tithes from these two places.

Shield:- **Richard Poore** was a brother of Herbert Poore, Bishop of Sarum 1194-1217. He was Dean, holding also the prebend of Bere & Cherminster from 1197 to 1215 and played a large part in the founding of the present cathedral. He became Bishop of Chichester in 1215 and Bishop of Sarum from 1217 to 1228, holding the prebend of Major Pars Altaris from 1217 to 1219, when it was exchanged for the prebend of Horton. He became Bishop of Durham in 1228. (Fig. 42.)

Blazon:- Argent a fess azure between three mullets gules. [On a silver shield, a blue horizontal band between three red, pierced five pointed stars.]

Psalter:- The portion of the psalter allotted to the prebend is Psalm 119 (49-128)

Holders of the prebend:-

James of Vercelli (c.1226/7-?) was fined for non-residence in 1227, was abroad in 1228 and was probably absent in 1233.

John de Kirkeby (c.1284) held the prebend in 1284. He was Treasurer of the Exchequer, Archdeacon of Coventry, Bishop-elect of Rochester in 1283 and Bishop of Ely in 1286.

Reimund de Ferrariis (c.1290-c.1297/9) first occurs as a canon going abroad on the business of King Edward I in 1290. He was the King's clerk, held stalls at Beverley and Bridgnorth and was Dean of St Severin, Bordeaux. He died between 19 August 1297 and 24 August 1299.

Gilbert Lovel (1298-?) held the prebend of Preston from 1298 until being succeeded in 1304. He held the prebends of Fordington & Writhlington from ? to 1311 and Grantham Australis from 1311 to 1332. In 1305 Simon de Gandavo, Bishop of Sarum 1297-1315, conceded to him the house of residence called 'Aula Plumbea' (Leadenhall) previously occupied by the late William Burnel, Prebendary of Horton (1298-1304).

Francis de Sancto Alberto (?-1330) held the prebend in 1304 and despite grants to William de Ayremynne and Robert de Patrica, continued to hold the prebend until his death in 1330.

William de Ayremynne (1317) received the prebend by royal grant in 1317 but Francis de Sancto Alberto continued to occupy it. He held stalls at St Paul's, York and Lincoln. In 1324 he was one of King Edward II's Commissioners to negotiate peace with Robert the Bruce. He became Bishop of Norwich in 1326, Chancellor of England in 1327 and Treasurer of England in 1331. He died on 27 March 1336.

Robert de Patrica (1320) was granted the prebend of Preston in 1320 but this was revoked in the same year. He then held the prebend of Stratford from 1321 until exchanging it in 1327 with Nicholas de Lodelowe for the prebend of Stretton in the royal free chapel of Penkridge, Staffs.

John de Kirkeby (1334-1338) was Rector of Keevil in 1333 and held the prebends of Preston from 1334 to 1338 and Minor Pars Altaris from 1338 to ?. He was probably the same person who was Precentor of Lichfield from 1332 to 1339. He was a Canon Residentiary and Archdeacon of Dorset from 1340 to 1346, holding with the dignity the church of Gussage, and died in 1346.

Nicholas Branche (or Branor de Urbe) (1338-?).

Robert Thresk (?-1351) died whilst holding the prebend in 1351.

John Gogh (1351-1361) received a royal grant of the prebend of Chardstock in 1350, King Edward III having recovered the right of presentation from Roger Wyville, Bishop of Sarum 1330-1375, and was installed in 1351. He was nominated to the prebend of Preston in 1351 and despite claims by John de Buckingham and Henry de Blakebourn, he was installed in 1352. The prebend of Preston was then claimed in 1357 by Thomas de Socton but John Gogh held it in 1360 and probably died whilst still holding it in 1361.

John de Buckingham (1351) was given the prebend of Preston in 1351 but it was claimed by two others. He then held the prebend of Stratton from 1361 to 1362 before becoming Bishop of Lincoln in 1362.

Henry de Blakebourn (1351) claimed the prebend in 1351 but John Gogh was installed.

Thomas de Socton (1357) claimed to have been nominated to the prebend and this was confirmed by the Pope in 1357. John Gogh however, continued to hold it.

Ralph de Codeford (1361-?).

John de Northwode (1366) who had expectations of a prebend in 1363, claimed the prebend of Preston in 1366 but Richard de Ravenser appears to have held it.

Richard de Ravenser (?-1367) held the prebend of Ruscomb from 1362 to ? and, having had expectations of a prebend in 1363, appears to have held the prebend of Preston from 1366? to 1367. He exchanged this with John de Withornwick for the free chapel of Tickhill, Yorkshire. He was the Chaplain to King Edward III, held stalls at St Paul's, Hereford, St David's and the collegiate church of St Stephen, Westminster and was Provost of Beverley.

John de Withornwick (1367-?)

Richard Beverley (?-1387) received the prebend of Coombe & Harnham by royal grant in 1372 and held the prebend of Preston from ? until exchanging it in1387 with John Carp for the prebend of Whitgreave Parva in the royal free chapel of Stafford.

John Carp (1387-?) held the prebend in 1395.

Walter Medford (?-1402) BCL, was Archdeacon of Sarum in 1397, Chancellor of Sarum from 1402 to 1404 and a brother of Richard Medford, Bishop of Sarum 1396 to 1407. In 1404 he exchanged the dignity with Henry Chichele for the Archdeaconry of Sarum and the prebend of Fordington & Writhlington, exchanging this dignity a few days later for the Archdeaconry of Berks. He probably exchanged this Archdeaconry with Peter Alcobasso for the deanery of Wimborne in 1417. He held the prebends of Major Pars Altaris from 1396 to 1397, Yetminster Prima in 1397, Faringdon from 1397 to 1400, having been excommunicated but later absolved, when he exchanged this prebend for the Treasurership of St Paul's. He held the prebend of Netherbury in Ecclesia in 1401, followed by Preston, which he exchanged with Richard Derham for Netherbury in Ecclesia in 1402. He held the prebends of Fordington & Writhlington from 1404 to 1407 and Bedwin from 1407 until his death in 1423.

Richard Derham (1402-1412) DTh, held the prebend of Netherbury in Ecclesia, despite litigation, from 1401 to 1402 when he exchanged it with Walter Medford for the prebend of Preston, which he held from 1402 to 1412.

John Macworth (1412-1451) was Chancellor of Henry, Prince of Wales, afterwards King Henry V. He held a stall at Lincoln in 1404 and was Archdeacon of Dorset from 1406 until exchanging the dignity in 1437 with John Hody for the church of Tredington, Worcestershire. He held a stall in York in 1436 and is believed to have been Archdeacon of Norfolk in 1408, Dean of Lincoln in 1412 and to have died in 1451.

William Nessingwick (1450-1454) was a Notary Public and held the prebends of Preston from 1450 to 1454, Stratton from 1454 to 1459 and Faringdon from 1459 to c.1486. He was Subdean of Sarum from 1459 to 1476, exchanging the office in 1476 with Giles Stanbridge for the church of Milston, which he held until 1487. A Canon Residentiary, he acted as locum tenens for the Dean of Sarum on more than one occasion, presiding in chapter as locum tenens not Subdean and visiting the prebends in 1463.

John Reedhill (1454-1473) BCn&CL, held the prebends Grantham Borealis from 1450 to 1454 and Preston from 1454 to 1473. He died early in 1473.

Edmund Audley (1473-1475) DTh, was a member of the family of Tuchet, Barons Audley and Earls of Castlehaven who in 1640 owned what is now Church House in Crane Street, Sarum. He held a stall at Hereford in 1464, before he was of age for ordination, and then held stalls at Lincoln and Windsor in 1472, Lichfield in 1474, Wells in 1475, London in 1476 and York in 1478. From 1473 to 1475 he held the prebend of Preston, in 1475 he was Archdeacon of the East Riding and while holding that office, was appointed to the rectory of Berwick St John. In 1479 he was Archdeacon of Essex and, in 1480, became Bishop of Rochester, only then giving up the remainder of his prebends. He became Bishop of Hereford in 1492 and was promoted to be Bishop of Sarum in 1502. He died at Ramsbury on 23 August 1524 and was buried in his chantry chapel in the cathedral.

George FitzHugh (1475-?) held the prebend in 1483.

Simon (or George) **Harcourt** (?-1493) resigned the prebend in 1493.

Edward Hawtrey (1493-1517) resigned the prebend in 1517.

Edmund Hawtrey (1517-?).

Richard Arche (?-1524) BCL, held the prebend of Preston from ? to 1524, resigning to assume the prebend of Faringdon in 1524, which he resigned a month later. He then received the prebend of Hurstbourne & Burbage which he held from 1524 until resigning in 1552. Two years later he was appointed to the prebend of Minor Pars Altaris but may not have received it before being deprived of all benefices early in 1555. He was Vicar of Avebury and held a stall at Windsor from 1538 until deprived in 1555. He was a Canon Residentiary from 1527 to 1554 and Treasurer of Sarum from 1551 to 1555 during which time the Commissioners appointed to survey Church Goods and Chantries visited the cathedral.

John Mason (1524-1548) BMus, held the prebends of Stratford from 1523 to 1524 and Preston from 1524 to 1548. He died in 1548.

Richard Petre (1548-1570) BA, was deprived of the prebend in 1570.

Anthony Brasier (1570-1595) MA, resigned in 1595.

Richard Johnson (1595-1622) MA, died in 1622.

Edward Thornborough (1623-1645) MA, was a son of John Thornborough, Bishop of Worcester, and was a Canon Residentiary from ? to 1645. He was Archdeacon of Worcester and died in 1645.

Thomas Triplett (1645-1662) MA, went to Ireland during the Commonwealth. At the Restoration he was reappointed but resigned in 1662 to assume a stall at Westminster. He died in 1670.

Jerameel Tarrant (1662-1677) MA, died in 1677.

John Martin (1677-1690) MA, held the prebends of Yatesbury from 1668 to 1677 and of Preston from 1677 until he was deprived as a non-juror in 1690. Because of his learning and temperament, Gilbert Burnet, Bishop of Sarum 1689-1715, gave him the equivalent of a stipend for life, from his own pocket. He died on 10 November 1693.

Robert Townsend (1691-1721) MA, was Rector of Devizes. He died in 1721 and was buried at Devizes St Mary.

John Shuttleworth (1721-1750) MA, died in 1750.

Henry Hawes (1750-1759) MA, died on 13 March 1759.

John Fisher (1759-1779) MA, was the father of John Fisher, Bishop of Sarum 1807-1825. He was Vicar of Preston and resigned the prebend in 1779.

John Spicer (1779-1784) MA, died on 27 November 1784.

Reynold Gideon Bouyer (1785-1826) LLB, died on 30 January 1826.

Edward Bouverie (1826-1874) MA, was Vicar of Coleshill, Berks from 1808 to 1874. He died on 22 July 1874.

Dacres Olivier (1874-1919) MA, was Domestic Chaplain to the Earl of Pembroke in 1865, Rector of Wilton with Netherhampton from 1867 to 1912 and Rural Dean of Wilton from 1885 to 1897. He died on 7 January 1919

Wyndham Arthur Scinde Merewether (1919-1929) MA, was Vicar of North Bradley from 1885 to 1908, Vicar of Bradford-on-Avon from 1908 to 1914 and of St Thomas, Sarum from 1914 to 1922. He died in 1929.

Edward Hungerford Goddard (1929-1944) MA, FSA, was an archaeologist. He was Vicar of Clyffe Pypard from 1883 to 1935 and resigned the prebend in 1944.

George David Archer (1945-1969) MA, was a Chaplain to the Forces from 1915 to 1919, Vicar of Broadstone from 1921 to 1965 and Rural Dean of Poole from 1949 to 1954.

Douglas John Strickland (1970-1981) held a stall at Birmingham from 1964 to 1966, was Vicar of Wimborne Minster from 1966 to 1980 and Team Rector of Wimborne and Holt from 1980 to 1981.

David Caldwell Ritchie (1981-1985) MA, was Priest-in-Charge of Bradford-on-Avon from 1973 to 1975, Vicar from 1975 to 1981 and Rural Dean of Bradford from 1980 to 1984. He was Vicar of Winsley from 1981 to 1984, Custos of St John's Hospital, Heytesbury from 1984 to 1985 and an Honorary Canon of Papua New Guinea from 1985.

John Anthony Phelps Standen-McDougal (1986-1994) AKC, was Rector of Tollard Royal with Farnham from 1970 to 1981, Priest-in-Charge of Gussage St Michael and Gussage All Saints from 1971 to 1976, Rector from 1976 to 1981, Rector Tollard Royal with Farnham, Gussage St Michael etc from 1982 to 1986, Rural Dean Milton & Blandford from 1981 to 1986, and Team Rector of the Bride Valley from 1986 to 1994.

Michael Anthony Ward (1995-) was Team Vicar of Swanborough from 1974 to 1977, Priest-in Charge Chute with Chute Forest, and of Shalbourne with Ham from 1977 to 1979, Team Rector Wexcombe from 1979 to 1986 and Vicar of Southbroom from 1986 to 1999. He became Team Rector of Alderbury in 1999.

FORDINGTON & WRITHLINGTON

Prebend:- In 1086, Fordington was in the royal manor of Dorchester in Dorset, while Writhlington in Somerset was held in 1066 and 1086 by Brictuuoldus, thegn of King William I. The church of Fordington St George was granted in 1091 to the canons by Osmund, Bishop of Sarum 1078-1099. The prebend, consisting of the churches of Fordington and Writhlington, was in existence by 1151.

Shield:- **Hubert Walter** was a Royal Justice and Dean of York. He was Bishop of Sarum, holding the prebend of Major Pars Altaris from 1189 to 1193, although absent from England with King Richard I on the Third Crusade from early 1190 to early 1193. He was enthroned as Archbishop of Canterbury in 1193 and died on 13 July 1205. (Fig. 43.)

Blazon:- Quarterly azure and argent a cross or between in dexter chief and sinister base five mullets of the second and in sinister chief and dexter base an eagle displayed sable. [On a shield divided into four quarters, a gold cross. The top left and bottom right; on blue, five silver pierced five pointed stars. The top right and bottom left; on silver, a black spread eagle.]

Psalter:- The portion of the psalter allotted to the prebend is Psalms 94, 95, 96 and 97.

Holders of the prebend:-

Laurence de Sancto Nicholao (c.1222-c.1233) was a Roman papal subdeacon. He was fined for non-residence in 1227 and was absent in 1233. He donated a pall to the cathedral and he held stalls at Lincoln, Chichester and York, where he was Subdean.

Ralph le Waleys of Brightwell (?-c.1284) was Precentor of Sarum from c.1288 to c.1294/5 and was only in deacon's orders at the time of his appointment. He received a papal dispensation, notwithstanding his being the son of a subdeacon, to become Archdeacon of Wilts from c.1283 to c. 1287, although the Archdeaconry was probably already in the hands of Ralph of Leicester in 1283. He held the prebend of Fordington and Writhlington from c.1275 to c.1284.

Gilbert Lovel (?-1311) held the prebends of Preston from 1298 until being succeeded in 1304. He held the prebends of Fordington & Writhlington from ? to 1311 and Grantham Australis from 1311 to 1332. In 1305 Simon de Gandavo, Bishop of Sarum 1297-1315, conceded to Gilbert Lovel the house of residence called 'Aula Plumbea' (Leadenhall) previously occupied by the late William Burnel, Prebendary of Horton (1298-1304).

Henry de la Wyle (1311-1313) DTh, held the prebends of Minor Pars Altaris in 1309, Durnford from 1309 to 1311 and Fordington & Writhlington from 1311 to 1313. He was Chancellor of Sarum from 1313 to 1329 and in 1326 he founded a chantry at the altar of St Peter and the rest of the Apostles at the east end of the north aisle of the cathedral. In 1329 he left to the Chapter his house near Leadenhall in the Close and died in June 1329.

John Hakeney (1313-1317) held the prebends of Durnford from 1311 to 1313 and Fordington & Writhlington from 1313 to 1317. He was Vicar of Bremhill and Rector of Fonthill in 1299, and was Rector of Compton Chamberlayne.

William de Fresapanis (?-1331) claimed the prebend of Blewbery in 1316 but withdrew it a year later. He held the prebend of Fordington & Writhlington in 1320 and exchanged it in 1331 with Peter de Galicia for a benefice in Agen, France.

Peter de Galicia (1331-1334) exchanged the prebend in 1334 with Richard de Chaddesley for the portion of Imber in Romsey conventual church, Hampshire.

Richard de Chaddesley (1334-1348) DCnL, received the prebend in 1334 and despite Robert de Askeby being nominated in 1345, he continued to hold it until his death in 1348.

Robert de Askeby (1345-?) was nominated in 1345 on the death of Peter de Galicia but Robert de Chaddesley continued to hold the prebend.

Richard de Spridlington (?-1361) held the prebend of Fordington & Writhlington from ? to 1361, exchanging it with William of Wykeham for Yetminster Prima which he held from 1361 until exchanging this in 1376 with John Turk for the prebend of Offley, Lichfield.

William of Wykeham (1361-1366) held the prebend of Yetminster Prima in 1361, before he was in holy Orders, exchanging it in the same year with Richard de Spridlington for Fordington & Writhlington, which he held from 1361 to 1366. He was appointed to the prebend of Bedminster & Redcliffe in 1361 but may have returned to Fordington & Writhlington. He became Bishop of Winchester in 1367 and was the founder of New College, Oxford and Winchester College.

Reginald de Cobham (?-1379) exchanged the prebend in 1379 with Richard Postell for the church of Northfleet, Kent.

Richard Postell (1379-1400) was a Canon Residentiary who died in 1400.

Henry Chichele (1400) DCL, was appointed to the Archdeaconry of Dorset in 1397 and after two years' litigation at the curia over the claims of Nicholas Bubwith, he was declared technically an intrusor, but was reinstated in 1399, although collation to Bubwith was made a year later. He held the prebends of Rotesfen in 1397, Yetminster Prima from 1397 to 1400, Fordington & Writhlington in 1400, Yetminster Secunda from 1400 to 1402 and Bedminster & Redcliffe from 1402 to 1404, when he exchanged with George Westby for the prebend of Fordington & Writhlington. After litigation, he became Archdeacon of Sarum in 1402, exchanging this and the prebend in 1404 for the dignity of Chancellor of Sarum which, following his consecration as Bishop of St David's in 1407, he continued to hold by papal indulgence until 1409. At one time he held the living of Melcombe Bingham and he became Archbishop of Canterbury in 1414. He was the founder of All Souls, Oxford and died on 12 April 1443.

John Scarle (1400-1403) held the prebends of Minor Pars Altaris from 1395 to 1400 and Fordington & Writhlington from 1400 to 1403. He died in 1403.

George Louthorp (1403-1404) was Rector of St Thomas, Sarum and held the prebend of Netherbury in Terra from 1393 to 1403. He exchanged this with George Westby for the prebend of Fordington & Writhlington in 1403 and in 1404 exchanged this for the dignity of Treasurer of Sarum, which he held until 1427. He was a Canon Residentiary

George Westby (1404) held the prebend of Netherbury in Terra from 1403 to 1404, becoming Treasurer of Sarum in 1404. A day later, he exchanged the dignity for the prebend of Fordington & Writhlington and within the same year exchanged this for the prebend of Bedminster & Redcliffe, which he in turn exchanged for Major Pars Altaris, which he then exchanged for Axford, resigning the last in the autumn of the same year.

Henry Chichele (1404) see above. He resigned in December 1404 after four months.

Walter Medford (1404-1407) BCL, was Archdeacon of Dorset in 1397, Chancellor of Sarum from 1402 to 1404 and a brother of Richard Medford, Bishop of Sarum 1396 to 1407. In 1404 he exchanged the dignity with Henry Chichele for the Archdeaconry of Sarum and the prebend of Fordington & Writhlington, exchanging the dignity a few days later for the Archdeaconry of Berks. He probably exchanged this Archdeaconry with Peter Alcobasso for the deanery of Wimborne in 1417. He held the prebends of Major Pars Altaris from 1396 to 1397, Yetminster Prima in 1397, Faringdon from 1397 to 1400, having been excommunicated but later absolved, when he exchanged the last for the Treasurership of St Paul's. He held the prebend of Netherbury in Ecclesia in 1401, followed by Preston, which he exchanged with Richard Derham for Netherbury in Ecclesia in 1402. He held the prebends of Fordington & Writhlington from 1404 to 1407 and Bedwin from 1407 until his death in 1423.

John Wakering (1407-1415) held the prebend of Bedwin in 1407, exchanging it in the same year with Walter Medford for the prebend of Fordington & Writhlington which he held from 1407 to 1415. He became Bishop of Norwich in 1416.

John Longville (1416-1426) held the prebend of Axford from 1404 until exchanging it in 1411 with William Werkeman for the prebend of Bedford Major at Lincoln cathedral. He held the prebend of Fordington & Writhlington from 1416 to 1426, held a stall at Windsor and died in 1426.

Alexander Sparrow (1426-1433) BCn&CL, held the prebends of Axford from 1423 to 1426 and Fordington & Writhlington from 1426 to 1433. He was Archdeacon of Sarum from 1426 to 1432 when he became Archdeacon of Berks until 1433. He was Treasurer of St Paul's in 1423 and died in 1433.

John Frank (1433-1438) held the prebend of Rotesfen in 1406, exchanging it with Reginald Braybroke for Beminster Prima which he held from 1406 to 1415. He then held the prebend of Chisenbury & Chute from 1415 to 1433 and Fordington & Writhlington from 1433 to 1438.

Fulk Bermyngham (1438-1443) held the prebends of Torleton in 1438, Fordington & Writhlington from 1438 to 1443, Bedwin from 1443 to 1459 and Teynton Regis from 1459 to 1461, exchanging the last with Roger Keys for Netherbury in Ecclesia in 1461 until resigning in 1464.

William Walesby (1444-1458) MA, was Chaplain to King Henry VI and also held a stall at Lincoln in 1449. One of his name was Archdeacon of Chichester from 1440 to 1454. He died in 1458.

John Morton (1458-1476) DCL, and held the prebends of Fordington & Writhlington from 1458 to 1476 and Horton from 1476 to 1478. He was a native of Milborne St Andrew and in 1453 was Principal of Peckwater's Inn at Oxford. He was afterwards an advocate at the Court of Arches. He was Archdeacon of Winchester in 1474 and held a stall at Wells in 1475. For short periods between 1475 and 1477 he would also seem to have held the Archdeaconries of Chichester, Huntingdon and Leicester. He was Archdeacon of Berks from 1476 until 1478 when he was consecrated Bishop of Ely. In 1486 he became Archbishop of Canterbury, being created Cardinal-Priest of St Anastasia in 1493. He died on 12 October 1500 at the age of 90 and was buried in Canterbury cathedral.

Thomas Chippenham (1464-?) DCnL, was installed in the prebend in 1464 although it was still held by John Morton. He apparently held it in 1466 and 1468, but it was John Morton who resigned the prebend in 1476.

Richard Martyn (1476-1482) BCnL, held the prebends of Rotesfen from 1473 to 1476 and Fordington & Writhlington from 1476 to 1482. He held a stall at St Paul's in 1471 and would appear to have been Archdeacon of London in 1469 and of Hereford in 1476. He was Archdeacon of Berks from 1478 until 1482 when he was consecrated Bishop of St David's. He resigned when Richard, Duke of Gloucester, later King Richard III claimed the crown.

William Chauntry (1482-1485) held the prebend of Warminster from 1472 until resigning in 1475. He then held the prebend of Fordington & Writhlington from 1482 until his death in 1485.

Robert Langton (1485-1488) was a nephew of Thomas Langton, Bishop of Sarum 1485-1493. He was Archdeacon of Dorset from 1486 to 1514 and held the prebends of Fordington and Writhlington from 1485 to 1488 and Bere & Cherminster from 1488 to 1524. He also held stalls at Lincoln from 1483 to 1516, at Southwell from 1514 to 1517 and at York from 1514 to 1524. He appears to have been Treasurer of York from 1509 to 1514 and Chancellor of Lichfield in 1516. He died in 1524.

John Forster (1488-1490) Sch.Th, held the prebends of Grantham Borealis from 1487 to 1488 and Fordington & Writhlington from 1488 until resigning the prebend in 1490.

John de Gigliis (1490-1497) DCn&CL, held the prebends of Major Pars Altaris from 1489 to 1490 and Fordington & Writhlington from 1490 to 1497. He was an active politician in the time of King Henry VII, held a stall at St Paul's and was Archdeacon of London in 1482. He was consecrated to the see of Worcester in 1497.

Thomas Jane (1497-1499) DCnL, became Bishop of Norwich in 1499.

Gonsalvo Ferdinand (?-1513) held the prebend in 1503 and died in 1513. He was Precentor of St Paul's.

Andrew Ammonius (1513-1517) was Rector of Christian Malford in 1510. He was collector for the Pope in England, Latin Secretary to King Henry VIII and a favourite with Hadrian, Bishop of Bath & Wells, obtaining a stall at Wells. In 1512 he held a stall at Westminster and was naturalised in 1514. He died in 1517.

Edward Finch (1517-1518) DM, was well endowed with prebends holding in succession those of Yatesbury from 1514 to 1515, Chardstock from 1515 to 1517, Wilsford & Woodford in 1517, Fordington & Writhlington from 1517 to 1518, Grimston from 1518 to 1519 and Faringdon from 1519 to 1521, exchanging the last with William Webbe for the church of Ross on Wye, Hereford. He then held the prebends of Bishopstone from 1521 to 1522, Teynton Regis from 1522 to 1524 and Bere & Cherminster from 1524 to 1539. He was Archdeacon of Wilts from 1522 until 1539. He died in 1539 and was buried in the cathedral.

George Sydenham (1518-1524) BCn&CL, held the prebends of Yetminster Secunda from 1502 to 1518 and Fordington & Writhlington from 1518 to 1524. He was Archdeacon of Sarum from 1503 to 1524 and was Chaplain to King Henry VII and King Henry VIII. He died in 1524 and was buried in the cathedral.

John Stone (1524-?) BCL, held the prebends of Axford from 1509 to 1511, Warminster from 1511 to 1517, Chardstock from 1517 to 1524 and Fordington & Writhlington from 1524 to ?.

Richard Basinge (1534-1566) was a fugitive living in Strasbourg in the reign of Queen Mary I. He died in 1566.

Augustin Bradbridge (1566-1567) MA, was Chancellor of Chichester in 1560 and Treasurer of Chichester in 1562. He died in 1567.

John Cottrell (1567-1572) DCL, became Archdeacon of Dorset in the diocese of Bristol in 1551. He held a stall at Bristol in 1545, was Archdeacon of Wells in 1554 and held a stall at Lincoln in 1555. He was a Canon Residentiary from 1569 to 1572 and died in 1572.

Thomas Dilworth (1572-1588/9) held the prebend of Fordington & Writhlington from 1572 to 1588/9 and was Subdean of Sarum from c.1577 to 1589. He was a Canon Residentiary from 1578 to 1588/9 and acted as locum tenens, not as Subdean but by special commission from the Dean. He had died by 23 January 1589.

William Souch (1589-1608) DD, was Precentor of Sarum from 1584 to 1608. He held the prebends of Netherbury in Terra from 1586 to 1589 and Fordington & Writhlington from 1589 to 1608. He appears to have been the subject of a Visitation over the Precentor's rights to the common fund and a house of residence.

Henry Cotton (1608-1612) MA, was a son of Henry Cotton, Bishop of Sarum 1598-1615. He was appointed Precentor of Sarum in 1614 but Francis Souch was presented by the King and instituted by the Archbishop in 1620. He held the prebends of Fordington & Writhlington from 1608 to 1612, Bitton from 1612 to 1615 and Highworth from 1615 to his death, while still Precentor, in 1622/3.

Humphrey Gwyn (1612-1641) BA, died in 1641 and was buried at East Hendred, Berkshire.

Edward Onslow (1641-1667) MA, was married to a niece of John Davenant, Bishop of Sarum 1621-1641. He died in 1667.

Thomas Wyatt (1667-1726) DD, was a Fellow of St John's College, Oxford, Vicar of Melksham in 1662, Rector of Bromham in 1668 and a Canon Residentiary from 1706 to 1726. He died on 18 February 1726 aged 93 and was buried in the cathedral.

Richard Younger (1726-1757) MA, died on 14 February 1757.

John Allen (1757-1765) MA, held the prebends of Beminster Prima from 1753 to 1757 and Fordington & Writhlington from 1757 to 1765. He died in 1765.

John Taylor (1765-1772) DD, held the prebends of Bishopstone from 1762 to 1765 and Fordington & Writhlington from 1765 to 1772, and was a Canon Residentiary with the house of Leadenhall from 1766 to 1772. He was well known in the literary world, was Chancellor of the Diocese of Lincoln in 1744, Archdeacon of Buckingham in 1753 and held a stall at St Paul's from 1757 to 1766. He died on 29 August 1772 and is buried in the south transept.

Arthur Coham (1772-1799) MA, held the prebends of Netherbury in Terra from 1771 to 1772 and Fordington & Writhlington from 1772 to 1799. He was Vicar of Potterne from 1781 to 1793, Rector of Brixton Deverill and Archdeacon of Wilts from 1779 to 1799. He died on 14 February 1799 and is commemorated at Brixton Deverill.

William Douglas (1799-1819) MA, was a son of John Douglas, Bishop of Sarum 1791-1807. He was Archdeacon of Wilts from 1799 to 1804, a Canon Residentiary from 1799 to 1819 and Precentor of Sarum from 1804 to 1819. He held the prebends of Coombe & Harnham from 1792 to 1799 and Fordington & Writhlington from 1799 to 1819. He was also Chancellor of the Diocese, Master of St Nicholas Hospital, Sarum in 1792, and Rector of Brixton Deverill and Vicar of Potterne. He died on 19 March 1819.

John Fisher (1819-1832) BA, was a nephew of John Fisher, Bishop of Sarum 1817-1825, receiving the prebend of Hurstbourne & Burbage in 1812, one month after his ordination as a deacon. He continued to hold this prebend to 1819 and Fordington & Writhlington from 1819 to 1832, and was Vicar of Osmington and Vicar of Gillingham. He was Archdeacon of Berks from 1817 to 1832 and a Canon Residentiary, occupying the house of Leadenhall, from 1819 to 1832. He died on 25 August 1832 and is commemorated at Osmington.

Charles Buchanan Pearson (1832-1881) was Prior of St John's Hospital, Wilton and died on 7 January 1881

Charles Adams Houghton (1881-1915) MA, was Vicar of East Harnham from 1868, and Secretary of the Diocesan Synod from 1871 to 1875. He was Rector of St Peter's, Marlborough from 1875 to 1887 and died on 15 October 1915.

St John Basil Wynne Willson (1915-1916) MA, DD, was Master of Haileybury College from 1905 to 1911, Master of Marlborough College from 1911 to 1916, Dean of Bristol from 1916 to 1921 and Bishop of Bath & Wells from 1921 to 1937. He died in 1946.

William Augustine Heygate (1916-1927) MA, was Vicar of Leigh, Dorset, from 1884 to 1890, Vicar of Burbage from 1890 to 1899, Vicar of Gillingham with East & West Stour and Milton from 1899 to 1905 and Rural Dean of Shaftesbury from 1899 to 1905. He resigned the prebend in 1927.

Gerald Burton Allen (1927-1936) MA, DD, was a Fellow, Dean and Chaplain of Pembroke College, Oxford, between 1910 and 1920, a Chaplain to the Forces from 1917 to 1918 and a Chaplain RAF from 1918 to 1919. He was Principal of St Edward's Hall, Oxford from 1920 to 1928 and Bishop Suffragan of Sherborne from 1928 until resigning in 1936. He was an Assistant Bishop of Oxford from 1936 to 1939 and again from 1952 to 1956, Archdeacon of Oxford, holding a stall at Christ Church, from 1936 to 1952 and Bishop Suffragan of Dorchester from 1939 to 1952. He died on 27 March 1956.

Harold Nickinson Rodgers (1937-1947) MA, was Archdeacon of Portsmouth from 1927 to 1936, Bishop Suffragan of Sherborne from 1936 to 1947 and Archdeacon of Dorset from 1940 to 1947. He died on 22 June 1947.

John Maurice Key (1947-1959) MA, DD, was Bishop Suffragan of Sherborne from 1947 to 1959, Bishop of Truro from 1959 to 1973 and Assistant Bishop of Exeter from 1975 to 1984. He died on 21 December 1984.

Victor Joseph Pike (1960-1976) CB, CBE, DD, MA, was a Chaplain to the Forces from 1932 to 1960 (mentioned in despatches) and Chaplain General from 1951 to 1960. He was an Honorary Chaplain to King George VI from 1948 to 1952 and to Queen Elizabeth II from 1952 to 1953. He held a stall at Canterbury from 1951 to 1960 and was Chaplain to Queen Elizabeth II from 1953 to 1960. He was Bishop Suffragan of Sherborne, holding the stall of Fordington & Writhlington from 1960 to 1976 and he died on 25 February 1986.

David John Letcher (1979-1999) was Rector of Odstock with Nunton & Bodenham from 1964 to 1972, Vicar of Downton from 1972 to 1985 and Rural Dean of Alderbury from 1968 to 1973 and 1977 to 1982. He was a Team Vicar of Dorchester with the church of Fordington St George from 1985 to 1997, and Rural Dean of Dorchester from 1989 to 1995. He resigned his prebend in 1999.

(Gangway)

Shield:- **Osmund** was believed to have been a younger son of a member of the Norman ruling class and was Chancellor to King William I. He was Bishop of Sarum from 1078 to 1099 and completed the building of the cathedral at Old Sarum, which was consecrated on 5 April 1092. He died on 3 December 1099 and was buried in the cathedral, being transferred to the new cathedral in 1226. He was canonised on 1 January 1457. (Fig. 44.)

Blazon (attributed):- Or a saltire sable. [On a gold shield, a black X.]

DURNFORD

Prebend:- The estate of Durnford in Wiltshire was held by William of Eu in 1086, whose lands were confiscated in 1093. The church was endowed by Isabel de Tosny, widow of Walter son of Richard and was granted by her to the cathedral before 1158. The prebend, consisting of the church of Durnford was probably in existence by c.1150 and certainly by 1220.

This stall was endowed with £1,000 under the Will of Montague Frederick Alderson, Prebendary of Durnford 1943-1962, who died on 14 July 1962.

Canopy statuette and shield:- **Richard Beauchamp** DCnL was a brother of William Beauchamp, Lord St Amand, and was Archdeacon of Suffolk. In 1448 he was appointed to the see of Hereford, being translated to Sarum in 1450. In 1477 he became also Dean of Windsor, rebuilding the collegiate chapel of St George and receiving the office of Chancellor of the Order of the Garter for him and his successors. Whilst at Sarum he saw the canonisation of St Osmund and he built onto the cathedral the Beauchamp chapel, later to be removed, in which he was buried following his death on 18 October 1481. (Fig. 45.)

Blazon:- Gules a fess between six martlets or within a bordure argent entoyre of mitres sable. [On a red shield, a gold horizontal strip between six gold martlets. The whole shield surrounded by a silver border with black mitres on it. (The mitres could perhaps be bells).]

Psalter:- The portion of the psalter allotted to the prebend is Psalms 90, 91, 92 and 93.

Holders of the prebend:-

Henry Tessun (c.1226/7-c.1243) was Chaplain to the Abbess of Wilton c.1191 and held the prebends of Durnford from c.1220 to c.1243 and Bedminster & Redcliffe from c.1243 to c.1254. He founded a chantry at St Mary Redcliffe and was successively Archdeacon of Bath by 1243 and Precentor of Wells by 1248. He was a brother of Nicholas Tessun who held the prebend of Blewbery c.1246.

Roger (c.1245) was Succentor of Sarum from c.1227 to c.1245 and held the prebend of Durnford c.1245.

Berard of Naples (c.1284-c.1295) was a professor of civil law, a papal subdeacon, chaplain and notary and was the uncle of Matthew de Carozolis, Prebendary of Wilsford & Woodford (c.1275-1305). He was Prior of Andover in 1250, held a stall at York and was Treasurer of Tours. He had died by 13 December 1295.

Monaldus de Camerino (c.1296-1297) may have held this prebend when elected Bishop of Fossombrone in the district of Ancona in 1296. He died in 1304.

John of Droxford (1297-1309) was Rector of Urchfont and also Keeper of the Wardrobe to King Edward II. He held stalls at London, Wells, York, St Martin le Grand, Dublin, Kildare, Bishop Aukland and Darlington He was elected Bishop of Bath & Wells in 1309.

Peter de Periton (1309) DCnL, held the prebend of Yetminster Prima from 1303 to 1310, was appointed to but declined the prebend of Durnford in 1309, and held the prebend of Bedminster & Redcliffe from 1310 to 1321. He was Archdeacon of Dorset from 1316 to 1321 and died in 1321.

Henry de la Wyle (1309-1311) DTh, held the prebends of Minor Pars Altaris in 1309, Durnford from 1309 to 1311 and Fordington & Writhlington from 1311 to 1313. He was Chancellor of Sarum from 1313 to 1329 and in 1326 he founded a chantry at the altar of St Peter and the rest of the Apostles at the east end of the north aisle of the cathedral. In 1329 he left to the Chapter his house near Leadenhall in the Close and died in June 1329.

John Hakeney (1311-1313) held the prebends of Durnford from 1311 to 1313 and Fordington & Writhlington from 1313 to 1317. He was Vicar of Bremhill and Rector of Fonthill in 1299, and was Rector of Compton Chamberlayne.

Robert de Worth (1313-1316) was Subdean of Sarum from 1309 to 1320 and held the prebends of Alton Australis from 1309 to 1313, Durnford from 1313 to 1316 and Chisenbury & Chute from 1316 to 1349. He was a Canon Residentiary, resigning the office of Subdean on 25 November 1320 to become Rector of Bradford-on-Avon. During his time, the office of Confessor was permanently added to that of Subdean.

Nicholas Wardeden (1316-?) DTh, was fined for non-residence in 1320.

William de Herlaston (1329) received a royal grant of the prebend of Highworth in 1326 but Walter de London was in occupation. He then received a royal grant of the prebend of Durnford in 1329.

Thomas de Garton (1330-?) was granted the prebend in 1330.

Elias de Sancto Albano (1334-1340) held the prebend of Durnford from 1334 to 1340 when he became a Canon Residentiary and Chancellor of Sarum. He was wrongly reported dead in 1350 so that Thomas de Trillek was appointed Chancellor. In 1352 the Pope permitted him to resign the dignity in exchange for the prebend of Stratford which he does not appear to have occupied and the church of St Thomas, Sarum, held by John de Wilton.

John Wyville (1340-1346) exchanged the prebend in 1346 with John de Chesterfield for the prebend of Chalke in Wilton conventual church.

John de Chesterfield (1346-?).

Lambert Threkingham (?-1387) exchanged the prebend in 1387 with John Shillingford for the Chancellorship of Chichester cathedral.

John Shillingford (1387-1406) DCL, exchanged the prebend in 1406 with Simon Membury for the chapel of Athelhampton.

Simon Membury (1406-1423) was Rector of Collingbourne Abbas and a Canon Residentiary. He died in 1423 and desired to be buried in the cathedral.

Edward Prentys (1423-1446) BCL, was Precentor of Sarum from 1419 to 1446. He exchanged the prebend of Grantham Australis which he held in 1406 with Richard Prentys for the prebend of Stratford which he held from 1406 until 1423. He held the prebend of Durnford from 1423 to his death in 1446. He was a Canon Residentiary and occupied the house called Leadenhall in the Close.

William Byconyll (1446-1447) DCL, held the prebends of Durnford from 1446 to 1447 and Netheravon from 1447 to 1448. He died in 1448.

William Normanton (1447-1448) held the prebends of Yatesbury from 1443 to 1445, Warminster from 1445 to 1446, Bishopstone from 1446 to 1447, Durnford from 1447 to 1448, Chisenbury & Chute from 1448 to 1449 and Faringdon from 1449 to 1459. He died in 1459.

Robert Langrish (1448-1454) held the prebends of Ruscomb from 1446 to 1448 and Durnford from 1448 to 1454.. He was a Canon Residentiary and Rector of Newbury and died in 1454.

William Brygon (1454-1459) BCn&CL, held the prebends of Minor Pars Altaris from 1447 to 1448, Ruscomb from 1448 to 1454, Durnford from 1454 to 1459 and Stratton from 1459 to 1469. He died in 1469.

Thomas Winterborne (1459-1478) DCL, was Archdeacon of Canterbury in 1468 and Dean of St Paul's from 1471 to 1478. He died in 1478.

Laurence Cokkys (1478-1479) DCnL, held the prebends of Durnford from 1478 to 1479, Netheravon from 1479 to? and Grimston in 1490. He was Rector of Winterbourne Basset in 1485, of Fisherton Anger in 1490 and was a Canon Residentiary in 1497. He died in 1501.

John Cooke (1479-1482) DCL, resigned the prebend in 1482.

John Arundel (1482-1489) BTh, held the prebend of Durnford from 1482 to 1489 and Beminster Secunda from 1489 to 1496. He was Dean of Exeter in 1483, Bishop of Coventry & Lichfield in 1496 and Bishop of Exeter in 1502. He died in 1504.

William Higham (1489-1490) DTh, died in 1490.

John Bostock (1490-1500) BCnL, held the prebends of Minor Pars Altaris from? to 1490 and Durnford from 1490 to 1500. He was Rector of Okeford Fitzpaine, a Canon Residentiary and the Commissary of the Chapter for visiting various prebends during a vacancy in the deanery. He died in 1500.

Richard Rawson (?-1503) DCnL, resigned the prebend in 1503.

John Colet (1503-1519) DTh, was Dean of St Paul's in 1505 and founded its school. He died in 1519.

John Pinnock (1519-1520) was consecrated Bishop Suffragan of Syene in 1518 to assist Edmund Audley, Bishop of Sarum 1502-1524, within the diocese which he did until 1535. He held the prebend of Durnford from 1519 to 1520, exchanging it with Nicholas Inglescent for the vicarage of Highworth and the prebend of Axford. He held the prebend of Axford from 1520 to 1524, exchanging it in 1524 for the prebend of Chardstock which he held until 1537. He died in 1537.

Nicholas Inglesent (1520-?) MA, held the prebend of Axford from 1511, exchanging it and the vicarage of Highworth in 1520 with John Pinnock for the prebend of Durnford.

Richard Dudley (?-1536) DTh, was Precentor of Sarum from 1507 to 1536 and held the prebends of Minor Pars Altaris from 1508 to 1517, Yatesbury from 1517 to ? and Durnford from ? (holding it in 1535) to 1536. He died in 1536.

Thomas Thebolde (?-1550) held the prebend in 1539 and died in 1550.

Henry Stansby (1550-?) DM, may have been deprived; he was at Wells cathedral in 1556.

Richard Reade (1557-1565) died in 1565.

John Thompson (1565-1571) BD, died in 1571.

William Cole (1571-1600) BD, died in 1600.

John Humphrey (1600-1613) MA, resigned the prebend in 1613.

Frederick Vaughan (1613-1663) died on 10 February 1663 and was buried in the cathedral where he is commemorated.

Edmund Sly (1663-1677) MA, held the prebends of Slape from 1661 to 1663 and Durnford from 1663 until his death on 19 August 1677. He was Rector of Sherrington from 1670 to 1677 and is commemorated in the cathedral.

Edward Pocock (1677-1693) MA, was Rector of Mildenhall from 1692 to 1727 and held the prebends of Winterbourne Earls from 1675 to 1677, Durnford from 1677 to 1693 and Netherbury in Ecclesia from 1693 to 1726. He died on 27 December 1726.

James Canaries (1693-1696) held the prebends of Durnford from 1693 to 1696 and Hurstbourne & Burbage from 1696 to 1698.

Timothy Topping (1696-1708) MA, held the prebends of Alton Australis from 1672 to 1696 and Durnford from 1696 to 1708. He was Rector of Chilton Foliat where he was buried following his death in 1708.

John Craig (1708-1726) MA, held the prebends of Durnford from 1708 to 1726 and Gillingham Major from 1726 to 1732. He died in 1732.

Thomas Pyle (1726-1757) MA, was a Canon Residentiary from 1741 to 1757. He died on 5 January 1757.

George Watts (1757-1766) MA, held the prebends of Major Pars Altaris from 1754 to 1757 and Durnford from 1757 until resigning the prebend in 1766.

George Watts (1766-1810) MA, died on 2 February 1810.

Arthur Edward Howman (1810-1848) MA, was Master of St Nicholas Hospital, Sarum in 1819 and died on 28 September 1848.

Edward Elliott (1848-1861) BD, was Vicar of Norton Bavant and died on 1 November 1861.

Edward Paroissien Eddrup (1861-1905) was the first Principal of Sarum Theological College from 1861 to 1868. He held the prebend of Durnford from 1861 to 1905, which included the period 1864 to 1905 during which he was Chancellor of Sarum and should have received the prebend of Bricklesworth. This had however been retained by Francis Lear upon his move to the dignity of Precentor of Sarum. He was Vicar of Bremhill with Foxham and Highway from 1868 to ? and was Rural Dean of Avebury. He died on 13 November 1905 and is commemorated in the north choir aisle of the cathedral.

Charles Myers (1905-1926) MA, held the prebend of Durnford from 1905 to 1926 and was a Canon Residentiary from 1915 to 1927. He was Subdean of Sarum from 1919 to 1926 and Treasurer of Sarum from 1926 until resigning the dignity in 1937. He died in 1948.

Charles Dixon Hoste (1926-1929) MA, was Rector of St Peter & St Paul and Vicar of St Mary's, Marlborough from 1917 to 1929 and Rural Dean of Marlborough from 1925 to 1929. He resigned the prebend in 1929.

Arthur Edward George Peters (1930-1943) MA, was Domestic Chaplain to John Wordsworth, Bishop of Sarum 1885-1911, Vicar of St Mary's, Marlborough from 1905 to 1917 and Rural Dean of Marlborough from 1911 to 1917. He was Vicar of Bremhill with Foxham & Highway from 1917 and Rural Dean of Avebury from 1925.

Montague Frederick Alderson (1943-1962) MA, BMus, was Rector of Fugglestone with Bemerton from 1918 to 1947. He was a friend of Sir Sydney Nicholson, founder of the Royal School of Music, and was a Fellow of St Michael's College, Tenby to which the RSCM moved during World War II. He died in 1962 having endowed this stall in his Will.

Edward Stephen Wakefield (1962-1979) BSc, was Vicar of Winterbourne Stickland with Turnworth and Rector of Winterbourne Houghton from 1955 to 1961 and Rural Dean of Milton from 1959 to 1961. He was Rector of Tockenham and Vicar of Clyffe Pypard and also Rural Dean of Avebury from 1961 to 1965 and was Rector of Pewsey from 1965 to 1975. He died in April 1980.

John Lionel Reynolds (1980-) JP, BTh, MA, was Vicar of Chiseldon and Draycott Foliat from 1968 to 1974, Rector Ridgeway Team and Rural Dean of Marlborough from 1974 to 1976, Vicar of Calne & Blackland from 1976 to 1989, Rural Dean of Calne from 1977 to 1986 and Vicar Woodford Valley from 1989.

GRANTHAM BOREALIS

Prebend:- Grantham in Lincolnshire was a royal manor in 1086 and its churches were given to the canons in 1091 by Osmund, Bishop of Sarum 1078-1099. The two prebends were probably in existence c.1150, Grantham Australis and Borealis consisted of the churches of South and North Grantham and before 1226 an interest in Stratford-sub-Castle which was later given to the office of Succentor in order to make better provision for the daily mass of the Blessed Virgin. Grantham Australis included the churches of Gonersby, Harlaxton, Cotsworth and Stoke.

Canopy statuette and shield:- **Lionel Woodville** was brother-in-law to King Edward IV, being the son of Richard, Earl Rivers, whose daughter Elizabeth, co-foundress with Margaret of Anjou of Queens' College, Cambridge, was married to the King. He held a stall at Lincoln in 1465, the prebends of Coombe & Harnham from 1467 to 1478 and of Bere & Cherminster from 1478 to 1482. He was also Archdeacon of Oxford and Dean of Exeter, becoming Bishop of Sarum from 1482 to 1484. His death in June 1484 was said to have been hastened by grief at the downfall of his family on the accession of Richard III, and the execution at Salisbury of Henry Stafford, Duke of Buckingham, his brother-in-law. He was buried in the cathedral. (Fig. 46.)

Blazon:- Argent a fess and canton conjoined gules. [On a silver shield, a horizontal red strip with a red square in the top left corner joined to it.]

Psalter:- The portion of the psalter allotted to the prebend is Psalms 25, 26, 27 and 28.

Holders of the prebend:-

Hugh de Puiset (12c.) was a son of Hugh du Puiset, Bishop of Durham 1153-1195, and was Chancellor of the King of France from c.1179-c.1185. He was said in a case of 1228 to have held this prebend and was said in 1189 to have died.

John of Coutances (c.1188/1196) was a nephew of Walter of Coutances, Bishop of Lincoln 1183-1184 and Archbishop of Rouen 1184-1208. He was Treasurer of Lisieux, Dean of Rouen and by 1187 was Archdeacon of Oxford. He became Bishop of Worcester in 1196.

Richard (c.1219) was Chaplain to Richard Poore, Bishop of Sarum 1217-1228.

William de Linden (before 1219-c.1222).

William of Ingoldsby (c.1222-c.1230/1) had been succeeded in the prebend before 20 December 1232 but there may have been two people of this name.

Benedict (1231/2-c.1242) was a papal chaplain and chamberlain who held a stall at London. He was probably still alive in 1240 but had died by 20 May 1242.

Marinus of Eboli (c.1246-1271) was a papal vice-chancellor who in 1246 unsuccessfully claimed the dignity of Treasurer of Sarum. He continued to hold the prebend whilst Bishop-elect of Capua and while still holding the prebend had died by 21 December 1271.

Stephen de Gurunvile (1271-1272) held a stall at Hereford and was Precentor of Sarum from 1270 to 1272. He briefly held the prebend of Teynton Regis which was then joined to this dignity, from 1270 to 1271. He then held the prebend of Grantham Borealis from 1271 until his death before 30 August 1272.

John de Burton (1272-c.1287) was Subdean of Sarum from c.1262 to 1269 and Warden of de Vaux College, Sarum from September 1269 until his death. He was Precentor holding also the stall of Grantham Borealis from 1272 to c.1287. He had charge of the diocese during the vacancy in the see prior to the appointment of Walter Scammel, Bishop of Sarum 1284-1286, and had died by 16 November 1287.

William de Berges (1288-1313) was Archdeacon of Berks from c.1287 to c.1311/13 and had died by 10 March 1313.

Alexander de Hemingby (1313) held the prebend of Slape from 1304 and although Robert de Winchcombe was appointed in 1313, this was revoked four months later and he continued to hold the prebend until 1316. He was appointed to the prebend of Grantham Borealis in 1313 but this was also revoked four months later on the appointment of Tydo de Varesio. He held the prebend of Hurstbourne & Burbage from 1316 to c.1328.

Tydo de Varesio (1313-1331) was given the dignity of Chancellor of Sarum in 1311, although William de Bosco was in occupation. He held the prebend of Grantham Borealis from 1313 to 1331 and on appointment by the Pope, was Archdeacon of Berks from 1313 to 1331, despite an ineffective royal grant being made to Gilbert de Stapleton in 1317. He died in 1331.

Gilbert de Stapleton (1317) received the dignity of Archdeacon of Berks by royal grant in 1317 but this was apparently ineffective since Tydo de Varesio was in possession at his death in 1331. In the same year he was appointed to the prebend of Grantham Borealis but Tydo de Varesio was in occupation.

John de Langebergh (1331-1349) was appointed to the prebend in 1331 but Matthew de Briselee was nominated twice in 1347. In 1348 there was a royal inquiry into the persons who ejected him from the prebend and the Chapter refused to install Matthew Briselee pending a decision of the Court in Rome. He died in 1349.

Matthew de Briselee (1347-1350) twice received nomination in 1347 however the Chapter refused to install him in 1349 as a case was pending in the Roman Court. His position was confirmed later in the year following the death of John de Langebergh. He died in 1350.

Robert Canley (1347) was nominated in 1347 but less than a month later Matthew de Briselee was nominated for the second time.

John de Brian (1350) received the prebend of Torleton by royal grant in 1343 but a grant was subsequently made to John de Makelesfeld. He was nominated to the prebend of Grantham Borealis in 1350 but a royal grant of this prebend was made to William de Retford.

William de Retford (1350-1373) died in 1373.

John de Sleford (1373-?).

John deYerdeburgh (?-1395) resigned in 1395.

Guy Mone (1395-1396) was granted the prebend of Yetminster Secunda in 1388. He held the prebends of Grantham Borealis from 1395 until resigning in 1396, and Faringdon in 1397. He held a stall at St Paul's and was Treasurer of that cathedral from 1394 to 1397 when he became Bishop of St David's. He twice held the office of Treasurer of England.

John Elvet (1396-1404) died in 1404.

Roger Coringham (1404-1412) DTh, died in 1412.

John Fyton (1412-1416) MA, BTh, was also Archdeacon of Stafford and held the prebends of Ruscomb from 1410 to 1412, Granthan Borealis from 1412 to 1416 and Highworth from 1416 to 1422. He exchanged the last with John Stafford for the dignity of Chancellor of Sarum which he held from 1422 to 1432, dying in 1432.

Edmund Dutton (1416-1450) held the prebends of Torleton in 1416 and Grantham Borealis from 1416 to 1450, exchanging the latter with John Reedhill in 1450 for a prebend in St Chad's collegiate church, Shrewsbury.

John Reedhill (1450-1454) BCn&CL, held the prebends of Grantham Borealis from 1450 to 1454 and Preston from 1454 to 1473. He died early in 1473.

Richard Andrew (1454-1477) DCL, was Archdeacon of Sarum from 1441 until resigning in 1444. He held the prebends of Faringdon from 1447 to 1449, Stratton from 1449 to 1454 and Grantham Borealis from 1454 to 1477. He was a friend of Archbishop Chichele and first Warden of All Souls, Oxford, founded by him in 1437. He was Dean of York in 1451 and Chancellor of Canterbury. He died in 1477.

Ralph Shaa (1477-?) DTh.

Christopher Bainbridge (?-1486) LLD, held the prebends of Grantham Borealis from ? to 1486, Chardstock in 1486 and Horton from 1486 to 1508. He was Master of the Rolls in 1504. After holding many preferments, amongst them those of Provost of Queen's College, Oxford and Dean of York, he was made Bishop of Durham in 1507 and Archbishop of York in 1508. He was created Cardinal-Priest of St Marcellinus & St Peter in 1508 and of St Praxedes in 1511. He led a military expedition against Ferrara, was poisoned by his steward, an Italian priest, on 14 July 1514 and was buried at the English College, Rome. Sylvester Gigliis, Bishop of Worcester, was suspected of having instigated the murder but was declared innocent by the Pope.

Richard Fox (1486-1487) BCL, held the prebends of Bishopstone from ? to 1486 and Granthan Borealis from 1486 to 1487. He became Bishop of Exeter in 1487, of Bath in 1492, of Durham in 1494 and of Winchester in 1501. He was the Keeper of the Great Seal to King Henry VII and King Henry VIII and founded Corpus Christ College, Oxford. He died in 1528.

John Forster (1487-1488) Sch.Th, held the prebends of Grantham Borealis from 1487 to 1488 and Fordington & Writhlington from 1488 until resigning the prebend in 1490.

Edward Willoughby (1488-1508) MA, was Rector of Berwick St John.

William Gray (1508-1514) MA, would appear not to have been ordained before 1510 when he became Archdeacon of Berks, holding the dignity until 1522. He held the prebends of Grantham Borealis from 1508 to 1514, Horton in 1514, Faringdon from 1514 to 1515 and Teynton Regis from 1515 to 1522. He held a stall at Hereford from 1512 to 1522. He died in 1522 and asked to be buried in Ramsbury church.

John Baker (alias Elton) (1514-1519) BCn&CL, held the prebends of Grantham Australis from 1512 to 1514, Grantham Borealis from 1514 to 1519 and Grimston from 1519 until his death in 1547. He was Rector of St Peter's, Marlborough in 1510 and of Sherston in 1511. In 1513 he exchanged the living of Marlborough for the Wardenship of St Catherine's Hospital, Ledbury. He was presented to the living of Mildenhall in 1514. In 1515 he held a stall at Hereford and in 1519 became Rector of Childrey, Berks. In 1534 he gave lands in Oxfordshire and Gloucestershire to found a fellowship at Brazenose College, Oxford and in the same year was Vicar of Yetminster. Later he became Chancellor of Hereford.

William Pykenham (1519-1535) BCL, held the prebends of Yatesbury from 1515 to 1517, Ruscomb from 1517 to 1518, Yetminster Secunda from 1518 to 1519, Grantham Australis in 1519 and Grantham Borealis from 1519 to 1535. He died in 1535.

Matthew Wotton (1535-1551) BD, held the prebend of Grantham Borealis from 1535 to 1551, was a Canon Residentiary from 1537 to 1551 and was Treasurer of Sarum from 1550 to 1551. He died in December 1551.

Rowland Middleton (1551-1555) MA, died in 1555.

John Griffith (1555-1558) BCn&CL, died in 1558.

John Boxall (1558-1559) DD, was a Fellow of New College, Oxford and Principal Secretary to Queen Mary I. He became Warden of Winchester in 1554 and Archdeacon of Ely in 1556. In 1557 he was appointed Dean of Peterborough and shortly afterwards of Norwich. He was Dean of Windsor in 1557 and Registrar of the Order of the Garter. He was a great promoter of the catholic faith in the time of Queen Mary I but was deprived of his preferments in 1559 and died in retirement c.1571.

Walter Wright (1559-1561) DCL, held the prebend, despite the presentation of Edward Barnard by Queen Mary I. He held a stall at Winchester, was Archdeacon of Oxford and died on 10 May 1561.

Edward Barnard (1559) was presented to the prebend by Queen Mary I because it had become vacant by deprivation. It was, however held by Walter Wright.

James Proctor (1561-1584) BD, was a Canon Residentiary from 1561 to 1584. He died in 1584.

Abraham Conham (1584-1613) BD, held the prebends of Yetminster Prima in 1584 and Grantham Borealis from 1584 to 1613. He was Rector and Vicar of Bishopstone and died in 1613.

John Still (1613-1662) MA, was a son of Bishop Still of Bath & Wells and held a stall at Wells. He held the prebends of Yetminster Prima from 1611 to 1613 and Grantham Borealis from 1613 to 1662, was Rector of Christian Malford and died in 1662.

William Grove (1662-1666) MA, was Rector of Poulshot.

Richard Hyde (1666) DCL, held the prebend of Warminster from 1660 to 1666, the office of Subdean of Sarum from 1661 to 1664 and the prebend of Grantham Borealis in 1666. He held a stall at Winchester in 1662 and died in 1666.

Richard Hill (1666-1683) MA, was Rector of East Knoyle from 1662 to 1695. He held the prebends of Grantham Borealis from 1666-1683 and Alton Borealis from 1683 to 1695. He was a Canon Residentiary from 1665 to 1671. He died on 20 March 1695 and was buried in the cathedral near the door of the Consistory Court.

William Dowse (1683-1697) MA, died in 1697.

John Jolland (1697-1726/7) MA, had died by 17 January 1727.

Thomas Wishaw (1727-1756) MA, was a Canon Residentiary with the house of Leadenhall from 1727 to 1756. He died on 7 May 1756.

Richard Easton (1756-1786) MA, held a stall at Lincoln and died on 1 January 1786.

George Barrington (1786-1802) MA, resigned in 1802. He held a stall at Durham.

Joseph Smith (1802-1825) MA, was Vicar of Melksham and died on 3 June 1825.

William Potchett (1825-1859) was Vicar of Grantham and died on 13 November 1859.

John David Hastings (1860-1869) was Rector of Trowbridge from 1841 to 1869.

Charles Woodcock (1869-1898) was Vicar of Chardstock from 1833 to 1875 and Rector of Chardstock All Saints from 1875 to 1898. He died on 6 March 1898.

Thomas Neville Hutchinson (1898-1899) MA was Vicar of Broad Chalke from 1882 until his death on 6 May 1899.

Arthur Barugh Thynne (1899-1917) MA, was Curate in Charge of Wilsford from 1869 to 1873, Vicar of Seend from 1873 to 1917 and Rural Dean of Potterne from 1896 to 1916. He died in December 1917.

Robert Crowther Abbott (1918-1927) MA, was Assistant Master, Marlborough College from 1892 to 1907 and Principal of Sarum Theological College from 1907 to 1913. He was Vicar of Holy Trinity, Weymouth and Rural Dean of Weymouth from 1914 to 1916, Vicar of Gillingham with East & West Stour from 1916 to 1925 and Rural Dean of Gillingham from 1917 to 1925. He held the prebends of Chardstock from 1907 to 1913 and Grantham Borealis from 1918 to 1927. He was a Proctor in Convocation and was the first Bishop Suffragan of Sherborne from 1925 to 1927, dying on 25 November 1927.

James William Sackett Tomlin (1928-1929) MA, was Principal of Queensland Theological College from 1906 to 1910 and held a stall at Brisbane from 1906 to 1911. He was Principal of St Boniface College, Warminster from 1914 to 1929 (Chaplain to the Forces 1916) and Rector of Bishopstrow from 1921 to 1924. He was Warden of St Augustine's College, Canterbury from 1929 to 1940 and held a stall at Canterbury from 1941 to 1958. He died on 3 November 1959.

Archbald Leslie Keith (1929-1937) MA, was Vicar of Wimborne Minster from 1920 to 1946 and Rural Dean of Wimborne from 1928 to 1946. He held the prebends of Grantham Borealis from 1929 to 1937 and Netheravon from 1938 until resigning in 1948. He died in 1956.

Wilfred Marcus Askwith (1938-1941) MA, DD, was a Fellow of Corpus Christi College, Cambridge. He was Rector of Stalbridge from 1920 to 1925, Vicar of Sherborne with Castleton & Lillington from 1932 to 1939 and Rural Dean of Sherborne from 1934 to 1939. He held a stall at Ripon from 1941 to 1942, was Bishop of Blackburn from 1942 to 1954, Prelate of the Order of St Michael & St George from 1951 to 1962 and Bishop of Gloucester from 1954 until his death on 16 July 1962.

John Percival Willoughby Lovett (1941-1962) MA, held a stall at Liverpool from 1928 to 1939 and was Vicar of Sherborne with Castleton & Lillington from 1939 to 1947. He was Rector of Gussage St Michael and of Gussage All Saints from 1947 to 1952, Rector of Mapperton from 1952 to 1958 and Vicar of Melplash from 1952 to 1959. He resigned the prebend in 1962.

Albert Jesse Gauntlett Chard (1962-1975) was Vicar of Collingbourne Kingston from 1940 to 1943 and Vicar of Figheldean with Milston from 1943 to 1948. He was Vicar of Winterborne Whitechurch with Winterbourne Clenstone from 1948 to 1950. He was Rector of Holy Trinity, Dorchester from 1950 to 1964 and Perpetual Curate of St Thomas', Sarum from 1964 to 1969. He died before 31 July 1989.

Reginald James Albert Askew (1975-1987) MA, was Principal of Salisbury & Wells Theological College and Chairman of the Southern Dioceses Ministerial Training Scheme from 1973 to 1987, and was Dean of King's College, London from 1988 until his retirement in 1993.

John Kingsmill Cavell (1988-) MA, held a stall at Exeter from 1967 to 1972 and was Bishop Suffragan of Southampton also holding a stall at Winchester from 1972 to 1984. He was Bishop to HM Prisons from 1974 to 1985 and became Assistant Bishop of Sarum in 1988.

HIGHWORTH

Prebend:- The church of Highworth in Wiltshire was part of a royal manor in 1086 and the churches of 'Worda' were granted to the canons in 1091 by Osmund, Bishop of Sarum 1078-1099. The prebend was probably in existence by c.1150, being known as 'Worth', but 'Hauteworthe' in 1291.

Canopy statuette and shield:- **Thomas Langton** BTh, held a stall at Wells in 1478 and was later Provost of Queen's College, Oxford. He was translated from the see of St David's to that of Sarum in 1485 but it appears that on the accession of King Henry VII, he was imprisoned and deprived of the revenues of the see for a period of less than a month. He was translated to the see of Winchester in 1493 and was elected in 1501 to be Archbishop of Canterbury but died on 27 January, five days afterwards. He was buried in Winchester cathedral. (Fig. 47.)

Blazon:- Or on a cross quarterly azure and gules five roses argent. [On a gold shield, a cross, the top left and bottom right red, the top right and bottom left blue, with on it five silver roses.]

Psalter:- The portion of the psalter allotted to the prebend is Psalms 32, 33 and 34.

Holders of the prebend:-

Geoffrey (?-1226/27) witnessed a deed c.1224 by which the prebend of Calne was joined to the dignity of Treasurer. He was Precentor of Sarum from c.1224 to c.1226/7 and held the prebend of Highworth in 1226/27.

William de la Corner (c.1284-1288) had been elected Archbishop of Dublin in 1279 but the election was set aside. He was a papal chaplain, proctor and royal envoy who held the prebends of Teynton Regis from 1270 to 1274 and Highworth from c.1284 to 1288, and was Precentor of York and Archdeacon of Northumberland. He failed to be elected to the see of Sarum in May 1288 but was successful six months later. He was Bishop of Sarum from 1289 until his death probably on 10 October 1291. He was buried in the middle of the quire 'nearly under the eagle'.

Peter of Savoy (1289-1297) was a kinsman of King Edward I and held the prebend of Highworth from 1289 to 1297, stalls at York in 1290 and Hereford, was Precentor of Lincoln, Dean of Bridgnorth and of St Martin le Grand, London, and was Treasurer of Llandaff. He was Dean of Sarum from 1297 to 1308 but went to Rome in 1298 and was mostly non-resident. He protested in 1301 against the Bishop's claim to jurisdiction over the canons and others of the cathedral. In 1304 he was summoned into residence but soon after obtained formal licence to live abroad. He became Archbishop of Lyon in 1308 and had died by November 1332.

Amadeus of Savoy (1297-?) was a brother of Peter of Savoy and a kinsman of King Edward I. He held stalls at Lincoln, Lyons and Dublin, was Archdeacon of Oxford, Dean of Bridgnorth and Archdeacon of Rheims.

William of Savoy (?-c.1305) vacated the prebend some time before 1305.

John de Frescobaldis (1305) was nominated to the prebend on the death of William of Savoy but Richard de Bello gained possession.

Richard de Bello (?-1326) held in turn, during 1298, the prebends of Beminster Prima and Grantham Australis, and also Coombe & Harnham from 1298 to 1305. He was then given the prebend of Highworth although John de Frescobaldis had already received a papal nomination. The Pope tried to restore Frescobaldis to the prebend but the Bishop prevented the Dean from oppressing Richard de Bello. Eventually, in 1308, there was a papal dispensation allowing de Bello to retain the prebend which he did until 1326. He was Archdeacon of Berks in 1313 and, in 1315, had charge of the diocese while the see was vacant on the death of Simon de Gandavo, Bishop of Sarum, 1297-1315. He would seem also to have held a stall at Hereford in 1305 and to have been Rector of Poulshot in 1313. He died in 1326.

Walter de London (1326-1350) held the prebend despite a royal grant to William de Herlaston in 1326. He died in 1350.

William de Herlaston (1326) received a royal grant of the prebend of Highworth in 1326 but Walter de London was already in occupation. He then received a royal grant of the prebend of Durnford in 1329.

Lewis son of Lapus de Ruspis (1350).

Ramond Pelegrini (1350-1365) held the prebend of Bishopstone from 1350 to 1363. He was nominated to the prebend of Highworth in 1350 but Henry Walton was also appointed. In 1365 however, he exchanged this prebend with Peter Boniface for the chapel in the palace of the Bishop of London but it appears that the exchange was out of order as the prebend was later said to be vacant due to his death on 16 September 1365.

Henry de Walton (1350-1352) was nominated to the prebend of Yetminster Prima in 1348, installed in 1352 and had resigned by 25 June 1358, the same date that Dalmacius de Monte Florum was also said to have resigned. He held the prebend of Highworth from 1350 to 1352.

Peter Boniface (1365) received the prebend by exchange but Ramond Pelegrini's death may have rendered it ineffective.

John Ketene (1365-?) was appointed to the prebend in 1365 but three months later Thomas Paxton was nominated.

Thomas Paxton (1365) DCL, claimed to have been nominated Archdeacon of Berks but probably did not gain possession. He resigned the Archdeaconry in 1365 on receiving nomination to the prebend of Highworth.

William de Agrifolio (?-1371) was a nephew of Pope Clement VI and was created Cardinal-Priest of St Stephanus in 1367 at the age of 28 years. He returned with Pope Urban V to Avignon in 1370 and became Dean of Anti-Cardinals. He held the prebend of Highworth from ? to 1371, was Archdeacon of Taunton and was Archdeacon of Berks in both 1371 and 1384. He was nominated to the prebend of Bere & Cherminster in 1371, but Henry de Wakefield remained in possession. He held a stall at Lincoln from 1397 to 1384 and died of the plague on 13 January 1401 in the College of St Martial..

Bertrand Atgerius (1371-?) was a native of the Auvergne, probably a Franciscan and a nephew of Pope Gregory XI. He became Bishop of Assisi in 1357 and of Glandéves in the Alpes Maritime in 1368. He became Vicar General of the Minorites in 1372, Cardinal-Priest of St Prisca in 1371 and Cardinal-Bishop of Ostia in 1378. Dying at Avignon on 15 November 1392, he was buried in the church of the Franciscans there. He was given the prebend of Highworth by the Pope in 1371 and probably still held it in 1381.

Richard Medford (?-1387) received the prebend of Bere & Cherminster in 1386 by royal grant, he having exchanged the prebend with Thomas Stowe for the prebend of Highworth, but the Dean's locum refused to install him. Despite charges by Ralph Ergum, Bishop of Sarum 1375-1388, and Nicholas Doberham against William Byde and Thomas Stowe for intrusion into the two prebends and fraudulent exchanges, the exchange between Thomas Stowe and Richard Medford was ratified in 1387, the latter assuming the prebend of Highworth. He held stalls at Windsor in 1381 and at York in 1386. He was imprisoned for some time at Bristol by the Parliament as a supporter of King Richard II. He was Archdeacon of Norfolk in 1385 and in 1390 was appointed by the Pope to the see of Chichester. He was translated to the see of Sarum in 1395 and was Bishop until his death on 3 May 1407. He was buried in St Margaret's Chapel in the south west transept of the cathedral and left a small sum to keep the tower and spire in repair which indicates that they had been completed before his death.

Thomas Stowe (1387-1405) DCL, as a result of the exchange of the prebend of Highworth with Richard Medford, claimed the prebend of Bere & Cherminster in early 1386 but the Dean's locum tenens refused to install him and Nicholas Doberham was installed. In 1387 he received the prebend of Highworth by royal grant and died whilst holding the prebend before 19 November 1405.

Richard Felde (1392) received a royal grant of the prebend of Chardstock in 1389, which was probably ineffective since John Cheyne had incorrectly been reported dead. He was granted the prebend of Highworth in 1392, although Thomas Stowe was in occupation but was appointed to the prebend of Lyme & Halstock a month later, resigning it in 1400.

John Medford (1405) was Rector of Huish in 1401 and held the prebends of Coombe & Harnham in 1404, Highworth in 1405 and Yetminster Prima from 1405 to 1407. He died in 1407

John Catryk (1405-?) Lic.CnL, was nominated to the prebend in 1405 but John Medford was already in possession.

Ralph Lovell (1405-1413) held the prebends of Yetminster Prima from 1402 to 1405 and Highworth from 1405 to 1413.

John Ixworth (1406) DCL, was nominated to the prebend of Highworth in 1406 but apparently failed to gain possession.. He was Archdeacon of Worcester in 1412, held stalls at St Paul's and Chichester and held the prebend of Beminster Prima from 1420 until his resignation in 1431.

Gilbert Hallum (1413-1416) held the prebends of Netherbury in Terra from 1410 to 1413, Highworth from 1413 to 1416 and Netherbury in Ecclesia from 1416 to 1449. He died in 1449.

John Fyton (1416-1422) MA, BTh, was also Archdeacon of Stafford and held the prebends of Ruscomb from 1410 to 1412, Granthan Borealis from 1412 to 1416 and Highworth from 1416 to 1422. He exchanged the last with John Stafford for the dignity of Chancellor of Sarum, which he held from 1422 to 1432, dying in 1432.

John Stafford (1422-1424) DCL, was Archdeacon of Sarum from 1419 to 1420 and Chancellor of Sarum from 1420 to 1422. He exchanged the dignity of Chancellor for the prebend of Highworth, becoming Bishop of Bath & Wells in 1424 and Archbishop of Canterbury in 1443. He died 25 May 1452.

William Hayton (1425-1435) held the prebends of Wilsford & Woodford from 1419 to 1425 and Highworth from 1425 to 1435. He died in 1435.

William Ingram (1435-1464) was a Canon Residentiary and Comunar in 1456. He held the prebends of Torleton from 1427 to 1435 and Highworth from 1435 to 1464. He died in 1464.

Thomas Kirkeby (1464-1476) held the prebends of Yatesbury from 1445 to 1446, Warminster from 1446 to 1448, Netheravon from 1448 to 1449, Ramsbury from 1449 to 1464 and Highworth from 1464 to 1476. He also held the prebend of Stanton Berners of Wilton Abbey and died in 1476.

John Segden (1476-?) DTh, was Master of Balliol College, Oxford and Archdeacon of Gloucester. He held the prebends of Netheravon from 1470 to 1476 and Highworth from 1476 to ?. He also held a stall at Worcester and died in 1482.

Stephen Bereworth (?-1507) DMus, was Archdeacon of Berks from 1493 and resigned both the prebend of Highworth and the dignity in 1507. He again held the prebend and the Archdeaconry of Berks from 1509 until resigning in 1510.

Christopher Twyneho (1507-1509) held the prebends of Axford from 1504 to 1505 and Chardstock from 1505 to 1507 and the Archdeaconry of Berks together with the prebend of Highworth from 1507 to 1509. He appears also to have held a stall at Hereford from 1480 to 1509. He had died by 20 December 1509.

Stephen Bereworth (1509-1510) see above.

James Deynton (1510-1533) DCn&CL, was a Chaplain to King Henry VIII. He held prebends at York, Lincoln and Windsor and became Dean of Lichfield in 1521, holding it with the Archdeaconry of Cleveland.

Guy Jenetto (1533-?) received the prebend in 1533 and although William Austin was installed in 1561, he held the prebend in 1562. John Bente was installed in 1572 but Guy Jenetto was still in occupation in 1577.

William Austin (1561) was installed in 1561 but Guy Jenetto continued to hold the prebend.

John Bente (1572) was installed in 1572 but Guy Jenetto continued to hold the prebend.

Hugh Munsfield (1582-1604) MA, died early in 1604.

Peter Lilly (1604-1615) MA, BD, received the prebend of Hurstbourne & Burbage in 1594 and held it for less than a year. He held a stall at St Paul's in 1599, was Archdeacon of Taunton and occupied the prebend of Highworth from 1604 until his death in 1615.

Henry Cotton (1615-1622/3) MA, was a son of Henry Cotton, Bishop of Sarum 1598-1615. He was appointed Precentor of Sarum in 1614 but Francis Souch was presented by the King and instituted by the Archbishop in 1620. He held the prebends of Fordington & Writhlington from 1608 to 1612, Bitton from 1612 to 1615 and Highworth from 1615 to his death whilst still Precentor in 1622/3.

Thomas Fuller (1623-1632) died in 1632.

Robert Tounson (1632-1633) MA, was the eldest son of Robert Tounson, Bishop of Sarum 1620-1621. He died in 1633.

John Tounson (1633-1687) was a son of Robert Tounson, Bishop of Sarum 1620-1621, and was Vicar of Bremhill. He died on 24 July 1687 having held the prebend for over fifty three years and is commemorated at Bremhill.

Edmund Scarborough (1687-1705) died in 1705 and was buried at Upwey.

Joseph Kelsey (1705-1710) BD, held the prebends of Netherbury in Terra from 1674 to 1695, Grantham Australis from 1695 to 1705 and Highworth from 1705 to 1710. He was Rector of Newton Tony from 1669 to 1710 and of Fugglestone from 1681. He was Warden of St John's Hospital, Heytesbury in 1686 and was a Canon Residentiary and Archdeacon of Sarum from 1695 until his death on 1 November 1710. He was buried in the cathedral.

George Stevens (1710-1733) MA, held the prebends of Stratton from 1708 to 1710 and Highworth from 1710 to 1733. He died in 1733.

Thomas Eyre (1733-1753) MA, was Rector of Fovant where he died in 1753 and was buried.

Robert Gilbert (1753-1776) MA, was Chancellor of Llandaff in 1744, and Rector of Compton Basset and West Kington in 1750. He held the prebends of Alton Australis from 1749 to 1753 and Highworth from 1753 to 1776. He died on 30 November 1776 and is commemorated in the cathedral.

James Benson (1777-1785) DCL, died on 19 September 1785.

Francis Rowden (1785-1822) BD, died on 29 December 1823.

Richard Francis Onslow (1823-1849) MA, was Archdeacon of Worcester in 1815. He held the prebends of Beminster Prima from 1803 to 1823 and Highworth from 1823 to 1849. He died on 18 October 1849.

Sir William Palmer Bt (1849-1858) resigned the prebend on succeeding to the baronetcy in 1858.

William Renand (1858-1903) MA, was Curate-in-Charge of St Thomas, Sarum from 1844 to 1863 and Rector from 1863 to 1874. In 1874 he was offered the living of Poulshot but instead went to Winchester Diocese until returning to Sarum in 1899. He died on 15 April 1903 and was buried in the cloister garth..

Francis Briggs Sowter (1903-1927) MA, was Rector of Corscombe from 1878 to 1884, Vicar of Holy Trinity Weymouth from 1884 to 1890 and of Fleet from 1886 to 1890. He was Rector of Holy Trinity, Dorchester and Rural Dean of Dorchester from 1895 to 1898. He was Archdeacon of Dorset from 1889 to 1902, held the prebend of Highworth from 1903 to 1927 and was a Canon Residentiary from 1910 until resigning in 1916. He died on 10 September 1928 and bequeathed his valuable library to Church House.

Arthur Leonard Helps (1927-1960) MA, was a Chaplain to the Forces in South Africa from 1900 to 1902, Vicar of Puddletown with Athelhampton & Burleston from 1906 and was a Chaplain to the Forces from 1914 to 1918, being mentioned in despatches He was Rural Dean of Bere Regis from 1912 to 1956.

Frank Ernest Pratt (1960-1968?) AKC, was Rector of Wyke Regis from 1943 to 1967 and Rural Dean of Weymouth from 1964 to 1967. He was Rector of St Martin's, Sarum from 1967 to ?.

Ralph Edward Hughes Dudley (1970-1981) was Perpetual Curate of Edington with Imber from 1954 to 1968 and Vicar from 1968 to 1981. He was Curate-in-Charge of East Coulston from 1966 to 1967 and Rector from 1967 until his retirement in 1981. He died in 1990.

Wilfred Samuel Down (1983-1991) MA, was Rector of Monkton Farleigh with South Wraxall from 1969 to 1976 and was Team Rector of Marlborough from 1976 until his retirement in 1991.

[**Charles Christopher Gordon Ross** (1995-) FIMgt, Lieutenant Colonel and Lay Canon. He served in the 14th/20th King's Hussars from 1951 to 1979, and was Diocesan Secretary, Secretary to the Diocesan Synod, and Secretary and Treasurer of the Diocesan Board of Finance from 1979 to 1996, whilst also holding parochial appointments. He occupies Highworth as a courtesy stall.]

MAJOR PARS ALTARIS

Prebend:- A portion of the gifts at the high altar were included in a grant by Osmund, Bishop of Sarum 1078-1099, to the cathedral. From this, Jocelin de Bohun, Bishop of Sarum 1142-1184, created two prebends the greater being Major Pars Altaris and the lesser Minor Pars Altaris. The former was originally joined to the bishopric but as the income was variable and not very large, it was relinquished on 11 April 1219 in exchange for the prebend of Horton.

Canopy statuette and shield:- **John Blyth** DCL, was Archdeacon of Stow in 1477 and of Huntingdon in 1478. He held stalls at Lincoln in 1481 and at York in 1484, was Archdeacon of Richmond in 1488 and Master of the Rolls in 1492. His brother, Geoffrey Blyth, was Bishop of Lichfield in 1503 and his uncle, Thomas Rotherham, was Archbishop of York in 1480. He was Bishop of Sarum from 1493 until his death in August 1499. He was buried behind the high altar, beneath the confessional chair and was commonly called the thwart-over bishop from his body lying north and south, perhaps to allow his body to be under the chair. (Fig. 48.)

Blazon:- Ermine three bucks trippant gules. (On an ermine shield, three red walking bucks.]

Psalter:- The portion of the psalter allotted to the prebend is Psalms 1, 2, 3, 4 and 5

Holders of the prebend:-

Jocelin de Bohun (1142-1184) was a brother of Richard de Bohun who was Dean of Bayeux by 1144 and Bishop of Coutances 1150/51-1179, and was the father of Reginald Fitz Jocelin who was Archdeacon (of Wilts) 1161-1191? and Bishop of Bath 1174-1191. He had been an Archdeacon in Winchester diocese by 1139 and was Bishop of Sarum from 1142 to 1184. During his episcopacy, he was suspended by Archbishop Becket in 1166, absolved by the Pope in 1168, excommunicated by Archbishop Becket in 1169 and absolved early in the following year. He resigned to become a monk at Forde Abbey, Dorset, in 1184 and died on 18 November 1184.

Hubert Walter (1189-1193) was a Royal Justice and Dean of York. He was Bishop of Sarum from 1189 to 1193, although absent from England with King Richard I on the Third Crusade from early 1190 to early 1193. He was enthroned as Archbishop of Canterbury in 1193 and died on 13 July 1205.

Herbert Poore (1194-1217) was probably the son of Richard of Ilchester, Bishop of Winchester 1174-1188. He was Archdeacon of Canterbury and held stalls at Lincoln and Wells. He was ordained priest on 4 June, consecrated bishop on 5 June and enthroned Bishop of Sarum on 12 June 1194. He went to Scotland when debarred from exercising his ministry between 1209 and 1213, and died in 1217, probably on 7 January.

Richard Poore (1217-1219) was a brother of Herbert Poore, Bishop of Sarum 1194-1217. He was Dean of Sarum, holding the prebend of Bere & Cherminster from 1197 to 1215 and played a large part in the founding of the present cathedral. He became Bishop of Chichester in 1215 and Bishop of Sarum from 1217 to 1228, holding the prebend of Major Pars Altaris from 1217 to 1219 when it was exchanged for the prebend of Horton. He became Bishop of Durham in 1228.

Reginald Sinibaldi (c.1226/7) held the prebend in 1226/7.

William of Chardstock (c.1284-c.1295) was the Penitentiary by 1276 and a canon by 1277/8. He was a canon, presumably with another, unidentified, prebend in 1302.

Peter de Sancto Mauro (c.1295-c.1296) was Archdeacon of Surrey both in 1258 and from 1264 until his death in 1296. He appears to have died on 23 June 1296.

Ralph de Stanford (c.1297-1309) held a stall at London and was a royal clerk and a chaplain to King Edward I. He died holding the prebend before 5 March 1309.

Nicholas Tyngewicke (1309-1312) MA, held the prebend of Major Pars Altaris from 1309 to 1312 and in 1312 was appointed to the prebend of Bedwin. He was in possession of Bedwin in 1320 despite the appointment of both Rigaud and Bertrand de Asserio.

Iswin de Gandavo (1312-1314) was Rector of Beechingstoke in 1304 and of Preshute in 1312. He held the prebends of Major Pars Altaris from 1312 to 1314 and Coombe & Harnham from 1314 to ?. He was Precentor of Sarum in 1323, holding the dignity with the church of Westbury annexed to it, and was Archdeacon of Wilts from 12 March 1326 until resigning fifteen days later.

John de la Grave (1314-1321) exchanged the prebend in 1321 with Robert de Ayleston for the church of Buckland, Berkshire.

Robert de Ayleston (1321-1322) held the prebend of Major Pars Altaris from 1321 to 1322, exchanging it in 1322 with John de Winchelsea for the prebend of Bitton. He was Archdeacon of Wilts from 1326 to 1331 and of Berks from 1331 to c.1333 and was in the same year Archdeacon of Bath. He was Rector of Wootton Basset in 1322 and held a stall at Lincoln in 1331.

John de Winchelsea (1322-1326) MA, was a distinguished theologian who exchanged the prebend of Bitton in 1322 with Robert de Ayleston for the prebend of Major Pars Altaris which he held from 1322 to 1326. He then became a Franciscan friar at Sarum.

William de Lobenham (1329-1330) was Subdean of Sarum and held the prebend of Major Pars Altaris from 1329 to 1330, exchanging both office and prebend with his successor for the rectory of Norton, near Twycross in Lincolnshire.

Ralph de Querendon (1330-1358) was Subdean of Sarum and a Canon Residentiary from 1330 to ? and held the prebend of Major Pars Altaris from 1330 to 1358. He was Archdeacon of Wilts from 1331 to c.1333 and died in 1358.

William de Ayston (1332) claimed the prebend of Major Pars Altaris in 1332 but it was held by Ralph de Querendon. He claimed the office of Subdean in 1333 but the Chapter considered that he had intruded into it, contrary to statutes.

John de Offord (1359-1375) was, it is presumed, the same who held a stall at St Paul's in 1331, was Archdeacon of Ely in 1335, Dean of York in 1343 and Keeper of the Great Seal in 1345. He was nominated by Pope Clement VI to the Archbishopric of Canterbury but died in 1375, before his consecration.

Thomas of Sudbury (1375-1396) died in 1396.

Walter Medford (1396-1397) BCL, was Archdeacon of Dorset in 1397, Chancellor of Sarum from 1402 to 1404 and a brother of Richard Medford, Bishop of Sarum 1396 to 1407. In 1404 he exchanged the dignity with Henry Chichele for the Archdeaconry of Sarum and the prebend of Fordington & Writhlington, exchanging the dignity a few days later for the Archdeaconry of Berks. He probably exchanged this Archdeaconry with Peter Alcobasso for the deanery of Wimborne in 1417. He held the prebends of Major Pars Altaris from 1396 to 1397, Yetminster Prima in 1397, Faringdon from 1397 to 1400, having been excommunicated but later absolved, when he exchanged the last for the Treasurership of St Paul's. He held the prebend of Netherbury in Ecclesia in 1401, followed by Preston, which he exchanged with Richard Derham for Netherbury in Ecclesia in 1402. He held the prebends of Fordington & Writhlington from 1404 to 1407 and Bedwin from 1407 until his death in 1423.

John Lincoln (1397-1404) received a royal grant of the prebend of Ramsbury in 1392 but this was probably ineffective. He held the prebends of Major Pars Altaris from 1397 to 1404 and Bedminster & Redcliffe from 1404 to 1415. He was a Canon Residentiary and held stalls at Lincoln and Wells. He died in 1415.

George Westby (1404) held the prebend of Netherbury in Terra from 1403 to 1404 becoming Treasurer of Sarum in 1404. A day later he exchanged the dignity for the prebend of Fordington & Writhlington and within the same year exchanged this for Bedminster & Redcliffe which he in turn exchanged for Major Pars Altaris, which he then exchanged for Axford, resigning the last in the autumn of the same year.

John Tydeling (1404-1406) BCL, was a Canon Residentiary and held the prebend of Axford from 1401 until exchanging it with George Westby for the prebend of Major Pars Altaris in 1404; this he held until 1406. He then held the prebends of Warminster from 1406 to 1418, Yetminster Secunda in 1418, Beminster Prima from 1418 to 1420 and Stratton from 1420 to 1437, exchanging the last with John Symondsburgh for the prebend of Yatesbury in 1437. This he exchanged with John Morton for the prebend of North Leverton in Southwell collegiate church, Nottinghamshire.

Philip Newton (1405-?) was nominated to the prebend in 1405 but it was held by John Tydeling until he exchanged it in 1406.

Robert Ragenhull (1406-1407) was a Canon Residentiary and Archdeacon of Dorset from 1388 to c.1390. He held the prebend of Bishopstone in 1393, exchanging it with Richard Holme for the prebend of Warminster which he exchanged with John Tydeling in 1406 for the prebend of Major Pars Altaris, holding the last until 1407. He was Provost of St Edmund's College, Sarum in 1395 and died in 1407.

John Parker (1407-1408) resigned the prebend in 1408.

William Rede (1408-1411) died in 1411.

Thomas Ayleward (1411-1413) died in 1413.

Thomas Teynton (1413) held the prebend for a month before exchanging it with John Haket for a stall at Exeter.

John Haket (1413-1423) DCL, was appointed to the prebend of Chardstock in 1406 but a royal grant was made to John Bathe. He held the prebends of Major Pars Altaris from 1413 to 1423 and Yetminster Secunda from 1423 to 1442 and died in 1442.

Oliver Dyneley (1423-1431) held the prebends of Yatesbury from 1416 to 1423 and Major Pars Altaris from 1423 to 1431. He was a Canon Residentiary, Rector of Fittleton and died in 1431.

Robert Beaumont (1431) BCn&CL, held the prebends of Major Pars Altaris in 1431, Beminster Secunda from 1431 to 1432 and Teynton Regis from 1432 until his death in 1459.

Nicholas Upton (1431-?) BCn&CL, was co-author of *Survey of churches, lands and tenements belonging to the church of Sarum* and was an author of treatises on war and heraldry. He received the prebend of Major Pars Altaris in 1431 and still held it in 1435. He was Rector of Stapleford from 1434 to 1442, Master of St Nicholas Hospital, Sarum in 1442 and Precentor of Sarum from 1446 to 1457. He died in 1457.

William Estcourt (?-1438) Sch.Th, is said to have held the prebend of Major Pars Altaris in 1438 and held the prebend of Ramsbury from 1438 to 1447. He died in 1447.

Robert Hall (?-1464) DCnL, held the prebends of Major Pars Altaris from ? to 1464 and Ramsbury from 1464 to 1481.

Richard Hayward (1464-1472) DCL, held the prebends of Major Pars Altaris from 1464 to 1472, Axford from 1472 to 1477 and Lyme & Halstock from 1477 to 1493. He died in 1493.

William Sheriff (1472-?) MA, held the prebends of Major Pars Altaris from 1472 to ? and Chardstock in 1481.

William Bolton (?-1489) BCL, died in 1489.

John de Gigliis (1489-1490) DCn&CL, held the prebends of Major Pars Altaris from 1489 to 1490 and Fordington & Writhlington from 1490 to 1497. He was an active politician in the time of King Henry VII, he held a stall at St Paul's and was Archdeacon of London in 1482. He was consecrated to the see of Worcester in 1497.

Richard Newport (1490-1492) BCL, held the prebends of Major Pars Altaris from 1490 to 1492, Wilsford & Woodford in 1492 and Faringdon from 1492 to 1514. He was Rector of Mildenhall and Vicar General to Edmund Audley, Bishop of Sarum, 1502-1524. He died in 1514 and desired to be buried in the cathedral.

William Cosyn (1492-?).

Edward Fox (?-1535) DTh, was Master of Sherborne Hospital and held a stall at York in 1527. He was Almoner to King Henry VIII who sent him to Rome as his 'Orator' with Stephen Gardiner in dealings over the validity of the King's marriage with Catherine of Aragon. In 1528 he became Provost of King's College, Cambridge and held the prebend of Major Pars Altaris from ? to 1535. He was Archdeacon of Leicester in 1533 and Archdeacon of Dorset from 1533 to 1535 when he became Bishop of Hereford. He died in 1548.

William Turner (1535-1545/6) died in 1545/6.

Richard Chaundeler (1546-1558) was Rector of Cheverell Magna and held the prebends of Major Pars Altaris from 1546 to 1558 and Grimston from 1558 to 1582/3. From 1554 to 1582/3 he was Archdeacon of Sarum and from 1557 to 1582/3 a Canon Residentiary. He died in 1582/3 and was buried in the cathedral.

Thomas Bird (1558-?).

Robert Moody (1560-1613) was Rector of Fovant where he died in 1613 and was buried.

Robert Bower (1613-1664) BA, was Rector of Wylye and of Wishford Magna from 1637and died on 13 June 1664.

Richard Kent (1664-1679) MA, held the prebends of Major Pars Altaris from 1664 to 1679 and Chisenbury & Chute from 1679 to 1692. He was Subdean of Sarum from 1668 to 1692 and died in 1692.

Timothy Morton (1679-1687) MA, held the prebends of Yatesbury in 1679 and Major Pars Altaris from 1679 until resigning in 1687. He was Vicar of St Martin's, Sarum.

Nathaniel Spinks (1687-1690) MA, was Rector of St Martin's, Sarum but was suspended in 1689 and deprived in 1690 for failing to swear the oath of allegiance to King William & Queen Mary.

Thomas Smith (1691-1694) MA, held the prebend of Major Pars Altaris from 1691 to 1694, was Subdean of Sarum from 1692 to 1694 and was Rector of St Edmund's, Sarum.

Peter Terry (1694-1727) MA, held the prebend of Major Pars Altaris from 1694 to 1727, was Rector of St Martin's, Sarum and was Succentor of Sarum from 1703 to 1727. He died on 7 June 1727 and is commemorated at St Martin's, Sarum.

John Nourse (1727-1754) MA, was Vicar of Damerham. He died in 1754.

George Watts (1754-1757) MA, held the prebends of Major Pars Altaris from 1754 to 1757 and Durnford from 1757 to 1766. He resigned the latter in 1766.

William Bowles (1757-1788) MA, was a Canon Residentiary from 1773 to 1788. He was Rector of Milston from 1757 until resigning in 1761 after inheriting Milston and Brigmerston manor. He was Vicar of Stratford-sub-Castle and died on 22 November 1788.

John Dobson (1788-1805) MA, was Vicar of Market Lavington and of Longbridge Deverill from 1750 to 1805 and died in 1805.

William Lisle Bowles (1805-1850) MA, poet and antiquary, held the prebends of Stratford from 1804 to 1805 and Major Pars Altaris from 1805 to 1850. He was Rector of Chicklade from 1795 to 1797, Vicar of Bremhill and was a Canon Residentiary from 1828 to 1850. He died on 7 April 1850 and was buried in the south choir aisle of the cathedral.

Edward Wyndham Tufnell (1850-1858) was Rector of Beechingstoke from 1846 to 1857 and of St Peter's Marlborough from 1857 to 1858. He held the prebends of Major Pars Altaris from 1850 to 1858 and Bedminster & Redcliffe from 1858 to 1859. He was Bishop of Brisbane from 1859 to 1873.

Moss King (1858-1864) was Rector of Long Crichel and died in 1864.

Henry Parry Liddon (1864-1870) MA, DD, DCL, LLD, was Vice Principal of Cuddesdon Theological College from 1854 to 1859 and Vice Principal of St Edmund's Hall, Oxford from 1859 to 1864. He was Chancellor of St Paul's in 1886, becoming a Canon Residentiary and Ireland Professor of Exegesis at Oxford from 1870 to 1890. He was a Bampton Lecturer in 1866 and was instrumental in the founding of Keble College, Oxford in 1870. He died on 9 September 1890 and is commemorated in the south choir aisle of the cathedral.

Sir James Erasmus Philipps Bt (1870-1912) was Vicar of Warminster from 1859 to 1897, during which time he founded St Boniface College and St Denys' Home. He was a Proctor in Convocation from 1874 to 1885 and Rural Dean of Warminster from 1895 to 1899. He died on 21 February 1912.

Gordon Bolles Wickham (1912-1920) MA, was Vicar of Bradford Abbas with Clifton Maybank from 1886 to 1920? and Rural Dean of Sherborne from 1906 to 1920. He died on 19 December 1921 and was buried at Bradford Abbas.

Michael Ward Kinloch (1921-1942) OBE, MA, was Rector of West Stafford with Frome Billett from 1896 to 1902 and Chaplain to the Duke of Westminster from 1904 to 1911. He was Rector of Holy Trinity, Dorchester, from 1911 to 1916 and a Chaplain to the Forces from 1914 to 1919 (mentioned in despatches). He was Rector of St Edmund's, Sarum from 1919 to 1923 and Rector of Moreton from 1930 to ?. He died in 1942.

Alexander Ross Wallace (1943-1950) MA, was Headmaster of Sherborne School from 1934 to 1950 and was Dean of Exeter from 1950 to 1960. He died on 26 August 1982.

Basil Aston (1950-1957) DSO, MA, was a Chaplain to the Forces from 1915 to 1919 (twice mentioned in despatches). He was Vicar of Melksham from 1919 to 1933 and Rector of Great Chalfield from 1926 to 1933. He died in 1957.

Pendennis John Hayes (1958-1971) was Perpetual Curate of Derry Hill from 1931 to 1938, Vicar of St Thomas', Sarum, from 1938 to 1963 and Rural Dean of Wilton from 1948 to 1954.

Robert George Chaffey Moore (1972-) was Rector of Compton Abbas from 1949 to 1973, Rural Dean of Shaftesbury from 1958 to 1963 and 1968 to 1973 and Team Vicar of Shaston from 1973 to 1977.

CALNE

Prebend:- Calne in Wiltshire was one of the pre-Conquest episcopal estates of Sherborne. The church of Calne was given to the canons of the cathedral by Osmund, Bishop of Sarum 1078-1099 and the prebend was probably in existence by c.1150. Between 1220 and 1227 this prebend was permanently joined to the dignity of Treasurer of Sarum. At an early period an attempt was made to over-ride this decision but it was successfully resisted.

Canopy statuette:- **Henry Deane** was a member of the order of Augustinian canons, Prior of Llanthony, near Gloucester and in 1499 Chancellor of Ireland. For his services to King Henry VII, especially with regard to the rebellion by Perkin Warbeck, he was made Bishop of Bangor while also holding the Priory. In 1500 he became Bishop of Sarum, being advanced to the see of Canterbury in May 1501 and appointed Papal Legat. He died of the plague at Lambeth on 15 February 1503 and was buried at Canterbury.

Shield:- **Edmund Rich** (of Abingdon) was Treasurer of Sarum from c.1222 to 1234, being the first to hold the prebend of Calne joined to the dignity. He became Archbishop of Canterbury in 1234, died on 16 November 1240 and in 1246 he was canonised by Pope Innocent IV as St Edmund of Canterbury. In the same year the central of the three chapels on the east side of the north-west transept of the cathedral was founded as a chantry chapel in his memory. (Fig. 49.)

Blazon (attributed):- Azure three suns in splendour or each charged with an annulet gules. [On a blue shield, three gold suns with rays, each sun having a red ring on it.] (These are the arms of St Edmund's Hall, Oxford).

Psalter:- The portion of the psalter allotted to the prebend is Psalm 18.

Holders of the prebend:-

Nigel of Calne (c.1107/16) may have been the son of Nigel Medicus and brother of Archdeacon Everard of Calne.

Richard of Calne (c.1151/64) may have held this prebend.

Richard Grosseteste (c.1221) was Archdeacon of Wilts from c.1199 to c.1222/23.

The Treasurer of Sarum for the time being (c. 1220-)

Gwendoline Margaret Hitchings (1987-1993) Lay Canon, was President of the Diocesan Mothers' Union from 1976 to 1982 and a member of the General Synod from 1983 to 1990. She has held parochial, deanery and diocesan positions and became Lay Chairman of Chalke Deanery in 1993. She was appointed to the Close Chapter from 1987 to 1993 and occupied Calne as a courtesy stall.]

[**Martin Marriott** (1993-) MA, Lay Canon. He was an Education Officer in the Royal Air Force from 1956 to 1959; an assistant master at Heversham Grammar School, Cumbria from 1959 to 1966, HouseMaster, Second Master and Acting Master of Haileybury College from 1966 to 1976 and Headmaster of Canford School from 1976 to 1992. He was Chairman of the Headmasters' Conference in 1989, was appointed to the Close Chapter in 1993 and occupies Calne as a courtesy stall.]

WINTERBOURNE EARLS
(olim Rotesfen)

Prebend:- One hide of land at Rotesfen, otherwise Ratfyn, near Amesbury in Wiltshire was given to the cathedral by Hervey of Wilton and confirmed by King Henry I. The prebend was probably in existence by c.1150.

The prebend of Winterbourne Earls was established by Act of Parliament in 1545, as a result of the exchange between the Earl of Hertford and John Salcot, Bishop of Sarum 1539-5557, of the land at Rotesfen and part of the estate of Winterbourne Comitis, or Earls, Wiltshire.

Canopy statuette and shield:- **Edmund Audley** DTh, was a member of the family of Tuchet, Barons Audley and Earls of Castlehaven who owned a house, now Church House in Crane Street, in 1640. He held a stall at Hereford in 1464, before he was of age for ordination, and then held stalls at Lincoln and Windsor in 1472, Lichfield in 1474, Wells in 1475, London in 1476 and York in 1478. From 1473 to 1475 he held the prebend of Preston, in 1475 he was Archdeacon of the East Riding and while holding that dignity was appointed to the rectory of Berwick St John. In 1479 he was Archdeacon of Essex and in 1480 became Bishop of Rochester, only then giving up the remainder of his prebends. He became Bishop of Hereford in 1492 and was translated to be Bishop of Sarum in 1502. He died at Ramsbury on 23 August 1524 and was buried in his chantry chapel in the cathedral. (Fig. 50.)

Blazon:- Gules a fret or. [On a red shield, a gold hollow diamond interlaced with two gold strips.]

Psalter:- The portion of the psalter allotted to the prebend is Psalms 103 and 104.

Holders of the prebend of Rotesfen:-

Thomas of Ebbesbourne (c.1226/7) held the prebends of Rotesfen in c.1226/7 and Grantham Australis from 1226/7 to c.1246 and was Subdean of Sarum from c.1237 to c.1240. He died or had resigned by 6 November 1246.

Richard de Clifford (c.1284-c.1294) held a stall at York from c.1270 to c.1295 and was Precentor of Chichester in 1271.

Stephen of Ramsbury (?-1305) was a beneficiary and executor of the will of Nicholas Longespee, Bishop of Sarum 1292-1297. He was Warden of de Vaux College, Sarum from 1296/7 to 1303 and resigned his prebend in 1305.

William de Foderingeye (1305-1311) died in 1311.

William Coleshulle (1311-1316) MA, held the prebend of Rotesfen from 1311 to 1316, although receiving the prebend of Netherbury in Terra for a four month period in 1313. He was Rector of St Peter's, Sarum in 1298 and died in 1335.

William de Mepham (1313) was appointed to the prebend of Rotesfen in 1313 but this was subsequently revoked as William de Coleshull was already holding it. He held the prebends of Minor Pars Altaris from 1313 to 1316, Beminster Secunda from 1314 to 1316 and Slape in 1316.

Henry de Harkeley (1316-1317) DTh, died in 1317.

Paul de Testa (1317-1327).

Thomas de Astley (1327-1349) was Chaplain to King Edward III and held stalls at Lichfield, Exeter and St Paul's, He was Archdeacon of Middlesex and Treasurer of St Paul's and died in 1349.

Thomas de Luco (1349) was installed in the prebend of Netherbury in Ecclesia in 1329. Despite a royal grant to Andrew Offord in 1345, he continued in the prebend to 1349. In the same year the prebend of Rotesfen was reserved to him but he died before occupying it.

Reginald de Brian (1349) BCL, had expectation of a prebend in 1348 and unlawfully occupied the prebend of Netherbury in Ecclesia the following year despite Elias de Pelegrini being nominated to it. He was then nominated to the prebend of Rotesfen and this was confirmed despite it being reserved to Thomas de Luco who died before occupying it. Later in 1349 he became Bishop of St David's.

John Oliver (1349-?) was installed in the prebend in 1349 on the death of Thomas de Luco but on Reginald de Brian relinquishing the prebend in the same year John de Gatagie was nominated.

John Gatagie (1349-1351) resigned the prebend in 1351.

Gasbert de Cusornio (1351-?).

William de Driffield (?-1357) exchanged the prebend in 1357 with Peter de Gildesburgh for the prebend of Tarvin in Lichfield.

Peter de Gildesburg (1357-1362) received the prebend of Beminster Prima by royal grant in 1351 and held the prebend of Rotesfen from 1357 to 1362, when he exchanged it with Robert Walsham for the prebend of St Martin-le-Grand, London.

Robert Walsham (1362-?) held the prebend of Rotesfen from 1362 to c.1372 and was Precentor of Sarum from ? to 1385. He died in 1385.

John Upton (1387-1397) was a Canon Residentiary and died in 1397.

Henry Chichele (1397) DCL, was appointed Archdeacon of Dorset in 1397 and after two years' litigation at the curia over the claims of Nicholas Bubwith, he was declared technically an intrusor, but was reinstated in 1399, although collation to Bubwith was made a year later. He held the prebends of Rotesfen in 1397, Yetminster Prima from 1397 to 1400, Fordington & Writhlington in 1400, Yetminster Secunda from 1400 to 1402 and Bedminster & Redcliffe from 1402 to 1404, when he exchanged the last with George Westby for the prebend of Fordington & Writhlington. After litigation, he became Archdeacon of Sarum in 1402, exchanging this and the prebend in 1404 for the dignity of Chancellor of Sarum which, following his consecration as Bishop of St David's in 1407, he continued to hold by papal indulgence until 1409. At one time he held the living of Melcombe Bingham and he became Archbishop of Canterbury in 1414. He was the founder of All Souls, Oxford and died on 12 April 1443.

Richard Maudeleyn (1398) seven months after receiving this prebend he exchanged it, together with the prebend of Gillingham in Shaftesbury conventual church, with Thomas Hetersete for the Archdeaconry of Sudbury.

Thomas Hetersete (1398-1406) DCL, died in 1406.

John Frank (1406) held the prebend of Rotesfen in 1406, exchanging it with Reginald Braybroke for Beminster Prima which he held from 1406 to 1415. He then held the prebend of Chisenbury & Chute from 1415 to 1433 and Fordington & Writhlington from 1433 to 1438.

Reginald Braybroke (1406-1407) held the prebends of Beminster Prima from ? to 1406 and Rotesfen from 1406 to 1407 when he exchanged the latter with Roger Attehurn for St Radegund's chapel in St Paul's crypt.

Roger Attehurne (1407) exchanged the prebend, in the same month as receiving it, with John Tyssebury for the portion of Astley in Bromyard church, Hereford but this was apparently ineffective and he exchanged it four months later with Simon Sydenham for the church of Sherston.

John Tyssebury (1407) BCL, received the prebend by an exchange which was apparently ineffective.

Simon Sydenham (1407-1415) DCL, incorrectly accepted nomination to the Archdeaconry of Berks in 1404 but was pardoned and exchanged it for the Archdeaconry of Sarum which he held from 1404 to 1418. He held the rectory of Sutton Veny from 1417 to 1421 and the prebends of Rotesfen from 1407 to 1415 and Yetminster Secunda from 1415 to 1418 and was Dean of Sarum from 1418 to 1431. Although in 1426 he was elected to the see of Sarum, the Chapter on the recommendation of King Henry VI, gave way to a papal provision in favour of Robert Neville. In 1431 he was consecrated as Bishop of Chichester.

Richard Lentwardyn (1415-1425) resigned in 1425.

John Chaundeler (1425-1431) exchanged the prebend in 1431 with Thomas Brouns for the Treasurer's prebend in South Malling collegiate church, Kent.

Thomas Brouns (1431) DCn&CL, seems to have been Archdeacon of Stow in 1418. He was Archdeacon of Berks from 1427 to 1431 and early in 1431 held the prebend of Rotesfen. He was the Dean of Sarum from 1431 to 1435, being present in 1433 at the Council of Basle. He became Bishop of Rochester in 1435 and Bishop of Norwich the following year.

Robert Ampleford (1431-1432) MA, held the prebends of Rotesfen from 1431 to 1432 and Beminster Secunda from 1432 to 1467, exchanging the latter with William Osgodby for the prebend of Bishopstone which he held from 1467 until his death in 1468.

John Cranborne (1432-1435) BCL, held the prebends of Rotesfen from 1432 to 1435, Coombe & Harnham from 1435 to 1452 and Hurstbourne & Burbage from 1452 to 1474. He died in 1474.

Robert Frend (1435) died within three months of receiving the prebend.

Draco Malafortini (1435-1455?) MA, appears to have died in 1455.

John Harnham (1455-1473) BCn&CL, died in 1473.

Richard Martyn (1473-1476) BCnL, held the prebends of Rotesfen from 1473 to 1476 and Fordington & Writhlington from 1476 to 1482. He held a stall at St Paul's in 1471 and would appear to have been Archdeacon of London in 1469 and of Hereford in 1476. He was Archdeacon of Berks from 1478 until 1482 when he was consecrated Bishop of St David's. He resigned when Richard, Duke of Gloucester, later King Richard III claimed the crown.

Robert Thacham (1476-1481) died in 1481.

Henry Sutton (1481-1486) DM, held the prebends of Rotesfen from 1481 to 1486 and Chisenbury & Chute from 1486 until exchanging the latter in 1495 with Geoffrey Blythe for the dignity of Treasurer of Sarum which he held until 1501.

Robert Day (1486-1489) held the prebends of Axford from ? to 1486, Rotesfen from 1486 to 1489 and Grantham Australis from 1489 to 1506. He died in 1506.

Thomas Holes (1489-1498) BCL, held the prebends of Rotesfen from 1489 to 1498 and Bitton from 1498 to 1531. He was Rector of Dinton and died in 1531.

Henry Hawte (1498-1508) died in 1508.

John Estmond (1508-1509) MA, held the prebends of Axford from 1507 to 1508, Rotesfen from 1508 to 1509, Coombe & Harnham from 1509 to 1514 and Minor Pars Altaris from 1517 to 1519 He died in 1519.

Edward Lee (1510-1530) DTh, held the prebend of Rotesfen from 1510 to 1530 and was Chancellor of Sarum from 1530 to 1531. He was Archdeacon of Colchester in 1523 later becoming Almoner to King Henry VIII and being consecrated Archbishop of York in 1531. He is described as a furious papist and opponent of the Reformation. He died in 1544 and was buried in York Cathedral.

Richard Duck (1530-1539) DTh, was Vice-Chancellor of Oxford in 1517, held a prebend at Wells in 1537 and was Archdeacon of Sarum from ? to 1539. He died in 1539.

John Gough (1539-1543/4) DD, was Provost of St Edmund's College, Sarum and had died by 17 January 1544.

Robert Okinge (1544-1554) LLD, was Archdeacon of Sarum from 1546 to 1554 and a Canon Residentiary from 1547 to 1554. He had been Commissary to John Salcot, Bishop of Sarum 1539-1557, when Bishop of Bangor. In the convocation of 1547 he voted against allowing the marriage of clergy but married as soon as this was permissible. He held the prebend of Rotesfen from 1544 to 1545 when an Act of Parliament dissolved the prebend. He was probably deprived of his livings in 1554.

Walter Mugge (1556) was appointed to the prebend in 1556, presumably irregularly.

Holders of the prebend of Winterbourne Earls:-

John Goodman (1552-1561) BCn&CL, was a Canon Residentiary from 1552 to 1561 and was Rector of Winterbourne Gunner. He died in 1561.

Richard Hughes (1561-?) MA.

Thomas Greneway (1563-?) BD, had died by August 1571.

Robert Hooper (?-1571) MA, was a Canon Residentiary from 1569 to 1571. He held the prebend of Chardstock from 1564 until at least 1568, and is thought to have held the prebend of Winterbourne Earls from ? to 1571. He died in 1571 whilst holding a prebend but this may have been Chardstock. He was Rector of Fyfield.

Adam Squire (1571-?) MA, had died by 26 October 1558.

John King (1589) MA.

Thomas Holland (1590-1612) DD, was a Fellow of Balliol College, Oxford in 1573. He was Regius Professor of Divinity in 1589 and Rector of Exeter College, Oxford in 1592. He was one of the translators of the Bible appointed in 1604 by King James II and died on 17 March 1612.

Henry Seward (1612-1640) BD, was a Fellow of Brasenose College, Oxford held the prebend of Winterbourne Earls from 1612 to 1640, was Succentor of Sarum from 1609 to ? and was Vicar of Britford. He was a Canon Residentiary from ? to 1640 and died in 1640.

Bartholomew Shapley (1640-?) MA.

John Gregory (1643-1647) MA, held a stall at Chichester. He was the author of *Episcopus Puerorum* (The Boy Bishop) and died on 13 March 1647.

Hugh Nashe (1660) MA.

John Gurgany (1660-1675) BD, died in 1675.

Edward Pocock (1675-1677) MA, was Rector of Mildenhall from 1692 to 1727 and held the prebends of Winterbourne Earls from 1675 to 1677, Durnford from 1677 to 1693 and Netherbury in Ecclesia from 1693 to 1726. He died on 27 December 1726.

Joshua Sacheverell (1677-1685) MA, was a Fellow of Magdalen College, Oxford, and Rector of St Peter's, Marlborough. He died in 1685 and was buried at Marlborough.

Farwell Perry (1685-1723) MA, died in 1723 and was buried at St Peter's, Marlborough.

Charles Naylor (1723-1729) MA, was Chancellor of the Diocese and resigned the prebend in 1729 apparently on becoming Dean of Winchester.

George Frome (1729-1770) BCL, died in 1770 and was buried at Tollard Royal.

Nathaniel Hume (1770-1777) MA, was Precentor of Sarum from 1774 to 1804. He held the prebends of Winterbourne Earls from 1770 to 1777, Yetminster Prima from 1777 to 1804 and the livings of Bremhill in 1782 and Brixton Deverill in 1799. He died on 28 April 1804.

Phipps Weston (1777-1794) BD, died on 20 April 1794.

Humphrey Sumner (1794-1814) DD, held the prebends of Stratford from 1782 to 1794 and Winterbourne Earls from 1794 to 1814. He was Provost of King's College, Cambridge from 1797 to 1814 and died on 23 March 1814.

John Salter (1814-1833) MA, was Vicar of Stratton St Margaret in 1808 and died on 19 March 1833.

Sir Henry Robert Dukinfield Bt (1833-1856) MA, resigned the prebend in 1856 becoming Vicar of St Martin-in-the-Fields, London.

William Beadon Heathcote (1856-1862) BCL, was a Fellow of New College, Oxford, Precentor of Sarum from 1854 to 1862 and held the prebend of Winterbourne Earls from 1856 to 1862. He was Vicar of Sturminster Marshall in 1858 and died on 21 August 1862.

Alexander Broadley (1862-1894) was Vicar of Bridport from 1838 and also Vicar of Walditch from 1839, to 1844. He was Vicar of Bradpole from 1844 and Rural Dean of Bridport from 1848 to 1870. He died on Advent Sunday 1894.

John Augustus Beazor (1894-1909) was Rector of St George's, Portland from 1872 to 1909. He died on 21 January 1909 and was buried on Portland.

Joseph Pulliblank (1909-1912) MA, was a professor at Queen's College, Liverpool and Chief Inspector of Schools from 1886 to 1895. He was Vicar of Rampisham and Diocesan Inspector of Schools from 1895 to 1912. He died in 1912.

Frederick William Macdonald (1912-1924) MA, was Vicar of Stapleford from 1877 to 1895 and Berwick St James from 1880 to 1895. He was Rector of Wishford Magna from 1895 to 1924 and Rural Dean of Wylye from 1893 to 1920. He died on 24 November 1928 and was buried at Wishford Magna.

Herbert William Allen (1925-1940) BA, ARCO, was Curate-in-Charge of Broadstone, Canford Magna, from 1901 to 1904 and Rector of South Perrott with Mosterton from 1904 to 1917. He was Vicar of St Paul's, Fisherton Anger from 1917 to 1930, Rural Dean of Wilton from 1929 to 1930 and Vicar of Alderbury from 1936 to 1940. He was Succentor of Sarum from 1938 to 1944 and held the prebends of Winterbourne Earls from 1925 to 1940 and Ufcomb from 1940 to 1944. He was Vicar of the Close from 1940 until his death in 1944.

Frank Harold Sangster (1940-1951) MA, held a stall at Wakefield from 1930 to 1933. He was Vicar of Melksham from 1933 to 1946, Rector of Great Chalfield from 1934 to 1943, Rural Dean of Bradford from 1937 to 1939 and Rector of Great Chalfield from 1945 to 1946.

Charles Carew Cox (1951-1964) AKC, MA was Perpetual Curate of West Moors from 1922 to 1927, Vicar of Lyme Regis from 1927 to 1953 and a Proctor in Convocation from 1935 to 1948.

Harold Wilson (1965-1970) MA, DD, was Principal of Sarum Theological College from 1965 to 1971, a Canon Residentiary from 1968 to 1973, Chancellor of Sarum from 1971 to 1972 and Principal of Salisbury & Wells Theological College from 1971 to 1973. He held the prebends of Winterbourne Earls from 1965 to 1970 and Netherbury in Terra in 1972. He was a Canon Residentiary and Chancellor of St Paul's from 1973 to 1975 and died on 2 November 1975.

Rex Albert Wells (1972-1977) MA, was Vicar Choral from 1937 to 1944. He was Vicar of Branksome St Aldhelm from 1944 to 1951, of Iwerne Minster with Sutton Waldren from 1951 to 1975 and of the Iwernes and Sutton Waldren from 1975 to 1977. He became Warden of the College of St Barnabas, Lingfield in 1977.

Kenneth Edward Brown (1977-1987) MA, was Vicar of Southbroom from 1969 to 1983, Team Vicar of Tisbury from 1983 to 1987 and a Proctor in Convocation from 1980 to 1985.

Stanley Michael Royle (1989-) MA, BD, AKC, was Rector of Milton Abbas, Hilton with Cheselbourne and Melcombe Horsey from 1981 to 1986 and Diocesan Adviser on Ministry from 1986 to 1998. He became Diocesan Director of Ordinands in 1986 and in 1998 Senior Chaplain to David Staffurth Stancliffe, Bishop of Sarum 1993- .

CATHEDRAL CHAPLAIN
(formerly Succentoris)

Office:- From 1226/28 a farm at Stratford-sub-Castle in Wiltshire belonged to the Succentory. The office of Succentor fell into disuse in 1968. In 1987, upon the ordination of women to the diaconate, the office of Cathedral Deacon was created. Later, on the admission of women to the priesthood, it was renamed Cathedral Chaplain.

Canopy statuette and shield:- **Laurence Campeggio** was married and had a son who became a cardinal. On the death of his wife he took Holy Orders and was made Bishop of Feltre in 1512, of Bologna in 1523, of Huesca in 1530 and of Parenzo in 1533. He was created Cardinal-Priest of St Thomas in Parione in 1518, of St Anastasia in 1519 and of St Maria trans-Tiberim in 1528. He succeeded to the see of Sarum by papal bull in 1524, being enthroned by proxy, and in 1528 was created Papal Legat for England. He was one of the delegates appointed by the Pope to hear the question of the divorce of Henry VIII from Catherine of Aragon and appears in Shakespeare's play King Henry VIII as 'Cardinal Campeius'. In March 1534 he and the Bishop of Worcester were deprived of their sees by Act of Parliament, for non-residence but Campeggio was considered by Rome to be Bishop of Sarum until his death in August 1539. He became Cardinal-Bishop of St Albano in 1534, of Sabina in 1537 and of Praeneste in 1538. He died at the Roman Court on 15 January 1539. For some time after this, an independent succession was maintained by the Pope for both Sarum and Worcester. (Fig. 51.)

Blazon:- Argent an eagle displayed parti per pale issuant from the sinister side sable impaling argent a wolf salient sable. [A shield divided down the centre. The left silver with, issuing from the dividing line, the left half of a black spread eagle. The right half silver with on it a black wolf springing forward.]

Psalter:-

Holders of the office of Succentor:-

Roger (before 1153) was Succentor of Sarum and held the prebend of Wilsford & Woodford before 1153.

Walter (c.1155/1189) held the office of Succentor of Sarum and the prebend of Axford.

John (c.1193-1197/1215) was Succentor of Sarum between c.1193 and 1197/1215 and held the prebend of Ruscomb c.1197/1215. He gave a cope and ornaments to the cathedral.

Anastasius (c.1209/15-1226/27) held first an unidentified prebend and then the prebend of Stratford from ? to c.1226/27. He was Succentor of Sarum from c.1209/15 to c.1226/27.

Roger (c.1227-c.1245) was Succentor of Sarum from 1227 to 1245 and held the prebend of Durnford c.1245.

Walter de la Wyle (c.1248-c.1262) was Succentor of Sarum from c.1248 to c.1262 and Bishop of Sarum, holding the prebend of Pottern, from 1263 until his death on 3 January 1271. In 1269 he founded the College of St Edmund, in Sarum for a provost and twelve secular canons. He was buried by the altar of the chapel of St Edmund in the cathedral.

John de Middleton (c.1268-c.1290/1) is named in the 1268 foundation charter of the College of St Edmund, Sarum as the Rector of St Thomas, Sarum. He held the prebend of Yatesbury and was Succentor of Sarum c.1268 to c.1291.

Simon de Derham (1319-1323) was Subtreasurer in 1294 and Succentor of Sarum by 1319.

Gilbert de Wythenham (1323-c.1334) held this office with the rectory of Ebbesbourne Wake which was attached to it. He died in or before the year 1334.

Edmund de Granton (1334).

Thomas de Lanynton (1350-?).

Adam Gore (1361-1401) died in 1401.

Robert Peers (1401-?).

Peter Benham (1418-1424) died in 1424.

William Malton (1424-1435) resigned the office in 1435.

William Berwick (1435-?) arbitrated in 1441 between the rival claims of the Chapter and the Provost of St Edmund's College, Sarum to certain tithes in the city.

William Cockes (1467-?) is shown at the head of a list thirty-one Vicars Choral present at the Visitation of the cathedral in 1468.

John Leche (1472-1473) resigned in 1473.

John Tykell (1473-1486) died in 1486.

Robert Pusey (1486-1498) died in 1498.

William Tofte (1498-1502) died in 1502.

William Barton (1502-1509) was Succentor of Sarum from 1502 to 1509. He was consecrated Bishop of Saloniensis c.1509 to assist Edmund Audley, Bishop of Sarum 1502-1524, within the diocese, which he did from 1509 to 1517. He held the prebends of Ruscombe in 1509, Beminster Prima from 1509 to 1515 and of Grimston from 1515 to 1518. He died in 1518.

Francis May (1509-?).

Edmund Lotteshall (?-1532) died in 1532.

Edward Mitchell (1532-?).

William Walker (1554-?) incurred protests against his appointment from two of the Vicars Choral.

Henry Brither (1561-1564) died in 1564.

Nicholas Poole (1564-1566) died in 1566.

John Sheppard (1566-?).

Adam Hill (1584) MA, was a Fellow of Balliol College, Oxford in 1568, held the prebend of Gillingham Minor from 1582 to 1595 and was Succentor of Sarum in 1584. He was a noted and eloquent preacher, becoming the Vicar of Westbury and Rector of Gussage St Michael. He died in 1594 and was buried in the cathedral.

Thomas Crump (1595-1602) was Succentor of Sarum from 1595 until resigning in 1602. He held the prebend of Gillingham Minor from 1595 until resigning the prebend in 1604.

Nicholas Martin (1602-1609) died in 1609.

Henry Seward (1609-?) BD, was a Fellow of Brasenose College, Oxford, held the prebend of Winterbourne Earls from 1612 to 1640, was Succentor of Sarum from 1609 to ? and was Vicar of Britford. He was a Canon Residentiary from ? to 1640 and died in 1640.

William Cartwright (1642-1643) died on 29 November 1643.

Robert Joyner (1643-?) was deprived during the Commonwealth.

John Stephens (1660-1675) died in 1675.

William West (1675-1683) held office at the time when a "preaching turn" was first given to the Succentor, and died in 1683.

Samuel Filer (1683-1703) was Rector of Stockton and died in 1703.

Peter Terry (1703-1727) MA, held the prebend of Major Pars Altaris from 1694 to 1727, was Rector of St Martin's, Sarum and Succentor of Sarum in 1703. He died on 7 June 1727 and is commemorated at St Martin's, Sarum.

John Squire (1727-1759) MA, held the prebend of Yatesbury from 1721 to 1759 and was Succentor of Sarum from 1727 to 1759. He died on 2 July 1759.

Charles Tarrant (1759-1791) MA, was Subdean of Sarum from 1755 to 1759 and Succentor of Sarum, holding the prebend of Yatesbury from 1759 to 1791. He died on 22 February 1791.

John Selwyn (1791-1823) BCL, LLB, was Rector of Ludgershall from 1777 to 1823 and of East Coulston. He was Bailiff of the borough of Ludgerhall in 1791, Succentor of Sarum from 1791 to 1823 and Rector of Coulston from 1798. He died on 28 October 1823, was buried at the spire crossing and is commemorated in the south transept of the cathedral.

George Ingram Fisher (1823-?) was Rector of Winfrith Newburgh, Dorset.

John Daubney (1865-?) MA, was Succentor of Sarum from 1865 to ?, Chancellor of Sarum from 1868 to 1877, Principal of Sarum Theological College from 1868 to 1878, and Precentor of Sarum from 1877 to ?.

Charles Tower (1869-1877) was Rector of Chilmark from 1843 to 1880, Rural Dean of Chalke from 1863 to 1872 and Succentor of Sarum from 1869 to 1877. He held the prebend of Gillingham Major from 1877 to 1890. He died on 12 June 1890 and was buried at Chilmark.

Henry Thomas Armfield (1877-1879) was Vicar Choral in 1863 and Succentor of Sarum from 1877 until resigning the office in 1879.

Storer Marshall Lakin (1879-1909) MA, was a Vicar Choral from 1856 to 1897, Cathedral Librarian from 1875 to 1909, Vicar of the Close from 1879 to 1888 and Succentor of Sarum from 1879 to 1909. He died on 1 April 1909.

Ernest Edward Dugmore (1909-1925) MA, author, was Vicar of Parkstone from 1872 to 1910 and Succentor of Sarum from 1909 to 1925. He held the prebends of Gillingham Major from 1890 to 1917 and Netheravon from 1917 to 1925. He died in 1925.

Henry Robert Whytehead (1925-1931) MA, was Rector of St Peter's & St Paul's, Marlborough from 1887 to 1897, Vicar of Warminster from 1897 to 1915 and Rural Dean of Heytesbury from 1914 to 1919. He held the prebends of Minor Pars Altaris from 1917 to 1925 and Netheravon from 1925 to 1937 and was Succentor of Sarum from 1925 to 1931. He died in 1937.

Arthur Gordon Robertson (1931-1937) MA, was Headmaster of Sarum Choir School from 1900 to 1930, a Vicar Choral from 1900 to 1937 and Succentor of Sarum from 1931 to 1937. He held the prebend of Lyme & Halstock from 1931 until his death in 1940.

Herbert William Allen (1938-1944) BA, ARCO, was Curate in Charge of Broadstone, Canford Magna from 1901 to 1904 and Rector of South Perrott with Mosterton from 1904 to 1917. He was Vicar of St Paul's, Fisherton Anger from 1917 to 1930, Rural Dean of Wilton from 1929 to 1930 and Vicar of Alderbury from 1936 to 1940. He was Succentor of Sarum from 1938 to 1944 and held the prebends of Winterbourne Earls from 1925 to 1940 and Ufcomb from 1940 to 1944. He was Vicar of the Close from 1940 until his death in 1944.

Peter Nourse (1947-?) MA, was a Vicar Choral from 1944 and died in November 1992.

Keith Wedgwood (1955-1968) MA, was Succentor of Derby from 1949 to 1952, Vicar Choral of Sarum from 1952 to 1968 and Succentor of Sarum from 1955 to 1968.

[The office has remained vacant since 1968]

Holders of the office of Cathedral Deacon:-

Christine Marion Farrington (1987-1993) MA, was Director of Pastoral Studies at Lincoln Theological College from 1986 to 1987, Cathedral Deacon and Director of the Sarum Christian Centre from 1987 to 1993, and held a stall at Ely from 1993.

Holders of the office of Cathedral Chaplain:-

Ann Carol Philp (1995-) MA(Ed), MIPD, became Cathedral Chaplain in 1995, was Director of the Sarum Christian Centre from 1993 to 1998, and assumed responsibility for the Congregational Centre in 1998. She is the Bishop's Adviser for Non-stipendiary Ministry.

(Gangway)

Canopy statuette and shield:- **Nicholas Shaxton** DTh, was a benefactor of Gonville Hall, Cambridge. He was Treasurer of Sarum from 1533 to 1535 and about the same time held the rectory of Fugglestone with Bemerton. He was Bishop of Sarum from 1535 until resigning in 1539. He had been silenced and afterwards condemned with Latimer but recanted and preached a sermon proclaiming his apostacy when Ann Askew was burnt. He afterwards acted as a bishop suffragan in Ely diocese. (Fig. 52.)

Blazon:- Or three chaplets in bend gules. [On a gold shield, three red chaplets slanting from top left to bottom right.]

SHERBORNE
(previously the stall of the Archdeacons of Berks and Sherborne)

Until 1977 each Archdeacon had a stall of his dignity in a position of prominence close to one of the four principal persons; these stalls have now been renamed. Particulars of the Archdeacons are given first, followed by the particulars of the prebend the name of which the stall now bears.

Canopy statuette and shield:- **John Salcot** (or Capon) DD, was Abbot of St Benet's Hulme, Norfolk. He was an active supporter of King Henry VIII over the King's divorce from Catherine of Aragon, becoming Abbot of Hyde, near Winchester in 1530 and Bishop of Bangor in 1534, whilst still holding the Abbey. As King's Commissioner under Henry VIII, he sent several people to the stake but he became a Protestant under King Edward VI, changing again under Mary and then sitting as a judge on the trial of Bishop Hooper and John Rogers. He was Bishop of Sarum from 1539 to 1557 and condemned several Protestants to the stake. King Henry VIII described him as "a great clerk and singularly learned in divinity", and he was no doubt a very able but unscrupulous man, both in the constant change in his opinions and his administration of the estates of the see, impoverishing his bishopric but enriching himself. He died on 24 August 1542 and was buried in the south choir of the cathedral behind the bishop's throne. (Fig. 53)

Blazon:- Argent on a chevron between three trefoils sable as many escallops of the first. [On a silver shield, a black chevron with on it three silver scallop shells, between three black trefoils.]

ARCHDEACON OF BERKS

The dignity: The second senior Archdeaconry, comprising the entire county of Berkshire with its deaneries of Abingdon, Newbury, Reading and Wallingford. In 1836, the Archdeaconry was added to the Diocese of Oxford.

The property of the Archdeaconry was originally the churches of Wantage and Hungerford and the chapel of Shalbourne. These were given to the Abbot of Le Bec Hellouin to provide the prebend of Ogborne and in compensation, the church of North Moreton, Berkshire, was given to the Archdeaconry.

Holders of the dignity:-

Roger (c.1150/51-c.1156) held a stall at Lincoln.

Geoffrey de Vernun (c.1173-c.1197/1205)

Alberic (c.1206/7-c.1215)

Geoffrey (c.1204/20-c.1222)

William de Merton (c.1224-c.1236) may have been the father of Walter of Merton, Bishop of Rochester and founder of Merton College, Oxford. He held the prebend of Faringdon from c.1219 to 1237/8, was the Official to Richard Poore, Bishop of Sarum 1217-1228, Archdeacon of Berks from c.1224 to 1237/8 and Dean of Wells in 1237.

Clement (c.1236)

William de Ralegh (c.1236-c.1237) is believed to have been Treasurer of Exeter and to have held a stall at London. He was a royal justice from 1229 until becoming Bishop of Norwich in 1239.

Giles of Bridport (1237-c.1255) was Archdeacon of Berks from 1237 to c.1255 and Dean of Wells in 1253. He appears to have held the office of Master of St Nicholas Hospital, Sarum from 1259 to 1260, was Bishop of Sarum, holding the prebend of Pottern, from 1257 to 1262 and founded de Vaux College, Sarum in 1262. It was during his episcopate that the present cathedral was completed. He died on 13 December 1262 and was buried "in the south side of the choir in the chapel of St Mary Magdalen, under an arch that has a beautiful white marble tomb, wrought as a model of the outside of the tower".

William (c.1262) died as Archdeacon of Berks and Rector of Lewknor, Oxford before 3 November 1262.

Simon of Bridport (c.1262-c.1263) may have been a brother of Giles of Bridport, Bishop of Sarum 1257-1262. He was Archdeacon of Dorset from ? to 1262, Archdeacon of Berks from c.1262 to c.1263 and Treasurer of Sarum from c.1265 to c.1267.

William (c.1265).

Walter Scammel (c.1266-1274) was Archdeacon of Berks from c.1266 to 1274 and Clerk & Collector to King Henry III from 1267 to 1268. He was Treasurer of Sarum and held the prebend of Calne from 1267 to 1271 when, on becoming Dean from 1271 to 1284 he also held the prebend of Heytesbury. He was elected Bishop of Sarum in 1284, died on 20 September 1286 and was buried at the north side of the presbytery in the cathedral. It is believed to have been in 1280 that the prebend of Heytesbury became permanently joined to the deanery.

Stephen of Newbury (c.1275-c.1281).

William de Berges (?-1313) was Archdeacon of Berks from c.1287 to 1313, held the prebend of Grantham Borealis from 1288 to ? and had died by March 1313.

Richard de Bello (1313) held in turn during 1298 the prebends of Beminster Prima and Grantham Australis, and then Coombe & Harnham from 1298 to 1305. He was then given the prebend of Highworth although John de Frescobaldis had already been nominated by the Pope. The Pope tried to restore Frescobaldis to the prebend but the bishop prevented the Dean from oppressing Richard de Bello. Eventually, in 1308, there was a papal dispensation allowing de Bello to retain the prebend, which he did until 1326. He was Archdeacon of Berks in 1313 and in 1315 had charge of the diocese while the see was vacant on the death of Simon de Gandavo, Bishop of Sarum, 1297-1315. He would seem also to have held a stall at Hereford in 1305 and to have been Rector of Poulshot in 1313. He died in 1326.

Tydo de Varesio (1313-1331) was given the dignity of Chancellor of Sarum in 1311, although William de Bosco was in occupation. He held the prebend of Grantham Borealis from 1313 to 1331 and on appointment by the Pope, was Archdeacon of Berks from 1313 to 1331, despite an ineffective royal grant being made to Gilbert de Stapleton in 1317. He died in 1331.

Gilbert de Stapleton (1317) received the dignity of Archdeacon of Berks by royal grant but this was apparently ineffective since Tydo de Varesio was in possession In the same year he was appointed to the prebend of Grantham Borealis but Tydo de Varesio was in occupation.

Robert de Ayleston (1331-?) held the prebend of Major Pars Altaris from 1321 to 1322, exchanging it in 1322 with John de Winchelsea for the prebend of Bitton. He was Archdeacon of Wilts from 1326 to 1331 and of Berks from 1331 to c.1333 and was in the same year Archdeacon of Bath. He was Rector of Wootton Basset in 1322 and held a stall at Lincoln in 1331.

Edmund de la Beche (1334,1359) received the prebend of Ramsbury by royal grant in 1335 but in 1355 there was a papal mandate for his removal and the appointment of John de Stretley. He was Rector of Compton Chamberlain in 1315 and Archdeacon of Berks in 1334 and 1359.

Thomas Paxton (?-1365) DCL, claimed to have been nominated Archdeacon of Berks but probably did not gain possession. He resigned the Archdeaconry in 1365 on receiving nomination to the prebend of Highworth.

John de Harewell (1365-1366) BCL, became Bishop of Bath & Wells in 1366.

William de Agrifolio (1371, 1384) was a nephew of Pope Clement VI and was created Cardinal-Priest of St Stephanus in 1367 at the age of 28 years. He returned with Pope Urban V to Avignon in 1370 and became Dean of Anti-Cardinals. He held the prebend of Highworth from ? to 1371 and was Archdeacon of Taunton. He was Archdeacon of Berks in both 1371 and 1384. He was nominated to the prebend of Bere & Cherminster in 1371 but Henry de Wakefield remained in possession. He held a stall at Lincoln from 1379 to 1384 and died of the plague on 13 January 1401 in the College of St Martial.

Thomas Yokflete (1389-?)

Andrew Bontempi (?-1390) was a canon of Perugia becoming Bishop of Perugia in 1354 and Cardinal-Priest of St Marcellinus & St Peter in 1378. He held the Archdeaconry of Berks from ? to 1390, was Legate to Umbria and the Marches and died on 16 July 1390.

Christopher Marini (1390-1395) became Arch-Priest of the Vatican, holding with this dignity the Abbey of St Boniface and St Alexis in the Aventine. He became Bishop of Isernia, Lower Italy in 1327 and was created Cardinal-Priest of St Cyriacus in 1329. He was nominated to the dignity of Archdeacon of Berks in 1390 but not having gained possession he resigned the dignity to the Pope and exchanged it in 1395 with Walter Cook for the prebend of Warthill in York. He was nominated to the prebend of Faringdon in 1398 but Walter Medford continued to hold it. He died in Rome on 4 December 1404 and was buried in St Peter's.

Walter Cook (1395-1397) received the Archdeaconry of Berks by exchange in 1395, apparently holding it until 1397 when he was nominated to the prebend of Faringdon but Walter Medford was installed. He may have received the prebend of Netherbury in Ecclesia c.1399 by papal grace but he was deposed in the same year.

John Southam (1395-1404) Lic.CL, received a royal grant of the Archdeaconry of Berks in 1395, apparently holding it until 1404 when he exchanged it with Thomas Southam for the Archdeaconry of Oxford. He held the prebend of Grantham Australis from 1416 to 1441 and had died by March 1441.

Ralph Repyngton (1395) had a royal grant of the Archdeaconry of Berks in 1395 but John Southam was holding it in 1404. He also received the prebend of Wilsford & Woodford by royal grant in 1398 but Henry de Winterton did not vacate it until his death in 1400.

John Wynwyk (1395) received a royal grant of the Archdeaconry of Berks in 1395 but John Southam held it until 1404.

Thomas Southam (1404) Lic.CL, held the prebend of Coombe & Harnham from ? to 1404. He exchanged the Archdeaconry of Oxford for the Archdeaconry of Berks with John Southam two months before his death on 15 March 1404.

John Fraunceys (1404) BCnL, claimed the prebend of Bere & Cherminster in 1402 and received a royal licence to accept nomination in 1404. He was Archdeacon of Berks and held the prebend of Coombe & Harnham, both in 1404.

Simon Sydenham (1404) DCL, incorrectly accepted nomination to the Archdeaconry of Berks in 1404 but was pardoned and exchanged it for the Archdeaconry of Sarum which he held from 1404 to 1418. He held the rectory of Sutton Veny from 1417 to 1421 and the prebends of Rotesfen from 1407 to 1415 and Yetminster Secunda from 1415 to 1418 and was Dean of Sarum from 1418 to 1431. Although in 1426 he was elected to the see of Sarum, the Chapter on the recommendation of King Henry VI, gave way to a papal provision in favour of Robert Neville. In 1431 he was consecrated as Bishop of Chichester.

Walter Medford (1404-1417) BCL, was Archdeacon of Dorset in 1397, Chancellor of Sarum from 1402 to 1404 and a brother of Richard Medford, Bishop of Sarum 1396-1407. In 1404 he exchanged the dignity with his successor for the Archdeaconry of Sarum and the prebend of Fordington & Writhlington, exchanging a few days later for the Archdeaconry of Berks. He probably exchanged this Archdeaconry with Peter Alcobasso for the deanery of Wimborne in 1417. He held the prebends of Major Pars Altaris from 1397 to 1397, Yetminster Prima in 1397, Faringdon from 1397 to 1400, having been excommunicated but later absolved, when he exchanged this prebend for the treasurership of St Paul's. He held the prebend of Netherbury in Ecclesia in 1401, followed by Preston, which he exchanged with Richard Derham for Netherbury in Ecclesia in 1402. He held the prebends of Fordington & Writhlington from 1404 to 1407 and Bedwin from 1407 until his death in 1423.

Peter de Alcobasso (1417-1427) received the Archdeaconry of Berks by exchange in 1417 and died in 1427.

Thomas Brouns (1427-1431) DCn&CL, seems to have been Archdeacon of Stow in 1418. He was Archdeacon of Berks from 1427 to 1431 and early in 1431 held the prebend of Rotesfen. He was the Dean of Sarum from 1431 to 1435, being present in 1433 at the Council of Basle. He became Bishop of Rochester in 1435 and Bishop of Norwich the following year.

John Castell (1431-?) DTh, held the prebends of Yetminster Prima from 1428 to 1432, Teynton Regis in 1432 and Bere & Cherminster from 1432 to 1436. He was Archdeacon of Berks from 1431 to 1432?

Alexander Sparrow (1432-1433) BCn&CL, held the prebends of Axford from 1423 to 1426 and Fordington & Writhlington from 1426 to 1433. He was Archdeacon of Sarum from 1426 to 1432 when he became Archdeacon of Berks until 1433. He was Treasurer of St Paul's in 1423 and died in 1433.

John Norton (1433-1462) DCnL, held the prebends of Beminster Secunda from 1429 to 1431 and Horton from 1431 to 1462. He was Archdeacon of Sarum from 1432 to 1433 and Archdeacon of Berks from 1433 until his death in 1462.

Richard Ewen (1462-1464) died in 1464.

Robert Stillington (1464-1465) DCL, held the prebend of Chardstock in 1464 and was Archdeacon of Berks from 1464 to 1465 when he became Bishop of Bath & Wells.

John Russell (1466-1476) DCnL, held the prebends of Yatesbury from 1461 to 1462 and Horton from 1462 to 1476. He was Archdeacon of Berks from 1466 to 1476 and held a stall at St Paul's in 1474. He became Bishop of Rochester in 1476 and of Lincoln in 1480. He was Chancellor of Oxford from 1483 to 1494 and Chancellor of England under Kings Edward V and Richard III. He died in 1494.

John Morton (1476-1478) DCL, held the prebends of Fordington & Writhlington from 1458 to 1476 and Horton from 1476 to 1478. He was a native of Milborne St Andrew and in 1453 was Principal of Peckwater's Inn at Oxford. He was afterwards an advocate at the Court of Arches. He was Archdeacon of Winchester in 1474 and held a stall at Wells in 1475. For short periods between 1475 and 1477 he would also seem to have held the Archdeaconries of Chichester, Huntingdon and Leicester. He was Archdeacon of Berks from 1476 until 1478 when he was consecrated Bishop of Ely. In 1486 he became Archbishop of Canterbury, being created Cardinal-Priest of St Anastasia in 1493. He died on 12 October 1500 at the age of 90 and was buried in Canterbury cathedral.

Richard Martyn (1478-1482) BCnL, held the prebends of Rotesfen from 1473 to 1476 and Fordington & Writhlington from 1476 to 1482. He held a stall at St Paul's in 1471 and would appear to have been Archdeacon of London in 1469 and of Hereford in 1476. He was Archdeacon of Berks from 1478 until 1482 when he was consecrated Bishop of St David's. He resigned when Richard, Duke of Gloucester, later King Richard III claimed the crown.

Oliver King (?-1492) DCn&CL became Bishop of Exeter in 1492.

Stephen Bereworth (1493-1507) DMus, was Archdeacon of Berks from 1493 and resigned both the prebend of Highworth and the dignity in 1507. He again held the prebend and the Archdeaconry of Berks from 1509 until resigning in 1510.

Christopher Twyneho (1507-1509) held the prebends of Axford from 1504 to 1505 and Chardstock from 1505 to 1507 and the Archdeaconry of Berks, together with the prebend of Highworth, from 1507 to 1509. He appears also to have held a stall at Hereford from 1480 to 1509. He had died by 20 December 1509.

Stephen Bereworth (1509-1510) See above

William Gray (1510-1522) MA, would appear not to have been ordained before 1510 when he became Archdeacon of Berks, holding the dignity until 1522. He held the prebends of Grantham Borealis from 1508 to 1514, Horton in 1514, Faringdon from 1514 to 1515 and Teynton Regis from 1515 to 1522. He held a stall at Hereford from 1512 to 1522. He died in 1522 and asked to be buried in Ramsbury church.

Robert Audley (1522-1545) held the prebend of Ramsbury from 1514 to 1545 and was Archdeacon of Berks from 1522 to 1545. He died in 1545 and asked to be buried in the cathedral near his uncle Edmund Audley, Bishop of Sarum 1502-1524.

John Crayford (1545-1547) DD, held the prebend of Alton Borealis from 1542 to 1544 and was permitted to be simultaneously Chancellor of Sarum from 1544 to 1547 and Archdeacon of Berks from 1545 to 1547, becoming Master of University College, Oxford in 1546. He became a Canon Residentiary in 1547 and died the same year.

William Pye (1547-1557) BD, died on 3 September 1557.

Thomas White (1557-1588) DCL, held the prebends of Yatesbury from 1553 to 1565 and Ufcomb from 1565 to 1571. He was Warden of New College, Oxford from 1553 to 1573, Chancellor of Sarum from 1571 to 1588, Archdeacon of Berks from 1557 to 1588 and Chancellor of the Diocese. He died on 12 June 1588 and was buried in the Morning Chapel of the cathedral.

Martin Culpepper (1588-1605) DM, died in 1605 and was buried at Feckenham, Worcestershire.

Lionel Sharp (1605-1631) DD, died in 1631.

Edward Davenant (1631-1634) DD, held the prebends of Torleton in 1623, Ilfracombe from 1624 to 1632 and Chisenbury & Chute from 1632 to 1634. He was Treasurer of Sarum from 1634 to 1680, Rector of Poulshot and, in 1625, of Gillingham. He was appointed by his uncle, John Davenant, Bishop of Sarum 1621-1641, to the Archdeaconry of Berks from 1631 to 1634. He died in 1680 at the age of 84.

John Ryves (1634-1665) BCL, was a son-in-law of Robert Tounson, Bishop of Sarum 1620-1621. He held the prebend of Gillingham Major from 1626 to 1665, was Archdeacon of Berks from 1634 to 1665 and a Canon Residentiary from 1662 to 1665. He also held a stall at Winchester. He was Rector of Tarrant Gunville where he is commemorated following his death on 19 August 1665.

Peter Mews (1665-1673) DCL, became Bishop of Bath & Wells in 1673.

John Sharp (1673-1689) MA, became Dean of Canterbury in 1689.

William Richards (1689-1698) MA, resigned in 1698.

Jonas Proast (1698-1710) MA, died in 1710 and was buried at St Mary Magdalen, Oxford.

Richard West (1710-1716) DD, died on 2 December 1716.

Edward Talbot (1717-1720) MA, was installed on 17 May as both Treasurer of Sarum and Archdeacon of Berks, which dignities he held from 1717 to 1720, and four days later he became a Canon Residentiary until 1720. He was a son of William Talbot, Bishop of Sarum 1715-1721, a Fellow of Oriel College, Oxford and was Rector of East Hendred, Berkshire. He died of small-pox on 9 December 1720.

Martin Benson (1721-1735) held the prebends of Yetminster Prima from 1720 to 1721 and Ilfracombe from 1721 to 1727. He was Archdeacon of Berks from 1721 to 1735, holding a stall at Durham in 1724. In 1735 he became Bishop of Gloucester and died on 30 August 1752.

Samuel Knight (1735-1746) DD, died on 9 December 1746.

John Spry (1747-1763) BD, died on 21 October 1763.

William Dodwell (1763-1785) MA, held the prebend of Grantham Australis from 1748 to 1785, was a Canon Residentiary from 1754 to 1785, Archdeacon of Berks from 1763 to 1785 and also Vicar of Shottesbrooke cum Waltham and Bucklesbury. He died on 23 October 1785 and is buried in the south transept of the cathedral.

Arthur Onslow (1785-1817) DD, died on 15 October 1817.

John Fisher (1817-1832) BA, was a nephew of John Fisher, Bishop of Sarum 1817-1825, receiving the prebend of Hurstbourne & Burbage in 1812, one month after his ordination as a deacon. He continued to hold this prebend to 1819 and Fordington & Writhlington from 1819 to 1832, and was Vicar of Osmington and Vicar of Gillingham. He was Archdeacon of Berks from 1817 to 1832 and a Canon Residentiary, occupying the house of Leadenhall, from 1819 to 1832. He died on 25 August 1832 and is commemorated at Osmington.

Edward Berens (1832-1836) MA, was Vicar of Shrivenham in 1804 and Rector of Englefield Green in 1818 and held the prebend of Slape from 1829 to 1859. He was Archdeacon of Berks in Sarum diocese from 1832 to 1836, when the Archdeaconry was transferred to Oxford diocese by Order in Council dated 5 October 1836. He continued as Archdeacon of Berks in Oxford diocese from 1836 until his resignation in 1855. He died on 7 April 1859.

(In 1836 the Archdeaconry of Berks was transferred to Oxford Diocese.)

ARCHDEACON OF SHERBORNE

The dignity: - In 1916, it was determined that the Archdeaconry of Dorset had become too large a responsibility and it was divided. The rural deaneries of Shaftesbury, Milton, Stalbridge, Sturminster Newton, Blandford, Wimborne, Poole and Purbeck were retained and the rural deaneries of Lyme Bay, Beaminster, Dorchester, Weymouth and Sherborne formed a new Archdeaconry of Sherborne.

Holders of the dignity: -

Frederick Wallis (1916-1919) DD, was a Fellow of Caius College, Cambridge, and Dean of Caius from 1878 to 1891. He was Bishop of Wellington, New Zealand from 1895 to 1911, Archdeacon of Wilts from 1911 to 1912, held the prebend of Beminster Secunda from 1913 to 1928 and was Archdeacon of Sherborne from 1916 to 1919. He died on 24 June 1928.

Albert Ernest Joscellyne (1919-1941) DD, was Co-adjutor Bishop of Jamaica from 1905 to 1913. He was Vicar of St Mark's, Sarum, from 1913 to 1919, Vicar of Chardstock from 1919 to 1930 and Vicar of Preston from 1930 to 1937. He held the prebend of Yatesbury from 1915 to 1941 and was Archdeacon of Sherborne from 1919 to 1941. He resigned his Archdeaconry in 1941 and died on 3 May 1945.

John Challoner Chute (1941-1961) MA, was Rector of Piddlehinton from 1938 to 1957 and Archdeacon of Sherborne, holding the prebend of Yatesbury from 1941 to 1961. He died on 12 September 1961.

David Rokeby Maddock (1961-1966) MA, was Vicar of Wilton from 1943 to 1947, Rector of Wareham with Arne from 1947 to 1961, Curate-in-Charge of Grange from 1950 to 1961 and Rural Dean of Purbeck from 1948 to 1961. He held the prebend of Warminster from 1956 to 1967, was Archdeacon of Sherborne and Rector of Bradford Peverell with Stratton from 1961 to 1966, Bishop Suffragan of Dunwich from 1967 to 1976 and Provost of Bury St Edmund from 1976 to 1980. He died on 14 August 1984.

Edwin James Greenfield Ward (1968-1984) LVO, MA, was a Chaplain to Queen Elizabeth II from 1955 to 1990 and an Extra Chaplain from 1995, was Archdeacon of Sherborne and Rector of West Stafford with Frome Billet from 1968 to 1984 and held the prebend of Netherbury in Ecclesia from 1968 to 1985. He retired in 1985.

(In 1977 the Archdeacons' stalls were discontinued, the stall of the Archdeacon of Sherborne being used for the prebend of Sherborne.)

SHERBORNE

Prebend:- The prebend consisted of the parish church of Sherborne in Dorset, the tithes, the chapels of Compton and Folke, and lands held by the Abbots of Sherborne.

In the time of Henry VIII, with the dissolution of the monasteries, the prebend was dissolved and its income dealt with as part of the possessions of the Abbey. In 1997 it was decided to revive this and three other titular prebends, using the Archdeacons' stalls for this purpose.

Psalter:- The portion of the psalter allotted to the prebend is Psalms 44, 45, 46, 47 and 48.

Holders of the prebend:-

Hubald (c.1078/99-c.1122) was an Archdeacon who was described as being trained in the liberal arts.

The Abbot of Sherborne for the time being (1122-c.1540). Occupied as his prebendal residence the house in the Close later known as The King's House (No. 65).

John Dudley Galtrey Kirkham (1977-) MA, was Domestic Chaplain to the Archbishop of Canterbury from 1972 to 1976 and Bishop Suffragan of Sherborne from 1976 to 1981, becoming Area Bishop of Sherborne in 1981. He was Archbishop's Advisor to the Headmasters' Conference from 1990 to 1992 and became Bishop to HM Forces in 1992.

THESAURARII

Dignity:- The Treasurer has the care of the sacred vessels, vestments, furniture and ornaments of the cathedral and is to endeavour to promote its beauty and dignity. (Note: The stall plaque should read "Thesaurarii").

Canopy statuette and shield:- **John Jewel** BD, was Fellow of Corpus Christi College, Oxford from which he was expelled chiefly on account of his relationship with Peter Martyr who had been Regius Professor of Divinity. He was Archdeacon of Chichester in 1551 but went to Germany to escape the troubles. He returned in 1557, becoming Bishop of Sarum from 1559 to 1571. He was a friend and patron of Richard Hooker who regarded him as the "worthiest divine that Christendom had had for the space of some hundreds of years." His best known work was *Apology for the Church of England.* He quarrelled with Dr Thomas Harding, Treasurer of Sarum over his right to hold a visitation of the Cathedral and died on 23 September 1571 in his 50th year. He was buried in the cathedral before the bishop's throne in the quire. (Fig 54.)

Blazon:- Or on a chevron azure between three pinks gules stalked and leaved vert a woman's head proper hair dishevelled of the first a chief sable charged with a lure two-stringed or between two falcons argent beaked and legged of the first. [On a gold shield, a blue chevron with on it a natural coloured woman's head with gold dishevelled hair, between three red 'pinks' with green stalks and leaves. Above it, on black, a gold two-stringed lure between two silver falcons with gold beaks and legs.]

Holders of the dignity:-

Harding (c.1122).

Jordan (c.1154/5-c.1159/60).

Savaric (c.1174/88-c.1191) was a son of Geldwin who was probably second cousin of Jocelin, Bishop of Sarum 1142-1184. He was Archdeacon of Sarum from c.1174 to c.1184 and of Northampton from 1175 to 1192 He held the prebend of Heytesbury c.1183, was Treasurer of Sarum in c.1174/88 and possibly holder of the prebend of Beminster Prima at about the same time. He became Bishop of Bath & Wells in 1192. He held the rectories of Godalming and Hill Deverill in 1180. He died in 1205 and was buried in Bath.

Ranulf (c.1193-c.1205) was a member of the household of Hubert Walter, Archbishop of Canterbury 1193-1205, and was a witness to a deed giving the Treasurer of Sarum jurisdiction over Figheldean and Alderbury.

A ------ (1206/7).

Thomas (c.1209-c.1215) gave a chasuble for his burial.

Ralph (c.1215/27).

Abraham of Winchester (1214-c.1222) was Treasurer of Sarum from 1214 to c.1222 and held the prebend of Chardstock between 1215 & 1220.

Edmund Rich (of Abingdon) (c.1222-1234) was the first Treasurer of Sarum to hold the prebend of Calne joined to the dignity. He became Archbishop of Canterbury in 1234, died on 16 November 1240 and in 1246 he was canonised by Pope Innocent IV as St Edmund of Canterbury. In the same year the central of the three chapels on the east side of the north-west transept of the cathedral was founded as a chantry chapel in his memory.

John of St Quentin (alias St Albans) (1234-c.1238) resigned the Deanery of St Quentin in 1234.

Henry de Lexington (c.1239-c.1245) became Dean of Lincoln in 1245, and Bishop of Lincoln in 1254. He died on 8 August 1258.

Robert de Cardeville (c.1246-1264) built a chapel at Figheldean dedicated to St Edmund of Abingdon and died as Treasurer on 2 September 1264.

Adam (1236/57).

Simon of Bridport (c.1265-c.1267) may have been a brother of Giles of Bridport, Bishop of Sarum 1257-1262. He was Archdeacon of Dorset from ? to 1262, Archdeacon of Berks from c.1262 to c.1263 and Treasurer of Sarum from c.1265 to c.1267.

Walter Scammel (1267/8-1271) was Archdeacon of Berks from c.1266 to 1274 and Clerk & Collector to King Henry III from 1267 to 1268. He was Treasurer of Sarum and held the prebend of Calne from 1267 to 1271 when, on becoming Dean of Sarum from 1271 to 1284, he also held the prebend of Heytesbury. He was elected Bishop of Sarum in 1284, died on 20 September 1286 and was buried at the north side of the presbytery in the Cathedral. It is believed to have been in 1280 that the prebend of Heytesbury became permanently joined to the deanery.

Nicholas Longespee (before 1275-1291) was the fourth son of William Longespee, who in the right of his wife Ella, the foundress of Lacock Abbey, became Earl of Salisbury. He was Treasurer of Sarum from before 1275 to 1291 and was Bishop of Sarum from 1292 until his death on 18 May 1297. He was buried in the cathedral, with his heart at Lacock and his viscera at Ramsbury.

Louis de Beaumont (?-1317) was referred to as 'his cousin' by King Edward I. He may have held the prebend of Blewbery in 1284, was Treasurer of Sarum from c.1293 to 1317, held stalls at Le Mans, York, Wells and Bishop Aukland and became Bishop of Durham in 1317.

James de Via (1317) was a nephew of Pope John XXII and brother of Arnald de Via. He was elected Bishop of Avignon in 1313, was created Cardinal-Priest of St John and St Paul in 1316 and became Treasurer of Sarum in 1317. He died at Avignon on 13 June 1317, having not apparently been consecrated.

Arnold de Via (1318-1336) was a nephew of Pope John XXII and brother of James de Via and was, perhaps, Bishop of Avignon. He was created Cardinal-Deacon of St Eustace in 1317, was Treasurer of Sarum from 1318 to 1336 and had died by 11 April 1336.

Ralph de Stratford (1336-1340) BCL, was a nephew of John de Stratford, Archbishop of Canterbury. He held stalls at St Paul's and in 1332 at Lincoln. He received the prebend of Blewbery by exchange in 1335 holding it until 1336, when he served as Treasurer of Sarum from 1336 to 1340. He gave to the cathedral an image of our Lady in silver and gilt with precious stones. In 1340 he became Bishop of London and died on 7 April 1354.

Walter Wyville (1340-1345) was Rector of Kingsclere in 1330 and held the prebends of Minor Pars Altaris from 1334 to 1338 and of Bere & Cherminster from 1338 to 1340. He was Treasurer of Sarum and a Canon Residentiary from 1340 to 1345 and died in 1345.

Gaillard de la Motte (1345) was a nephew of Pope Clement V and was made Cardinal-Deacon of St Lucia in Silice in 1316. He was nominated to the dignity of Treasurer of Sarum but John de Bredon gained possession and he died at Avignon on 20 December 1356.

John de Bredon (1345-1350) was excommunicated.

Bartholomew de Bradden (1351) held the prebend of Axford from 1344 to 1350, claimed the dignity of Treasurer of Sarum in 1351 but the case was referred for judgement. He received papal confirmation of the prebend of Warminster in 1350 and resigned it in 1361. He was Rector of St Peter's Marlborough from 1334 to 1336 and was Rector of Barford St Martin.

Francis de Aptis (1357-1361) was made Bishop of Monte Cassino in 1353 and became Cardinal-Priest of St Mark's in 1356. He died at Ponte Sorgia on 4 September 1361.

John de Blandiaco (1361-?) was made Bishop of Nimes in 1348, Cardinal-Priest of St Mark in 1361 and Cardinal-Bishop of Sabina in 1372. He deserted Pope Urban VI for the Anti-Pope Clement VII and died at Avignon on 8 January 1379.

Nicholas Caraccioli (1380) was Cardinal of Naples and in 1380 Archdeacon of Dorset.

Francis Prignani (?-1394) 'an unworthy and immoral' nephew of Pope Urban VI, was created Cardinal-Priest of St Eusebius in 1378 and before 1390 Cardinal-Bishop of Palestrina. He had a royal licence to receive possession of the dignity of Treasurer of Sarum in 1383 but there were three other claimants; Hugh Farington by grant in 1386, Henry Bowet who was said to be Treasurer of Sarum in 1388 and a person called Peter, Cardinal of Pisa, in 1390. Despite these, Francis Prignagni held the dignity in 1391 and died at Assisi on 6 February 1394.

Hugh Farington (1386) received a grant of the dignity in 1386 but does not appear to have assumed it.

Henry Bowet (1388) DCn&CL, was said to be Treasurer of Sarum in 1388 but Francis Prignani seems to have retained the dignity in 1391. He also claimed the prebend of Bere & Cherminster in 1390 but three months after Robert Bloor was installed he was said to be still litigating about prebends.

Bartholomew Mezzaracca (1394-1395) LLD, was consecrated Bishop of Ostuni, Lower Italy in 1374 and was translated to Rieti in 1378. He was created Cardinal-Priest of St Marcellus in 1378 but was deprived as a fomentor of disturbances by Pope Urban VI in 1383 whereupon he fled to the Anti-Pope Clement VII at Avignon. In 1389 Pope Boniface IX restored him as Cardinal of St Martin's and he became Treasurer of Sarum from 1394 to 1395. He died in Rome on 29 January 1396 and was buried in the Church of St Magdalene. At the death of Pope Urban VI, he had been a candidate for the papacy.

Henry Harburgh (1394) was Treasurer of Sarum for three days in 1394 when he exchanged the dignity with John Chaundeler for the prebend of Netherbury in Ecclesia. This he exchanged in 1395 with Ralph Selby for the prebend of Alton Borealis. He relinquished this latest prebend in 1403, receiving that of Slape. This he held until 1415 when he received the prebend of Beminster Prima. In 1416 he became Precentor of Sarum, he relinquished his prebend in 1418 and in the same year exchanged the dignity of Precentor for the prebend of Bere & Cherminster, which he held until 1432. He had died by 22 September 1432.

John Chaundeler (1394-1404) held a stall at Lincoln in 1405 and the prebend of Netherbury in Ecclesia from ? to 1394, exchanging it for the dignity of Treasurer of Sarum which he held until 1404. He was Dean of Sarum from 1404 to 1417 and Bishop of Sarum from 1417 until his death on 16 July 1426.

George Westby (1404) held the prebend of Netherbury in Terra from 1403 to 1404, becoming Treasurer of Sarum in 1404. A day later, he exchanged the dignity for the prebend of Fordington & Writhlington and, within the same year, exchanged this for the prebend of Bedminster & Redcliffe, which he in turn exchanged for Major Pars Altaris which he then exchanged for Axford, resigning the last in the autumn of the same year.

George Louthorp (1404-1427) was Rector of St Thomas, Sarum and held the prebend of Netherbury in Terra from 1393 to 1403. He exchanged this with George Westby for the prebend of Fordington & Writhlington in 1403 and in 1404 exchanged this for the dignity of Treasurer of Sarum which he held until 1427.

William Glym (1404) was excommunicated in 1399 for disobeying a decision of the papal court, which had confirmed John Cheyne's possession of the prebend of Chardstock. He received, however, a royal grant of the prebend in 1402 but appears to have failed to gain possession. In 1404 he claimed the dignity of Treasurer of Sarum by virtue of a royal licence of May 1404. There was an inquiry in 1408 at which he was imprisoned but he was pardoned in 1410.

Gilbert Kymer (1427-1449) DM, BCL, was Treasurer of Sarum from 1427 to 1449, Chancellor of Oxford in 1446 and Dean of Sarum from 1449 to 1463. He was also Dean of Wimborne between 1447-1463. He died 16 May 1463 and asked to be buried in the Cathedral.

John Symondesburgh (1449-1454) BCL, was Archdeacon of Wilts from 1423 to 1449 and Treasurer of Sarum from 1449 to 1454. He held the prebend of Yatesbury from 1423 to 1437, exchanging it with John Tydeling for the prebend of Stratton which he held from 1437 to 1449. He held the Rectory of Dinton in 1433 and was Canon Treasurer of St Paul's from 1420 to 1423. He died in 1454 and asked to be buried before St Margaret's altar in the cathedral.

Thomas Mannynge (1454-1462) BCnL, was Treasurer of Sarum from 1454 until resigning in 1462. He held a stall at St Paul's in 1459 and may have been the person of the same name who was Dean of Windsor from 1452 to 1462.

Richard Whitby (1462-1494) BCn&CL, was Treasurer of Sarum from 1462 to 1494 and held the prebends of Slape from 1451 to 1457, Chisenbury & Chute from 1457 to 1459 and Bedwin from 1459 to 1462. He was a Canon Residentiary and not infrequently locum tenens of the Dean. He died in 1494 and was buried in the chapel of St Edmund in the cathedral.

Geoffrey Blythe (1494-1495) BTh, was a brother of John Blythe, Bishop of Sarum 1494-1499. He was Treasurer of Sarum from 1494 to 1495, exchanging the dignity for the prebend of Chisenbury & Chute which he held from 1495 to 1498. He was Archdeacon of Sarum, holding the prebend of Stratton, from 1499 to 1503 and would seem to have been Dean of York in 1497 and Provost of King's Hall, Cambridge in 1499. In 1503 be was consecrated Bishop of Lichfield and died in 1533.

Henry Sutton (1495-1501) DM, was the Master of St Nicholas Hospital, Sarum in 1478. He held the prebends of Rotesfen from 1481 to 1486 and Chisenbury & Chute from 1486 to 1495 when he exchanged the latter for the dignity of Treasurer of Sarum which he held from 1495 to 1501.

Richard Hilley (?-1533) BCnL, died on 1 September 1533 and was buried near the entrance to the quire in the cathedral.

Nicholas Shaxton (1533-1535) DTh, was a benefactor of Gonville Hall, Cambridge. He was Treasurer of Sarum from 1533 to 1535 and about the same time held the rectory of Fugglestone with Bemerton. He was Bishop of Sarum from 1535 until resigning in 1539. He had been silenced and afterwards condemned with Latimer but recanted and preached a sermon proclaiming his apostacy when Ann Askew was burnt. He afterwards acted as a bishop suffragan in Ely diocese.

Richard Sampson (1535-1540) DCn&CL, held a stall at Lincoln in 1527, was Archdeacon of Suffolk in 1528, Dean of Windsor from 1522 to 1536, of Lichfield from1533 to 1536 and of St Paul's from 1536 to 1540. He was Treasurer of Sarum from 1535 to 1540, becoming Bishop of Chichester in 1536 but was sent to the Tower in 1540. In 1543 he was translated to Lichfield and died on 25 September 1554.

Thomas Robertson (1540-1548) MA, prepared, in 1536, an *'Inventory of the Jewels and Riches belonging to the Cathedral Church of Sarum'*. He was Treasurer of Sarum from 1540 until resigning the dignity in 1548.

Thomas Stevens (1548-1550) died in September 1550.

Matthew Wotton (1550-1551) BD, held the prebend of Grantham Borealis from 1535 to 1551, was a Canon Residentiary from 1537 to 1551 and was Treasurer of Sarum from 1550 to 1551. He died in December 1551.

Richard Arche (1551-1555) BCL, held the prebends of Preston from ? to 1524, Faringdon in 1524 and Hurstbourne & Burbage from 1524 to 1552. He was Vicar of Avebury and held a stall at Windsor from 1538 until deprived in 1554. He was Treasurer of Sarum from 1551 to 1555 during which time the Commissioners appointed to survey Church Goods and Chantries visited the cathedral. It is presumed that he was deprived of this dignity in 1555, as being married.

Thomas Harding (1555-1559) DD, was made Treasurer of Sarum at the request of Stephen Gardiner, Bishop of Winchester, whose chaplain he was, and he held the dignity from 1555 to 1559. He became a Canon Residentiary from 1558 to 1559. He was a great opponent of John Jewell, Bishop of Sarum 1557-1571, with whom he disputed the right of the bishop to hold a Visitation of the cathedral. Described as "a violent maintainer of the Popish religion", he was deprived by November 1559 and died in 1562.

Thomas Lancaster (1559-1583) BD, was Treasurer of Sarum from 1559 to 1583 and a Canon Residentiary from 1560 to 1566. He continued to hold the dignity of Treasurer of Sarum when becoming Bishop of Kildare in 1550 and Archbishop of Armagh in 1568. He died in December 1583.

John Sprint (1584-1590) DD, was Dean of Bristol in 1571. He held the prebend of Bitton from 1573 to 1578, was Archdeacon of Wilts from 1577 to 1590, being also Treasurer of Sarum from 1584 to 1590. He died in 1590.

Thomas White (1590-1624) DD, held stalls at St Paul's in 1588, Christ Church, Oxford in 1591 and Windsor in 1593. He was Treasurer of Sarum from 1590 to 1624, founded a Professorship of Moral Philosophy at Oxford in 1621 and was founder of Sion College, London. He died on 1 March 1624.

John Lee (1624-1634) BD, held the prebend of Alton Australis from 1616 to 1624, was Treasurer of Sarum from 1624 to 1634 and was a Canon Residentiary from ? to 1634. He was Rector of Wylye from 1619 to 1634 and in 1629 of Little Langford, both of which he held with the Treasurership. He died on 16 November 1634.

Edward Davenant (1634-1680) DD, held the prebends of Torleton in 1623, Ilfracombe from 1624 to 1632 and Chisenbury & Chute from 1632 to 1634. He was appointed by his uncle, John Davenant, Bishop of Sarum 1621-1641, to the Archdeaconry of Berks from 1631 to 1634 and was Treasurer of Sarum from 1634 to 1680. He was Rector of Poulshot and in 1625 of Gillingham. He died in 1680 at the age of 84.

Thomas Jeames (1680-1687) DD, was Warden of All Souls, Oxford from 1665 to 1686 and died on 5 January 1687.

Seth Ward (1687-1690) MA, was a nephew of Seth Ward, Bishop of Sarum 1667-1689. He was Archdeacon of Wilts from 1675 to 1681, Chancellor of Sarum from 1681 to 1687 and Treasurer of Sarum from 1687 to 1690. He held the prebend of Coombe & Harnham from 1672 to 1681, died on 11 May 1690 aged 43 and was buried in the cathedral near the grave of his uncle.

Peter Allix (1690-1717) DD, had been a minister of the reformed church at Charenton in France, came to England because of the persecution of the French Protestants and was Treasurer of Sarum from 1690 to 1717. He died on 21 February 1717.

Edward Talbot (1717-1720) MA, was a son of William Talbot, Bishop of Sarum 1715-1721, a Fellow of Oriel College, Oxford and Rector of East Hendred, Berkshire. He was both Treasurer of Sarum and Archdeacon of Berks from 1717 to 1720, four days after his installation he was made a Canon Residentiary, a post he held until 1720. He died of small-pox on 9 December 1720.

Thomas Rundle (1721-1735) BCL, held the prebends of Gillingham Minor from 1716 to 1717 and Ilfracombe from 1717 to 1721. He held the Archdeaconry of Wilts from 1720 to 1735 together with the dignity of Treasurer of Sarum from 1721 to 1735 and was consecrated Bishop of Derry in 1735.

John Lynch (1735-1760) DD, was Master of St Cross Hospital, Winchester, Dean of Canterbury from 1734 to 1760 and Treasurer of Sarum from 1735 to 1760. He died on 25 May 1760.

Francis Dodsworth (1760-1806) MA, held a stall at York and died on 18 October 1806.

Thomas Henry Hume (1806-1834) MA, was the only son of John Hume, Bishop of Sarum 1766-1782, and nephew of Nathaniel Hume, Precentor of Sarum 1774-1804. He held the prebends of Yatesbury from 1795 to 1799 and of Bitton from 1799 to 1806. He was a Canon Residentiary from 1803 to 1834 and Treasurer of Sarum from 1806 to 1834 Amongst others, he held the livings of Broad Hinton, Stratford-sub-Castle and Brixton Deverill. He died on 6 January 1834 and is buried in the south transept of the cathedral.

Liscombe Clarke (1834-1841) MA, held a stall at Hereford in 1821. He was Archdeacon of Sarum from 1827 to 1836 and Treasurer of Sarum from 1834 to 1841. He held the prebends of Minor Pars Altaris from 1827 to 1828 and Netheravon from 1828 to 1834 and was Vicar of Downton. He died on 17 April 1841.

Walter Kerr Hamilton (1841-1843) DD, was in 1833 a Fellow of Merton College, Oxford. In 1834 he held a stall at Wells, becoming a Canon Residentiary with the house of Leadenhall, and Treasurer of Sarum from 1841 to 1843 and Precentor of Sarum from 1843 to 1854, also holding the prebend of Torleton from 1843 to 1854. He was Bishop of Sarum from 1854 until his death on 1 August 1869. Whilst at Sarum he founded Salisbury Theological College and contributed to the debate on cathedral reform. He was buried in the cathedral beside his predecessor, Edward Denison, Bishop of Sarum 1837-1854.

*[**No Appointment** (1843-1854) the dignity becoming disendowed under the Cathedral Acts 1840, the revenues being transferred to the Ecclesiastical Commissioners.]*

Robert Bickersteth (1854-1857) MA, held the prebend of Torleton in 1854. He was Treasurer of Sarum and a Canon Residentiary from 1854 to 1857 and Bishop of Ripon from 1857 to 1884. He died on 15 April 1884.

The Hon Samuel Waldegrave (1857-1860) MA, DD, was the 2nd son of the 8th Earl Waldegrave. He was a Fellow of All Souls, Oxford from 1839 to 1845 and was Rector of Barford St Martin from 1844 to 1860. He was Bampton Lecturer in 1854 and Treasurer of Sarum, a Canon Residentiary and a Proctor in Convocation from 1857 to 1860. He was Bishop of Carlisle from 1860 until his death on 1 October 1869 and was buried at Carlisle Cathedral.

The Hon Douglas Hamilton Gordon (1860-1901) MA, was a son of the fourth Earl of Aberdeen, Prime Minister from 1852-1855. He was a Chaplain in Ordinary to Queen Victoria from 1857 and Honorary Chaplain to King Edward VII from 1901. He was Treasurer of Sarum from 1860 to 1901 and a Canon Residentiary from 1860 until resigning due to failing health in 1898. He was Prior of St John's Hospital, Burcombe from 1894 and died on 6 December 1901 being buried in the cloisters.

George Hugh Bourne (1901-1925) BA, DCL, was Headmaster of St Andrew's School Chardstock from 1866 to 1874, Warden of St Edmund's College, Sarum from 1874 to 1885, Subdean of Sarum from 1887 to 1901 and Treasurer of Sarum from 1901 to 1925. He died on 1 December 1925 and left his property, St Edmund's College in Bourne Hill, Salisbury, to the diocese for religious purposes.

Charles Myers (1926-1937) MA, held the prebend of Durnford from 1905 to 1926 and was a Canon Residentiary from 1915 to 1927. He was Subdean of Sarum from 1919 to 1926 and Treasurer of Sarum from 1926 until resigning the dignity in 1937. He died in 1948.

Robert Quirk (1938-1949) MA, was an Assistant master of Winchester College from 1905, Chaplain to the Forces 1914 to 1918, HouseMaster from 1919, to 1938. He was Treasurer of Sarum and a Canon Residentiary from 1938 to 1949, being provided with the South Canonry as his official canonical residence. He died in March 1949.

Walter John Barton (1949-1955) MA, was Headmaster of Epsom College from 1914 to 1922 and of Portsmouth Grammar School from 1926 to 1936. He was Domestic Chaplain to Ernest Neville Lovett, Bishop of Sarum 1936-1946, held the prebend of Shipton from 1937 to 1949 and was Treasurer of Sarum from 1949 until resigning in 1955. He was a Canon Residentiary from 1944 resigning in 1951 as the donor, believed to be his sister, who had made it financially possible to revive the canonry for seven years, had been unable to renew the donation.

Lancelot Farquharson Addison (1955-1956) was Vicar of Cranborne with Boveridge from 1921 to 1947. He was Archdeacon of Dorset from 1947 to 1956, held the prebend of Grimston from 1947 to 1955 and was Treasurer of Sarum from 1955 until his death in 1956.

Arthur Frederick Smethurst (1956-1957) MA, PhD, BSc, held the prebend of Shipton from 1949 to 1953. He was a Canon Residentiary from 1949 to 1957, Chancellor of Sarum from 1953 to 1956 and Treasurer of Sarum from 1956 until his death on 15 September 1957.

Ralph Sigismund Dawson (1958-1968) MA, was Treasurer of Sarum and a Canon Residentiary from 1958 to 1968 He died in 1968.

Stephen Basil Wingfield-Digby (1971-1978) MBE, MA, was Curate-in-Charge of St George's Conventual District of Oakdale from 1938 to 1946 and Minister from 1946 to 1947. He was Chaplain to the Forces from 1940 to 1945 and was mentioned in despatches. He was Vicar of Sherborne with Castleton and Lillington from 1947 to 1968 and held the prebend of Grimston from 1955 to 1971. He was Archdeacon of Sarum and Canon Residentiary from 1968 to 1979 and Treasurer of Sarum from 1971 to 1978. He died on 22 January 1996.

Rhys Derrick Chamberlain Walters (1979-1983) OBE, BSc, was Diocesan Missioner from 1974 to 1983, Priest-in-Charge of Burcombe from 1974 to 1979, held the prebend of Ogborne from 1977 to 1979 and was Treasurer of Sarum and a Canon Residentiary from 1979 to 1983. He was Dean of Liverpool from 1983 to 1999.

Richard George Askew (1983-1990) MA, was Treasurer of Sarum, a Canon Residentiary and Diocesan Advisor on Mission and Ministry from 1983 to 1990 and a Proctor in Convocation from 1985 to 1990. He became Rector of Bath Abbey with St James in 1990 and held a stall at Wells from 1992.

John Roberton Stewart (1990-1995) was Rector of Langton Matravers from 1970 to 1984 and Rector of Kingston, Langton Matravers and Worth Matravers from 1984 to 1990, and Rural Dean of Purbeck from 1982 to 1989. He held the prebend of Loders from 1983 to 1990 and was Treasurer of Sarum and a Canon Residentiary from 1990 to 1995.

June Osborne (1995-) BA, MPhil, was Deaconess, Deacon and Priest-in-Charge of Old Ford St Paul & St Mark, London from 1984 to 1995 and a Proctor in Convocation from 1985 to 1995. She became Treasurer of Sarum and a Canon Residentiary in 1995 and from 1995 to 1998 also acted as "chief of staff" to David Staffurth Stancliffe, Bishop of Sarum 1993- .

PREBENDS IN SUSPENSE

There are no stalls named in the quire for these prebends.

BLEWBERY

Prebend:- The churches of the royal manors of Blewbery in Berkshire and Marlborough in Wiltshire were held by William Beaufou, Bishop of Norwich in 1086 and were granted to the canons of Sarum in 1091 by Osmund, Bishop of Sarum 1078-1099. The prebend was probably in existence by c.1150, the churches being conferred as a prebend by King Henry II in 1158. Between 1142 and 1184 both churches were part of the communal estate of the canons but were conferred as a prebend in 1181/85 by Pope Lucius III although the patronage was in the hands of the Sandford family and an interest was maintained by the Knights Hospitallers and Knights Templars. The church of Preshute in Wiltshire was added to the prebend by 1223 but both this and the churches of Marlborough St Mary and St Peter were removed from the prebend in the same year, becoming part of the bishop's jurisdiction.

In 1542, the holder of the prebend, Thomas Paston Esq, exchanged the prebend with John Salcot, Bishop of Sarum 1559-1557, for the bishop's manor of Godalming, Surrey, and the prebend was dissolved by Act of Parliament.

Psalter:- The portion of the psalter allotted to the prebend was Psalms 35 and 36.

Warin of Sandford (before 1184).

Robert of Sandford (c.1213/4-after 1219) is likely to have held this prebend as he would appear to be a relative of Warin of Sandford.

Luke (c.1226/7-?) was fined for non-residence in 1227. He was Dean of St Martin-le-Grand, London in 1225 and is therefore identified as Chaplain to King Henry III and the Senior Clerk of the King's Wardrobe. He was Chancellor of Lichfield, became Archdeacon of Norwich in 1226 and held a stall at London. Despite a papal decree that he was not to be elected a bishop, he was elected Archbishop of Dublin in 1228 and was consecrated in 1230.

Nicholas de Tessun (after 1246) held the prebend some time after 1246. He was Archdeacon of Bath by 1247 and held a stall at Lincoln. He was a brother of Henry Tessun, who held successively the prebends of Durnford and Bedminster & Redcliffe.

Louis de Beaumont (c.1284-1293?) was Treasurer of Sarum from c.1293 to 1317 and was referred to as 'his cousin' by King Edward I. He held stalls at Le Mans, York, Wells and Bishop Aukland and became Bishop of Durham in 1317.

John de Berwick (1292-1312) was presented to the prebend by the Prior of the Order of St John of Jerusalem in England but was ordered twice, in 1299 and 1300, to give up the prebend in favour of Nicholas de Orsini, son of Napoleone son of Ursi de Urbe but he continued to retain it until his death on 30 June 1312. He was Keeper of Queen Eleanor's Gold in 1285 and Keeper of the Queen's Wardrobe from 1287 to 1290. He held stalls at Exeter, Lichfield, London, Wells and York.

Adam de Osgodby (1312-1316) was Master of the Rolls, and held stalls at York and Lincoln. He died in 1316.

Roger de Northborough (1316) was presented by King Edward II to the prebend of Blewbery in 1316 but Richard de Osgodby was presented by the Prior of St John of Jerusalem. He held the prebend of Yatesbury from 1318 to 1322 when he became Bishop of Lichfield.

Richard de Osgodby (1316) was presented by the Prior of St John of Jerusalem but William Rothewell revived a claim from a previous vacancy.

William de Rothewell (1316) claimed the prebend from his presentation by the Prior of St John of Jerusalem at a previous vacancy in 1312 but there was a dispute over the right of presentation over which he appealed to the Court of Canterbury.

Hubert le Conestable (1316) was presented by Denise de la River who claimed the right of presentation, but was taken to court.

Henry de Clif (1316-1334) was presented by the Prior of St John of Jerusalem but claims were made by William de Fresapanis and Thomas Charlton. The decision of the Court at Rome in 1326 was that his claim should be accepted. He held the prebend in 1333 and died in 1334.

William de Fresapanis (1316-1317) claimed the prebend of Blewbery in 1316 but withdrew his claim a year later. He held the prebend of Fordington & Writhlington in 1320 exchanging it in 1331 with Peter de Galicia for a benefice in Agen.

Thomas de Charlton (1317-1326) DCL, was Vicar of Downton in 1318. He was granted the prebend by Roger de Mortival, Bishop of Sarum 1315-1330, on the grounds that the right of presentation had lapsed to the see. In 1321 the bishop received a request from the Prior of St John of Jerusalem to remove Thomas de Charlton and admit Henry Clif. The dispute was taken to the Court of Arches and then to Rome, the decision in 1326 being that Henry de Clif's claim should be accepted.

Cassaleto de Tibertis (1334-1335) received the prebend on the death of Henry de Clif and exchanged the prebend in 1335 with Ralph de Stratford for the prebend of Urchfont in the conventual church of St Mary, Winchester.

Ralph de Stratford (1335-1336) BCL, was a nephew of John de Stratford, Archbishop of Canterbury. He held stalls at St Paul's and in 1332 at Lincoln. He received the prebend of Blewbery by exchange in 1335, holding it until 1336, when he served as Treasurer of Sarum from 1336 to 1340. He gave to the cathedral an image of our Lady in silver and gilt, with precious stones. In 1340 he became Bishop of London and died on 7 April 1354.

John Geraud (1336-?) held the prebend in 1366.

William de Salisbury (1376-?) received a royal grant of the prebend but it was claimed by David Calveley and he was later ousted and imprisoned.

David Calveley (1380) claimed to have been nominated to the prebend but a royal mandate was issued for his arrest for suing William de Salisbury. He was imprisoned in 1381 but escaped from Marshalsea Prison later in the year.

Richard Clifford (1387-1400) held the prebend of Blewbery from 1387 to 1400, was Archdeacon of Canterbury in 1397 and Bishop of Worcester in 1401. He became Bishop of London in 1407 and in 1414 introduced the Use of Sarum into his cathedral.

Angelo Acciaiuoli (1401-1408) was consecrated Bishop of Rapolla in 1375 and was translated to Florence in 1383. In 1385 be became Chancellor of the Holy Roman Church, Arch-Priest of the Vatican and Cardinal-Priest of St Laurentius in Damaso, becoming Cardinal-Bishop of Ostia in 1397. He was nominated to be Dean of Sarum on the death of Thomas Ursinus in 1390 but had resigned by 30 July 1391 and Thomas Montacute was nominated. He received a royal licence to take possession of the prebend of Blewbery in 1401 and died on 31 May 1408.

John Grendon (1400-1431) was presented to the prebend by the Prior of St John of Jerusalem but when he was not admitted to it by Richard Medford, Bishop of Sarum 1396-1407, an archbishop's inquiry was held. On the death of Angelo Acciaiuoli, John Grendon's possession was confirmed and he held the prebend in 1431.

John Burdet (1432-1449) died in 1449.

Roger Keyes (1449-1457) BCnL, held the prebend of Blewbery from 1449 to 1457, exchanging it with John Druell for the prebend of Netherbury in Ecclesia which he held from 1457 until 1461 when he exchanged the latter with Fulk Bermyngham for the prebend of Teynton Regis, holding the last until 1477 in which year he died.

John Druell (1457-1469) DCn&CL, held the prebends of Alton Australis from 1441 to 1445, Netheravon from 1445 to 1447, Ramsbury from 1447 to 1449 and Netherbury in Ecclesia from 1449 to 1457, exchanging the last with Roger Keyes for the prebend of Blewbery which he held from 1457 until 1469. In 1449 he was Rector of Steeple Langford and he died in 1469.

John Newton (1470-1479) died in 1479.

Thomas Davy (1479-1503) resigned in 1503.

John Docwra (1503-1511) died in 1511.

John Tynmouth (or Maynelyn) (1511-1524) resigned in 1524.

John Docwra (1524-1536) died in 1536.

Sir Thomas Cromwell (1536-1540) conducted under Cardinal Wolsey in 1525 the most unpopular suppression of a number of small monasteries to allow Wolsey to endow two proposed colleges at Ipswich and Oxford. He became Secretary to Wolsey and is believed to have made the suggestion to King Henry VIII that the King should become head of the church. He was a Privy Counsellor in 1531, Chancellor of the Exchequer in 1533, Secretary to the King in 1534, General Visitor of the Monasteries in 1535 and Baron Cromwell of Oakham in 1536, in which year he received, although not ordained, the prebend of Blewbery followed by the Deanery of Wells and the Knighthood of the Garter in 1537. In 1539 he became Lord Great Chamberlain and in the following year Earl of Essex. Two months later he was accused of treason and heresy. He was found guilty of treason and was beheaded on 29 July 1540.

Thomas Paston (1540-1542), although a layman, received the prebend by royal grant in 1540 and was admitted by proxy to the prebend but he was not installed as a canon. He exchanged the prebend in 1542 with John Salcot, Bishop of Sarum 1559-1557, for the bishop's manor of Godalming, Surrey and the prebend was dissolved by Act of Parliament.

FARINGDON

Prebend :- Faringdon in Berkshire was a royal manor in 1086, of which Osmund, Bishop of Sarum 1078-1099, held one hide, together with the church which he had given to the canons of Sarum by 1091. The prebend was certainly in existence by 1220 and there was an establishment of four priests in the church of Faringdon and the chapel of Coxwell in 1227.

In 1551, the prebend was transferred to William Honnying Esq, to be held of the King.

Psalter:- The portion of the psalter allotted to the prebend is Psalms 143, 144, 145 and 146.

Holders of the prebend :-

William de Teise (?-1227) died, holding the prebend, before 3 October 1227.

William de Merton (c.1219-1237/8) may have been the father of Walter of Merton, Bishop of Rochester and founder of Merton College, Oxford. He held the prebend of Faringdon from c.1219 to 1237/8, was the Official to Richard Poore, Bishop of Sarum 1217-1228, Archdeacon of Berks from c.1224 to 1237/8 and Dean of Wells in 1237.

Ancher Pantaléon of Troyes (c.1264-c.1284?) was a nephew of Pope Urban IV who became Archdeacon of Laon and held a stall at Bayeux. He became Cardinal-Priest of St Praxedes in 1261, held the Prebend of Faringdon from c.1264 to c.1284? and a stall at York. He died on 1 November 1286.

John Walwayne (1315-?) DCL.

Pandulf de Sabellis (?-1328) held the prebend in 1318 and died in 1328.

Itherius de Concoreto (1328-?) BCn&CL, was nominated to the prebend of Warminster in 1328 although Thomas de Bocton had received it a year earlier. Six months later he was nominated to the prebend of Faringdon which he was holding in 1337, despite a royal grant in 1335 to William de Excestre. He was Archdeacon of London, held a stall at St Paul's, and was Chancellor of Ely. He had married by June 1343.

William de Excestre (c.1335) DTh, had a royal grant of the prebend in 1335 but Itherius de Concoreto was occupying it in 1337.

Henry de la Dale (1340-1349) died in 1349.

Nicholas Hethe (1349-1351) was nominated to the prebend in 1349 but Richard de Brankescombe who had had expectations of a prebend in 1343 was installed. Nicholas Hethe continued to claim the prebend but in 1351 swore not to do so.

Richard de Brankescombe (1349) had expectations of a prebend in 1343 and despite Nicholas Hethe being nominated in 1349, he was installed and probably died holding the prebend.

Roger de Cloune (1349-1350) held the prebend of Faringdon from 1349 until it was given to John de Edington by royal grant in 1350 when he then received the prebend of Grimston holding it until at least 1366. He was Archdeacon of Sarum from 1361 until at least 1375 and was a Canon Residentiary.

John de Edington (1350-1397) BCL, received the prebend by royal grant in 1350 and continued to hold it until his death in 1397, Nicholas Hethe having sworn not to pursue claims to the prebend.

Guy Mone (1397) was granted the prebend of Yetminster Secunda in 1388. He held the prebends of Grantham Borealis from 1395 until resigning in 1396 and Faringdon in 1397. He held a stall at St Paul's and was Treasurer of that cathedral from 1394 to 1397 when he became Bishop of St David's. He twice held the office of Treasurer of England.

Walter Cook (1397) was Archdeacon of Berks from 1395 to 1397 when he was nominated to the prebend of Faringdon but Walter Medford was installed. He may have received the prebend of Netherbury in Ecclesia c.1399, by papal grace, but he was deposed in the same year. He finally received the prebend of Faringdon in 1400 and resigned in 1422.

Walter Medford (1397-1400) BCL, was Archdeacon of Dorset in 1397, Chancellor of Sarum from 1402 to 1404 and a brother of Richard Medford, Bishop of Sarum 1396 to 1407. In 1404 he exchanged the dignity with Henry Chichele for the Archdeaconry of Sarum and the prebend of Fordington & Writhlington, exchanging the dignity a few days later for the Archdeaconry of Berks. He probably exchanged this Archdeaconry with Peter Alcobasso for the deanery of Wimborne in 1417. He held the prebends of Major Pars Altaris from 1396 to 1397, Yetminster Prima in 1397, Faringdon from 1397 to 1400, having been excommunicated but later absolved, when he exchanged the last with Walter Cook for the Treasurership of St Paul's. He held the prebend of Netherbury in Ecclesia in 1401, followed by Preston, which he exchanged with Richard Derham for Netherbury in Ecclesia in 1402. He held the prebends of Fordington & Writhlington from 1404 to 1407 and Bedwin from 1407 until his death in 1423.

Christopher Marini (1398) became Arch-Priest of the Vatican, holding with this dignity the Abbey of St Boniface and St Alexis in the Aventine. He became Bishop of Isernia, Lower Italy in 1327 and was created Cardinal-Priest of St Cyriacus in 1329. He was nominated to the dignity of Archdeacon of Berks in 1390 but not having gained possession he resigned the dignity to the Pope and exchanged it in 1395 with Walter Cook for the prebend of Warthill in York. He was nominated to the prebend of Faringdon in 1398 but Walter Medford continued to hold it. He died in Rome on 4 December 1404 and was buried in St Peter's.

Walter Cook (1400-1422) (see above).

Reginald Kentwood (1422-1441) BCL, was Dean of St Paul's in 1421. He died in 1441.

Robert Aiscough (1441-1447) DTh, held the prebends of Netheravon from 1440 to 1441, Faringdon from 1441 to 1447, Grantham Australis from 1447 to 1448, Chisenbury & Chute in 1448 and Bere & Cherminster from 1448 to 1449. He was Archdeacon of Dorset from 1447 to 1449 and had died by 14 February 1449.

Richard Andrew (1477-1449) DCL, was Archdeacon of Sarum from 1441 until resigning in 1444. He held the prebends of Faringdon from 1447 to 1449, Stratton from 1449 to 1454 and Grantham Borealis from 1454 to 1477. He was a friend of Archbishop Chichele and the first Warden of All Souls, Oxford founded by him in 1437. He was Dean of York in 1451 and Chancellor of Canterbury. He died in 1477.

William Normanton (1449-1459) held the prebends of Yatesbury from 1443 to 1445, Warminster from 1445 to 1446, Bishopstone from 1446 to 1447, Durnford from 1447 to 1448, Chisenbury & Chute from 1448 to 1449 and Faringdon from 1449 to 1459. He died in 1459.

William Nessingwick (1459-?) was a Notary Public and held the prebends of Preston from 1450 to 1454, Stratton from 1454 to 1459 and Faringdon from 1459 to c.1486. He was Subdean of Sarum from 1459 to 1476, exchanging the office in 1476 with Giles Stanbridge for the church of Milston, which he held until 1487. A Canon Residentiary, he acted as locum tenens for the Dean on more than one occasion presiding in chapter as locum tenens not Subdean and visiting the prebends in 1463.

Ralph Heathcott (?-1492) BCn&CL, held the prebends of Chardstock from ? to 1486 and Bitton from 1486 to 1487, Faringdon from 1487? to 1492 and Hurstbourne & Burbage from 1492 to 1493, exchanging the last with Adrian de Bardis in 1493 for the prebend of Ramsbury and the church of Wroughton, holding this prebend from 1493 until his death in 1499. He was Rector of St Peter's, Marlborough in 1481.

Richard Newport (1492-1514) BCL, held the prebends of Major Pars Altaris from 1490 to 1492, Wilsford & Woodford in 1492 and Faringdon from 1492 to 1514. He was Rector of Mildenhall and Vicar General to Edmund Audley, Bishop of Sarum 1502-1524. He died in 1514 and desired to be buried in the cathedral.

William Gray (1514-1515) MA, would appear not to have been ordained before 1510 when he became Archdeacon of Berks, holding the dignity until 1522. He held the prebends of Grantham Borealis from 1508 to 1514, Horton in 1514, Faringdon from 1514 to 1515 and Teynton Regis from 1515 to 1522. He held a stall at Hereford from 1512 to 1522. He died in 1522 and asked to be buried in Ramsbury church.

James Bromwich (1515-1519) BCnL, held the prebends of Axford from 1505 to 1507, Coombe & Harnham in 1507, Grimston from 1507 to 1515, Faringdon from 1515 to 1519 and Hurstbourne & Burbage from 1519 to 1524. He was Chancellor of Hereford in 1518 and became Archdeacon of Sarum in 1524, dying a month after his appointment.

Edward Finch (1519-1521) DM, was well endowed with prebends holding in succession those of Yatesbury from 1514 to 1515, Chardstock from 1515 to 1517, Wilsford & Woodford in 1517, Fordington & Writhlington from 1517 to 1518, Grimston from 1518 to 1519 and Faringdon from 1519 to 1521, exchanging the last with William Webbe for the church of Ross on Wye, Hereford. He then held the prebends of Bishopstone from 1521 to 1522, Teynton Regis from 1522 to 1524 and Bere & Cherminster from 1524 to 1539. He was Archdeacon of Wilts from 1522 until 1539. He died in 1539 and was buried in the cathedral.

William Webbe (1521-1523) MA, held a stall at Hereford and was Chancellor of that diocese. He was Archdeacon of Salop and of Hereford and died in 1523.

Henry Rawlyns (1523-1524) BCL, was well provided with prebends. He held Yatesbury from1513 to 1514, Grantham Australis from 1514 to 1519 and Coombe & Harnham 1519 to 1521. He resigned the last in May 1521, was succeeded by Cuthbert Tunstall who then became Dean of Sarum, and was again collated to the prebend later in the same year. The prebend then passed to Richard Pace but was assumed by Henry Rawlyns for the third time in 1523. He then held Faringdon from 1523 to 1524, Hurstbourne & Burbage in 1524 and Teynton Regis, together with the Archdeaconry of Sarum from 1524 to 1526. He was Rector of Christian Malford, died in 1526 and is buried in the cathedral near Bishop Audley's chantry.

Richard Arche (1524) BCL, held the prebend of Preston from ? to 1524, resigning to assume the prebend of Faringdon in 1524, which he resigned a month later. He then received the prebend of Hurstbourne & Burbage which he held from 1524 until resigning in 1552. Two years later he was appointed to the prebend of Minor Pars Altaris but may not have received it before being deprived of all benefices early in 1555. He was Vicar of Avebury and held a stall at Windsor from 1538 until deprived. He was a Canon Residentiary from 1527 to 1554 and Treasurer of Sarum from 1551 to 1555 during which time the Commissioners appointed to survey Church Goods and Chantries visited the cathedral.

Edward Molineux (1524-1535) held the prebends of Minor Pars Altaris from 1519 to 1522, Bishopstone from 1522 to 1524 and Faringdon from 1524 to 1535.

Guy de Cavalcante (1535,1551) was a Florentine and was Parson of Faringdon in 1542. Although his rights were preserved, the prebend was transferred in 1551 to William Honnying Esq to be held of the King and it ceased to exist.

HORTON

Prebend:- The manor of Horton is in Gloustershire. The church was given to the cathedral by Agnes wife of Ralph de Bellofago, the gift being confirmed by King Henry II in 1158. The prebend was probably in existence by c.1150 and it was joined to the bishopric on 11 April 1219, in place of the prebend of Major Pars Altaris, on account of the uncertain income of the latter. In 1255 the bishopric assumed the prebend of Pottern and relinquished that of Horton.

On 9 July 1547, the prebend was dissolved and was granted by King Edward VI to Edward, Duke of Somerset. On Somerset forfeiting his estate on sentence of death, it was granted to Clement Paston.

Psalter:- The portion of the psalter allotted to the prebend is Psalms 52, 53, 54 and 55.

Holders of the prebend:-

Gilbert de Bellofago (before 1155) was described as a son of Agnes, wife of Ralph de Bellofago.

Robert de Bellofago (c.1155/61-c.1193) was presumably related to Gilbert de Bellofago.

Richard Poore (1219-1228) was a brother of Herbert Poore, Bishop of Sarum 1194-1217. He was Dean of Sarum, holding the prebend of Bere & Cherminster from 1197 to 1215 and played a large part in the founding of the present cathedral. He became Bishop of Chichester in 1215 and Bishop of Sarum from 1217 to 1228, holding the prebend of Major Pars Altaris from 1217 to 1219, when it was exchanged for the prebend of Horton. He became Bishop of Durham in 1228.

Robert de Bingham (1229-1246) was fined for non-residence in 1227. He was the founder of St Nicholas Hospital, Sarum and is said to have built Ayleswade Bridge over the River Avon beside the Hospital. He held the prebend of Slape from c.1226/7 to 1229 when he became Bishop of Sarum from 1229 to 1246, holding with the bishopric the prebend of Horton. He died on 2 November 1246 and was buried in the still unfinished cathedral.

William of York (1247-1254) was Provost of Beverley and held stalls at Lincoln, London and York.. He was a royal justice and is described as "a courtier from his childhood, and better versed in the laws of the realm, which he had chiefly studied, than in the laws of God." He was Bishop of Sarum from 1247 to 1256 and held the prebends of Horton from 1247 to 1254 and Pottern from 1254 to 1256. He died on 31 January 1256 and was buried in the cathedral, on the 'south side of the chancel, near St John's altar under a gilt tomb'.

Ralph of York (c.1273-c.1288) was a canon of Sarum as early as 1244 when he witnessed the foundation deed of the Hospital of St Nicholas, Sarum and was a great benefactor of the cathedral library. From c.1273 to c.1288 he held the prebend of Horton and was Chancellor of Sarum from 1288 to 1309. He became Archdeacon of Sudbury, Norfolk, in 1284. He died on 21 November 1309.

Henry de Esse (1289-1297/98) held the prebends of Chardstock from before 1281 to c.1297 and Horton from 1289 to 1297/98. He had died by 20 January 1298.

William of Abingdon (1298) was Precentor of Sarum from c.1296 to 1298 and held the prebend of Horton for less than four months in 1298 despite it having been given by the Pope to George Saluzzo, his successor as Precentor. He was Archdeacon of Wilts from ? to c.1295/6 and died by 5 May 1298.

William Burnel (1298-1304) Lived in the house called Leadenhall in the Close. He held the prebend of Bedminster & Redcliffe from c.1284 to 1298 and also held stalls at Exeter, Lichfield, St David's and York. He was Provost of Wells by 1289, Dean of Wells from 1292 to c.1295 and Archdeacon of Taunton from 1294 to 1298. He was a nephew of Robert Burnel, Bishop of Bath & Wells 1275-1292. He transferred to the prebend of Horton in 1298, holding it until his death before 4 November 1304. He occupied the house, Leadenhall, in the Close.

Walter Burdon (1304-1308) MA, was a distinguished theologian and a former Chancellor of Oxford University, who was Archdeacon of Gloucester from 1295. He held the prebends of Alton Australis from 1298 to 1304 and Horton from 1304 to 1308.

Richard de Abingdon (1309-1322) held a prebends of Minor Pars Altaris from 1305 to 1309 and Horton from 1309 to 1322 and died in 1322.

Pontius de Varesio (1309) claimed the prebend of Horton in 1309 although Richard de Abingdon had been appointed to it in the same year. The case was taken to the Roman Court but before it was settled he claimed the prebend of Grantham Australis. This was questioned and he resigned his claim before the end of 1310. Also in 1309 he claimed the dignity of Chancellor of Sarum but the Bishop appealed against this papal grant. Protection was granted to William de Bosco in 1310 and, following the death of Pontius de Varesio in 1310, Tydo de Varesio was appointed.

John de Fonteneye (1322) held the prebend of Horton in 1322, exchanging it with Gilbert de Middleton for the prebend of Netheravon which he held from 1322 to ?.

Gilbert de Middleton (1322-1330) held the prebends of Netheravon from 1315 to 1322 and Horton from 1322 to 1330. He was also well endowed with other prebends, simultaneously holding stalls at St Paul's, Lincoln, Chichester, Hereford and Wells. He became Archdeacon of Northampton in 1316 and held the church of Edington. In 1321 King Edward II "granted him that he should not be disturbed in any of his benefices." He died in 1330/31.

Peter de Berkeley (1331-1342) received the prebend by royal grant in 1330 but this was revoked seven months later as it was already held by Gilbert de Middleton. A further grant was made in 1331 and he was installed. He died in 1342.

Richard de Bury (or d'Aungerville) (1331-1333) received a royal grant of the Archdeaconry of Sarum in 1330 but this was revoked and the dignity given to Robert Luffenham. He held the prebend of Beminster Secunda from 1330 to 1333, was nominated to the prebend of Horton in 1331 but it was already occupied by Peter de Berkeley and he became Bishop of Durham 1333 without having had possession of the prebend. He is also believed to have held a stall at Lichfield in 1330 and been Dean of Wells in 1332. He was Chancellor of England in 1334 and died in 1335.

Stephen de Mucheldevere (1342-1344) DCL, had expectations of a prebend since 1342 and took possession of the prebend of Horton on the death of Peter de Berkeley but he sued Richard Thormerton who had also been appointed. He died in 1344 at Rome during the court case.

Richard Thormerton (1342-1347) BCn&CL, was appointed to the prebend in 1342 but was not admitted until 1344, following the death of Stephen Mucheldevere. He died c. June 1361.

William Farley (1346-1363) received the prebend by royal grant in 1346 and held it until his death in 1363.

William Langborough (1363-1365) was nominated to the prebend of Horton in 1363, following the death of Richard Thormerton but although Nicholas de Louth was granted the prebend on the death of William Farley, he retained possession of the prebend, exchanging it in 1365 with Nicholas de Louth for a prebend at St Asaph.

Nicholas de Louth (1363-?) obtained the prebend of Horton in 1363 on the death of William Farley but William Langborough was in possession and he had to receive it by exchange in 1365. He still held it in 1383.

William Farewelle (1385) held the prebend in 1385.

Giles Wenlock (1388) received the prebend in 1388 by royal grant, as did Guy de Roucliffe on the same day. He was installed in September but Guy de Roucliffe was installed a month later.

Guy de Roucliffe (1388-1392) received the prebend by royal grant on the same day as Giles Wenlock. Despite the latter being installed before him, he held the prebend until his death in 1392.

Roger Walden (1392-1397) received a royal grant of the prebend of Beminster Prima in 1389 and held the prebends of Bishopstone from 1391 to 1392 and Horton from 1392 to 1397. He was consecrated Archbishop of Canterbury in 1397 but his claim was refused by King Henry IV. He became Bishop of London in 1405 and died a year later.

Nicholas Daniel (1397-1424) was nominated to the prebend in 1397 but despite the nomination of Henry de Beaufort he continued to hold the prebend until his death in 1424.

Henry Beaufort (1397-1398) was a son of John of Gaunt, Duke of Lancaster and held a stall at Lincoln both in 1389 and 1391. He was nominated to the prebend of Horton in 1397 but became Dean of Wells in the same year and Bishop of Lincoln a year later and of Winchester in 1404. He became Chancellor of Oxford University in 1399 and of England in 1403 and 1413. In 1426 he was raised to the rank of Cardinal-Priest of St Eusebius. He crowned King Henry VI as King of France and was at the Councils of Florence in 1417 and Basle in 1433. He died on 10 April 1447.

John Burton (1424-1431) died in 1431.

John Norton (1431-1462) DCnL, held the prebends of Beminster Secunda from 1429 to 1431 and Horton from 1431 to 1462. He was Archdeacon of Sarum from 1432 to 1433 and Archdeacon of Berks from 1433 until his death in 1462.

Thomas Beauchamp (1462) resigned four months after his installation.

John Russell (1462-1476) DCnL, held the prebends of Yatesbury from 1461 to 1462 and Horton from 1462 to 1476. He was Archdeacon of Berks from 1466 to 1476 and held a stall at St Paul's in 1474. He became Bishop of Rochester in 1476 and of Lincoln in 1480, was Chancellor of Oxford from 1483 to 1494 and Chancellor of England under Kings Edward V and Richard III. He died in 1494.

John Morton (1476-1478) DCL, held the prebends of Fordington & Writhlington from 1458 to 1476 and Horton from 1476 to 1478. He was a native of Milborne St Andrew and in 1453 was Principal of Peckwater's Inn at Oxford. He was afterwards an advocate at the Court of Arches. He was Archdeacon of Winchester in 1474 and Prebendary of Wells in 1475. For short periods between 1475 and 1477 he would also seem to have held the Archdeaconries of Chichester, Huntingdon and Leicester. He was Archdeacon of Berks from 1476 until 1478 when he was consecrated Bishop of Ely. In 1486 he became Archbishop of Canterbury, being created Cardinal-Priest of St Anastasia in 1493. He died on 12 October 1500 at the age of 90 and was buried in Canterbury cathedral.

Robert Morton (?-1486) MA, resigned the prebend in 1486 on becoming Bishop of Worcester. In 1485, "during the time that Maister Robert Morton, the King's rebel, standeth out of the King's grace" his prebend was put towards the construction of St Osmund's shrine.

Christopher Bainbridge (1486-1508) LLD, held the prebends of Grantham Borealis from ? to 1486, Chardstock in 1486 and Horton from 1486 to 1508. He was Master of the Rolls in 1504. After holding many preferments, amongst them those of Provost of Queen's College, Oxford and Dean of York, was made Bishop of Durham in 1507 and Archbishop of York in 1508. He was created Cardinal-Priest of SS Marcellinus & Peter in 1508 and of St Praxedes in 1511. He led a military expedition against Ferrara, was poisoned by his steward, an Italian priest, on 14 July 1514 and was buried at the English College, Rome. Sylvester Gigliis, Bishop of Worcester, was suspected of having instigated the murder but was declared innocent by the Pope.

Matthew Lang (1508-1517) was Latin secretary to the Emperor Maximilian and became Bishop of Gurcke in Hungary in 1501 and of Carthagina in Spain in 1510. He was Co-adjutor to the Archbishop of Saltzbourg and Cardinal-Deacon of St Angelo in 1512, and Cardinal-Bishop of Albano in 1538. He held the prebend of Horton from 1508, although reported dead in 1514, until resigning it in 1517, when he was given a pension 'to preserve him from want and mendicancy in his old age.' He held converse with Erasmus, in 1525 he was besieged in his castle at Saltzbourg by Lutherans, and dying at Saltzbourg on 30 March 1530 was buried there.

William Gray (1514) MA, would appear not to have been ordained before 1510 when he became Archdeacon of Berks, holding the dignity until 1522. He held the prebend of Grantham Borealis from 1508 to 1514, was given the prebend of Horton in 1514, and held the prebends of Faringdon from 1514 to 1515 and Teynton Regis from 1515 to 1522. He held a stall at Hereford from 1512 to 1522, died in 1522 and asked to be buried in Ramsbury church.

William Knight (1517-1541) DCL, became Bishop of Bath & Wells in 1541.

James Lomelyne (1541-1547) was the last official holder of the prebend which was dissolved on 9 July 1547.

John Billing (1557-1560) BD, was instituted to the prebend by Archbishop Pole, under protest by the Chapter. He died in 1560.

SHIELDS FIXED TO THE REAR OF THE STALLS

The shields start on the south side with the prebendal stall of Ilfracombe and continue from west to east to the Chancellor's stall.

1

2

3

4

5

6

7

8

9

10

11

12

13

14

15

16

17

18

19

20

21

22

23

24

25

26

27

The shields start on the north side with the prebendal stall of Teynton Regis and continue from west to east to the Treasurer's stall

28

29

30

31

32

33

34

35

36

37

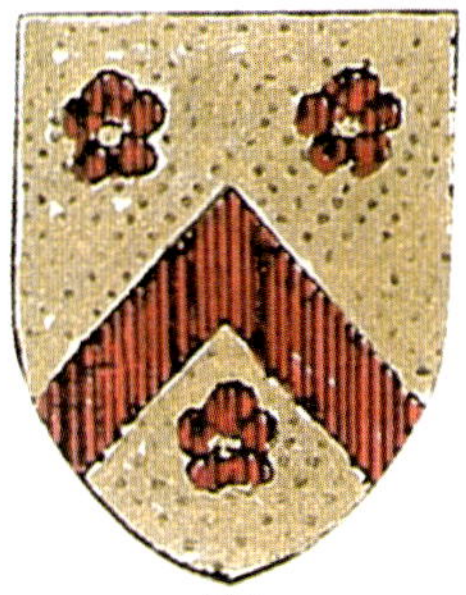
38

39

40

41

42

43

44

45

46

47

48

49

50

51

52

53

54

HOLDERS OF THE SHIELDS

PRINCIPAL SOURCES

Fasti Ecclesiæ Sarisberiensis, William Henry Jones, Brown & Co Salisbury 1879/1881.

Fasti Ecclesiæ Anglicanæ 1066-1300 IV Salisbury, Diana E Greenway, University of London Institute of Historical Research 1991.

Fasti Ecclesiæ Anglicanæ 1300-1541 III Salisbury Diocese, Joyce M Horn, University of London Institute of Historical Research 1962.

Fasti Ecclesiæ Anglicanæ 1541-1875 VI Salisbury Diocese, Joyce M Horn, London University Institute of Historical Research 1986.

"Salisbury Cathedral ", Kathleen Edwards, *Victoria County History, A History of Wiltshire vol III*, R B Pugh & Elizabeth Crittall, Oxford University Press 1956.

Statutes and Customs of the Cathedral Church of the Blessed Virgin Mary of Salisbury, Chr Worsworth & Douglas Macleane, William Clowes & Sons London 1915

The English Secular Cathedrals in the Middle Ages, Kathleen Edwards, Manchester University Press 1949.

"Orders and Rank in the Cathedral of Old Sarum", Diana Greenway, *Studies in Church History vol 26, The Ministry - Clerical & Lay*, W J Shiels & Diana Wood, Blackwell, Oxford 1989.

"Cardinals Beneficed in Salisbury Cathedral", Revd Dr C Moor, *Wiltshire Archeological & Natural History Magazine*, vol 50, 1942-44.

"Obituary of Canon Rich-Jones", ACS, *Wiltshire Archeological & Natural History Magazine*, vol 22, 1885.

The New Bells Cathedral Guides - Salisbury Cathedral, Roy Spring, Unwin Hyman London 1987.

Barchester - English Cathedral Life in the Nineteenth Century, Philip Barrett, SPCK London 1993

Salisbury Cathedral, Roy Spring, Dean & Chapter Salisbury Cathedral 1991

Extracts from Salisbury Cathedral Chapter Acts Books 1878-1971 and 1975-1995.

Osmund Bishop of Salisbury 1078-1099 and Founder of the Cathedral at Old Sarum, Diana Greenway, RJL Smith & Associates, Much Wenlock 1999.

The Victoria History of Wiltshire, University of London Institute of Historical Research.

Heraldry Notes for Guides, Part I - Shields in the Choir, by Ronald Mathieson

Masters of St Nicholas Hospital - a framed list in the Hall of the Hospital.

Salisbury Diocesan Gazette.

Sarum Diocesan Directory.

Salisbury Diocesan Year Book.

Crockford's Clerical Directory.

Burke's Peerage

The Dictionary of National Biography.

Who's Who.

The Times Newspaper - Obituaries.

INDEX OF PERSONS

A

B

C

D

G

H

I

J

K

L

N

O

P

Q

R

S

T

U

V

W

Y

Z